THE REFORMATION OF THE CONSTITUTION

This book revisits one of the defining judicial engagements in English legal history.

It provides a fresh account of the years 1606 to 1616 which witnessed a series of increasingly volatile confrontations between, on the one side, King James I and his Attorney-General, Sir Francis Bacon, and on the other, Sir Edward Coke, successively Chief Justice of Common Pleas and Lord Chief Justice.

At the heart of the dispute were differing opinions regarding the nature of kingship and the reach of prerogative in reformation England. Appreciating the longer context, in the summer of 1616 King James appealed for a reformation of law and constitution to complement the reformation of his Church.

Later historians would discern in these debates the seeding of a century of revolution, followed by another four centuries of reform. This book ventures the further thought that the arguments which echoed around Westminster Hall in the first years of the seventeenth century have lost little of their resonance half a millennium on. Breaks with Rome are little easier to 'get done', the margins of executive governance little easier to draw.

The Reformation of the Constitution

Law, Culture and Conflict in Jacobean England

Law, Culture and Conflict in Jacobean England

Ian Ward

·HART·

OXFORD · LONDON · NEW YORK · NEW DELHI · SYDNEY

HART PUBLISHING

Bloomsbury Publishing Plc

Kemp House, Chawley Park, Cumnor Hill, Oxford, OX2 9PH, UK

1385 Broadway, New York, NY 10018, USA

29 Earlsfort Terrace, Dublin 2, Ireland

HART PUBLISHING, the Hart/Stag logo, BLOOMSBURY and the Diana logo are
trademarks of Bloomsbury Publishing Plc

First published in Great Britain 2024

A catalogue record for this book is available from the British Library.

A catalogue record for this book is available from the Library of Congress.

Library of Congress Control Number: 2024931025

ISBN: HB: 978-1-50995-775-0
        ePDF: 978-1-50995-777-4
        ePub: 978-1-50995-776-7

Typeset by Compuscript Ltd, Shannon

To find out more about our authors and books visit www.hartpublishing.co.uk.
Here you will find extracts, author information, details of forthcoming events
and the option to sign up for our newsletters.

TABLE OF CONTENTS

Introduction: Irony and Rhyme

History is momentary, or rather it can often seem so. In their brilliant pastiche of English historiography, *1066 and All That*, Sellar and Yeatman suggested that just two dates in English history really mattered. The first, when that history begins, is 55 BC. The second, as the title foretells, is 1066. After which, to layer the irony, they eschew any more. It is, of course, the writing of history which makes it seem momentary. The stitching together of incidents to create narratives. Sometimes the stitching is tighter, and brighter; the preference of the Whiggish historian. Sometimes it is looser, ragged even, and sceptical: a history of ironies and contingencies. A 'chain of conjectures', as Carlo Ginzburg puts it.[1] This book is ironic in the sense Ginzburg conceives. Something else that history can be is resonant. The moments might recur. It is sometimes surmised that history repeats, or at least, to adopt Mark Twain's neat aphorism, rhyme. This book is also about the 'playfulness' of rhyming history.[2] Before we get to our particular history, which turns around an event in summer 1616, we should contemplate further the idea of irony and resonance in our inscription of the past.

Irony and Anecdote

The essence of ironic history is the appreciation of conversation and contingency. Keith Jenkins identifies two leading exponents of ironic history.[3] The first is Hayden White. In his *Tropics of Discourse*, White suggests that history should be conceived as an exercise in 'ironic reflection', rather than scientific 'discovery', a matter of taking situational 'incidents' and writing 'stories', something that necessarily requires the deployment of the 'figurative imagination' in the writing of the past.[4] At the same time, the endemic 'discontinuities' of the past necessitate a 'realistic' reconciliation with the fact that 'chaos is our lot'.[5] There is an evident affinity here with ideas of post-modernist philosophers such as Jean-Francois Lyotard. In his *The Differend*, Lyotard treated the idea of justice as fashionable in each sense of the word, as an *accoutrement* and an art form.[6] Derridean deconstruction adopted

---

[1] Ginzburg (2002) 40.
[2] The term borrowed from Rorty (1989).
[3] Jenkins (1995).
[4] White (1978) 4–6, 27–29, 73–74, 82–83, 104–07.
[5] White (1978) 49–50, 107–11.
[6] Lyotard (1989).

a similar pose. In his *Specters of Marx*, Derrida raised 'generations of ghosts', intangible 'spectres' flitting about the historical imagination.[7]

The second exemplary ironist is Richard Rorty. Here again the acceptance of both textuality and contingency is central to Rorty's idea of historical 'ironism'. In a renowned passage in his *Contingency, Irony, and Solidarity*, Rorty suggested that:

> To say that truth is not out there is simply to say that where there are no sentences there is no truth, that sentences are elements of human languages, and that human languages are human creations.[8]

The consequence is simple and arresting: 'The world does not speak. Only we do'.[9] The 'certaintist' historian, as Jenkins terms them, is likely to be disconcerted by the implication; that history is nothing other than conversational practice, and judgement simply the product of this discursive engagement. The creed of the 'certaintist' supposes that the kernel of history is discovery not discourse. A century ago, John Robert Seeley warned his fellow historians against dissolving their discipline into a species of '*belles lettres*'.[10] A generation on, taking particular aim at two centuries of Whig historiography, Herbert Butterfield famously railed against history as told by 'strolling minstrels'.[11] Rorty's embrace of ironic and empathetic textuality insinuates something very different.

The supposition is that because we get to write the text, we create our own morality, our own politics, and our own history. The 'contingency of selfhood', as Rorty terms it, the 'philosophy of us'.[12] Critical here is the appreciation that no incident is described just once, even if there is only one so-called 'original source'.[13] There will always be descriptions and re-descriptions, and it is here that the contingencies are created, where these vying narratives come into interpretive contact. The historian will try to fashion some coherence from these contingencies, to construct Ginzburg's 'chain of conjectures'. There is nothing wrong in this. Edward Gibbon famously confessed the need to 'deviate from the conditional into the indicative mood' at times, where only 'conjecture and analogy' could hold the narrative together.[14]

But it is important that we appreciate the artistry, and its implications. Here Rorty invokes the 'strong poet', someone who embraces this responsibility in order to mediate the contingencies of 'self' and 'community', appreciating that all that they can do is refashion what 'certain poets and revolutionaries of the past' have

---

[7] Derrida (1994) xviii–xix.

[8] Rorty (1989) 5.

[9] Rorty (1989) 6.

[10] Howsam (2004) 525.

[11] Butterfield (1931) 11–13, 39–41, 64.

[12] On the 'philosophy of us', see Rorty (1989) 54–56. For a more general consideration of the 'contingency of selfhood', see (1989) ch 2. For White's comment on the 'accident' of history, see (1978) 29.

[13] See here Ginzburg (2013) xxiv–xxv.

[14] Chapter 31 of History of the Decline and Fall of the Roman Empire, quoted in Ginzburg (2012) 67.

earlier created.[15] Incident building on incident, chance on chance.[16] And there is a further dimension, as Richard Brown observes: for every history is not only a history of chance, but is also written 'by chance'.[17] Ginzburg futher unsettles the picture, suggesting that incidental history inheres an elemental 'self-deception'.[18] There is 'no direct access to historical reality', just the delusions and impressions of the past.[19]

It is possible to mediate the margins of certainty and irony. Lara Putnam recommends the art of the judicious 'side-glance'.[20] Richard Evans gestures likewise in his *In Defence of History*. History needs direction, which is why it creates it, but the historian should stay alert to all the incidents and oddities lurking 'in the verges and ditches by the highway'.[21] All the contingencies that previous historians had ignored or cast aside because they did not fit the preferred narrative. There is just as much history here as there is in the middle of the road; a resolution which brings us to the idea of anecdotal history. The art of the inveterate side-glancer.

The anecdotalist takes the insights of the Rortian ironist, the conversational and the contingent, and aligns them with the incidental impulses of the micro-historian. The motif here is supplied by William Blake:

To see the World in a grain of sand

And a Heaven in a wild flower

Hold Infinity in the palm of your hand

And Eternity in an hour.[22]

The closer we look at something, the more we can see the beauty. Along, of course, with the incongruities; indeed it is in the incongruities that the beauty is discovered, and the authenticity. A 'true' diamond always has tiny imperfections or 'inclusions'; a fake diamond has none.

The responsibility of the micro-historian is to focus on the closer moment or incident, to discern the inclusions. The contention in micro-historical scholarship arises where the perspective broadens, to contemplate the macro-historical.[23] The idea that global trade flows might be anticipated in the market preferences of first-century Roman vintners, or coffee shop patrons in Georgian London. Norbert Elias famously supposed that the practice of early renaissance state-building might

---

[15] As opposed to the 'warrior, the priest, the sage, or the truth-seeking "logical" scientist'. See Rorty (1989) 53, 60–61.

[16] Ginzburg refers to 'dispersed' fragments of the past 'reaching us by chance' (2013) xxxii.

[17] Brown (2003) 3.

[18] See Ginzburg (2015) 448–50, 459; and for similar, White (1978) 59–60, 84–85.

[19] Ginzburg (2002) 17.

[20] Putnam (2016) 377–78.

[21] Evans (2000) 244.

[22] Blake, *Auguries of Innocence* ll. 1–4 (1977) 506.

[23] See here Brown (2003) 14–15; Trivellato (2023) 19–25; and Ghobrial (2019) 4–5, supposing that 'micro-history', in its interest in the lives of 'everyday' persons, might save 'macro-history' from accusations that it ignores the fate of 'others'.

be traced to the introduction of the fork.[24] Micro-histories like to play with such 'conjectures'. In his *Pickett's Charge*, George Stewart reviewed an entire civil war through the lens of a desperate 20-minute charge at the battle of Gettysburg in 1863.[25] James Chandler revisits the 'Peterloo massacre' of August 1819 to prophesy an entire century of English cultural radicalism.[26] In his *The Cheese and the Worms*, Ginzburg reads the mind of a sixteenth-century Italian miller in order to comprehend the reach of the Catholic Inquisition.[27] What this requires of course is a willingness to exercise the 'imagination'; the most important quality, as Fernand Braudel confirmed, of any historian.[28] Reading 'beyond the edge of the page', as Giovanni Levi puts it.[29] Ginzburg terms it 'inductive reconstruction'.[30]

We too will be trying to read minds in the coming chapters, even if the minds in question have had rather more to say about themselves, in a directly testamentary sense at least, than Ginzburg's miller. Our three were inveterate self-fashioners, constantly reaching for their quills in order to tell us about themselves, what they thought and what they did, and why. James Stuart, Edward Coke and Francis Bacon were, in this sense, definitively gentlemen of Stephen Greenblatt's renaissance.[31] We will also, as advertised, be seizing a moment as the pretext to exploring some larger movements, in our case in early modern English constitutional history. Ours will, accordingly, be a discursive engagement, not just with the past, but in the past. In doing all of this, concentrating on minds and moments, conversing with past and present, imagining our chains of conjecture, we will be adopting the pose of the ironic historian.

English constitutional history tempts us with plenty of higher-octane moments from which to choose: 1215, 1689, 1867. Rather less familiar perhaps is 1616, struggling for attention amidst a century of seemingly endless constitutional crises across the 'three kingdoms' which would, at the beginning of the century to come, presume themselves to be 'united'. Not that our concern is with 1616 alone. Moments, as we have already inferred, can be long or short. Quite how far forward we move, and how far back, and how widely we range across the constitutional landscape, is up to us. The only margins are those which inhibit our imagination. We will start with only the slightest trip over the margin, drifting back just a couple of months to the previous autumn, and the decision of a couple of Staffordshire landowners to commence legal proceedings challenging the validity of a writ of *commendam*.

---

[24] Elias (1939), recommended in Levi (1992) 96.
[25] Stewart (1959). It is commonly agreed that Stewart was the first to use the term 'microhistory' in the Anglo-American context. For an overview of the parallel development of continental and American micro-history, see Ginzburg (1993) 10–20.
[26] Chandler (1998).
[27] Ginzburg (1992).
[28] Quoted in Andrade (2011) 591.
[29] Levi (2019) 41.
[30] Ginzburg (2003) 666.
[31] Greenblatt (2005).

Consecrating Justice

A *commendam* was a means of transferring an ecclesiastical benefice in trust to the custody of a bishop; in this case the Bishop of Coventry and Lichfield. The grant was in the gift of the Governor of the Church of England, in other words the King, and was supposed to facilitate the continued governance and the exaction of tithes in parishes temporarily divested of incumbent vicars. Somewhat arcane, then, but also lucrative. And ordinarily, not especially controversial. On this occasion, however, it would precipitate a constitutional crisis which would end with the removal from office of the Lord Chief Justice of England and Wales, Sir Edward Coke. And which also, with the benefit of hindsight, might be supposed to have mapped out four centuries of prospective constitutional contention.

The *Case of Commendams*, as it would become known, was remitted to the Court of Exchequer sitting as a deliberative assembly.[32] The King, James I of England and VI of Scotland, despatched the bishop of Winchester to spy on the proceedings. He returned a disturbing report. On being advised that a *commendam* could only be issued in cases of 'necessity' and, the implication ran, this was hardly that, the Lord Chief Justice had been seen to nod. A series of letters were despatched, drafted by the Attorney General, Sir Francis Bacon, asking that judgment be deferred until the King 'be first consulted with'. Whilst admitting that it seemed 'a little strange', Bacon assumed it was sufficient. He was wrong. The case, the judges returned, was of 'private interest', and so nothing to do with the King.[33]

A further flurry of correspondence, in which James confirmed that whilst he 'never studied the common law of England', he was 'not ignorant of any points which belong to a King to know', resolved nothing.[34] And so, on 6 June 1616, the judges were summoned to attend the Privy Council at Whitehall, for a serious dressing-down. An event foretold, in a whimsical sense. A few years earlier, William Shakespeare had completed *Cymbeline*; perhaps the most problematic of his so-called later 'problem' plays.[35] Towards the end of which the Roman God Jupiter descends from Olympus to chastise the 'petty spirits of region low' for the mess they have made (5.4. 93). Of the many things which have become 'mangled' in Cymbeline's realm is the law. The play was set in Roman Britain, and Cymbeline was struggling to accommodate 'our laws' with Roman law (3.1. 55–58).[36] A prescient dilemma, as we will see.[37] And a prescient intervention. The Roman Emperor

---

[32] *Colt and Glover v Bishop of Coventry and Lichfield* (1615–17) 1 Rolle Rep 451, reprinted in Sheppard (2003) 1310.

[33] See Smith (2014) 281–82; and Jardine and Stewart (1998) 370–72.

[34] Jardine and Stewart (1998) 372.

[35] A play of 'unresisting imbecility', according to Samuel Johnson. See James (1997) 151, 154. The dating of composition is especially difficult with *Cymbeline*. The critical consensus is somewhere between 1608 and 1610.

[36] By 'our laws', Cymbeline meant those laws established by Mulmutius, the first King of the Britons, according to Holinshed, which had then passed down to Gildas and King Arthur.

[37] For recent discussions of the literary jurisprudence discovered in *Cymbeline*, see Raffield (2017) ch 4; and Ward (2022).

Augustus liked to model himself on Jupiter and liked his poets to do the same. Ovid famously obliged at the close of his *Metamorphoses*. James Stuart, in turn, liked to model himself on Augustus, and again appreciated the help of his poets. We will revisit *Cymbeline*.

Meanwhile, we might imagine James descending on his judges that June morning in much the same mood as Shakespeare's Jupiter. 'Express impatience, lest you stir up mine'. (5.4. 112). The King's brief that day had again been drafted by Bacon, who would be sworn in as a Privy Counsellor 72 hours later, in effect replacing Coke. They had, the assembled judges were informed, 'entertayned' a too 'greater boldness to dispute the heigh pointes of his Majesty's prerogative'. A 'reverend' body, James admitted of his judiciary, but also 'corrigible', as 'all subjects are'. And now overreaching themselves, misusing a common law that had 'growne so vast and transcendent'. More particularly, 'ever since comeinge to this Crowne the popular sorte of lawyers have bene men that most affrontedly in all Parliament have trodden upon his prerogative'. The bane of the 'activist' lawyer, a familiar refrain. The 'supreme and imperial power' was not, James concluded, something to be disputed in 'vulgar argument', in court or out.[38]

The judges had probably sensed what was coming. It was reported that they duly 'fell downe upon their knees' and 'asked pardon for their error'. Except, it seems, for Coke, who explained that the King's request to defer judgment had threatened a 'delay of justice' and was itself 'contrary to law'. All he could promise was that he 'would doe that should be fit for a judge to do'.[39] It was reported that the King moved to strike his Lord Chief Justice, but was dissuaded by Lord Chancellor Ellesmere. There would, though, be a reckoning.

The judges were called back a fortnight later for further admonishment, and another lecture on the nature of 'settled' kingship. With a particular emphasis, this time, on matters of jurisdiction. That 'in all well settled Monarchies, where Law is established formerly and orderly, there Iudgement is deferred from the King to his subordinate Magistrates; not that the King takes it from himselfe, but gives it unto them'.[40] And again: 'As Kings borrow their power from God, so judges from Kings: And as Kings are to accompt to God, so Judges unto God and Kings'. Continuing:

> And as no King can discharge his accompt to God, unless he make conscience not to alter, but to declare and establish the will of God: So Judges cannot discharge their accompts to Kings, unless they take the like care, not to take upon them to make the Law, but joyned together after a deliberate consultation, to declare what the Law is. For as Kings are subject unto God's Law, so they to mans Law. It is the Kings Office to protect and settle the trew interpretation of the Law of God within his Dominions: And it is the Judges Office to interpret the Law of the King, whereto themselves are also subject.[41]

---

[38] In Sheppard (2003) 1316. See also Baker (2017) 424–25.
[39] Sheppard (2003) 1318–19.
[40] King James (1994) 205.
[41] King James (1994) 206.

After which, James proceeded to reinvest some variants on what had, over the previous few years, become a familiar theme. First, on the 'diversity' of laws between nations. It was a 'foolish Querke of some Iudges' that the design of a 'Great Britaine' was precluded by the seeming difference between English and Scots law. The very idea of a 'Great' Britain was contestable, of course, then as now. A subject to which we will again return. In the meantime, James was keen to affirm that God had gifted his kings with the ability to 'settle' civil law precisely so that 'particularity' might be properly accommodated within the broader ambit of 'universall' law.[42] Whilst he 'loved' the common law, James wished to remind his judges that:

> There is another Law, of all Lawes free and supreme, which is God's Law: and by this all Common and Municipall Lawes must be governed: And except they have dependence upon this Law, they are uniust and unlawfull.[43]

The principle of natural law, of general application across the *res publica*. And lest anyone continue to harbour any doubts as to James's ability to comprehend the common law, he confirmed that he had invested seven years 'to learne my selfe the Lawes of the Kingdome'. For which reason he was perfectly capable of intervening in cases of 'great cause'.[44] As God intended.

Perfectly capable, too, of appreciating the parlous state of English law, 'too much neglected', made worse by the propensity of his judges to render judgments against 'common sense and reason'. And then, worse still, to 'meddle with the King's Prerogative'.[45] Despite so many warnings, on both counts. The consequence of this 'incertaintie and noveltie' is both metaphysical and practical. In touching upon the prerogative, the judges 'take away the mystical reverence, that belongs unto them that sit in the Throne of God', whilst their erratic judgments sow confusion amongst the King's subjects. The prerogative courts especially have been much 'shaken of late'. Henceforth respective courts must 'keepe' within their 'owne bounds, and nourish not the people in the contempt of other Courts'. If they did there would be 'sweete harmonie' once more.[46]

In order to expedite this 'reformation' of the laws, James confirmed that he would, in the future, be holding his judges much closer to account, demanding regular 'accompt of their labours'. A 'good ancient custome' that 'hath likewise been too much slacked of late'. That way he would be better able to distinguish the 'good and bad justices'.[47] And be better placed to dispense with the latter. Six days later, Coke was charged with corruption, and suspended from Privy Council. On 15 November, he was fired; receiving his writ of dismissal, it was reported,

---

[42] King James (1994) 205.
[43] King James (1994) 210.
[44] King James (1994) 207.
[45] King James (1994) 213. For a commentary, see Burgess (1996) 155–57.
[46] King James (1994) 217.
[47] King James (1994) 220–22. By way of a heads-up, James provided a typology of 'bad' justices, to include the 'idle Slowbellies', the 'busie-bodies', the corrupt, doing favours for friends, and those consumed by 'their owne conceite'.

'with dejection and tears'.[48] When his successor, Sir Henry Montagu, offered to buy his collar of esses, as custom supposed, Coke churlishly declined. He might have gotten wind of Montagu's investiture, at which Ellesmere had given what Bulstrode Whitelock described as a 'very bitter invective'.[49]

The end of a glittering career, a first part at least. 'Four Ps', John Chamberlain declared, 'have overthrown and put him down – that is Pride, Prohibitions, Praemunire and Prerogative'.[50] Too many 'enemies', he further supposed.[51] A perception shared by Henry Calthorpe, who singled out the peculiar enmity of the Attorney General, the 'ill-will' of the Archbishop of Canterbury, and the 'implacable malice' of the Lord Chancellor.[52]

Whatever the reason, it was a brute conclusion to an increasingly bitter controversy which moved around James's more poetic evocations of *dominus* and divine right.[53] And what might have seemed a remarkable irruption; a 'year to consecrate justice', Bacon triumphantly proclaimed.[54] Perhaps, but the tectonic plates had been shifting for some time. The *Commendams* ended a sequence of contentious constitutional cases which stretched back the best part of a decade. We will encounter many of them in the coming pages. It is our shorter history.

Our longer reaches much further back; to where precisely is a matter of choice. At least a century, perhaps a millennium. We will, on occasion, stretch back that far. Meanwhile, 80 years has a tempting symmetry: one that places 1616 at a pivot-point in a longer history of reformation and revolution. It was 80 years earlier that King Henry VIII had given his assent to an Act extinguishing the authority of the Bishop of Rome, a statutory capstone to the Reformation 'settlement'. It confirmed that anyone who:

> By writing, ciphering, printing, preaching or teaching, deed or act, obstinately or maliciously hold or stand with to extol, set forth, maintain or defend the authority, jurisdiction of power of the Bishop of Rome ... shall incur or run with the dangers, penalties, pains and forfeitures ordained and provided by the statute of provision and *praemunire* made in the sixteenth year of the reign of the noble and virtuous prince King Richard II.[55]

---

[48] His closing advice, though undoubtedly sage, doing little to lighten the mood; 'Remember the removing and putting down of your late predecessor'. In Baker (2017) 439.

[49] In Jardine and Stewart (1998) 391.

[50] In Baker (2017) 435.

[51] Jardine and Stewart (1998) 384.

[52] Baker (2017) 436–37. Suffolk was Lord Treasurer, and would himself appear before Star Chamber, a couple of years later, on charges of corruption. Never one to neglect a grudge, Coke took the opportunity to argue stridently for a crippling fine of £100,000, plus imprisonment. In the end, it was set at £30,000. The Earl, and his wife, spent 10 days in the Tower, whilst the fine was further remitted, to £7,000. By this time, the Earl's son had absconded to Paris, to join Coke's daughter, Frances. A discomforting scandal for both fathers, but most especially for Coke; as Frances had only recently married Viscount Purbeck, the half-mad brother of the King's favourite, Sir George Villiers.

[53] See Monateri (2018) 92.

[54] Baker (2017) 410.

[55] 28 Hen.VIII c.10.

We will come across the said 'noble and virtuous prince' in due course, and maybe raise a quizzical eyebrow. It was the *praemunire* statute that Henry liked. A convenient tool of terror with which he had already browbeaten his parochial clergy into submission.[56] To similar end, a few months earlier, Henry had assented to a first dissolution statute, the Suppression of Religious Houses Act.[57] Three years before that he had kicked things off with a Statute in Restraint of Appeals.[58] The longer cause of the crisis of 1616 can be traced back to these statutes, and their failure.

The symmetry is completed if we move eight decades on from 1616. Though we need to be a bit shiftier with our numbers. The Act of Settlement, passed in 1701, was likewise supposed to seal yet another constitutional settlement, this time of the 'happy and glorious' revolution of 1688.[59] The end of a series of revolutions, it has been conjectured, the origins of which can be traced precisely to 1616.[60] Noting that the present monarch, King William III, was childless and unlikely to remarry, and that his natural successor, Princess Anne, was no more likely to have children, the Act of Settlement prescribed that the succession would, in time, pass to the nearest 'in the protestant line', which was identified in the moment in the person of the Electress Sophia of Hanover, the granddaughter of King James I.[61] The main point was, though, in the converse. The Act was also devised for 'extinguishing the Hope of the pretended Prince of Wales and all other Pretenders and their open and secret Abettors'. An Act purposed, we might say, for getting the Reformation done, finally.

A familiar resonance throughout English constitutional history. Two centuries on, Lord Macaulay would sell the 1832 Reform Act on the promise of 'finality'. If Parliament passed his Act, there would be no need for further franchise reform; at least not until 1867, and then 1884 and 1918 and 1928. It is a familiarity which might be expected to breed an appropriate measure of contempt for those politicians who continue to promise that constitutional reformations can be readily 'done'. But discerning an echo from history is not the same as listening to it; still less learning from it. A thought to which we will return in our final chapter.

The Rhyme of History

The temptation to look back, in the hope of making better sense of the present, and the future, is something to which most historians fall prey. For good reason. History is just as much in the present as the past. As Viscount Bolingbroke

---

[56] In 1530. For commentaries, see Scarisbrick (1956); and Guy (1982).
[57] 27 Hen.VIII c.28.
[58] 24 Hen.VIII c.12.
[59] 12 & 13 Will.III c.2.
[60] Coquillette (1992) 175.
[61] Anne's only remaining child, Prince William, Duke of Gloucester, had died in August 1700. Eight months earlier, her final pregnancy had ended with a stillborn son.

observed in his *Letters on the Study of History*; history as 'conversant about the past', rather than set in it.[62] A quintessentially ironic sentiment. The only difference between vying 'schools' of history is how much the temptation to craft coherence might be resisted. Whiggish and Marxist histories are especially susceptible, in their differing ways, to the narrative lure, liking to suppose that the future is predicated on the past. It lends a sense of security, as well as predictability. It also tends to bring out the story in history. The ironic historian, as we have already intimated, wonders particularity and moment, and the disruptions of contingency. History as narrative still, but resisting the drive towards a happy ending; or any ending. It is not, however, a resolution which is likely to appeal to the 'certaintist', as Sellar and Yeatman intimated. The 'certaintist' likes her history to come to a 'full stop'. But there are, as Ginzburg intimates, no full stops, just commas and semi-colons, moments in which to take a breath.[63]

In this context, the idea of history repeating also become contentious. In one sense, contingency embraces recurrence, appreciating an affinity with history as a redescriptive process. On the other, it doubts the insinuation of precision. It is here that Twain's aphorism appears to resonate, even as it mixes our sensory metaphors: 'History doesn't repeat itself, but it often does rhyme'. Something else oddly apt about Twain's aphorism is its uncertain provenance. A 'certaintist' might again find this disconcerting. Less so an ironist, appreciative of Voltaire's notorious report of a witty exchange between the future King Louis XIV and his father on the subject of princely performance. It too lacked provenance, as Voltaire conceded, but was far too good not to become history.[64]

The Enlightenment was, in many respects, the age of anecdote and rhyme. Horace Walpole reduced history to little else. 'I draw characters, I preserve anecdotes', Horace proudly proclaimed, 'which my superiors, the historians of Britain, may enclose into their weighty annals or pass over at the pleasure'.[65] His contemporary Edmund Burke penned one of the most brilliant histories of the French Revolution in like spirit. What was different about his *Reflections on the Revolution in France* was the pretence that it was anything else. Readers really were supposed to believe that Marie Antoinette had been raped by a gang of 'ruffians' at Versailles on 5 October 1789. A little poetic licence, as Burke confessed, designed to bring 'tears' to the eyes of his readers. Burke was an empathetic ironist, and he expected his readers to be the same.[66] He also expected them to spot the resonances, for *Reflections* was as much about England in 1789, and 1689, and by inference America in 1787. He wanted them to note what struck a bell and, more importantly, what did not. The French Revolution was a 'terror' wrought by proletarian

---

[62] Kramnick (1972) 25.

[63] Ginzburg (2002) 21–22, 152–54.

[64] Gossman, citing Burkhardt (2003) 160.

[65] In Mowl (1996) 257. Walpole developed his liking of the *petite histoire* following a tour round France, during which he met Voltaire.

[66] Burke (1986) 164, 175. For commentaries on the ironic in Burke's 'history', see White (1978) 96–97; and Ward (2018) 29–36.

yobs; the English and American revolutions were the business, in the most literal sense, of gentlemen.

The implication is that any narrative coherence is discovered as much in the historian as the history. If you want to know the history, as EH Carr affirmed, you first need to know the historian.[67] A second Twain quote, this time of more certain provenance, reverts the metaphor, and twists the insight:

> There is no such thing as an original idea. It is impossible. We simply take a lot of old ideas and put them into a sort of kaleidoscope. We give them a turn and they make new combinations indefinitely; but they are the same old pieces of glass that have been in use throughout the ages.[68]

History as an impressionistic discipline, every historian shaped by the prejudices of their predecessors. Refashioning the poetry of the past, as Rorty avers. Absent originality, history can only rhyme.

From the Greek *rhythmos*, to flow. In classical Greece, the term was originally applied to dancers, as they moved through momentary poses. It would become more familiar in sculpture, appraising the ability to capture movement whilst creating something inevitably static. Not that any of this precludes the reason of history. 'Here is rhyme, not empty of reason', as Ben Jonson put it.[69] But it does make us rethink how reason is created, and history. We create the history, just as the sculptor creates the sculpture, and in the process we shape its reason. The play-wright David Hare refashions the metaphor. Referring more closely to the writing of *verbatim* or docu-drama, Hare likens himself to a beachcomber: 'You find the driftwood on the beach, but you carve the wood and paint it to make it art'.[70]

The purpose of this book is then to revisit the history of 1616, the shorter, the longer, and the longer still. We might have picked a different moment, as we have already noted. English constitutional history is hardly short of crises. We have alighted on 1616 in part because it has tended to assume a more modest place in English constitutional history. Absent the drama of usurped kings, or the appella-tion of 'great' reform acts, 1616 inhabits a place of relative neglect. But also, because there is a proposition to explore, consonant with Frederick Maitland's supposi-tion that Coke's writings represent a 'great dividing line' between the medieval and the modern.[71] The intimation of a critical moment, where the 'modern' history of Anglo-British constitutional law begins.[72] Akin perhaps to the so-called 'Philadelphia moment' in American constitutional history, or the seeding of a European 'union' in 1958.[73] And something else too, priced into the same

---

[67] Carr (2001) 38.
[68] Paine (1912) 2.251.
[69] *Volpone*, Prol.4, in Wilkes (1999) 229.
[70] Hare (2005) 29.
[71] See Allison (2007) 129.
[72] For the inference, see Sedley (2015) 123–24.
[73] See Siedentop (2011).

supposition. If 1616 was that kind of moment, it should be possible to 'trace' its presence, to follow its 'trail' as Ginzburg puts it.[74] To look for its rhyme and its reason, to vary the metaphor, so that we might better comprehend then and now, and the considerable in-between.

And then something more, a contingent conceit to which we have already gestured. The events of summer 1616 brought into collision three minds: those of James Stuart, Edward Coke and Francis Bacon. We need to read these minds, or at least try to, in part because it might help us to better appreciate what happened in that moment. But also because these same minds articulated differing ways of thinking about the constitution of England, literal and figurative. Ways that were rooted in their own histories, personal and intellectual, and which indeed import their own histories. But also, ways which have, once again, continued to resonate down the centuries. Our longer history continues to this point.

Crises are, by definition, discontinuous. They come and go; otherwise they would not really be crises. For which reason the temptation to revisit previous constitutional crises tends to press most when we feel ourselves to be living amidst another. Like today.[75] Context shifts of course. But even the briefest of comparisons between the England of 1616 and the 'great' Britain of today tempts us to suppose that there might be some cadence; the shifting nature of monarchy and the abuse of prerogative powers, the consequence of English exceptionalism and another 'break' with Rome, the vying claims of historical and scientific reason in the realms of what Bacon liked to term 'policy', the practice of law and governance. We will see.

It remains to signpost more precisely where we will be going on our journey into England's distant, and more recent, past. This book is about the perceptions of three men in summer 1616. The identification of the moment is our conceit. To an extent we are doing what Stewart did when he tried to read the mind of George Pickett, or Ginzburg in the case of Mennochio, his unfortunate miller. We have already recognised a significant difference. A collateral aspiration of anecdotal history is the desire to retrieve quieted voices.[76] It is not the case here. Whilst much of what we know of Pickett is filtered through the reminiscences of his devoted wife, and in Menocchio's case courtesy of an inquisitorial clerk, our three wrote copiously, chiefly about themselves.

Our first chapter sets course, taking us back to Reformation England. We will find a people both blessed and cursed, chosen by God to lead a crusade against the papal anti-Christ, but seemingly unable to find tranquillity in their calling. So many changes, from the experience of Sunday morning worship, to the very idea of English kingship. The Reformation was as much a cultural and constitutional, as it was a theological, experience. Having orientated ourselves, we will

---

[74] Ginzburg (2012) 1.

[75] See Esler (2021) 221, suggesting that the UK is 'sliding at a glacial pace into a constitutional crisis'; maybe not that glacial.

[76] Lepore (2001) 131, 141.

then concentrate our attention on our three protagonists. Starting with James Stuart. The succession of a new monarch was always a challenge in medieval and early modern England, a new dynasty more so still. The succession of James Stuart was no exception. It was not simply the difficulty of succeeding Gloriana, Queen Elizabeth I, the hardest of acts to follow. It was the fact that James seemed so very foreign and had written so many unsettling things about kingship and law. He was only invited because there was no one else.

A dozen years lay between the coronation of King James I of England, and his decision to dispense with the services of his Lord Chief Justice. Not all were difficult, but too many became so. We will trace this history from Coke's perspective in our third chapter, where we will encounter a Chief Justice who increasingly felt himself to be embarked on his own crusade, not just against the Church of Rome, but against its mutant legal culture. Coke did not fear the despatch of the common law by the civil, at least not in the simpler sense. But he did fear that England's new King rather fancied himself in the garb of a Roman emperor, still more the idea of ruling like one. A suspicion very probably shared by Sir Francis Bacon. Less troubled though, in part because he rather admired the Romans; the way they thought and wrote, and got things done. What mattered to Bacon was what worked, and why. Rather more a man of the theatre too, appreciative that politics is just as much a matter of art as it is of reason, natural or historical. We will take a closer look at Bacon, his politics and his thinking, in our fourth chapter.

After which we will turn our attention to matters of elevation and the afterlife. Each of our protagonists craved an apotheosis, to be raised in our imagination and estimation. Posterity is, though, fickle. As Bacon recognised in his unfinished essay 'Of Fame', bemoaning the likelihood that future 'poets' would paint an inconstant and unflattering image. The 'Poets make Fame a Monster', writing the 'false' alongside the 'true'. So 'many Tongues; so Many Voyces'.[77] Ironic and prescient. Over the course of four centuries Bacon's ideas on matters of law, and everything else, would evolve. As would those of James Stuart and Edward Coke. Rethought, reimagined, rewritten by coming generations, variously in admiration and not. Any afterlife is necessarily speculative, and the intellectual is no exception. But that is in the nature of ironic and inferential history. It requires a willingness to speculate, to reach back into a past that is always, to the greater degree, imagined.

After which we will, finally, catch up with the present. To contemplate the 'condition' of early-twenty-first-century Britain, as it staggers uncertainly and ill-temperedly forwards. Stretched to its geopolitical breaking-point, ravaged by another plague, struggling to make constitutional, as well as cultural, sense of another 'break' with Rome. We might, as we proceed, recall Jean-Baptiste Alphonse Karr's familiar adage. It was Karr, renowned dahlia-cultivator and minor French novelist of the mid-nineteenth century, who coined the phrase '*Plus ca change, plus c'est la meme chose*'. Another evidently attracted towards the idea of rhyming

---

[77] Bacon (1985) 256.

history. A lover of the theatre too.[78] Which is where we will start, albeit a London theatre, rather than a Parisian, and in a rather different moment. On 29 June 1616 in fact, just three days after James had ordered Coke's removal from the Privy Council, at the Globe Theatre, on the south bank of the Thames. In the company of England's greatest playwright, arguably its greatest Queen, a renowned diplomat, and a very careless stage-manager.

---

[78] And the pretty actresses who walked its stage. Karr was one of the many lovers of the scandalous Juliet Drouet. Shortly after they met, Drouet was catapulted to stardom, playing the role of the murder-ous Princess Negrozi in Victor Hugo's *Lucrezia Borgia*, which premiered at La Scala in Milan early 1833. At which point she dumped Karr for Hugo. A winsome Juliet can still be seen in a pencil sketch from 1832, just before fame hit. A rather stonier Juliet can also be seen in the Place de la Concorde in Paris. Representing 'Strasbourg' in the imagination of the sculptor James Pradier, another *amour*. The lovelorn Karr, meanwhile, retired to the south of France and started cross-pollinating his dahlias.

1

Reformation

On the late afternoon of 29 June 1613, Sir Henry Wotton took his seat in the Globe Theatre, to watch a 'new' play written by William Shakespeare. It was entitled *King Henry VIII*, and carried the subtitle *All is True*. It would prove to be a peculiarly exciting performance, for the reason which Sir Henry subsequently reported to a friend:

> Now, King Henry making a Masque at Cardinal Wolsey's House, and certain canons being shot off at his entry, some of the Paper, or other stuff wherewith one of them was stopped, did light a thatch, where … it kindled inwardly, and ran round like a train, consuming within less than an hour the whole House to the very grounds.[1]

The more superstitious might have sensed a portent. Sir Henry, very much a man of the world, was probably not one of them. A diplomat by profession, remembered for the aphorism that 'an ambassador is an honest gentlemen sent to lie abroad for the good of his country'. We can reasonably assume that Sir Henry was well attuned to the art of dissimulation; he had also trained as a barrister before becoming 'our man' in Venice.[2] For which reason we might further wonder just how much of *Henry VIII* he really thought was 'true'. It moved, he attested, around 'some principal pieces' of the King's reign. We shall contemplate which 'pieces' very shortly.

Before we do, though, we might ponder congruity. Few histories of England spend long in 1613. A couple of marriages might catch the eye. First, towards the end of the year, that of the King's favourite, Robert Carr, Earl of Somerset, to Frances Howard, the very recently divorced wife of the Earl of Essex. Sadly, not a happy marriage, as we will see. Frances would end up in the Tower on charges of murder, along with Robert. The other was the marriage of the Princess Elizabeth to the Elector Palatine, Prince Frederick. The seeding of the Hanoverian succession, and a match which was supposed to reinforce England's presence at the vanguard of the protestant cause; albeit an essentially non-combative presence. It has been surmised that *Henry VIII* might have been written in celebration of the event. The more percipient legal historian might also note a judicial appointment in the early

---

[1] Smith (1907) 2.32.
[2] Ambassador at the palace of the Doge, from 1604 to 1624, with a couple of short breaks, including from 1613 to 1614, during which time he was able to enjoy some of London's theatre life. We will, by a coincidence which is not that strange in truth, return to Venice later in the chapter.

autumn of 1613. That of Sir Edward Coke as Lord Chief Justice of England and Wales. The pinnacle of a career, it might be assumed. Not by Sir Edward, though, reported to have been reduced to tears at the prospect.

The years 1613 to 1616 frame our shorter history. The longer, as we have already intimated, stretches back rather further, at least a century, perhaps a millennium. Our present purpose is to reconcile these histories. An aspiration which brings us back to *The Famous History of the Life of King Henry the Eight*, as it was entitled in the First Folio edition of Shakespeare's plays, published in 1623. One of the last of the Bard's plays, by common account, and almost certainly a joint composition with his protégé, John Fletcher.[3] The only 'history' that Shakespeare wrote following the death of Queen Elizabeth, and necessarily tendentious, because the play was at least as much about Gloriana as it was her father. Which meant that it could only be reflective of her successor too. As was the case with all the 'histories', the choice of moment was pivotal, and the 'principal pieces' about which Shakespeare chose to write moved around Henry's divorce from his first wife Katherine of Aragon. There were alternatives. He might, most obviously perhaps, have written a romantic 'tragedy' about the fall of Anne Boleyn. But instead, he preferred to focus the attention of his audience on the colder constitutional ramifications of the Henrician Reformation.[4]

The historical background to the divorce is familiar, and can be briefly recounted. Henry met Anne in summer 1525. She was charming and pretty, he was irascible, and used to getting his own way. Anne made it plain that she would not become his mistress, only his wife, which meant that Henry must divorce Queen Katherine. A tricky situation for a variety of reasons, foremost of which was securing papal approval; from a Pope who was, in the moment, cowering in Castel Sant'Angelo in Rome, besieged by the army of Charles V, the Holy Roman Emperor and Katherine's nephew.[5] Resolving the 'great matter', as Henry termed it, fell to Cardinal Thomas Wolsey.[6] The Pope, Clement VII, agreed to establish a Legatine Court. What he did not agree to was a decretal commission which would vest full authority in Wolsey to determine the 'matter'.[7] Worse still, he decided to despatch Cardinal Lorenzo Campeggio to help out. Just the man for the job, a serial procrastinator who had managed to prevent the Diet of Nuremberg from resolving anything in 1524, and would do so again at the Diet of Augsburg in 1530, in the process driving Melanchthon to despair.[8]

---

[3] On the question of authorship, see Mincoff (1961) 239–61; and Ward (2018).

[4] The only 'history' in which there are no battles either; if indeed it can be properly termed a history.

[5] Only a few weeks earlier, a horrified Clement had watched the Emperor's troops, under the command of the Duke of Bourbon, sack the city. Confined to the Castel for over a year, Clement would eventually extricate himself to Orvieto, handing over some of his cardinals as hostages.

[6] The term was recorded by Sir Thomas More, following a conversation with the King whilst walking the gardens of Hampton Court, in late 1527. See Ackroyd (1998) 262–63.

[7] Precluding any appeal to Rome.

[8] It is thought that Campeggio might have carried a decretal commission with him, to grant Wolsey at his discretion.

Campeggio set off for England, very slowly, in early 1529, falling ill as soon as he landed at Dover. Finally arriving in London, he made it clear that his first recourse was to attempt some kind of reconciliation, or failing that negotiate a separation settlement.[9] He wondered if Katherine might like to take a vow of chastity and enter a nunnery. She would not; 'stiff and obstinate', it was reported.[10] A four-hour interview with Henry was no more productive, as Campeggio reported back to Rome. An 'angel descending from Heaven would be unable to persuade' the King to reconcile. His love for Anne was 'quite pitiable' and 'on it depends his life, and the destruction or survival of the kingdom', or so Henry maintained.[11] Henry claimed that his marriage to Katherine had offended God, for which reason they were unable to have children. Leviticus 18:16: 'Thou shalt not uncover the nakedness of thy brother's wife, it is thy brother's nakedness'. Reinforced at 20:21: 'If a man shall take a brother's wife, it is an impurity; he hath uncovered his brother's nakedness; they shall be childless'.[12] Katherine had previously been married to Henry's elder brother, Arthur, who had died in 1502.[13]

There was no compromise to be negotiated. The scene was set, literally. The Legatine Court convened at Blackfriars on 15 June 1529. The star-turns appeared on 21 June. Henry sat beneath a canopy of gold, Katherine fell to her knees and pleaded wifely devotion. And then departed, ignoring the request of the court-crier to return. Instead, she invoked a right to appeal to Rome. Precisely what Campeggio expected and Wolsey dreaded. The Court went into recess, on the grounds that it was time for the summer holidays. Henry was reported furious.[14] Wolsey was dismissed from Privy Council a few months later.[15] Meanwhile Campeggio went home. Leaving the seminaries of Catholic Europe to contemplate the more esoteric matters of legatine jurisprudence.[16] Three and a half years

---

[9] For a comment on Campeggio's strategy, see Loades (2009) 198–201.

[10] Wolsey had reportedly begged on his knees, in the same cause. See Scarisbrick (1997) 194, 214–15.

[11] Gwyn (1990) 513; and also Ives (1988) 115.

[12] As ever, there is counter-testament. In Deuteronomy 15:5: 'When brethren dwell together, and one of them dieth without children, the wife of the deceased shall not marry another, but his brother shall take her, and raise up seed for his brother'.

[13] For which reason Henry had only married Katherine, seven years later in 1509, under papal dispensation. His father, Henry VII, had briefly considered stepping into the breach and marrying Katherine. But in the end, left it to his son.

[14] His anger was conveyed to Campeggio by the Dukes of Norfolk and Suffolk in person. The King had given 'a great clap on the table and said "by the Mass, now I see that the old said saw is true, that there was never legate nor cardinal that did good in England"'. See Scarisbrick (1997) 227; and Bernard (2005) 35–40.

[15] In the October, when he was further served with a writ of *praemunire*, having derogated from the sovereignty of the King by the very fact of sitting on the Legatine Commission. Having scurried away to York, the following spring he was called to London to answer charges of treason, dying along the way in Leicester.

[16] It was possible that the bull of dispensation, issued by Pope Julius in 1503, was ultra vires, thus making the marriage void. There was also the question as to whether Katherine's marriage to Arthur had been consummated. She said 'no'. Others wondered why two perfectly healthy teenagers would have decided not to consummate for the full seven months they were married, and living together. Moreover, there was authority in St Thomas Aquinas for the principle *societas conjugalis*, which supposed that simply living together was enough to construct consummation.

passed, until it was discovered that Anne was pregnant. They married in secret in January 1533. An event the legality of which was confirmed by an obliging Archbishop Cranmer on 28 May 1533, five days after the formal annulment of Henry's marriage to Katherine. The 'great whore', as the Spanish Ambassador called her, was crowned on 1 June. Four months later she gave birth to the 'little whore', the Princess Elizabeth. The marriage would last a thousand days, ending when Anne was convicted, and executed, on charges of adultery, witchcraft and incest. Led astray by a 'frail and carnal lust'.[17] By then Henry had broken with the Church of Rome, and established his own in its place; a revolution to which we will shortly turn our attention.

Once we have taken a closer look at what Shakespeare made of it all. There are two scenes in *Henry VIII* which warrant our particular attention. The first describes the events of 21 June, presented in the form of a judicial masque in Act 4 Scene 2.[18] Reconvened for two related purposes. The first is to decry the processes, and the pretence, of a 'Romish' legatine court. The second is to bear witness to where 'mightiness meets misery' (Prol 30). The human consequence of political machination; a 'good queen', of 'sweet gentleness', betrayed, not so much by her husband as by her Church (2.1. 158; 2.4. 135). It is Katherine who steals the scene, calmly arguing her case whilst Henry blusters, and the two Cardinals try to hide their embarrassment.

The second scene of especial interest comes at the close, with Cranmer's speech in which he prophesies the 'wonders' of the coming reign of the infant Elizabeth (5.4. 55). Hardly her first appearance in the canon, as we shall see. But Shakespeare had never said, quite so plainly, what he had Cranmer say:

> This royal infant (heaven still move about her)
>
> Though in her cradle, yet now promises
>
> Upon this land a thousand blessings …
>
> In her days every man shall eat in safety
>
> Under his own vine what he plants, and sing
>
> The merry songs of peace to all his neighbours.
>
> God shall be truly known, and those about her
>
> From her shall read the perfect ways of honour,
>
> And by those claim their greatness, not by blood (5.4. 17–20, 33–38).

Gloriana in her all her prospective glory. And a remarkable intervention, written not just for the likes of Sir Henry Wotton, and his fellow theatre-goers, but for Elizabeth's successor. James is not quite forgotten. Elizabeth will 'leave her blessedness' to a successor who will be known by the 'greatness of his name' (5.4. 43, 51). But still, it is pretty obvious to whom God had first turned, to finish His reformation.

[17] Guy (1988) 141.
[18] With the most extensive stage directions in the canon.

Reformation

It is understandable if the Henrician Reformation was thought to be a princi-pally religious experience. God certainly mattered. But who mattered most, in the moment, was Henry's Secretary of State, Thomas Cromwell, and the team of lawyers he pulled together to write it up. There is a broader context here. An appreciation, that 'divers Laws' had 'now grown insufficient and imperfect', as Sir Thomas More had put it on assuming office as Lord Chancellor in 1529. That too many of these laws, as another Lord Chancellor, Sir Thomas Audley, shortly after agreed, were so 'perfectly unknown' as to be of 'no small hurt of the republic'.[19] England needed a reformation of its laws, it seemed, just as much as it needed a reformation of its church.[20] And, it transpired, a constitutional renaissance. A process which would, in the end, consume centuries.

Stacks of Statutes

Starting with a legislative blitz. The 'stacks of statutes' which William Lambarde would later account, in his *Eirenarcha*. The passage of an Act in Restraint of Annates in 1532 set the tone.[21] A taste of the likely financial cost if the Pope did not grant Henry his divorce. Followed a year later by an Act in Restraint of Appeals.[22] Henceforth, any appeal made from an English court to the 'Bishop of Rome' would 'incur and run into the dangers and pains, and penalties contained and limited in the Acts of Provision and Praemunire'.[23] Maitland would suppose that the Acts 'in restraint' affirmed the exclusivity of common law jurisdiction in English law.[24] So far as Church courts continued to operate, they would, as Henry reminded the Bishop of Durham, do so at 'our sufferance'.[25] And just to impress the fact, Henry had a number of senior clergy served with cautionary writs of *praemunire*; a gesture which persuaded Convocation to make a humble 'submission', and offer up a subsidy of £100,000.

The lawyers did not, however, stop there. In March 1534, Parliament passed a Succession Act which confirmed that, in the event of any subsequent male heir, the Crown would pass to Princess Elizabeth, rather than her elder, but conspicu-ously Catholic sister, Mary.[26] Eight months later, an Act Respecting the Oath to the

---

[19] Shapiro (2019) 13–14.

[20] See here Shapiro (2019) 11–13, 39–41.

[21] 23 Hen.VIII c.20. The Act limited to 5% the amount of annates that could be remitted to Rome; the rest to be diverted to the Exchequer. An annate was effectively a Church tax.

[22] 24 Hen.VIII c.12.

[23] The penalties to include escheat, confiscation of chattels, and imprisonment at the 'king's pleasure'.

[24] Maitland (1898) 92.

[25] Scarisbrick (1997) 279–80.

[26] 25 Hen.VIII c.22. The fall of Anne Boleyn necessitated a hasty revision, a second Act of Succession in 1536, bastardising Elizabeth. A third Succession Act, of 1543, tried to tidy matters up, restoring the natural succession, from Prince Edward to Princess Mary to Princess Elizabeth.

Succession was passed, designed to flesh out the recalcitrant.[27] For the especially recalcitrant there was a reinvested Treason Act, encompassing not only those who 'maliciously wish, will or desire by words of writing' to harm the King, but any who seek to 'deprive' him of his 'dignity' by pronouncing him to be a 'heretic, schismatic, tyrant, infidel or usurper of the crown'.[28] An Act Extinguishing the Authority of the Bishop of Rome, passed in 1536, was similarly directed towards anyone who 'by writing, ciphering, printing or teaching, deed or act' sought to 'defend the authority, jurisdiction or power of the Bishop of Rome'.[29]

Still the statutes flowed. A couple more intended to starve papal coffers further. Albeit only a little in the case of an Act Concerning Peter's Pence and Dispensations, which deprived Rome of a customary parochial collection of £200.[30] An Act Concerning Ecclesiastical Appointments and the Absolute Restraint of Annates removed the remaining 5 per cent of annates payments that might be remitted to Rome. More importantly, perhaps, it entrusted all Church appointments to the Crown.[31] Successive Dissolution Acts added a bit of legislative gloss to the pillaging of the monasteries. The capstone of the settlement was the Act of Supremacy, passed in November 1534.[32] And then, two years later, came the first of a series of dissolution statutes, designed to break monastic resistance and resuscitate the Exchequer.[33]

Henry VIII died on 28 January 1547, his conscience apparently wracked. He was succeeded by his nine-year-old son, Edward, and a regency council, led by his uncle, the Duke of Somerset. Ardent protestants both. Unlike Edward's sister Mary, who succeeded in 1553. Loyal to her mother's faith, 'bloody' Mary, as she would be famously characterised in Foxe's *Book of Martyrs*, instigated a Counter-Reformation designed to return England to Rome. A project cut short by Mary's death in autumn 1558, and the succession of her 25-year-old sister, Elizabeth.[34] Just as Cranmer prophesied, half a century later.

At the top of the new Queen's lengthy 'to-do' list was the pressing matter of countering the effects of Counter-Reformation. To which purpose two new statutes were drafted. The first was an Act of Supremacy. Passed within a matter of months, and not that new in truth. A quarter of a century earlier, a similar Act had confirmed Henry as 'Supreme Head' of the newly established Church, vested with authority to 'repress' all 'errors, heresies ... and enormities'. The Act

---

[27] 26 Hen.VIII c.2.

[28] 26 Hen.VIII c.13.

[29] 28 Hen.VIII c.10.

[30] 25 Hen.VIII c.21. 'Peter's pence' was an annual levy collected by English parishes, limited by custom to £200.

[31] 25 Hen.VIII c.20.

[32] 26 Hen.VIII c.1.

[33] A first wave of dissolutions, following the first Act in 1536, realised around £100,000, together with £32,000 pa income. Cromwell established a Court of Augmentation to help with the auditing. A second Dissolution Act followed in 1539.

[34] Conspicuously absent amongst the *dramatis personae* of *Henry VIII*, Princess Mary was 17 at the moment in which the play is set.

of 1558 was necessary because Mary had repealed the 1534 Act. The new Act of Supremacy duly confirmed that Elizabeth was 'Supreme Governor' of the English Church, enjoying 'all honours, dignities, pre-eminences, jurisdictions, privileges, authorities, immunities, profits and commodities to the said dignity'.[35] Put simply, everything that had been formerly owed to the Pope, was now owed to her. The second of the new statutes, enacted a few months later in early 1559, was the Act of Uniformity. Here again, the idea was not entirely new. Similar Acts had been passed in 1549 and 1552, both purposed to enshrine the liturgy prescribed in the *Book of Common Prayer*.[36] The Elizabethan Act added provisions intended to address church attendance, establishing an escalated system of penalties for non-attenders, starting with fines of 12 pence and finishing with life imprisonment.[37]

In essence, Elizabeth's lawyers simply traced over the original statutory template, emphasising the bits that mattered most: that she was the 'supreme governor' of the Church, and that all her subjects were expected to worship in the same way. The order of worship set by a 'common' *Book of Prayer*, the matter of conformity reaffirmed in the various homilies and sermons read out each and every Sunday to captive parishioners. Where the reasoning was presented in both lighter and darker tones. The *Homilie against disobedience and wilfull rebellion* drew on Romans 13: 1–7 and Peter 2: 13–18 to confirm that 'it was most evident that kings, queens and other princes (for He speaketh of authority and power be it in men or women) are ordained of GOD, are to be obeyed and honoured of their subjects; that such subjects, as are disobedient or rebellious against their princes, disobey GOD and procure their own damnation'.

Before endorsing what everyone was supposed to know already, that 'the nearer and nearer that an earthly prince doth come in his regiment the greater blessing of GOD's mercy is he unto that country and people over whom he reigneth'. The *Sermon of Obedience*, meanwhile, made very clear the contrary consequence: 'all abuse, carnall libertie, enormitie, synne and Babilonical confusion'. Thus the need for a 'supreme governor', chosen by God, to ensure the 'uniformity' of the secular and the spiritual. In the 'very solemnities and rites' of office, as the clerical jurist Richard Hooker put it, applicable from prince to parish priest.[38]

Hooker's Harp

We might pause to take a closer look at Hooker, and more especially at his *Laws of Ecclesiastical Polity*, the first four volumes of which were published in 1594, a fifth three years later, and the final three posthumously in 1600. Hooker was a

---

[35] 1 Eliz.1 c.1.
[36] 1 Eliz.1 c.2.
[37] A fine of 100 marks awaiting anyone discovered attending a Mass; double the amount for anyone giving a Mass.
[38] Hooker (1989) 147.

man of the cloth, who had spent much of his career in London, serving latterly as rector of the Temple church in the Inns of Court since 1585. An exciting, if undoubtedly wearying position, as assorted Presbyterian ministers mounted an increasingly bitter assault on High Church ritualism. The so-called 'battle of the pulpits'; between those who continued to devour the 'garlicke and onions of Aegypt' and those who preferred the 'milk and honey' of Christ's testament.[39] The words of John King, future Bishop of London; very much a 'milk and honey' man.

Whilst he might have eschewed anything that smacked of confrontation, Hooker would likewise have identified himself on the 'milk and honey' side of the argument. Above all, though, he was a man of the 'established' Church. Protégé of Edwin Sandys, Archbishop of York, to whom he owed his preferment, and John Jewel, Bishop of Salisbury, author of the 1562 *Apology of the Anglican Church*. There was a lot of Jewel's *Apology* in Hooker's *Laws*.[40] Most obviously the tone of assurance. The purpose of the *Laws of Ecclesiastical Polity* was to settle, the nerves of the 'chosen' people, and the body of their constitution. Written, in other words, in aid of getting the English Reformation done, finally; or more accurately, persuading its readers that it was already done.

In 1595, Hooker had moved to the rather more peaceable surroundings of Bishopsbourne on the Kentish Weald. A place more conducive to his greater ambition, which was to complete a comprehensive defence of the Elizabethan settlement, whilst at the same time lending some clarity to the constitutional law of Reformation England. The need for the latter was implicit in the burgeoning market for commentaries, abridgements and various ancillary texts on matters of common and Church law, all advertising themselves as handbooks, not just for lawyers, but for interested gentlemen. Texts such as Lambarde's *Eirenarcha*, Fraunce's *Lawyer's Logicke*, and Plowden's *Commentaries* and *Abridgement*. The latter was a particular inspiration for Sir Edward Coke, whose similarly purposed writings we will shortly revisit. As we will those of Sir Francis Bacon, who was just as much impressed by Plowden's ambition, if not so much his product.

Others still, such as Rastell's *Exposition of the Terms of the Laws of England*, Pulton's *Abstract of all the Penal Statutes*, and Barker's *Collection in English, of all the statutes now in force, from Magna Carta to the third year of Elizabeth's reign*, revealed a collateral concern. The idea that statutory law was in urgent need of tidying up resonated most especially amongst common lawyers of a more grudging disposition, many of whom detected in the use of statutes a strategy designed to buttress government by prerogative. The complaint was not so much about the statutes which comprised the Reformation 'settlement', as the tone that had been set. A culture of casual disregard for the sanctity of the common law which,

---

[39] Walsham (2012) 924.

[40] Just as there was a lot of Melanchthon's *Augsburg Confession* in Jewel's *Apology*, and a lot of Luther's *Babylonian Captivity* too. The latter being useful for its ringing denunciation of Catholic abuses. The *Apology* was, though, a much more political commentary, geared to defending the particular virtues of the English Reformation.

according to the more neurotic, or maybe perspicacious, meant that little stood between England and Catholic absolutism. Aside, that is, from the sagacity of a particular monarch. All of which added an edge to the growing realisation that the age of Gloriana was approaching its close.

It was this anxiety which Hooker set out to moderate, by assuring his readers of the constitutional integrity of the Reformation settlement. The attention of the legal historian is directed more closely to the first book of the *Laws*, which treats 'laws in general', and the last book, on matters of civil governance. And there is nothing, in a sense, especially controversial here. Which was the point. The purpose of the *Laws* was to confirm a 'natural' affinity between divine injunction and the historical reason of English law. The jurisprudential foundation is discovered in the Aristotelian 'common good', and the assertion that people 'naturally' crave 'commonwealth' because they are 'induced to seek communion and fellowship with others'.[41]

Hooker was hardly alone in seeking recourse to classical, more specifically Aristotelian, authority. Thomas Smith did likewise in his *Commonwealth of England*, and Sir Thomas Elyot in his *Boke named the Governor*, albeit preferring the term 'public weal'.[42] Both specifically purposed for Reformation England and hugely influential. As were Sir John Fortescue's treatises on *The Governance of England* and *In Praise of the Laws of England*, which would be freshly printed in 1567, 1573 and 1599. In Fortescue's opinion, the English constitution was not only 'good, but the very best'. First, because it was governed *dominium regale*, by law and king. And second, because its 'common law' had evolved in accordance with Aristotelian principles of equity and natural justice.[43] And it is with this premise in mind, Hooker affirmed, that the laws of Reformation England were written; the closest approximation of civil to natural law, rational and 'measured' too. They are 'the very soul of a political body, the parts whereof are by the law animated, held together, and set on work in such actions as the common good requireth'.[44]

Critical here is the role of the Crown, as head of both the civil and the spiritual state. In a truly Christian state, the interests of Church and commonwealth are necessarily aligned, and it is the principal responsibility of an English monarch to ensure that this is so. For which reason, the logic runs, so too must this monarch enjoy a supervening juridical authority. Here again Aristotle was deployed to add assurance. A measured legal system needs an 'equitable' jurisdiction. But the measure also bounds the King. Equity, Hooker emphasises, is an expression of natural law, given by God, framed by human reason. Which, in England, means the common law. The Reformation settlement, at least that described in Hooker's *Laws*, pivoted on this point.

---

[41] Hooker (1989) 79–80.

[42] On the ground that the 'common weal … signifieth only the multitude wherein be contained the base and vulgar inhabitants not advanced to any honour or dignity'. In Briggs (1997) 19.

[43] Fortescue (1997) 26–27, 83–87.

[44] Hooker (1989) 87–88.

The necessary implications are drawn in the eighth chapter of the final book of the *Laws*. Following a brief discourse on the risks of reducing equitable discretion to 'private persuasion', as exemplified by certain later Roman emperors, Hooker glowingly endorsed the 'better' settlement of a 'reformed' England:

> In this respect therefore we must needs think the state of our own laws have with far more certainty prescribed bounds unto each kind of power. All decisions of things doubtful and corrections of things amiss are proceeded in by order of law, what person soever he be unto whom the administration of judgement belongeth. It is neither permitted unto Prelates nor Prince to judge or determine at their own discretion, but law hath prescribed what both shall do. What power the king hath he hath it by law, the bounds and limits of it are known. The entire community giveth general order by law how all things publicly are to be done and the King as the head thereof the highest authority over all causeth according to the same law every particular to be framed and ordered thereby.[45]

The law 'frames' the king. A point worth repeating:

> The whole body politic maketh the laws which laws give power unto the King and the King having bound himself to use according unto law that power, is to falleth out that the execution of the one is accomplished by the other in most religious and peaceable sort.[46]

Isaak Walton, Hooker's first biographer, would later record the admiration of King James I. 'I observe that there is in Mr Hooker no affected language, but a grave, comprehensive, clear manifestation of reason and that backed with the authorities of the Scriptures, the fathers and schoolmen, and with all law both sacred and civil', James is said to have remarked. On every page of the *Laws* could be found 'such pictures of truth and reason, and drawn in so sacred colours, that they shall never fade, but give an immortal memory to the author'.[47] It might, at first glance, seem an incongruous statement. As we will see in the next chapter, James did not much like the idea of 'prescribed' kingship. Hooker's comment, a little earlier in the same chapter, that any royal 'grant' made 'contrary to law is void', might have made him blanch too.[48]

There was some room for interpretive manoeuvre, as we have already noted. And a renowned metaphor, to ease the mood:

> Happier the people whose law is their king in the greatest things that that whose King is himself their law. Where the King doth guide the state and the law the King, that commonwealth is like an harp or melodious instrument, the strings whereof are tuned and handled all by one hand, following as laws the rules and canons of Musical science.[49]

---

[45] Hooker (1989) 217.

[46] Hooker (1989) 217.

[47] Morley (1888) 67. James even asked about the possibility of meeting Hooker, when he arrived in London in 1603. Not realising that Hooker had died three years earlier. In truth, it was the theological commentary that James especially admired.

[48] Hooker (1989) 147.

[49] Hooker (1989) 146–47.

A touching choice, the harp was said to be Elizabeth's favourite instrument, famed for its tonal purity. As for James, no shortage of similar pleas for harmony in various writings and speeches, as we will shortly see. Less evidence of fine-tuning though. All of which leaves us to ponder the place of Hooker's *Laws of Ecclesiastical Polity*, and the point. A text which can be read as a testament to both the aspirations of the Elizabethan Reformation, and the anxieties. Metaphors of resonance playing against moments of dissonance and doubt.

Grinding Courts

Hooker's *Laws*, like indeed the various homilies that were regurgitated every Sunday morning, were written to assure. Uniformity, though, required more than mere persuasion. It also needed enforcement. To this end the Act of Uniformity also established a regulatory body, the High Commission, for the purpose of rooting out:

> All and singular heretical opinions, seditious books, contempts, conspiracies, false rumours, tales, seditions, misbehaviours, slanderous words or shewings, published, invented or set forth by any person or persons against us, or contrary or against the laws and statutes of this realm.

Commonly referred to as a court by the 1580s, recognised explicitly as such in the 1593 Seditious Secretaries Act, the jurisdiction of the High Commission was bitterly resented by puritans, and their lawyers.[50] Not least because its sessions were commonly held *in camera*, with the accused obliged to subscribe an ex officio oath. Catholic inferences too easily laid; an 'ungodly and intolerable inquisition', as James Morice put it in his 1578 Middle Temple lecture.[51] We will, in due course, revisit some High Commission cases, and encounter plenty of embittered puritans.

The establishment of the High Commission is testament to a familiar truth about revolutions: they mutate, often alarmingly. The reformation of the law might have been intended to simplify. But its immediate consequence was more law, more litigants and more lawyers; the 'vipers of the commonwealth', as Lord Chancellor Ellesmere famously disparaged them.[52] Many squabbling over the ill-gotten gains which followed the dissolution of the monasteries, others cashing in on emergent markets at home and abroad. In 1560 there was roughly one lawyer for every 20,000 subjects. In 1640, it was one for every 25. More courts too.[53] In his *Reports*, Coke would list around a hundred, many smaller and regional. Some older, but plenty newer, such as the courts of Augmentation, First Fruits

---

[50] Baker (2017) 133–35.
[51] See Shapiro (2019) 45–46; and Baker (2017) 272.
[52] Brooks (1986) 139.
[53] Sir Geoffrey Elton famously referred to Cromwell's 'court-making industry'. See Elton (1973) 141–42.

and Tenths, and Wards and Liveries, each established in 1540 as part of the wider Reformation 'settlement'.

The greater constitutional controversies, though, moved around the central courts. There were three common law courts, King's Bench, Common Pleas, and Exchequer. King's Bench dealt with pleas of the Crown, its Lord Chief Justice appointed *in persona regis*. The role of Common Pleas, as confirmed in Article 17 of *Magna Carta*, was to hear disputes between subjects. The origins of Exchequer, as its name intimated, lay in revenue disputes. Barons of Exchequer were selected, as needed, from King's Bench and Common Pleas. In 1585, Elizabeth had further created an Exchequer Chamber, to hear appeals from the Exchequer Court and King's Bench.[54] The central courts would sit during four terms of approximately three weeks, sharing the load between 12 judges.[55] During the summer recess, the judges would go on 'assize', visiting the provinces to dispense justice and the King's 'majesty'.

In addition to the common law courts could be found an array of 'prerogative' courts, purporting to draw their authority from the person of the King. Some were more niche, such as the Court of Requests. Others assumed a greater presence. The origins of the Court of Chancery could be traced to the Norman *curia regis*, but had assumed a more familiar shape in the wake of the Black Death.[56] Presided over by the Lord Chancellor, the Court dispensed equitable relief, most commonly in property and trust cases. Something which made it seem a lot like a court of appeal. Common lawyers tended to view Chancery with at least suspicion, if not downright hostility. A place, Timothy Tourneur confirmed, of 'infinite vexation'.[57]

A view attested, from the alternative perspective, by Lord Chancellor Ellesmere who castigated a generation of gaming lawyers in his *Memorials*, trying to set 'verditte agaynst verditte, and by judgement agaynst judgement, and by manifoulde sutes in severall Courtes for one and the self same cause'. The end result was an increasingly fractious profession serving an ever more vexatious clientele. A legal system, Ellesmere resolved, brought to its knees by an 'infinite multiplycitye of sutes'.[58] Tourneur and Ellesmere were not natural allies, indeed they would have probably blamed each other. On this though they were in agreement, the reformation of English law had become an unholy mess, literally. The matter of operational chaos and jurisdictional dispute were inextricably bound.

And it was not just Chancery. The Reformation had resuscitated a second prerogative court, and founded a third. Whereas Chancery concerned itself with

---

[54] The Chamber would commonly recruit two judges each from the Exchequer Court and King's Bench. In the celebrated, and rather later, 1686 case of *Godden v Hales*, Justice Herbert would liken it to a supreme court, which would 'never suffer' to have its rulings 'disputed or drawn in question again'. See Jones (1971) 50.

[55] Usually sitting in benches of three. Though, in more serious cases, occasionally sitting as a full bench.

[56] Palmer (1993) 130–31.

[57] Smith (2014) 243.

[58] Smith (2014) 45.

private disputes, these other two courts assumed a more public responsibility, designed to secure the safety of the realm. In a later chapter, we will discover Bacon deploying classical terminology to recast this distinction; between the 'Praetorian' Chancery and the 'Censorian' prerogative courts. We have already come across one of these courts, the newly minted High Commission. The other was Star Chamber. Established as the judicial arm of the King's Council in 1485, and originally purposed to hear allegations of abuse in public office, Star Chamber had broadened its remit over the intervening century, most notably to include cases of alleged seditious dissent.

John Milton would later categorise these Censorian courts in predictably disparaging terms. The 'grinding courts' of the popish counter-reformation, peddling their 'thir gibrish laws'.[59] Both Star Chamber and High Commission would be abolished in 1641, for having 'undertaken to punish where no law doth warrant'. A brute political solution to a seemingly intractable jurisprudential contention, which had pressed ever more closely since the 1530s: the relation of the King, his conscience, and the common law of England.

The Conscience of the King

The pragmatics of prerogative jurisdiction were inextricably bound up in these more esoteric matters, of equity and conscience. King James certainly perceived his Chancery Court in these terms. A court of 'conscience', where he could 'mixeth Mercy with Justice, as it preserves men from destruction'.[60] Hake took a similar view in his *Epieikeia*, identifying a distinctive legal equity, 'drawne owte and derived allonly from the conscience of the Lord Chauncellor or Lord Keeper'.[61] So too, Bulstrode Whitelock, in his *Memorials*, published later in the seventeenth century. Whereas 'judges of the Common Law have certain rules to guide them; a Keeper of the Seals hath nothing but his own conscience to direct him'.[62] A king, a satirist, and a Cromwellian Commissioner of the Great Seal, each betraying the same appreciation, albeit evincing differing levels of enthusiasm.[63] And each reflecting further on the constitutional consequence of reformation.

The Length of the Chancellor's Foot

The history of English equity law is often told in these terms: the mutation of a canonist 'culture of equity' into a rule-based jurisprudence.[64] A process

---

[59] Milton (1991) 4–8.
[60] King James (1994) 214.
[61] Klinck (2010) 2.
[62] Klinck (2010) 3.
[63] The office of Commissioner of the Great Seal replaced that of Lord Keeper during the 1650s.
[64] Fortier (2005) 11.

complemented by the protestant denunciation of Catholic 'casuistry', and the investment of a 'grounded conscience', of the kind recommended by the likes of William Perkins and Richard Bernard, discovered in the laws of God, nature, and 'reason'.[65] Before the Reformation, Lord Chancellors were commonly drawn from the Church and, familiar with texts such as the *Summa Confessorum* and the *Summae de Casibus Conscientiae*, had conceived their role as a species of confessional. Guided by twin principles of canon law. First, to 'to know the will of God, as near as one reasonably can', as Fortescue put it. And second to discover the 'within' of every litigant, as Reginald Pecock alleged in his *Reule of Chrysten Religioun*.[66] The principles which Sir Thomas More famously proclaimed on succeeding to the Chancellorship. He would serve his King, but 'obey his God' first.

Few of his successors made so bold. In a reading given at the Inner Temple in 1526, Thomas Audley, who succeeded More as Chancellor, dismissed 'law called conscience, which is always uncertain and depends for the greater part on the *arbytrement* of the judge in conscience'.[67] Archbishop Cranmer agreed; a 'lesbian rule'. Christopher St German likewise; a mere 'pretence' of justice.[68] It was St German who mapped out the direction of travel in his treatise, *Doctor and Student*; a text which would exercise a profound influence on coming generations of common lawyer.[69] Henceforth, 'conscience' would be secured in the public person of the King, and English law interpreted in accordance with intrinsic principles of equity. So that equity 'foloweth the intent of the lawe' rather 'then the words of the lawe'.[70] A recommendation which bore a closer resemblance to the *aequitas* of Roman jurisprudence.[71] This was not to deny the 'swetnes of mercy' in the judgement of the King and his Chancellor, but recourse to equity will only succeed if it is 'reinforced by some subsidiary maxim of the law'.[72]

An elegant resolution, seemingly; the idea that equity should be present in all English law, Chancery existing simply to ensure that its presence is properly appreciated, and to cover the odd glitch, the occasional 'Oppression, Wrong or hard Conscience', as Ellesmere put it in the *Earl of Oxford's Case*.[73] It would find various similar expression in Hake's *Epieikeia*, for example, in the 'helpe that Chancery gyveth', and Robert Snagg's renowned Middle Temple reading in 1591.[74] There must be 'common' laws, Snagg acknowledged, otherwise the 'Golden Rule

---

[65] Klinck (2010) 114.

[66] See Klinck (2010) 17, 37; Coing (1955) 225; and also Simpson (1975) 377, 401. For a more cautious view, see Haskett (1996) 257, wondering about the extent to which medieval chancellors remained wedded to 'canonist' orthodoxy, at least in its more rigorous form.

[67] Guy (1985) 79–80.

[68] Guy (1985) 102; and Klinck (2010) 41–42.

[69] A first edition appeared, in Latin, in 1523. A second, judiciously amended and in English, appeared in 1530. By the turn of the century, it had gone through at least 20 reprints.

[70] Guy (1985) 99.

[71] A possibility discussed in Klinck (2010) 48–49.

[72] Guy (1985) 79.

[73] (1615) I Ch Rep 1; 21 ER 485.

[74] Klinck (2010) 102.

of Law' might become a 'Leaden Rule' bent to the 'will' of individual judges. There again, so too must there be a facility to 'mitigate where the Rule of Law would light too hard', where 'mischiefs' would otherwise flourish.[75]

The problem was, of course, perceptual; Chancery as complement or corrective? It might be a court dedicated to securing the natural justice discovered in the common law, or it might be the 'roguish thing' famously identified by John Selden, sustaining the whimsies of Catholic absolutism. Equity 'according to the conscience of the Chancellor', and nothing more, no more measurable than the length of his 'foot'.[76] A court of inquisition indeed, like Star Chamber and the High Commission, forever prying into the private consciences of Englishmen and women in order to discern their deeper 'intent'. So much depended on the 'good conscience' of the 'prince', as Elizabeth readily acknowledged, or so Coke would later recall, glowingly.[77] And that of his judges.

The Jacobean Justice, Sir John Doderidge, was certainly acute to the danger. Whilst 'conscience' might qualify the law, it must:

> Stand upon permanent Rules, as of Iron not to be bent or broken upon this or that occasion, or to be infringed upon this or that occurrence (for else there need be no Court of Law but all should be one with the Court of Conscience, and have their proceedings framed according to the Arbitrary conceipt of the Judge.[78]

Jurisprudential reservations, to be shaped and reshaped by political imperatives, a century of constitutional crises to come. There would be distractions, but the direction of progress remained steady. The last clerical appointment to the office of Lord Keeper was John Williams, Bishop of Lincoln, who succeeded Bacon in 1621. A man of God in his Church perhaps, and his soul, but in his office very much a man of law, fully appreciating that rules are necessary 'to keep the Keeper from Extravagancies of his own Fancies and Affections, and to hold him really to Conscience'. A position echoed a generation on by the Cromwellian Justice, Sir Matthew Hale. Conscience 'doth of necessity presuppose a Rule or Principle given unto Man'.[79]

The invocation of *scientia* sharpened the tone. '*Ubi non est scientia, non est conscientia*', Coke is said to have said. Even Restoration Tory clerics such as John Nalson agreed that here must be '*scientia* before *conscientia*'.[80] And Restoration Chancellors. 'There is some Science necessary', Lord Clarendon conceded, 'where there is Pretence to Conscience'.[81] By the close of the century, impelled by the needs of market stabilisation as well as political principle, the idea that equity

---

[75] In Klinck (2010) 90.
[76] Selden (1716) 37.
[77] Comments recalled from his interview with Elizabeth when appointed Attorney General in 1594. In Baker (2017) 148–49.
[78] In Klinck (2010) 153.
[79] Klinck (2010) 174, 189.
[80] Klinck (2010) 194.
[81] Klinck (2010) 259.

should be rule-bound was unarguable. So much that Lord Chancellor Nottingham could confirm that 'equity itself would cease to be Justice if the rules and measure of it were not certain and known'.[82] Matters of *conscientia politica et civilis* were his domain; those of *conscientia naturalis and interna* were for the philosophers and the priests.[83]

And maybe the poets. The task of crafting fictions to guise political fault-lines usually falls to them. Later medieval literature had tended to inscribe conscience as a purgation. In *Piers Plowman*, for example, where the king deploys 'Sir Conscience' to help dispel Worldly Wisdom and Cunning from his courts. The poets of the English Renaissance were tasked with something rather trickier: to provide a cultural accompaniment to constitutional revolution. A grand project, as we will see, at the centre of which was the inscription of kingly conscience, public and private. Shakespeare played with the dilemma repeatedly. In *Hamlet*, tasking his eponymous prince with the responsibility to 'catch the conscience of the king' (2.2. 537). In *Richard III*, creating a villain who is defined by his determination to reject the same:

> Conscience is a word that cowards use,
>
> Devised at first to keep the strong in awe.
>
> Our strong arms be our conscience, swords our law (5.3. 310–12).

A famously bad call. A year or so after he had dealt with the third Richard, Shakespeare turned his attention to the second, and wrote what is perhaps his most nuanced reflection on the nature of early modern kingship: the *Tragedy of King Richard II*.[84]

The Balm of an Anointed King

In which the Bard solicits his audience to reflect on various aligned aspects of the relation of conscience and prerogative. A first is the narrower jurisprudential debate, on the nature of early modern kingship. Here, as is commonly noted, Shakespeare is riffing on the idea of the 'king's two bodies', popular in later medieval political theology.[85] It supposed that the king had a 'body natural' and a 'body politic'. The latter being, in essence, his public office, and accordingly determined in what we might today term 'public' law. Whilst these bodies did not map precisely, there was a clear inference in regard to Crown prerogative. Thus, as Coke recognised in his prosecution of the Earl of Essex in 1601, an English monarch had 'two

---

[82] *Earl of Feversham v Watson*, 1678, reported in Yale (1961) 2.639. There were dissenting voices in the House of Lords, but Nottingham's view prevailed.

[83] *Cook v Fountain*, 1676, reported in Yale (1961) 1.371.

[84] Dating Shakespearean plays is rarely easy. The general consensus is that *Richard II* was probably completed in 1597. *Richard III*, is trickier still, but most likely written around 1595.

[85] The definitive statement found in Kantorowicz (1957). For a more recent commentary on the thesis in Shakespearean context, see Raffield (2010) 89–90.

kinds of prerogative, the one absolute and the other ordinary'. The first attaches to the person and is 'obeyed without dispute', and includes such matters as 'directing' wars, whereas the latter is 'decided by the laws of the realm'.[86] An echo could be heard a few years later, in Chief Justice Fleming's opinion in *Bate's Case*. The 'king's power is of two kinds, ordinary and absolute'. The former 'tends to the utility of every private subject by punishing offences', and is known to 'civilians' as 'private law, though in truth it is the common law itself'. The 'absolute power', conversely, is a matter of 'state and policy' rather than law, and is determined by the 'wisdom of the king, for the common good'.[87]

A second dimension of kingship upon which Shakespeare wants his audience to concentrate is the human dimension, the contingency of how particular kings weigh their public and private consciences. The charges brought against Richard Plantagenet alleged behaviour 'contrary to justice and the laws of his realm, and his oath'.[88] High on the list was corruption of judicial process.[89] Of the kind which Shakespeare writes into Act 1 Scene 3 of *Richard II*, when Richard intervenes to bring a hasty conclusion to the 'trial by combat' between his favourite Mowbray, and Bolingbroke. So 'that our kingdom's earth should not be soil'd/ With the dear blood that it has fostered' (1.3. 125–26). Both combatants, duly banished, feel that they have been unjustly treated, whilst Bolingbroke's father, John of Gaunt, perceives a further portent of the 'Devouring pestilence' which will shortly ravage the kingdom (1.3. 284). The figurative disease of the body-politic, a pandemic of constitutional and political chaos on the way.

The import of the scene can be read differently. At a more prosaic level, it can be interpreted as a critique of medieval customary justice. Arcane and ineffacious, and certainly not the way to settle disputes which touch the royal estate; not then, and not now. The mistake was not so much curtailing it, as encouraging it in the first place. It is tempting to wonder if Shakespeare was aware of James Stuart's notoriously dim view of duelling. In his *Basilicon Doron*, published in Scotland in early 1599, James soberly advised:

> Neither commit your quarrell to bee tried by a Duell: for beside that generally all Duell appeareth to be unlawful, committing the quarrel, as it were, to a lot; whereof there is no warrant in the Scripture, since the abrogating of the olde Lawe: it is specially moste unlawful in the person of a King; who being a publicke person hath no power therefore to dispose of himselfe, in respect, that to his preservation or fall, the safetie of wracke of the whole commonweale is necessarily coupled, as the body is to the head.[90]

We will revisit the *Basilicon*, and its various similar admonishments, in due course.

There is a more nuanced, and allusive, interpretation of Richard's intervention. It supposes that the customary law of trial by combat serves as *locum tenens*

---

[86] In Baker (2017) 145.
[87] (1606) 2 St Tr 371.
[88] In Baker (2017) 63.
[89] Chrimes (1956) 365–90.
[90] King James (1994) 32–33.

for the common law. Part of the law of the land which should not be abrogated at princely whim. Not that Richard would have thought it whim, but rather part of his divine right to rule. Later in the play, as he slowly comes to terms with his pending deposition, Richard muses on the nature, and 'brittle glory', of his kingship (4.1. 287). It is, in poetic terms, his finest moment. Invoking a succession of Christological images, Richard accuses those who have conspired his removal of 'cracking the strong warrant of an oath,/ Mark'd with a blot, damn'd in the book of heaven' (4.1. 235–36). Alluding to the anointing oil which confirmed his coronation, he declares that his 'own tears' will 'wash away my balm' (4.1. 207). And thus he will be 'unking'd'. By brute force, and by his own delusion. Trapped by his own magic, in a sense, his inability to distinguish his corporeal body from his kingly. It is only when he 'dashes' the 'flatt'ring glass' to the ground that Richard is released from his own spell (4.1. 279). And by then it is far too late. Act 1 Scene 3 is an early portent of what might happen when a prince fails to properly understand the relation of conscience and prerogative. Act 4 Scene 1 is the confirmation.

We might ponder a couple of anecdotes, both of which touch on the sensitivities of princely conscience. The first is more allusive, and invites us to wonder what, had he been alive, Shakespeare might have made of the 'tragedy' of King Charles I. If he had been moved to write it up, the fall of the Earl of Strafford would surely have caught his eye. More particularly still, the moment when Charles, agonising over whether he should give his assent to the Earl's attainder, had sought spiritual advice from his Archbishop of York, and former Lord Keeper, John Williams.[91] Williams reminded Charles that a king has both a 'Private and a Publick Conscience', and that the latter might, on occasion, 'oblige him to do that which was against his Private Conscience as a Man'.[92] About as close to casuistry as a reformed churchman could get, but politic. A few weeks later, Strafford was dead.

The second anecdote, which revisits *Richard II*, touches more closely on the sensitivities of Elizabeth Tudor. The antiquarian William Lambarde recorded Elizabeth visiting the Tower of London in August 1601. Five months had passed since the collapse of the Essex 'rebellion', but Elizabeth was evidently still living the moment. Their conversation 'fell upon the reign of Richard II', at which point Elizabeth exclaimed 'I am Richard II, know ye not that?' Lambarde would have muttered something emollient. Brooding a little longer, Elizabeth had continued, 'He that will forget God, will also forget his benefactors; this tragedy was played forty times in open streets and houses'.[93] The allusion was to a performance of *Richard II* commissioned by Essex the evening before his ill-judged meander along the Strand.[94] Not an intelligent move, for a variety of reasons. Not least because it confirmed what Cecil already suspected: that the Earl planned an insurrection.

---

[91] Williams had stepped down as Lord Keeper in 1625, on the death of James I.

[92] In Klinck (2010) 176.

[93] For commentaries on Lambarde's account of the event, see Barroll (1988); and Schoenbaum (1987) 217–19.

[94] Essex apparently sent a servant with £40 to persuade the Company.

It also placed Shakespeare, and his actors, in a potentially awkward situation. A couple of days later, Shakespeare was summoned to an interview with the Queen's 'Extraordinary Counsel', Francis Bacon.

A few months earlier, John Hayward had found himself in a similar predicament when Elizabeth had taken similar umbrage at passages written into his *Life and Reign of Henry IV*. Hayward had compounded his error by dedicating his *History* to Essex. Bacon could find no evidence of treason in Hayward's text, or demeanour; though there was plenty of 'felony', by which he meant shameless plagiarism, chiefly from the Roman historian Tacitus. Two things especially troubled Elizabeth about these histories of fated predecessors. First, that it might be a fate shared, the inference that princes can be so readily deposed. Second, that they insinuated something unsettling about the art of kingship: that performance is everything. Under interrogation, one of the conspirators admitted that the Earl had commissioned the performance precisely so that people should see how easily a 'sovereign of England could be deposed'.[95]

Life in Fairyland

We will stay with Shakespeare a little longer. In October 1600, the bookseller Thomas Fisher registered a play entitled *A Midsummer Night's Dream* at the Stationer's Office. Probably written four or five years earlier, it moves around the idea of parallel worlds, a real city-state and an enchanted forest, the realms of sense and sensibility.[96] Over both rules an 'imperial votress'. *Midsummer Night's Dream* is emblematic of the Elizabethan age, or at least how we perceive it. But it also speaks to the uncertainties which beset the closure of this age, to the fear that when everyone woke from their dream, the reality might seem altogether less enchanting. The extent to which each of Shakespeare's earlier comedies speaks to this anxiety, like indeed his earlier histories, remains moot. For now, we will contemplate two which most certainly did.

This Other Eden

After we first pay a quick visit to a field outside Tilbury in Essex. Where we will find Elizabeth Tudor looking very splendid, seated on a huge white warhorse, wearing a long flowing velvet gown overlaid by a shiny silver cuirass. Walking in front is the Earl of Ormonde, carrying the sword of state. The Earl of Leicester, her

---

[95] For an account, see Raffield (2010) 86–87.

[96] At a variant an upside-down world, and a right-way-up. Part of the festival of Midsummer's Day would commonly see communities elect lords of misrule to preside over various activities, including mock-courts.

commander-in-chief and long-term 'favourite', is holding the bridle. Just behind is a page with a plumed helmet. Elizabeth carries a gold marshal's baton. It is 19 August 1588, and Elizabeth is there to inspire her troops, assembled in preparation for the approaching Spanish Armada. And to make a spectacle of herself, literally.[97] One sentence has resounded: 'I know I have the body but of a weak, feeble woman; but I have the heart and stomach of a king, and a king of England too'. Affirming her trust 'under God' and having placed 'my chiefest strength and safeguard in the loyal hearts and good-will of my subjects', Elizabeth is ready for battle.[98] England's very own Pallas Athena, goddess of war. Its Britomart, at a variant, the Redcrosse Knight's Amazonian bodyguard in Edmund Spenser's *Faerie Queene*. More of Britomart shortly.

The remembrance of Elizabeth at Tilbury is that of an England merry in its militancy. Embracing its destiny as the 'only nation almost that doth openly and solely profess the true religion of God', as the puritan divine William Whately put it. A sentiment shared by Bishop Aylmer. It was clear for all to see: 'God is English'.[99] John Lyly too. Conscious of 'so tender a care that' God 'always had of that England, as of a new Israel, his chosen and peculiar people'.[100] That the English were chosen was hardly to be doubted. It was, after all, foretold in Bede's *Ecclesiastical History*, and then confirmed in so many glorious, God-given victories.[101]

And would be again, with the entirely predictable help of some rotten weather. The Lord blew up a storm, scattering the Spanish fleet and sending it on a perilous voyage around the coasts of Scotland and Ireland, before its battered remnants limped back to the Iberian Peninsula. Another stunning victory, achieved with barely a cannon shot. And shortly after commemorated in oil in the famed *Armada Portrait*. Elizabeth centre, of course, her hand on a globe, wearing a large pearl, a customary symbol of chastity. In the background are two panels: a first depicting English fire-ships sailing out to engage the Armada, and a second describing the storm-tossed Spaniards.

The Armada may have been the most spectacular threat to Elizabeth's crown, but it was certainly not the only. Only a year earlier, her cousin Mary Queen of Scots had been executed at Fotheringay Castle, implicated in the Babington 'plot'. And we have already revisited the fallout from the Essex rebellion. In the end Bacon found nothing treasonous in Shakespeare's gullibility, and a few weeks later, on the eve of Essex's execution, the Lord Chamberlain's Men presented a performance of *A Midsummer Night's Dream* at court. Soaked in regal sycophancy, it was an obvious choice, and a very public act of forgiveness. Shakespeare could count himself fortunate. A more neurotic prince might have acted very differently. At the

---

[97] John Neale supposed that she must have looked like an 'Amazonian empress'. In Neale (1934) 296.

[98] There are various accounts of the speech, the original version of which appears to have been recorded by a subaltern attached to the camp of the Earl of Leicester. The possibility that Elizabeth wrote the speech herself is considered in Green (1997).

[99] Collinson (1988) 4–5, 8.

[100] Kumar (2003) 107.

[101] Ackroyd (2002) xix, 37–40.

same time, though, the role of a poet in massaging sovereign power was incalculable. Elizabeth needed her poets, along with providence, her spy-masters and her army of food-tasters.

For whilst the lawyers might have built up the statutory edifice, and God assured it, the matter of decorating the English Reformation fell to these poets. The affinity of *reformatio* and *renovatio*. A task they resolved at the more allusive level by rewriting English history, and at the more prosaic by making the English feel better about themselves, giving them a sense of greater purpose, and ensuring that they were properly aware of just how lucky they were in having such a queen. In essence, doing for Reformation England what Virgil had done for classical Rome; fashioning a poetic of national destiny that was rooted firmly in a past of 'blessed memory', as John Foxe put it.[102]

The destiny which Shakespeare famously put into the mouth of the dying John of Gaunt in *Richard II*:

> This royal throne of kings, this scept'red isle,
>
> This earth of majesty, this seat of Mars,
>
> This other Eden, demi-paradise,
>
> This fortress built by Nature for herself
>
> Against infection and the hand of war,
>
> This happy breed of men, this little world,
>
> This precious stone set in a silver sea,
>
> Which serves it in the office of a wall,
>
> Or as a moat defensive to a house,
>
> Against the envy of less happier lands;
>
> This blessed plot, this earth, this realm, this England (2.1. 40–50).

A people ruled by kings, Gaunt continues, alluding to this crusading history, 'Renowned for their deeds far from home,/ For Christian service and true chivalry' (2.1. 53–54). Except, of course, that this destiny is about to be corrupted by the venal Richard Plantagenet. History turns, and turns again. Something to ponder in the England of spring 1601.

We will encounter the English poetic repeatedly in the coming chapters. For now, we can simply state the unarguable; that everything Shakespeare and his fellow poets wrote was intended, in one way or another, to celebrate this 'other Eden'. And, perhaps, to bolster its confidence. The Armada might have seemed a wonderful victory to the English, but across Europe it was treated as a strange aberration, in a longer history of decline. The binding narrative being one in which, since its break from Rome, England was a nation damned for its godless

---

[102] For a discussion of the relation between past and present in the writing of the English reformation, see Walsham (2012) 902–04.

impudence and destined to fall. A small offshore kingdom which, absent a voice in Europe, mattered rather less.[103] And which, as a consequence, felt an ever more pressing need to assure itself that it really was chosen.

The birth of English exceptionalism; another dividend of the English Reformation, or a blight? We will see: there is a further prescience here. Celebrated in the Prologue to Shakespeare's *Henry V*. 'A kingdom for a stage, princes to act/ And monarchs to behold the swelling scene' (Prol 3–4). Which is, again, why the brilliance of its monarch mattered so much. The 'art of imitation', as Sir Philip Sidney put it in his *Defence of Poesy*, which distinguishes the dazzling magistrate from the dull and dimly remembered.[104] And a defining metaphor. 'We princes', Elizabeth proclaimed, 'are set on stages in sight and view of all the world duly observed'.[105]

We will discover her successor saying something very similar shortly; not that he was anything like so accomplished a performer. As was customary, during her coronation pageant the young Elizabeth had been invited to watch a series of carefully choreographed performances and show her appreciation. A contemporary remarked on the 'perpetual attentiveness in her face', as she would clasp her hands and lift her eyes to heaven, or smile benignly at the actors and bestow gifts.[106] A few months later, embarking on the first of her many progresses around the realm, Elizabeth entered York, and 'ravished' the assembled crowds with her 'loving answers and gestures'.[107] Elizabeth did not progress in order to see her realm; she progressed so that her realm could see her.

The Imperial Votress

'I have no dealing with the Queen', the MP Thomas Norton confirmed to his son in 1582, 'but as with the image of God'.[108] The image of so many things in truth.[109] Rarely had England lived quite so figuratively, or so romantically. Britomart at Tilbury, or maybe Pallas Athena. And then, at the merest slip of a pen, refashioned as 'Good Queen Bess' or Belphoebe or Diana the moon-goddess, or Cynthia, as she appeared in Lyly's 1588 play *Endymion* and then again in Jonson's *Cynthia's Revels*: 'Queen and huntress, chaste and fair'.[110] Or Astraea, the goddess of justice

---

[103] See Wormald (2021) 247–48, 406.

[104] Sidney (1989) 21–27, 220–23, 226–31. For a commentary, see Worden (1996) 227–39.

[105] Greenblatt (1985) 44; and Pye (1990) 63.

[106] For accounts of the coronation celebrations, see Neale (1934) 64–67; and McCaffrey (1993) 43–44.

[107] For commentary on the performativity of Elizabeth's progresses, see here Greenblatt (2005) 166–69; and Talbert (1962) 83–88.

[108] Collinson (1987) 409.

[109] As Christopher Haigh has suggested, 'the public Elizabeth was not a real person, but a cluster of images'. See Haigh (1984) 5.

[110] See Donaldson (2011) 165, quoting Jonson's later renowned aside; that 'Queen Elizabeth never saw herself after she became old in a true glass'.

whose return was prophesied by Virgil, and celebrated, at a variant, by William Byrd as the 'beauteous Queen of second Troy'.[111] The 'Lady of the Common Law', at a suggestive variant; the 'Laws of the Second Venus', as Selden put it, inverting the variant. The Elizabeth of the 'Coronation portrait', which looks an awful lot like the renowned wood-panel painting of Richard II; the Justinian *Imago Dei*.[112] Orb in one hand, sceptre in the other. The prefiguring, at yet another variant, of the frontispiece which would famously decorate Hobbes's *Leviathan*.

Or the 'Virgin Queen', of course, perhaps the most familiar of all. The 'imperial votress' who crosses the night sky in *A Midsummer Night's Dream*, immune to 'Cupid's fiery shaft/ Quenched in the chaste beams of the wat'ry moon' (2.1. 161, 163).[113] An allusion to the Vestal Tuccia, who miraculously managed to carry water in a sieve; an iconography captured in the so-called 'sieve portraits' of Elizabeth painted by George Gower and Quentin Metsys the Younger. Augmented by an array of familiar painterly motifs, from the self-regenerating phoenix, to pure white ermine, dripping pearls and translucent veils. The diaphanous collars too, of the kind spectacularly apparent in the *Rainbow Portrait*, looking very much like fairy-wings. Precisely what a Fairy Queen might be expected to wear.

Which brings us to what is perhaps the most renowned of Elizabethan poetics. Edmund Spenser's *The Fairie Queene*, dedicated to 'the most excellent and glorious person of our soveraine the Queene and her kingdome in Faery land'.[114] The greater aspiration of the *Faerie Queene*, to burnish the reformed English nation-state, and celebrate its crusading spirit, was written into the first three books. The first, dedicated to the virtue of 'Holiness', emphasised the crusading destiny of the English people, the 'new Hierusalem, that God has built' for those 'that are chosen his' (1.10. 57).[115] A quest undertaken by the 'Redcrosse Knight', the personification of the English Church, his 'Despair' assuaged by Una the 'royall virgin' who affirms the assurance of 'greater grace' (1.9. 53; 1.10. 19, 61). The second book addresses Temperance, telling the story of Sir Guyon, a knight whose shield bears the image of Gloriana, the model of measured government, and whose mission is to sack the Bower of Bliss; a caution against licence of any kind, but the carnal especially. A theme taken up in the third book, on Chastity, where the laudably resilient Florimell flees from one potential ravisher to another, whilst the redoubtable Britomart rescues the Redcrosse Knight from the clutches of the Roman 'beast'. Much as Elizabeth saved the English from the rapine of the Spanish Armada.

---

[111] In his *Sweet and Merry Month of May*, published in Thomas Watson's *First Sett, of Italian Madrigals*, in 1590.

[112] The latter being the earliest surviving portrait of an incumbent English monarch. The extent to which the Coronation Portrait is modelled on the Ricardian wood-panel remains a matter of academic conjecture, see *Digest* 1.3.2. For a broader commentary on the legal iconography, see Raffield (2010) 111.

[113] According to Louis Montrose, Elizabeth's 'cultural presence was a condition' of the play's 'imaginative possibility'. See Montrose (1983) 62, 81–82.

[114] As he confided to Sir Walter Raleigh. In Waller (1994) 101.

[115] Internal references from Spenser (1980).

The second set of books was published in 1596: six years later, during which time Spenser's mood had evidently darkened. The first of this set is dedicated to Friendship, a virtue cherished by Aristotelian humanists, but which Spenser prefers to contemplate in terms of dissimulation and equivocation. A similar ambiguity shrouds the sixth book, on Courtesy. Another virtue which can too easily be corrupted by inauthenticity. It is the fifth book, on Justice, which catches the eye of the literary jurist. It describes the arraignment of the 'foule Duessa', an allusion to the summary trial of Mary Queen of Scots. Justice effected, albeit on the terms prescribed by Astraea. Where, for reason of law's sometime limitation, a godly magistrate must employ 'equitie to measure out along/ According to the line of conscience,/ When so it needs with rigour to dispence' (5.1. 7). Dancing along the margins of law.

Spenser originally devised a set of 12 books. But time took its toll. Two cantos of a projected seventh book, 'on Mutabilitie', were published posthumously in 1609. An extended muse on 'man's decay' (7.6. 1). Intimations of death, his own and that of his Fairy Queen too, perhaps. Together with a growing sense that closet Romish 'remoaners' were stopping the reformation from getting properly 'done'. The Blatant Beast is loosed again, embarked upon a seditious rampage across Fairyland. As Spenser had anticipated in his *Teares of the Muses*, published back in 1591:

> And beside sits ugly Barbarisme
>
> And brutish Ingnorance, ycrept of late
>
> Out of dredd darknes of the deep Absyme,
>
> Where being bredd, he light and heaven does hate
>
> They in the mindes of men now tyrannize,
>
> And the faire Scene with rudeness fould disguise (187–92).[116]

Spenser died in 1599. Three and a half years before Elizabeth. History conjectures the passing of a generation, and the birth of a new cynicism. In the moment, George Chapman was busy redrafting *Bussy D'Amboise*, in which the Duke of Guise ridicules the English for 'making ... of their old Queen/ An ever-young and most immortal goddess' (1.2. 11–13). A decade later Jonson would dress his Doll Common as the 'Faery Queen'.[117] Gloriana faded away, leaving a memory that would grow ever more whimsical with time.

What she did not leave was a natural heir. The downside of being a 'virgin' queen, as Thomas Sackville and Thomas Norton had intimated in their *Gorboduc*, first performed at Court in January 1561. There was time then to hope that a hint dropped might give the young Elizabeth pause for thought. Not 40 years on. We will take a closer look at Gloriana's successor, a monarch with a very different idea of kingship, very shortly. First, though, we will consider another late Elizabethan

---

[116] Published in 1591. In Spenser (1980) 482.
[117] Doll is one of the three con artists around which Jonson wrote *The Alchemist*.

text, darker still in tone; one which spoke directly to the sense that, underneath all the glitter, there was something not quite right about the life, and indeed the law, of late Elizabethan England. The fate foretold, perhaps, by the exiled Thomas Becon back in 1554: 'We have abhorred the light of Goddes worde, therefore we are how justly overwhelmed with the darkenes of mens tryffeling tradicions and develishe decrees'.[118]

The Case of the Hapless Merchant

It involves the case of a hapless merchant by the name of Antonio, around whose fate Shakespeare wrote his most overtly jurisprudential, play, *The Merchant of Venice*. The facts can again be briefly told. Antonio has over-extended his credit, borrowing the considerable sum of 3,000 ducats from a Jewish moneylender named Shylock, in order to finance another commercial venture.[119] The play opens with a forlorn Antonio 'Piring in maps for ports, and piers and road:/ And every object that might make me fear/ Misfortune to my ventures' (1.1. 19–21). The terms of the 'bond' stipulate that if Antonio is unable to pay back the loan, plus interest, he will forfeit a 'pound of flesh'.[120] His venture having failed, his ships 'all miscarried' (3.2. 322), Antonio is taken to court, where Shylock, who harbours a series of private grudges, makes plain that he intends to enforce the terms of the bond strictly. And where, most alarmingly, it becomes apparent that the Duke, who presides over the court, seems to have little idea what to do in order to mitigate the consequence.[121]

Antonio's luck is, though, about to take a turn for the better. In the person of Portia, who arrives from nearby Belmont to rescue him, as well as the Duke. There are three things to note about Portia.[122] First, she is not a lawyer. Second, she proves to be a brilliant jurist. And third, she should not have been needed. We will come to the brilliance shortly, and the lack of qualifications. As to the need, a

---

[118] Walsham (2012) 923.

[119] It is always difficult to project current value to sums such as this; but fun all the same. On current value, a gold ducat would be worth around £125, suggesting a total value equivalence of £375,000. A fair sum to be able to lend; which would in all probability have been offset. The fact that Shylock refuses to give up his action, when offered twice the amount, says something about the depth of his grievance, as well as his ability, potentially, to soak up the capital loss.

[120] The 'pound of flesh' bond was borrowed, most likely, from Ser Giovanni's *Il Pecorone*. Which, in turn, was an adaption from the 'flesh-bond' discovered in the Roman law of the *Twelve Tables*. It permitted creditors to take shares in the corpse of an insolvent debtor.

[121] Venice had a reputation, at the time, for the severity with which it enforced the law, however unjust the consequence might seem. See Klotz (2011) 388.

[122] At least. Something else is her name; quite possibly intended to resonate with the *lex Porcia*, a law which forbad the scourging of Roman citizens, and which served as shorthand for the mitigation of punishment. See here Watt (2008) 240. It might also be noted that she is independently wealthy, and unmarried; both qualities suggesting that her pressing need is to find a husband and produce an heir, so as to release the family estate from the restrictive terms of her father's will. Belmont needs an infusion of Venetian capital, which will arrive courtesy of Bassanio.

familiar cultural trope. Dick the Butcher's notorious suggestion, in *Henry VI Part 2*, that they 'kill all the lawyers', inheres a teasing irony, in large part because of Dick and his profession (4.2. 71).[123] But the sentiment would not have horrified many in Shakespeare's audience. The reputation of lawyers is rarely high anywhere, at any time. But rarely has it been lower than it was in Shakespeare's England.

A gang of 'upstart *Rabulae Forenses*', according to the poet Abraham Fraunce, 'which under pretence of Lawe, become altogether lawless, to the continual molestation of ignorant men, and general overcharging of the country'.[124] The most grafting of professions in Phillip Stubbes's *Anatomie of Abuses*. We have already encountered the shared anxieties of Ellesmere and Tourneur, bringing into alignment the jurisdictional and professional consequences of the Reformation. In their *Looking-Glass for London and England*, Thomas Lodge and Robert Greene reminded their readers of the fate that very nearly befell Ninevah in the *Book of Jonah*, saved only because it got rid of its lawyers, and usurers, and turned instead to God. Hardly surprising if King James felt much the same, for reasons we have already intimated. In 1615, James was treated to a performance of George Ruggle's *Ignoramus*. It was all about common lawyers in training to rip off their clients; a fair number of the former presumably covering their blushes in the audience, including, it was reported, a scowling Sir Edward Coke.[125] A fair number of the clients too perhaps. The King was, though, much more impressed, loudly expressing his admiration. As was Sir John Chamberlain, also in attendance. A play 'full of mirth', he reported, albeit rather spoilt by being six hours long.

A decade on, the English theatre-goer would be invited back to Venice, to witness the downfall of another venal lawyer, Voltore, in Ben Jonson's *Volpone*. Whilst critics have liked to assume that the eponymous Volpone might be a caricature of Sir Robert Cecil, Voltore has proved more elusive.[126] The eager recommendation of torture as a means of getting to the 'truth' might have struck a chord perhaps: 'I have heard,/ The rack hath cured the gout, faith, give it him' (4.6. 32–33).[127] The strategy which Coke happily deployed, as Attorney General, to extract confessions from the surviving 'powder' plotters. Maybe, maybe not. Either way, we can safely conclude that the venal lawyer was a familiar enough figure on the Jacobean stage.

---

[123] It is possible that, by putting the words into the mouth of a plebeian, and chaotic, revolutionary, Shakespeare meant to damn the sentiment. It is also possible that he did not. See here Raffield (2010) 153.

[124] A Fraunce, *The Lawyer's Logicke, exemplifying the praecepts of Logicke by the practise of common law*, quoted in Raffield (2010) 156.

[125] The play, performed during James's visit to Cambridge, was written to lampoon the recorder of Clare College, Francis Brackyn. Brackyn, a common lawyer, was engaged in a long-running dispute with university officials regarding the teaching of civil law. The hallmark of being an 'ignoramus' is not having much Latin.

[126] Albeit a risky caricature if so. See Donaldson (2011) 233.

[127] A recommendation preceded by lines that admit a distinctively Inquisitorial tone; 'Best try him, then, with goads, or burning irons;/ Put him to the strappado' (4.6. 31–32).

Men

> that could speak
>
> To every cause, and things mere contraries,
>
> Til they were hoarse again, yet all be law;
>
> That, with most quick agility, could turn,
>
> And return; make knots, and undo them;
>
> Give forked counsel; take provoking gold
>
> On either hand, and put it up (*Volpone* 1.3. 53–59).

Along with the gullible perhaps, and the conceited.[128] If it is not Voltore trying to con his way into a fortune, it is Dapper being conned out of another.[129]

It might be supposed that Shakespeare created Portia, precisely because the presence of an honest lawyer on his stage would have been incredible. Certainly, her lack of formal qualifications is no hindrance, and neither is her gender. Arriving disguised as a 'fine braggart youth', Portia lures Shylock into a trap. At first, she appeals to 'the quality of mercy', that 'droppeth as the gentle rain from heaven' (4.1. 180–81). Glancing, we might imagine, from Shylock to the Duke:

> 'Tis mightiest in the mightiest, it becomes
>
> The throned monarch better than his crown.
>
> His sceptre shows the force of temporal power,
>
> The attribute to awe and majesty,
>
> Wherein doth sit the dread and fear of kings:
>
> But mercy is above this sceptred sway,
>
> It is enthroned in the hearts of kings,
>
> It is an attribute to God himself;
>
> And earthly power doth then show likest God's
>
> When mercy seasons justice (4.1. 184–93).

The ambiguity moves, of course, around the seasoning. The rhetoric immediately suggests a Christian mercy. But this does not preclude the possibility that Portia might be alluding to the more 'rational' Senecan variety.[130] The metaphor intimates a tempering facility, of the kind most readily familiar in the exercise of prerogative; and to which Portia will shortly allude in the context of mitigating Shylock's fate. The kind which, it might have been expected, of which the Duke was already aware. But apparently not. Meanwhile, Shylock simply asserts his claim: 'I crave

---

[128] For the idea that something of both can be seen in the *avocatore*, who try to make sense of the variously conned in *Volpone*, see Klotz (2011) 394–405.

[129] Dapper the lawyer's 'clerk' being one of Subtle's victims in *The Alchemist*.

[130] An essay particularly admired by King James, as we will see in the next chapter. For an appreciation of the possibilities here, see Watt (2009) 214.

the law,/ The penalty and forfeit of my bond' (4.1. 202–03). Another man inclined to see 'conscience' as something 'cowards use'.

Having anticipated Shylock's recalcitrance, Portia changes tack. And guise. The 'excellent young man' becomes the 'learned judge' (4.1. 242, 300, 309). Reading the bond literally, Portia notes that it does not permit Shylock to take any more than the 'pound of flesh'. More particularly he must 'Shed' no 'blood' (4.1. 321). If he does he will have breached the terms of the bond himself. Spotting the danger, and realising that he has already, in threatening the life of a Venetian, transgressed existing anti-alien laws, Shylock tries to negotiate. It is, though, too late. Shylock has already 'refus'd' those terms in 'open court' (4.1. 334). Thus, his fate 'lies in the mercy' of the Duke (4.1. 351–52). Not as an exercise of 'conscience' alone, as Portia makes clear, but because it is 'enacted in the laws of Venice' (4.1. 343). Shylock's life is spared, even as he loses his money and his dignity.[131] The 'sweet harmony' of the commonwealth is restored: not by abrogating, even mitigating, the law, but by enforcing it (5.1. 57).[132] Hooker would have been proud.

The public law of Venice tends then to justice, even if the extent to which it tends to equity is less sure. And its Duke seems less sure still. There is 'no lawful means can carry me', Antonio despairs at the opening of the trial scene; another statement from which the Duke fails to demur (4.1. 9). He has 'ta'en pains to qualify' the law, but can do nothing more (4.1. 25). To an extent, this might be ascribed to generic predisposition. Most of Shakespeare's 'comic dukes' seem to struggle with the nitty-gritty of governance, especially when dealing with overly strict laws. The Duke in *Comedy of Errors*, for example, only partially mitigating a statute which threatens the life of another luckless merchant, Egeon. The Duke in *Measure for Measure* similarly bemused as to why his 'biting' laws do not seem to be working. The King of Navarre in *Love's Labours Lost*, Prospero in *The Tempest*, Leontes in *The Winter's Tale*; three more princes in urgent need of sharpening up. Princes should know better; and will, the imputation runs, if they attend enough of Shakespeare's plays.[133]

The setting of the *Merchant* creates some poetic distance, of course. A place of 'Popery', 'whoredom' and demonic consumerism, the puritan Richard Baxter declared of Venice.[134] But also a centre of renaissance learning, with a vibrant market economy. Not many in late Elizabethan England would have openly admired its republican principles, nor the popery, but they would have admired plenty else. Moreover, few in the audience would have missed the juridical inference. Antonio might be a Venetian merchant, and the Duke a Venetian magistrate, but it is the law of England which is on trial. As for the particular court, the

---

[131] The mitigation is further dependent on Shylock's conversion to Christianity: 'He shall do this, or else I do recant/ The pardon that I late pronounced here' (4.1. 378–79).

[132] See Ward (1999) 130–31.

[133] See here Watt (2009) 213–14, noting the sheer number of Shakespearean plays to which James was treated in his first year or so on the English throne.

[134] Baxter (1994) 136.

stage setting for Act 4 Scene I is a 'Court of Justice' attended by the Duke, the 'Magnificoes', a courtesy title given to leading Venetian nobility, and the interested parties. Whilst it could impute the Court of Chancery, or even Admiralty, given its maritime dimension, the closer resemblance is with the Star Chamber of the King's Council sitting in Whitehall. A court which, as we have already noted, evinced an emerging interest, not just in cases which threatened the 'peace' and security of the realm, but in the resolution of commercial disputes.[135]

The place, ironically, where Coke would be hauled two decades later, to be dismissed by King James. Another prince, some supposed, who never properly appreciated his responsibility to secure, above all else, the integrity of the common law. On that we will reserve judgement. For now, we can conclude that Portia at least manages to work things out in the particular instance of Antonio's case, and the law acquits itself, albeit with very little thanks to the Duke and his coterie of counsellors. Or any real lawyers. Something for the audience to ponder as they tramped back home along the muddy, rat-infested streets of late Elizabethan London. But then they probably already knew that, 60 years on, they were not much nearer to getting the reformation done, of Church or law. But at least they got to spend a couple of hours hurling abuse at an odd-looking immigrant.[136]

---

[135] Perhaps the most famous example being *Twyne's Case* 76 ER 809; 3 Co Rep 80b, which involved a sham 'transfer' of livestock intended to frustrate the terms of the Fraudulent Conveyances Act of 1584.

[136] Much as Shylock claims that he is treated, by Antonio and his mates: 'You call me a misbeliever, cut-throat dog,/ And spet upon my Jewish gabardine'. A gabardine was an ankle-length coat commonly worn at the time by Hasidic Jews. It would normally be coloured with particular stripes; usually white and yellow in England. Anti-alien sentiment, specifically anti-Semitic, ran high through much of the closing years of the sixteenth century. Widespread rioting in London was recorded in 1588, 1593 and 1595, the latter spiced by the infamous Lopez trial.

2

The Aspirations of James Stuart

James Stuart arrived in London in April 1603, his succession to the throne plotted by his predecessor's Secretary of State, Sir Robert Cecil. A bit odd; dynastic switches were supposed to be murderous and hectic. James had spent four leisurely weeks meandering south, hanging a thief along the way, doling out knighthoods and collecting plenty of nice presents from assorted aristocrats in whose homes he had bed and breakfasted.[1] The mood was soured slightly on receiving a 'millenary' petition from a bunch of angst-ridden puritans.[2] But hopes were otherwise high, with some serious celebrations planned. The coronation, on 25 July, was supposed to be the culmination of a month of partying and 'puking', to plagiarise Pepys.[3] Sadly, though, London was riven with plague, which meant that whilst there was plenty of puking, there was less facility for partying. The celebrations, at the centre of which was to be a grand 'Triumph' through the streets of the London, were cancelled.[4] By way of small consolation, James had a coronation medal struck. It depicted the new King wearing a laurel wreath and bore the inscription, in translation, 'James I, Caesar Augustus of Britain, Caesar heir of Caesars'.[5]

As London emerged from its lockdown in early 1604, thoughts turned once again to the planned 'Triumph'. James's thoughts especially. The big day out was rescheduled for 15 March 1604. Hoisted onto a splendid white steed, at around eleven in the morning, James was sent on his way from the Tower to 'make his royall passage through the Citie, having a Canopie borne over him by 8 knights', along with a cavalcade of doting courtiers and fawning prelates, musicians and artists, including Shakespeare's newly warranted, and liveried, Company of King's Men.[6] The route passed through seven vast Roman arches, upon which could be found assorted scriptural and classical verse. At each of the arches, James was

---

[1] The hanging of the thief caused some consternation, not least we might assume on the part of the thief. It was politely pointed out to the new King that even thieves were entitled to due process in English law. An intimation perhaps, of what was to come.

[2] So named because there were, apparently, a thousand signatures to the petition.

[3] For Pepys's account of the partying and puking which characterised the week leading up to the coronation of King Charles II, see Latham (1993) 12–13.

[4] For an account of the coronation, and the necessarily abbreviated ceremonies, see Jack (2004).

[5] Kernan (1995) 12.

[6] James had issued the warrant within months of arriving in London in spring 1603, evidently keen to recruit Shakespeare's services. Whether the Company joined the parade, or lined the streets somewhere, or maybe even took part in one of the pageants, remains a matter of speculation.

invited to pause and watch a performance on the theme of why he was chosen by God to rule, and how lucky the English were to have a king so wise.[7]

The pageant masters were Thomas Dekker and Ben Jonson.[8] The inspiration, for Jonson at least, was William Camden's *Britannia*, in which London was imagined as the 'seat' of a nascent 'British empire'. Modelled indeed on Virgil's Rome.[9] The very first arch, designed by Jonson, was dedicated to the idea of 'union'. It presented an image of the King seated beneath the twin crowns bearing an orb carrying the motto '*Orbis Britannicus, Divisus ab orbe*', to 'shew', as Jonson said, 'that this empire is a world divided from the world'.[10] The destiny Virgil had foretold, now realised by James.

The largest arch, paid for by the Dutch Company, was set up at the Royal Exchange, and measured 87 feet. It was there that God passed the 'Raynes of thy Kingdome in his owne hand'.[11] For which reason, by the time that James reached Fenchurch, centre stage had been ceded to the 'deified Augustus', the paragon of civil magistracy. As Jonson's script confirmed:

> Long maist thou live, and see me thus appeare,
>
> As ominous a comet, from my spheare,
>
> Unto thy raigne; as that did auspicate
>
> So lasting glory to AUGUSTUS state.[12]

As he duly passed through the arch, presided over by *Monarchia Britannia*, James was heralded 'King of Great Britain'. The very last arch was at Temple Bar, modelled on the Temple of Janus in the Forum, where James was handed an olive wreath and laurel crown.[13] The architect Stephen Harrison, who designed the arches, left an account of the day, confirming how much everyone had admired both his work and his King. And how much they had drunk, 'claret wine' flowing 'merrily' through the streets, filling the 'bellies' of all who had turned out to smile

---

[7] See Bergeron (2000) 147–63.

[8] Four days later, Jonson registered the 'pageant' in the Stationer's Register. Not that Dekker and Jonson got on especially, even though they collaborated on a number of occasions. Jonson caricatured Dekker as Demetrius Fannius in his *Poetaster*, the 'dresser of plays'. Dekker's account of the 'pageant', *The Magnificent Entertainment*, makes only 'grudging' acknowledgement of Jonson's contribution. See Donaldson (2011) 196–97.

[9] Which had 'reared her head as high among all other cities as cypresses oft do among the bending osiers'. See Donaldson (2011) 28 and also 78, noting Jonson's especial admiration of Livy, along, of course, with Horace.

[10] In Wormald (2021) 355.

[11] Bergeron (2002) 223. The Royal Exchange arch, paid for by the Dutch Company, was the largest at 87 feet. Some of the smaller were around 20 feet.

[12] In Wortham (1996) 105.

[13] The Temple was famous for its doors, which would be ceremonially closed at the end of a war. In the *Res Gestaie Divi Augusti*, which he was purported to have written, Augustus proudly claimed that the doors had been shut three times during his *princeps*, more than in any previous period. The presentation of the model Temple spoke, very obviously, to James's particular desire to assure a *pax Britannia*. See Bergeron (2002) 222.

and wave.[14] Gilbert Dugdale's *The Time Triumphant* left similar account, albeit focusing more on how brilliant James had looked, and less on all the drinking. As did Dekker in his *The Magnificent Entertainment*.

Such, at least, was the authorised version of the day's entertainment. There are reports that James in fact looked rather bored by the end of what must have been a wearying day. 'He endured the day's brunt with patience', Arthur Wilson recalled, 'being assured he would never have another'. Very unlike 'his predecessor', Wilson added, who 'with a well-pleased affection met her people's acclamations'.[15] James, though, was not a natural actor. More the 'poor player', perhaps, 'That struts and frets his hour upon the stage'.[16] Nor, by admittedly scurrilous contemporary report, was the new King much of a presence either.

Some tried to be kinder. Roger Wilbraham recommended his 'ready and pith speech', and Bacon was predictably cloying, as we will see.[17] But history has tended to prefer the notorious account left by Anthony Weldon in his *The Court and Character of King James I*. A man 'naturally of timorous disposition', his 'eyes large, ever rolling after any stranger that came into his presence', his 'tongue too large for his mouth, which ever made him speak full in the mouth' and dribble a lot, his beard 'very thin', like his legs, so much so that he was 'ever leaning on other men's shoulders; his walk was ever circular, his fingers ever in that walk fiddling about his cod-piece'.[18] Hardly prepossessing, and all adding to a growing disquiet in regard to the propriety of the new King, and his court; a subject to which we will also return.

Not much interested in the arts either, at least according to the French Ambassador Fontenoy, despatched to Edinburgh in 1584.[19] The young King 'hates dancing and music in general', Fontenoy reported back. He was also 'rude' and 'uncivil in speaking', by which he meant inelegant.[20] It was certainly true that James preferred private pursuits, liking nothing better than escaping to the country to slaughter its wildlife.[21] There is, though, reason to be wary of disdainful courtiers with axes to grind. James's Court in Edinburgh was renowned for its artistic patronage, of the 'Castalian poets' especially. He even wrote some poetry himself.[22]

---

[14] Entitled *The Arches of Triumph*, already printed and available for sale on the day of the pageant.

[15] See Stewart (2003) 173; and Hopkins (2021) 478–80.

[16] *Macbeth* 5.5. 24–26.

[17] Stewart (2003) 171–72.

[18] A French ambassador attested to similar, during a visit to Edinburgh in 1584; 'his gait is bad, composed of erratic steps'. See Stewart (2003) 75, 270.

[19] Denmark House, where his wife Queen Anna held court, came to fill the void as an artistic salon, attracting the likes of Donne, Jonson and Inigo Jones, amongst many. Unlike her husband, Anna loved masques too.

[20] In Stewart (2003) 75. Fontenoy especially noted James's rudeness around women; surmising that it might have been a consequence of spending his formative years surrounded by lots of similarly 'rude' men. The Ambassador was even more 'astonished' by James's seeming disinterest in the fate of his mother, Mary Queen of Scots.

[21] To excess, some concluded. In 1616, Queen Anna's chaplain Geoffrey Goodman gave a necessarily pointed sermon on the evils of hunting. See Stewart (2003) 175–79.

[22] Styling himself a 'Prentice in the Divine Art of Poesie'. The most renowned of the Castalians were Alexander Montgomery, who arrived from France, replete with assorted literary affectations, in 1579,

A veritable 'Homer', according to a fawning Gabriel Harvey.[23] What put paid to James Stuart the poet, it seems, was the travail of kingship, English particularly.

It was public performance that James evidently liked less, even as he appreciated its necessity.[24] Thus the case, however energy-sapping, for a flashy coronation. And for a cult. Where his predecessor had Gloriana and the variously Fairie and Virgin queens, James preferred a select group of Old Testament kings, Solomon foremost.[25] Alongside some carefully cultivated Roman emperors. Augustus very much the favourite, the epitome of *pax Romana*, Antoninus Pius occasionally, for much the same reason, and, at a variant intended for the fawning prelates, Constantine, the midwife of Roman Christianity.[26] The admixture of wisdom, faith and majesty. If things went well.

Sadly, they did not, at least not as well as James had hoped. *Pax Jacobus* hardly fitted the image of a crusading nation, whilst the politics of a 'greater' Britain would prove altogether harder than the performance. Neither did many of those sitting in James's new Parliament at Westminster seem especially sympathetic to the ideas of kingship articulated in his various writings on the subject. We will see quite how unsympathetic shortly. First, though, we need to read James's mind. Something which should be made easier by the fact that he was so keen to let everyone know what was in it.[27] A man of so many opinions, and ever inclined to publicise them, in conference, in print, at dinner.

The Wisest Fool

John Hacket recorded that James liked to have a couple of divines standing in attendance whilst he dined publicly, so that he might debate 'some point of controversy in philosophy'. A 'trial of wits', Hacket termed it.[28] Some were impressed by a king who, in the words of Thomas Howard, 'doth wondrously covet learned discourse'.[29] Even Fontenoy admitted that England's new King was undoubtedly

---

and Patrick Hume of Polwarth, who assumed the ceremonial role as 'bard' during James's Edinburgh coronation pageant. Another, William Fowler, spent much of his spare time translating various Renaissance poems and essays into Scots, including Petrarch and Machiavelli. See Wormald (2021) 176–78.

[23] Wormald (2021) 441–44.

[24] See Wormald (2021) 185, 451–52.

[25] The centrepiece of his entry into Edinburgh in 1577, his first public appearance, was a performance of 'The Judgement of Solomon'. The 13-year-old James was apparently entranced; probably more so than he was with the harangues of various ministers of the Kirk which interspersed his big day.

[26] Such as Lancelot Andrews, who gave an obliging Court sermon on James as Constantine in 1606. See Fincham and Lake (1985) 169. A different Rome then, of course.

[27] Not that it does, of course. The sheer welter of writing, literary and political, only serving to obscure the writer. See Wormald (2021) 442.

[28] Stewart (2003) 190.

[29] Writing to Sir John Harrington, published in *Nugae Antiquae* (1779) 2.271. In Blakemore Evans (1998) 193.

'learned'.[30] So too William Barlow, Dean of Chester: 'Surely whosoever heard his Majesty, might justly think; that title did more properly fit him, which Eunapius gave to that famous rhetorician, in saying he was a living library, and a walking study'.[31] Others were less sure. Amongst those who supposed that the Hampton Court conference was called just so that he might show off, was Sir John Harrington. The King, he recorded, 'rather used upbraidings than arguments'.[32] And it is the pejorative impression that has tended to stick; the 'wisest fool in Christendom'.[33] If we want to get a better understanding of what James thought about kingship, and why it created such a negative impression amongst so many of his prospective English subjects, we might revisit three treatises which he had already written; *Basilicon Doron*, *Daemonology* and *The Trew Law of Free Monarchies*. Variations on a theme: that theme being the divinely ordained authority of a 'true' Renaissance prince.

The Education of Princes

In 1577, George Buchanan published a short treatise on Greek drama, entitled *Baptistes*, dedicated to his 11-year-old charge, James Stuart. It was, the dedication advertised, purposed 'to the imitation of antiquity and to the study of piety'.[34] More closely still, it was intended to educate prospective princes, like James. 'Sovereignty needs counsel: learning affords it', as Jonson put it.[35] The young James duly spent every morning learning Greek, every afternoon reading Latin. Day after day of Herodotus and Livy. 'They gar me speik Latin ar I could speik Scotis', he later recalled.[36] We have already encountered plenty of improving Renaissance literature and will do so again. Our immediate concern is, though, with a particular genre of *specula*, or mirror, literature which was purposed specifically to furthering magisterial education.

   By the time that Buchanan was setting his reading lists, the temper of 'mirror' literature was already mutating.[37] Early examples, such as Boccaccio's *De casibus virorum illustrium* and Lydgate's *Fall of Princes*, had limited themselves to plainer accounts of wicked magistracy.[38] The more nuanced imitative edge arrived with

---

[30] In Stewart (2003) 75.

[31] In Stewart (2003) 191–92.

[32] Stewart (2003) 200.

[33] There is no direct attribution for the epithet. It is commonly thought to have been either King Henry IV of France or his Chief Minister the Duc de Sully. On the unfairness of the pejorative, see Wormald (2021) 32.

[34] In Stewart (2003) 44–45.

[35] Donaldson (2011) 169, 265.

[36] See Wormald (2021) 11, commenting on Buchanan's 'heavily classical' syllabus and also Stewart (2003) 39.

[37] For a discussion of the evolving nature of 'mirror' literature, from later medieval to Renaissance, and suggesting its particular affinity with the Inns of Court during the latter period, see Winston (2016) 127–48.

[38] Boccaccio's *De casibus* appeared around 1358; Lydgate's *Fall of Princes* at some point in the 1430s.

texts such as Erasmus's *Education of a Christian Prince*, published in 1516, and Machiavelli's *The Prince* which first appeared in 1532.[39] 'Men', the latter confirmed, 'nearly always follow the tracks made by others and proceed in their affairs by imitation'.[40] Machiavelli's other renowned contribution to the genre was his *Discourses on Livy*. Another Roman historian to whom Renaissance scholars looked in the hope of better discerning the future was Tacitus, whose *Annals* advertised a sobering story on a theme no less unsettling for being familiar: the 'ruin of innocence'.[41] Never an easy read, and certainly not in 1603. There would be a lot of Tacitus in early Jacobean England. Seneca likewise. Chroniclers of moral and political dissolution both.

Plenty of opportunity for dramatic reflection too. Within 10 days of arriving in London, James had signed patents confirming royal patronage of the restyled Company of King's Men.[42] Managed by a man with an established reputation for writing cautionary plays about the fall of tyrannous English kings, *King John*, *Richard II*, *Richard III*. Any thoughts that 'our bending author' would compose something suitably fawning by way of thanks was quickly dispelled.[43] The first play that Shakespeare wrote for his new King was *Measure for Measure*, a dark piece about a dithery duke and a very wicked counsellor. We will take a closer look at the play in the next chapter, as it sets a context for one of Coke's most renowned opinions on the reach of royal prerogative. For the present, we can note some pointed commentary on the subject of princely performance. Unable to comprehend why his commonwealth is descending into lawlessness, Shakespeare has his duke abdicate for a period and go about in disguise. A strategy adopted by James, who famously visited the Exchange *incognito* in 1604; albeit everyone knew he was there. A risky venture, playing the 'fantastical duke of dark corners', as the courtier Lucio puts it (4.3. 156). And certainly not something that Elizabeth would ever have done. She might have wearied of life in a 'stage-play world', as Raleigh famously termed it, so 'false and dureless'.[44] But she never showed it.

Unlike James, and notwithstanding the fact that he made so much of princely performance in his own contribution to the *specula* genre, *Basilicon Doron*. Composed in 1599 as an 'instruction' to his eldest son, Prince Henry, the 'argument' of the *Basilicon* was affirmed in its dedicatory sonnet: 'God giues not Kings the stile of Gods in vaine/ For on his Throne his Scepter doe they swey'.[45] And it is

---

[39] Albeit Machiavelli had completed *The Prince* rather earlier, around 1513.

[40] Machiavelli (1995) 15–17.

[41] In Bacon (1998) xvi.

[42] The original patent naming eight 'sharers', Shakespeare listed at the top. For a commentary, see Syme (2019).

[43] *Henry V*, Epil. 2. Bending meaning moving under the weight of expectation.

[44] Briggs (1997) 8.

[45] King James (1994) 1. The composition of the *Basilicon* was evidently inspired by the *Political Testament* which Charles V wrote for his son Philip. James had received a copy of the *Testament* from the Italian scholar and fugitive from the Inquisition, Giacomo Castelvetro, in 1591. Further inspiration coming from Aurelius's *Meditations* and Alfred's *Boethius*, both of which he had encountered during Buchanan's tutelage.

for this very reason that He vests in them a 'glistering wordly glorie', so that they may 'shine before their people'.[46] As a 'mirror' indeed, 'viue and faire'.[47] Put simply, a king 'is as one set upon a stage', and if he does not look kingly, he can hardly expect to earn the love, and the awe, of his subjects.[48]

Not that things should otherwise be taken to excess. A good prince also appreciates the benefit of a balanced diet and sensible dress-wear. His food should be 'simple, without composition or sauces' and he should learn to 'eate in a manlie, round and honest fashion'. And not to dress 'like a Candie souldier or a vaine young Courtier'.[49] He will also appreciate the benefits of 'honest' exercise, hunting especially. James loved hunting.[50] The benefits of writing poetry too, particularly that which is 'rich in quicke inventions', rather than merely rhymes 'right'.[51] The younger James fancied himself as a bit of a poet, as we have already noted. Conversely, avoid getting into scraps of any kind, including duelling, a practice against which James would issue a Proclamation in 1604. Or bear-baiting, which just annoyed the bears. All very sensible, if hardly fitting the image of a warrior-prince.[52] But then James was not, by inclination, the warrior type. More the paranoid, posting bodyguards around his Bedchamber, wearing double-quilted jackets, in case of knife-wielding assassins, and liking a good ruff too for much the same reason. More of the ruffs in due course. The younger James had dodged enough assassination attempts to make the older borderline neurotic.[53]

But there was more than just advice on princely behaviour in the *Basilicon*. Alongside the chatter about dress sense and bear-baiting, could be read assorted commentary on matters of public philosophy, on the responsibilities of kingship and the nature of 'divine right', on the duties which attend to a prince who is also the 'conserver of Religion'.[54] More particularly the exercise of 'conscience', so that a king might discharge his 'Office ... in the points of Justice and Equitie'.[55] It is indeed the 'highest honour' and 'greatest suretie', in having subjects know in their

---

[46] King James (1994) 13.

[47] King James (1994) 1.

[48] King James (1994) 49.

[49] King James (1994) 50–52. A French ambassador despatched by King Henri IV in 1584, reported back that James had a peculiar dislike of earrings. See Stewart (2003) 75.

[50] King James (1994) 56 and also 202, stressing the need to ensure that the forests are kept properly stocked too.

[51] King James (1994) 55.

[52] The 'most cowardly man I ever knew', an unimpressed Sir John Oglander later recalled, having spent the day hunting with his new King. A staunch royalist, and copious diarist, Oglander was later High Sheriff of Hampshire. See Stewart (2003) ix.

[53] The Ruthven 'raid' and Gowrie 'conspiracy' being perhaps the most notable of many hairy moments prior to James removing to England; after which, in quick succession, came the Bye and Main plots and, of course, the Gunpowder. The fate of James's parents would hardly have done much for the nerves either. His father Lord Darnley murdered at Kirk o'Field on the outskirts of Edinburgh in 1567, most likely strangled, his mother, Mary Queen of Scots, executed at Fotheringay castle in 1587. To which might be added the knowledge that two kings of France had been recently assassinated, two Guise brothers, and William of Orange.

[54] King James (1994) 17.

[55] King James (1994) 20.

'hearts' that their prince is the 'contrarie' of 'an usurping Tyrant'.[56] Plenty then for the *specula* enthusiast to enjoy. A 'law-booke and a mirrour', as the *Basilicon* advertised itself.[57] In essence, a practical guide to magistracy, of which just seven copies were printed in 1599, for a very select private circulation.

And then hundreds more in spring 1603, when it was reprinted, along-side another of James's musings on the nature of kingship, *The Trew Law of Free Monarchies*. In combination, a manifesto for a prospective King of England, a job application almost. Bacon was certainly impressed, and everyone else, or so he later recalled. The 'book falling into every man's hand filled the whole realm as with a good perfume or incense before the King's coming in'.[58] We will encounter some more doubting voices very shortly, when we take a closer look at the *Trew Law*. First, though, another piece of advice, of immediate pertinence to men like Sir Francis Bacon.

Sick and Spewing

The matter of choosing the right counsellors. 'Choose then all for these Offices, men of knowen wisedome, honestie, and good conscience', the *Basilicon* advises, and who are furthermore 'well practised in the point of the craft, that yee ordaine them for'. Above all, make sure they are 'free of that fllthie vice of Flatterie, the pest of all Princes'.[59] Sound advice, commonly recommended, not so often followed, and not much by James. Nor by the Duke in *Measure for Measure*, or the King of Denmark in *Hamlet*, or the eponymous Othello, or Leontes in *The Winter's Tale*. The blight of Shakespeare's variously problematic Jacobean princes is that of bad counsel. We can only surmise how much of a hint James took from their vari-ous misfortunes. As might be imagined of another play presented at Court within months of James arriving in his new realm.

Drawn, its author advertised, from Lipsius's edition of *Tacitus*, supplemented with some juicy bits of Suetonius, Ben Jonson's *Sejanus* dramatises the 'fall' of Tiberius's eponymous, and notorious, *praetorian* prefect.[60] Another text written in the 'mirror' tradition, ushering a distinctly Machiavellian, as well as Roman, historiography onto the Jacobean stage.[61] The murderous Sejanus flourishes for

---

[56] King James (1994) 20.

[57] King James (1994) 34.

[58] Bacon (1998) 219. And it does seem to have fallen into quite a few hands. It has been estimated that successive reprints, over the first few years alone, would have amounted to around 16,000 copies, making it 'one of the runaway bestsellers of the Renaissance'. See Stewart (2003) 149; and also Wormald (2021) 209–10.

[59] King James (1994) 37.

[60] 'Preface', in Wilkes (1999) 104. For a comment on Jonson's extensive use of Tacitus in *Sejanus*, see Donaldson (2011) 186–88. Intriguingly, it has been surmised that Shakespeare might have played the role of Tiberius in the original production of the play.

[61] See MacLeod (2021) supposing that the writing of *Sejanus* was presaged in the 'apologeticall Dialogue' which Jonson attached to his *Poetaster* a year or so earlier. The turn from comic satire to a very deadly historical seriousness.

a dangerous while because the environment is conducive. A place of 'soft and glutinous' flatterers, and 'black secrets' (1.8. 15).[62] Where the only 'way to rise, is to obey and please' (3. 735). All played out against a backdrop in which better minds cast back to happier days, before Tiberius, an 'emperor only in his lusts', before indeed there were any emperors pretending to 'divine election' (4. 376, 5. 332). Ironically, Jonson liked to see himself as something of a poetic counsellor, a Horace to his Augustus.[63]

Patronage could, though, be a mixed blessing. As the sorry demise of George Villiers, Duke of Buckingham, confirmed. 'Steenie', as James took to calling him; after St Stephen, for reason of having the 'face of an angel'. Some cracking legs as well, by common repute the shapeliest as well as the springiest in England. It was reported that James paid £1,500 for a masque on Twelfth Night in early 1615, just so that he could admire Steenie's 'jumps'.[64] James had become quickly besotted. 'Christ had his John, I have my George', he proclaimed.[65] Neither saintly allusion impressed an emergent opposition 'junto' in the Commons. It preferred a different caricature. When the Duke was assassinated in the summer of 1628 his assailant alluded to accounts of heated parliamentary debate in which Steenie was likened to Sejanus.[66] There was, the insinuation ran, only one way to get rid of a Steenie.

As the years rolled on, Jacobean drama became obsessed with the seamier side of courtly life. The corpse-strewn close of *Hamlet* setting the scene, not just for Shakespeare's own later tragedies, *Antony and Cleopatra* and *Othello*, but for a refined genre of 'revenger' plays, associated with the likes of Middleton and John Webster, in which princely courts invariably become havens of satanic depravity. The very opening of Webster's *The Duchess of Malfi*, first performed in 1614, left nothing, and everything, to the imagination:

> a prince's court
>
> Is like a common fountain, whence should flow
>
> Pure silver drops in general: but of't chance
>
> Some curs'd example poison't near the head,
>
> Death, and disease through the whole land spread (1.1. 11–15).[67]

---

[62] Internal references from Wilkes (1999). It has been suggested that references to 'black secrets' and similar might allude to recusant life. It is thought that Jonson might have converted to Roman Catholicism whilst in Newgate over the winter of 1598 to 1599. He was awaiting trial for having killed a fellow actor in a duel.

[63] Relations with his Augustus would be stretched just that little too far in 1605, with the production of *Eastward Ho!*, co-written with John Marston and George Chapman. A few too many anti-Scottish jokes would see all three co-authors spending some time at 'His Majesty's Pleasure'.

[64] Adding rather pointedly, that Steenie 'jumped higher than ever Englishman did in short a time, from a private gentleman to a dukedom'. In Stewart (2003) 268.

[65] Stewart (2003) 281–82.

[66] Buckingham was stabbed through the heart by a disgruntled officer named John Felton, who claimed that the Duke had promised him promotion and back pay, and then reneged. Under torture, Felton admitted having read reports of parliamentary debates closely.

[67] Internal references from Webster (1986).

By then it had become only too obvious that the idea of magistracy recommended in the *Basilicon* and the reality of life at the Court of James Stuart were barely congruent. A place of 'riot and excess', according to Jonson's friend, Sir Nicholas Roe, who managed to get himself ejected from Court for protesting too loudly at a performance of Samuel Daniels's masque, *The Vision of the Twelve Goddesses*.[68] Sir Dudley Carleton took an equally dim view of a performance of the *Masque of Blackness*, performed as part of the Twelfth Night celebrations at Whitehall in 1605. Sir Dudley questioned the wisdom of presenting so many ladies of the court like 'blackamoors' and oriental courtesans. Another Inigo Jones and Ben Jonson production, at a cost of £3,000 for the evening.[69] James might have liked a good masque, but it was never a genre that sat particularly well with the more puritanical sentiment, at Court or anywhere else.

No contemporary report of courtly debauchery, though, quite matches that left by Sir John Harrington, who attended an evening of celebrations in honour of the visit of James's brother-in-law, Christian IV of Denmark, in July 1606. On the theme of *Solomon his Temple and the coming of the Queen of Sheba*. Suitably cloying, for reasons with which we are already familiar. James rather fancied himself as Solomon. He also rather liked a drink, as it seemed did the Queen of Sheba, and her various attendants, most of whom turned out to be prostitutes. At least Chastity remembered her lines, an appalled Sir John reported, before joining Hope and Faith in the 'lower hall', rolling about 'sick and spewing'. Peace, meanwhile, 'much contrary to her semblance, most rudely made war with her olive branch'. 'I ne'er did see such a lack of good order, discretion, and sobriety as I have now done', Harrington concluded. More like 'Mahomet's paradise' than the court of a Christian prince, and so very different from what 'passed' in 'our Queen's days'.[70]

A sense enhanced with each scandal that beset James's Court, reaching a peak with the Overbury scandal in 1615.[71] Its origins could be traced back to 1607, when James first espied 20-year-old Robert Carr at a tilt.[72] Six years on Carr became Earl of Somerset as a precursor to marrying the recently divorced Countess of Essex, Frances Howard. The path of true love though rarely runs straight. Frances's first marriage had been ruined by sorcery, her husband rendered impotent by bewitchment.[73] Her second went awry when she decided to murder Sir Thomas

---

[68] See Donaldson (2011) 199.

[69] Roughly £400,000 today.

[70] Letter to Secretary Barlow, in *Nugae Antiquae* (1779) 2. 126–30. For accounts of the event, see Blakemore Evans (1988) 201–02; Briggs (1997) 233; and Stewart (2003) 236–37.

[71] For a pleasingly racy account of the 'case', see Somerset (1997).

[72] The story goes that Carr broke his leg at the tilt, and James decided to take personal responsibility for his rehabilitation, whilst also teaching him Latin.

[73] Evidenced, indeed, by the fact that he was only impotent in her presence. Not that witchcraft-induced impotence was an offence recognised in law or scripture, as Archbishop Abbott counselled his King. Only to be reminded of the fact that he was in the presence of an expert who had indeed written about it in 'my *Daemonologie*'. James stacked the investigating commission, as a precaution, and the divorce was duly secured.

Overbury. Formerly Carr's personal secretary, and lover, Sir Thomas had died in mysterious circumstances in the Tower a few weeks before the marriage.[74] And a few days after eating some suspicious 'tarts' made by a Mrs Turner, reputed to be a close confidante of the Countess. Eighteenth months of rumour concluded in the spectacular trial and conviction of Frances and her husband. At least they were saved from the gallows, by order of the King.[75] Unlike Mrs Turner, who had some sage advice for those who attended her final moments.[76] A court is a place of 'malice, pride, whoredom' where no one should ever 'put' their children. All very shocking, it might be thought. Albeit less so to anyone who had attended performances of *The Duchess of Malfi*. Webster's Antonio was very much of the same mind as Mrs Turner: 'Let my son fly the courts of princes' (5.4. 72). His stage-mate Vittoria likewise: 'O happy they that never saw the court' (5.6. 261).

It might be wondered why a spot of spewing matters so much, in the longer history of English constitutional reformation. The same might be wondered of all the debauchery and the skits ridiculing James's 'sodomitical' preferences. The reason is given in the *Basilicon*, as well as Webster's *Duchess*, and *Sejanus*, and *Measure for Measure*, and Machiavelli's *Prince* and his *Discourses*, and every other contribution to the *specula* genre. The appearance of majesty reflects on everyone. We might call it the 'party-gate' experience. Small wonder if God seemed so disappointed with his formerly 'chosen' people, that He kept sending plagues, and refused them the solace of religious and constitutional 'settlement'. No matter how hard a prince might protest his divine appointment, or his mandate from the people, to get things 'done'.

Rapt in Studies

No wonder, either, that the Devil seemed to be doing so well. In truth he had been doing well for a while, and not just in England. Protestant Europe was beset by his diabolical endeavours. There was, of course, no surprise in discovering that the Devil had a particular interest in England. It was, after all, where the 'chosen people' lived. Chief Justice Anderson was in no doubt as to the pressing danger, informing a jury in 1602 that 'the land is full of witches; they abound in all places'. There would, the Chief Justice inferred, need to be a new war against witchery,

---

[74] Overbury had actually died two years earlier, but evidence of wrongdoing was only attested in early 1615, following an investigation conducted by the new Secretary of State, Sir Ralph Winwood. His gangrenous body had apparently smelt so bad, that no one had fancied conducting a postmortem examination at the time.

[75] The prosecution was led by Bacon, as Attorney General, his job made easier by the fact that the Countess confessed and threw herself on the mercy of the Court, and King. The Earl was apparently more recalcitrant. After commutation of sentence the two were held, separately, in the Tower until 1622.

[76] The same fate awaited the Lieutenant of the Tower, Sir Gervase Elwes, and Thomas Weston, who Elwes had appointed as Overbury's 'keeper'.

'otherwise they will in a short-time over-run the whole land'.[77] A new king might help, particularly one who was an expert on the subject. So might some new law, which treated the matter with the seriousness it deserved.

The existing 1563 Act against Conjurations, Enchantments and Witchcrafts required evidence of harm caused 'whereby any person shall happen to be killed', before a witch might be convicted and executed. Far too slack. Emergencies require emergency law. 'Presumptions' sufficiently 'great', the Chief Justice advised, ought to be enough. A new Act against Conjuration, Witchcraft and dealing with evil and wicked spirits, passed in 1604, duly allowed for convictions based on evidence of mere conjuration or diabolic association, regardless of harm. It also transferred jurisdiction from namby-pamby Church courts to common law, witchery being so evidently a state crime.

After which it was time to get the poets on the job. Just over a year later, following the Devil's audacious attempt to blow up Parliament in November 1605, came a new play from the pen of the King's chief propagandist, within which could be found the most famous witches in English literature. If anyone had any doubts as to the damage that a coven of witches might do to the security of a commonwealth, they only need spend an hour or so with the 'midnight hags' of *Macbeth*. 'Double, double toil and trouble;/ Fire, burn, and cauldron bubble' (4.1. 10–11). Few literary witches have had better rhythm, or better ingredients: 'eye of newt, and toe of frog', a sprinkling of herbs and a 'pilot's thumb' (1.3. 28). Or indeed greater ambition: the 'sacrilegious murder' of a king (2.3. 66). 'Though this bark cannot be lost/ Yet it shall be tempest tossed'; one of the many allusions which the new King of England would undoubtedly have picked up (1.3. 26).[78]

Evidently thrilling, witches proved to be a predictably popular presence on the Jacobean stage. At the opposite end of the spectrum from Shakespeare's fabulous creations could be found the altogether earthier Elizabeth Sawyer raised in Dekker, Ford and Rowley's *The Witch of Edmonton*. Based on a 'true' account, Dekker and his co-writers presented their audience with a witch who, whilst undoubtedly possessed, was also 'spun' for 'the devil's own wearing' (4.1. 126).[79] The construct of an 'envious world' and the 'rubbish of men's tongues' (2.1. 1, 7). But more especially, the fear of women's, which is why Elizabeth must be hanged. Not just because she has a strangely behaving dog, but because she is 'too saucy and too bitter' (4.1. 82).[80] In modern vernacular, Elizabeth is a bit woke. When arraigned by the local justice, she launches into a diatribe against the assorted 'lechers' and 'men-witches' who steal the land and abuse young maidens (4.1. 107–08, 115–19, 134–38).

---

[77] Sharpe (1997) 216.

[78] Having only just survived a storm conjured by the 'North Berwick witches' in 1590. An adventure to which we will shortly return.

[79] Internal references to *The Witch of Edmonton* are from Wiggins (2008). The 'true' account of the 'wonderful discoverie' and subsequent trial of Elizabeth Sawyer was recorded by the Reverend Henry Goodcole.

[80] For an account of this construction, see O'Mahoney (2009); and Pearson (2008).

A variant theme is discovered in Jonson's *The Alchemist*, playing along the hazy margins that lay between conman and 'cunning man' (1.2. 8).[81] Another still in the Machiavellian sorcerers and schemers who wander John Webster's stage.[82] Webster, like Jonson, traded on gullibility. It did not necessarily make either a witchcraft-sceptic, but it insinuated that there was a fair bit of nonsense about. Jonson's *Masque of Queens*, performed at Court in 1609, owed much to Thomas Scot's earlier, and notoriously sceptical, *Discovery of Witchcraft*.

It was against Scot's 'damnable' *Discovery* that James had composed his own treatise on the subject, entitled *Daemonology*. Which, to an extent, shared Scot's concerns regarding false accusations. Witch 'crazes' must be distinguished, if witchery was to be properly 'discovered'.[83] James never doubted the existence of witches though. Published in 1598, *Daemonology* was inspired by James's personal involvement in the 'discovery' of a coven in North Berwick several years earlier.[84] A didactic piece, structured in the familiar 'doctor and student' style, it differed from other witchcraft treatises in that it focused more on the philosophical dimensions of witchery than on the pragmatics of 'discovery'. And more especially still, on the peculiar prerogatives vested in the King as investigating magistrate and judge. It is the latter which makes *Daemonology* a treatise not just on witchery, but on the political theology of kingship.[85]

A theology the origins of which lay, once again, in classical Rome. In the idea, more particularly, of the *dominus mundi*. 'I am master of the world'; *Digest* 14.2.9. A statement which was derived, according to Ulpian, from the 'rule' of the 'divine Augustus'.[86] And a sentiment which had long proved attractive to canon lawyers trying to flatter the absolutist pretensions of successive 'Holy Roman' emperors. Comprehended in its purest sense, it allowed an aspiring emperor to assume a

---

[81] It has been suggested that Jonson modelled his conman/alchemist Subtle on either, or both of, John Dee and Simon Forman. Both renowned in their moment, and able to advertise a range of key transferable skills. In the latter's case, to include 'astrology, geomancy, medicine, divination by facial moles, alchemy, and conjuring'. It was to Forman that Frances Howard turned in order to build her divorce case against her first husband, on the grounds of impotence-bewitchment. For a comment on the possible modelling of Subtle and his laboratory, see Donaldson (2011) 246–47.

[82] The most renowned example being the attempt to use faux-witchcraft to turn the mind of the Duchess in Act 4 Scene 1 of *The Duchess of Malfi*. For a commentary here, see Tricomi (2004).

[83] Though it was, otherwise, primarily written in rebuttal of Scot. The most famous example of James 'discovering' a false witchcraft accusation was the 'case' of Anne Gunter. For an account, see Sharpe (2001).

[84] Written, it has been supposed, in part for his own 'self-assurance'. See Wormald (2021) 182 and also 220–21. The coven was first discovered in 1590, following an enquiry into a series of abortive attempts to transport James's new wife Anna of Denmark across the North Sea. Blighted by storms which, it was discovered, were the Devil's work. For further commentary here, see Orr (2016) 140–41.

[85] For the suggestion that James's idea of kingship was founded on this political theology, see Monateri (2018) 87–99. For a similar argument, from a slightly different perspective, see Kernan (1995) 86–87, suggesting that *Macbeth* might be read a 'theatrical version' of a 'political strategy', more particularly affirming the peculiar capacity of kings to deal with witchcraft.

[86] And possibly earlier still. See Tuori (2016) 56–57, tracing the idea back to the dictatorship of Julius Caesar, and the inspiration of Alexander the Great, and also 282–87.

'divine' status, as the embodiment of God and His law. The 'manner and resemblance of Divine power upon earth', as James would remind his Westminster Parliament in 1610. Plenty of supportive scriptural referents. Proverbs 8:15, 'By me kings reign, and princes decree justice'. Psalms 82:6, 'I have said, Ye are gods'. Cultural referents too. The sixth canto of Dante's *Divine Comedy*, the parallel of God as *dominus* in heaven, and the monarch as *dominus* on earth. An intriguing possibility for a prospective *imperator* of a 'greater' Britain.

And 'saviour' of its people. The responsibility affirmed in the closing passages of *News from Scotland*, a contemporary account of James's role in the 'apprehension' of the 'North Berwick witches'. James as 'the child and servant of God', leading his people on a crusade to rid his realm of the Devil and all his minions.[87] Of all the responsibilities which God vested in his princely 'children', none were more important than this, the 'sharp persewing' of Satan.[88] It is why God further vested in his kings certain 'mysterious' prerogatives, as James called them, to help identify and destroy the anti-Christ and his minions.[89] The inspiration here was Jean Bodin's *Daemonomanie*, which James had read extensively.[90] The preface to *Daemonology* paid tribute to a text 'collected with greater diligence, then written with judgement, together with their confessions, that have bene at this time apprehended'.[91] At the heart of *Daemonology* was the thought, taken from Bodin, that witchery must be treated as a crime against the state, rather than a species of private nuisance. The antics of the North Berwick witches proved that much, with their devilish attempt to murder James and his new wife as they crossed the North Sea. It was high time to get tough on witchery, and the causes of witchery.

A view emphasised in the closing passages of the treatise, which discuss appropriate forms of legal process and punishment. The 'forme' of punishment was unarguable. Witches 'ought to be put to death according to the Law of God, the civill and imperial law, and municipall law of all Christian nations', for felony 'treason against the Prince' is nothing less than a 'high treason against God'.[92] Two collateral assumptions were taken from Bodin's *Six Livres de la Republique*.[93] First, that a crime committed against the 'manner and resemblance of Divine

---

[87] *News from Scotland* in King James (1924) 29.

[88] King James (1924) 48. See also Orr (2016) 142–43.

[89] Who might, as a consequence, be too easily gulled. For this reason, James poured scorn on those who believed that witches could fly, or take the form of werewolves. The claim to be the voice of reason is a curious twist, in the circumstances. See Orr (2016) 144; and also Monateri (2018) 3.

[90] As did the entire treatise, an essentially 'derivative' endeavour according to Christina Larner (1984) 16.

[91] King James (1924) xv. The same arguments could be found in Bodin's *Republique*. For further commentary here, see Monateri (2018) 108–11.

[92] Citing 1 Samuel 15, 'and not to strike when God bids strike, and so severelie punish in so odious a fault and treason against God, it is not only unlawful, but doubtlesse no lesse sinne in that Magistrate, nor it was Saul's sparing of Agar'. King James (1924) 77, 79.

[93] See Evrigenis (2019) 1074–77, noting that James kept a copy of the *Republique* in his library, and was, moreover, fluent in French.

power on earth' is a crime committed against that 'Divine power', and second that the consequential jurisprudence is an expression of 'natural' law, universally accepted amongst Christian nations. It was here that James found an authoritative affirmation of the political theology of the *dominus mundi*.[94]

Whilst his personal interest in witchery would wane, James never wavered in his aligned belief that witches existed and that, as King, he was entrusted with 'mysterious' prerogatives for the purpose of 'discovering' them.[95] 'The mysteries of the Kings power is not lawfully to be disputed', he reminded Star Chamber in 1616, for it 'would be to be take away' the 'mystical reverence that belongs unto them that sit in the Throne of God'. To do so, indeed, was a form of 'atheisme and blasphemy'.[96] Put simply, the 'presence of the Devil' legitimates the prerogative.[97] Indeed, it legitimates the very idea of rule by 'divine right'. A subject about which James was already writing another treatise, to appear just a few months later. Before we turn to that, however, we will close with a rather pointed poetic muse on the ups and downs of being a learned Renaissance prince peculiarly obsessed by witches.

The Tempest was the last play that Shakespeare is thought to have written, at least in substantive part. And it is all about a wise fool who masquerades, literally, as a wizard. So 'rapt in secret studies' that he becomes a 'stranger' to his more prosaic duties (1.2. 73, 76–77, 110). Another allusion that would have been difficult to miss. If he had not been a king, James once observed, 'I would be a University-man'. Geoffrey Goodman, Bishop of Gloucester noted how much his King 'did love solitariness, and was given to his study'.[98] As did Isaac Casaubon, albeit in more disapproving tones, bemoaning the fact that his King's mind was 'now so entirely taken up' with rebutting a particular 'letter' despatched by the Vatican that he neglected all else.[99] We will take a closer look at this letter very shortly.

Bacon likewise spotted the risk in his essay 'On Studies'. To 'spend too much time in studies is sloth; to use them too much for ornament is affection'. A 'learned' man is not the same as a 'ready man'.[100] Prospero is precisely this: learned, but unready. Which is why he has been deposed and is now discovered trying to impose his authority on an enchanted island. Order is restored only when Prospero abjures his 'rough magic' and turns his attention instead to the more pragmatic arts of magistracy (5.1. 50).[101] No longer just a sorcerer, but a stage-manager, directing himself and his subjects. In the final line pleading the 'indulgence' of his audience (Epil 20). Bringing the curtain down on a play which was all about the kingship, and the pretence, of James Stuart.

---

[94] Monateri (2018) 101–11.
[95] See Wormald (2021) 27–28; and Elmer (2016) 64–65.
[96] King James (1994) 213.
[97] Monateri (2018) 98–99, 138.
[98] Wormald (2021) 175.
[99] In Stewart (2003) 231.
[100] Bacon (1985) 209.
[101] Raffield (2017) 208–10.

God's Lieutenant

At the heart of the Reformation settlement was the plain fact that kings and queens of England were also *de jure* governors of its Church. In its original conception, a pragmatic, and lucrative, convenience. But also one that inhered a spiritual dimension, for a reformation English monarch was also a priest and confessor, the divinely chosen intermediary between the chosen people and their God. A responsibility that James Stuart certainly felt, and about which he wrote at considerable length, not just in his *Basilicon Doron*, but in his most concentrated reflection on the nature of kingship, the *Trew Law of Free Monarchies*.

The Trew Law

Again published in 1598, and again anonymously, the *Trew Law* opened in vaunting tones. Monarchy, 'as resembling Divinitie, approcheth nearest to perfection'.[102] The influence of Bodin once again, the *dominus* confirmed by divinity.[103] Written in the fashionable inductive style too, demolishing 'contrary propositions' first, before moving on to affirm the 'trew' law. The 'contrary propositions' that most troubled James were those found in texts such as *De jure regni apud Scotus*, written by his erstwhile tutor George Buchanan.[104] A species of early-day contract-theory, which would be proscribed by the Scottish Parliament in 1589, *De jure regni* imported the notion that subjects might retrieve sovereignty from a king who, in their opinion, had breached the terms of his covenant. Or a queen indeed, such as James's mother Mary, to whom Buchanan had also served as tutor. Not that either seems to have been much persuaded by the contention. The idea of covenanted rights, James confirmed, was absurd, for once 'privileges' have been renounced 'by your willing consent', they are renounced 'for ever'.[105] As for 'wicked princes', they must be remitted to the 'justice and providence of God', the 'sharpest schoolemaster'.[106] It is for this reason that St Paul urged his followers to 'pray' for Nero, rather than seek to 'shake' him 'off'.[107] The ideal of the 'Stoic subject', reinvested in the writings of humanists such as Lipsius and Machiavelli.[108]

---

[102] King James (1994) 63.

[103] For Bodin's influence on absolutist theory in general, and the *Trew Law* in particular, see Sommerville (1986) 38–39; and Evrigenis (2019) 1085.

[104] For a commentary on the presence of Buchanan in James's 'mind' as he wrote the *Trew Law*, see Burns (1996) 234; and Evrigenis (2019) 1083–84.

[105] King James (1994) 69. See Burgess (1996) 40-41, suggesting that the *Trew Law* was less a defence of absolutism than a counter to 'resistance' theory.

[106] King James (1994) 83.

[107] King James (1994) 79.

[108] It has been surmised that James was introduced to Stoic philosophy by Buchanan, and was, in truth, not much impressed. In *Basilicon Doron*, he would disparage its 'insensible stupidity'. The presence of the 'Stoic subject' in the *Trew Law* is though implicit. See Orr (2016) 139, 147–52; Burgess (1996) 52–55; and also Salmon (1989) 200–04, 223. For the surmise regarding Shakespeare and Stoicism, see Bate (2019) 154–58.

In refining his belief in 'divine right', James sought recourse in the same scriptural and classical authorities commonly deployed by successive Holy Roman emperors, and their scribes.[109] Thus the bold, and bald, statement, reworked from Psalms 82:6 and 101: 'Kings are called Gods by the propheticall King David, because they sit upon God his Throne in the earth'.[110] Repeated invocations of patriarchy too: 'By the Law of Nature the King becomes a natural Father to all his Lieges at his Coronation', and 'the stile of *Pater patriae* was ever, and is commonly used to Kings'.[111] Classical authority in the shape of Ulpian's affirmation, written into Justinian's *Digest*, *princeps legibus solutus est*; 'the Emperor is not bound by law' (*Digest* 1.3.31). And again, in perhaps its most renowned articulation, *Quod principi placuit, legis habet vigorem*; 'what pleases the prince has the force of law' (*Digest* 1.4.1).

The 'defining feature', as Seneca intimated in his *De clementia*, of the 'constitutional history' of imperial Rome, the 'law animate' in the person of the *deorum vice*, divinely appointed emperor.[112] The authority again of 1 Samuel 8:20, which centres the *Trew Law*: 'That we may also be like all the nations; and that our king may judge us, and go out before us, and fight all our battles'.[113] The congruence between 'divine right' and the species of absolutism discovered in these classical authorities, and in Bodin and other continental writers, may not be exact.[114] But it comes close. A king whose authority was derived from God, who ruled in his place, vested with certain prerogatives which placed him above the 'common' law, and without threat of removal by resisting subjects. It is here that James engaged the binding constitutional controversy of reformation political theology: the reach of prerogative discretion.

Prerogatives which were bestowed on kings to ensure that 'natural' justice will always be done. The argument of *Daemonology* reinvested. For which reason, there are specific courts designed to correct errors in the civil, or indeed 'common', law. The 'rolles of our Chancellery (which containe our eldest and fundamentall Lawes) that the King is *Dominus omnium honorum*, and *Dominus directus totius Dominii*'; direct lord of the whole dominium.[115] The principle which underlay James's splenetic address to his judges in 1616. For their failure to appreciate that 'the Chancerie tempers the Law with Equitie, and so mixeth Mercy with Justice, as it preserves men from destruction'. And 'thus (as I before told you) is the King's

---

[109] See Monateri (2018) 87–88.

[110] King James (1994) 64.

[111] King James (1994) 65, 76. James made similar recourse to the patriarchal analogy in his 1610 address to Parliament: 182–83.

[112] See Tuori (2016) 7–8, 130–42; and also Romm (2014) 89–91. In some ways *speculum principis* writing can be treated as a classical forerunner of the 'mirror for magistrates' literature which became so popular during the Renaissance. We will revisit some of the latter shortly.

[113] See Burns (1996) 233, discussing James's 'sermon', at the heart of the *Trew Law*, on 1 Samuel 8: 9–20.

[114] See here Russell (1990) 147, thinking the term 'absolutism' simply too broad; and also Burgess (1996) 17–21, 31–33, 63–66, 93–96.

[115] King James (1994) 73. For a commentary on this defining statement, see Evrigenis (2019) 1084.

Throne established by Mercy and Justice'.[116] A king must be above the law, in order to secure it. This does not mean that a 'good king' will do other than 'frame all his actions to be according to the Law'. But it does mean that, being 'above the law', he is not 'bound thereunto'.[117]

Foremost amongst these prerogatives, as Bodin again affirmed, is that of mercy. The exercise of *clementia*, the defining attribute of the *dominus*.[118] A prerogative derived from practical reason, even as it is recommended by history. And an 'adornment' which, following Seneca, would improve public 'morals' whilst also securing the empire, and emperor, by virtue of inspiring the 'love' of an appreciative citizenry.[119] The *princeps* that Seneca has more immediately in mind, of course, was the young Nero. But the precedent to which he recurred was Augustus. Both Suetonius and Dio likewise paid testament to Augustus's particular determination to exercise his prerogative of *clementia*.[120] Likewise Bodin, especially impressed by an account of Augustus being counselled by his friend Maecenas against giving judgement in anger, precisely because it would incline him less to *clementia*. In one case, Augustus 'finding himselfe transported with choler, and to bee too hastie in judgment, to stay his anger, forthwith brake up the court'.[121]

James underlined the passage in his copy of the *Republique* and paid oblique homage in both the *Trew Law* and the *Basilicon Doron*.[122] In the latter, advising that the first responsibility of a king, having 'setled' his realm, is to ensure 'all the daies of your life' to 'mixe Justice with Mercie'. Not simply 'pity', James advised, which would likely lead to 'heapes' of offences and petitions, nor merely to 'winke at faults', as he would later put it, but to 'forgive faults after they are confessed'.[123] Seneca's distinction precisely.[124] Too much winking leads to 'Tyrannie', too much rigour to 'injustice'. '*Nam in medio stat virtus*', justice lies in moderation.[125] Portia's resolution too, in the *Merchant of Venice*. A principle reinforced in the common law, even if it is not derived from it.

Back in early 1584, in the wake of the Ruthven 'raid', Queen Elizabeth had despatched her spy-chief Sir Francis Walsingham to Scotland, to try to pass on some advice, chiefly on the topic of choosing the right counsellors. Afflicted by 'some kind of distemperature', in other words a bit tipsy, James had suggested to Walsingham that he was 'an absolute king' and could do what he wanted. Unlike

---

[116] King James (1994) 214.

[117] King James (1994) 75. For a commentary, see Evrigenis (2019) 1082.

[118] Evrigenis (2019) 1079.

[119] In Seneca (2007) 193, 200, 209–12.

[120] A supreme capacity too, given the absence at the time of any other kind of recognised appeal process. See Suetonius (2000) 61–62; and also Tuori (2016) 90–91, 109–10.

[121] Bodin (1962) 577. The name Maecenas became shorthand for virtuous counselling. The poet Fulke Greville likened the deceased Prince Henry to Maecenas, 'both for wisdom and strength of body'.

[122] See here Evrigenis (2019) 1079–82.

[123] King James (1994) 22 and also 200, for the latter observation, which was made in his 1610 speech to Parliament.

[124] Seneca (2007) 215–17, distinguishing mercy from mere 'pity'.

[125] King James (1994) 43.

Elizabeth. An observation that could be interpreted in different ways. The more hopeful supposed that he recognised a difference in being King of Scotland and King of England. The *Trew Law* certainly reflected a distinctly Scottish idea of kingship, wherein the likes of Bodin and the residue of Roman public philosophy was more clearly inscribed.[126] Composed, moreover, as a particular rebuttal of Calvinist 'resistance' theory, which had rather greater traction north of the border.

For the present at least. But it was the future that worried the pessimists. And the closing intimation of James's treatise, that English and Scottish kingship was founded on 'the same ground'. The fact that the *Trew Law* had been published anonymously, with limited circulation, retained a margin of discretion. Perhaps it would stay in Scotland?[127] A fresh reprint within months of arriving in London, alongside a shiny new edition of the *Basilicon*, dispelled that illusion.[128] More likely, the new King of England imagined himself chosen by God to rule *dominus directus*; just as he did in Scotland. An interpretation endorsed by James Cowell, Professor of Civil Law at Cambridge. In case anyone had not yet read the *Trew Law*, Cowell summed up its central thesis. The King ruled *supra legem*, above the law, 'by his absolute power', in both his realms.[129]

Sitting in God's Throne

There was nothing peculiar in James assuming that he was chosen by God to rule England, or Scotland. His predecessor took 'delight' in the fact that 'God hath made me his instrument'.[130] It was the absolutist imputation that jarred, and from this James, once again, never wavered. It was, in his mind, the logic of reformation, which made him governor of both the Church and the civil state. 'No bishop, no King', as James kept on reminding assembled delegates at the Hampton Court conference. A governor, moreover, vested with a primary responsibility, not just to discover all the abounding witches, but likewise all the 'puritans and novelists … lurking within the bowels of this nation'.[131] How could a man vested by God with this peculiar responsibility be subject to the whims of his judges? A point he was at pains to make, not just in successive parliamentary addresses, and Privy Council harangues, but in other published writings, such as the *Triplici nodo, triplex*

---

[126] See here Wormald (2021) 35.

[127] For the supposition that the *Trew Law* was written in a specifically Scottish context, and that English parliamentarians and common lawyers made the mistake of taking the texts 'too seriously', see Wormald (2021) 196–97.

[128] The spring 1603 republication 'flooded the market', according to Wormald (2021) 36.

[129] Cowell was the author of a best-selling primer for law students, civil and common, entitled *The Interpreter*, wherein could be discovered numerous similar assertions. For commentaries on Cowell and his *Interpreter*, see Sommerville (1986) 121–22; and Monateri (2018) 90.

[130] Most notably in her 'Golden Speech', delivered to Parliament in 1601, in order to distract monopoly 'grievances'. See Baker (2017) 198–99.

[131] Speech to Parliament in 1604. In Jardine and Stewart (1998) 277.

cuneus; or Apologie for the Oath of Allegiance which appeared in 1608.[132] Just as Shakespeare was conceiving his Cymbeline and, very probably, his Prospero.

The purpose of the *Apologie* was to defend the imposition of a new oath of allegiance following the Gunpowder Plot, whilst also rebutting a 'letter' which had been despatched by Pope Paul V's intellectual hit-man, Cardinal Bellarmine, for the purpose of stiffening the resolve of the Catholic 'community' in England.[133] It was against this same letter that John Donne directed his first substantive piece of prose, *Pseudo-Martyr*. Sacrifice on the part of those who refused the oath was, Donne argued, a 'corrupt affectation of martyrdom'.[134] The *Apologie* went further still. Bellarmine's 'letter' had been despatched to sew 'seeds of jealousie' between the King and his subjects.[135] Unarguable evidence of the 'craft of the Devil', intended, not just to usurp the 'naturall Allegiance of Subjects to their Prince', but to sanction the 'killing of kings'.[136] The lexicon of witchery again, of 'light to darknesse, and heaven to hell', and the 'discovery' of Satan in the seat of St Peter.[137] Closing in tones designed to assure, but also to emphasise the danger. The English Church would indeed be finally reformed, 'purged and cleansed from corruption'.[138] At which point, it would innervate its God-given responsibility to liberate the rest of Europe from the Roman yoke. But only because it was blessed with a king like James; 'Sonnes of the Most High, nay God's themselves, The Lords anoynted, Sitting in God's throne', and doing His work.[139]

Resonant not just with the sentiment of the *Trew Law*, but with what he kept telling his Parliament and Council. In his address to Parliament in 1604, railing against the assumption of 'imperial civill power' in Rome, for the 'dethroning and decrowning Princes with his foot as pleaseth him'.[140] Counsel that the events of

---

[132] Published anonymously, it is uncertain precisely how much was originally drafted by James. But he clearly approved the sentiment.

[133] For a commentary on the oath and its reception, see Fincham and Lake (1985) 187–88; and also Hamilton (1992) 131–37.

[134] In Donaldson (2011) 258–59.

[135] King James (1994) 139.

[136] King James (1994) 93, 98, 111. The sanctioning of regicide being personally felt, of course; a ratcheting of the fact that the Pope had failed to condemn the Powder plotters, at least not to James's satisfaction.

[137] King James (1994) 130.

[138] King James (1994) 86, 139. Whilst the *Triplici* was a particular response to Bellarmine's 'letter', its tenor takes general issue with the longer-standing papal habit of publishing admonitions of God's temporal 'lieutenants'.

[139] King James (1994) 128. Published anonymously, precisely how much of the *Apologie* was James's work remains a matter of conjecture. The general consensus is that James most likely served in a supervening editorial capacity. Needless to say, the *Apologie* elicited another letter in rebuttal from Bellarmine, which was in turn rebutted by a *Reponsio ad apologiam cardinalis Ballarmini*, penned by Lancelot Andrews. Which came with a very long, slightly incongruous, preface written by James. Full of ribald jokes. How can we know the image of God, and paint it, when Moses 'never saw but his back parts'? And surely the Virgin Mary had better things to do with her time than 'make love to priests' and brawl 'with devils'? And as to purgatory, it had better have a 'fair green meadow', so that James can do some 'hawking upon it' while he awaits admission to heaven. Catholic Europe was suitably horrified. The Venetian Inquisition proscribed it, as of course did the Vatican, the Count of Florence burned his copy, Count Fuentes had his cut up. In Stewart (2003) 231.

[140] King James (1994) 140.

November 1605 had duly proved.[141] And in the 'directest contravention of the Will of God, for as any true Christian knows, a prince is appointed of God', not the Pope, his 'Supremacie' discovered in the 'word of God'.[142] James had been King of England for nearly five years when the *Apologie* was published. Long enough to appreciate that his idea of kingship was far from universally acclaimed amongst his new subjects. Not that he was inclined to give up.[143] On the contrary, all the more reason to intensify the argument. And, more urgently still, to bring into alignment the reformation of the English Church, and the reformation of English law.

Measured reformation of course. James's very first speech to Parliament talked of the need to think more 'wisely' about enacting new laws, to be 'warie about proposing novelties'. The 'life and strength of the Law' did not consist in 'heaping up infinite and confused numbers of Laws, but in the right interpretation and good execution of good and wholesome Laws'.[144] A sentiment inscribed in the *Basilicon Doron*. New laws should be 'seldome'. Better, in any legal order, for there to be 'few Lawes and well put in execution'.[145] In other words, making better sense of what is already there, of returning the law, like the Church, to its original principles. Likewise, in his speech opening Parliament in 1607, praising the 'grounds' of the common law, as the 'best of any Law in the world', whilst also taking pains to point out its inefficacies. The 'obscuritie in some points of this our written Law, and the want of fulnesse in others, the variations in Cases and mens curiosities breeding every day new questions and to the practice of bad'. All of which too readily led judges to 'unjust and partial' decisions. Accordingly, 'clearing and sweeping off the rust' of the common law was Parliament's most urgent responsibility.[146] That and giving him some money.

Moving on, James invited Parliament to focus its attention more closely on the need to reform the jury system. An 'excellent institution', provided it was populated by men 'of such qualities, credit' and 'understanding, as are worthy to be trusted with so great a charge'. But sadly, as with so much of the law, 'time and abuse' had taken its toll, so that 'many of the ablest and fittest persons' were being permitted to dodge service, to be replaced by the 'simple' and the 'ignorant'. Variations on a theme. Another year on, the focus was the prospective 'union of crowns', a recurring motif in James's addresses, to which we will shortly turn, and another opportunity to introduce a greater measure of coherence to English law.

---

[141] Though, for the sake of impressing the same point, an extensive passage in the *Triplici* duly chronicles a series of similar instances of popes undermining civil sovereigns, chiefly by means of issuing bulls or demanding contrary oaths. See King James (1994) 114–23.

[142] Or indeed studied Augustine, who is deployed as a particular authority for this point. See King James (1994) 93–94, 128.

[143] On the consistency of James's argument, before 1603 and for the duration after, see Wormald (2021) 75–103.

[144] King James (1994) 142–43.

[145] King James (1994) 21.

[146] King James (1994) 162–63.

In 1610, it was back to a broader denunciation of the confused state of the law, and Parliament's seeming inability, or unwillingness, to do much about it. A conciliatory start, as was customary at such moments. No law provided 'better or more advantages for a King' than the common law. But several 'things' in it must be 'purged and cleared'. Including linguistic affection. Henceforth English law should be written in English. Most worryingly, though, the law still had no 'settled Text', being discovered in a mess of 'old Customes, or else upon Reports and Cases of Judges'. The law should not depend 'upon the bare opinions of Judges, and uncertain Reports'. It was for Parliament, accordingly, to set down an 'exposition of the Law', along with an authoritative report of cases 'fit to serve for Law in all times hereafter'. Both sources, statutes and cases, should be 'maturely reviewed, and reconciled', and 'contraries … scraped out of our Bookes'. After which Parliament should enact a 'golden law'. A written constitution perhaps? It would, James pointedly concluded, represent nothing less than a 'reformation' of English law.[147] A view duly broadcast to the wider public in the form of a Royal Proclamation, which confirmed that a committee of 'discreet persons learned in the law' would be selected by Privy Council, tasked with a specific responsibility to collect the statutes and 'digest them into some orderly Method'.[148]

There was nothing aberrant in recommending a legal reformation. Coke would write his *Institutes* to similar purpose, as we will see. So too Bacon, in a stream of treatises, and just as many book proposals, constantly offering himself as just the man for the job. The consonance of Bacon's ideas and those articulated by his King is hardly surprising, given that his key transferable skill was to tell James precisely what he wanted to hear, and then tell everyone else. We will revisit Bacon's various offerings in due course, all part of grander project designed to rethink and reimagine pretty much everything. Meanwhile, a committee was established, tasked with reviewing the 'snaring' statutes.

But that was all, despite Lord Chancellor Ellesmere's constant nudging. If judges were not better informed as to the law, Ellesmere regaled the House of Lords, they could 'only follow their noses and grope at in the dark'.[149] Which, it seems, they were happy enough to do. We will contemplate judicial resistance to James's reform programme very shortly. As for James, it was a matter of waiting for the right moment, which would come in summer 1616: the moment to 'consecrate justice'. It certainly felt a decisive moment to Timothy Tourneur. The 'bias' of the King's speech was 'for raising his prerogative above the law of the realm', and thus bringing the common law 'into contempt'.[150] The judges bested, Tourneur looked to Parliament to save the common law.

It was all undoubtedly wearing, for all parties, reforming the Church and constitution, and law. But James was nothing if not stubborn, and he never

---

[147] Stewart (2003) 240.
[148] King James (1994) 186–88.
[149] In Shapiro (2019) 65.
[150] In Baker (2017) 420–21.

demurred in his belief that on this, as on pretty much everything else, he was right. The essential arguments would be revisited in 1615 in another diatribe against papal interference in civil governance, *A Remonstrance on the Right of Kings, and the Independence of their Crowns*.[151] God had vested in him a peculiar authority, as head of the spiritual and secular estate, and given him lots of prerogatives designed to purpose. God had also provided him with a remarkable opportunity, which could not be ascribed to mere coincidence. James Stuart could become a *dominus*, if not of the entire *mundi*, a fair bit of it. King of a 'united' England and Scotland, just so long as he could convince everyone else that it really was a good idea.

Dominus

We have already noted the imperial insinuation displayed in the coronation pageant of 1604. The coronation medal depicted the new King wearing a laurel wreath, 'James I, Caesar Augustus of Britain, Caesar heir of Caesars'. In a short while we will take a longer look at some splendid Rubens canvasses, set on the ceiling of the Banqueting Chamber in Whitehall. We will be there, primarily, to contemplate a poignant irony. For now, we can sneak a quick peak. There are three central canvasses, one of which is entitled *The Union of Crowns*. It depicts Mars ushering two female figures into James's presence, representing England and Scotland. At the same time, they hold two crowns above the head of the infant, there in turn to represent the nascent 'union'.[152] The *dominus* of James Stuart, and his progeny.

The Kings of Britain

Not the first to make the claim, of course. Athelstan took to styling himself *imperator*, as well as *Bretwalda*, 'wielder of the strength of Britons' and *rex totius Britanniae*, king of all the Britons, and 'King of Engaland'. The chronicler Aethewelweard tried to make sense of it all, declaring that 'Britain is now called England'.[153] A sleight of hand used by Geoffrey of Monmouth in his *History of the Kings of Britain*, and then again by Spenser in his *Faerie Queen*. By which time, the Act in Restraint of Appeals had confirmed that

> whereas by divers sundry and authentic histories and chronicles it is manifestly declared that this realm of England is an empire, and so hath been accepted in the

---

[151] The context, on this occasion, was the attempt of the new French King, Louis XIII, to impose an oath of obedience, and which was again opposed by the Catholic Church. Another example of the 'pernicious opinion; That Popes may tosse the French King his Throne like a tennis ball'. See Wormald (2021) 187.

[152] It has been speculated that the baby is modelled on the future Charles II. See Millar (2007) 103.

[153] Kumar (2003) 42.

world, governed by one supreme head and king, having the dignity and royal estate of the imperial crown the same.[154]

Only by being an empire could England assert its independence from Rome. Poetic invocation of an imperial Britain settled by the English was familiar enough. James, though, was the first to find himself in a credible position to transmute the poetry into a reality.

Something that Sir Robert Cotton surmised, very early on. Two days after Elizabeth was dead, Sir Robert produced a treatise which, based on various historical examples, suggested that union between England and Scotland was now inevitable.[155] He also suggested an appropriate name for this new imperial kingdom, or rather old. Why not 'Britannia', as the Romans used to call it? There were plenty of reasons why not, as we will see; not the least the fact that it was a Roman affectation. But the idea certainly chimed with the opinion of his new King, who assured his Scottish Privy Council that the case for a 'perfect and sincere union' was now unarguable.[156] Alexander Craig, one of the Castalian poets who travelled down with James, composed a sonnet in honour of the notion. A slightly different take on Cotton's, it might be noted. Craig imagined a 'Scoto-Britaine'.[157]

At much the same time, James established a Commission on Union, headed by Bacon and Ellesmere; partly to draft legislation, partly to provide PR.[158] Partly also, as Sir Edwin Sandys recommended, to advance the greater project of reforming English law, which was not anyway in 'high repute'.[159] The Commission returned three recommendations: abrogate 'hostile lawes', create a uniform commercial law, and establish a kind of common citizenship. At the same time, James issued a Proclamation on the Post-Nati. A *post-nati* was someone born in Scotland after James had succeeded to the English throne. Such a person, the Proclamation confirmed, should acquire rights in English, as well as Scots, law, by virtue of their birth. James also asked Parliament to approve a statutory change of title, so that he might restyle himself King of 'Great Britain'.

To which the answer was no. Here again, the idea of a 'greater' Britain was hardly new. The term was commonly used to distinguish England from the 'lesser' Britain discovered across the Channel in Brittany. James, however, had something altogether more unsettling in mind. The word 'Britain', it was pointed out in rebuttal, recalled a dark age of pagan savagery, whereas 'England' was an 'ancient name' of reverence. Undaunted, James issued another Proclamation, declaring himself King of 'Great' Britain and citing, by way of reason, cultural and religious commonality:

---

[154] A statement reaffirmed, the following year, in the 1534 Act of Supremacy. For a comment on the significance of Henry's imperial assertion, and the extent to which it served to develop a more conscious, and confident, 'England', see Greenfield (1992) 30–35, 50–51.

[155] Amongst the more pertinent, and recent, examples vouched by Cotton, and others, was the Spanish *monarchia*, bringing together Aragon and Castile.

[156] Stewart (2003) 209.

[157] In Wormald (2021) 355.

[158] The Commission comprised 48 Englishmen and 31 Scots.

[159] Shapiro (2019) 66.

'A communitie of language, the principall meanes of civil societie. An unitie of Religion, the chiefest band of heartie Union, and the surest knot of lasting Peace'.[160] What the Proclamation did not cite, notably, was legal commonality. As we will discover, James was a habitual issuer of proclamations; much preferable to all the bother of Parliament. And, on this occasion, a gesture of enduring significance. The 'tangle' of nomenclature which has, for four centuries, afflicted those who try to distinguish England from Britain can be traced to this moment.[161] We will catch up with this confusion in due course, for it might be about to end.[162]

The Proclamation also confirmed that there would be some shiny new coins celebrating the new 'union', starting with a 20-shilling piece, called the 'Unite'. 'James by grace of God King of Great Britain, France and Ireland', the obverse read. The reverse was inscribed with a no less hopeful bit of scripture. From Ezekiel 37:22, 'I will make them one nation'. A bit too hopeful, it transpired. Whilst there was little Parliament could do about the cultural refashioning, or the coinage, it could reject two bills which the Commission had proposed. A first would have added statutory heft to the Proclamation on the Post-Nati. The second was intended to naturalise the *ante-nati*. By way of compensation, it would, a few bitter months on, agree to a new flag; to become known as the 'Union Jack'.[163] But that was all that Parliament was prepared to concede.

The more judicious couched their concerns in tempered tones, wondering about the feasibility of a closer legal 'union', and the practicalities of a common citizenship. The less measured stood up in the Commons and voiced their opposition to the prospect of a nation of 'pedlars, infidels and pagans ... swarming' over the border.[164] The words of Nicholas Fuller. Not a man of easy temper, as we will shortly discover. Gervase Holles was just as troubled, noting that the Court, and more particularly still the Bedchamber, was full of swaggering Scotsmen sporting 'beggarly bluecaps'.[165] No wonder that the King was already broke, as John Haskyns rather tactlessly pointed out, given that he had spent the thick end of £100,000 on treats for all his fellow-swarmers.[166] Sir Christopher Pegge managed to get himself suspended from the House for claiming that there 'was as much difference between an English and a Scots man as between a judge and a thief'.[167]

---

[160] In Wormald (2021) 244.

[161] 'Whatever word we use lands us in a tangle', as a despairing AJP Taylor declared, in the 'Preface' to his volume of the *Oxford History of England* (1965) v. Jenny Wormald deploys a different metaphor to the same effect, 'slap-happy'. In Wormald (2021) 359.

[162] Along with the Union. For this latter surmise, see Wormald (2021) 69.

[163] Jack after *Jacobus*.

[164] The rhetoric of 'xenophobia', according to Wormald (2021) 90. See also Wright (2006) 184–88; and Stewart (2003) 214–15.

[165] Meaning woollen bonnets. The occupants of the Bedchamber were always a matter of peculiar concern, in every sense of the word.

[166] The King's 'cistern has sprung a leak', as Hoskyns put it to fellow Members. Around £90,000 in gifts and a further £10,000 in pensions. Not to be repeated, James tried to assure Parliament. See Wormald (2021) 47.

[167] Stewart (2003) 215.

The Scots, Pegge insinuated, were on the make. James would later express his contempt for those who carry 'an outward appearance of love to the Union, but indeed a contrary resolution in their hearts'.[168] At least Fuller, Holles and Pegge could not be accused of that.

In his address to Parliament in March 1604, James had set out his case in a 'discourse more particularly of the benefits that doe arise of the Union which is made in my blood'. Benefits that are 'naturall and Physicall', including the rather prosaic matter of being able to recruit bigger armies and improve national 'security'. But also benefits of the more spiritual kind, doing God's work. 'Hath not God first united these two Kingdomes both in Language, Religion and similitude of maners?' he enquired.[169] Not really, in truth, given that no one could understand his accent, that religion was about the last thing that might be said to be settled, and as for his manners, perhaps the less said the better.[170] James tried to work a metaphor made familiar, at a tangent, by his predecessor. 'What God that conioyned then, let no man separate. I am the Husband, and all the whole Island is my Wife'. The Virgin Queen had made much of her 'marriage' to her realm. James, in contrast, suggested that his apparent fertility was evidence of God's peculiar favour, and his desire that the new 'union' should be cast into 'perpetuitie'.[171] A *paterfamilias*, he insinuated, in a way that his predecessor could never have been.

Sadly, Parliament remained unpersuaded. Leaving its King to bemoan that it had evinced 'nothing but curiosity from morning to evening, to find fault with my propositions'.[172] It was even less persuaded of the case after the discovery of the Powder Plot, 18 months later. God had saved a Parliament full of Englishmen. James momentarily worried that there might be a link between the plot and his imperial aspirations.[173] Rightly, as we will discover. Not that he was daunted. James returned to the theme in his subsequent address to Parliament in March 1607. The 'union' as an 'eternal agreement' between the two 'crowns' would seal the security of the realm and its prosperity in 'perpetuitie'. It would also help to further the cause of a broader legal 'reformation'.[174]

Amongst those who now spoke loudest in his support was Sir Francis Bacon. We will take a closer look at his role as counsellor and parliamentary spokesperson in due course. But we can briefly note the argument Bacon supplied his King on this occasion, in a position-paper written sometime in early 1607. There were,

---

[168] King James (1994) 168.

[169] King James (1994) 134–35.

[170] How broadly this impression was shared, in the English Court and indeed the English Parliament, is debatable. Though anyone reading Weldon's account would have been left in little doubt. It has been thought that Ben Jonson's depiction of the court of Tiberius in his *Sejanus* might have been pointed, dangerously so. See Salmon (1989) 220.

[171] King James (1994) 135–37.

[172] Stewart (2003) 213.

[173] An instruction was passed to Fawkes's interrogators suggesting they check whether any of the conspirators were behind a recent lampoon of his aspiration to be 'King of Great Britain'.

[174] King James (1994) 164.

Bacon advised, 'two several kinds of policy in uniting states and kingdoms'. The first is 'to retain the ancient forms still severed, and only conjoined in authority'; which was pretty much how things presently stood. The second was to 'superinduce a new form agreeable to the entire state'. The former is easier, the latter 'more happy'. And here history provided a salient example. The 'best state of the world', and the happiest, was the Roman.[175] Look 'into the histories', Bacon advised the Commons a few weeks before James's address, and you will know what is best for the 'posterity', and the 'greatness', of the kingdom.[176] Get to the library, re-read the classics, Livy, Caesar, Tacitus. Better still, read him on Livy, Caesar and Tacitus.

Too Much Mangled

Go to the theatre too. Given the intensity of the King's interest in the subject, the engagement of his 'Players' was to be expected. Shakespeare repeatedly alluded to the 'matter' of union in his Jacobean plays. Most famously perhaps in *Macbeth*, composed in the immediate aftermath of the Gunpowder Plot. Amidst all the 'midnight hags' and slaughtered princes, Shakespeare was careful to insert some meaningful imputations regarding the legitimacy of the Stuart claim. 'Thou shalt get kings, though thou be none', the witches tell Banquo, the supposed founder of the Stuart clan.[177] The play of providence. A point emphasised by Bacon in his fragmentary *History of Great Britain*. James Stuart had not succeeded to the throne by accident. It was 'Divine Providence' bringing harmony to the people chosen by God to lead the protestant reformation; 'one of the most memorable accidents, that had happened a long time in the Christian world'.[178]

A point reiterated, in the negative, in *King Lear*. The break up of an existing union, at the urging of a couple more 'unnatural hags', Goneril and Regan, leading inexorably to a chaotic war of prospective succession. The great kingdom of 'Britain' reduced to a 'gor'd state' (5.3. 319). Pretty much what had happened half a century earlier in Sackville and Newton's *Gorbudoc*. And precisely what James repeatedly advised Parliament had always happened at such moments. In his 1604 speech, he had taken his audience back to the days of the Anglo-Saxon heptarchy, to illustrate just how badly things can go awry when a realm refuses to be 'united'. When 'this Kingdome of England was divided into so many little Kingdoms', which 'one of them behoved to eate up another, till they were united as one'.[179] An assurance which Shakespeare noticeably disdains in *King Lear*. *Macbeth* ends with an English army on the way to help, *Hamlet* with an obliging Norwegian king.

---

[175] See Wormald (1993) 154–55, making pointed comparison with Sparta, and its reluctance to extend rights of naturalisation.
[176] Wormald (1993) 155.
[177] Less said about Holinshed's Banquo the better, an accomplice in Macbeth's heinous enterprise.
[178] Bacon (1998) 216.
[179] King James (1994) 136–37.

King Lear closes with Albany musing on the 'general woe', Kent saying he is too old, and Edgar hedging.

It should have been easy to inscribe Albany as prospective saviour, invested with a dukedom familiarly held by scions of the Stuart Royal Family.[180] To chime with Bacon's idea of a 'union of love' designed to 'inculcate with the hearts and heads of the people that they are one People and nation'.[181] Instead Shakespeare invites his audience to ponder, one last time, the truly calamitous consequences of Lear's vanity; destroying not just his kingdom, but his family. To 'Speak what we feel, not what we ought to say' (5.3. 323). Holinshed estimated that his Leir had been King of Britain around 800 BC. Which implies two and half millennia of misery and enslavement to follow; encompassing successive Roman and Viking thralls, the Norman 'yoke', and the extended dominion of the papal anti-Christ. Alleviated only now by the successive reformations of the sixteenth century, and the prospect, finally, of reuniting a 'greater' Britain.

Whilst the union debate is most evidently engaged in *King Lear*, the Scottish theme in *Macbeth*, perhaps the most intriguing commentary is found in another of Shakespeare's later so-called 'problem' plays. We have already encountered *Cymbeline*. The story of another distant English king, who reigned over much of southern England during the reign of Augustus.[182] A play about a sort of break from Rome, but also a play about its residual cultural presence in Shakespeare's England. The necessary ambiguities of renaissance and reformation. And a play about the renaissance of English law too. For Cymbeline is a law-maker, with a mission:

> Our ancestor was that Mulmutius which
>
> Ordain'd our laws, whose use the sword of Caesar
>
> Hath too much mangled; whose repair, and franchise,
>
> Shall (by the power we hold) be our good deed,
>
> Though Rome be therefore angry (3.1. 55–59).

A passage which owed everything to Holinshed's confirmation that Mulmutius really had been the first king of the Britons, and the first to write up a set of English laws which were then preserved by Gildas, before being passed down to the care of King Arthur. And then inscribed in Bracton, most obviously perhaps in his accommodation of the *gubernaculum*, the *imperium* of Crown authority, with the *jurisdictio* of the common law.[183] So not a defence of Roman law, in the simpler sense. But importing an insinuation: that different legal orders might share certain common principles of natural reason. The accommodation of 'customary'

---

[180] Held indeed by James in his younger years, inherited from his father Lord Darnley. The dukedom had only recently been bestowed on Prince Charles.

[181] In *Certain Articles or Considerations Touching the Union of the Kingdoms of England and Scotland*, quoted in McEachern (1996) 140.

[182] See James (1997) 151, 154.

[183] See here McIlwain (1947) 86.

particularities within a 'generall Union of Lawes', as James recommended in his 1607 speech to Parliament: '*unus Grex et una Lex*'. We will discover Bacon writing a 'general' jurisprudence around this very principle shortly.

In the meantime, Shakespeare's portrayal of the long-forgotten King Cunobelinus was just what the *dominus* ordered. Only a monarch ruling by divine right could rise above the petty controversies of 'customary' jurisprudence and govern an empire. The theme of the closing scene, in which Shakespeare strives to straighten out his 'mangled' play.

> Nobly doomed!
>
> We'll learn our freeness of a son-in-law
>
> Pardon's the word for all (5.5. 421–23).

Cymbeline declares, exercising his Senecan *clementia* to forgive a motley crew of invading Roman soldiers and wandering Italian gentlemen. And so

> Let
>
> A Roman and a British ensign wave
>
> Friendly together (5.5. 480–82).

The *pax Augustus*, to be refashioned, a millennium and a half later, as the *pax Jacobus*.

The Case of the Deracinated Infant

The poetry helped. And the 'mappes', as James liked to emphasise, so many of 'great Antiquitie', wherein 'this isle is described'.[184] But ultimately, the possibility of union was a matter of politics, and law. In a rather compromised attempt to assuage anxieties, James repeatedly emphasised that he did not expect his two realms to adopt the same 'common' laws. Any more perhaps than he expected the same of their two churches, Anglican and Kirk. More congruity than conformity perhaps, 'customary' particularities accommodated within a 'generall Union of Lawes'.[185] To the benefit of both, as he reiterated in his speech to Parliament in 1607, but to the common law particularly, so much in it having such 'uncertaintie'.[186] In a pointed passage on the 'Coniuction of Nations', he further extrapolated how the civil law might work alongside the common. First, because the ability to 'make Aliens Citizens' flows from the 'Kings owne Prerogative'. Second, because 'wherein the law is thought not to be clear', then the matter falls to the King, 'for he is *Lex loquens*'.[187]

---

[184] In Wormald (2021) 381.
[185] For the idea of 'congruity' rather than 'conformity', in the closer context of church politics, see Morrill (1985) 7.
[186] King James (1994) 162–63.
[187] King James (1994) 171.

Comments with a purpose, for by then the case of a young Scotsman named Robert Colville was already making its way through the courts, to arrive at Exchequer Chamber in 1608.[188] Robert was just three-years old, the grandson of an otherwise much more interesting man, James Colville, the renowned 'Laird of Wemyss', mercenary, privateer, diplomat and prime mover in helping to secure the succession of James Stuart. And, by no coincidence, loud supporter of 'union'. Robert's life was nothing like as exciting. Except, perhaps, to legal historians, for it was in Robert's name that his guardians launched a legal action which would test the constitutional boundaries of the incipient 'union'. It would become known as *Calvin's Case*.[189] Little Robert was a *post-nati*, and the legal contention moved around whether, by reason of birth, he might thereby enjoy the legal rights of an Englishman. The precise issue which James had treated in his Proclamation on the Post-Nati, back in 1604. The converse argument supposed that he was an 'alien', whose status in English law would be dependent on some other form of naturalisation. This mattered, because if an 'alien' did not acquire this 'personality', Robert could not by right own or inherit property in England.

The case, 'the greatest that ever was argued in the hall of Westminster', according to Coke, was triggered by the seizure of some properties held in Robert's name in London.[190] His guardians issued writs for their recovery, arguing that they had been sequestered 'unjustly'.[191] The defendants claimed that the writs were inadmissible because Robert was an 'alien' in English law. Given that a positive resolution would add something tangible to his dream of a 'greater' Britain, the King signalled his interest. Appreciating the complexity of the case, and taking the hint, King's Bench and Chancery adjourned proceedings to the Exchequer, to sit in full bench. Fourteen judges, all but two of whom would give judgment for Robert and, at a remove, his King. Not, though, for the same reasons. Various reports of the case exist, but the most influential was that written up by Coke.[192]

The Chief Justice was, in fact, faced with something of a dilemma, inclined in this instance towards the King's wishes, but determined that the case should be decided on precedents and principles discovered in the 'common' law. Of which, he was keen to affirm, there were 'copious'. Thus no need to consult 'strange histories' or cite 'foreign laws'.[193] An impression not shared by Lord Chancellor Ellesmere, in whose opinion the matter was 'rare'.[194] A potentially helpful precedent was *Cobledike's Case*, disinterred from the reign of Edward I, which implied

---

[188] 77 Eng Rep 377 (KB 1608).

[189] Calvin being an English-ised corruption of Colville.

[190] 'Preface' to volume 7 of the *Reports*, iii.

[191] Two London properties in fact, one in Shoreditch, another in Bishopsgate.

[192] Who, predictably enough, only wrote up his own judgment. For a broader account, see Howell (1816) 2.559.

[193] Though there were precedents of the 'customary' kind, such as the 1351 statute De Natis Ultra Mare, certain passages from Bracton and so on. See here Price (1997) 92–93.

[194] Howell (1816) 2.612, 659.

that 'ligeance' was owed to the person of the King.[195] The counter-argument, drawn from the familiar political theology of the King's 'two bodies', suggested that allegiance was in fact owed to the 'public' rather than the private person of the King, *ad fidem Regis*. If this was correct, it would mean that a Scotsman owed allegiance to a Scottish king, and in return only enjoyed 'protection' of his Scottish assets. The citation of the Roman principle *cum duo jura*, in recent parliamentary debate gestured the same way.[196] In repelling this argument *Cobledike* was useful, but hardly sufficient.

It was for this reason that the Court was drawn towards more 'general' principles of jurisprudence. Easier for some than others. Whilst repainting various English 'precedents', Bacon, as Attorney General, made extensive recourse to Bodin and the principles of 'natural' law.[197] As, in the end, did Coke. The 'law of nature is that which God at the time of creation of the nature of man infused into his heart, for his preservation and direction; and this is *lex aeterna*, the moral law, called also the 'law of nature', and it is by this law that the 'faith, ligeance, and obedience of the subject is due to his Sovereign or superior'.[198] Here the authority of the common law was buttressed by the classical idea of the divinely inspired *communis sensus*. The title page of the first book of Coke's *Reports*, to which we will turn our closer attention in the next chapter, carried Cicero's renowned assertion: *lex est certa ratio e mente divina manans*.[199]

Subscribing to the idea that reason as a natural faculty was not incompatible with due reverence for the common law. Quite the converse. Selden likewise located the origins of government in 'natural' inclination.[200] No need for Bodin and his *Lettres*, the 'custom' of the 'common law' was anyway in accordance with 'nature', and 'immutable'.[201] Likewise Sir John Davies, in his *Le Primer Report des Cases*, published in 1615. The 'lawe of nature, which the schoolmen call *ius commune*' and 'which is also *ius non Scriptum*, being written only in the heart, is better than all the written laws in the world'.[202] The metaphor chosen, no doubt, to resonate. All of which meant that any who were 'born under one natural obedience while the realms were united under one sovereign, should remain natural

---

[195] 77 *Eng Rep* 388. The case involved a French woman's right to hold property in England. Which was upheld, the court gesturing towards the idea that her 'ligeance' was owed to the person of the King, not the English state.

[196] In full *cum duo jura concurrent in una persona aequum est ac si essent in diversis*; when two rights meet in one person, it is the same as if they were in different persons. The maxim was familiar to canon lawyers, recently discussed in *Acton's Case*, decided in the last year of Elizabeth's reign. An original formulation could be read in Justinian's *Digest*, 34.9.22. The maxim was ventured in Parliament by Sir John Bennet, a civil lawyer. Bacon touched on it in court, airily dismissing its applicability in the 'common' law. See Price (1997) 108–12.

[197] See Price (1997) 109–10; and more generally Kim (1996) 155–71.

[198] At 392.

[199] 'Law is unerring reason, adhering to a divine purpose'. For a comment, see Raffield (2005) 71.

[200] Most obviously in his *Jure Naturali*. See Burgess (1992) 37–38; and also Haivry (2017) 171, 225–35, 239–41.

[201] See Sommerville (1986) 19–20, 105–08.

[202] Raffield (2017) 159.

born subjects, and no aliens'.[203] The sketching, it has been alleged, of an 'imperial constitution'.[204]

The rooting of the judgment in an adaptive 'natural' law allowed Coke and his fellow justices to gesture towards principles of a 'general' jurisprudence, without having to flirt too obviously with their Roman origins.[205] We will, as already advertised, revisit the idea of 'general' jurisprudence when we take a closer look at Bacon's legal writing. Bacon was certainly keen on the idea, though similarly wary of too obvious a recourse to Roman precedent. For which reason, he was reluctant to flirt with principles discovered in civilian treatises such as Thomas Craig's *Unione Regnorum Britanniae Tractatus*. Craig, a Scots lawyer, and member of the Commission of Union, thought very much as his King. The 'sharing of offices, dignities and rights' was the surest way of ending the 'catastrophes' which had so long 'vexed the island'.[206] Something that was now readily achievable, given that the laws of England and Scotland enjoyed a common root in the *jus feudale*.[207] Bacon did not go that far, and neither, most certainly, did Coke. But, in the resolution of young Robert Colville's case, they went far enough. And as far as James might have reasonably hoped.

Not, though, far enough to persuade Parliament of the case for a statutory union. Thus, another pointed reference in James's 1610 address to Parliament, against those who continued to evince too 'great' an 'Antipathy of the Lawes and Customes' of England and Scotland and failed to appreciate the merits of a 'generall union' of laws. To this end, James treated his Parliament to a quick tutorial in Scots law. Of which there were three kinds: the law of tenures, wards and liveries, which was based on English Chancery law; statute law, which operated in the same way in both countries; and civil law. The latter is not observed 'absolutely', as might be the case in France, but is rather 'to supply such cases wherein the Municipall Law is defective'. A pertinent analogy thereafter, between civil law and Latin. When a scholar is unsure of the meaning of a word or phrase, he can, for guidance, seek recourse to 'the Latin tongue'. A 'good Chauncellor' will seek recourse to civil law in the same way.[208] It is this supervening authority, characteristic of both jurisdictions, which would make a 'union of laws' work. The particularities of English and Scottish law accommodated, perhaps in time erased. So James hoped, and his opponents feared.

It never came to pass, of course. In 1620, James would write a *Meditation upon the 27, 28, 29 Verses of the xxvii Chapter of St Matthew*. Predictably doleful, the

---

[203] At 409.

[204] Hulsebosch (2003) 468–69.

[205] See here Price (1997) 96, 100–02, 123–28, discussing the extent to which James and his counsel strove to distance themselves from too evident a reliance on 'Roman rule', as Bacon termed it.

[206] Price (1997) 128–29. Craig was a Scots civil lawyer of repute, who had also been invited to sit on the Commission of Union.

[207] Price (1997) 129–31, 136.

[208] King James (1994) 173–74.

'epistle dedicatory' confirmed that he was by now 'weary of controversies'.[209] Any lingering possibility of an immediate union of crowns would be extinguished a generation later on the battlefields of Marston Moor and Naseby. James could not have anticipated this. It is history which supposes that the imperial aspiration was, in the moment, 'hopeless'.[210] But he would, from the earliest days as King of England, have appreciated the controversy which his ambitions had engendered amongst so many of his new subjects.

When Guy Fawkes travelled to Spain in summer 1605, to solicit support for a prospective coup, he gave a particular reason as to why the moment was conducive. A 'natural hostility between the English and the Scots' had mutated into 'grievances' which it was no longer 'possible to reconcile'. Under torture a few months later, Fawkes would say the same. The plan was intended to have 'blown' James and his fellow-travellers 'back to Scotland'.[211] History has painted Fawkes as many things: mercenary, religious zealot, early-day terrorist. A case might be made for each assignation. Above all, though, Guy Fawkes was an early-day 'little Englander'.[212] We will take a look at this England in due course, to see what makes it quite so little. We will also revisit James Stuart, in his afterlife. And imagine what he might think of both 'little' England and 'great' Britain today. For now, though, we will leave him wrestling with his parliaments, and his disappointment. And with his judges, to one of whom we will now turn our closer attention.

[209] In Wormald (2021) 66.
[210] See Wormald (2021) 42.
[211] In Donaldson (2011) 214; and Wormald (2021) 340.
[212] See Wormald (2021) 339, concluding that the Powder Plot might be best understood as an early expression of English 'xenophobia'.

3

The Casebook of Sir Edward Coke

Spring 1615 found Richard Glanvil incarcerated in the Fleet prison. Not a great place to be at any time of the year. Bitterly cold through the winter, challengingly pungent as the bloom of spring approached. He had been placed there at the order of Lord Chancellor Ellesmere. It was not his first time behind bars. Richard Glanvil was a career conman. One of plenty in Jacobean England, as anyone who had attended a performance of Ben Jonson's *Bartholomew Fair* would have been well aware. A 'foul fair', in which the 'giddy-headed' multitude, as contemporaries such as Robert Dallington termed them, pitched up in the half-expectation of getting ripped off. Dallington was tutor to the future King Charles I, who loved shiny, pretty things, and was always getting ripped off. A passing irony.[1]

Glanvil was, in sum, a chancer. In a different moment he would have made his fortune trading Bitcoin or selling dodgy personal protective equipment to harassed NHS account managers. In due course, he would probably have ended up in the House of Lords. The Jacobeans were, though, less tolerant of chancers, at least those of the common variety. So instead, Glanvil spent much of 1615 in and out of the Fleet. Characteristically unrepentant, he despatched a couple of 'activist' lawyers to the Court of King's Bench armed with a writ of habeas corpus. His was, in truth, an unexceptional case, except for the fact that Glanvil was about to get lucky, in a manner of speaking. For the Lord Chief Justice of England and Wales, in 1615, was Sir Edward Coke, and he was about to have one of those days.

We might briefly consider the facts of the case. Amongst his variously dubious activities, Glanvil sold 'paste' jewellery to gullible gentlemen and their ladies. Most of whom, it seems, either never noticed, or just put it down to experience. Unfortunately for Glanvil, one of his clients took more serious exception to being conned. Mr Courtney had agreed to pay £360 for a presumably very nice diamond. Instead he received a piece of 'topaz', which in the right light looked like a diamond. There were reasons to wear topaz; good for curing lunacy, it was commonly believed, and warning off the 'evil eye'. But it was not what Courtney wanted, and it was not worth £360. Nearer to £20. Understandably perhaps he refused to pay up. Glanvil, hardly lacking in boldness, sued for payment in King's

---

[1] Beware of 'novelty', Dallington advised his teenage charge, more particularly those 'desirous' of it. Deaf ears. See Cressy (2015) 35.

Bench and secured an order. Courtney retaliated by suing in Chancery for rescission of the contract of sale.

And received judgment, Chancery issuing a declaration halting the judgment of King's Bench. Which, needless to say, Glanvil ignored. All very predictable, as was the consequence: a spell of bed and board in the Fleet. Another Lord Chief Justice might have left well alone. Glanvil was hardly deserving of judicial favour. Not Coke though. Glanvil's writ of habeas corpus was granted on the grounds that the reasons for the 'return' of Chancery were not stated. 'As long as I have this coif upon my head', Coke declared, 'I will not allow this'.[2] A triumphant Glanvil apparently returned to the Fleet, this time of his own volition, to encourage other incumbents to seek similar recourse. Ellesmere immediately ordered his rearrest, whilst making 'greevous complaint' to the King, and voicing his deeper suspicion. Not enough of what was going on seemed to surprise the Lord Chief Justice.

By this point Glanvil had adopted a new strategy, preferring bills of *praemunire* against Courtney and his lawyers, and a range of other legal officers, including the warden of the Fleet, and Serjeant Moore who had prosecuted his case. It was even rumoured that he was contemplating a bill against the Lord Chancellor himself. We have come across the Statute of Praemunire already, enacted back in the fourteenth century to regulate the remission of tax to Rome. A tool that Henry VIII had found useful for terrorising his Lord Chancellors, and plenty of others, but which was not intended to weaponise conmen with attitude. Still Glanvil was inclined to keep pushing his luck. So it was back to King's Bench, where Coke was invited to exercise his imagination. The thought that an action in Chancery might be analogous to an appeal to Rome was something of a stretch. But Coke, it seems, was persuaded.

Not though the jury, which declined to follow the direction of their Lord Chief Justice, despite repeated promptings. A furious Coke dismissed them as a bunch of 'varletts and knaves', and advised the sheriff to 'return a wiser jury the next term'. The court was further given 'faire warning' that his hand would 'fall heavy' on any who attempted to interfere with the run of a King's Bench writ. 'We must looke about or the common lawe of England will be overthrown', he concluded to his presumably startled audience of lawyers and clerks; or maybe they had heard it all before. Contemporary reports supposed that a 'war' had already broken out between Chancery and King's Bench. But the situation, Timothy Tourneur confirmed, was now 'much aggravated'. Shortly after, Glanvil found himself 'clogged' in 'irons' again, and hauled before Star Chamber, to answer some very awkward questions.[3] Chiefly about Coke. Who, it was wondered, might just have put him up to the whole charade.

There was no fine constitutional point at play in *Glanvil's Case*, at least nothing that was new. What intrigues is the temper of the court. And hindsight, which supposes that *Glanvil's Case* might represent the beginning of an end. Whilst

[2] I Rolle Rep 111.
[3] Knapfla (1977) 173–74; Smith (2014) 245–47; and Baker (2017) 418–19.

Coke was berating his courtroom on the hazard of empanelling a disobliging jury, he was also wrestling with a rather awkward conveyancing case involving an indigent Master and an enterprising property developer. We will return to the *Earl of Oxford's Case* shortly; another critical misstep. And then, a few weeks later, Messrs Colt and Glover pitched up at King's Bench with their writ challenging the *commendam* granted to the Bishop of Lichfield. During the ensuing proceedings, as the King turned the *Case of Commendams* into a trial of his Lord Chief Justice's fidelity, minds would return to Glanvil and his dodgy 'diamonds'. In his speech of 20 June, drafted by Bacon, the King would allude to the idea that a bill of *praemunire* might be laid against the Chancellor. To do so, James observed, would be to lay a bill against the person of the King. A chilling observation, and an imputation: that in Sir Edward Coke, Glanvil had discovered, not just a sympathetic judge, but a partner in crime.

For Coke, as we intimated earlier, it was a spectacular fall from grace. As spectacular as his rise. Solicitor General in 1592, promoted to Attorney General two years later, in which capacity he represented the Crown in a series of high-profile treason cases, including those of the Earl of Essex, Sir Walter Raleigh and the Gunpowder Plotters. Rewarded for the latter service, he was appointed Chief Justice of Common Pleas in 1606, and then Lord Chief Justice of the Kings Bench in 1613. The latter promotion recommended by Sir Francis Bacon. For two reasons: first, in the hope that it might curtail the number of vexatious civil suits against the Crown; and second, because the resultant shuffling of judicial appointments might secure Bacon's further preferment. The latter strategy proved the more successful, Sir Francis duly becoming Attorney General. The vexation, however, did not end. Indeed, it was reported that the new Lord Chief Justice was seen to be 'weeping' the morning he was ceremonially escorted across Westminster Hall, from Common Pleas to King's Bench; probably as much from frustration. Getting rid of Coke, it very quickly became apparent, would require something rather more determinative.

Thus summer 1616. Even then, Coke proved difficult to dispose. In the moment, Henry Calthorpe bemoaned the fact that 'so profitable a member of the common wealth should' now 'lie idle'.[4] He need not have worried. Eschewing the gentler pleasures of retirement, Coke did what any devotee of Shakespeare or Jonson might have anticipated, or indeed any scholar of Seneca or Tacitus. He plotted his revenge, to be inflicted, not on the father, but on the son. In 1628, firmly ensconced amongst the 'stirring men' in the Commons, Coke would draft a *Petition of Right*. A written constitution, in all but name, specifically designed to inhibit the absolutist aspirations of any coming king, Stuart or otherwise. And the prologue, it transpired, to civil war and the great 'alterations', as Tourneur put it, which would follow 'upon King Charles'.[5] We will revisit all of this in the coming

[4] In Baker (2017) 437.
[5] In Baker (2017) 437.

pages. First, though, we need to get a better sense of the 'mind', and the temper, of Sir Edward Coke.

The Temper of the Common Law

We can most readily access the thinking of Sir Edward Coke through his published writings. More particularly 13 volumes of *Reports*, which cease in 1613, and four volumes of *Institutes* which were completed during his 'retirement'. Which leaves a rather obvious gap, covering the years leading up to his tumultuous fall from grace in 1616. Here we are more dependent on the accounts of others. A necessary irony, given how evidently desirous Coke was to fashion his own history. For the *Reports*, most especially, are testaments to the author as much as the law they purport to chronicle, intended to be read in much the same way as John Foxe's *Book of Martyrs* and the myriad similar confessionals that would hallmark the English Reformation poetic.[6]

The Common Law Mind

We have already encountered some flashes of Coke's intellect, and his temper. Bacon took pains to record a few more. 'The less you speak of your greatness, the more I will think of it', he ventured on one such occasion, or so he would have us believe. Eliciting in reply 'a number of disgraceful words'.[7] In his *Letter of Advice*, Bacon was brusquer still. 'You make the law to lean a little too much to your opinion', such that 'you show yourself a legal tyrant'.[8] We will encounter further admonitions in the next chapter, when we turn our closer attention to Bacon and his various writings. The enmity was long-standing and ran deep, nurtured by years of professional jealousy.

And thwarted romance. Bacon had been a rival for the hand of the recently widowed Lady Elizabeth Hatton, a serious financial catch, young and beautiful too.[9] In the end she married Coke. A bit of a 'mystery', as one as contemporary noted.[10] Scurrilous rumour had it that she was already pregnant. A predictably tempestuous marriage collapsed predictably. By 1606 they were living apart. A bit of a rubbish dad too, as we will see, who would beat his teenage daughter into marriage with an insane nobleman in the hope that it might help his flagging

---

[6] Walsham (2012) 912–15.

[7] In Jardine and Stewart (1998) 254.

[8] In Knapfla (1977) 126.

[9] The widow of Sir William Hatton, herself a daughter of Lord Burghley's eldest son, Thomas. In addition to her connections, and reported beauty, Elizabeth also brought Ely House in London, Corfe Castle in Dorset and the Holdenby estate in Northamptonshire. It was from the latter that Charles I would be seized by the army in 1647; another passing irony.

[10] Jardine and Stewart (1998) 190.

career; or so, again, rumour would have us believe. 'We shall never see his like again', Lady Elizabeth remarked, on hearing of her husband's death in 1634, 'praises be to God'.[11] It had been a fair old wait. Coke was 84 when he passed on.

Not much liked in court either, or at Court. Caricatured, it has been surmised, in the shape of Shakespeare's pompous buffoon, Sir Andrew Aguecheek, in *Twelfth Night*.[12] Jonson's Voltore too, possibly, as we have already noted. Something of a gamble on either count, it might be thought. Especially so in the case of *Twelfth Night*, which was performed repeatedly at Court in 1601 and 1602. There again Shakespeare was probably reassured by the thought that there would be plenty in the audience who did not much like Sir Edward Coke. It would be pleasing, of course, to be able to draw a distinction between the brilliant public 'body' of Sir Edward Coke and the embittered private. But you never can; 'manners maketh man'.[13] Mind and temper are mutually constitutive. Something which brings us neatly back to the idea of a common law 'mind', and the possibility that it might, or might not, have an existence distinct from those who are supposed to have shaped it.

We have already touched on this mind, in the company of Richard Hooker most notably. Not a common law jurist as such, but someone who shared an appreciation that England was best governed in Socratic 'harmony', balancing the interests of the Crown with the principles and 'liberties' of the common law. A thesis which had assumed a greater urgency with the succession of James Stuart. The difference between a text such as Hooker's *Laws* and those written by various later Elizabethan and indeed Jacobean jurists was essentially sentimental. The authority to which Hooker turns is instinctively scriptural. The authority to which the jurists turned was, just as instinctively, historical. Indeed, we might trace the emergence of a distinctive breed of English legal historian to this moment. Lambarde might be counted one. Plowden another. William Fleetwood another still, author of a *Table to the Reports of Edmund Plowden* and *A Discourse upon Statutes*, together with a dedicated treatise on *Magna Carta*.[14]

The 'great' Charter assumed a transcendent place in Elizabethan 'histories' of the common law.[15] Chapter 29 was especially revered:

> No free person shall be taken or imprisoned, or disseised of any tenement or of his liberties or free customs, or outlawed or exiled, or in any way destroyed, nor shall we go

---

[11] In 1634, at the age of 82. For the quote, see Burgess (1996) 207.

[12] Gest (1909) 510–11, questioning the veracity of the suggestion, which was first advanced by Lord Campbell in his *Lives of the Chief Justices*, and was based on similarities between some of Sir Andrew's lines and Coke's speech in the trial of Sir Walter Raleigh. Raleigh's trial took place in 1603, after the first recorded performances of *Twelfth Night*. This does not preclude, of course, the possibility that Coke had used the same rhetorical devices in earlier treason cases.

[13] As someone once said, though sadly we are not sure who. The proverb is most commonly associated with William of Wykeham, fourteenth-century Bishop of Winchester and Lord Chancellor, and a fifteenth-century Eton schoolmaster named William Holman.

[14] For a discussion of Fleetwood's career, and his place as one of the first English legal historians, see Baker (2017) 216–48.

[15] A 'process of beatification', Baker suggests (2017) 261.

against him or send against him, except by the lawful judgment of his peers or by the law of the land; to no one shall we sell, to no one deny or delay, right or justice.

The inspiration for writs of habeas corpus, and so much else.[16] In his renowned 1681 Middle Temple lecture, Robert Snagge would voice a pervasive perception: that it was *Magna Carta*, enshrined in the Statute of Marlborough, which had started the process of liberating England from the Norman 'yoke'. James Morice had gestured similarly in his Middle Temple lecture three years earlier, in which he presented the Reformation settlement as a statutory revolution designed to liberate England from the thrall of Rome. And not yet 'done', at least not so long as the High Commission and Star Chamber were in operation.

The affinity of the Charter, the common law and an essential Englishness, found vaunting statement in Edmund Hake's *Epieikeia*:

> Of all the nations of the world I have read of, the English nation is a people most free ... for whereas peoples of other nations and kingdoms, for the most part, are ruled and governed by the absolute beck, will and power of their prince, only the English nation is ruled and governed by the laws of their country – or rather by their kings and rulers, whose rule and government is according to their law and not otherwise. And therefore the kings of England are said to rule (not to reign), I say, to rule by their laws and not to reign by their wills or absolute powers.

There was nothing especially novel here. Sir John Fortescue had said much the same in his renowned *Laws of England*, famously distinguishing between *dominium regale* and *dominium politicum et regale*. The former allowing a king to 'rule his people by such laws as he makes himself', the latter supposing that a king 'may not rule his people by other laws than such as they assent to'.[17] The temper again of the common law.

And the temper of Sir Edward Coke, the second book of whose *Institutes* was, in considerable part, a commentary on the great *Charta libertatum Regni*.[18] A text that warranted such reverence 'in respect' of its 'great importance, and weightiness'.[19] No part weightier than chapter 29, the sanctity of which Coke had already attested in a brief tract penned in 1604, inspired by a dispute regarding the presentation of habeas corpus writs in the Council of Marches. There was, Coke had confirmed, nowhere in England where chapter 29 did not run. Something for James to ponder as he settled into life in his new realm. As would have been the preface to the fourth book of *Reports*, which baldly stated that a king of England 'is under no man, but under God and the law, for the law makes the king'.[20] The echo of Hooker's harp, and the template, if read with a more whimsical eye, of the principal of legality.[21]

[16] See Baker (2017) 16.
[17] Fortescue (1997) 83.
[18] Albeit the document confirmed by King Henry III in 1225, not the original more famously 'signed' by his father King John 10 years earlier.
[19] Sheppard (2003) 2. 746.
[20] Sheppard (2003) 1. 102.
[21] On the affinity between Hooker and Coke, see Raffield (2005) 74–75.

Certainly as read by Coke, for whom, as for Fleetwood or Snagge or Morice, *Magna Carta* added historical solidity to something that was otherwise discovered in nothing more tangible than the 'mists' of time. Back to the Anglo-Saxons and the Witanagemot, then back past the Romans to the England of Brutus and Arthur. The raising of all things 'ancient'.[22] In the preface to the ninth volume of *Reports*, Coke talked of setting a 'frame of the ancient common laws of this realm', in deference most obviously to Bracton and Fortescue.[23] It was the 'great charter', and its subsequent affirmation 'by thirty-two parliaments at least', which gave the common law tangibility.[24] Not foundational in the modern sense of a written constitution, but an authoritative enactment of a customary law which had shaped the English for millennia; 'declaratory of the principall grounds of the fundamentall Laws of England', as Coke put it in the prologue to the second *Institutes*.[25] A generation on, Sir Matthew Hale would pay uxorious tribute to a common law which has been shaped by 'long experience and use', and which is for that very reason not only a 'very just and excellent law in itself', but is

> singularly accommodated to the Frame of the English Government and to the Disposition of the English Nation, and such as by long Experience and Use is as it were incorporated into their very Temperament, and, in a Manner, become the Complection and Constitution of the English Commonwealth.[26]

A feeling thing.

Coke's contemporary Sir John Davies spun a consonant metaphor. England was 'like a silk worm that formeth all her web out of herself onely'.[27] The spinning of English exceptionalism, threaded by two determining qualities: godliness and a reverence for the common law. As Coke confirmed in *Bulthorpe's Case*, there was nothing in the 'great charter' which was not already present in the customary law of Edward the Confessor. Rather it added statutory heft to historical reason. And, most importantly, it confirmed that the prerogative powers of an English king were encompassed in English law. A thesis which Coke would articulate, time and again, in court. As we will now see, starting with the case involving a peculiarly fractious barrister.

The Case of the Fractious Barrister

We have already come across Nicholas Fuller, barrister of Gray's Inn and Member of Parliament for the City of London. Another man of loud opinion,

---

[22] Though the familiar 'ancient constitution' was the invention of a later generation of historians.
[23] Sheppard (2003) 1. 292.
[24] As he put it in *Bulthorpe v Ladbrook* in 1607. Quoted in Baker (2017) 352–53.
[25] Sheppard (2003) 2. 748.
[26] Hale (1971) 30. For a commentary on Hale's adherence to the idea of a common law discovered in historical reason, see Postema (2019) 6–7, 21–26.
[27] In Pocock (1967) 34.

not much enamoured of the Scots or their King. A 'rash and headlong' man, Gardiner would later attest.[28] A lawyer of the 'activist' kind. A vehement critic of monopolies, Fuller had built a lucrative practice disputing patents. Hostile to anything which smacked of prerogative abuse, zealous in his faith and in his defence of both Parliament and the common law. It was the job of the latter, in Fuller's opinion, to 'tell the king of England what by the laws of England he may do'.[29] And if he forgot, it was the job of the courts to remind him. The common law 'mind' and the puritan 'conscience' hand in hand.[30] With a common enemy. Milton's 'grinding courts', Chancery, Star Chamber and, most especially, the High Commission.[31]

By the time that James succeeded to the throne in 1603, Fuller had become the barrister of choice for many harassed puritan preachers. The kind indeed who had butted in on James's progress south in spring 1603, to present their Millenary Petition.[32] Amongst the various abuses to which the petitioners objected was the use of the sign of the cross during baptism and the use of rings during marriage ceremonies, together with the wearing of surplices and caps.[33] The affections of papists and sorcerers and other Romish remainers that must, following the Corinthian injunction, be cast 'down' to the 'obedience of God'. And then 'buried', as the fiery Brownist John Penry urged, for otherwise the 'harlott' might rise once again.[34]

Smashing stuff up was a predictable consequence of serial reformations and counter-reformations. A political theology of endemic, if endlessly confusing, violence. Albeit Grace Palmer, of St Osyth in Essex, retained an earthier common sense. Grace, whose case was recorded in Foxe's *Acts and Monuments*, was turned in by her appalled neighbours when she declined to join a mini pilgrimage around the county. A total waste of time, Grace had responded to their kind invitation, trailing from one 'piece of timber painted' to another.[35] For most others of a puritan disposition, however, the matter demanded rather greater urgency. Men like Henry Sherfield, recorder of Salisbury, hauled before Star Chamber in 1631, accused of smashing a church window which depicted the Son of God wearing a blue frock-coat.[36] And women such as Lady Eleanor Davies, prosecuted for

---

[28] Gardiner (1886) 1. 329.

[29] In Wormald (2021) 47.

[30] See Wright (2006) 204–05.

[31] See Milton (1991) 4–8.

[32] The name from the Latin *millenarius*, of a thousand. The petition was reputed to have been signed by a thousand ministers.

[33] The petitioners also objected to confirmation ceremonies and the holding of livings in plurality. For an overview of the *Petition* and its consequence, see Craig (2008).

[34] In Walsham (2012) 908. Penry, who authored various tracts denouncing episcopacy, was convicted of sedition and hanged in 1593.

[35] Haigh (1993) 69.

[36] Sherfield had been alerted to the offending window, on seeing some women parishioners making 'low curtesies' to it. Sherfield had first asked parish officers to remove the window, but they had refused. See Underdown (1987) 51.

throwing a kettle of steaming 'puddle-water' over an arras-tapestry in Hereford Cathedral.[37]

Alert to the Word of God and prepared to do whatever it takes to ensure that the same was true of everyone else, Sherfield and Davies inhabited a place towards the radical edge of puritanism. We might imagine them today, in their element: blockading refineries, gluing themselves to government buildings, graffiti-ing colonial statues. The rhyme of apocalypse rebellion. There is a range of resonances here, of course. The zeal which attended the smashing of windows, and the window-smashers, was the same as that which fired the hunting of witches. It comes as no surprise to discover that witchcraft prosecutions commonly aligned the taking of the Black Mass with the taking of the Catholic.[38] Witchery, popery, wokery; all 'discovered' in the jaundiced eye of the beholder.

And all warranting the full attention of the state. James's first response was to call a conference at Hampton Court, in which he might beat the puritans with his wit. His second was more customary, to use the law to drive them off the streets, and out of their livings. There was law in place. The 'Three Articles' issued by Archbishop Whitgift in 1583, intended to reinforce the 'Thirty-Nine Articles' issued in 1563, and, perhaps more pertinently, an Act Against Seditious Sectaries passed, just a decade earlier, in 1593.[39] In the eye of its critics, however, the problem with Elizabethan anti-puritan legislation was the same as that which blighted inherited witchery law. It was not sufficiently prosecuted. Following the break-up of the Hampton Court conference, James determined that this insufficiency should be redressed.

So that the heresies of men like Richard Mansell and Thomas Ladd might be quieted. Ladd had put his name to a parliamentary petition which argued that the 1593 Act was contrary to *Magna Carta*. Mansell was accused of holding conventicles in Yarmouth. Deprived of their livings and imprisoned in 1607, both had turned to the obvious place for assistance, the offices of Nicholas Fuller.[40] Writs of habeas corpus were entered at King's Bench whilst Fuller let it be known that, in his opinion, the desire to imprison men 'without showing any cause or matter' was ultra vires, 'popish and antichristian'. 'Granted an ynch', Fuller warned, the officers of the Commission will 'take an ell'. On hearing report, the Commission had Fuller

---

[37] See Ward (2019) 36.

[38] A famous example being the prosecution of the Pendle witches, an account of which is provided in Thomas Potts's *The Wonderfull Discoverie of Witches in the Countie of Lancashre*, published in 1613. At the heart of which was a report of a Black Mass held at Malkin Tower, at which the Devil was guest of honour. See Lumby (1995) 42, 47–49, 102–06. For a broader commentary on the perceived affinity of witchery and popery, see Elmer (2016) ch 2.

[39] The 'Three Articles' required all ministers to swear an oath to observe the Thirty-Nine Articles, recognise episcopacy and approve the use of the Common Prayer Book.

[40] A couple of years earlier, Fuller had represented the notorious Thomas Cartwright, hauled before Star Chamber on similar charges.

committed for his 'offensive words' and 'schismatical and factious humour', and despatched to the Fleet.[41]

Released, and then arrested again, Fuller entered another writ, this time on his own part, requesting a prohibition to stay proceedings.[42] An 'evil' man looking for a fight, Lord Chancellor Ellesmere advised his King. A 'villain' indeed, James agreed, whose 'evil deserts' threatened the very foundations of the Crown; for 'whensoever the ecclesiastical dignity together with the King's government thereof shall be turned to contempt and begin to evanish in this kingdom, the king thereof shall not prosper long, and the monarchy shall fall to ruin'.[43] Time for a consultation with the judges, who sought to somehow cut a compromise. The jurisdiction of the Commission in matters of heresy was unarguable. But matters of 'scandal' and contempt against the 'King or his Government, Temporal or Ecclesiastical' fell to the common law courts. The Commission duly took the hint, and prosecuted Fuller for heresy, fining him £200.

Meanwhile James decided to press the matter with the judges, who were summoned to Privy Council on 10 November. Accounts vary as to the temper of the meeting, and precisely what was said.[44] Coke was certainly in no mood to be malleable, at least not according to his own report of the proceedings. Rather than seeking his King's forgiveness, he launched into a diatribe against the suggestion, made by Archbishop Bancroft, that the authority of the Commission was 'clear in Divinity'. Not so, Coke replied. The authority of the judges lay in the common law, and it 'protecteth the king'. To which James had apparently replied, in heated tones, that 'he was not defended by his laws but by God'. Which gave him the authority to 'maketh the Judges', and unmake them.[45]

Rarely averse to a bit of intellectual fencing, James then engaged Coke directly. Given that 'the law was founded on reason, and that he had reason as well as judges', he wondered why he should be precluded from assuming a judicial authority clearly invested in him by God. The answer was simple, but hardly tactful. Coke agreed entirely that reason was the 'life of the law'. But it was a particular kind of reason, an 'artificial perfection' that was only 'gotten by long study', by Englishmen, in an English Inn of Court, and then sitting on an English bench. None of which James had done, and thus a 'perfection' he could hardly be expected to have learned:

> True it was that God had endowed his Majesty with excellent science and great endowments of nature; but His Majesty was not learned in the laws of the realm of England; and causes which concern the life, or inheritance, or goods, or fortunes, of his subjects are not to be decided by natural reason, but by artificial reason and judgement of law, which requires long study and experience before that a man can attain to the cognizance

---

[41] See Wright (2006) 192–93; and Smith (2014) 194–95.
[42] (1607) 5 James I; 12 Co Rep 41.
[43] Stewart (2003) 234.
[44] See here Usher (1903) 667–75.
[45] Comments repeated in further accounts of the meeting. See Usher (1903) 669, 675.

of it; and that the law was the golden mete-wand and means to try the causes of his subjects; and which protected His Majesty in safety and peace.[46]

The idea that only judges might properly understand the law was not unusual. Selden intimated likewise, suggesting indeed that 'the Eternal and Sacred Scriptures themselves do more than once call Judges by that most holy name *Elohim*, that is, Gods'.[47] But still, to articulate as much to the man who thought that he was ordained to the same purpose was, to say the least, bold. And then closing with a famous bit of Bracton, to rub it in: 'The king ought not to be under any man, but under God and the law'. Coke liked to cite Bracton at such moments, when elevating opinion into something apparently beyond argument. Such a principle, he continued, 'delights the honour of the king, whose person they represent as they sit in justice'.[48]

James did not seem very delighted. On the contrary, the King was reported to be 'greatly offended'. Hardly surprising; the inference being that he was probably bright enough, but not sufficiently learned in English law. James wondered loudly if his Chief Justice was too 'full of craturity', his body of judges too ready to embellish the 'obscuritie' of their jurisprudence. Like the 'papistes' indeed, who 'alleadge scriptures and will interpret the same'. A dark insinuation.[49] Whatever, it was, James concluded, a 'traiterous speech'. According to one report, 'his Majestie fell into that high indignation as the like was never knowne in him, looking and speaking fiercely with bended fist, offering to strike' his Chief Justice. And was only pacified when Coke 'fell flatt on all fower; humbly beseeching his Majestie to take compassion on him and pardon him'. Along with the Lord Treasurer, Sir Robert Cecil, who likewise 'kneeled down' and 'prayed', the King forgave his wayward Chief Justice.[50]

If Coke was cowed, it was not for long. In *Roper's Case*, which followed shortly after, Coke would repeat his reservations regarding the High Commission. Superficially conciliatory language, the court as a 'fountain of sweet water to refresh all the earth', followed by confirmation that the Commission's propensity to meddle in matters *meum et tuum* was not 'convenient'.[51] Stick to the heretics, and leave the rest to Common Pleas. From which, in the meantime, writs of prohibition continued to issue. Displaced ushers, lazy parsons, tardy alimony-payers, alleged adulterers, assorted tithe-disputants; all fancying their chances of persuading the Chief Justice to reverse Commission rulings.[52] James licked his wounds. As for Fuller, released from the Fleet in January 1608, and 'very frolic' it was reported,

---

[46] A mete-wand was a measuring stick, most commonly used for describing boundaries.

[47] In Raffield (2005) 76.

[48] See Smith (2014) 249.

[49] A kind of legal reasoning found, apparently, in *De Legibus*. See Smith (2014) 154–55, 178, 203.

[50] See Usher (1903) 669; and Smith (2014) 176–77.

[51] In Baker (2017) 363–64.

[52] The displaced usher in *Fawne's Case*; the lazy parson in *Vinard's Case*; the tardy alimony-payer in *Bradstone's Case*; the alleged adulterer in *Sir William Chauncy's Case*.

by the end of the month he was back inside. More 'offensive words', chiefly found in a printed text entitled *The Argument of Nicholas Fuller*. Wherein, readers discovered, the 'laws of England are the high inheritance of the realm, by which both King and subjects are directed', chapter 29 of *Magna Carta* secures the 'liberty' of every subject, and 'kings are made for commonwealths, not commonwealths for kings'.[53] We will move on.

The Casebook

Fuller's Case and the *Case of Prohibitions* into which it mutated are discovered in the twelfth and thirteenth 'parts' of the *Reports*. The thirteenth is, in fact, the last of the books, completed in 1613; a dateline that precluded report of *Glanvil's Case*, and indeed the *Commendams*. The first 'part' of the *Reports*, which chiefly treats cases in which Coke acted as Attorney General, had appeared in 1600. Selective, of course, as we noted earlier: the cases which Coke wanted recorded for his posterity. Not all touched on matters of kingship and governance. But many did, not least because Coke twisted them this way. We will visit three more of Coke's most renowned cases, two of which assume a prominent place in the *Reports*. And a third which, for reason of timing once again, is discovered elsewhere.

The Case of the Floppy Ruff and the Overrunning Stew

Starting with the *Case of Proclamations*, the facts of which moved around the similarly vexed matters of floppy ruffs and overrunning stews.[54] Like most authoritarians, King James preferred to rule by prerogative decree, what we today call executive ordinances. Dozens a year. He even had all his proclamations published together in 1610, to add a veneer of authority. Just like the King of France, his critics were quick to observe. Subsequent reprints only got bigger. *The Case of Proclamations* touched on the legality of these ordinances.

And money, the blight of English kings. Or the saving, according to Sir John Fortescue. In his *Laws of England*, Fortescue had identified two particular characteristics of a country governed *dominium politicum et regale*. First, that the King ruled in accordance with the law. Second, that he could only levy taxes with the approval of Parliament. There could be no 'strange impositions'. The upside for the King was that his people would 'rejoice'.[55] The downside was that the King was commonly broke, and obliged to keep going to Parliament to beg a favour. Something that did not make James rejoice much. Like most Renaissance

---

[53] Wright (2006) 198–200; and Baker (2017) 357.
[54] (1610) 8 James I; 12 Co Rep 74.
[55] Fortescue (1997) 17.

princes, James liked to spend, copiously.[56] We have already noted his profligacy in handing out treats to those who had accompanied him south in spring 1603. A calculated, and evolving, benevolence. By 1611 he was selling baronetcies, by 1615 peerages.

Relations would sink to a new low following the collapse of negotiations regarding a proposed 'great contract' in 1610. Four years later, James sent the Bishop of Durham to Parliament with a different reading of Fortescue on fiscal policy. Impositions, Bishop Neile confirmed, were actually part of Crown prerogative, a *noli me tangere*. The Commons was having none of it. Sir Thomas Roe demanded that Neile be removed from his bishopric and prevented from ever seeing his King again, 'or to be among reasonable men, but to run away and bewail his estate in the woods amongst wild beasts'.[57] To the surprise of few, the 'addled' Parliament lasted just three months. Leaving James with a limited range of alternatives; ever more creative accountancy, or the granting of tax-raising licences under prerogative.[58]

Which brings us to two proclamations premiered a few years earlier, in 1607. Both tapped into growing markets and were intended to protect revenue streams which brought 'considerable sums' to the Exchequer.[59] The first was purposed to protect the Company of Starchmakers, which had been granted a monopoly in starch manufacture, and an authority to 'fine' imported starch. The Company would get half the 'fine', the Crown the other half. There was money in starch, alongside all the glycosidic bonds which made it so usefully sticky. Commonly used in baking, as well as fermenting and malting. And in the making of paper, an increasingly lucrative market. And in fashion. No self-respecting Jacobean gentleman could be seen wandering the streets of London with a floppy ruff. Originally designed to counter the hazards of the unbecoming dribble, the 'ruff of pride' had become quite the fashion item by the mid-sixteenth century.[60] Useful too, in the event of a knife-wielding assassin attempting to cut your throat. James, as neurotic as he was dribbly and vain, liked to sport a good ruff. When he really wanted to impress, he wore one that was nearly two feet wide in diameter.

The second proclamation addressed building regulation. There was a lot about his new realm that James rather liked. But London disappointed. A city of 'sticks', he observed on arriving in spring 1603, which he intended to replace with 'bricke, being a material farre more durable, safe from fire and beautiful and magnificent'.[61] Less likely to fall down or to promote the spread of disease too. The Proclamation of 1607 was aimed at a more particular kind of construction, though, which spoke

---

[56] He was the first Scottish king to introduce taxation, in 1581.

[57] In Donaldson (2011) 336.

[58] On the relation of revenue and prerogative in late sixteenth and early seventeenth-century England, see Baker (2017) 184–87.

[59] In effect, the Crown took a cut of all fines levied by the Company.

[60] 'That ruff of pride', as Ananias puts it in Jonson's *Alchemist* (4.7.51); lampooning not just the fashion for ridiculous ruffs, but also the pomposity of puritans such as Ananias.

[61] See Breward (2009) 26.

as much to crumbling morality as crumbling masonry. The conversion of existing houses into what we would now term multi-occupancy units, and for the housing of a particular kind of resident, prostitutes. For which reason the Proclamation served a useful collateral purpose, as a sop to puritan disquiet. The later Elizabethan commentator Thomas Nashe was not alone in regretting that his capital city should be a haven of 'six-penny whoredom'. A disdain which betrayed the deeper contention. There was money in prostitution.

A prosaic fact appreciated, not just by the prostitutes and their bawds, but by the gentlemen of the theatre. A half-hour fumble in a nearby brothel, followed by a slap-up dinner, and a couple of hours hurling abuse and rotten vegetation at a troupe of actors, was pretty much the definition of a cracking night out in Jacobean London. Both Phillip Henslowe and Edward Alleyne are known to have dabbled in the brothel market. Shakespeare too, it has been surmised. It was evidently on his mind in summer 1603, as he pondered the plotline of his first Jacobean 'comedy'. We came across *Measure for Measure* earlier, musing on the wisdom of princes who wander off-stage now and again. There is a reason, though, why the Duke of Vienna decides to disappear for a while. There is too much illicit sex going on, and he is not sure what to do about it.

There are three magistrates in *Measure for Measure*. The first is the Duke. Baffled by jurisprudence, his commonwealth possessed of 'strict statutes and most biting laws', but now 'more mock'd than fear'd' (1.3. 19, 27–29). For which reason he abdicates and goes about his commonwealth in disguise. Just as James liked to do. Risky though, as the courtier Lucio observes. Playing the 'fantastical duke of dark corners' (4.3. 156). The second magistrate is the Duke's brother Angelo. A strident puritan, in whom the Duke vests regency powers during his absence. The third magistrate is Escalus, the local Justice who struggles to impose some kind of order on the ground. We can only conjecture how James might have reacted to the resonances. A commonwealth drowning in a sea of sexual impropriety; threatening to 'oe'errun the stew' (5.1. 316–17). And a court that did not seem to be setting much of an example, as we have already noted. A 'nursery of lust and intemperance', as the very puritan Lucy Hutchinson would later describe the Court of King James. A place 'grown scandalous', Lady Anne Clifford agreed.[62]

Time perhaps for a royal proclamation that made it look like the new King cared. Remember though, as Lucio again observes, there is measure to be had: 'Grace is grace, despite of all controversy' (1.2. 24–25). For which reason it might be best to check with the judges. The legality of the two proclamations was tested, at the King's request, in 1610. Coke's account of what transpired was written up from notes taken of a conference in Privy Council, and published in the twelfth volume of *Reports*.[63] Called to join a starry bench, alongside Lord Chief Justice Fleming, Chief Baron Tanfield and Baron Altham. And greeted by a similarly

---

[62] Stone (1967) 188, 299.
[63] (1610) 12 Coke Rep 74.

starry cast of royal sycophants. Headed by Lord Chancellor Ellesmere who, on behalf of the King, requested an 'opinion' on the legality of the proclamations, and some pretended 'grievances' articulated in the House of Commons. His view, as 'keeper of the king's conscience', was predictable. He would enforce any 'decree accordingly'.

But the King wished to know that his judges would do similarly, that they too would respect the 'power and prerogative of the King', recognising that in 'cases in which there is no authority and president' they must 'leave it to the King to order in it according to his wisdome'. Otherwise the King would indeed be 'no more than the Duke of Venice'. The Lord Privy Seal chipped in with a familiar metaphor. A king, like a physician, is best placed to 'apply his Medecine according to the quality of the disease'.[64] Allusions, and questions, of the loaded variety. Which did not elicit an especially helpful response, as the King, deep down, probably feared.

Speaking on behalf of the four, Coke requested time to consult his judicial 'brethren'. The questions were of 'great importance', and touched on a matter of 'novelty'. Precedent appeared 'wanting', which necessitated 'great considerations'. He would though venture a preliminary 'opinion'. That a 'King cannot change any part of the Common Law, nor create any offence by his Proclamations, which was not an offence before, without Parliament'. Plenty of alarm bells ringing; for all concerned. A few weeks later Coke was back, having consulted with his 'brethren', his preliminary opinion now confirmed, and despite the 'novelty' apparently unarguable.[65] Authority discovered in Fortescue and Holinshed and various statutes, including a Henrician Act of 1539 which confirmed that proclamations enjoyed the same status as parliamentary Acts. Coke did not challenge the existence of the prerogative, but 'resolved that the King hath no Prerogative, but that which the Law of the Land allows him'. To rub it in a bit, Coke cited various proclamations which he had, on closer study, discovered to be 'utterly against Law and reason'. At least he did not list any of James's.

The Case of the Doubtful Doctor

Hindsight supposes that 1610 might be a watershed moment in the evolving constitutional and political crisis. The question of proclamations was hardly settled. The Commons duly presented a long petition of grievances to the King, making reference to 'a general fear conceived and spread amongst your majesty's people that proclamations will by degrees grow up and increase to the strength and nature of laws', something that could only diminish the 'ancient happiness' enjoyed by 'their ancestors', but also 'in process of time, bring a new form of arbitrary government upon the realm'. In the meantime, another litigant pitched up at Common Pleas,

[64] Sheppard (2003) 1. 487.
[65] Sheppard (2003) 1. 488–89.

looking to challenge the legality of another kind of prerogative proclamation. His name was Doctor Bonham; or maybe just Mr Bonham.[66]

There were two kinds of medic in Jacobean England. There were barber-surgeons, who advertised a number of key transferable skills, to include beard-shaving, boil-lancing, bloodletting and dental extraction. And there were members of the College of Physicians, who boasted university certificates. Barber-surgeons operated from commercial premises, commonly designated by a red and white striped pole. The physicians saw themselves a cut above, and were not much pleased by the competition, still less the comparison. Needless to say, whilst the King liked to imagine himself a 'physician' caring for the health of his commonwealth, his subjects tended to hold medics of either variety in much the same regard as they did lawyers. Their prejudices regularly fuelled by reported cases of variously venal, inept and downright devilish doctors.

Such as that of the notorious Dr Rodrigo Lopez, accused of trying to poison the Queen in 1594. It is thought that Lopez was in Shakespeare's mind when he came to fashion his Shylock. He would certainly have been in that of his audience. Likewise, anyone who attended performances of Jonson's *Sejanus*, which exhibited the peculiar talents of the 'skilful' Eudemus: physician, beautician, and prospective regicide (2.18). Another profession, as Jonson's Mosca elsewhere confirms, crammed with conmen ready to prescribe anything for a 'fee': from a 'cataplasm of spices' to an 'oil with wild cat's skins' to a 'lusty' young woman 'full of juice'.[67] Raising a smile, of the sicklier kind. Not that there was anything aberrant in a judiciously placed cataplasm. It was precisely what the doctors ordered for the ailing Prince Henry in 1612, comprised of 'warm cocks and pigeons newly killed', washed down with a swig of 'unicorn horn'.[68] Sadly ineffective.

The problem with Thomas Bonham moved around his qualifications. Bonham claimed to be a graduate of Cambridge University, and thus sufficiently skilled to seek a licence to practise surgery. Such licences were in the gift of the College of Physicians, under statutory authority granted in 1540 and reaffirmed in 1553. He was also a member of the Company of Barber-Surgeons, who had put his name to a petition to Parliament designed to end the College's perceived licensing monopoly. Not lacking in boldness, Bonham had then presented himself to the College for examination at the end of 1605. The interview did not go well, and Bonham was refused his licence. Whether he was much surprised is a matter of conjecture. A further interview in April 1607 did not go any better, and he appears not have bothered trying again. He did though continue practising, in defiance of an order to desist, and the threat of a £5 fine and imprisonment. Six months later, Bonham

---

[66] (1610) 7 James I; 8 Co Rep 113b.

[67] Mosca in *Volpone*, 2.4. 29–35, telling Corvino of the various remedies for his master's ailments, as supposedly recommended by the 'college of physicians', at 'extreme fees'. Corvino believes it ready enough. A conspicuous number of Jonson's conmen pretend to be medics. Witness Subtle in *The Alchemist*, with his various concoctions.

[68] Stewart (2003) 248. A cataplasm being a poultice.

was ordered to attend the College to explain himself. Failing to show up, he was duly fined £10. A month later he was arrested, and brought before the College, where he refused to give an assurance that he would cease practising. At which point he was hauled off to Newgate.

His lawyers, almost certainly funded by the Company, submitted a writ of habeas corpus at the Court of Common Pleas. Only four years earlier Chief Justice Popham had declared himself unable to 'bayle or deliver' a man imprisoned by order of the College of Physicians. Chief Justice Coke, however, had no such scruples and ordered Bonham to be released. The College immediately sought the advice of Lord Chancellor Ellesmere and met with a committee of judges. Having received their tacit support, the College sued for £60 damages in consequence of Bonham's unlicensed practising. The writ was entered in King's Bench. Bonham counter-sued, claiming £100 damages for trespass to his person and wrongful imprisonment 'against the law and custom of this kingdom of England'. The counter-suit was entered at Common Pleas; the obvious choice, given what had occurred a year and half earlier, and the obvious Chief Justice. Bonham's lawyers couched their case in terms of restraint of trade, arguing that the statutes in question empowered the College to punish the 'ill-using' of 'physic', not to 'make a monopoly'. In the meantime, the College won in King's Bench, and Bonham found himself returned to Newgate.

The stakes kept rising. Bonham, now something of a poster-boy for the broader anti-licensing campaign, agreed to become a Freeman of the Company. The Archbishop of Canterbury weighed in, wondering that a man so obviously 'well learned in the Greek and Latin tongue' should have been prosecuted at all, and threatening to 'move' the matter in the House of Lords.[69] The College sought to flatter the Archbishop out of the idea, suggesting that he might, instead, like to serve as a mediator. Compromise, though, proved elusive. Another message was despatched to Newgate, repeating that if Bonham dropped his counter-suit, the College would order his release. No deal. Bonham's writ arrived at Common Pleas in Hilary Term 1610.

Where Chief Justice Coke led a majority opinion, of three to two, in Bonham's favour. The 'doctor' was released once again and awarded £40 damages for trespass to his person. In dissent, Justice Walmsley deployed a prescient metaphor: the King was the 'physician to cure' the maladies of his subjects, and the justiciability of the College Charter fell within his prerogative discretion. Coke saw things very differently, starting from the premise that a statutory power to fine was different from a power to imprison. The first concerned illicit practice, the second malpractice. And there was no evidence presented of the latter. At which point Coke moved on to consider the larger questions of constitutional propriety. Namely whether the College authorities should act as 'judges' in their own interests, and the possible

---

[69] An unlikely ally, perhaps, Archbishop Richard Bancroft is chiefly renowned for supervising the completion of the 'Authorized Version' of the King James Bible.

voidability of statutes which might be deemed to be 'against common right and reason'.[70]

What followed would not have surprised anyone who had attended Coke's opinion in the *Prohibitions*; especially the bit about the King's limited comprehension of the common law. The College was a 'learned' body well capable of regulating itself, and assessing the suitability of prospective physicians. But it was not a body 'learned' in the law. And neither, in passing, was it the only body capable of judging the merits of likely doctors; the universities were just as readily equipped. Bonham was a university graduate, and there was no 'reason' to prevent him practising his profession. The College was wrong in both fact and law. Moreover, as Bonham's lawyers had argued from the start, the original statute was not intended to establish a monopoly position in matters of either practice or adjudication. Neither could it presume to oust the supervening jurisdiction of a common law court. Echoes of chapter 29.

There is a judicial rider to *Bonham's Case*. A troublesome tailor this time, whose case arrived at King's Bench in 1614, shortly after Coke's reluctant traipse across Westminster Hall to be installed as Lord Chief Justice. William Shening was another who wished to practise his trade, but who found his local regulatory body unhelpful. Fined £3 13s 4d by the Ipswich Corporation of Tailors for having begun trading before presenting his credentials and providing proof that he had completed his apprenticeship. The 1563 Statute of Artificers vested a wide authority in such corporations, not merely to regulate admission to various trades, but to control prices and wages. Shening threatened all of this, in his small way. Not that the *Case of the Tailors of Ipswich* assumed the same profile as *Bonham's Case*. It did though attract a predictably similar opinion on Coke's part. Dismissing the Corporation's writ of prohibition, Coke took the opportunity to lecture his court on the merits of the protestant work ethic: 'That at the Common Law no man might be forbidden to work in any lawful Trade, for the Law doth abhor idleness, the mother of all evil'. Monopolies and trade-restraints especially, which the 'Law doth abhor'.[71]

The Case of the Mendacious Master

The third of our cases moves us forward to 1615. The *Earl of Oxford's Case* involved a contested conveyance.[72] It also provided Lord Chancellor Ellesmere with the opportunity to make his most concerted defence of Chancery as a court of 'good conscience'. A position he had laid out repeatedly in his various writings on the subject. In *Certaine Observations Concerning the Office of the Lord Chancellor*

---

[70] For a commentary here, see Cook (2004) 142–49.
[71] (1614) 11 Co Rep 53a.
[72] (1615) 21 ER 485.

confirming that Chancery 'intermedleth only with matters of a conscience'.[73] And then again in his *Priviledges and Prerogatives of the High Court of Chancery*:

> It is *lex terrae*, that is, the Judges of the Common Law shall determine questions in Law, and *Pares & Iurors* to try matters in fact, so the Chancery is to order and decree matters of Conscience and Equity, which cannot be remedied by the strict rules of the common law.[74]

The distinction might have stretched Coke's patience, but it was not aberrant, for reasons we have already noted. The metaphysics of conscience grounded in public law, the *lex conscientiae politicae* as opposed to the *lex conscientiae Divinae*, where the 'offendor standeth at the judgment of God only' and 'in times past was said to be examinable' before his 'Confessor'. Now, instead, there is the confessional of Chancery, and a Chancellor, not only dispensing equity under the 'direction of his 'Conscience that lyeth hidden and concealed in his own breast', but also tasked to 'judge *secundum conscientiam*'.[75] A court, it might be supposed, designed for men like Edward Vere, 17th Earl of Oxford.

Not that Edward was an especially godly man, as we will shortly see. He was, though, in possession of some formerly monastic property in St Botolph Aldgate. Seven acres, to be precise, commonly known as the 'Great Garden of Christ Church'. Originally gifted by Henry VIII to his Lord Chancellor, Sir Thomas Audley, who had bequeathed it to Magdalene College Cambridge.[76] The property was then sold to Benedict Spinola, 'Merchant of Genova', whose rather unflattering gargoyle can still be seen clinging to a wall at Magdalene. Spinola was a wealthy man, creditor to both the College and the Queen. At Lord Burghley's recommendation, the College transferred the property to the Queen in freehold, who then passed it to a suitably grateful Spinola in discharge of debt. It was hoped that such a transfer would circumvent the provisions of a 1571 statute which voided such leases unless limited to a period of 21 years or three lives. At the time, the property was estimated to be worth around £15 pa.

Spinola then sold part of the land to the 17th Earl, who sublet to a property developer named Hamond. An extensive redevelopment saw 130 new buildings erected, at the considerable cost of around £10,000, resulting in a dramatic increase in rental value, to around £800 pa. A shrewd long-term investment that most likely owed everything to the de Vere trustees, and very little to the Earl, rather more the spender than the saver, whose principal pastimes were jousting and seducing royal maids-in-waiting. Admonished for 'unthrifyness' by the Queen in 1574, and then again seven years later for seducing one of the said maids, by 1586 the Earl was petitioning the Court for relief from 'distress'. He died in 1604, leaving his predictably encumbered estate to his son, Henry. And, it has been suggested, some

---

[73] In Klinck (2010) 158.
[74] In Klinck (2010) 158.
[75] Klinck (2010) 161, 163–64.
[76] In thankful return, the College changed the pronunciation of its name; to 'Maudelyn'.

of the greatest dramatic writing in English literature, if the 'Oxfordians' are to be believed.[77]

In the very same year that the 17th Earl died, Magdalene College elected a new Master. Barnaby Gooch was a civil lawyer and mathematician, not that it would have taken an accounting genius to appreciate that the College was in a parlous financial condition. In order to raise much-needed funds, Gooch decided to challenge the validity of the 1580 conveyance, in the hope of reclaiming the property. And so, in 1607 he provocatively leased one of the buildings to the College Bursar, Mr Smith. Hamond retaliated through a sub-tenant, Sir Francis Castillion, who leased the same property to a Mr Warren. Counsel was recruited, on the Earl's behalf, in the shape of the Attorney General, Sir Francis Bacon. And proceedings for the ejectment of the College Bursar commenced at King's Bench in late 1613.

Eighteen months later, the Court found for Gooch, confirming that the 1580 conveyance was indeed void. The Queen was the 'fountain of justice and common right', and it was thus inconceivable that she should be exempt from her own laws. The 1571 statute was good. Bacon immediately petitioned for relief in Chancery. Gooch and his bursar refused to reply to the Chancery bill, on the grounds that judgment had already been given, and were duly held in contempt by the Lord Chancellor and committed to the Fleet. A writ of habeas corpus was successfully preferred in King's Bench, Coke articulating his customary warning that it would 'tend to the downfall of the common law if judgments here given should be suffered to be called into question in courts of equity'.[78] On this occasion, though, Coke was disinclined to go further, advising Gooch's attorneys that it would be 'better for you if we hear no more of it'. Meanwhile, a 'breviate' on Chancery jurisdiction was published in September 1615, emphasising the particular importance of 'good conscience' in ejectment actions.

Finally, in June 1616, Ellesmere was ready to revisit the case of the mendacious master. The timing was of course propitious, albeit rotten for Gooch. A spot of scripture to start, intimating that the Lord was broadly supportive of property development. Deuteronomy 28:30, 'He that builds a House ought to dwell in it; and he who plants a Vineyard ought to gather the Grapes thereof'. After which followed a long discourse confirming that the Lord was also supportive of kings who ruled in 'good conscience' and in accordance with the 'original lawe of nature'; the sentiment of *Calvin's Case* revisited.[79] Indeed:

> The cause why there is Chancery is, for men's actions are so divers and infinite, that it is impossible to make any general law which may aptly meet with every particular Act, and not fail in some circumstance. The office of the Chancellor is to correct Mens consciences for frauds, breaches of trust, wrongs and oppressions, of what nature soever they be, and to soften and nullify the extremity of the law, which is called

---

[77] Which they should probably not; the works of Shakespeare being rather more likely written by Shakespeare.
[78] 1 Rolle Rep 227.
[79] See Klinck (2010) 159.

Summum Ius … By all which cases, it appeareth, that when a Judgment is obtained by oppression, wrong and hard conscience, the Chancellor will frustrate and set aside, not for any error or defect in the judgment, but for the hard conscience of the party.[80]

The Earl was vindicated. Along with the Attorney General, who was invited to draft a royal declaration on the subject, published on 14 July 1616:

For inasmuch as Mercy and Justice be the true Supporters of our Royal Throne, and that it properly belongeth unto us in our Princely Office to take care and provide, that our Subjects … should not be abandoned and exposed to perish under the Rigor and Extremity of our Laws.[81]

Ellesmere might have written it himself; in a sense he did. Coke was reported 'vexed'.[82]

Not least, perhaps, by the activities of his estranged wife. Who, in that very moment, was busy trying to engineer a match between their daughter Frances and the 18th Earl. Coke, though, had his eyes on a different prize: the intermittently demented John Villiers, prospective Viscount Purbeck, and far more importantly brother of the George, in the moment the King's very favourite favourite. An expedient route back to royal favour, Coke rather hoped. Frances was kidnapped from her mother's house, tied to a bedpost and whipped into submission; or so scurrilous rumour reported. As a consequence of which, barely a month after his suspension from office, Coke was summoned to Council to answer charges of 'riot and force'. A less traumatic audience this time, though.[83] The King was keen on the Villiers match.[84]

Coke duly stumped up a dowry of £10,000, and the big day finally arrived in September 1617, the distraught 15-year-old bride led down the chapel aisle at Hampton Court by a beaming, and apparently slightly tipsy, King. As for the rest of the original cast, the 18th Earl consoled himself with the hand of Diana, daughter of the 2nd Earl of Exeter, and a dowry of £30,000, whilst Gooch was elected MP for Cambridge University, where he strove, fruitlessly, to have the Chancery judgment overturned.[85] A rather grislier moment in English legal history awaited the 'Great Garden of Christ Church'; the discovery, in its grounds, in September 1888, of the mutilated remains of Catherine Eddowes, the fifth victim of 'Jack the Ripper'.

---

[80] (1615) 1 Ch Rep 1, 6–7, 10.

[81] (1616) 1 Ch Rep 49; 21 Eng Rep 65.

[82] For an account of the case, see Watt (2009) 67–72.

[83] At first the Council apparently contemplated sending Coke to answer before Star Chamber, whilst also admonishing Secretary Winwood for having granted the original search warrant used for retrieving Frances from her mother. At which point Winwood flourished a letter from the King confirming his support for the warrant. 'To which', the Secretary recorded, 'there was no reply'. In Jardine and Stewart (1998) 403.

[84] Disregarding Bacon's increasingly desperate urgings against it; fearing that it might indeed secure Coke's return to Court and royal favour.

[85] He died in 1626, having spent a number of years serving, not just as Vice-Chancellor of Cambridge University, but as Chancellor to the see of Exeter.

Retirement Plans

The marriage of Frances Coke and Viscount Purbeck proved to be predictably unhappy. In due course, they each hired astrologers to predict their differing futures, and sorcerers to shape them. And futile too, in the grander design of Sir Edward Coke. The subsequent trial of Frances on charges of witchcraft and adultery, before the High Commission, imported some fine ironies, and did little to help rehabilitate her father's reputation at Court.[86] Not that Coke seemed much inclined to help himself. Back in summer 1616, James had supposed that his disgraced Lord Chief Justice might like to spend some of his newly spare time correcting the 'manifold errors' which the Attorney General had spotted in his *Reports*, along with 'some peremptory and extra-judicial resolutions'. A 'scattering and sowing his own conceits', as the Lord Chancellor put it.[87] A predictably truculent Coke reported back that he had only found five errors, all 'minor'.

The Case of the Factious Knights

James might have cowed his bench, or at least gotten rid of his most troublesome judge, but the common lawyers were hardly bested. Writing in the immediate aftermath of Coke's suspension, Tourneur observed that unless 'these breeding mischiefs', by which he meant prerogative abuses designed by flattering 'favourites', be 'redressed by Parliament, the body will in a short time die in all the parts'.[88] A view affirmed, rather courageously it might be thought, by Francis Ashley in his Middle Temple Reading later that summer. On the familiar topic of chapter 29, under threat like never before. The 'law of laws', Ashley opined, and 'if it be a mere statute' then the 'statute of statutes'. The reason why 'we have property in our goods, title to our lands, for our persons, and safety for our lives'.[89]

In the meantime, Coke retired to his estate at Standon.[90] In the moment the home of his elder daughter Anne and her husband. Keeping himself busy with various matters, including selling off his other daughter, whilst also refining his

---

[86] Charged along with her lover Sir Thomas Howard, son of the Earl of Suffolk; by no coincidence one of Coke's most implacable enemies at Court. In the end Frances fled to France, disdaining to do the prescribed penance, which amounted to standing outside her house in a white sheet. In due course, she went to live in a convent, with her illegitimate son.

[87] Smith (2014) 278–79.

[88] In Baker (2017) 421.

[89] In Baker (2017) 428.

[90] One of many estates. Coke had made a fortune both as a lawyer and an investor, much of the latter in property. Corruption would be amongst the charges levelled against him in 1616. Coke's considerable property portfolio had long aggravated the King. During a sharp exchange the previous year, James had suggested that his Lord Chief Justice had rather more property than became for a 'subject'. To which, it is said, Coke had replied that there was only one more 'acre' that he wanted. After which he purchased Castle Acre in Norfolk.

Reports, forging new alliances most importantly with Sir Lionel Cranfield, shortly to be appointed Lord Treasurer, and plotting his revenge against Bacon, who had succeeded Ellesmere as Lord Chancellor in 1618. In early 1621, he presented a new bill in Parliament designed to limit the power of Chancery; a glancing blow. More direct was the instantiation of a joint House committee to enquire into allegations of corruption against the new Chancellor. We will revisit these in due course. Suffice to say, a few weeks later, Bacon was gone. Another cold revenge to enjoy. Not that Coke was finished. James Stuart breathed his last in March 1625. Not though before Coke could play a major role in the passage of the 1624 Monopolies Act which, despite certain notorious exceptions, generally voided all Crown monopolies.

For a brief moment, it was hoped that the new King Charles I would prove more conciliatory. A very brief moment. It was also hoped that he might spend less. Charles, though, loved pretty things, and kept making expensive promises. Within months of ascending to the throne he had offered to help his Uncle Christian, King of Denmark, in his struggle against the perfidious Hapsburgs. Hardly investable, having just suffered a crushing defeat at the battle of Lutter. But still, family is family, and there was honour to be met. So Charles asked his Parliament for a loan, for a war priced-up at just under £1 million. Parliament offered grants of roughly a fifth of that amount. All very frustrating, and not a little embarrassing. Which brings us to two cases which moved around the consequence of Charles's inability to budget sensibly. Coke did not participate directly in either, but his presence is undeniable. The first was the so-called *Case of the Five Knights*.[91]

The story begins in late summer 1626. Having already dissolved his second Parliament, on hearing news that it intended to impeach Steenie, now Duke of Buckingham, but still wishing to somehow help Uncle Christian, Charles looked about for a 'speedie way' of raising some cash. And alighted upon the idea of using his prerogative to 'force' a loan from some of his better-off subjects.[92] Thomas Crosfield, fellow of Queen's College Oxford, likened it to Spanish 'servility'.[93] Feeding the 'palate of absolute power', the Earl of Clare was heard to observe in agreement.[94] Lord Keeper Coventry counselled caution too. Mindful perhaps of a run in with the gentlemen of Kent at Maidstone Assizes, who had reminded him, in no uncertain terms, that such a tax was against the 'whole discourse of Fortescue'.[95] Charles, though, was undeterred. A proclamation was issued, and writs sent out. The reason being 'necessitie to which no ordinarie course can give the lawe'.[96] Some paid up.

---

[91] (1627) How St T 1.
[92] Willms (2006) 92.
[93] Sharpe (1992) 700.
[94] In Cressy (2015) 99.
[95] In Smith (1994) 34.
[96] Cust (1985) 219.

More did not. In March 1627, warrants were issued for the arrest of five particularly 'refractory' knights.[97] Along with the Earl of Lincoln, who had published a pamphlet which suggested that the 'loan' threatened the 'liberties' of Parliament.[98] The Earl was despatched to the Tower, as befitted his rank, the knights to the Fleet. None were actually charged with a crime. The dispute moved around the detention of the knights. On receiving a petition 'for their relief out of prison' in July, the King was said to be 'much moved'. Not, though, the hawks in the Privy Council, who urged him to bring the 'factious men' to heel.[99] So they stayed where they were, for the time being. Lawyers for the five duly issued writs of habeas corpus at King's Bench. The bailiff, unsure of the legal position, failed to present. The Attorney General secured a second writ, in the name of one of the knights, Sir Thomas Darnell, and the matter was returned to court.[100] In effect, a test-case on the reach of the prerogative.

Lead counsel for the knights was John Selden. Another barrister favoured by the more factious, especially those who were reluctant to pay their taxes. Revered man of letters too, author of a renowned *History of Tithes*, which argued that all Church law was held under common rather than canon law, together with myriad articles on Arabic poetry, Syrian architecture and the law of the Old Testament. Along with plenty more on the history of the common law, Chapter 29 of the 'great charter' especially. The reason why, Selden reminded King's Bench, the five knights had to be surrendered. For if they were not, their 'imprisonment shall not continue on for a time, but for ever; and the subjects of this kingdom may be restrained of their liberties perpetually'. An argument which elicited 'wonderful applause' in the galleries, 'even of shouting and clapping of hands'. Attorney General Heath was lower-key; simply arguing that Selden had vouched no precedents. A view approved by Lord Chief Justice Hyde, a couple of days later. Selden might have managed to 'inveigle' the galleries, but he had not charmed Hyde. Relief lay with the King and, being 'bound by law', the King will do what is right.[101]

So the 'factious' knights remained where they were; at least until the 2 January, when they were quietly released. A kind of victory for the King. Narrow though, and tainted. A few months later, Selden uncovered a dreadful plot. The judges had given a 'declaration of judgement', in effect an interlocutory ruling, but the Attorney General had apparently sought to enrol it, thus creating a precedent from a particular, 'for ever and ever'.[102] Secretly. A tyranny compounded. If the common

---

[97] Being Sir Thomas Darnell, Sir John Corbet, Sir John Heviningham, Sir Walter Earls and Sir Edmund Hampden. None have left much more of a mark on history. Though we will encounter Sir Edmund's nephew very shortly.

[98] The Earl would spend the 1630s helping his father-in-law, Lord Saye, to shape a distinctive parliamentary opposition 'junto'.

[99] See Cust (2007) 69, quoting William Laud.

[100] Ironically Darnell had, by then, withdrawn from the action.

[101] In fact, Hyde chastised both parties for the failure to bring in precedents. See Kishlansky (1999) 61–64 and 76.

[102] Kishlansky (1999) 74.

law was scripture, the Attorney General's subterfuge was sacrilege.[103] The newly returned House of Commons feigned horror, and established an investigative committee under Selden's chairmanship. In the context of the longer history of the English constitution, it is what happened next which matters most. Looking around for another brilliant jurist to help, ideally one with a grudge and some time on his hands, the Commons alighted on Sir Edward Coke. Who set about drafting what would, in due course, become one of the most important documents in English constitutional history, the *Petition of Right*.

The preliminary draft of the *Petition* took the form of four *Resolutions*. A first deploring prerogative taxation, and three more relating to conditions of detention; which could only be lawful, had to be under formal charge, and were subject to the run of habeas corpus.[104] When Charles demurred, it was suggested that the *Resolutions* be passed into law in the form of a petition. Which Coke duly presented in draft form to the House of Lords on 8 May 1628. Nothing that was especially new; which was the point, written in the past tense, summoning the ghosts of the 'ancient' constitution. The hallowed 'liberties' of *Magna Carta*, liberated from the 'yoke' of Norman tyranny and, by insinuation, the threatened yoke of Stuart absolutism. As Sir Dudley Digges assured the Commons, in blunt terms: 'Prerogative only has caused it'.[105]

Coke's *Petition* again identified four particular 'liberties': habeas corpus, prohibitions against billeting on private property and the imposition of martial law, to which was added, rather pointedly, confirmation that 'no person should be compelled to make any loans to the king against his will'. Charles offered to reaffirm *Magna Carta* instead. But that was precisely what Coke did not want. The *Petition* was a statutory reassertion, not a plea for 'pleasure'. And the lexicon had moved. These were 'rights', being 'liberties' now in the care of Parliament, not in the gift of the Crown. Which gestures to something else, rather more familiar today. The birthing of a defining principle of English constitutional law. Parliament asserting a legislative 'sovereignty'.[106] Or re-birthing, according to Coke, in his commentary on the 'High Court of Parliament', which appeared in the fourth volume of *Institutes*.[107]

Unsurprisingly Charles chafed at the idea of giving his assent to the *Petition*. Equally unsurprisingly, though, he had run out of money again. And made some more silly promises, this time to relieve the Huguenots, bottled up in La Rochelle. The Commons offered a sweetener, five subsidies worth £300,000. On 7 June Charles gave his assent, and the *Petition* passed into law. There is a longer history here, which we will revisit in due course, tracing the influence of the *Petition* down

---

[103] See Morrill (1993) 289, suggesting that Charles was seeking to establish 'legal tyranny'.
[104] These three principles would later find statutory authority, in the shape of the 1679 Habeas Corpus Act.
[105] Raffield (2004) 205–06.
[106] See Pocock (1967) 48–50.
[107] Sheppard (2003) 3. 1110–12, discussed in Burgess (1996) 177–81.

the centuries, pausing to include the drafting of an English Bill of Rights and an American Declaration. A closer consequence was the Army *Remonstrance* drafted by Sir Henry Ireton in November 1648, in essence the indictment of Charles Stuart preparatory to his trial six weeks later. Ghosted, we might say, by Sir Edward Coke. Another revenge of the colder variety, and a whimsy we will revisit. Now, though, we need to return to the 1630s; for history was about to rhyme once again.

The Case of the Fainting Farmers

Charles dissolved his third Parliament in March 1629 and embarked on an 11-year period of 'personal rule'. Not itself aberrant. Plenty of kings had preferred to rule without Parliament, not least his own father. It was the extent which was notable, and the consequence. It might have worked, provided the King had been careful. His Chancellor of the Exchequer, Sir Richard Weston, recommended a period of 'rest and vigilancy'.[108] Charles was though a restless man, and not remotely vigilant. Which brings us to our next case, seven years on from the dissolution of spring 1629. During which time Charles had urged further contentious Church reforms, engaged in some more silly wars, and bought some very nice paintings, most spectacularly perhaps the famed Gonzaga art collection, recently come to market in late 1627, comprising lots of Titian and Rubens, together with Mantegna's *Triumph of Caesar*. A bit pricey, at £21,000, but Charles was determined. Neither he, nor his Queen, seemed able to stop spending, chiefly on themselves. Expenditure on the royal wardrobe doubled during the first decade of Charles's reign, from £13 million a year to £27 million.

By 1633 the Exchequer was bankrupt. The City declined a loan, which did not say much for the security. Absent any more Crown property to sell or mortgage, the King sought familiar recourse: to prerogative taxation. The precedents were hardly encouraging, but the need was unarguable. Charles consulted his Attorney General, who suggested the idea of 'ship money', a tax to be levied on ports for the maintenance of the navy. The right to do so in times of emergency was not contested. But peace was different. The prerogative order issued in 1635 cited incidents of 'piracy'. But it was a stretch. There were always pirates around. Charles issued a declaration clarifying the need, 'for the good and safety of the Kingdom'. And emphasising that 'in such cases' he was the 'sole judge ... of the danger'. A variant on a familiar tension: the King's absolute authority to determine when he had absolute authority.

Which met with a similarly familiar, and entirely predictable, response. The 'most deadly and fatal blow' inflicted on the 'liberty of the subjects of England' in 'five hundred years last past', Sir Simonds D'Ewes observed. Before asking the equally familiar question: 'What shall free men differ from ancient bondsmen and

---

[108] Sharpe (1992) 23.

villeins' if 'their estates be subject to arbitrary taxes?' He closed by wondering if the 'disease' which presently afflicted the county might prove 'incurable'.[109] Sir Simonds was an inveterate worrier. But there was reason, and history, and Chapter 29. The lesson of the past was plain enough: princes short of cash tend to take chances. The levy was extended across the country, and the courtrooms of England filled with fractious cattle-owners suing writs of replevin.[110] And their lawyers, looking for a fight and a decent fee.

Counter-suits were pressed against constables attempting distraint. The London merchant Richard Chambers sued the Lord Mayor. When the latter checked with his lawyers, he received the disappointing advice that the levy probably was unlawful, and that settlement might be a good idea. Up in Nottinghamshire an attorney named Coude advised the gentlemen of the county along the same lines. Any distraint should be contested. Down in Somerset, Sir William Strode, wealthy cloth merchant and soon-to-be Parliamentarian colonel, was told the same. Another cow recovered. Over in Lincolnshire, a couple of oxen were sequestered from the estate of Lord Saye at Brumby.[111] Not for long though. Saye, a prominent member of the 'junto', was gearing up. In the summer of 1637, the Sheriff of Buckingham returned a list of non-payers. At the top of the list was the name of John Hampden. A writ of *scire facias* was issued, for failure to pay an assessment of 20 shillings. Hampden knew it was coming. The Sheriff was Saye's kinsman, and Saye and Hampden were mates. The matter arrived at the Court of Exchequer in early autumn.

Hampden's Case is amongst the most famous in English constitutional history; and the most muddled.[112] Hampden's counsel, Oliver St John, did not dispute prerogative power. But he did question the authority of the Crown to seize 'goods' without 'parliamentary assistance', or the presence of any 'special' case of emergency, in the absence of which 'by the fundamental laws of England, the King cannot, out of Parliament, charge the subject'. Attorney General Bankes retaliated metaphorically. The King 'is the first mover among these orbs of ours, and he is the circle of this circumference'. The power to 'defend' the realm 'absolutely inherent in the king's person'. The Solicitor General threw in some jurisprudence, of the marginally contentious kind. The King held a 'trust', which included a duty to do 'whatever tends to the preservation' of the realm at moments of 'danger'; and if need be deal with instances of 'refractoriness'.[113] Contemporaries sensed a close call, recognising the skill in St John's argument, but doubting whether a full bench would go against the King.

And so it proved. The 12 judges found themselves at considerable odds. Aside from a basic agreement that tax could only be raised through Parliament, except in

---

[109] Sharpe (1992) 692.
[110] Constables despatched to deal with non-payers were instructed to seize movable chattels. Usually livestock. Writs of replevin were issued for the recovery of wrongly distrained goods.
[111] Sharpe (1992) 718–19.
[112] (1637) 3 St T 826.
[113] Affirming the original questions presented to the Court by the King. See Cressy (2015) 107–08.

moments of credible 'necessity'; something that neither side disputed. Four justices inclined towards the King on grounds of principle. Most strongly, perhaps, Sir Robert Berkeley, in whose opinion, the law was 'of itself an old and trusty servant of the King', the 'instrument of means which he useth to govern his people by'. Any attempt to challenge the prerogative would be a kind of 'king-yoking' unknown in English law. Two justices leant just as strongly the other way. According to Justice Croke 'no necessity can procure this charge without a Parliament'. Justice Hutton affirmed, simply, that the 'king had no lawful power to levy the Ship Money'. The remaining judges dodged the larger questions altogether, preferring to immerse themselves in technical arguments regarding the execution of the writ, whether it was appropriate to a tax or a 'service'. Justice Bramston and Justice Davenport resolved that the King had the power to command the service, but not receive the money. Most thought that the judges had decided for the King by seven to five. But no one was entirely sure. The Venetian envoy thought it might be seven to four, with one abstention. Whitelock counted it ten to two.[114]

If it was difficult to be sure who had won, and by how much, it was clear who had lost. *Hampden's Case*, as Sir Edward Hyde later attested, 'grew the argument of all tongues'. And did far more 'credit' for Hampden than it did his King. At that moment, Hampden had the 'greatest power and interest' of any man 'in the kingdom'.[115] Hyde closed his potted biography of Hampden, who would later die fighting for Parliament in 1643, by noting that he had by then become 'much fiercer'. And by casting an intimation. If Charles had been rather more sensitive in his dealings with men such as John Hampden, he would never have gotten himself into quite such a mess. A perception shared by Sir Roger Twysden. Up until 1637, prerogative taxation was mere 'grating'. Something different now though. *Hampden's Case* had made Charles look like an 'absolute' tyrant, not dissimilar to the 'King of France or the Great Duke of Tuscany'.[116]

The tax would, in the end, raise around £750,000. But at what cost? In April 1640, having embroiled himself in another ruinously expensive war, this time against the Scots, which needless to say he lost, Charles found himself obliged to recall Parliament. Amongst the many 'grievances' which the 'Short' Parliament immediately began discussing was prerogative taxation. A threat to the 'inheritance' of every gentleman', Sir Nicholas Culpeper recalled, an idea that made 'the farmers faint and the plough to grow heavy'.[117] A moment of poetic fancy. Culpeper was the most loyal of the King's supporters. But even they drew a line; around what they owned. Two years later, England dissolved into a vicious civil war. Ending with the execution of King Charles and the establishment of a Republic. It did not last. But the principles survived and would, in due course, assume a more familiar form.

---

[114] See Sharpe (1992) 722–23; and Cressy (2015) 108.
[115] Clarendon (1978) 168. See also Sharpe (1992) 721–29.
[116] Sharpe (1992) 727–28.
[117] Russell (1990) 137.

The Case of the Tyrant King

We might, in closing, pause to contemplate the sad demise of Charles Stuart, in January 1649. By then, of course, Coke was dead by 15 years. But that does not mean that he was not present in spirit. We might indeed catch a glimpse of him peering eerily out of an upstairs window at his house in Stoke Poges in summer 1647. Another of his many estates, this time purchased in 1599, hastily refurbished for the visit of Queen Elizabeth two years later, and then, rather later, the marital home of the estranged Frances Coke. At the very end of his life, father and daughter were reconciled, and it is thought that Coke might even have drafted various sections of the *Petition* at Stoke Poges, and the final two volumes of *Institutes*.[118]

It is also said that the manor house, pleasingly decayed today, is haunted by Coke's ghost. Imagined by Sir Thomas Gray in his cryptic muse on the poetics of late Elizabethan England, *A Long Story*, which he completed in 1750 whilst staying nearby; a 'gloomy' mansion inhabited by 'ghostly prudes', full of 'Rich windows that exclude the light/ And passages that lead to nothing'.[119] It is certainly tempting to imagine it so when Charles paid an enforced visit in the company of a troop of New Model cavalry in late summer 1647. Recently seized at Holdenby House, the captive King was on his way to an inevitably tense meeting with Fairfax and Cromwell at Childerley. Another revenge served nice and cold. We might imagine the spectral Sir Edward smiling grimly through one of those 'rich windows' as the royal carriage clattered up the drive.

A year and a half later, Charles would be sitting in the middle of Westminster Hall on trial for his life. A show trial, of course. Amongst the audience, surely, was the same ghostly presence wearing the same grim smile. For the prosecution brief that week was, in considerable part, drafted by Sir Edward Coke. The decision to put the King on trial, reached by a small group of senior New Model officers, had been made most likely in late October 1648. The prime mover was Henry Ireton, barrister of Middle Temple, hero of Naseby, and Cromwell's son-in-law. It was Ireton who drafted the *Remonstrance of the Army*, which appeared on 15 November. It promised 'exemplary justice' in the 'shape of capital punishment upon the principal author and some prime instruments of our late wars, and the blood thereof expiated'.[120] It was Ireton who determined that there must be due process, as well as atonement. The despatch of Charles Stuart should not be something, as Colonel Thomas Harrison later boasted, 'done in a corner'.[121]

---

[118] In the immediate aftermath of his fall, Coke stayed with his other daughter Anne, at another family estate near Standon in Hertfordshire. Where, it is surmised, he touched up his *Reports*, and began work on the first volumes of *Institutes*.

[119] The 'prudes' being in fact Amazonian sorceresses in the service of Queen Elizabeth, chasing errant poets around the haunted imagination of the author. At the time, whilst staying in Stoke, Gray was composing the poem which would secure his place in the pantheon of eighteenth-century English poets, *An Elegy Written in a Country Churchyard*. Most of *A Long Story*, which was indeed very long, is now missing; the bulk of 500 stanzas.

[120] Braddick (2009) 556–58.

[121] Ward (2023) 150.

Thus the passage, on 6 January 1649, of an Act Establishing the High Court of Justice.

The risk was of course patent. Show trials can go both ways. Blighted by a speech impediment, perhaps, but Charles was trained in public performance and, unlike his father, was comfortable centre-stage. The trial of King Charles I was a calculated gamble. For which reason it was essential that the script was compelling and the cast imposing. We can only wonder how Coke might have reacted, had he been alive still, and offered the position of Lord President of the Court. Filling the post proved a struggle. Rumour supposed that Cromwell had first pressed his old friend, Bulstrode Whitelock, presently Lord Keeper. But he declined, preferring to retreat to his country estate in Buckinghamshire 'till this business be ended'.[122] The lucky man, in the end, was John Bradshaw, a Cheshire lawyer who had made his name defending the firebrand leveller John Lilburne in his 1646 treason trial.[123]

The draft indictment, entitled 'A Charge of High Treason, and Other High Crimes', was presented to the court of 'commissioners' on 19 January, by the newly appointed Solicitor General, John Cook. Another position that might, in a different moment, have fallen to a different Coke. Cook would lead the prosecution, assisted by the Dutch jurist Isaac Dorislaus.[124] The indictment bore the stamp of both, along with a very long list of battles at which Charles was alleged to have been in attendance. Closing in vaunting tones, that Charles Stuart was the 'author, and continuer of the said unnatural cruel and bloody wars; and therein guilty of all the treasons, murders, rapines, burnings, spoils, desolations, damages and mischiefs to this nation, acted and committed in the said wars'. A war criminal, a tyrant and a traitor, in bloody and evident breach of the responsibilities inscribed in the original 'compact' which bound king and commonwealth. A construction which facilitated the redetermination of treason as a crime, not just against the person of a king, but against the commonwealth.[125]

And which, accordingly, appealed to both the Calvinist resistance-theorist in Dorislaus and the common lawyer in Cook. A composite jurisprudence of the kind recommended in John Selden's *Mare Clausem*, which recognised in the common law 'such compact or covenant, passed in the very beginnings of private

[122] Taking his fellow Lord Keeper, Thomas Widdrington with him. Whitelock also declined an invitation to help draft the indictment. He would later agree to his reappointment as Lord Commissioner of the Great Seal during the Protectorate.

[123] And more recently appointed Chief Justice of Wales.

[124] Another set of appointments that had proved tricky. Amongst those who pleaded various excuses to dodge the gig, was the Attorney General, John Steele. A tummy-upset did for Steele. Perhaps a wise evasion, given what would happen, in due course, to Cook and Dorislaus. The latter assassinated by a royalist hit-squad in The Hague a few months later in May 1649, the former hanged, drawn and quartered in 1660. There was a third member of the prosecution team appointed, John Aske. Who appears to have contributed next to nothing. A distant relative of Fairfax, Aske would later be appointed a Serjeant and High Court judge. It is thought that the assassination of the diplomat Anthony Ascham, also in May 1649, by another royalist hit-squad, was a case of consequential identity confusion.

[125] An argument originally advanced at the attainder 'trial' of the Earl of Strafford back in 1641.

dominion'.[126] In Thomas Elyot's *Boke Named the Governor* too, invoking the 'public weal' as 'a body living, compact or made of sundry estates and degrees of men, which is disposed by the order of equity and governed by the rule and moderation of reason'.[127] And which can be found scattered around Coke's *Reports*, most notably perhaps in his account of *Calvin's Case*. Prior to even the most ancient of British kings, there had been an original 'covenant' between the people. At which moment the English had established their own version of the Roman *dictum*; *salus populi est suprema lex*.[128]

The idea of the mutually binding covenant was at the centre of the charge that Cook read out on the first morning of the trial, which confirmed that a King of England was:

> Trusted with a limited power to govern by and according to the laws of the land and not otherwise; and by his trust, oath and office being obliged to use the power committed to him for the good and benefit of the people, and for the preservation of their rights and liberties.[129]

A trust sealed in the 'coronation oath', and then so obviously broken when Charles Stuart had 'traitorously and maliciously levied war against the present parliament'. Thus, in case there was any doubt, the long list of battles.

And thus, also, the product of so many long hours spent by the young John Cook at Gray's Inn, pouring over 'reports' of *Prohibitions* and *Proclamations* and similar cases. An industry that was made evident in a pamphlet which Cook had published shortly after his successful defence of Lilburne in 1646, entitled 'The Vindication of the Professors and Profession of Law'. A reformist tract, determined to reinforce the importance of a proper education in the 'artifice' of the common law. Because 'that which we call the reason of the law is not every natural man's reason but a practical and studied experience acquired by much industry and long observation'.[130] The 'Vindication' also urged the statutory reinvestment of *Magna Carta* and the *Petition of Right*.

Charles was not allowed legal representation in court.[131] He did, though, have plenty of expert legal counsel, which came up with an aligned defence, challenging both the jurisdiction of the court, and the substance of the charge.[132] The jurisdictional argument was ventured on the first morning, before the trial proper had even started. 'I would know', Charles enquired, 'by what power I am called hither

---

[126] See Haivry (2017) 308–11.

[127] In Raffield (2005) 81.

[128] 'The welfare of the people is the supreme law'. The comparable moment in Roman legal history being the inscription of the Twelve Tables.

[129] Kesselring (2016) 32–33.

[130] For a commentary on Cook's education and the influence of his near-namesake, see Robertson (2006) 25–26, 80–81, 147–48.

[131] For the reason Coke confirmed in his *Institutes*: 3. 1012–13, that 'the testimonies and the proofs of the offence ought to be clear and manifest, as there can be no defence of it'.

[132] The defence team was headed by Orlando Bridgeman and John Vaughan, successive Restoration Chief Justices of Common Pleas.

... by what authority, I mean lawful'.[133] There was no precedent in history, or law. And neither was there any precedent for an English king to be charged with treason. The common law defined treason as a crime against the King, which made the charge a logical fallacy. In fact, the very idea that an English king could be subject to any of his own laws was, Charles opined, a nonsense. Ruling by 'divine right', he was answerable to God alone.

The substantive trial opened the following afternoon, with Cook outlining the prosecution case. Charles Stuart had begun a civil war with the sole intent of imposing a 'tyrannical power'. In doing so, he had broken the terms of his 'compact' with the commonwealth. The consequence was the 'highest Treason' that 'was ever wrought' in English legal history.[134] All very sensible, if rather ruined by the fact that Charles kept stealing scenes.[135] Dressed for the part too, immaculate, bedecked with the Order of Garter, the jewelled 'Great George' around his neck. James would have been proud. Sitting in splendid isolation in the centre of Westminster Hall, Charles might have been terrified, disoriented certainly, but he never flinched. Every inch the King.[136]

And so it continued, Charles refusing to recognise the judicial authority of the Commons, which, in the absence of the Peers, was 'never a court of judicature'. 'Show me precedent', he demanded. Bradshaw had none. When the Lord President intimated that he was before the court 'in the name of the people of England, of which you are elected', Charles immediately shot back that no English king in history had been 'elected'. His 'trust' was 'committed to me by God, by old and lawful decent'. The common law supported a hereditary crown. If Bradshaw could supply evidence to the contrary, then fair enough. Again, the Lord President was baffled. The first day of the trial ended early. The second was a Sunday, all parties investing their time in prayer. The lead sermon at Westminster was given by Joshua Sprigge, Fairfax's chaplain, taken from Genesis 9:6, 'He that sheds blood, by man shall his blood be shed'. Ambivalent at best.

The Monday picked up where Saturday ended, Charles still refusing to recognise the court or enter a plea. To do either would be to betray a responsibility implicit in the coronation oath. 'It is not my case alone, it is the freedom and liberty of the people of England, and do you pretend what you will, I stand more for their liberties'. 'You are before a court', a visibly angered Bradshaw repeated. 'I am before a power', Charles replied.[137] He was certainly that. Enough, Cromwell informed

---

[133] Kesselring (2016) 36.

[134] Kesselring (2016) 32–35.

[135] The moment when he ruined Cook's opening address, by stooping to pick up the head of his cane, is legendary. The head had fallen off when Charles had tapped Cook on the shoulder, to request he pause during the opening address. Cook stopped, if inadvertently. Charles, realising that no one was going to pick up the top, did so himself. It was reported that there was an audible exclamation across the hall.

[136] Not that there were many inches; at just under five feet tall. Another reason, it was surmised, for staying seated.

[137] Wedgwood (2011) 142–45.

Cook, was enough. A plea of *pro confesso* was entered on the King's behalf; a gesture which rather compromised another big day that Cook had planned, examining all his witnesses.[138] After which it was a matter of drafting the verdict, which was read out on the morning of 27 January.

A nervy 45-minute speech incorporating lots of Bracton and Coke, fashioning an odd parallel between Charles and the Roman Emperor Caligula, and then revisiting some tyrants of more recent memory, Edward II and Richard II, neither of whom had come close to the 'height and capitalness of crimes that are laid at your charge'. As to the jurisprudential gist, Bradshaw fell back on the breach of 'a contract and a bargain made'. The sentence was duly read, that 'Charles Stuart, as a tyrant, traitor, murderer and public enemy, shall be put to death by the severing of the head from the body'.[139]

All that remained was the execution of sentence three days later, on a specially constructed scaffold erected outside the Banqueting Chamber at Whitehall. And then the appeal. For by the time that New Model troopers were selling off bits of bloodstained timber to lingering spectators, the first edition of a book entitled *Eikon Basilike* was being hawked around nearby streets.[140] A regicidal lament in honour of a king whose fate was 'paralleled ... only in the murther of Christ'. Part testament, part hagiography, the *Eikon* purported to be the collected thoughts of a prospective martyr.[141] Within 10 days, it had sold out its third print-run. By then the appeal was won, at least according to its self-proclaimed author, John Gauden: 'In a word it was an army and did vanquish more than any sword did'.[142]

Parliamentarian apologists did what they could. Cook published a text entitled *King Charls, his case*. Revisiting the prosecution brief, fatally dull. The most renowned defences of the regicide came from the pen of John Milton. The following October he published a pointedly entitled *Eikonoclastes*. Along with a screaming denunciation of 'Romish guilded Portrature', Milton revisited the legal argumentation which Cook had struggled to articulate in Westminster Hall. It was the 'common law' which Parliament had fought to secure, 'so ingrav'd in the hearts of our Ancestors, and by them so constantly enjoy'd and claim'd, as it needed not enrouling'.[143] The execution of the tyrant King and the instantiation of the republic was not, despite appearances, a constitutional aberration. On the contrary, it reinvested the principles of the 'ancient' constitution. By the end of

---

[138] The witness evidence was still taken, over the following two days, but in committee. And then read out in court the day after. Thirty-three witnesses in total, most of whom were called simply to confirm Charles's presence at various battles.

[139] Kesselring (2016) 73.

[140] There would be 30 more by the end of the year.

[141] The renowned frontispiece presented the martyred King in prayer, clutching a crown of thorns, his earthly crown at his feet. Engraved by William Marshall, probably inspired by Titian's *St Catharine at Prayer*.

[142] See McKnight (1996) 139; and Ward (2023) 108–11. Gauden would become a restoration bishop of Worcester. His claim to authorship remains debated.

[143] Ward (2000) 108.

the year, *Eikonoclastes* had staggered into a second print-run. The *Eikon* was in its thirty-fifth.

Milton had already premiered the legal argument in a treatise entitled *The Tenure of Kings and Magistrates*, drafted in anticipation of the regicide, and ready to run in the first week of February. It emphasised that 'liberty' of conscience was rooted in the common law, and the purpose of the 'compact' between sovereign and subject was to secure these liberties. Much as *Magna Carta* had, or Coke's *Petition*; statements both of reinscription. The same urgent assertion; the power of a king is 'nothing else, but what is only derivative, transferr'd and committed to them in trust from the People, to the Common good of them all'.[144] Nothing that happened in January 1649 was contrary to either the law of God, or the law of England. On the contrary, everything was in accordance with the same common law that Coke, and Fortescue and Bracton before, had done so much to enshrine in the 'hearts' as well as the 'minds' of Englishmen. The execution of Charles Stuart had not confirmed a revolution; rather it had completed a reformation. A few weeks later, Parliament passed an Act Abolishing the Office of King. The spirit of Edward Coke could rest, for now at least; though how easily we can only surmise.

---

[144] Milton (1991) 10.

4

The Lives of Francis Bacon

There is an ideal way to run a commonwealth. Francis Bacon sketched the possibilities in an unfinished text entitled *New Atlantis* which was published posthumously in 1626 by his chaplain, William Rawley. *New Atlantis* was a contribution to a genre which had become very fashionable during the Renaissance. The 'utopian', after Sir Thomas More's original contribution published just over a century earlier in 1516. The purpose of a utopian treatise was to dream. Something which inevitably attracted dreamy poets. The 'insubstantial pageant' of Shakespeare's *The Tempest* is an obvious example: 'I would with such perfection govern, sir/ T'excel the Golden Age' (2.1. 163–64).[1] But which also attracted historians and philosophers, variously looking backwards and forwards for inspiration. Machiavelli's *Discourses on Livy* and *The Prince* can be likewise termed utopian.

The idea could, of course, be traced much further back, to Plato's account of 'Atlantis' most presciently.[2] Bacon characteristically trimmed the possibilities. As a much younger man, invited to contribute a masque to the Gray's Inn Revels in 1594, and keen to impress, he had devised a prototype; a 'palace of invention'.[3] Two decades on, he favoured something rather more structured, with lots of numbers. An exercise in what we might now term speculative modelling.[4] Half a millennium of experience has tempered our enthusiasm for such exercises; history too often describing the easy elision from the utopian to the dystopian. Back in 1623, though, when Bacon set about modelling his ideal world, it was still very much *a la mode*. Science made art.

Something else which chimed with the idea of renaissance was adventure. Not just discovering 'new' learning, but also 'new' lands. The further aspiration of the *Tempest*, the seed of empire, and a good way to make money. Not always, as the

---

[1] The latter line most likely alluding to the same age projected by Ovid towards the close of *Metamorphoses*. See Bate (1993) 256; and more broadly Raffield (2017) 198–200, 204–05.

[2] In his *Timaeus*. Bacon (1974) 226–27 makes reference to Atlantis in his story, dating back around three thousand years, and recounting its destruction during a 'deluge'; an image clearly taken from the Biblical Flood. And then supposing that it is now re-'discovered' as America.

[3] The revels were published as the *Gesta Grayorum, or the High and Mighty Prince: Henry Prince of Purpoole*. The 'prince' is a Christmas Lord, 'purpoole' a bastardised spelling of Portpool, the original name of the property upon which the Inns were built. An early performance of *Comedy of Errors* at the revels catches the eye of the Shakespearean scholar. Questions remain as to whether Bacon wrote the masque in its entirety. See Jardine and Stewart (1998) 167–68; and Coquillette (1992) 33, 259.

[4] For a renowned, and controversial, commentary on Bacon's 'scientific vision' and the extent to which it defined the 'Golden Age of Learning' which he 'envisioned', see Bowen (1963) 51.

hapless 'merchant of Venice' discovered, but often enough. Bacon was certainly intrigued, a prime mover in the establishment of colonies in both Virginia and Newfoundland.[5] The conceit in *New Atlantis* supposes precisely such an endeavour, albeit once again going slightly awry. A gang of 'adventurers' getting lost at sea, before finally alighting on a land called 'Bensalem'. The name, derived from the Hebrew, meaning 'son of wholeness', is suggestive. Sir James Harrington would base the governance of his *Oceana*, published later in 1656, on the Jewish Sanhedrin, and Bacon may well have been imputing the same. The seeming absence of a sovereign ruler in Bensalem likewise insinuating some kind of republican model of the kind which Harrington recommended. Maybe, maybe not.

Either way, what is most conspicuous about Bensalem is how settled it seems to be, and how happy its inhabitants. Having experienced its reformation long before. And its renaissance, for Bensalem is similarly conspicuous in its learning. In sum, a place of enviable 'piety and public spirit'.[6] Even immigration control seems welcoming; the 'care of desolate strangers' being God's work.[7] The renaissance dream, it might be supposed. But also, perhaps, its nightmare. For it becomes apparent that Bensalem is a land governed, at a remove, by an army of secretive scientists, operating out of 'Salomon's House'. Digging deep into the earth, fracking for resources, conducting genetic experiments, building ever-more effective weapons of war, wondering the possibility of human flight. There is even a dedicated home for its 'Compilers', the 'mathematical house'; somewhere in which to glean data for the Conservator of Health, and worry about plague responses, birth control and climate change.[8] Every modern polity needs its Compilers; or seems to think so.

Just as it needs its lawyers, and lawgivers. Here again Bensalem appears to have been strangely blessed. Originally by the endeavours of a king 'whose memory of all others we most adore; not superstitiously, but as a divine instrument, though a mortal man; his name was Solamona'. Another Soloman perhaps, or another James Stuart. A man of 'large heart, inscrutable for good', and 'wholly bent' to 'make his kingdom and people happy'. It was Solamona who established Salomon's House. Most importantly Solamona was a 'lawgiver', who designed his laws so that they 'preserved all points of humanity'.[9] He was also a king who found time to write a series of brilliant treatises, on theology and natural history. And design a sort of

---

[5] Providing a report on the Virginian colony in 1609, and securing a charter for a 'company of adventurers' and a colony in Newfoundland the year after.

[6] With some laudable absences; 'no stews, no dissolute houses, no courtesans, nor any thing of that kind'. See Bacon (1974) 219, 235.

[7] Bacon (1974) 218–19. The sailors are first taken to the appropriately named Strangers' House, to confirm that they are indeed Christian, and not pirates. The House is run by a 'Christian priest'. After which they are assured that they will 'want nothing'. Resources are hardly stretched, it must be admitted, no one else having pitched up on the coastline of Bensalem for 37 years.

[8] A 'tower' of the House is put aside for those whose principal responsibility is to check changes in weather patterns, together with 'engines' for changing wind-speed. A 'Chamber of Health', part laboratory, part clinic, deals with matters of disease control.

[9] Bacon (1974) 228.

written constitution, entitled the 'King's Charter'. The Charter creates a patriarchal hierarchy of commonwealths, variously familiar in the writings of Hooker, and, a little later, Sir Robert Filmer. So brilliantly devised is this Charter that there seems to be no need of any more kings; just a counsel of wise men, to sift through all the data.

Law and science fascinated Bacon, the relation of the two especially. Complementary means by which humanity might be saved, not least from itself. Ironically, it was the particular faith in science which killed him, or so goes the story related in John Aubrey's *Brief Lives*.[10] Journeying home through the snow one day, accompanied by the King's physician, Bacon stopped his carriage to buy a fowl. He had pondered the idea that meat might be preserved by 'artificial freezing', both in *New Atlantis* and his essay *De Augmentis*.[11] Now was the time to find out. So Bacon stuffed his fowl with snow, 'that so chilled him that he immediately fell so extremely ill, that he could not return to his Lodging'. And was taken instead to the nearby home of the Earl of Arundel, where he was placed in a damp bed.[12] A couple of days later he was dead, 'of suffocation'. In a last letter composed to the Earl, Bacon likened himself to the elder Pliny who could not resist taking a closer look at the erupting Vesuvius.[13] The letter is though slightly elusive, making reference to other experiments regarding the 'conservation and induration of bodies'.[14] It might have been a stuffed fowl that did for Bacon, or it might have been an afternoon poking the plague-ridden. Either way, the 'great apostle of experimental philosophy', as Macaulay put it, was prophetically 'destined to be its martyr'.[15]

Bacon had started work on *New Atlantis* shortly after his dismissal from office as Lord Chancellor in 1621.[16] It was one of 24 pieces that he would compose during his enforced retirement; around a third of his entire canon. We will revisit much of this, as we will the circumstance of his 'retirement', in the coming pages. In doing so we will discover a common denominator: the determination to found a 'universal' theory of knowledge, or more precisely a common methodology. In a sense, *New Atlantis* represented the epitome of this aspiration. James Spedding, who edited a definitive collection of Bacon's *Works* in the nineteenth century, supposed

---

[10] Aubrey claimed that his source for the account was Thomas Hobbes, then serving as Bacon's secretary. The extent to which Hobbes might have played a more creative role in some of Bacon's late writings remains a matter of conjecture.

[11] Referencing the idea to the Dutch scientist Cornelius Drebbel, who had conducted experiments on the effects of air-conditioning. A team of scientists at Salomon's House is tasked with investigating the same.

[12] Arundel was a long-time friend, with a shared interest in scientific experiments. Amongst his many projects, the Earl supported William Gilbert's work on magnetism.

[13] Pliny, a Roman admiral, left comparative safety to see if he could effect a rescue of those trapped at the port of Stabiae. It has been surmised that natural curiosity was a collateral factor in persuading him to make his fateful decision.

[14] Jardine and Stewart (1998) 504–05.

[15] Macaulay preferred the stuffed fowl theory. See his 'Lord Bacon' (1837) 63.

[16] Most likely sometime in 1623.

that there was 'no single work' which had 'so much of himself in it'. A 'vision' of what 'our own world' might be 'if we did our duty by it'.[17]

As we will see, there was much about Bacon's sudden fall from grace which resonates with that of his great antagonist Sir Edward Coke. Even the retirement hobby chimes; the life of the mind. Very different minds though. Coke's was consumed by revenge, Bacon's by the urge to dream. It might say something about character, as well as circumstance. A 'man of pity and compassion', Rawley would attest, entirely 'free from malice', neither a 'revenger of injuries', nor a 'defamer of any man'.[18] Which, if true, made him pretty much unique amongst Jacobean courtiers. There again, Rawley was a close personal friend, as well as chaplain. We will see what others have thought of Bacon too. Opinions tend to be mixed, and not infrequently perplexed. Lytton Strachey famously. 'Who', Strachey wondered, has ever really 'explained Francis Bacon?'[19]

Renaissance Man

We will start with Bacon's professional 'life'. A not unfamiliar career arc; much the same as Coke's, only half a step back. Building a reputation at the bar, gaining preferment at Court, rising to the highest legal offices in the land. From which he would fall spectacularly. Impeachment, followed by a retirement during which time Bacon nursed his gout, wrote copiously, and experimented with poultry. He might have even written 'Shakespeare'; a candidacy no more likely than that pressed by the 'Oxfordians'.[20] We will chart the legal and political career first, before turning our attention to the 'man of letters'.

Learned Counsel

Born into a legal family, his father was Elizabeth's first Lord Keeper, Bacon's career choice was hardly surprising. Admitted as an 'utter' barrister of Gray's Inn in 1582, a year after securing a seat in the Commons, the young Francis quickly resolved that the readiest way to preferment was by seeming clever and saying the right things. My 'young Lord Keeper', he proudly recorded Queen Elizabeth as saying, when she first met the precocious 14-year-old during a visit to Cambridge. He would have

---

[17] Coquillette (1992) 257–58. Spedding also produced a *Life and Letters*.

[18] Not, it must be admitted, the most impartial of commentators. Rawley would continue to serve his master after his death, editing a collection of flattering memorials, the *Manes Verulami*. He also supervised a variety of posthumous publications, including *New Atlantis*, and the necessarily poignant *History of Life and Death*.

[19] Zagorin (1998) 4.

[20] The idea that Bacon might have written 'Shakespeare' was something of a nineteenth-century fad, founded chiefly on a few coincidental textual references, and the possibility that Bacon, who was interested in ciphers, might have encrypted his identity within some of the plays.

practised a suitably flattering response. Bencher in 1586, reader in 1587, Francis cultivated lots of the right friends. A first patron was Robert Devereux, Earl of Essex.[21] The importance of patronage was something else that the young Bacon would have gleaned from early readings of Machiavelli.[22] Along with a need for patience. Devereux promised to secure the position of Attorney General in 1594, but it went to Coke.[23] As did the hand of Lady Elizabeth Hatton. Bacon would wait until 1606 before marrying Anne Barnham, daughter of a wealthy City merchant. Sadly, the wedded life of the Bacons would prove to be little happier than that of the Cokes.[24] He was also beaten to the Solicitor-Generalship, in 1595; this time by Sir Thomas Fleming, reportedly on Coke's recommendation.[25] Years later, in his essay 'Of Great Place', he would reflect on the 'pains' of rising to public office, and the 'indignities'.[26]

Ever sensitive to changes in the political climate, Bacon managed to detach himself from Devereux just in time.[27] Though 'much bound unto him', Bacon explained to the Earl of Northampton, he was not 'servile' to his erstwhile patron.[28] In due course, he would join Coke's prosecutorial team for the Earl's trial, and then write up the 'official' report.[29] A strange coupling it might be thought, thrown together by chance. We have already encountered various fiery exchanges between the two, in court and in print. Some, as Bacon complained, so 'insulting' as 'cannot be expressed'.[30] Shortly after their notorious exchange in Exchequer in 1601, Bacon sent a personal 'letter of expostulation', accusing Coke of taking 'a liberty

---

[21] Becoming, as Coquillette puts it, the Earl's 'ghost writer' (1992) 31.

[22] See Zagorin (1998) 18–21.

[23] Reportedly telling Sir Robert Cecil that 'it is the attorneyship that I must have for Francis, in that I will spend all my power, mine authority, and amity'. In Jardine and Stewart (1998) 15.

[24] Bacon was 31 years older than his then 14-year-old wife. He admitted to having first taking a shine to the 'handsome' Alice three years earlier. Alice earned a considerable reputation for extravagance, and in due course adultery. She married Bacon's usher John Underhill within weeks of his death in 1626, after which, according to admittedly scurrilous rumour, she made the poor man 'deaf and blind with too much of Venus'. Even so, not the most interesting Barnham sister. Her elder sister, Elizabeth, would gain still greater notoriety, as the wife of Mervyn Tuchet, 2nd Earl of Castlehaven, executed in 1631 for sodomy and rape. The sodomy being with his page, the rape being that of his wife, in which he had allegedly conspired with his servants. Tuchet maintained that the entire case was stitched-up by his bored wife and estranged son, the soon-to-be 3rd Earl. A view shared by the page, who was also executed. In his opinion, Elizabeth Barnham was the 'wickedest woman in the world'.

[25] Esteemed by Coke for his 'great judgements, integrity and discretion', Fleming would later serve as Lord Chief Baron of the Exchequer and Lord Chief Justice.

[26] Bacon (1985) 90.

[27] Sensing a turning of fortunes, following the Earl's disastrous Irish campaign in 1599.

[28] Jardine and Stewart (1998) 15.

[29] Entitled a *Declaration of the Practices and Treasons attempted and committed by Robert late Earl of Essex and his Complices*. A first print in April 1601, swiftly followed by a second, Elizabeth having taken exception to the designation 'my Lord of Essex' in the original. The second print-run replaced 'my Lord of' with 'Earl of'. The French Ambassador supposed that Bacon had been a prime mover against the Earl since 1599; an insight which led King Henri IV to conclude that Bacon must be a man of great 'perfidy'. In Jardine and Stewart (1998) 230–31.

[30] In Jardine and Stewart (1998) 254.

to disgrace and disable my law, my experience, my discretion', and traducing him at Court.[31]

Having dumped Devereux, Bacon sought out the steadier patronage of Sir Thomas Egerton, later Lord Chancellor Ellesmere. It was Egerton who secured Bacon the consolatory position of Queen's Counsel 'extraordinary' in 1597.[32] Meanwhile, Bacon was busy establishing a considerable reputation for himself at the bar; a 'hired gun' in high-profile cases such as *Slade* and *Chudleigh*.[33] All of which meant that he was nicely positioned when the new King James succeeded to the throne in 1603. Possessed, indeed, of three essential qualities: evidently capable, just as evidently willing to please, and usually broke.[34] His status as King's 'counsel' reaffirmed, a knighthood bestowed, Bacon duly set to work as the King's point-man in the Commons. An obliging servant, with an obliging tongue. 'It was the voice of God in man', he reported to his fellow parliamentarians, of one audience with his new master, 'I do not say the voice of God, and not of man: I am not one of Herod's flatterers'. But still, a king of such 'eloquence', so full of 'bounty and amity' and of such 'good nature'.[35]

And of such 'rare sufficiency', he added in another 1604 speech, spotting that what James really liked was someone flattering his intellectual pretension.[36] Some helpful writing too, composed 'not as a man born in England, but as a man born in Britain'.[37] And taking immediate shape in *A Brief Discourse Touching the Happy Union of the Kingdoms of England and Scotland*, followed swiftly by *Certain Considerations Touching the Better Pacification and Edification of the Church of England*. Amongst its proposals was the idea of a cross-border court modelled on the Council of the Marches, exercising a jurisprudence that was 'mixtly' derived, from England and Scotland, under the supervening authority of the prerogative.[38] A man seemingly after the King's heart; liking the idea of union, and an expansive prerogative, but not liking incessant religious bickering. Echoes of Hooker too, in recommending the 'golden mediocrity', in the establishment of that which is sound'.[39] In other words, an established Church.[40]

---

[31] Most obviously in the matter of the contested Solicitor-Generalship. See Jardine and Stewart (1998) 254–55.

[32] The first such designation in English legal history.

[33] He would later write up four of these early engagements in a text entitled *The Arguments of Law … in Certain Great and Difficult Cases*. Along with *Slade's Case* (1598) 4 Co Rep 92b, 76 ER 1074; and *Chudleigh's Case* (1623) 145 ER 199, Bacon revisited his arguments in *Bowle's Case* 11 Co Rep 79b (1616) and the *Council of the Marches Case* reported in Spedding (1857/2011) 7. 567. The sensitivity of the latter probably precluded publication during the author's lifetime, and the collection was not published until 1730. The term 'hired gun' is deployed in Coquillette (1992) 2 and 128.

[34] Bacon was actually arrested for debt in 1598. By 1603 he owed a colossal £3,700 on his own credit, and a further £1,700 on that of his recently deceased brother.

[35] In Jardine and Stewart (1998) 279.

[36] In Jardine and Stewart (1998) 282–83.

[37] See Wormald (1993) 387.

[38] Coquillette (1992) 72.

[39] In Jardine and Stewart (1998) 273.

[40] A thesis which Bacon would affirm in one of his later essays, 'Of Unity in Religion'.

The *Council of Marches Case*, which reached court in 1606, furnished Bacon with the opportunity of refreshing his thesis. Whilst in the process defending the jurisdictional reach of the King's prerogative as something held not 'from the law but immediately from God, as he holdeth the Crown'; part of which is to 'delegate' to the judges, the rest 'inherent in his own person'. History showed, Bacon advised, that monarchies 'do often degenerate' when their kings are 'made accomptable and brought before the law'.[41] Not just history either, but scripture too, and Bracton, and the author of the *Trew Law of Monarchies*; a nicely turned bit of flattery.[42] Typically, Bacon rounded out his principled argument with a more prosaic injunction. The Council was necessary in order to deal with an infestation of papists and 'disorderly' Marcher lords.

The following year Bacon argued the case for the 'Greatness of Britain' during the heated Commons debate in which Fuller railed against the influx of Scottish 'pedlars'. Reward came shortly after, appointed Solicitor General, with a salary of £1,000 pa. It was in this capacity that he would represent the King in *Calvin's Case*, reminding everyone that hereditary monarchy was the only natural form of government, as the very brilliance of James Stuart proved. Shortly after, Bacon composed a *Preparation for the Union of Laws*. He could hardly have done more, but patience was still the order of the day. Early in 1611, he wrote to the King noting how many 'preferments of the law fly about mine ears', and praying that he was not 'forgotten'. He wanted 'the Attorney's place'.[43] Which he got, finally, in 1613, when the incumbent, Sir Henry Hobart, was appointed Chief Justice of Common Pleas in place of Coke.

A busy four years followed, during which Bacon would be tasked with orchestrating Coke's downfall in summer 1616. The case *De Rege inconsulto*, a few months earlier, setting the tone.[44] Defending the integrity of a writ *non procedendo rege inconsulto*, which supposed that a king must be first consulted before the appointment of certain public office-holders. The King 'were better to lose his castle of Windsor than his privilege of inhibiting proceedings by this writ', Bacon obligingly opined. It was an immediate Crown interest, recognised in the common law. It was also the proudest two and half hours of his life, or so Bacon reported back to his King. A weary Coke was less impressed: 'Justice knows no such strange prerogative to shut up the mouth of the subject'.[45] As the *Commendams* loomed, Bacon also found himself immersed in the Overbury scandal, leading the prosecution of Carr and his wife. Only three years earlier, he had organised their wedding reception, now he was tasked with managing a show trial. Part Crown prosecutor, part *impresario*, in the office of Attorney General Bacon had found his *metier*.

---

[41] See Spedding (1861) 3. 368–82, for the printed version of his argument in the *Council of Marches Case*.

[42] See Wormald (1993) 140–41.

[43] Jardine and Stewart (1998) 323–24.

[44] (1615–16) *Brownlow v Mitchell and Cox* 1 Rolle Rep 188.

[45] Baker (2017) 422–23.

He had also found a new patron, in Sir George Villiers. It was 'Steenie' who recommended Bacon's appointment to the Privy Council.[46] And then again, as Lord Keeper, when Ellesmere died in March 1617. Receiving his seal of office, King James ordered him to 'contain the jurisdiction' of his court 'within the true and due limits, without swelling or excess'.[47] Raised to the peerage the next year, as Baron Verulam, Bacon duly became Lord Chancellor.[48] The top of the greasy pole, at last. All those years of saying the right things. An exultant Bacon spent £700 on a lavish feast to celebrate his inaugural speech in Chancery, given on 7 May 1618.[49] The theme was 'reformation' of the law, to root out the 'brambles that grown about justice'.[50] Exactly what his King would have wanted to hear.

As was Bacon's consistent defence of an encompassing prerogative. Affirmed as early as 1601:

> For the prerogative royal of the prince, for my own part I ever allowed of it, and it is such as I hope I shall never see discussed. The queen, as she is our sovereign, hath both an enlarging and restraining liberty of her prerogative; that is, she hath power by her patents to set at liberty things restrained by statute law otherwise; secondly, by her prerogative she may restrain things which be at liberty.[51]

And then again three years later:

> The king holdeth not his prerogative of this kind mediately from the law, but immediately from God, as he holdeth his crown; and though other prerogatives, by which he claimeth any matter of revenue or other right pleadable in his ordinary courts of justice, may be there disputed, yet his sovereign power, which no judge can censure, is not of that nature.

In fact, polities 'degenerate' when 'prerogatives are made envious or subject to the construction of laws' or where 'law as an oracle is fixed to place'.[52] A sentiment reiterated in 1610, when Bacon reminded the Commons that any 'diminution' of the prerogative would bring the country 'speedily to confusion and dissolution'.[53]

---

[46] In return for his support over the counsellorship, Bacon loudly approved the idea of raising Steenie to the peerage. Bacon personally drew up the patent for 'Viscount Villiers', arguing that the personalised name would further elevate the honour. Villiers duly became a Viscount in July 1616. Earl of Buckingham the following year, Marquess in 1618, Duke in 1623.

[47] To which Bacon replied that he would indeed treat the 'tumour of this court of Chancery'. A reference not to principle, but to inefficiencies. An odd choice of metaphor, all the same. See Klinck (2010) 168.

[48] Ennoblement was a precondition of becoming a Lord Chancellor. In the absence of which the appointee was made Lord Keeper. In 1621, Bacon would be elevated in the peerage, created Viscount St Albans.

[49] Living up to the philosophy which opened his essay 'Of Expense'. 'Riches are for spending; and spending for honour and good actions'. See Bacon (1985) 145.

[50] Along with genetic predisposition. Apparently Bacon devoted much of his address to assuring the audience that he was, quite literally, born to the role. See Jardine and Stewart (1998) 397.

[51] Defending monopoly licences against a bill was brought by Laurence Hyde. See Baker (2017) 197; and Jardine and Stewart (1998) 255–26.

[52] Baker (2017) 305–06.

[53] In Zagorin (1998) 165.

And precisely what might be expected of a Lord Chancellor. A couple of weeks after his own elevation, he used the appointment of a new Baron of Exchequer as an opportunity to remind his fellow judges that their principal duty was to 'maintain the King's prerogative'.[54] Bacon would remain Chancellor for four years. Still saying all the right things, appraising his King as the 'Uniter of Britain' in Star Chamber, the man who had finally brought peace to the Church and supervised the much needed purgation of his courts.[55] Not, of course, that the latter 'reformation' could be said to be done. Nor indeed that corruption was a thing of the past, ironically. There was a poetic justice in the fact that Bacon should be brought down on charges of corruption, not dissimilar to those which ended Coke's career. And there is certainly no surprise in discovering that Coke was a prime mover in the Chancellor's fall.

Articles of impeachment were laid in early 1621; 23 separate charges, mostly allegations of bribery. The stakes were high, as Bacon was reported to have advised his master: 'Those that strike at your Chancellor, its much to be feared, will strike at your crown'.[56] Particular attention was paid to Bacon's role in massaging, for a fee, a patent for gold and silver thread, the profits of which were shared by Steenie and the King. Bacon put up little resistance in the end, beseeching his peers to be 'merciful to a broken reed', and hoping that 'my penitent submission may be my sentence'. He had taken the money, but it had not affected his judgement. Sir Simonds D'Ewes was not much impressed. The falling Sir Francis was an 'eminent scholar, and a reasonable good lawyer', but also 'immoderately ambitious, and excessively proud', and prone to 'injustice and bribery'.[57] Venal and flash, put simply.

A fine of £40,000 plus committal to the Tower, at 'his Majesty's pleasure', did not seem especially merciful.[58] But it was all a charade. Having obligingly sacrificed himself, Bacon was released after a couple of days, his fine remitted by order of the King.[59] The benefit of an encompassing prerogative; another irony. He was, though, barred from public office. Embracing his fate, his health anyway failing, Bacon seemed reconciled, likening himself to Demosthenes and Seneca, fellow geniuses brought low by the 'slings and arrows' of political fortune. Years earlier, as an aspiring barrister, he had confided that the only reason 'to follow the practice of

[54] Jardine and Stewart (1998) 399. The new Baron was Sir John Denham, formerly Exchequer Baron in Ireland. Denham would be amongst the 'dissenters' in *Hampden's Case*; something which rather supposes that Bacon's counsel fell on deaf ears. His son, also named John, would become an admired 'cavalier' poet.
[55] At the trial of the Earl of Suffolk in late 1619.
[56] In Stewart (2003) 310.
[57] In Jardine and Stewart (1998) 464.
[58] For an account of the process, see Jardine and Stewart (1998) 455–63.
[59] The idea that Bacon was sacrificed to save Steenie in particular is discovered in an account left by his servant Thomas Bushell. In characteristically blunt terms, James told Bacon that he was done for; but that, if he was obliging, he could be confident that the King would show mercy. Doubts as to the reliability of Bushell's account remain. There is less doubt that both Steenie and James were genuinely concerned. See Coquillette (1992) 222–23.

law' was financial. Otherwise, it 'drinketh too much time, which I have dedicated to better purposes'.[60] The life of the mind, and time now to indulge it.

The Life of the Mind

The Renaissance looked both ways. It reached back, more specifically to a classical and Roman past, in order to reinvest the present; and then forward, to chart a surer course into an enlightened future. At Cambridge University, to which he was despatched in 1573, Bacon had been placed under the watchful eye of John Whitgift, Master of Trinity, his reading list replete with all the classics of Renaissance humanism, Plato, Aristotle, Cicero, Sallust. The result, ironically,was a deep suspicion of Aristotelian metaphysics.[61] Three years later, he was sent to France to improve his knowledge of Roman law.[62] At the behest of his father, who had long maintained that any man destined for public service should have a sound knowledge of both civil and common law. And a decision which chimed, not only with the didactic spirit of the Renaissance, but with Bacon's own philosophy of learning:

> Studies serve for delight, for ornament, and for ability ... They perfect nature, and are perfected by experience, for natural abilities are like natural plants that need poyning by study; and studies themselves do give forth directions too much at large, except they be bounded in by experience.[63]

The marriage of learning and experience; the core of what would become familiar as the 'Baconian renaissance'.

Learning mattered to Bacon for two reasons. First, because he regarded education as his principal responsibility as a writer. And second, because he constantly strove to uncover the encompassing. Never wanting for ambition, the young Bacon had written to his uncle, Lord Burghley, in 1592, confirming that he had 'vast contemplative ends ... for I have taken all knowledge to be my province'.[64] To recover nothing less than a 'true model of the world, such as it really is', which might in turn reframe 'human understanding'.[65] His prospective *Great Instauration* would imagine a 'total reconstruction of science, arts and all human understanding' which would be 'raised upon proper foundations'.[66] The fact that it was never completed, not even nearly, comes as no surprise.[67] But that does not detract from

---

[60] See Jardine and Stewart (1998) 18, suggesting that hitherto Bacon's legal career had 'constantly interfered' with his intellectual; see also 179.

[61] See here Zagorin (1998) 30, 131.

[62] To stay with the English Ambassador to the French Court, the fiercely puritan Sir Amias Paulet.

[63] Bacon (1985) 209.

[64] Spedding (1861) 1. 109.

[65] Spedding (1857/2011) 8. 156.

[66] Spedding (1857/2011) 4. 8.

[67] See Wormald (1993) 274–75, noting the vast *Catalogue of Particular Histories by Titles* that Bacon published alongside his *Novum Organum* in 1620, virtually all unwritten and to remain so. The only exceptions being a *History of Winds*, a *History of Life and Death*, and a *History of Dense and Rare*.

the aspiration; to invest a new way of thinking.[68] It was for this reason that the 'maxim' so appealed to Bacon. Simple axioms of general application, context-resistant, and easy to learn.[69] In the Preface to his *Maxims of the Common Law*, published in 1596, he stated that whilst he might have adopted a 'more admired' form, 'more cunning and more deep', he chose the maxim because 'we see all the ancient wisdom and science was wont to be delivered in that form', as well as the 'precedent of civil law'.[70]

The *Maxims* is amongst the earliest of around 80 pieces of writing which comprise the Baconian canon, nearly a third of which, as we have already noted, were 'composed' during his retirement; the 'greater part of his books and writings', as Rawley put it.[71] Composed, rather than completed, because in many cases Bacon never reached a conclusion, constantly returning to revise and rewrite.[72] An endless process of self-reformation, it might be said. Any Baconian scholar is necessarily obliged to make some choices, geared most likely by subject-range. Anyone interested in Bacon's legal writing will, as a consequence, militate towards his *Reading on the Statute of Uses*, his *Elements of the Common Law*, along with various of his *Essays*, and the *Maxims*. But there is also much to be learned about the practice of law and governance in Bacon's various historical essays on civil 'policy'. Most notable here, in the reformation context, is his *History of the Reign of Henry VII*, published in 1622. We will focus our closer attention on these writings, legal and historical, very shortly. In the meantime, a necessarily selective survey of the broader critical landscape will help to orient us, on what might otherwise seem to be a rather daunting venture.

A chronological compass will help. Starting indeed with the *Maxims*. Followed by a first volume of 12 *Essays*, which appeared a year later, to be significantly expanded in later editions, to 38 in 1612, and 58 in 1625. Composed 'but as recreation to my other studies', Bacon later supposed, but no less seriously intended. Again very much *a la mode*, the essay-genre found distant inspiration in the likes of Pliny and Seneca, and then more recently in the testamentary musings of leading continental humanists such as Lipsius, Montaigne and Machiavelli.[73] Bacon's ever-expanding collection of *Essays* ranged over a variety of topics 'civil and moral'.[74] Written for the discerning Jacobean gentlemen, so that they might be

---

[68] According to Zagorin, Bacon's 'entire natural philosophy might be described as the quest for a method'. See (1998) 31.

[69] For a commentary here, see Jardine and Stewart (1998) 176–77.

[70] Spedding (1857/2011) 7. 321.

[71] In Jardine and Stewart (1998) 476. Another draft text, possibly redrafted during Bacon's retirement, was provisionally entitled *Aphorismi de Iure gentium maiore*. Principally reworking his earlier *Maxims*.

[72] Many of those writings 'composed' during retirement were also already in existence, even if fragmentary. Of the nine substantial works started between 1603 and 1613, only four could be said to have been completed.

[73] Voltaire appreciated the didactic aspiration of the genre, Bacon's contribution especially, supposing the *Essays* to be 'written in order to instruct rather than to please'. In Wormald (1993) 27.

[74] As the title page declared.

better able to 'weigh and consider'.[75] And with the defining renaissance question in mind: how should such an improving gentleman improve? More gardening, possibly. 'Of Gardens' recommended the meditative benefits of gentlemen and their ladies spending their afternoons digging over tubers and pricking out roses; or at least watching their servants doing so. Or making money, and maybe giving some of it away, as suggested in 'Of Riches'. Bacon was fascinated by money, possibly because he never seemed to have enough. We will contemplate a few more of the finer possibilities in due course.

The larger aspiration, to describe a 'general' theory of natural and civil history, would start to take shape in the *Interpretation of Nature*, published in 1603; commonly read as a groundwork for his first encompassing 'scientific' work, *The Advancement of Learning*, which appeared two years later. Strategically dedicated to the King, the *Advancement* was written in two parts. The purpose of the first was to advise the importance of learning in matters of governance or 'policy', helpfully concluding that the better princes are the more obviously learned. It is they who 'approacheth nearest to the similitude of the divine rule'.[76] The second part presented a critical survey of the state of learning across Europe, along the way distinguishing three faculties, history, poetry and philosophy, to be mapped respectively onto the faculties of memory, imagination and reason.[77] A categorisation reaffirmed in a second edition of the *Advancement*, which appeared in 1623. The reworking of the text, to make it 'more of a science of government', was habitual.[78] Bacon wrote organically, constantly redeveloping original arguments, as he strove towards the completion of the greater ambition.

Which was the *Great Instauration*; of which the *Advancement* was to be the first part. A project designed to reinvest the pursuit of knowledge for generations to come. Bacon thought of it as a 'reformation' of learning. A second part would appear in 1620, entitled *New Method*, or *Novum Organum*, which advanced a new 'universal' theory of inductive logic, rooted in empirical observation.[79] After which he envisaged four more parts: a natural history, a 'ladder of the intellect', and then an 'anticipation' and realisation of a 'second philosophy'. The 'vast contemplative ends' he had advertised to Burghley.[80] Too vast, it transpired.[81] The final four parts remained fragmentary.[82] But there is enough in the *Advancement* and the

---

[75] Bacon (1985) 209–10.

[76] Coquillette (1992) 82.

[77] Spedding (1857/2011) 3. 329.

[78] See Wormald (1993) 164.

[79] The product of 'near thirty years' of work, he informed King James. The title alluded to Aristotle's treatise on logic, the *Organum*. We can only conjecture how impressed James might have been, if that is, he understood much of it. On receiving his dedicated copy, James quipped that it was like God in that it 'passeth all understanding'. See Stewart (2003) 183. For a commentary on the origins of Bacon's inductive method, and the influence of contemporary dialectics, see Jardine and Stewart (1998) 1–11, 17–19, 35–43.

[80] Zagorin (1998) 121.

[81] See Zagorin (1998) 75, referring to an 'unrealized dream'.

[82] The *Advancement* advertised the possibility that a 'history' of the emotions might have been a substantial part of the greater project; a treatise on 'different characters of dispositions'.

Novum Organum, along with ancillary writings, to give us a clear sense of what Bacon had in mind. Which was the overcoming of metaphysical 'abstraction' with the physical experience of 'nature'; in essence to encourage people to stuff poultry with snow rather than just think about it.[83] A 'true Physics' to replace a discredited 'Metaphysics', as he confided to one correspondent.[84]

Metaphysics was the clear loser in Bacon's 'conflict of the faculties'.[85] One of four 'idols', or intellectual distractions, identified in *Novum Organum*; the 'deepest' and most 'pernicious' of 'fallacies'.[86] In the *Advancement*, he talked of 'cobwebs of learning, admirable for the fineness of thread and work, but of no substance or profit'.[87] The 'true model of the world' was 'such as it really is, not as man's reason would like it to be'.[88] It was for this reason that Bacon was so effusive in his praise of Machiavelli, who wrote 'openly and unfeignedly' about 'what men do, and not what they ought to do'.[89] In 1608 he composed a treatise entitled *Redargutio Philosophiarum*, the 'refutation of philosophies', mainly Aristotelian.[90] Replete with another airing for the cobweb metaphor, this time contrasted with the endeavour of empirical 'ants', and the more measured strategy of the bee, who draws 'her material from the flowers of the garden or the field, but transforming it by a faculty peculiar to herself'. Such, he concluded, 'should be the activity of a genuine philosophy'.[91]

In the second part of the *Advancement*, Bacon further identified three kinds of 'philosophy': natural, revealed, and scientific. A distinction that required discretion, the nature of revealed philosophy especially. The '*placets* of God', as he termed them, 'positive upon authority and not upon reason', and the close study of which was an essential part of learning.[92] But the Erastian in Bacon was at pains to emphasise that abstract theology should not be allowed to corrupt matters of ecclesiastical 'policy'; the insinuated error of Calvinism. The 'greatest of scandals' is schism, the 'greatest vicissitudes amongst men', the 'vicissitudes of sects and religions'.[93] Whilst he would compose various essays on religious texts, Bacon tended to eschew deeper matters of theological controversy.[94] Revealed

---

[83] See here Jardine and Stewart (1998) 70–72.

[84] To Father Barazan. In Spedding (1861) 7. 377.

[85] The phrase is borrowed from Kant's famous treatise of the same name, published in 1798.

[86] Spedding (1857/2011) 4. 120–21, 431. The idol of the 'theatre', as he termed it. The other three idols were of the 'tribe', common to humanity, of the 'den', peculiar to the individual, and of the 'marketplace', which was communicative confusion.

[87] Coquillette (1992) 81.

[88] In Zagorin (1998) 89.

[89] Bacon (1974) 157. For commentaries on Bacon's admiration for Machiavelli, see Zagorin (1998) 132–39.

[90] Unpublished, perhaps wisely, given James's known admiration for Aristotle. The suggestion that only those 'lacking in experience, or poisoned by partisanship, or just lazy' still took Aristotle seriously might have grinded. Coquillette (1992) 95.

[91] Coquillette (1992) 96.

[92] Coquillette (1992) 87.

[93] Bacon (1985) 67, 230. On Bacon's *Erastianism*, see Zagorin (1998) 168–69.

[94] Foremost amongst these religious musings were *Meditations Sacrae* in 1597, *Prayers* in 1603, and the later *Translation of Certain Psalms into English* which he completed in 1624.

philosophy delicately detached, Bacon found the 'root' of civil 'science' in 'the unity of nature'.[95] The same distinction would be reinvested in *De Augmentis Scientiarum*, published in 1623 and designed to be a refined version of the first part of the *Instauration*. It included a fresh section entitled the 'Art of Empire or Civil Government', the theme of which was the foundation of prospective empires on universal principles of governmental practice. We will take a closer look at what Bacon had to say about this possibility very shortly.

It might be supposed that Bacon would castigate the imagination in much the same way as he did abstract thought. In fact, the contrary was true. Human activity is 'incited by imagination', which serves as a principal 'messenger' transmitting sensory experience to the rational faculty.[96] Essentially inductive, both in the present and the past, 'poesy conduces not only to delight but also to magnanimity and morality'.[97] As he affirmed in the *Advancement*, 'the monuments of wit and learning are more durable than the monuments of power', precisely because the 'images of men's wits and knowledge remain in books, exempted from the wrongs of time and capable of renovation'. Indeed, so much so that 'neither are they fitly to be called images, because they generate still, and cast their seeds in the minds of others, provoking and causing infinite actions and opinions in succeeding ages'.[98] In *Novum Organum*, he referred to the human mind as an 'enchanted glass'; a defining renaissance metaphor, if ever so slightly distorted.[99]

No one appreciated better than Bacon that politics is a textual and discursive art, a matter of fashioning impressions.[100] It was for this reason that he elevated poets alongside the 'writers of history' as the 'best doctors' of knowledge, sharing that same ability to determine how the 'affections are kindled and excited, and how pacified and restrained'.[101] Best placed, too, to present *exempla*, in the form of parables, proverbs, or similar species of 'poesy'.[102] *New Atlantis* might seem to be his most imaginative work, but only in the conspicuous sense. Everything Bacon wrote was dressed to impress. The *Essays* were intrinsically ironic in their styling, a series of artistic 'insinuations'.[103] Wisdom has an inherent value, but it is 'eloquence which prevails most in action and common life'.[104]

Unsurprisingly, Bacon took considerable pride in his own oratorical skills. With good reason, according to Jonson: 'His hearers could not cough, or look aside from him, without loss. He commanded where he spoke; and had his judges

---

[95] Spedding (1857/2011) 4. 339.
[96] Spedding (1857/2011) 4. 405–06.
[97] Spedding (1857/2011) 4. 315–16.
[98] Zagorin (1998) 221.
[99] Coquillette (1992) 1.
[100] Jardine and Stewart (1998) 12.
[101] Spedding (1857/2011) 5. 23.
[102] As he argued forcefully in *De Sapienta Veterum*, in which he took the opportunity to interpret certain famous Greek myths, in order to retrieve their insights, moral and political.
[103] See Jardine and Stewart (1998) 248, concluding that an 'appeal to reason is no part of the strategy of the *Essays*'.
[104] Spedding (1857/2011) 4. 454–55.

angry and pleased at his devotion. No man had their affections more in power'.[105] Another who, in a self-reflective moment, likened himself to a musician, searching for 'sweet accord'.[106] Playing Hooker's harp. Bacon knew how to work a metaphor, in court or on the page, and he knew the reason. For, as Solomon observed, 'he that is sweet of speech shall encompass greater things'.[107]

The Histories of Francis Bacon

It was Bacon's firm opinion that in the study of 'policy' the 'pre-eminent' discipline was history. No other discipline could so 'make learned men wise in the use and administration of learning'.[108] 'Stand in the ancient ways but look into present experiences to see whether in the light of this experience, ancient ways are right', he informed the Commons on one occasion, quoting from the book of Jeremiah, and 'if they are found to be so, walk in them'.[109] The 'reduction of things to their ancient and true institution'; the essence of renaissance, and reformation.[110] Everything about the present, and the future, could be read in the past; an insight that applied to the study of law as to the study of anything else. Any assessment of Bacon's legal thinking must first revisit his writings on history.

On History

'I come next to Civil History', Bacon announced in his 1623 edition of the *Advancement*, 'properly so called, whereof the dignity and authority are pre-eminent among human writings. For to its fidelity are entrusted the examples of our ancestors, the vicissitudes of things, the foundations of civil policy, and the name and reputation of men'.[111] It was this concentration on civil history which distinguished the 1623 edition. The basic dichotomy of history was though unaltered from the 1605 edition: 'Natural History treats of the deeds and works of nature; Civil History of those of men'.[112] The former was factual and non-interpretative, the latter the converse:

> For to carry the mind in writing back into the past, and bring it to sympathy with antiquity; diligently to examine, freely and faithfully to report, and by the light of words to

---

[105] In Jardine and Stewart (1998) 16.
[106] Spedding (1857/2011) 3. 230.
[107] Spedding (1857/2011) 4. 454–55.
[108] Spedding (1857/2011) 3. 330; 4. 302.
[109] Spedding (1857/2011) 4. 183.
[110] Spedding (1857/2011) 4. 285.
[111] Spedding (1857/2011) 4. 302.
[112] Spedding (1857/2011) 4. 293. For a commentary on the greater concentration on civil history, see Wormald (1993) 214–15.

place it as it were before the eyes, the revolution of times, the characters of persons, the fluctuations of counsels, the courses and currents of actions, the bottom of pretences, and the secrets of governments; is a task of great labour and judgment.[113]

The stuff of life, in other words. Knowledge, as he elsewhere affirmed, in rather earthier terms, that is 'drenched in flesh and blood'.[114]

Interpretive, but grounded in historical reality. 'All history walks the earth', as Bacon put it, unlike philosophy, or poetry indeed, the mere 'dream of learning'.[115] In contrast to metaphysics, and even 'poesy', which too easily leads to 'irresolution' and 'pertinacity'. It is for this reason that the study of history 'deserveth least taxation'.[116] The reader can be sure of a historian, or at least surer. Exceptions, of course, those who let their 'passions' run wild, but otherwise, a gentleman can pick up a copy of Herodotus or Tacitus and be pretty sure that they will learn something, not just of ancient Greece or Rome, but about life in Jacobean England.[117] Above 'all other books', Bacon advised the young Earl of Rutland, about to go 'on his travels' in 1596, read 'histories'. They 'will best instruct you' and 'ripen and settle your judgement'.[118]

There were other histories and historians, of course. But when it came to retrieving instructive *exampla*, none could match the 'ancient histories', Roman especially; 'worth more' than 'all' other histories 'combined'.[119] The Tacitus reinvested in Lipsius's *Politicorum libri sex*, for example, all cynicism and secrecy, and Bacon's favourite Roman as readers of his *Essays* would have quickly realised. And fellow Members of the Commons who heard Bacon defend the 'King's Sovereignty' in 1610. If they had properly read Tacitus's account of the fall of Nerva, there would have been no need to waste parliamentary time chewing over the reach of Crown prerogative.

Or maybe if they had read their Machiavelli, whose *Discourses on Livy* Bacon likewise revered. Someone 'concerned with composite bodies, such as are states and religious institutions' and determined to recover the means for 'their conservation which lead them back to the start'.[120] In his *Advancement*, Bacon confirmed that the 'form of writing which all of others' can best 'supply' a 'pattern for action' is that 'which Machiavel chose wisely and aptly'; 'namely discourse upon histories and examples'.[121] A sentiment repeated in a renowned homage:

---

[113] Spedding (1857/2011) 4. 302.
[114] Spedding (1857/2011) 3. 383.
[115] Spedding (1857/2011) 4. 336.
[116] Spedding (1857/2011) 6. 17–18.
[117] Spedding (1857/2011) 4. 302.
[118] Spedding (1857/2011) 9. 12–13. Five years later, the young Earl managed to embroil himself in the Essex rebellion, as a consequence of which he spent several months in the Tower, and was fined a colossal £30,000; a sum which broke the family estate. If only he had read his Tacitus more closely.
[119] Spedding (1857/2011) 3. 335. See also Wormald (1993) 294, quoting from his *Refutation of Philosophies*.
[120] Machiavelli's 'most eminent English disciple', according to Lord Acton. In Wormald (1993) 323.
[121] Spedding (1857/2011) 3. 453.

So that we are much beholden to Machiavel and others, that they write what men do and not what they ought to do. For it is not possible to join serpentine wisdom with columbine innocency, except men know exactly all the conditions of the serpent; his baseness and going upon his belly, his volubility and lubricity, his envy and sting, and the rest; that is, all forms and nature of evil. For without this virtue lieth unfenced.[122]

The stuff of life again, and the necessary lesson of any history.

Like anything else, there is a correct way of writing history, and an incorrect. 'Perfect', history is narrative in form, rather than merely 'memorial' or 'antiquarian'.[123] Here again, Bacon drew inspiration from the 'wiser historians', and from those who had written in their honour; the usual suspects, Livy, Tacitus, Machiavelli.[124] They knew how to tell an instructive 'story' without becoming distracted by the 'moths' of history.[125] 'Ruminated history', he termed it, at a variant, history as 'speaking pictures'.[126] Needless to say, Bacon further subscribed to Polybius's injunction, that the only historians worth reading were those who appreciate that 'practical experience is of the first importance for historical composition'.[127] Something echoed by Montaigne; the 'only good histories are those written by men who were themselves at the head of affairs'.[128] A quality that might have excluded Livy in truth, though not Tacitus, or Montaigne or Machiavelli. And certainly not Francis Bacon.

On Counsel

The principal purpose of history is to inform 'policy'; a recommendation necessarily premised on the assumption that history at least rhymes.[129] Here again Bacon would repeat the claim that just as 'men of affairs' are best placed to write history, so too are they best placed to write treatises on counsel. 'I consider history and experience', Bacon confirmed in the second edition of the *Advancement*, to be the 'same thing'. Men who had acquired 'universal insight and experience of the affairs of the world', who 'have learned about human dispositions, compulsions and habits by much practice and attentive reading, listening and observation' are those who should look to govern it.[130] Behind every successful prince are the right

---

[122] Bacon (1974) 1157. For a commentary here, see Coquillette (1992) 89.

[123] Spedding (1857/2011) 3. 333, characterising antiquarian as the 'remnants of history'.

[124] Naming three in particular, Tacitus, Livy and Herodian, and a fourth by clear implication, Julius Caesar. In Spedding (1857/2011) 5. 21. For commentary, see Wormald (1993) 52–55, 114, 223–24.

[125] A distinction that led to a disdainful dismissal of the 'superstitious conceits' that attend the 'histories' of King Arthur, but not the origins of Rome discovered in the opening pages of Livy. See Spedding (1857/2011) 3. 334, 361.

[126] Spedding (1857/2011) 3. 339; and (1861) 3. 249–50.

[127] See Wormald (1993) 60.

[128] Montaigne, *Essays*, quoted in Wormald (1993) 308.

[129] Wormald (1993) 64, 69.

[130] Spedding (1857/2011) 5. 36.

counsellors, however garbed; an Escalus or a Gonzalo, a Feste or a Fool.[131] Or a Francis Bacon.

A sentiment likewise discovered in his earlier *Essays*, many of which were drafted to the same purpose, to inform those gentlemen destined to govern, how to govern. Species of 'civil philosophy', as Bacon termed it, as opposed to the airier variety.[132] Thematically driven, more in the spirit of Suetonius than Tacitus perhaps, but again written in the familiar *specula* spirit. Some tangential, as we have already noted, recommending the benefits of gardening, travel and a balanced diet, avoiding the excesses of passion, envy and indigestion.[133] A healthy constitution making for a healthy counsellor. Others more direct, such as 'Of Counsel', which first appeared in the 1612 edition. The 'greatest trust between man and man', confirmed in scripture. Isaiah 9:6: 'For unto us a child is born … and his name shall be called Wonderful, Counsellor'. Proverbs 21:18: 'Every purpose is established by counsel'. Hazards, of course, not least in the venality of prospective counsellors. But if a king looks hard enough, he can always find a Francis Bacon.

And again, in 'Of Simulation and Dissimulation', exploring some of the darker arts. Opening with Tacitus, proceeding with Machiavelli, in order to contemplate when a 'habit of secrecy' might be 'both politic and moral', and concluding that the 'best composition and temperature is to have openness in fame and opinion, secrecy in habit, dissimulation in seasonable use, and a power to feign, if there is no remedy'.[134] A sentiment revisited in 'Of Cunning', which provides a practical guide to the various ruses which a counsellor might deploy in counselling their prince. The consequences revealed differently in 'Of Great Place', 'in corruption, roughness and facility', and then again in 'Of Seditions and Troubles', reflecting on what happens when 'reverence of government is lost'.[135] Empirical evidence courtesy, once again, of Tacitus and his *Annals*. The importance of timing is affirmed in 'Of Boldness'. Act expeditiously, but not with that 'boldness that is ever blind'.[136] Another perception that would have resonated with the habitually cautious James Stuart, everything in harmony and just measure.[137] Otherwise, the making of policy might as well be left to the 'reeling of a drunken man'.[138] The lessons, once again, of Machiavelli's *Discourses*: 'Certain it is, that nothing destroyeth authority so much as the unequal and untimely interchange of power pressed too far, and relaxed too much'.[139]

---

[131] Escalus in *Measure for Measure*, Gonzalo in *The Tempest*, Feste in *Twelfth Night*, the Fool in *King Lear*.

[132] Spedding (1857/2011) 4. 373.

[133] The key to a good diet being the avoidance of sudden changes. See 'Of Regiment of Health' in Bacon (1985) 156–57.

[134] Temperature meaning temperament. See Bacon (1985) 77–78.

[135] Bacon (1985) 92, 102.

[136] Bacon (1985) 95.

[137] The lesson once again of the Rome discovered in Machiavelli's *Discourses*. See Wormald (1993) 192–93.

[138] Spedding (1861) 6. 423.

[139] Walker (1950) 1.41.2.

Good counsel underpins 'Of the True Greatness of Kingdoms and Estates' too; or, more accurately, bad counsel. Citing the example of the boastful Themistocles, Bacon reiterated the importance of kings knowing which counsellors to employ, and which to avoid, those who seem 'sufficient' on a day-to-day basis, but who 'are so far from being able to make a small state great'. Worse still, those who 'can fiddle very cunningly', but 'add nothing to the safety' of the state.[140] The insinuation was directed at the recently deceased Lord Treasurer, the Earl of Salisbury, presently blamed for the failure of the negotiations surrounding the mooted 'Great Contract'.[141] The ostensible subject of the essay was, in fact, foreign policy, more particularly when to make a 'just' war. One of the essential questions posed in Machiavelli's *Discourses*, and which was easily answered in Reformation England; a 'just' war is a war against papists.[142] As for the idea of war itself, very 'healthful'; a philosophy which chimed nicely with the idea of imperial expansion, even if King James tended to be wary of expensive military ventures. In 'the great frame of kingdoms and commonwealths, it is in the power of princes or estates to add amplitude and greatness to their kingdoms'.[143] Better still, establish 'plantations'. Not just 'heroical' and godly, but also profitable.[144]

On Kings

There is no surprise, given his predilection for the 'wiser historians', that Bacon should be drawn to 'persons', especially important persons.[145] Popes, emperors, counsellors, kings; capturing the 'history of times' in the lives of those who mattered most.[146] Requiring some sensitivity, of course. Drama helped to provide some cover, thus allowing Shakespeare to craft his Richard Plantagenet, Spenser his Faerie Queene and Jonson his Sejanus. Time likewise. Thus, Shakespeare's *Henry VIII*, just long enough ago to be discreetly revisited. And Bacon's *Henry VII*, his most substantive work of 'ruminated' English history, and one of the first he undertook on his 'retirement'.[147] Not that Bacon appears, in the moment, to have ruminated that long; no more than about four months from

---

[140] Bacon (1985) 147.

[141] See Wormald (1993) 152–53, quoting Rawley's report of Bacon in conversation with King James, and suggesting that Salisbury would 'never have made his Majesty's estate better'.

[142] Such wars he characterised as being defensive and pre-emptive, founded on a 'just fear' of invasion. Looking back through history, Bacon alighted on the account of the Lacedaemonian war against Athens, recounted in Thucydides, along with the more recent example of Christendom repelling the Ottomans. The thesis was advanced in an earlier treatise entitled *Considerations Touching a War with Spain*. For a commentary, see Wormald (1993) 180–81.

[143] Bacon (1985) 155.

[144] Bacon (1985) 162.

[145] Spedding (1857/2011) 5. 21.

[146] Spedding (1857/2011) 3. 334.

[147] His 'longest' and most 'deliberated exercise in civil history writing', according to Wormald (1993) 49.

first line to last.[148] A courtesy draft was presented to the King for a preview in October 1621, barely six months after his dismissal from office.

The existence of various printed sources helped expedite the writing, notably the final volumes of Polydore Vergil's *Historia Anglia*, and Sir Thomas More's *History of King Richard III*. As did the assistance of fellow habitues of the Cotton collection, most notably John Selden.[149] Ruminated history still needed some facts, around which to weave the narrative.[150] Selden would duly appraise Bacon's *Henry VII* as one of only two contemporary histories worth reading; the other being Camden's *Annals of Queen Elizabeth*. Three centuries later, Ranke would recommend *Henry VII* on similar terms, as 'one of the finest examples of exact investigation of details combined with reflective treatment'.[151] In short, a quintessentially Renaissance history, full of plot, prejudice and proposition.[152]

And written in the style of the historian who most impressed Renaissance historians, who came closest indeed to having written the 'perfect' history advertised in the *Advancement*, and whose histories best 'worked' character 'into the narrative'.[153] 'Of all the histories', Bacon advised a young Fulke Greville, 'I think Tacitus the best'.[154] He admired Suetonius too, but differently. Suetonius wrote 'incredible' histories.[155] Tacitus's were entirely credible. We are left to conjecture what Bacon might have made of his projected 'history' of Henry VIII, of which only fragments remain; or indeed which Roman historian might have provided the greater inspiration. The Neronian son and the Augustan father, the two 'lives' would have made for an intriguing 'mirror'.[156]

There is certainly an Augustan sobriety to Bacon's *Henry VII*. He had 'nothing in him of vain-glory', though he 'kept majesty to the height'.[157] There is also a fair bit of James Stuart. Godly, 'merciful', a man of 'wisdom' and 'dexterity', forever anticipating 'perils' and thereby delivering himself, and his country, from them. 'Affable', but also 'reverend', cautious by nature, a planner attentive to detail, checking his accounts, and his accountants. Bacon liked his princes to be cautious. His granddaughter, Elizabeth Tudor, is praised for the same.[158] Attentive to the

---

[148] Though scattered drafts of other histories, some stretching back 15 years, attest to a longer-term interest in his subject.

[149] Along with John Burrough, an old friend from Gray's Inn, who served as one of Bacon's secretaries. In time, Burrough would become Garter King of Arms, and principal herald under Charles I. Here again, Bacon had used the Cotton collection before, on numerous occasions. Selden's knowledge of the collection was, though, unparalleled.

[150] In the margin of the text, for example, Bacon noted having access to a previously unpublished proclamation issued by the 'pretender' Perkin Warbeck. See Vickers, 'Introduction to Bacon' (1998) vii.

[151] In Wormald (1993) 59.

[152] See here Clark (1974); and Zagorin (1998) 214–15.

[153] Spedding (1857/2011) 5. 21.

[154] Spedding (1861) 9. 25.

[155] Spedding (1857/2011) 2. 365–66.

[156] Wormald (1993) 248.

[157] Being 'sensible that majesty maketh the people bow'. See Bacon (1998) 199.

[158] For her 'extreme caution' indeed. See Bacon (1998) 218.

present too.[159] In his *Example of a Summary Treatise on the Extension of Empire*, and then again in his essay 'Of the True Greatness of Kingdoms and Estates'. Bacon paid particular tribute to Henry's land reforms, hauling England out of the Middle Ages, and establishing the foundations of empire.[160] In 1597, Bacon introduced two bills in the Commons to reinvest a statute of 1489, which had sought to regularise enclosure on the grounds that it led to 'depopulation' and 'idleness'.[161] Measured reform, driven by pragmatics, in this Henry Tudor was very much Bacon's kind of king. Even if the venality is troubling, and the fact that Henry used the law to asset-strip his nobility set an awkward precedent; for a son who would later employ an army of lawyers to asset-strip his Church.

It is though the legalism which Bacon most admires in Henry Tudor, even more than the financial acumen, the assiduity and the cunning. Henry is another lawgiver, the 'Salomon of England'.[162] It is the quality which defines a great king, and it is here that Henry Tudor did 'excel'.[163] Just as it is the appreciation of this quality which defines the 'wiser' historian. For 'in my judgment it is some defect even in the best writers of history, that they do not often enough summarily deliver and set down the most memorable laws passed in the times whereof they write, being indeed the principal acts of peace'.[164] A sentiment reiterated a year later in his *Summary Treatise on Universal Justice or the Fountains of Equity*. It is a 'misfortune even of the best historians, that they do not dwell sufficiently upon laws and judicial acts'.[165] It is hardly surprising if a prince fails to appreciate the importance of good laws, if the history he reads neglects to remind him. There is a lot of law in Tacitus.

And there is a lot in *Henry VII*; so much that Bacon apologises for their 'long insisting'.[166] We have already encountered his land law reforms, to which might be added the 'excellent moral law' against the abduction of heiresses, reform of the law of murder, 'politic laws' against usury, the 'charitable law for the admission of poor suitors', price-controls for the 'drapery' trade, and various measures purposed to better regulate international commerce.[167] In the round, 'good and wholesome laws', many of which 'yet continue to this day'.[168] In each instance, though, what

---

[159] Bacon (1998) 202–04.

[160] Bacon (1985) 149–50.

[161] Approved in *Henry VII* as measures not designed to detract from the necessary 'improvement of the patrimony', but to mitigate the 'consequence', most especially the depopulation. See Bacon (1998) 97.

[162] Bacon (1998) 196. And also 6 suggesting that the same quality is the only redeeming feature of his predecessor, Richard III; albeit outweighed by all the 'cruelties and parricides'.

[163] Bacon (1998) 198.

[164] Spedding (1857/2011) 6. 97.

[165] Spedding (1857/2011) 5. 94.

[166] Bacon (1998) 68–69.

[167] Bacon (1998) 58–68 and 123–24. The reform of the law of murder was designed to expedite proceedings, removing the common law provision that public prosecutions could only commence after a year and a day; 'experience' suggesting that families were, during this period, commonly bribed to discontinue their suit, to the wider detriment of the commonwealth.

[168] Bacon (1998) 56, 60.

Bacon really admires is the fact that Henry is reinvesting established law, rather than dreaming up new. A reformer in the truest sense of the word. And it is this which, ultimately, confirms Henry as 'one of the most sufficient kings' in English history:

> Certainly his times for good commonwealth laws did excel; so as he may justly be celebrated for the best lawgiver to this nation after King Edward the First. For his laws (whoso marks them well) are deep and not vulgar; not made upon the spur of a particular occasion for the present, but out of providence for the future; to make the estate of his people more and more happy, after the manner of the legislators in ancient and historical times.[169]

The planner again. Bacon does not say that Henry VII would have eschewed reforming the English Church. But it is difficult to imagine his Henry breaking with Rome in a fit of pique, and then crashing into its barely imagined consequence. An event that did 'so much busy the world', Bacon observes in somewhat understated tones.[170]

The legal commentary necessarily speaks to the issue of kingship. Immediately upon seizing the throne, Henry Tudor determined that he should hold it 'by the law of nature and descent of blood', rather than mere conquest and the 'civil act of estates'.[171] Something confirmed at his coronation. A later passage, tucked into an account of the Parliament of 1495, provides an intriguing perspective. An act passed to 'void' any later attempt to impeach any who had fought for the King at the battle of Bosworth and intended to 'draw him into the love and hearts of his people', some of them at least. But also 'illusory', for a 'supreme and absolute power cannot conclude itself' and 'neither can that which is in nature revocable be made fixed'.[172] An early statement of what a Diceyan jurist might recognise as 'continuing' sovereignty. To Bacon, it was just common sense. No king can guard against his posterity.

And evidence that paranoia might, in the moment, overcome the most percipient of princes. Otherwise, though, Henry was assiduous in ensuring the integrity of his constitution, so 'that as he governed his subjects by his laws, so he governed his laws by his lawyers'.[173] Even if he did 'sometimes strain up his laws to his prerogative'.[174] Bacon opens his encomium on Henry the 'lawgiver' with a particular, and approving, account of his reinvestment of the prerogative courts. Chancery, 'the Pretorian power for mitigating the rigour of the law, in case of extremity, by the conscience of a good man'. And more particularly Star Chamber, amongst 'the sagest and noblest institutions of this kingdom', the 'Censorian power'

---

[169] Bacon (1998) 64.
[170] Bacon (1998) 171.
[171] Bacon (1998) 8.
[172] Bacon (1998) 121–22. For a comment here, see Zagorin (1998) 151–52.
[173] Bacon (1998) 119.
[174] Bacon (1998) 197.

in which is vested the 'high and pre-eminent power' of the Crown for the purposes of securing the 'commonwealth'.[175]

There was then much to admire in Bacon's Henry. A 'wonder for wise men', and appreciative of them too. 'Governed by none', but to counsel 'he did refer much ... knowing it to be the way to assist his power and inform his judgment; in which respect also he was fairly patient of liberty both of advice and of vote, till himself he declared'.[176] The fact that he picked the wrong counsellors, the 'hated' Cardinal Morton, the 'horse-leeches' Dudley and Empson, who 'turned law and justice into wormwood and rapine', did not detract from the principle.[177] It simply supposed an inability to 'discern a busy nature from a willing mind'.[178] In Henry Tudor, though, a flaw. One of a few that Bacon, writing an earthier, personal history, feels obligated to note. Otherwise mostly excesses. Thus the financial acumen too often ran to venality, the caution to dither, warranted suspicion to consuming paranoia. He was 'indeed full of apprehensions and suspicions'.[179] Careless in his treatment of nobility too.[180] Things, Bacon imputes, for princes to avoid.

In his dedication to Prince Charles, Bacon was keen to stress that he had not 'flattered' his subject unduly. Which was probably just about true. But still, in enough ways, an admirer. When it came to choosing models of kingship, the young Charles could do no better than look to the 'living pattern, incomparable, of the King your father'.[181] But the *History of the Reign of King Henry VII* was high in the list of supplementary reading. Whether it left much impression is moot. One thing that can be safely said of Charles Stuart is that he was not overly careful with his money, nor with the exercise of his prerogative.

On Law

Whilst Bacon had much to say about matters of law and governance in his various writings on civil history and 'policy', he also composed a variety of specifically legal and jurisprudential writings. Most obviously, there were treatises on specific legal issues, from esoteric 'readings' on advowsons and statutory uses, to more encompassing commentaries on the legal consequence of Union. Along, of course, with the more reflective *Essays*, and the earlier collection of legal *Maxims*. Common to

[175] Bacon (1998) 57.

[176] Bacon (1998) 196–97.

[177] Bacon (1998) 165, 175. Morton was Archbishop of Canterbury, 'wise' and 'eloquent' but 'in his nature harsh and haughty'. Dudley and Empson were Henry's so-called Counsellors Learned in the Law, in effect glorified debt-collectors. Within months of Henry's death in 1509 they would be accused of treason and executed as a sop to public indignation.

[178] Bacon (1985) 174.

[179] Bacon (1998) 202. A perception revisited in his essay 'Of Suspicion'; a 'defect' which can afflict the 'stoutest' of kings.

[180] A concern reiterated in his essay 'Of Nobility'.

[181] Bacon (1998) 3.

each, albeit variously, was an abiding interest in legal reformation, the possibility of 'universal' principles, and the nature of judgement. We will follow this thematic route, along the way wondering the extent to which Bacon was really looking forward, or in fact looking back.

On Reformation

Bacon's reformist instincts were evident from his very earliest parliamentary speeches.[182] In 1592 praising Queen Elizabeth for a 'course taken by her own direction for the repealing of all heavy and snared laws'.[183] An argument decorated, two years later, in his Gray's Inn masque, identifying the urgent need to 'purge our multiplicitie of laws, clear the uncertainty of them, repeal those that are snaring and press the execution of those that are wholesome and necessary', as well as 'define the jurisdiction' of the courts and 'repress all causeless and vexatious suits'.[184] We have already noted his sitting on parliamentary committees in the later 1590s, tasked with discovering what laws were 'burdensome' to the commonwealth and should, as a consequence, be 'cutt off'.[185] Service which likely helped to secure his preferment as the Queen's 'extraordinary' Counsel.

Bacon's *Maxims of the Common Law*, composed in the mid-1590s, opened with the same approbation of Elizabeth's plans for a 'general amendment of the state of laws', and for reducing 'them to more brevity and certainty'.[186] Something which, the author supposed, would be aided by the refinement of a set of maxims which might collect the 'rules and grounds dispersed throughout the body of the same laws'. Another quintessential genre of renaissance writing, the 'delivery of knowledge in aphorisms' was explicitly recommended in the *Advancement*, 'the pith and heart' of intellectual enquiry.[187] Both St German and Fraunce had done similarly, as had Sir John Dodderidge in his popular *The Lawyer's Light*. Readers of Starkey's *Dialogue* and Plowden's *Commentaries* would have likewise discovered something familiar in tone. As might readers of Justinian's *Digest*.[188] And, needless to say, Machiavelli's *Discourses*. In his writing, as in his dress and haberdashery, Bacon was nothing if not fashionable.[189]

Numbering 25 in all, 'some of them ordinary and vulgar', the maxims were purposed for dispelling 'unprofitable subtlety', whilst creating a 'more sound'

---

[182] A 'reformer to his very bones', according to Zagorin (1998) 193.

[183] Spedding (1857/2011) 8. 130.

[184] Bacon (1968) 54.

[185] Shapiro (2019) 41.

[186] Spedding (1857/2011) 8. 316. The *Maxims* were not published until 1631, but were evidently part of legal conversation amongst Bacon's circle at least.

[187] Coquillette (1992) 83.

[188] Title 50, section 17 especially, which presented 'abstract principles of a more general nature originating in jurisprudence or in an imperial enactment'.

[189] We will contemplate the dress and haberdashery shortly.

understanding of the 'very nature and complexity of the whole law'.[190] Eschewing the temptation to venture a comprehensive codification of English law, Bacon preferred to leave his readers 'free to turn and toss'. Nevertheless, the *Maxims* can be read as a groundwork for such an enterprise, a way of thinking differently about law, how it might be improved, and rewritten.[191] Notably, Bacon drew his maxims from both common and 'civil Roman' law, reasoning that the latter often founded the former. *Regula XI*, for example, was directly lifted from *Digest* 50.17.8. The maxim, the 'rights of the blood cannot be destroyed by provision of the civil law', to which Bacon appended a commentary on the common law of attaint. The very idea of maxims derived from the law was itself Roman, of course; and necessarily inductive. As Paulus put it, the 'law many not be derived from a rule, but a rule must arise from the law as it is'.[192] And very different from the common law discovered in texts such as Coke's *Institutes*, much of which was derived from custom.

Bacon would spend the rest of his professional life building on this groundwork. Penning his sovereign's various pronouncements on the subject, composing further treatises, drafting legislation, setting up commissions. A year after his appointment as Attorney General, he introduced a bill for the appointment of commissioners to 'review the state of penal laws, to the end that such as are obstacle and snaring may be repealed, and such as are fit to continue and concern matter may be reduced retrospectively into one clear form of law'.[193]

A *Memorial Touching the Review of Penal Laws and Amendment of the Common Laws* duly followed, which proposed measures for 'taking away many cases obsolete and of no use', along with those which are 'but iterations', associated 'idle Queries, which serve but for seeds of incertainty', and the too many which are 'erroneously reported'. Reference to the 'worthy endeavours of the Lord Dier and the Lord Coke' was rather compromised by the blunt caveat that 'great judges are unfit persons to be reporters, for they have either too little leisure or too much authority'. Dier's efforts in the end amounting to little more than a 'kind of notebook', Coke's holding 'too much *de proprio*'.[194] In other words, made up. In their place there would be a 'digest of Books of competent volumes'.[195] Bacon did not say to be written by him, but might as well have done. Two years later, he composed another memorandum for his King on the subject, confirming that whilst he had no desire to alter the 'matter of the law', there was an urgent need to address the 'manner of their registry, expression, and tradition: so that it giveth

---

[190] Spedding (1857/2011) 8. 316, 220.

[191] See Coquillette (1992) 38–39 and also 47, suggesting that the *Maxims* was a 'first step in attempting to discover, out of the individual statements of the *leges* of English law, the harmony of scientific *regulae*'.

[192] Coquillette (1992) 45.

[193] In Shapiro (2019) 70.

[194] Coquillette (1992) 102. Sir John Dyer was Chief Justice of Common Pleas from 1559 until his death in 1582. His *Reports* covered the years 1513 to 1582.

[195] Shapiro (2019) 71.

them rather light than any new nature'. He would 'dare advise to cast the law into a new mould'.[196]

Shortly after his appointment as Privy Counsellor, in early 1616, Bacon produced another reforming treatise, entitled *A Proposition to His Majesty Touching the Compilation and Amendment of the Laws of England*. A legal variant of the *Redargutio*, arguing the case for a 'productive middle', between the 'cobwebs' of abstract legal philosophy and the pure instrumentalism of the empirical 'ant'. A year later, in his inaugural *Speech on Taking His Seat in Chancery*, Bacon presented himself as a prospective reforming Keeper, to police 'jurisdictions', to 'retrench all unnecessary delays', and to root out the 'brambles that grow about justice'.[197] Right up to the bitter end of his tenure as Lord Chancellor, Bacon was still urging the King 'to go on with the reformation of your courts of justice', a process which 'your Parliament has entered into'.[198] A plea eagerly rejoined, for there were indeed 'many new crimes and abuses that do daily creep unto this kingdom'.[199]

As he contemplated his enforced retirement, Bacon resolved to finally write up a long-imagined *corpus iuris* of English law. In a letter to King James, thanking him for his mitigation of sentence in March 1621, he included a book proposal, for a text entitled *An Offer to the King of a Digest to be Made of the Laws of England*; very probably fleshing out the template discovered in his *Propositions*. Unlike his great antagonist, however, who managed to produce his four-volume *Institutes*, Bacon got distracted. There would be no *Digest*. There would, though, be plenty of opportunities to rail against the dilapidated state of English law, 'patched up from time to time according to occasions, without frame or model'.[200]

In *De Augmentis Scientarum*, Bacon would make familiar reference to the 'excessive accumulation of laws', and the consequential decline in judicial standards. The suggested solution was for an aligned set of texts. A 'compressed and abridged' digest of case-reports, wherein judgments were recorded 'word for word'; of the kind that Coke had produced, only better, and absent all the 'conceits'. To be complemented by an 'institutes', comprising a set of commentaries intended to train the young legal mind. A 'good and careful treatise on the rules of law', presented in the form of rules or maxims 'gathered from the harmony of laws and decided cases'.[201] What King James needed was what the Emperor Justinian had realised that he needed: some brilliant jurists. Or maybe just the one. Perhaps a former Privy Counsellor and Lord Chancellor with time on his hands? The familiar insinuation; better a 'man of affairs' than a 'pettyfogging' lawyer or an airy philosopher.[202]

---

[196] Shapiro (2019) 71–72.
[197] Coquillette (1992) 197.
[198] Spedding (1857/2011) 13. 289.
[199] See Shapiro (2019) 74. The peculiar abuses of usury would be addressed in a newly drafted contribution to the 1625 edition of *Essays*, replete with some discomforting anti-Semitic asides. It is 'against nature for money to begat money'. See Bacon (1985) 183.
[200] Coquillette (1992) 117.
[201] Shapiro (2019) 87–88.
[202] Spedding (1857/2011) 13. 60–64.

On Universality

Bacon's reformist impulse was rooted in a genuine belief in the need to improve legal practice and 'policy'. At the same time, though, it resonated with a fundamental belief that any system of laws might be reduced to certain 'universal' principles; and that this reduction would, of itself, abet the reform of English law.[203] 'There are in nature', readers of the *Advancement* discovered, 'certain fountains of justice, whence all civil laws are derived but of streams, and like as waters do take tinctures and tastes from the soils through which they run, so do civil laws vary accordingly' to whatever 'regions and government'. Even as they 'proceed from the same fountains'.[204] An argument we have already encountered in Bacon's essays on Union, of both State and Church, and then again in his brief in *Calvin's Case*. And an argument which, as we also noted, chimed very nicely with that of his King. For law, as for any other matter of civil 'policy', it was possible to distinguish a general model and particular variants. The common law of England and the civil law of Scotland were precisely such variants, and there was nothing to preclude their more 'general' recalibration.

Something Bacon argued, most eloquently perhaps, in his *Preparation for the Union of Lawes*, wherein he proposed the establishment of a commission to refine the *ius privatum* of English and Scots law; not in terms of reducing it, but of better appreciating differences:

> For that which concerneth the private interest of *meum* and *tuam*, in my simple opinion, is not at this time to be meddled with; men love to hold their own as they have held, and the difference of this law carrieth no mark of separation. For we see in any one kingdom, which is most at unity with itself, there is a diversity of custome for the guiding of property and private rights.[205]

In the immediate term, therefore, Bacon focuses on the 'union' of *ius publicum*, which was divided into four parts: 'criminal causes'; 'causes of the Church'; causes 'concerning magistrates, officers, and Courts, wherein falleth the consideration of your Majesty's royal prerogative'; and 'certain special politic laws' purposed for the 'public peace, strength, and wealth of the kingdom'. In these matters, Bacon impressed, it would be to the benefit of both nations if 'some uniformity' might be secured.[206] The rhetoric, once again, of *Calvin's Case*.

Unsurprisingly Bacon was keen to impress that the idea of a 'universal' jurisprudence, like indeed that of Union, was not a matter of idle speculation. It was, on the contrary, a matter of 'policy', comprehended by history.[207] And of the various

---

[203] See Coquillette (1992) 4, and also 289, suggesting that the more Bacon pondered the reformation of English law, the more he was persuaded by the possibilities of a 'universal' jurisprudence.

[204] Zagorin (1998) 189; and Coquillette (1992) 85–86.

[205] Coquillette (1992) 74.

[206] Coquillette (1992) 74–75.

[207] See Briggs (1997) 4; and Zagorin (1998) 190.

histories which suggested themselves in these terms, one stood out. Just as Latin served as a 'universal' language, so too might Roman law provide the model for a universal jurisprudence.[208] Bacon was not, of course, the first to impute as much. Starkey's *Dialogue* had ended up recommending something akin to a bespoke English civil law, wherein 'all those laws should be brought into small number, and be written also in our mother tongue, or else put into Latin.'[209] The *Maxims*, as we have already noted, was likewise conceived in this spirit, albeit more modest in its reach; a set of axioms of prospectively universal application, which might then be shaped in the particular.

At the same time, the same modesty forbad Bacon recommending the incorporation of substantive principles of Roman law into the English common law. As he affirmed in his *Advancement*, despite 'their defect', the 'laws of England' could not 'but excel the civil laws in fitness for government' in 'your Majesty's' realm. The English Reformation was, after all, about securing the autonomy of an English Church, and English law. Bacon never questioned this, despite the later insinuations levelled by the likes of Macaulay, and notwithstanding his stated admiration for the 'learned' civil lawyers who populated Doctors Commons. Nor was there a need to incorporate. It was the 'general learning', the categorical methodology of the Roman jurists, the 'order' they brought, which attracted Bacon, as it had Machiavelli; not the temptation to 'intermingle' substantive principles of civil and common law.[210] 'Men', he sensibly concluded, 'will never agree about that.'[211]

The desire to bring 'order' to English law did not necessarily mean codification. Bacon evaded the proposition on pragmatic grounds; it would be 'too long a business to debate whether *lex scripta aut non scripta*'.[212] The better solution would be a set of authoritative commentaries and reports, written not by sitting judges with an eye to posterity, but by jurists of impeccable integrity, focused on the present need for reform, and with time on their hands. And who knew about history. The task which Bacon would recommend in 1621, and which he had recommended on plenty of occasions previously. In 1614, for example, in his *Memorial Touching the Review of Penal Laws*, and then again two years later, in the third part of the *corpus iuris* mapped out in the *Proposition*; a treatise entitled *De regulis iuris*, inspired by Justinian's *Institutes*, and more closely still by the *De diversis regulis iuris antiquai* in the fiftieth book of the *Digest*. A concise list of governing rules of law, to be given aphoristically. A 'model towards a great building', as Bacon put it.[213]

Which would remain unbuilt. In *De Augmentis*, which was again addressed to his King, Bacon made a now familiar promise. A new section on the benefits of Union advertised a prospective *Treatise on Universal Justice or the Fountains of*

---

[208] Wormald (1993) 18.
[209] Starkey (1989) 80–82, 126–27, 131.
[210] See Coquillette (1992) 86; and Wormald (1993) 110.
[211] Coquillette (1992) 107, 109.
[212] Spedding (1857/2011) 6. 67.
[213] Coquillette (1992) 113; and Wormald (1993) 62–63.

Equity, by Aphorisms. A 'narrative of the laws' comprised of all the major cases.[214] We can glean a sense of what Bacon intended from the draft *Aphorismi*, likely composed at much the same time:

> There is little doubt that there are certain fountains of natural equity from which spring and flow out the infinite variety of laws which individual legal systems have chosen for themselves. And as veins of water acquire diverse flavours and qualities according to the nature of the soil through which they flow and percolate, just so in these legal systems through natural equity is tinged and stained by the accidental forms of circumstances, according to the site of territories, the disposition of peoples, and the nature of commonwealth.[215]

The same riparian metaphor deployed in the *Advancement*, and for the same purpose. To present equity as a mechanism for ensuring the principles of universal justice. In the *Treatise*, he revisited the distinction between Censorian courts, for criminal matters, and Praetorian, for civil. The purpose of Praetorian courts, wherever they are found, is to administer the King's 'conscience' and deal with any 'monstrous' injustices which emanate from the Censorian courts. A court of Chancery, in all but name. But now elevated, as the epitome of 'higher' legal 'science'.[216]

It was not a matter of discovering substantive precepts of law 'common' to different polities, though some might, along the way, be observed. It was about advancing a common method of legal 'learning' that was inductive and empirical; the close study of particulars, from which general precepts of civil justice might be ventured. A 'law of laws', Bacon termed it, 'whereby we may derive information as to the good or ill set down and determined in every law'.[217] In recommending his prospective *Digest* to King James, Bacon styled it an 'instauration of the laws'; a comprehensive project of 'renewal', for the purpose of reinvesting the 'certainty of laws', founded on 'universal' principles of juristic method.[218]

On Judgment and Judges

The idea that a closer understanding of legal method, and principle, could inform the finer reformation of English law was something that Bacon explored in various more discrete legal essays and treatises, many of which he composed earlier in his career. Such as a *Brief Discourse upon the Commission of Bridlewell*, probably composed in 1587. It came replete with an introduction on the sources of English law, and the urgent need for their clarification in terms of 'maxims, customs

---

[214] Spedding (1857/2011) 5. 104.
[215] In Coquillette (1992) 239.
[216] See Klinck (2010) 170–71; and Coquillette (1992) 238.
[217] Coquillette (1992) 244.
[218] Coquillette (1992) 252–53.

and statutes'.[219] Later in the same year he gave his first 'reading' at the Inns, on advowsons. A more substantive work, albeit only fragments remain, was a second 'reading' *Upon the Statute of Uses*, which appeared in 1600. There were various motivations. Not least was a characteristic desire to show off; something clever on uses was a rite of passage for ambitious young barristers. There was also the experience of *Chudleigh's Case*, in which Bacon had appeared, and which had confirmed the need for reform in the particular area of law; evidently corrupted, Bacon insinuated, by hoards of common lawyers looking for tax-dodging loopholes. Such that litigants drifted from court to court, 'like a ship upon the sea' desperately seeking a 'haven'. Basing the case for reform on efficacy, and a well-turned metaphor, was definitively Baconian.[220]

Whilst the *Treatise* might seem a relatively esoteric piece, it also spoke to matters of greater constitutional propriety. Most obviously it can be read as a paean to Chancery, and its duty to treat matters of justice and 'conscience'. Thus 'the chancery looketh farther than the common law, namely, to the corrupt conscience of him that will deal with land knowing it in equity to be another's'.[221] A solicitation, hindsight might suppose, for the position which Bacon would finally secure in 1618. As the 'Sanctuarie to Conscience', as William Worship put it, dedicating his *Christian's Jewell* to the newly installed Lord Chancellor.[222] The draft *Treatise on Universal Justice* waxed lyrically about the importance of courts that could 'determine, by the judgment and discretion of a conscientious man, when the rule of law is deficient'. Without such 'supreme' courts, there could be no sensible appreciation of 'universal' jurisprudence.[223]

Just as there could not, without a refined appreciation of judgment, be a reformation of English law. The central argument of Bacon's most jurisprudential essay, 'On Judicature'. Starting from a familiar premise, the tangible decline in professional standards, 'On Judicature' provided a taxonomy of egregious lawyering. The first of 'four bad instruments' was the 'sower of suits, which makes the court swell, and the country pine'. The second were those who 'engage courts in quarrels of jurisdiction'. Bacon called them '*parasiti curiae*'. Third came the 'nimble and sinister' tricksters, who 'bring justice into oblique lines and labyrinths'. And then finally, the 'polluter and exacter of fees'.[224] Which was not, of course, how it was supposed to be. As Bacon had observed in the Preface to the *Maxims*:

> I hold every man a debtor to his profession; from the which as men of course do seek to receive countenance and profit, so ought they of duty to endeavour themselves, by way of amends, to be a help and ornament thereunto. This is performed in some

---

[219] Coquillette (1992) 27.
[220] Leaving some commentators, looking for a clearer Baconian position on 'conscience', somewhat frustrated. See Klinck (2010) 166–67; and also Coquillette (1992) 52–59, 131.
[221] Spedding (1857/2011) 7. 405.
[222] In Klinck (2010) 109.
[223] Coquillette (1992) 247.
[224] Bacon (1985) 224–25.

degree by the honest and liberal practice of a profession ... but much more ... if a man be able to visit and strengthen the roots and foundation of the science itself; thereby not only gracing it in reputation and dignity, but also amplifying it in perfection and substance.[225]

An aligned obligation, to maintain the integrity of law, and to improve it. Shared by all those who practise law, but most especially by those who matter most. Men like Bacon wanted to be; 'learned' counsel, Crown attorneys, judges and chief justices. In private correspondence, he confirmed that, 'because the life of the laws lies in the execution and administration of them', the 'choice of good Judges' was a principal duty of magistracy. Such men must be God-fearing, 'of courage' and 'hating covetousness'. As 'chaste as Caesar's wife', he elsewhere confirmed, a recommendation which suggests a selective approach to the history of imperial Rome.[226]

If the reformation of law and legal practice describes the broader context, the narrower focuses on judicial responsibility. And it is here that the larger constitutional questions resurface. Most obviously in the vexed matter of judicial interpretation, where 'negligent and ill-ordered methods of interpreting law' had become habitual, alongside a corrosive 'inconsistency of judgments'.[227] Such that:

> Judges ought to remember that their office is *ius dicere*, and not *ius dare*; to interpret law, and not to make law, or give law. Else will it be like the authority claimed by the Church of Rome, which under pretext of exposition of Scripture doth not stick to add and alter, and to pronounce that which they do not find, and by show of antiquity to introduce novelty.[228]

The pretence of precedent. It is not difficult to imagine which judge Bacon had in mind. Similar might be supposed of his ensuring injunction, that an 'over-speaking judge is no well-tuned cymbal'.[229]

So too should they 'remember the conclusion of the Roman Twelve Tables; *Salus populi suprema lex*'. The law belongs not to them, but to the commonwealth:

> Therefore it is a happy thing in a state when kings and states do often consult with judges; and when judges do often consult with king and state ... For many times the things deduced to judgment may be *meum* and *tuum*, when the reason and consequence thereof may trench to point of estate: I call matter of estate, not only the parts of sovereignty, but whatsoever introduceth any great alteration or dangerous precedent; or concerneth manifestly any great portion of people. And let no man weakly conceive that just laws and true policy have any antipathy; for they are like the spirits and sinews, that one moves with the other.[230]

---

[225] Coquillette (1992) 100.
[226] Letter to George Villiers, in Coquillette (1992) 104–05.
[227] Shapiro (2019) 87.
[228] Spedding (1857/2011) 6. 509–10.
[229] Bacon (1985) 223.
[230] Spedding (1857/2011) 6. 509–10.

The rhetoric of harmony and measure once again. So Bacon said in 1612, when the first version of the essay appeared. And so it remained in 1625, when the revised version was published. This time, though, with a famous rider:

> Let judges also remember, that Solomon's throne was supported by lions on both sides: let them be lions, but yet lions under the throne; being circumspect that they do not check or oppose any points of sovereignty.[231]

A strategically flattering analogy, drawn from the first Book of Kings; Solomon, as we have already noted, being an especial favourite of James Stuart.[232] And an intriguing editorial, in tone and in resonance. It is to Bacon and his lions that Sir Stephen Sedley has sought recourse four centuries on, to theme some contemporary reflections on public law in modern Britain.[233] Some things, as we will now see, have changed over the intervening four centuries. Others have not. Amongst the latter can be included a range of familiar relational uncertainties, between Crown and courtroom, 'universal' jurisprudence and the 'common' law, of England and everyone else.

---

[231] Bacon (1985) 225.
[232] 1 Kings 10: 19–20.
[233] Sedley (2015).

5

Apotheoses

A King, or indeed a Lord Chief Justice or a Lord Chancellor, had a couple of options, if they were keen to shape their posterity; and most were. It was, after all, the Renaissance, the age of 'self-fashioning'.[1] They could leave a written testament purposed for instructing their successors, and maybe persuading generations of coming historians. Both aspirations were evidently in the mind of James Stuart when he wrote his *Basilicon Doron*. Likewise, Sir Edward Coke, constantly recrafting his *Reports* and then dedicating much of his retirement to composing a four-volume *Institutes*. Testaments to the brilliance of the common law, and their author, or so he hoped. And then again, Sir Francis Bacon, another copious writer, with a still greater ambition. Coke might have limited himself to completing a comprehensive account of English law, Bacon accepted no such inhibition. The 'great instauration' would be a comprehensive account of everything.

Another possibility was to hire a decent artist, in the hope that he could make you look suitably magisterial and brilliant. A good couturier too, to get the decoration right. After which it was simply a matter of wearing the right expression and adopting a persuasive pose. Painterly impressions of each of our three protagonists remain. Rather more of James Stuart, as might be expected. Most familiar, perhaps, is the rather washed-out looking *dominus* who gazes blankly out of Daniel Mytens's portrait, painted around 1621. Not the first Mytens monarch to look a bit blank.[2] Fifteen years earlier, John de Critz painted a sober-looking James, dressed pretty much as prescribed in the *Basilicon*. The antithesis of a 'candie' soldier, albeit with a rather splendid jewel pinned to his hat, known as the 'mirror of Greater Britain'. The portrait, commissioned in 1603, to celebrate the Union of Crowns, is part of a series of de Critz canvasses, in each of which James looks a bit distracted. He apparently disliked having to pose for long periods, or short.

A later series would be painted by the Flemish artist Paul van Somer, who arrived in London in 1616. Amongst these is a portrait of James in his coronation robes, with the Banqueting House in the background, seen through a window.

---

[1] Greenblatt (2005).

[2] Which is why Charles would have him rapidly pensioned off, when he came to throne. The last straw being an attempted portrait of Charles and Henrietta Maria, from around 1630. It is thought that van Dyck was asked to amend the Mytens, in order to try to make the couple look a little more engaged, not least with each other. But he gave up, and instead painted his own *King Charles I and Henrietta Maria*. The King leaning forward towards his wife, she looking like she has noticed.

King-proud and house-proud, even if the house was not actually finished.[3] Another attributed to van Somer is held in the Royal Collection. Intriguing in a different way, absent the finery, aside from a striking ruff, hooded eyes, greying beard. James looking as 'weary' as he commonly said he felt. But then it had been a wearying few years. Long gone is the mop of bright red hair which can be seen in the portraits of the young King of Scotland captured nearly half a century earlier. The most renowned of these, reworked by Rowland Lockey, presents a bright-eyed eight-year-old, looking very smart in voluminous green breeches, buff doublet and pink hose, natty feathered hat on his head and obedient falcon on his hand. Every inch, so many as there were in that moment, a prospective king.

As for Sir Edward Coke, a few largely invariable images. The earliest of which presents the newly elected Recorder of Norwich in 1586. Displaying all the customary features of late Elizabethan civic portraiture, bearing his office and robes with an equal dignity.[4] Another younger Coke is captured by Cornelius Janssen, celebrating his appointment as Solicitor General and Speaker of the Commons in 1592.[5] Embossed with the family motto *Prudens Qui Patiens*, 'he who is prudent and patient'. The latter tended to wear thin, as we know. But few have doubted the prudence of Sir Edward Coke. Two decades on Marcus Gheeraerts the younger captured Coke at the pinnacle of his legal career, as Lord Chief Justice, resplendent in all his finery, ermine-lined red gown, black cap, chain of office proudly displayed. By convention, outgoing Lord Chief Justices would pass on their chain, for a cursory sum, to their successors. A custom which, as we have noted, Coke sourly disdained. Another, painted at much the same time by Gilbert Jackson, celebrates Coke's election as High Steward of Cambridge University. Another classic piece of civic portraiture; different finery, same pose. Coke never looked other than finely dressed, confident and ready for the fight.

As might, to a considered extent, be said of the painted Bacon. Differences though, not least in the kind of image the sitter preferred. Coke liked to look important. Bacon liked to look fashionable, as well as important. Something that van Somer managed to capture in a painting commissioned to recognise Bacon's appointment as Lord Keeper in 1617. Hat at a rakish angle, beautifully embroidered ruff and sleeve. Another study in vanity and vaunting ambition. Captured too by William Larkin, who painted numerous iconic portraits of the Jacobean court.[6]

---

[3] The Banqueting House was completed in 1622. Van Somer died the year before. It is thought that the portrait was was most likely painted in 1620, possibly completed by a student. Making the painting more a record of what the architect, Inigo Jones, hoped the House would look like.

[4] With his hand placed on a skull, clearly intended as a referent to earthly mortality. The presence of the skull, though not uncommon in much civic portraiture of the period, is conspicuous in a number of paintings of Norwich dignitaries. The identity of the painter of the series remains unknown. For an overview of the genre, noting the particularities of the Norwich collection, see Tittler (1998).

[5] Perhaps. Though given that Janssen was only born the following year, it required some imagination and, presumably, another portrait already in existence. The attribution accompanies a reworked version, by the nineteenth-century artist Thomas Athew. Part of a collection of former Speakers which still adorn the walls of the Speaker's House in Westminster.

[6] Though, not it seems, any portraits of James; or at least there is no record.

Material detail was Larkin's speciality, so just the man for anyone who did, in fact, rather like the idea of dressing up as a 'candie' soldier.[7] Good at carpets and curtains too.[8] A particularly impressive set of red curtains frame Larkin's Bacon, probably painted at some point around 1612, just as the prospective Attorney General was starting to measure up.

So much for the painters. We will contemplate some more artistic impressions in due course, sculptural particularly. Suffice to say that, in regard to posterity, there was not much else to be done really. Commission some flattering portraits, along with some fawning poets, and then hope that critics will be kind, especially if you have gone out of your way to venture lots of opinion about things. This chapter is about the shaping of reputations, because anything we presently think about James Stuart or Edward Coke or Francis Bacon is determined, in considerable part, by what others have thought of them.

It is not, though, a matter of reputation only. There is also rhythm. The year 1616 is a snapshot moment; providing, in our case, a glimpse into a much longer conversational history. A conversation which would continue to evolve over the coming four centuries. Sometimes resonating loudly, sometimes softly. Sometimes, where it is barely discernible, we will need to use our imagination that little bit more. It is, as we noted before, what historians do. The conceit which underpins this book is the thought that the constitutional crisis of 1616 was representative of an emergent, and ultimately defining, divergence in English, British and indeed American public philosophy. Time then to take a peek into the future. To follow the 'traces and the trail they leave'.[9] Starting where James, for sure, would have wanted us to start: with him.

Apotheosis

Though not perhaps in quite the way he would have wanted. By recalling his singular, and lingering, lack of stage presence. Howard Brenton found a place for him in his recent historical drama *Anne Boleyn*. The support for 'the whore who changed England'.[10] Earthy, slightly snide, inquisitive; a fair impression perhaps. A 'Bad King' with a 'tidy mind', it has been surmised of James Stuart, tongue only partly in cheek.[11] But then circumstances were hardly conducive. No Armada, no Naseby, no need for flashy speeches rallying the troops at Tilbury or embracing

---

[7] All of Larkin's sitters tend towards the 'candie'. Amongst his most striking portraits is that of the infamous Frances Carr, Countess of Somerset. Replete with the kind of plunging neckline that would, half a century on, become synonymous with Sir Peter Lely's 'Windsor Beauties', and perhaps the most spectacularly odd ruff of all the many odd ruffs painted during the reign of James Stuart.

[8] The 'carpet-master', as the art historian Sir Roy Strong has termed him.

[9] Ginzburg (2012) 1.

[10] Brenton (2010) 82. The play sees Anne as the animating force behind the English Reformation; a mess which James is still trying to sort out.

[11] Sellar and Yeatman (1993) 72–73.

martyrdom on the scaffold. A passing irony. The *pax Jacobus*, of which James was so proud, made for a more peaceful nation, relatively, but a much duller king. Or so posterity has supposed.

Solomon Sleeps

James Stuart died in March 1625. His final year had been plagued with ill-health, culminating in a malaria-like fever known as the 'tertian ague', the commonest symptoms of which were incessant convulsions and vomiting. His physicians suggested various remedies, lots of bloodletting of course, and the usual tinctures. James, though, preferred to keep his hands immersed in cold water, and drink lots of beer. We will contemplate the hazards of medical practice in Jacobean England shortly. Suffice to say that the beer probably did more to alleviate the pain than either the bloodletting or the tinctures. It did not though prevent the inevitable. And so 'Solomon slept', as Lord Keeper Williams concluded his account of James's final hours. A stroke, it seems, or maybe a dodgy julep concocted by one of Steenie's servants.[12]

We have just taken a glance at the painted Solomon, at various stages in his life, from the 'cradle king' through to the middle-aged. A bit drab, at least when compared with his predecessor. Or indeed his son Charles who, something of an aesthete himelf, had the good sense to hire the services of Anthony van Dyck, to make himself look a bit prettier, and a lot taller.[13] And commission the studio of Peter Paul Rubens in Antwerp, to see if it could make his recently deceased dad seem a bit grander and more divine. A commission which realised a set of nine canvasses, arriving eventually in 1634, to decorate the ceiling of the newly completed Banqueting Chamber in Whitehall palace.[14] The three central canvasses were entitled *The Apotheosis of James I*, *The Union of Crowns* and *The Peaceful Reign of James I*. A considerable tribute, and probably more than James was entitled to expect. He and Charles were not especially close; it has been surmised that the latter's pronounced stammer might, to an extent, have been a consequence of living in fear of his father's unpredictable temper.[15]

---

[12] The rumour that Steenie did for 'dear Dad' was quickly circulating. The allegation was redirected towards Charles I at his trial in January 1649.

[13] Arriving in 1632, to replace Mytens. Van Dyck had previously visited England in 1621, but left shortly afterwards for Italy, after which he moved back to the Low Countries, before returning to England, at the invitation of King Charles.

[14] The contract appears to have been signed in 1630, whilst Rubens was in London as part of a mission despatched by King Philip IV of Spain. It took a further two years after their arrival for the canvasses to be finally installed. It being discovered, rather belatedly, that a Flemish 'foot' is longer than an English, and there would need to be a lot of very careful trimming. Despite the delay, Charles expressed himself delighted, and sent the artist a gold chain by way of thanks, along with the original fee of £3,000. For an account, suggesting that much of the painting was most likely completed by Rubens's students, see Millar (2007).

[15] Though also heritable. James was commonly reported to have a milder version of the same speech impediment.

We have already encountered one of the canvasses, *The Union of Crowns*. We might briefly sketch the other two. The centrepiece is *The Apotheosis*. King James seated in the middle, glancing up towards a laurel wreath held by the figure of Mercury. It will replace the symbols of his earthly authority, the crown and sceptre; an eerie portent of the frontispiece to the *Eikon Basilike*, albeit a familiar enough image in late medieval and Renaissance portraiture. His feet are planted on an eagle and an imperial globe, ready to be raised by Justice, escorted by Religion and Scriptural Truth. A slightly detached Victory flutters a nearby approval. Again, there is nothing unusual in the familiar blend of the classical and the Christian, certainly not to any student of Rubens.

The third canvas, entitled *The Peaceful Reign of James I*, was intended to celebrate the inauguration of the *pax Jacobus*, not just at home, in the shape of the Union, but across Europe. Thomas Middleton had imagined similarly in his play *The Peace-Maker*. James as Solomon, the 'great' king to whom all the bickering princes of Europe would come for counsel and conciliation.[16] Mytens too, in his portrait of James, placing his subject before a tapestry embossed by the Tudor rose with the words *beati pacifici*, 'blessed are the peacemakers'. Rubens, though, took things to a different level entirely. James, seated in the centre once again, is shielding Peace and Plenty, whilst Minerva casts down Mars, the god of war. The goddess of wisdom, Minerva was the obvious support for a king who so prided himself on his intellect. Spectacular.

And again poignant, and tragic. For if we move forward 15 years, to the morning of 30 January 1649, we will find King Charles I sitting beneath the very same canvasses. Waiting patiently, by all accounts, for his own execution.[17] It turned out to be a longer wait than expected, by around three hours. The execution of the King, it was belatedly realised, would not itself bring the monarchy to an end. An Act prohibiting the proclaiming of any person to be King of England or Ireland was hurried through the Commons late morning.[18] As he waited Charles took a glass of claret and some bread. We might surmise that he glanced upwards, to admire the Rubens. Whether he appreciated the attendant ironies is another matter. His had hardly proved to be a 'peaceful reign'. We might also wonder if, in a fraught moment, he was inclined to blame his dad. Not least for instilling in his impressionable son's mind the fantastical idea that he might become king of a 'greater' British empire, blessed by God, above the law, and beyond reproach. The 'right divine', as Alexander Pope would later put it, 'of kings to govern wrong'.[19]

It was reported that Charles showed commendable courage that morning, as he had the preceding few days. Immersed in George Herbert's *Devotions*, embracing

---

[16] The authorship of the play, which first appeared in 1618, is generally ascribed to Middleton. Plenty more flattering references to James's 'union', as an exemplar of how peace might be secured between nations. Along with a sub-text on dangers of alcohol-induced disorder at home.

[17] To take place on a scaffold constructed outside the first floor windows.

[18] No explicit mention of Scotland, though there is reference to 'dominions thereof'.

[19] Pope (1978) *Dunciad* 4. 188.

his fate. Already wondering his own apotheosis very probably. As for James, looking down on the scene, we can assume a measure of sadness. His son about to butchered on a public stage, the dream of a great British *dominum* dashed; for now, at least. The nagging thought that it was perhaps this dream that got his son into trouble in the first place. A 'war of three kingdoms' started in August 1640, with a Scottish army marching south and sweeping aside Charles's forces at the battle of Newburn. And then ended eight years later with another Scottish army, this time defeated by Cromwell, at the battle of Preston. After which would come the trial of the tyrant king, and the events of 30 January.

To a considerable extent memorials of James would be shaped by the ensuing appeal in the case of the tyrant king. The Whig Charles Stuart could hardly be other then venal and murderous, and the Whig James Stuart written to fit the same narrative. The 'wisest fool' pejorative has certainly stuck. 'Shrewder than his son', in Winston Churchill's *History of the English Speaking Peoples*, but no more principled. A 'Scottish pedant' with 'fixed ideas' about kingship and 'pretensions to be a philosopher'.[20] A caricature that owed much to previous Whig excoriations, nowhere more notorious than that inscribed by Lord Macaulay. Which, in turn, owed everything to the accounts left by contemporaries such as Harrington and Weldon. A king cursed by 'his rolling eye, his rickety walk, his nervous tremblings, his slobbering mouth', who

> enraged and alarmed his Parliament by consistently telling them that they held their privileges merely during his pleasure, and that they had no more business to inquire what he might lawfully do than what the Deity might lawfully do. Yet he quailed before them, abandoned minister after minister to their vengeance, and suffered them to tease him into act directly opposed to his strongest inclinations ... His cowardice, his childishness, his pedantry, his ungainly person and manners, his provincial accent, made him an object of derision.[21]

Knackered too, by his own frequent admission, 'wearied' by disappointment. In his address to Parliament in 1621, on the endlessly vexed subject of Union, he sounded a note of both resignation and apology: 'I never meant to weary myself or you with such tedious discourses as I have done heretofore'.[22] Unlike his son, James at least knew when his race was done. But it hardly made for a hero.

Even Tory historians struggled to rehabilitate James Stuart. 'Many virtues, it must be owned, he was possessed of', David Hume ventured, 'but scarce any of them pure, or free from the contagion of neighbouriing vices'. To wit, 'His generosity bordered on profusion, his learning on pedantry, his pacific disposition on pusillanimity, his wisdom on cunning, his friendship on light fancy and boyish fondness'.[23] Sir Walter Scott republished a collection of other people's prejudices in

---

[20] Churchill (1956) 2. 117–22.
[21] Macaulay (1837) 147, 167, 195–96.
[22] In Wormald (2021) 91.
[23] Hume (1778) 3. 89.

1811, entitled the *Secret History of the Court of James the First*. All the most salacious rumours.

A century after James's death, White Kennet, Bishop of Peterborough, shrewdly observed that where Elizabeth 'had a Camden', and Charles his Clarendon, 'poor King James I has had I think none but paltry scribblers'.[24] The poets had tried to oblige, as we have already noted. 'How, best of Kings, does thou a scepter bear!/ How, best of Poets, dost though laurel wear!' Jonson fawned. There again, Jonson was desperately trying to make up for the aspersions written into *Eastward Ho!* and *Sejanus*. Not the only instance of poetic ambivalence either. Impatient and ill-tempered in *Cymbeline*, vain and distracted in *The Tempest*; neither can be said to flatter.

The reformation of James Stuart has required a discerning eye. It is possible to spot glimpses across the centuries. The 'most wise' king appraised by Thomas Hobbes.[25] The 'Learned King', acknowledged by John Locke, who 'well understood the Notions of things'.[26] The approbation of the viscerally conservative Hobbes is less suprising; that of Locke, the architect of the 'glorious' revolution, its settlement at least, is more. Later on, and just five years after Scott's *Secret History* appeared, Isaac D'Israeli pubished his *Inquiry into the Literary and Political Character of James I*. Writing in the fashionable perspective of the *petite histoire*, D'Israeli resisted the simpler Whig caricatures, correctly spotting that it was the *pax Jacobus* that did for James Stuart. Lacking 'military character', too determinedly unheroic.[27] Again hardly flattering. But a portent perhaps of the revisionist James Stuart to come. No less absolutist, but nothing like so much the fool. The James Stuart presented most recently by Jenny Wormald. An altogether more nuanced, and intriguing king, or kings, distinguishing a Scottish from an English, and an imperial. The former commendably capable, the latter progressively shattered, the one in between a fish out of water.[28]

Acts of Union

Having contemplated how James might have felt about his son's sorry predicament in January 1649, we might also wonder what he would have thought of his two great-granddaughters, Mary and Anne. Mixed feelings, most likely. Mary crushed one of his dreams, Anne realised the other. Mary arrived in England, a few weeks after her husband, William of Orange, in late 1688, invited by a select group of Whig peers to become Queen of England in succession to her father, the newly exiled James II. With certain terms and conditions, written into a 'declaration' to

---

[24] In Wormald (2021) 80.
[25] Hobbes (1985) 251.
[26] Locke (1924) 218–300.
[27] See Ferris (2006) 73–76.
[28] Wormald (2021) particularly 75–103.

be read out at her coronation. A reworked draft of Coke's *Petition of Right*, which would be reworked again into a Bill of Rights. We will revisit these documents very shortly. There would be no more English kings, or queens, ruling by divine right, certainly none presuming to rule above English law. Or outside the English Church. A sentiment reinforced a dozen years later in the Act of Settlement of 1701, which expressly barred the succession to any who did not 'join in communion with the Church of England'. An echo of the blunt statement discovered in the Bill of Rights, that 'it hath been found by experience that it is inconsistent with the safety and welfare of this Protestant kingdom to be governed by a papist prince'. It was no longer for God alone to decide who ruled England, or Scotland.[29]

There would though be a 'greater' Britain, enshrined in an Act of Union, to which Mary's sister, Queen Anne, granted her assent in 1707. The summation of half a century of English 'expansionism', as the late Victorian historian, and proud imperialist, John Robert Seeley confirmed.[30] Vested with constitutional precedence, courtesy not of divine providence, but of the deepening credit facility of the Bank of England. 'Bought and sold for English gold', as Robert Burns famously put it. More precisely £398,015 10s; the sum guaranteed in Article 15 of the Union Treaty. Known as 'The Equivalent', it was designed to offset acquired liability for a share of the English national debt, whilst providing some shorter-term capital fluidity to an economy brought to its knees by the Darien 'scheme'.[31] Other Scots evinced greater enthusiasm. 'May we be Britons, and down go the old ignominious names of Scotland, of England', the Earl of Cromarty declared in 1707, 'Britain is our true, our honourable denomination'.[32] Probably a tad too much enthusiasm for James in truth, and it might anyway be argued that the Union was designed as much to perpetuate as to erase these distinctions, carefully demarcating a Scottish church and Scots law.[33] But he would have appreciated the sentiment.

And the supporting pretence, which intimated, if not quite realised, a British empire. An ad hoc overseas, or 'outer', empire was already taking form by the time that Gloriana had departed the scene. This is not the place to embark on an extended history of this empire. Suffice to say that James was an enthusiastic imperialist, liking the grandeur and the profit-margins. An enthusiasm to which

---

[29] The fact that the Act expressly provided that the succession should pass to another granddaughter, Princess Sophie of Hanover, might have provided some consolation. Sophie would predecease Queen Anne, for which reason when the latter died, in 1714, the throne was offered to Sophie's son, George.

[30] Seeley (1971) 64–65. Originally published in 1883, Seeley's *History* was an instant bestseller, shifting 80,000 copies in its first two years. The 'bible of British imperialists', according to Gooch (1959) 346–47. Amongst its most ardent admirers could be counted the arch-imperialists Joseph Chamberlain and Lord Rosebery.

[31] Plus, around £20,000 in targeted bribes. The scheme, supported by the Scottish government, was purposed to establish a colony in the Gulf of Darien, in present day Panama, to be named New Caledonia. It was backed by the Company of Scotland, and drew investments totalling around 20% of national value. The scheme collapsed, following years of mismanagement, disease and war with Spain.

[32] Cromarty was Secretary of State in Scotland from 1702 to 1704, afterwards Lord Justice General, and a consistent advocate of union, not least because he had invested heavily in the Darien scheme.

[33] For which reason it 'did not create anything that resembled a united British nation', according to Levack (1987) 23.

Shakespeare famously gestures once again in his *The Tempest*. The 'brave new world' welcomed by Miranda, wherever it might be; the Bermudas, the Virginias, Ireland (5.1.183).[34] Variously beautiful and savage, ladened with exploitable natural resources, ready to be civilised. All Prospero's island needs is Prospero. A reformed Christian prince who can oust the malevolent, pseudo-papist witch Scyorax and despatch her would-be rapist son Caliban. Bringing law and order, and a protestant God, and in short order lots of eager merchant-adventurers.[35] England's destiny.

And Britain's in due course. The extent to which the British Empire became a vehicle for English expansionism and, perhaps ironically, English exceptionalism, remains moot. In her study of a nascent British identity, Linda Colley traced the seeding of empire, inner and outer, to the same protestant poetic we encountered earlier, the England of Foxe's martyrs and Bunyan's pilgrim. And Hogarth's *Roast Beef*, at a more a cynical variant. Still more cynical was the 'true-born' Englishman dreamt up by Daniel Defoe.[36] The stupefying concoction of faith, poetry and money. Tom Nairn reaches a similar conclusion, supposing that the same logic applies to the inner empire as it does the outer. The establishment of the Anglo-British state as the 'organic expansion of the English identity'.[37] A logic, moreover, which asks a pregnant question: absent an empire, does Britain mean anything? We will contemplate some possible answers shortly.

In the meantime, the English fleeced much of the rest of the world, as God had instructed them to do, importing vast amounts of raw materials, and making mouth-watering profits. 'Butchered half the world, and bullied t'other', as Byron put it.[38] In return for which it exported, amongst other things, a particular way of thinking about law. A history anticipated by the author of the *Maske of Flowers*, presented to the 'gentlemen of Gray's Inn' in 1613 to celebrate the marriage of the Earl and Countess of Somerset. That author was Sir Francis Bacon, the theme entirely predictable: how much the godless natives will benefit

---

[34] For a commentary on the physical possibilities here, see Raffield (2017) 195–96, 221–26. Antonio's comment, that they will receive no news from Naples 'till new-born chins/ Be rough and razorable' suggests that Prospero and his party have travelled a considerable distance from the Mediterrean (2.1. 244–45). A passing allusion to the 'still-vexed Bermoothes' might be intended to give us a further clue (1.2. 229). There was much contemporary interest in the Bermudas, stimulated to no small extent by Silvester Jourdain's *A Discovery of the Bermudas, Otherwise Called the Ile of Devils*, published in 1610, the opening of which resonates, very obviously, with the shipwreck which opens *The Tempest*. Ultimately, of course, the physical possibilities matter rather less than the imaginative.

[35] The kind of missionary alignment recommended by William Strachey in his *Lawes Divine, Morall and Martiall*, published in 1611, designed to stiffen the resolve of the Lords of the Council of Virginia, as they anticipated the hostilities of the Anglo-Powhatan war. To 'imitate your maker in his will/ To have his truth in blackest nations shine'. In the moment, the Virginia Company was disinclined to purchase more land from the native population, assuming that it had a literally God-given right just to take it. The Powhatans were unpersuaded. A portent of things to come, across North America, and much of the rest of the still-to-be 'discovered' world. On the broader alignment, of godly and mercantile imperatives, in the play, see Raffield (2017) 207–08, 219–20, 227–28.

[36] Colley (1994) 19–22, 27–35.

[37] Nairn (2002) 33.

[38] Byron (1980) 'Don Juan' 10.81.

from being conquered by 'God's lieutenant on earth', and governed by his laws.[39] Beneficience beyond argument, as Charles Darwin would confirm two centuries on, in his *The Descent of Man*, deploying an unimpeachable authority; 'as Mr Bagehot has well shown'.[40] By then the darker side of colonialism had been long exposed, even if it did not bother Darwin much, or Bagehot.

Two years after the publication of Darwin's *Descent*, in 1874, the British Empire would finally assume statutory form in the shape of a Royal Titles Act which recognised Queen Victoria as empress of India.[41] Given the extent of the British 'Empire' at the midpoint of the nineteenth century, it is perhaps as close as any English monarch had come to making a credible claim to be *dominus mundi*. James would have been impressed. Less so, perhaps, with the unravelling of this empire. Here again, though, the pretence would linger. As recently as 1954, Churchill could inform a State Department audience that 'only the English-speaking peoples count' and that 'together they can rule the world'.[42] He had even written a four-volume history on the theme.[43] Classically Whig, classically warped. Two years later, came the Suez crisis. The very same year that Seeley's *Expansion of England* finally went out of print; not much of a coincidence.

Even then the delusion was not entirely ended. In place of an empire, there would be a 'commonwealth of nations', ever-diminishing in scale and purpose, along with some remaining 'territories' scattered around the globe: a couple of islands off the coast of Argentina; a large 'rock' in southern Spain; a few other bits and pieces.[44] Less tangible are the countervailing sentiments of nostalgia and guilt also left behind. And the stigma of illegality, recently, and resoundingly, affirmed by the International Court of Justice in its advisory opinion in the case of the Chagos islanders.[45] Even the remembrance is soured.

The Hidden Republic

We might again ponder the need for the Royal Titles Act. In practical terms, it meant nothing. In terms of adding a little glitter, and cheering up Queen Victoria,

---

[39] See Raffield (2017) 232–35.

[40] Darwin (1974) 125–27.

[41] In return she made him Earl of Beaconsfield.

[42] In Haseler (1996) 125.

[43] Or at least put his name to it. The writing of Churchill's *History* has assumed a certain notoriety, not that much of the final draft actually being written by Churchill.

[44] See Heffer (1999) 75, dismissing the Commonwealth as a 'preposterous placebo' for nostalgic imperialists. For a further commentary on the collapse of empire, and its consequence, not least the peculiar struggles which the UK has experienced in coming to terms with the reality, see Garton Ash (2004) 7–24.

[45] The Chagos Islands sit off the coast of Mauritius. On the independence of Mauritius in 1968, the UK unilaterally decided to retain the Chagos Islands, removing its habitants and then leasing islands to the US for military purposes. Successive legal challenges to this retention, over the intervening six decades, are recounted in Sands (2022). In 2019, the International Court of Justice provided an advisory opinion confirming the illegality of the retention, and recommending that the

it meant everything. The previous 15 years had proved difficult for all concerned. A distraught Victoria, unable to come to terms with the death of her beloved Prince Albert in 1861, had drifted into a kind of retirement. There 'are other and higher duties than those of mere representation which are now thrown upon the Queen, alone and unassisted', she had observed in an ill-advised letter to *The Times*.[46] She could not have been more wrong, as Gladstone curtly reminded her. Representation was precisely her job; her only job. A view accorded by Disraeli, only more politely. Thus, the fawning missives addressed to his reluctant 'Fairy Queen', and the Royal Titles Act. Which seemed to do the trick. Victoria became fascinated in all things Indian, eating curries, hiring Indian servants, even learning a few words of Urdu.[47] More importantly, she started to perform again. Opening Parliament, inspecting troops, so long as they were nearby.[48] Hardly Gloriana, barely smiling; but something at least.

Someone else who readily appreciated the performance of majesty was Walter Bagehot. Indeed, Victoria's peremptory retirement was a principal motivation for writing the essays which comprised his *English Constitution*. 'The use of the Queen, in her dignified capacity, is incalculable', Bagehot declared, and 'Without her in England, the present English government would fail and pass away'.[49] It was the very essence of being a constitutional monarch.[50] The dignity of the Crown and the efficiency of government existed in a state of mutual dependence. And not just the Crown. By the time that Bagehot was writing, it was just as apparent that Parliament had been reduced to the same purpose. The 'instrument of power', as Lord Radcliffe would later confirm, 'instead of being its holder'.[51]

The idea that power shifted from the monarch to the Crown in the early eighteenth century was argued by William Anson a century ago. A prosaic consequence of the early Hanoverian kings not speaking English.[52] 'Ministers', George II complained in 1744, 'are the kings in this country'.[53] And whilst it was possible to identify moments of seeming judicial resistance over the intervening century and a half, in *Wilkes Case* for example, or *Entick v Carrington*, it did not fool Bagehot.

UK cease administration of the islands as 'rapidly as possible'. The UN General Assembly duly adopted Resolution 73/295 welcoming the opinion. The UK has refused to respect either the opinion or the Resolution.

[46] Strachey (1971) 184.

[47] Victoria's favourite curry dishes were chicken and daal, preferably cooked by her 'munshi', Abdul Karim. Needless to say curries quickly became *a la mode* amongst middle-class Victorian England. In her *Modern Cookery for Private Families*, the celebrated Eliza Acton thoughtfully provided some advice. Nothing wrong with a curry, Eliza observed, but if the ingredients are not completely fresh, it might taste a bit rubbish. And getting the right fresh vegetables and herbs in England was not easy. If in doubt, stick to a lamb cutlet with potatoes; which was, Eliza confirmed, Victoria's favourite 'British' dish.

[48] Aldershot being 22 miles from Windsor, and so comfortably done in a day.

[49] Bagehot (2001) 34.

[50] See here Bogdanor (1998) 30–34.

[51] Radcliffe (1952) 59. Radcliffe was a former Law Lord and prime mover in the partition of India.

[52] Anson (1980) 2.1.41.

[53] Bogdanor (1998) 11.

A 'republic', he famously concluded, had 'insinuated itself beneath the folds of a monarchy'.[54] And neither should it fool us. Executive power in the United Kingdom remains disguised and 'untrammelled'.[55] A century ago Lord Chief Justice Hewart spoke of a 'new despotism'.[56] A generation on, Lord Hailsham alluded to the practice of modern government as 'elective dictatorship'.[57] The curse of Cassandra was to foresee the future, but to have no one believe it. Bagehot's curse was to foresee the future, and make it only too believable, but have no one care enough to change it.

Meanwhile, as Bagehot also predicted, Britain would retain its monarchy, so long as it continued to bewitch. The 'charmed spectacle' of an 'antique', and antic, democracy.[58] And so it has proved, the 'new Elizabethans' as happily enchanted as the old.[59] Tripping the edge of sanity in the moment of the second Elizabeth's passing in summer 2022. The coincidence of nomenclature was, of course, barely resistible. But there is more to it than quaint fortuity. The English like playful princesses, that 'certain spectacle of beautiful women' on the throne, as Bagehot put it.[60] Elizabeth I was the first English monarch to regularly 'progress' around her kingdom. Elizabeth II was the second. There is, of course, a downside to the adoration. Aside from simple silliness, there is also the familiar bane of succession anxiety.

A subject treated in Mike Bartlett's critically acclaimed play *King Charles III*, which anticipates a conspicuously brief reign of its eponymous hero.[61] Deposed, in the end, because he did properly understand his Bagehot, more especially the renowned passage which confirms the 'rights' of a modern monarch, to be consulted, to encourage, and 'most importantly the right to warn' (103).[62] Bartlett's Charles thinks this gives him licence to interfere more directly in the matters of state. He has an overarching responsibility to 'protect/ This country's unique force and way of life' (27). It is why he has a 'conscience' and a prerogative, and why he declines to give his assent to a proposed bill to tighten press regulation (49–50).

It is the defining error which leads to his deposition. Helped on his way by a scheming Princess Kate; rather more Lady Macbeth than valiant Britomart. There not 'simply' to 'help my husband in his crown/ But wear one of my own' (92). And not much helped by his sons either, William or Harry. And certainly not by his

---

[54] Bagehot (2001) 44. For *Wilkes's Case*, see (1770) 19 How ST 1075; 98 ER 2, 327, and for *Entick v Carrington* (1765) 19 How ST 1029; 95 ER 807.

[55] Bogdanor (2021) vi.

[56] Remarkably, perhaps, whilst in office, and then published as indeed *The New Despotism*. For a commentary on Hewart's 'extraordinary step', see Sedley (2015) 29–31.

[57] In his 1976 Richard Dimbleby lecture. See Hailsham (1976).

[58] See Nairn (2002) 152.

[59] Haseler (1996) 55.

[60] Bagehot (2001) 41.

[61] Bartlett (2014).

[62] The original is found in Bagehot (2001) 60. The 'right to be consulted, the right to encourage, and the right to warn'. To which Bagehot famously adds and a 'king of great sagacity would want no others'.

first wife Diana, the 'beshrouded lady' flitting about in the shadows who riddles him with the idea that he might prove to be the 'greatest King we ever had' (71). Another enchantress who had threatened to bring the monarchy to its end. The inadvertent herald of republicanism, some supposed, in the febrile moment of her death. But who, with the benefit of a fonder remembrance, would be transformed into a 'Queen of Hearts'. Bartlett's Diana is more the seer than the sorceress; a bit like Bagehot. She does not conjure the deposition of her former husband, but she can see it coming. He sadly cannot.

But then depositions commonly seem to surprise their victims. Take Shakespeare's Richard Plantagenet, an evident source for Bartlett's play.[63] The essential theme of which is plain enough. Monarchies are fragile, especially those secured by nothing more than an 'insubstantial pageant' (*Tempest* 4.1. 155). For which reason so too are the constitutions which they are supposed to found. An insight that would not have been lost on James Stuart. Still less his son Charles; at least not by the end. We can only conjecture what either would have thought of Bartlett's whimsy. Or Bagehot's *Constitution*. The basic demarcation, between the 'dignified' and the 'efficient', would have chimed, though the idea of being little more than puppet princes would have been somewhat discordant. The idea that modern Britain was embracing a 'new despotism' would surely have appealed. And the same can be said of a more obviously presidential style of governance which has emerged over the last quarter century. As for the 'repopulation' of Whitehall by 'ministerial placemen', a concern of some modern commentators, it is reasonable to suppose that neither James nor Charles would have been anything like so worried.[64] Just like old times; a court of fawning sycophants.

Which brings us nicely to the still-evolving succession of the 'real' King Charles III, if such a thing exists. No shortage of fawning to be sure. Or spectacle. The coronation in May 2023 was priced at £100 million, to be paid from the public purse, during the deepest economic recession in a century. The £20,000 spent on James I in 1603 raised a few eyebrows at the time, being around a fifth more than that of his predecessor. The equivalent of around £2.5 million today, it looks a bargain in comparison. As for the new Caroline age, or Caroleon as some would prefer, still in the infancy of its writing, only time will tell how it will unfold.[65] But we all know how the first Caroline age ended. 'Uneasy lies the head that wears a crown'.[66] Behind every fawning sycophant, a wicked counsellor lurks; inside every wise king, a fool. The 'republican opportunity', finally?[67] We will see.

---

[63] For a comment on the Shakespearean sources evident in Bartlett's play, including *Richard II*, see Ward (2021) 117–26.
[64] For the concern, see Sedley (2015) 192.
[65] A Caroleon age being deemed more hopeful than a Caroline.
[66] Shakespeare (1966) 3.1.31.
[67] See Hutton (1995) 285–97.

The Old Laws

Having traced the longer presence of James Stuart, we can now proceed to do the same for his Lord Chief Justice. The man who stood, almost alone, in defending England and its common law against the recurring rapine of Roman tyranny. At least in the imagination of Cass Gilbert and John Donnelly, who designed the bronze reliefs which decorate the doors to the US Supreme Court. Coke barring James from the 'King Court' is one of the eight scenes selected across a long history of the rule of law, starting with the Shield of Achilles and ending with *Marbury v Madison*.[68] Of course, Coke never physically barred his King from anywhere. It is the impression that counts, literally and figuratively.

The Oracle

Not every historian has been persuaded by Coke. Not even every Whig historian, at least not entirely. 'Pedant, bigot and savage', in Macaulay's opinion, a man of 'half-suppressed insolence' and 'impracticable obstinacy', albeit also a man of undoubted courage. The ambiguity captured in the surmise that Coke 'had qualities which bore a strong, though a very disagreeable, resemblance to some of the highest virtues which a public man can possess'.[69] It is the heroic Coke which better fits the sweep of Whig history, and historiography, the man who saved *Magna Carta* from shameful neglect. The 'sacred text', as Maitland put it, and the sainted jurist.[70] The 'greatest lawyer in English history', whose writings 'established the common law on its firm foundations'.[71] The champion of the 'ancient' constitution, and chronicler of its 'mind', according to John Pocock, writing half a century ago.[72] A 'constitutional entrepreneur' who refitted Chapter 29 of the great Charter for the coming age of political economy, at a variant.[73] No shortage of Whiggish adulation amongst contemporary jurists either. A herald of jurisprudential 'modernity', according to Sir Stephen Sedley, 'one of the shaping forces' of the British constitution.[74] Perhaps 'the most influential English jurist of all time', in the opinion of Lord Bingham.[75]

---

[68] The Court itself was designed by Cass Gilbert. A bit of a Whig, and a lot of a classicist, Gilbert designed the Court as a Roman temple in the Corinthian style; to represent two thousand years of political, and jurisprudential, progress.

[69] Macaulay (1837) 35–36.

[70] In Sumption (2021) 28.

[71] Gest (1909) 506; and Berman (1994) 1675.

[72] The seminal commentary here being Pocock (1967), particularly chs 2 and 3. For a more recent critical assessment, see Burgess (1992) 21–22, 72–78.

[73] Who 'built a new constitutional order based on the operation of markets under the rule of law', according to Yandle (1993).

[74] Sedley (2015) 2, 124.

[75] Bingham (2010) 75.

Time, like absence, makes the heart grow fonder. But there were plenty of contemporaries prepared to vouch much the same. A 'judge of great integrity, much sincerity, great reading, happy memory and indefatigable industry', according to Henry Calthorpe.[76] Likewise the puritan polemicist, William Prynne; the 'patron and pillar of the common law', the man whose 'quotations' are 'received, and relied on by a mere implicit faith, as infallible oracles'.[77] Sir Matthew Hale too, whose *History of the Common Law of England* and later *Analysis of the Law* owed so much to the same infallibility. And his *Reflections on Hobbes's Dialogue*, confirming that the common law was indeed the construct of a peculiar historical reason.[78] Even Bacon was prepared to concede that English law had 'been almost like a ship without ballast' until Coke started compiling his *Reports*. An invaluable resource, even though they contained so many 'errors' and 'peremptory and extra-judicial resolutions'.[79]

Shakespeare mght have had his doubts, as we have already surmised, Jonson too. It is the poet's prerogataive to play the ironist. There again, it is possible to read George Chapman's *The Tragedie of Chabot Admirall of France* as an altogether more glowing dramatic testament.[80] Chapman's Chabot defending the integrity of the law against the venal Chancellor Poyet; a depiction which does little reciprocal credit to his allusive persecuter Sir Francis Bacon. It was not the first time that Chapman had sought cover in recent French history because its English equivalent was too hot to touch. We have already come across his *Bussy d'Amboise*, with its veiled critique of the collected mythologies of Gloriana. Another, the *Conspiracy and Tragedy of Biron*, revisited the trial of the Earl of Essex. Registered at the Stationer's Office in 1608, a percipient moment to remind England of how lucky it had then been to have, in Sir Edward Coke, an Attorney General of such rectitude.

A conclusion revisited in 1634, as Robert Codrington reflected on the recent passing of the same man:

The Nymphes that haunt the neighbouring woods and hilles,

That guard the valleys, and that guide the Rilles,

Resound his losse and honourd name and show

The boundles Rage of their impatient woe

In so distracting and so saddle a cry,

As if with him the Northern World did dye.

An Arcadian referent, of the kind which Culpepper's fainting farmers might in that moment have appreciated. Coke as the personification of jurisprudential integrity,

[76] Baker (2017) 437.

[77] In an essay entitled 'To All Ingenuous Readers', cited in Weston (1991) 375–76.

[78] See Cromartie (1995) 101–09, 119–20.

[79] Coquillette (1992) 109.

[80] The date of composition of the play is uncertain. A wider ambit between 1611 and 1624, a narrower between 1617 and 1622.

the guardian of the natural and common law of the English 'world'. And now gone, finally. Looking back through Coke's career, Codrington alighted on 1616 and discerned a martyr struck down in a manner which would have resonated with anyone who knew their Ovid, or their *Cymbeline*: 'The Bolts were flying, and the Brow of heaven/ Did ake with the thunders'.[81]

The continuing adoration of revolutionary England is unsurprising. The voice of the common law, Marchamont Nedham supposed, against the delusions of 'dreaming rabbies'.[82] The Long Parliament ordered printings of the second volume of the *Institutes* in 1642, and the third and fourth volumes two years later. A generation of disciples discovered in the likes of Algernon Sidney, whose *Discourses Concerning Government* confirmed that the Crown 'has no other power that what the law allows'.[83] And the Leveller John Lilburne. Who, just a few months after the execution of King Charles I in January 1649, marched into the Guildhall to answer charges of sedition, brandishing his copy of the *Institutes*. It was, he declared, the 'great Oracle of the Laws of England'.[84] The jury was apparently impressed, even more so when the roof fell in. The Hand of God, the ultimate in critical approval.

And a piece of theatre replayed a century later by John Adams, who likewise strode into the Carpenter's Hall in Philadelphia in 1784, to argue the case for 'natural rights', again carrying a copy of the *Institutes*. Revolutionary America was just as impressed with Coke as revolutionary England; a starring role in the longer narrative which imagined the former as completing the latter.[85] A 'sounder Whig never wrote', according to Thomas Jefferson. James Otis cited Coke's report of *Bonham's Case* when contesting crown writs in the 1760s. Hamilton similarly in *Rutgers v Waddington* in 1784.[86] Back at Westminster, John Wilkes liked to bait his parliamentary opponents with the line that the Americans were fighting for the 'best constitution on earth', whereas the English were fighting for a bunch of German princelings and their placemen.[87] Edmund Burke did not go quite that far in his support for the colonial 'cause', but he went far enough. Coke as one of defenders of 'liberty according to English ideas and English principles', in whom the 'fierce spirit of liberty is stronger' than 'any other people of the earth'.[88]

A perception which became ever more deeply embedded in Whiggish histories of the American Revolution, and its consequence. A century later, Sir William Holdsworth would recommend the US Supreme Court as the 'tribunal' which, more 'than any other in the world', respects 'Coke's ideal of the supremacy

---

[81] See Raffield (2005) 69–70, discussing Codrington's verse.

[82] Nedham had in mind, more particularly, the kind of millenarians who would, for a brief moment, govern England as members of the 'Barebones' Assembly in 1653. The Semitic allusion refers to the perception that the Assembly was modelled on the Old Testament Sanhedrin.

[83] Sidney (1996) 222.

[84] Loewenstein (2001) 28; and also Raffield (2005) 72.

[85] Hart (2002) 86–87, 92–97.

[86] Geobel (1969) 1. 357–58.

[87] In Colley (1994) 150–51.

[88] Bohn (1854–56) 1. 464.

of law'.[89] The man who, in retrieving *Magna Carta* and templating the English Bill of Rights, inspired the writing of the American 'declaration'. A surrogate 'framer' his stamp perhaps most evident in the due process clauses in the Fifth and Fourteenth Amendments; both of which were modelled on Chapter 29 of the 'great charter', or more accurately Coke's interpretation of it.[90]

On these grounds alone, it has been surmised that Coke's *Institutes* might have been the most influential legal treatise published during the seventeenth century.[91] Treated by his fellow students as the 'first universal law book', Jefferson confirmed, the unargued source of 'what is called British liberties'.[92] And thus, at remove, the source of American liberties too; the 'empire of liberty', as Jefferson liked to imagine it.[93] The common law may only have ruled in the newly crafted republic by grace of congressional approval, but that did not diminish its authenticity.[94] A view supported, just as strongly, by fellow 'framer', and *Institutes*-brandisher, John Adams.

In devoting himself to a 'deep reading in the common law tradition', and more especially in Coke's *Reports* and *Institutes*, the young Jefferson followed a path laid out by generations of pre-revolutionary Virginians.[95] He did not always agree with what he read, of course. Most obviously, he was much more persuaded of the case for incorporating principles of equity in the common law; an idea discovered in the likes of Blackstone and Kames, and the court of Lord Mansfield. But he agreed with a lot, most importantly the need for strong courts and legislatures which could counter executive overreach. In his *Parliamentary Pocket-Book* Jefferson alighted on 1621 as another defining moment in English constitutional history, when the Commons, egged on by Coke, decided the time was right to remind its King James that the 'liberties, franchises, privileges, and jurisdictions of Parliament are the ancient undoubted birthright and inheritance of the subjects of England'.[96] Jefferson rather wondered if the road to civil war and revolution, English and American, started here.

Hitherto, we have concentrated our attention rather more on Coke's *Reports*, for the simple reason that they chronicle events leading up to 1616. The *Institutes* so admired by Jefferson were the consequence of these events, and tend to loom larger in the prospective. The textbook a complement, in a sense, to the casebook that was presented in the *Reports*, and intended to do for England what Justinian's jurists had done for Rome. Sharing the same didactic aspiration, whilst also providing a testament intended for the benefit of posterity; to both their author,

---

[89] Holdsworth (1938) 131.
[90] Hulsebosch (2003) 441–44.
[91] Shapiro (2019) 90.
[92] Lipscomb (1903–04) 12.iv.
[93] An idea he shared with his close friend James Madison. See Crow (2019) 182–84.
[94] 'Our laws', he admitted, 'are so deeply laid in English foundations, that we shall nevere cease to consider their history as part of ours'. See Crow (2019) 227–29.
[95] Crow (2019) 9–16, 36–47, 51–54, 75–79.
[96] Crow (2019) 249.

and the law he inscribed.[97] Only rather more briefly. Justinian's *Institutes* stretched to 50 volumes. Coke condensed his into four.

The first of which, commonly known by its subtitle as Coke's 'Commentary on Littleton', revisited Sir Thomas Littleton's *Treatise on Tenures*, published around 1481.[98] A vehicle which allowed its author to vent his disdain for a particular source of confusion in English law, the introduction of newly devised statutory uses. A 'monstrous brood carved out of mere invention and never known to the ancient sage of the Law', the consequence of which was 'infinite troubles, questions, suits and difficulties'.[99] A common enough opinion. The preface to Pulton's 1577 *Abstract of all the Penal Statutes* had said the same. And not the first time that Coke had pressed the need for a cleansing pen. The Preface to the first volume of *Reports* was likewise written for the 'quieting' of confusion against the hazards of 'slippery memory', and to purge English law of 'many absurd and strange opinions'.[100] A familiar refrain, and metaphor. Plowden's *Commentaries* advertised the same determination to correct 'unfaithful and slippery' remembrance.

Something else that evidently attracted Coke to Littleton's *Treatise*, as opposed to many other similarly intended commentaries on late medieval property law, was its dogged determination to eschew any reference to principles of civil law. The *Treatise* was a paean to English law, and so, accordingly, was Coke's 'commentary'. As were the three volumes which followed. The second of which was given over to reinvesting *Magna Carta*, along with 'many ancient and other statutes'. It was this volume which so inspired Lilburne, Adams and Jefferson, and which has sustained Coke's place in the pantheon of determinedly English jurists. In searching for an English identity, Keith Thomas alighted on *Magna Carta*, along with Parliament, roast beef and plum pudding.[101] Coke could make reasonable claim to having saved at least two of these.

The third volume of the *Institutes* turned its attention to matters 'concerning high treason and other pleas of the crown and criminal causes', whilst the subject of the fourth concerned 'the jurisdiction of the courts'. Whilst the first volume had appeared in 1628, the latter three would wait until the early years of the Civil War. Seizing a moment of revolutionary fervour, on the battlefield and in the printing industry. To be read together, not just as reforming texts, but as reformation texts. Confirmation that if anything defined the reformed English it was, along with its new Church, its old laws.[102] And confirmation too, that rather than being dreamt up by a 'few learned, or unlearned ignorant men' the common law was a refined 'study of reason'.[103] More especially the reason of English history. All the way from

---

[97] See here Simpson (1981) 666.

[98] The likely year of its author's death. Littleton had risen through the profession to serve as a Justice of Common Pleas, appointed during the reign of Edward IV in 1466.

[99] Of which the most 'monstrous' are 'perpetuities'.

[100] Sheppard (2003) 1. 4.

[101] In Haseler (1996) 21.

[102] Colls (2002) 13–19.

[103] Hobbes (1971).

Malmutius to *Magna Carta*, to *Prohibitions, Proclamations* and the *Petition of Right*. A jurisprudence which justified the past, made sense of the present, and fitted out a truly chosen people for a future which was surely blessed. The England of Shakespeare, Spenser and Sidney.

The Old Laws

And Percy Shelley. Who, in summer 1819, found himself staying on the Ligurian coast, at the Villa Volsovano. Shrouded in 'melancholy', having just buried his youngest child, his wife Mary enduring another bout of manic depression, Shelley's consolation was a large glass tower, to which he could escape, to stare over the bay, and read the newspapers.[104] Mary spoke of a 'listless' moment. The papers took around two weeks to arrive from London. So it was not until 5 September that he read an account of a gathering at St Peter's Fields in Manchester, which had taken place 19 days earlier.

Around 60,000 had turned up to listen to the famed Henry 'Orator' Hunt; arguing the case for franchise reform. Many from miles around, marching in organised groups, with bands and banners, carrying mottoes such as 'Liberty and Fraternity' and 'Unity and Strength'.[105] Affronted by the presence of the rioters, fearing that the situation might run out of control, the magistrates had ordered the Riot Act to be read. A handful might have heard it, not many. No one moved. So the magistrates sent in the yeomanry to disperse the crowds. To no avail. At which point they ordered in six troops of Hussars, waiting outside the 'fields'. A few minutes later, 11 lay dead, hundreds injured.[106] The press dubbed it the 'Peterloo massacre'. Many of the Hussars had fought at Waterloo, and wore their battle medals as they charged into the crowd. Not so much to be proud of here, the insinuation ran, hacking down unarmed women and children.

The day after reading the report, Shelley wrote to his friend, Thomas Love Peacock, attesting to the 'torrent of indignation … not yet done boiling in my veins'. He waited 'anxiously to hear how the Country will express its sense of this bloody murderous oppression of its destroyers'. The 'dread lighting' of vengeance.[107] Meantime he would write one of the greatest poems of political protest in the English language.[108] He called it *The Mask of Anarchy*. Ninety-one stanzas, in three

---

[104] He was presently struggling with redrafts of his verse-drama *The Cenci*.

[105] A number of early-day Women's Suffrage banners too. The reporter Samuel Bamford noted that the stage upon which Hunt was to speak was ringed by some of the 'handsomest girls'. Compelling, if very different, accounts of the Peterloo 'massacre' can be found in Thompson (1991) 734–68; and Chandler (1998) 15–21.

[106] The precise number of consequential deaths, in the longer term, is unknown. The official tally was 11 dead and 421 injured, 162 with sabre-wounds.

[107] Holmes (1994) 329–30.

[108] Composed over what his biographer Richard Holmes terms the 'most creative eight weeks of his whole life' (1994) 532.

sections. The first 34 tore into the government of Lord Liverpool. A series of caricatures, as would be written into a Court masque.[109] The poem reaches its brilliant
crescendo in the ninth stanza, with the arrival of Anarchy; the figure before which
all the ministerial sycophants cower:

> Last came Anarchy: he rode
>
> On a white horse, splashed with blood;
>
> He was pale even to the lips,
>
> Like Death in the Apocalypse.
>
> …
>
> And he wore a kingly crown;
>
> And in his grasp a sceptre shone;
>
> On his brow this mark I saw –
>
> I AM GOD AND KING AND LAW! (ll. 30–37).[110]

Anarchy meant something different then. Shelley had written about it in his epic
poem on the French Revolution, *The Revolt of Islam*.[111] He had read Edmund
Burke too, and imbibed the idea that 'terror' is the principal weapon with which
the modern state assures itself. By 1819, the 'aesthetics of terror' was the defining presence in Shelley's writing, his mind turned by William Godwin's *Enquiry
Concerning Political Justice*, at the heart of which was a simple thesis.[112] First,
violent anarchy is found not in those who presume to protest, but in those who
fear the protest. Which in August 1819 was the Manchester magistrates, and their
masters in London, the 'tyrants' sitting around Liverpool's Cabinet table who had
'first shed blood'.[113]

Second, 'rational anarchy', as Godwin termed it, is the 'love of liberty'. And law.
The point which Shelley makes in the third set of stanzas, which paint a rather
brighter picture, of a distinctly English sensibility:

> The old laws of England – they
>
> Whose reverend heads with age are gray,
>
> Children of a wiser day;
>
> And whose solemn voice must be
>
> Thine own echo – Liberty! (ll. 333–35).

---

[109] Murder, Fraud and Hypocrisy, respectively Castlereagh, Eldon and Sidmouth. Beset by myriad
Chancery disputes regarding estate succession and child custody, Shelley harboured a peculiar animus
towards Lord Chancellor Eldon. 'Thy country's curse', as he put it in the opening line of his 'To the Lord
Chancellor'.

[110] All internal references from Shelley (1971).

[111] The revolution was the 'master theme of the epoch in which we live', he confirmed in
correspondence with Byron: Holmes (1994) 346.

[112] In the early 1790s, Godwin had been at the forefront of English Jacobinism. He was also Shelley's
father-in-law. Mary Godwin was Shelley's second wife, and author of *Frankenstein*. For Godwin's influence on Shelley, see Chandler (1998) 28–29; and also Holmes (1994) 261.

[113] Holmes (1994) 531.

It was the juristic complement to Thomas Gray's *Elegy Written in an English Country Churchyard*, composed a generation earlier, with its invocations of 'Some village Hampden, with his dauntless breast', and a 'mute, inglorious Milton' (ll. 57, 59):[114]

> Ev'n from the tomb the voice of Nature cries,
> Ev'n in our ashes live their wonted fires (ll. 91–92).

The raising of quieted voices. Shelley closes in like tones:

> Shake your chains to earth like dew
> Which in sleep had fallen on you –
> Ye are many – they are few (ll. 370–72).

And thus make England merry once more. A place where the 'churchyard' is always 'full of laughter', as the Elizabethan poet Nicholas Breton had liked to imagine it, where a 'hearty welcome fills the wassail bowl', and where 'pipe and tabor made as merry glee as at a may-pole one would wish to see'.[115] Shakespeare's 'other Eden'.

And as Alfred Lord Tennyson imagined it too, half a century on from Shelley's assault. Remembering

> the land that freemen till,
> That sober-suited Freedom chose,
> The land, where, girt with friends of foes
> A man may speak the thing he will;
> A land of settled government,
> A land of just and old renown,
> Where Freedom slowly broadens down
> From precedent to precedent (ll. 5–12).[116]

Less anger. But the same familiar fantasy; old England and its 'old laws'.

Less irony too perhaps. The renaissance 'masque' was all about the restoration of order. A first part depicting the 'state of nature', and its consequence, and a second during which calm is restored by a wise magistrate; albeit with the turn of a neatly placed heel, rather than the flash of a sabre-blade.[117] Shelley knew this. It is why he selected the governing metaphor, and disrupted the sequence. The spectacle of government, purposed to awe. A masque of terror. With, in the end, a simple enough message: strip away the mask, and beneath lies the familiar face of tyranny.

---

[114] All internal references from Turner (1998).
[115] A tabor being a sort of tambourine or snare-drum. See Hutton (1996) 104–10, 137, 169–70.
[116] 'You ask me, why, tho' ill at ease', in Tennyson (2009).
[117] The masque is commonly associated with the early Stuart Court. Charles I was a particular enthusiast.

An exhausted Shelley despatched a finalised draft of the *Mask* to his friend Leigh Hunt, editor of the *Examiner*, at the end of the month. The news, when it finally filtered back, was disappointing. Threatened with prosecution for sedition, Hunt could not publish.[118] It was the wrong moment.

The right moment, it transpired, was 1832, amidst the feverish conversation which anticipated the passage of the 'great' Reform Act; the 'finality' as Macaulay advertised it, to the project begun in 1689, and 1616, and 1536, and 1215. In celebration of the 'great' Act, Thomas Coke, 1st Earl of Leicester, commissioned Sir Francis Chantrey to sculpt something suitably imposing for the entrance hall at Holkham, the ancestral home acquired long ago by his distant relative, Sir Edward. Chantrey chose the signing of *Magna Carta*, overseen by the various heroes of 1832, including Thomas.[119] The *alpha* and the *omega* of English constitutional history, the beginning and the 'finality'. The reformation done at least, the break with Rome completed. For now.

We can move forward, to 1884, and the passage of what would prove to be the third in a sequence of 'reform' acts. And the year which followed, which saw the publication of the first edition of a text entitled *An Introduction to the Study of the Law of the Constitution*. The authorised version of the 'modern' Anglo-British constitution, at the heart of which was the argument that, in the absence of a written document, the attention of the law student should be redirected towards certain principles. Two in particular, parliamentary sovereignty and the rule of law. And both supposedly enshrined by the close of the seventeenth century. The author of the *Study*, Albert Venn Dicey, was a Tory in his politics. In his history, though, he was entirely the Whig.

And a bit of fantasist, at least according to his revisionist critics, his *Study* a testament to nothing more than high 'Victorian self-assurance'.[120] Traduced by the advance of globalisation, time has not been kind to Dicey. It is 'difficult, if not impossible', as Francis Jacobs has recently averred, 'to identify a State in which a sovereign legislature is not subject to legal limitations on the exercise of its powers'.[121] A thought to which we will shortly return. But if parliamentary sovereignty has lost some of its charm, outside Westminster at least, the same cannot be said of the rule of law. In the absence of which it remains almost impossible to talk sensibly of constitutional legality. Dicey, famously, gave the rule three meanings. First, that 'no man is punishable ... except for a distinct breach of law established in the ordinary legal manner'. Second, that 'no man is above the law'. And third, that the rule pervades the 'general principles of the constitution'.[122] In a rare moment of poetic fancy, Dicey supposed that the rule of law preserved the 'legal spirit' of

---

[118] Hunt sought to ameliorate a difficult situation by supposing that Shelley's prospective 'public had not become sufficiently discerning to do justice to the sincerity and kind-heartedness of the spirit that walked in this flaming robe of verse'. In Shelley (1971) 345.

[119] Thomas takes centre-stage on the freize, just in front of Lord Grey.

[120] Sedley (2015) 271.

[121] Jacobs (2007) 5.

[122] Dicey (1959) 188–95.

the British constitution. It is difficult to imagine Dicey and Shelley having much in common, politically or temperamentally. This though.

A Common Law Constitution

And not a sentiment from which many contemporary jurists have demurred. On the contrary, a principle which 'must exist in a democratic society', according to Lord Hoffmann.[123] Lord Bingham similarly, supposing that the rule of law is the 'nearest we are likely to approach a secular religion'.[124] A principle, moreover, discovered in the reason of a particular history which can be traced back to *Magna Carta*, and which then encompasses an array of familiar 'constitutional' statutes, including Coke's *Petition*, the English Bill of Rights, and the American. A 'lineal' descent, as Bingham puts it.[125] The same descent that Sir Stephen Sedley revisits, struck by the 'continuity of the river of jurisprudence which flows from' Coke and his judicial colleagues 'to us'.[126]

Dicey's imputation again, supposing that the interpretive principle of legality is a 'special attribute' of English constitutional history. Voiced by Lord Wilkinson in the *Fire Brigades Union* case:

> The constitutional history of this country is the history of the prerogative powers of the Crown being made subject to the overriding powers of the democratically elected legislature as the sovereign body.[127]

An imputation, moreover, which tempts Sedley to make a rather greater claim. That whilst all laws might be procedurally 'equal', some are 'constitutionally more equal than others'.[128] Something that Dicey might have relished rather less. But which has also gained judicial traction in recent years. In cases such as *HS2*, for example, in which Lord Neuberger and Lord Mance recognised the primacy of certain 'constitutional instruments', the rule of law especially.[129]

There is a more reserved position here, and a less. The more reserved supposes that certain principles of 'legality' might hold, unless expressly denied by statute. The intent to override such principles must, as Lord Sumption puts it, be 'squarely' declared.[130] The less reserved supposes that they hold regardless. As Lord Steyn imputed in *Jackson*, recognising in parliamentary sovereignty the 'general principle

---

[123] *R (Alconbury Developments) v Secretary of State for the Environment, Transport and the Regions* [2001] UKHL 23, para 73.

[124] Bingham (2010) 174.

[125] Bingham (2010) 17.

[126] Sedley (2015) 2, 124.

[127] *R v Secretary of State for the Home Dept ex p Fire Brigades Union* [1995] 2 AC 513 (HL) 552.

[128] Sedley (2015) 118.

[129] *R (on the application of HS2 Action Alliance) v Secretary of State for Transport* [2014] UKSC 3, 207–08.

[130] Sumption (2020) 35–36.

of our constitution', but confirming that it was at root a 'construct of the common law' and a 'principle' that 'judges' had 'created'. Before moving on to suppose that, in 'exceptional circumstances', where a Parliament looked to 'abolish' a 'constitutional fundamental', the 'new Supreme Court may have to consider' the possibility of striking down that legislation.[131] In blunt terms, in 'such exceptional cases, the rule of law may trump parliamentary supremacy'.[132] A 'silent step' towards a British *Marbury v Madison*, Sedley teases.[133]

Or back, perhaps, to *Prohibitions* and *Proclamations*. History calibrates the idea of a 'common law constitution', realising the 'historical and practical wisdom of the common law', as Trevor Allan puts it.[134] A Burkean resonance, of course. The English constitution as the 'collected reason of ages'.[135] Echoes of Shelley too, 'children of a wiser day', and Tennyson, and Coke. There is a surface difference, considerable and not, between the rationale deployed in cases such as *Proclamations* and the reasoning discovered in *Jackson*. The former presumed to protect the King, in essence from himself. The latter presumed to protect Parliament, in essence from itself.[136] For the reason Lord Hope expressed in *Jackson*, that parliamentary sovereignty becomes an 'empty principle if legislation is passed which is so absurd or so unacceptable that the populace at large refuses to recognise it at large'.[137] We might recall Lord Acton's renowned adage; 'power corrupts, and absolute power corrupts absolutely'. A sentiment which has lost little of its prescience over the last century and a half, and which we will revisit in due course, when we drop in on the Supreme Court in late summer 2019, on this occasion to see how ready it was to protect Parliament against an executive which sought to 'abolish' another kind of 'constitutional fundamental'. Very ready, it transpired.

The idea that principles of 'legality' might be discovered in a species of 'common law constitutionalism' chimes, as we have already imputed, with the thought that these same principles might be entrenched in certain 'primary' statutes. Something which imports a collateral supposition: that, consonant with their elevated status, such statutes might only be repealed expressly. At which point there is a parlour game to be enjoyed, hazarding which statutes might fall into this category. Coke would surely have vouched for *Magna Carta* and, more than likely, his own *Petition*, and its offspring, the Bill of Rights. The lineal descent favoured by Bingham too, as we have already noted. And Maitland, who cited the 'great Charter' as the 'nearest approach to an unrepealable fundamental statute that England ever had'.[138] Other possibilities, from various moments in constitutional

---

[131] [2005] UKHL 56, para 102. By way of example, Steyn cited any attempt to abolish judicial review. For discussions here, see Sedley (2015) 145–46; and also Allan (2011) 156–57, 161–62.

[132] Bogdanor (2021) 164.

[133] See Sedley (2015) 149. Allan prefers a more abrasive metaphor, suggesting that Steyn was 'driven to threaten a judicial revolt'. In (2011) 156.

[134] Allan (2001) 20.

[135] Burke (1985) 116–18.

[136] Allan (2011) 160–62.

[137] Para 120.

[138] In Sumption (2021) 28.

history, might include the original Act in Restraint of Appeals, and the successive reform acts of 1832 and 1867.

And then various more recent candidates. Such as the 1972 European Communities Act. The thought was raised, perhaps most strikingly, by Lord Justice Laws in *Thoburn*, the case of the so-called 'metric martyrs'. Laws defined a 'constitutional statute' as one which 'conditions the legal relationship' of 'citizen and state', or 'enlarges or diminishes the scope of what we would now regard as fundamental constitutional rights'.[139] The 1972 Act is gone now, of course, for which reason it is difficult to assess the extent to which it might have represented a 'quantum leap' from a historical to a legal constitution. In its moment perhaps.[140] There again, history will likely confirm that it was, at the end of the day, just another statute that came and went.

Other possibilities might be discovered amidst the 'stack of statutes' which comprised the constitutional reform package introduced by the 'new' Labour government in 1998. To include a series of devolution statutes, a Freedom of Information Act, a House of Lords Act, and a Human Rights Act. The latter, which incorporated the European Convention on Human Rights, is perhaps best placed to make a claim to elevated 'constitutional' status, seeming to entrench a series of 'fundamental rights' in UK law.[141] The 'cornerstone' of a 'new constitution', it has been supposed.[142] Or maybe an old, a revitalised 'historical constitution'.[143] Either way, creating, as Lord Steyn put it, a 'rights-based democracy':

> Parliament does not legislate in a vacuum. Parliament legislates for a European liberal democracy founded on the principles and traditions of the common law and the courts may approach legislation on the initial assumption.[144]

If anyone was much surprised by what Lord Steyn had to say seven years later in *Jackson*, they had not been paying attention. Likewise Lord Bingham's warm embrace of a 'thick' conception of human rights, the court as 'guarantor of legality and individual right' in even the most testing of moments.[145] Though whether the 1998 Act did anything more than provide statutory reinforcement for rights already enshrined in the common law is another question. Indeed, it has been suggested that the longer history of the Human Rights Act might be traced back to a now familiar place: the writings of Sir Edward Coke.[146]

Seven years after the Human Rights Act came the Constitutional Reform Act. Amongst its provisions was the establishment of a Supreme Court, removed from the House of Lords. A piece of stage-dressing designed to bring UK judicial

---

[139] [2003] QB 151, para 62.
[140] As suggested by Bogdanor (2021) 85–86.
[141] See Sumption (2020) 55–56.
[142] McConalogue (2020) 47–48.
[143] Allison (2007) 221–28.
[144] *R v Secretary of State for the Home Dept ex p Pierson* [1998] AC 539.
[145] See Bingham (2010) 66–84.
[146] See Sedley (2015) 194–97, noting the 'incremental' adaptation of 'human rights' in English law prior to 1998, and again at 207–08, tracing a longer history back to Coke.

procedure in line with Article 6 of the Convention, the right to a 'fair trial' held before an 'impartial tribunal'. In the spirit of Chapter 29 of *Magna Carta*, as well as later notions of 'separate powers' championed by the likes of Locke and Montesquieu.[147] There can be 'no liberty', the latter famously supposed, 'if the power of judgment be not separated from the legislative and executive powers'.[148] There was no evidence that the presence of the 'Law Lords' in the House of Lords had resulted in any substantive injustice, but it looked wrong.[149] Thus section 3 of the Constitutional Reform Act, establishing the new Court. And section 8 too, which makes specific mention of the rule of law as a defining 'constitutional principle'.[150] And the possibility that Parliament might have enacted another constitutional statute which matters that little bit more.

We might wonder what Dicey would have made of it all, Coke too. Dicey, famously, rejected the idea that some statutes mattered more than others. In his opinion, 'neither the Act of Union with Scotland, nor the Dentists Act 1878, has more claim than any other to be considered a supreme law'.[151] Coke might have taken a different view, particularly with statutes which appeared to affirm principles already discovered in the common law, such as his cherished *Magna Carta*, or his own *Petition*. He would certainly have appreciated the thought that it is for the judges to make the pick. As he would the sentiment discovered in William Wade's rejoinder. That the 'seat of sovereign power is not to be discovered by looking at the Acts of any Parliament but by looking at the courts and discovering to whom they give their obedience'.[152] A species of what might be termed 'judicial sovereignty', or maybe just plain common sense.[153]

In this context, we might reflect upon one relatively recent instance of judicial assertiveness which could, in part perhaps, be attributed to raising the spirit of legality. It engages a fear that was very familiar in Jacobean England: that of the religiously motivated terrorist.[154] James had his witches and his 'Powder' plotters, we have our Islamic 'fundamentalists'. Evidently abounding in the wake of '9/11', and certainly scary enough to warrant a range of draconian counter-terrorist measures. To include, on this side of the Atlantic, the shooting of darker-skinned men wearing unseasonable clothing, and the enactment of legislation intended

---

[147] For a comment on the place of *Magna Carta* in our 'constitutional culture', and more particularly chapter 29, and the idea of 'separate powers', see Sedley (2015) 177–78.

[148] Montesquieu (1989) 135–36.

[149] As indeed the European Court of Human Rights had inferred. See *McGonnell v UK* (2000) 30 EHRR 289.

[150] Section 1 provides that nothing in Act should be taken as compromising the principle, whilst section 17.1 requires the Lord Chancellor to take an oath, in assuming office, to protect it. For a comment here, see Bingham (2010) 7.

[151] Dicey (1959) 145.

[152] Wade (1955) 196.

[153] McConalogue (2020) 50.

[154] As Sunstein concludes, by 'its very nature, fear is selective'. See (2005) 224. And also Stampnitzky (2013) 3–5, noting that we are just as readily terrorised by the 'counter-terrorist' as by the 'terrorist'. A riff on the discomforting truism that 'one man's terrorist is another man's freedom fighter'.

to permit the indeterminate detention of suspected terrorists without trial.[155] Amongst the latter, who found themselves incarcerated under the terms of section 2.12 of part 4 of the 2001 Anti-Terrorism, Crime and Security Act, were the so-called 'Belmarsh detainees', who decided to challenge their detention, as being in breach of Articles 5 and 14 of the European Convention.[156] With a certain leap of historical imagination, we might imagine them in much the same predicament as the clients in whose cause Nicholas Fuller pleaded in 1607, or the 'five knights' whose case caused such a commotion two decades later.

Whilst the Appeal Court demurred in the case of the 'Belmarsh detainees', the House of Lords delivered a blistering ruling against the government, the rhetoric of which reached far beyond the supposed breach of the Convention Articles in question. The statutory provisions were an evident affront to the rule of law and centuries of 'libertarian tradition', according to Lord Bingham.[157] 'Stalinist', according to Lord Scott.[158] The 'antithesis of the right to liberty', according to Baroness Hale, adding that 'unwarranted declarations of emergency' are the 'familiar tools of tyranny'.[159] But it was Lord Hoffmann's opinion that really resounded:

> The real threat to the life of the nation, in the sense of a people living in accordance with its traditional laws and political values, comes not from terrorism but from laws such as these. That is the true measure of what terrorism may achieve. It is for Parliament to decide whether to give the terrorists such a victory.[160]

Lord Hoffmann already had form, in the shape of his renowned opinion in *Simms*. The 'principle of legality', means that 'fundamental rights cannot be overridden by general or ambiguous words'. Absent 'express language or necessary implication to the contrary' a court must 'presume that even the most general words were intended to be subject to the basic rights of the individual'.[161]

It might be fanciful to suppose that the ghost of Sir Edward Coke could be seen smirking in the background, as the House delivered its opinion. Coke was happy enough torturing terrorists when the circumstances demanded.[162] But he would surely have admired the rhetoric. Invocations of the 'great' Charter could be heard across the Atlantic too, in similar post-9/11 cases which reached the US Supreme Court. Justice Souter musing in *Hamdi*, for example, Justice Stevens in

---

[155] The tragic fate of the Brazilian electrician Jean-Charles de Menezes, shot dead on the London Underground by armed police in 2005, because he was wearing an anorak on a warm day, and looked a bit dodgy.

[156] Article 5 protects the 'liberty' and security' of individuals, whilst Article 14 prohibits discrimination on a variety of grounds, including gender, race and religion. The detainees were held at Belmarsh prison in north London.

[157] *A, X and Y v Secretary of State for the Home Department* [2002] EWCA Civ 1502, paras 36, 41.

[158] Para 155.

[159] Paras 222, 226.

[160] Para 97.

[161] *R v Secretary of State for the Home Dept ex p Simms* [2000] 2 AC 115 (HL).

[162] The extent to which Coke might have been party to the 'examination' of captured Powder plotters remains a moot. He was certainly happy to use evidence gleaned from these examinations in court. A tactic of otherwise dubious legality. Torture was, in theory at least, forbidden in the common law.

Padilla affirming that 'unconstrained executive detention for the purpose of investigating and preventing subversive activities is the hallmark of the Star Chamber'. Government must not be allowed to 'wield the tools of tyranny', no matter how great the threat.[163]

Fine words, on a familiar loop. As a previous Supreme Court Justice, William Brennan, had noted nearly 40 years before. Each time a crisis is perceived, the instinct of modern government is to panic, and brush aside 'civil liberties'. And then, a little later, when it realises that doing so was 'unnecessary' and wrong, it will express a degree of tacit remorse.[164] Leaving everyone to wait for the next time, when it will do exactly the same again. The next terrorist attack, the next nasty virus, the next flotilla of immigrant-laden dinghies.

The New Jurisprudence

James has his Rubens, Coke his bronze relief. If we want a different impression of Sir Francis Bacon, we might pay a visit to Stowe gardens, more precisely its Temple of British Worthies, completed in 1736. Where we will find 16 demi-busts of great Britons, selected by the then owner of the estate, Sir Richard Temple. Eight warriors and eight thinkers. Bacon is amongst the latter, along with the likes of Shakespeare, Milton and Pope. Temple was a Whig, but his Worthies are a various bunch, the selection criteria evincing some historical latitude. In Bacon's case, the reputation for progressive thinking mattered more than the political prejudice. As did the seeming prophetic acuity. The apologist for absolutism had, by the early eighteenth century, become a prospective hero of the Enlightenment, and beyond. 'Prophetic of a world', as Pierre Zagorin surmises, 'in which science was to become a great power in shaping humanity's course'.[165]

The Seeker

Bacon too had his contemporary admirers. We noted his secretary's glowing testimonial earlier. Jonson likewise, effusive in his 'reverence' for 'one of the greatest men, and most worthy of admiration'. Like many, impressed by Bacon's rhetorical skills: 'No man ever spake more neatly, more pressly, more weightily'.[166] Darling of the courtroom, and the Court; at least up until 1621. It is even possible to read Shakespeare's *Tempest* as a testament to a 'brave new' intellectual as well as

---

[163] See *Hamdi v Rumsfeld* 124 S Ct 263 (2004) 2655, 2659; and *Rumsfeld v Padilla* 124 S Ct 2711 (2004) 2735.

[164] Brennan (1988) 11.

[165] Zagorin (1998) 124.

[166] Jonson was a consistent friend, enjoining Bacon's determination to sweep away the 'cobwebs' of the schoolmen. See Donaldson (2011) 378–79.

physical world. There again, it might be just as easily read as a caution against a species of 'rough magic' which seems little distinguishable from the darker arts of witchery.[167] Others, disapproving of character, were rather more acerbic in their recollection of Sir Francis Bacon. An inveterate 'pederast', according to Aubrey, like his King. Sir Simonds D'Ewes took similar exception, condemning a man of 'stupendous vices', of which the seduction of young boys was only the 'most abominable'.[168]

As the generations passed, a particular feint would become familiar. There may have been much in the politics, and the personality, of Sir Francis Bacon which was less than endearing, to historians of a Whiggish persuasion particularly, but the mind was worth saving. Albeit not to Churchill, who tartly dismissed a toady whose 'theories were unreal and widely unpopular'. The template was set by Lord Macaulay, in a long essay published in 1837, reviewing Basil Montagu's 16-volume *Collected Works of Francis Bacon*.[169] Recognising the foremost legal philosopher of his age, whilst admitting his 'lamentable' lack of personal integrity, his 'coldness of heart and meanness of spirit', Macaulay tried to detach Bacon 'seeking for the truth' from Bacon 'seeking for the Seals'. Sadly, Bacon the lawyer fell into the latter category, a man who perverted 'the laws of England' to 'the vilest purposes of tyranny'.[170] The 'years during which Bacon held the Great Seal', Macaulay concluded, taking particular exception to his role in the execution of Sir Walter Raleigh, 'were among the darkest and most shameful in English history'.[171] If the educated Victorian gentleman wanted a comparable figure drawn from classical history, Macaulay suggested that they might consider Seneca. An allusion Bacon would have appreciated, even if he did not appreciate much else in Macaulay's extended character-assassination. He also suggested that if Bacon had been more 'moderate' in his 'civil ends', he might have been 'the Joshua of philosophy'.[172] Sadly, he was not, in either regard.

The ghost of Francis Bacon continued to walk the jurisprudential landscape of seventeenth-century England. Raised by Benjamin Nicholson in his *Lawyer's Bane*, published in 1647, which recommended the establishment of a permanent parliamentary commission for the 'Reformation' of the law, a thing for which all lawyers 'cry aloud'.[173] Present in both republican and restoration England too. A *Vindication of the Law as it is now Established*, published in 1659, recommended

---

[167] When Prospero wants to force matters, he seeks recourse to precisely the same strategy as the North Berwick witches; raise a storm and sink a ship. For the ambivalences which attent to Prospero's 'magic', see Raffield (2017) 209–13.

[168] See Zagorin (1998) 12.

[169] In the letter to the editor of the *Edinburgh Review*, Macaulay apologised for the 'interminable length' of his essay on Bacon. But he had 'never bestowed such care on anything that I have written'. There is a necessary irony in the fact that, in reviewing someone who tried to write too much, Macaulay ended up doing precisely the same. See Wormald (2021) 19.

[170] Macaulay (1837) 23, 30, 35.

[171] Macaulay (1837) 42.

[172] Macaulay (1837) 103–04.

[173] In Shapiro (2019) 114.

a distinctly Baconian programme of moderate reform. A process of 'pruning and grafting the Law', rather than ploughing 'and planting it again', to be celebrated in a concise set of reports and supplementary texts purposed for the 'Study and Science of the Law'.[174] A year later, a text entitled *New Atlantis begun by Lord Verulum* appeared, pretending to finish Bacon's original work which had been interrupted by an 'interregnum of tyranny and oppression'. Charles II, the author supposed, now presented as 'our Solomon, our second Justinian'.[175] Tangential reference, too, in another anonymous tract entitled *Ius Gentium or England's Birthright*, published in the same year, which recommended a reinvestment of King James's reform programme, in order to rid the law of 'delay, overburdening and deluding litigants'.[176]

Here again, it was a matter of detaching the progressive, and indeed prophetic, Bacon. Lauded by Vico, gently parodied in Swift's *Gulliver's Travels*, precisely for his faith in progress.[177] The 'father of modern science' according to Voltaire.[178] Guiding light of the Royal Society, the 'hero' of the 'scientific revolution' admired by Robert Hooke.[179] Bishop Sprat's *History of the Royal Society of London*, published in 1667, started with the author of *New Atlantis*, the man who had projected the possibility of reasoning all human endeavour.[180] And who, Edward Gibbon intimated, might also have founded modern jurisprudence: a thought to which we will shortly return. Gibbon compared him to the Roman jurist Tribonian, *quaestor* of the palace under Justinian, a man who 'embraced as his own all the business and knowledge of his age'.[181] A reasonable comparison. We can certainly imagine Bacon embracing an invitation to help write up the *Digest*, particularly if he was in charge. And Gibbon can be forgiven for looking a long way back in order to anticipate the future. His *Decline and Fall of the Roman Empire* was supposed to be read in the present tense.

The idea that law might be comprehended as a science was hardly new of course, as we have already noted. Not just '*scientia*' but '*scientificissima*', as Sir Henry Finch put it.[182] A suggestive emphasis, resonant, but also requiring of some mediation. Zeal rarely appeals to modern sensibilities, liberal especially, and Bacon was no less zealous in his jurisprudential faith. An 'authoritarian, not a totalitarian', it has been hazarded, in slightly compromised mitigation, pioneer

---

[174] In Shapiro (2019) 157–58.
[175] In Shapiro (2019) 181.
[176] Shapiro (2019) 181.
[177] The parody more closely centred on *New Atlantis*. For Vico's admiration, see Wormald (1993) 338, 342–46.
[178] An appraisal moderated by his collateral observation that whilst 'Bacon proposed new sciences; but Copernicus and Kepler invented them'. See Wormald (1993) 26; and also Zagorin (1998) 31.
[179] Whose laws of elasticity and displacement, and very long equations, have survived to torture generations of physics students. For a questioning commentary on Bacon as the 'father' of modern science, and Hooke's admiration for the 'incomparable Verulam', see Wormald (1993) 1, 26–27, 361.
[180] Porter (2000) 131–32.
[181] In Wormald (1993) 136.
[182] Klinck (2010) 181.

of a jurisprudence that is resolutely 'secular, utilitarian and progressive'.[183] And not always fashionable. For which reason Bacon needs periodic refurbishment. Thus a 'universalist' too, a cosmopolitan perhaps; another claim to which we will shortly return.[184] Far more appealing. As was the voice of reason appreciated by Ranke, who particularly admired the 'calm wisdom' found in the *Essays*.[185] Writing in much the same moment, as the nineteenth century drew to a close, Samuel Rawson Gardiner limited himself to the historical Bacon, granting him a walk-on part in his magisterial *History of England from the Accession of James I to the Outbreak of the Civil War*. Gardiner's Bacon was a man who had 'entered into the spirit of the future growth of the constitution'; by which he meant someone who had appreciated an incipient principle of separate constitutional powers.[186] A harbinger of revolution even.[187]

Holdsworth was more effusive still. A 'more complete lawyer than any of his contemporaries', Coke included. A 'great juridical thinker', who comprehended the law, common and civil, 'scientifically and critically'.[188] Another near-contemporary, Roscoe Pound, likewise credited Bacon with making the 'first tentative' step 'towards systematic generalization'. Rather than simply recovering scattered bits of law, Bacon had determined that there should be 'general principles for legal reasoning, reached by analysis and comparison of the rules, and by which the rules themselves must presently be tried'.[189] By the end of the twentieth century it was possible to suppose that Bacon's idea of law was not only redeemable, but truly prophetic. Someone who appreciated, from bitter personal experience, the hazards of uppity judges, but who also recognised that 'the state itself must operate within the law'.[190] Almost a Whig it might be said, well worth a niche and a demi-bust.

The Science of Law

In 1739, David Hume published the first part of his *Treatise of Human Nature*. The subtitle was 'An Attempt to Introduce the Experimental Method of Reasoning into Moral Subjects'.[191] A paean to the 'Baconian programme', so Roy Porter supposes, and the greater ambition of the Enlightenment.[192] Heralding the age of the rationalist. And the age of the sceptic. People even started wondering if

---

[183] Coquillette (1992) 286, 291.
[184] See Coquillette (1992) 295, suggesting that Bacon was one of only two genuine early modern English cosmopolitans. The other being Hooker.
[185] A 'treasure for the English nation', he added. See Wormald (1993) 212.
[186] Wormald (1993) 22.
[187] Trevor-Roper (1967) 84.
[188] Holdsworth (1903) 5. 239.
[189] In Coquillette (1992) 47–48.
[190] Sedley (2015) 124.
[191] Harris (2015) 84–85.
[192] Porter (2000) 56–57, 131–32.

witches really existed. Sorcery hardly made sense, save perhaps for the economic. In the *Spectator*, Joseph Addison recalled a not-so-distant past when the country had been possessed 'with extravagant Fancies, imaginary Distempers, and terrifying Dreams', and inclined to declare any old woman a witch once she had become 'chargeable to a Parish'.[193] The age of the rule-maker too. Samuel Johnson published his *Dictionary* in 1754. Seven years later, Joseph Priestley published *The Rudiments of Grammar*, so that everyone could string all the words together. Fifteen years on, the Marylebone Cricket Club confirmed its first set of 'rules'. The year 1728 saw Batty Langley's *New Principles of Gardening* first appear; more rules, and lots of measurements. Nineteen years later, Langley published *Gothic Architecture, Improved by Rules and Proportions*. Rules for everything. Scientific, political, economic, even poetic. A young Shelley declared himself 'completely captivated' by the 'new' science, and set about writing 'Prometheus Unbound'.[194]

Likewise a young Jeremy Bentham, thoroughly excited by a 'philosophy' which was so evidently suited to the 'busy age', and which held out the possibility of finding a 'method of becoming master of everything'.[195] Another avowed Baconian; '*fiat lux* were the words of the Almighty – *fiat experimentum*, were the words of the brightest genius he ever made'.[196] Even happiness might be calibrated, according to Bentham, by means of a 'calculus of felicity'.[197] The law improved too, as 'perfectible' as anything else.[198] And in such evident need. He famously likened the common law to 'dog law'; because like dogs, the poor only discovered what they had done wrong when they were beaten by their masters.[199] In his *Fragment on Government*, published in 1776, Bentham concentrated his ire on 'Mother' Blackstone and his *Commentaries*. More especially still, on the belief that 'everything' was 'as it should be'.[200] A complacency founded on the myriad historical 'fictions' which comprised the common law.[201] The 'yoke of custom'.[202]

Bentham's disdain for those who would set the law in historical aspic was matched by his disdain for those who would have it pronounced by moral philosophers, or worse still 'religionists'.[203] Thus the famous observation, reminiscent of

---

[193] In Porter (2000) 220–21.

[194] In Porter (2000) 143.

[195] Bentham (1988) 3; and also Porter (2000) 14 and 421–22, commenting on the 'bouyant pragmatism' of the moment.

[196] Mack (1962) 129.

[197] Bentham (1982) 38–41.

[198] Even if it meant that once the law had aided in the 'perfectibility' of society, it would no longer be needed. The irreducible logic of William Godwin, darling of the English Jacobins, and author of *An Enquiry Concerning Political Justice*. See Ward (2019) 277–79.

[199] For a commentary here, see Postema (2019) 192–93, 277.

[200] Bentham (1988) 10, 74–75.

[201] Bentham (1982) 8–9. For a commentary on Bentham's disdain for legal fictions, see Postema (1986) 271–73, 286.

[202] As he would later term it in his 1817 *Plan of Parliamentary Reform*. In Porter (2000) 417–18. See also Postema (1986) 286.

[203] Who would prefer to leave matters of law and governance in the 'hands of a splenetic and revengeful Deity'. See Bentham (1982) 18–21.

Machiavelli, that the jurist should be interested in what law is, rather than what it 'ought' to be.[204] The positive jurist acting as a 'censor', not an 'expositor'. There was nothing wrong with contemplating the morality of law. But it was something for moral philosophers to do, not lawyers. Law should make present sense, not a sense discovered in a hazy past, or a still hazier metaphysics. And it was certainly not something given by God, or kings. Or indeed history, at least not in an uncritical sense.[205]

Most urgently, if law was to be properly 'perfected' for the utility of its users, and comprehended by them, it must be clearly stated. Ideally codified. There was little Bentham enjoyed more than writing a draft legal code.[206] So that no judge should ever have to make Lord Goff's renowned admission in 1993: knowing that there was supposed to be a 'boundary' between the respective jurisdictions of the judge and legislator, but confessing that he was 'never quite sure where to find it'.[207] A measure of interpretive latitude might be accepted in any jurisprudence, but endemic confusion could not. If Bentham had won the argument, English law might have looked very different today, the constitution too. But he did not. The moment was inauspicious, the intellectual Enlightenment perceived by many to be the midwife of political revolution.

Writing in the immediate context of the French Revolution in 1789, Edmund Burke inscribed a fierce defence of the common law constitution. An 'entailed inheritance', the binding expression of a 'partnership not only between those who are living, but between those who are living, those who are dead, and those who are to be born'. A constitution which enshrines a 'presumption in favour' of a 'settled scheme of government against any untried project'.[208] A stark contrast with the new French Constitution, which had been designed by 'money-jobbers' in 'giddy coffee-houses'. An exercise in 'abstract perfection'. Modelled in other words.[209] We can conjecture what he might have made of Sir Robert Peel's later citation of Bacon's *Proposition* in support of criminal law reform in 1828. The 'lapse of 25 years', Peel informed his fellow parliamentarians, 'has increased the necessity of the measure which Lord Bacon then proposed, but it has produced no argument in favour of the principle, no object adverse to it, which he did not anticipate'.[210]

---

[204] Bentham (1982) 13.

[205] Postema (1986) 165, 304.

[206] At various stages offering his service, more commonly for the drafting of penal codes, to Greece, Columbia, Grenada, Guatemala and the Argentine. For a comment on Bentham's belief in the value of 'comprehensive' legal codes, see Postema (1986) 424–26.

[207] *Woolwich Equitable Building Society v Inland Revenue Commissioners* [1993] C 70, 173.

[208] Burke (1985) 119, 194–95. For a broader commentary on Burke's 'prescriptive' constitution, see Pocock (1960).

[209] Burke (1985) 138, 150–51, 164 and 294–96, for a merciless ridiculing of the constitutional modellers.

[210] Coquillette (1992) 115.

The conversation would rumble on through the nineteenth century. We can catch a differing glimpse in the constitutional writings of Bagehot and Dicey. What is most notable, at first glance, is the extent to which both seem to be persuaded by utility. A matter of national character, according to Bagehot, the English being 'perhaps the least a nation of pure philosophers'.[211] As for history, whilst there are various referents scattered about his *English Constitution*, and a closing essay that chases through a thousand years of assorted events, there is certainly no reverence of the kind which saturates Burke's *Reflections*. Bagehot's *Constitution* is an exercise in comparative legal science. As is Dicey's *Introduction to the Study of the Law of the Constitution*, albeit with less evident interest in comparativism.[212] But to suppose that neither was inclined to adopt an historical methodology, is not to say that their writings were anything other than historical.

On the contrary, both were steeped in the collected prejudices of two centuries of Whig historiography. Celebrations of the 'friends of freedom', as Dicey termed the 'glorious' revolutionaries of 1688, who had triumphed against both the 'tyranny of the Stuarts' and the 'fanatics for the common law'.[213] Moreover, both treatises were products of historical moment as well as historical prejudice. Bagehot wrote the first edition of his *Constitution* to counsel against the risks which attached to another reform bill, as well as a retiring monarch. Five years later, in 1872, he bolted a vituperative 'Preface' onto the second edition just so that he could tell everyone he was right. Dicey published his *Constitution* in the immediate aftermath of the third Reform Act, which had been passed by Parliament the year before, in 1884. It was not tempered in quite the same way as Bagehot's 'Preface', but it was supposed to be read in the same spirit. The last thing Dicey wanted was further reform, to anything: the right to vote, the rights of women, the rights of workers.

Moments of crisis, or so they were perceived by their contemporaries. Like 1616, or 1688, or 1787, the so-called Philadelphia 'moment'. Or 1790 of course, the moment which reduced Burke to splenetic fury.[214] Or 1992, perhaps, the moment when the European Union invented itself, proclaiming the next stage in an 'ever closer union among the peoples of Europe'.[215] Or 2016, when the United Kingdom decided to reverse the process: a moment, and a consequence, we will revisit very shortly.[216] The pending collapse of the 'united' kingdom, another prospective to which we will return, providing a further prospective stimulus. A moment of constitutional renewal, driven by necessity if not design. Like each and every other moment of constitutional renewal in Anglo-British history.

---

[211] Bagehot (2001) 42.

[212] Allison (2007) 8.

[213] Dicey (1959) 379–80. For a commentary on Dicey's 'highly selective' use of history, see Allison (2007) 157, 166–76, surmising the particular influence of Samuel Rawson Gardiner.

[214] Siedentop (2011).

[215] The phrase 'ever closer union', found in original form in the European Community Treaty of 1957, was reinvested in the Preamble to the Treaty on European Union in 1992. The difference being the emphasis on the 'peoples' rather than nation-states.

[216] See Bogdanor (2021) 245, 273–78.

There is, though, an attendant risk to which we have already averted. Moments are precisely that, transient and contingent.[217] Moreover, they like to enshrine themselves; the 'glorious' revolution of 1688, the 'glorious cause' of 1776. Something which invites a collateral risk; the dead hand of the past reaching into the present. The ferocity of the debate which continues to move around the role of the 'Framers' in the interpretation of the US Constitution is testament to the difficulties which can ensue when a reasoned appreciation of the past slips into blind devotion. No constitution, written or other, can be preserved in the aspic of the past. History forbids it.[218] An abiding irony.

General Jurisprudence

In recent decades it has become fashionable to contemplate, once again, the possibilities of a 'general' jurisprudence. The familiar temptation to somehow transcend contingencies, and to do so by means of concentrating on matters of methodology. The familiar sleight too, dependent on accepting that such matters can be detached from knottier questions of moral and political substance. Here again, later generations of legal positivists have commonly felt obliged to admit what Herbert Hart famously referred to as a 'minimum content' of natural law in their jurisprudence.[219] A partial concession, at least, to arguments considered in his renowned engagement with the American jurist Lon Fuller in the 1957 *Harvard Law Review*. In considering the 'legality' of 'bad' law, Hart and Fuller seized on the example of anti-Semitic legislation enacted in Nazi Germany. Was this still law?

Not according to Lord Simon in the case of *Oppenheimer v Cattermole*: 'In my mind a law of this sort constitutes so grave an infringement of human rights that the courts of this country ought to refuse to recognise it as a law at all'.[220] It is of course a variant of the question which exercised Lord Hoffmann in the 'Belmarsh detainees' case, and which has exercised jurists for millenia, ever since Aristotle tempted posterity with the thought that the purpose of law, like indeed the purpose of life, was to 'aim at some good'.[221] And the collateral supposition, more famous still, that 'justice' is itself a necessary good, 'not a part of virtue but the whole of it'.[222] Law that fails to facilitate this good is not, therefore, law at all. Not for reasons that are visceral, but for reasons that are rational.

The extent to which Bacon might be termed a natural lawyer remains contested; as indeed is the case with Coke. He certainly approved Aristotelian natural philosophy, and the scientific method which underpinned Aristotelian ethics.

---

[217] Sumption (2021) 216–17.
[218] See here Allison (2007) 235; and also, commenting more closely on the sacral veneration of the US Constitution, O'Brien (1996) 323.
[219] Hart (1961).
[220] [1976] AC 249, 277–78.
[221] Aristotle (1976) 63.
[222] Aristotle (1976) 174.

For which reason the logic that aligns law, justice and procedural fairness might have appealed, the application of so-called principles of 'natural justice'. And given what we know of Bacon's intellectual ambition, there is little surprise in discovering that he was attracted to the idea of a 'law of laws'. In *De Augmentis*, moreover, he wrote approvingly of the merits of washing the 'laws of particular states' in the purifying 'fountain of justice'. So that 'we may derive information as to the good or ill set down and determined in every law'.[223] As ever, though, it is a matter of practice and comparative experience; of the *a posteriori* rather than the *a priori*.[224] The job of the jurist is to determine which laws work best. At this point we might reasonably wonder if Bacon would have found as much to admire in Bentham as in Blackstone.

It is this thought which invites us to contemplate the idea of 'general' jurisprudence. Not least because a first 'modern' expression is commonly discerned in Bentham.[225] And then fleshed out in the *Province of Jurisprudence Determined*, the collected lectures of his star pupil, John Austin, published in 1832, and the text which, we are told, 'established the study of jurisprudence in England'.[226] No less contemptuous of the 'senseless fictions' of the common law, Austin advised that any who embarked on its study should gird themselves for a journey into an 'empire of chaos and darkness'.[227] An injunction that presumably rather depressed the lecture-hall mood. To which he added the rider that the shock would be especially grievous to any who had been previously schooled in the 'exact conceptions' of Roman law. Unpatriotic, as well as dampening. The only way to make sense of the law, common or other, is to embrace the spirit of Enlightenment, and Justinian's jurists. More precisely to embrace the 'rapid advancement of science', to observe, to analyse and, on that basis, to reform.[228] It comes as no surprise to discover that Austin was as keen to recommend codification as his mentor. The merest glance at the 'great defects' and 'monstrous evils' of the common law was 'amply sufficient to demonstrate' that 'codification is expedient'. Ultimately, codified rules should be 'the only positive law obtaining in a community'.[229]

As to the renewed interest in 'general' jurisprudence, William Twining puts it down to the experience of globalisation.[230] Whilst the myriad political cultures and philosophical prejudices described in the 'new world order' might seem rather more post-modern, in reality the 'increasingly cosmopolitan' and interconnected

---

[223] Coquillette (1992) 288–91.

[224] Of 'method and utility', as Francis Coquillette puts it, rather than 'charitable intent' (1992) 290.

[225] See Twining (2000) 65–66, 102.

[226] According to Herbert Hart at least. In his introduction to the 1954/1982 edition of the *Province*. For commentaries here, see Rumble (1981) 986–89; and also Tamanaha (2011) 287–88.

[227] A conclusion reached having spent two years in Germany studying comparative civil law. Vogenauer (2005).

[228] Austin (1995) 61–62, 73.

[229] Austin (1985) 2. 669–704.

[230] For an early discussion, quite literally, of the meaning of globalisation, as a political as well as social and economic force, see Hutton and Giddens (2000) 1–51. The need for a strengthened regulatory regime and 'framework of law' is, they conclude, unarguable.

nature of twenty-first-century life makes the 'revival of a more general jurisprudence' entirely consonant. More than ever 'we need a jurisprudence that can transcend jurisdictions and cultures, so far as that is feasible and appropriate, and which can address issues about law from a global and transnational perspective'.[231] Some have supposed that such an exercise might help to facilitate a greater enterprise: the evolution of a sense of 'global citizenship'. This is, though, a rather thicker conception of what a 'brave new world' might look like.[232] The reinvestment of 'general jurisprudence' is more empirical than aspirational, in essence an exercise in comparative modelling.[233] The Baconian tone is more pronounced still in Brian Tamanaha's determination to analyse the 'elements and concepts common to all systems' of law.[234]

The controversy, as ever, attends the drift from methodology to practice. It is one thing to model a 'universal' jurisprudence, another to decorate it with things such as 'universal' rights. Mindful perhaps of George Bernard Shaw's pithy takedown of Immanuel Kant's renowned categorical imperative: 'Do not do unto others as you would that they should do to you. Their tastes may not be the same'.[235] Only the enlightened natural lawyer is really comfortable in going against this advice, even if the approach is couched as a 'metalegal inquiry that concerns universal legal thought, talk and reality'.[236] And there is no evidence that Bacon, notwithstanding his embrace of the 'brave new world', would have gone that far. Neither his broader approval of the idea of *ius gentium*, nor his more particular statements in the case of little Robert Colville, allow us to assume differently. To be less 'insular' in his legal thinking than many of his contemporaries does not make Bacon a Kantian in classical guise.[237]

It just means that he was more interested in how others might get things to work better, or indeed had managed to do so in the past. Especially, it might be supposed, in years 'to consecrate justice'. When, in other words, crises come to a head. Which leads us nicely to our final venture, a journey into our very troubled present, during which we will encounter plenty that would have been familiar to Francis Bacon. Not just some more modellers, but a fair scattering of wicked counsellors and evil witches too, and Roman insurgents. A plague, of course; there is always a plague. And a constitution in crisis. *Plus ca change, plus c'est la meme chose.*

---

[231] Twining (2000) 3, 49.

[232] See Sandel (1996) 341–42.

[233] Twining (2000) 137–40, and also (2002) 99–100 confirming that 'we are in an important sense all comparativists now'.

[234] Tamanaha (2001) xiii, 154–55, 209–11.

[235] Shaw (2004) 251.

[236] For the recalibration of 'general' jurisprudence as a 'meta-legal' endeavour, see Plunkett and Shapiro (2017) particularly 44–51.

[237] On the comparative 'intellectual insularity' of Coke, see Kelley (1974) 32.

Epilogue

We started in England in 1616. It was, Bacon supposed, a 'year to consecrate justice'. Our purpose has been to wonder the enthusiasm and its reason. The simple answer is the resolution of the *Case of Commendams*. The enthusiasm though suggests something more: something that is both personal and political. On the one hand, the events of summer 1616 represented a personal triumph, against a long-standing antagonist. In the moment, Bacon might have reasonably assumed that the career of Sir Edward Coke was finished. In a sense, as we have seen, it was; even if his most important work, in terms of changing the course of English history, was still to come. At the same time, Bacon might also have surmised that the resolution of the case closed an encompassing argument regarding the 'constitution' of England. A moment when perhaps the Reformation settlement was finally 'done', settled in the terms he had advocated on his King's behalf. An 'oven-ready' settlement, we might say.

We might, still more ambitiously perhaps, characterise it as the triumph of the renaissance conception of English kingship over the reformation. Both Bacon and Coke had looked to history for inspiration and authority. But they had looked to different histories. Bacon, following his King, or perhaps leading him, had returned to classical Rome, to recover the spirit of its jurisprudence. James Stuart as the new Augustus, English law as a *ius civile* tempered by principles of *ius gentium*. Coke had looked back into a mistier past, to reinvest the precedents of an 'ancient', and distinctively English, common law. An 'artificial' law fashioned by English judges and English history. The fact that the argument was resolved, in the moment, by brute force would not have diminished Bacon's sense of satisfaction. On the contrary, it vindicated it. James did as Augustus would have done. And, for much the same reason, neither would it perhaps have surprised Coke that much.

It was not, though, simply an argument about England's past or its present. It was also about its future. We have tracked this future through the following three centuries. An impressionistic history of course, like any, because we are looking for something. Or, to revisit another metaphor which we advanced at the outset, we are listening for something, for rhythm and resonance. An ambition which, as we also advertised, tempts us to venture into the still riskier terrain of the present. Four centuries on, is there anything about England in 1616 which resonates today? It is the supposition which, as we noted at the start, animates the endeavour of the micro and anecdotal historian. How far can we reach, how strong is the 'chain of conjecture'?

To engage these questions, we might reacquaint ourselves with a text entitled *A Tour Through the Whole Island of Great Britain*, which appeared between 1724 and 1726. The author was Daniel Defoe, and the *Tour* was devised as an early-day gentleman's 'travel companion', of the kind anticipated in Camden's similarly topographical *Britannia*. A hybrid genre, as Ginzburg has observed, tripping the margins of history and literature, fact and fiction, commonly drawn to anecdote and curiosity.[1] Later contributions would include Boswell's *Journal of a Tour to the Hebrides with Samuel Johnson LLD*, published in 1785, and Laurence Sterne's more whimsical *Sentimental Journey to France and Italy*, which had appeared 17 years earlier.[2] Horizons would, over time, grow. For Defoe in the mid-1720s, however, geographical reach was described by political purpose. The *Tour* was written to introduce the English to their new empire, the 'Kingdom by the Name of Great Britain' as it was proudly described in the recently enacted Act of Union. A constitutionalised 'union of crowns' at last, the dream of James Stuart. Providing its readers with a 'description of the most flourishing and opulent country in the world', the *Tour* sought to make sense of a difficult past, whilst projecting a brilliant future.[3]

We might then wonder what Defoe would have thought of England, and its 'inner' empire, today. Retracing just three journeys, in an appropriately ironic spirit, might give us a clue.

A Reckless Moment

Our first takes us to Kent, the 'garden of England' as Henry VIII termed it.[4] The city of Rochester to be precise. We might, for reasons which will become apparent, have started in Eastleigh or Rotherham or Wythenshawe or South Shields. But Defoe skipped them all. He did though pay a visit to Rochester. The city itself was 'little remarkable', except for 'the ruins of a very old castle, and an ancient but not extraordinary cathedral'. Chatham docks, nearby, was a different matter; ran 'like a well-ordered city'. Defoe was fascinated. If anyone wanted to understand how 'great' Britain managed to run an empire, they only need to spend an afternoon at Chatham docks.[5] Our closer interest is, however, in what happened in Rochester on the late evening of 20 November 2014.

Earlier that day, the inhabitants of Rochester and Strood had voted for a new MP. And they chose Mark Reckless, representing the UK Independence Party. The only thing new about Reckless, in truth, was his party affiliation. He had previously

---

[1] Ginzburg (2012) 116–18.

[2] Boswell would also publish accounts of journeys to *Germany and Switzerland*, and *Italy, Corsica and France*.

[3] Defoe (1986) 43.

[4] Reputedly. The story goes that Henry was so taken by a locally sourced bowl of cherries when visiting Flanders on one occasion, that he ordered the cultivation of a 'garden' dedicated to cultivating English fruit, and suggested Kent.

[5] Defoe (1986) 123–25.

represented the constituency as a Conservative MP. Now though he had defected to a party which, if not exactly new, could certainly be said to be 'up and coming'. Just a month earlier UKIP, as it was more familiarly known, had won its first ever by-election, at Clacton.[6] But Defoe did not go there either. So, Rochester works better for us, our conceit being that there is a common thread running through these various English towns. They all experienced by-elections between 2013 and 2016, and more importantly witnessed significant successes for UKIP. So significant that the governing Conservative Party, and its leader David Cameron, sensed an existential threat. Back in 2006, Cameron had airily dismissed UKIP as a gang of 'fruitcakes, loonies and closet racists'. Perhaps. But the age of the fruitcake, it seemed, had arrived, and the loonies and the closet racists.

Cameron firmed up on a vaguer promise, made the previous year, to hold a referendum on continued membership of the European Union, which was duly enshrined in the manifesto for the 2015 general election.[7] Hindsight supposes a considerable gamble, not just on Cameron's own future, but that of his party, and the country. Cameron though was confident that his compatriots would vote to remain in the European Union.[8] At which point, UKIP would be wizarded away. Perhaps the most significant political misjudgement in British politics since the Suez Crisis, maybe even the Munich Agreement.[9] Not simply because Cameron misread the room, but because referenda are a rubbish way to govern, snapshot glimpses of public opinion, rarely able to present prospective voters with questions that can reflect the complexity of tendentious issues. Referenda are designed, in essence, for those disinclined to think very long or very hard. Dangerous too, 'absolutist' even, in their preference for reaching past established mechanisms of constitutional legitimacy.[10] The process was dodgy, the politics reckless.

This is not the place to indulge an extended history of the European Union, or the UK's membership of it.[11] Suffice to say that, whilst post-Imperial Britain has been obsessed with the emergent European 'union', it has never been sure what to think of it; probably because it is so obsessed.[12] Churchill famously recommended

---

[6] Re-electing its formerly Conservative MP, Douglas Carswell, with an overwhelming majority of 60%.

[7] Made in his so-called 'Bloomberg Speech' in January 2013. As recently as 2011, Cameron and his Foreign Secretary, William Hague, had both rejected calls for a referendum, on the grounds that there was no question which could encompass the complexity of the issue. See Adam (2020) 50–51.

[8] He loudly announced his intention to negotiate a 'better deal' for Britain; a proclamation met with icy disdain in Brussels. This deal secured, Cameron assumed, his compatriots would see the wisdom in remaining.

[9] 'Startling and catastrophic', according to the former Chancellor, Ken Clarke. In Burton (2021) 104. Or maybe not that startling. See Tombs (2022) 56–59, noting opinion surveys revealing a growing Euroscepticism in key demographics in the years leading up to the referendum, and concluding that the only thing that was surprising about the result was that so many people seemed so surprised.

[10] A 'bald, prerogative-based constitutional power grab', according to Mark Elliott (2017) 282. See also Sumption (2020) 30–32; and Adam (2020) 113–18.

[11] Histories of the latter are legion. Young (1998) is a classic, albeit increasingly dated. A more recent summation can be found in Bogdanor (2021) ch 1.

[12] McConalogue (2020) 1.

the idea of a 'United States' of Europe.[13] But he did not expect Britain to be part of it. More enthused was the renowned Bagehot scholar, Norman St John Stevas, who hoped that Queen Elizabeth II might become 'Empress of Europe'.[14] The United Kingdom joined the European Economic Community on 1 January 1973, but to St John Stevas's chagrin was not immediately put in charge. Even those who admitted the need, principally economic, to join the incipient union were hardly enthusiastic. 'We have not overcome the Divine Right of Kings', Harold Macmillan declared, 'to fall before the divine right of experts'.[15]

The technocracy bothered some. Others worried about constitutional consequence, especially the seeming diminution of parliamentary sovereignty. Achieved by statutory sleight of hand in section 2 of the 1972 European Communities Act, which supposed that sovereignty would be ceded in matters pertaining to European law, but otherwise retained.[16] A feint that was designed to accommodate the competing principle of legal 'supremacy' which was presently being refined in the European Court of Justice.[17] The more jurisprudentially perceptive further wondered if the 1972 Act might have somehow bound future parliaments, at least to the 'manner and form' of later repeal; a position intimated in an early 'integration' case, *Macarthy's v Smith*.[18] A constitutional 'revolution' some surmised.[19] A proper 'mess', according to others.[20] Reconcilable opinions. At the least, further evidence that certain statutes might indeed assume an elevated constitutional status.

The seriously overwrought supposed that the legislative sorcery masked a more prosaic truth, that sovereignty was in the process of being lost, maybe for ever; a particular instance, perhaps, of the broader fear that globalisation might be 'hollowing out' democratic institutions.[21] The idea that sovereignty might have been 'pooled' failed to convince.[22] Instead, what mattered was getting it 'back'

---

[13] In his 'Zurich speech', given in September 1946. 'Great Britain' and the 'British Commonwealth of Nations', Churchill assured his audience, along with 'mighty America', would be 'friends and sponsors' of this 'new Europe'. In Adam (2020) 1.

[14] In Haseler (1996) 130. Norman St John-Stevas, a prominent Conservative politician, served as Lord President of the Council and the Leader of the House of Commons. An unlikely ally of Margaret Thatcher too, it might be thought, until it is remembered that the latter was, in the earlier part of her career, a fervent pro-European, who never wavered from her support for the single market.

[15] In Adam (2020) 4.

[16] A piece of trickery that has elicited differently toned critical comment. A 'skilful form of pragmatism', according to Bogdanor (2021) 63.

[17] In cases such as *Costa v ENEL* 6/64 [1964] ECR 585; and *Simmenthal* 106/77 [1978] ECR 629.

[18] [1979] 3 All ER 325. Supposing that repeal might, in the circumstances, need to be 'express', as opposed to simply 'implied'. See here Allan (2011).

[19] See Bogdanor (2021) 87. A perception shared by Sir Malcolm Jack, former Clerk to the House of Commons, commenting in the preface to the twenty-fourth edition of *Erskine May*, in 2011. Whilst the British constitution has never been 'immutable', the pace of recent change, accelerated most obviously by membership of the EU, has been 'remarkable'. See Jack (2011) viii.

[20] See King (2007) 99.

[21] Loughlin (2019) 443, 450.

[22] A defining fiction of EU public law, 'pooled' sovereignty supposes that each Member State relinquishes some of its domestic sovereignty in order to share EU sovereignty.

before it was too late. It is, of course, a matter of perception; like all constitutional fictions.[23] Engagement with any international commercial order necessitates some sharing of legal sovereignty. It did in the Roman Empire and the Hanseatic League, it does in the European Union and the World Trade Organization. The constitutional was not, however, the only fiction exercising the British public.

Others were fixated by numbers and shapes. The 'Vote Leave' campaign conjured up a figure of £350 million a week that might be saved if the United Kingdom left the European Union.[24] Money that could be invested in the NHS, and which might come in very handy in the event of a viral pandemic. No one wants to be unprepared when one of those arrives. Quotas too, of fish and humans. Too little of the former, it seemed, all being nicked by the Spanish. And far too many of the latter. Britain was already at 'breaking point', and now there was the likelihood of 74 million more immigrants pitching up at St Pancras International, brandishing their shiny new EU passports and specimen social security forms.[25] The Hun at the platform barriers, again.[26] Brexit was not all about immigration, and it would be a mistake to assume that every 'Leave' voter was a racist. But it is reasonable to suppose that every racist voted to leave.[27] And then there was all the shape-shifting, of fruit and veg especially. The future British Prime Minister Boris Johnson made his name as the man to lead Britain through Brexit on the back of a series of brilliant articles on 'bendy bananas'. In truth, there are few more ridiculous pieces of EU legislation than Regulation 2257/94.[28] There again there are few more ridiculous reasons for breaking up an economic and political union.

Cameron lost his gamble. On 23 June 2016 the United Kingdom held its 'Brexit' referendum: 36 per cent of the adult population voted to leave; 35 per cent voted

---

[23] See Bogdanor (2021) 1, on the facile 'illusion' of 'taking back control'.

[24] The figure was, of course, nonsense, as the chair of the UK Statistics Authority immediately countered. The real figure was nearer to £180 million, and readily offset by incoming subsidies.

[25] The figure premised on the prospect of Turkey joining the EU. The Breaking Point image was taken from a photograph of asylum seekers crossing the Croatia–Slovakia border in 2015, white faces covered over or erased, just leaving black. In front of which the UKIP leader Nigel Farage happily posed. The template was a Nazi anti-Jewish poster from the 1930s. The storm it duly raised only helping to advertise the essential message. See Esler (2021) 156.

[26] In truth, internal EU migration had increased significantly following the most recent expansion in 2004, which added 10 new members. But most of those who made their way to the UK were looking for generally lower-skilled employment, not handouts. And were indeed vital to the functioning of the UK economy; as became apparent after Brexit, when it was discovered that there were not enough prospective workers to pick fruit, or service care homes, or restaurants, or to make the airports work properly, or the ferries. A case can indeed be made for supposing that the economic 'boom' which the UK enjoyed during the half decade leading up to the start of the Great Recession in 2008 was, to a considerable extent, a consequence of free movement of migrant workers. See Burton (2021) 36–37.

[27] It can even be argued that the referendum mutated into a vote on immigration policy. See Burton (2021) 169–70; and also Adam (2020) 299, commenting on the tragic death of the MP Jo Cox, just a week before the referendum. Murdered, her assailant declared, because she was a 'passionate defender of the EU and a traitor to white people'.

[28] The Regulation sought to categorise bananas in terms of shape. A Class 1 banana would suffer only 'slight defects of shape', if any. A Class 2 banana might be riddled with any number of unshapely 'defects'. They should though all taste the same; which most people might reasonably conclude is all that matters.

to stay; and 29 per cent did not vote at all.[29] A narrow defeat for apathy, a still narrower victory for 'Vote Leave'. Enough, though, to plunge the United Kingdom into constitutional crisis. The result had brought into open view a fundamental 'gulf between two nations', or maybe three. A 'deep and bitter cultural divide'.[30] It also meant that there was, not for the first time in Anglo-British history, a break with Rome to get 'done'.[31] And no one, it became quickly apparent, had bothered to do much by way of contingency planning.[32] Just as nobody had thought to put a 'lock' on the referendum, or make provision for a confirmatory referendum down the line.[33] There again, the United Kingdom has little experience of organising referenda; something which might, with the benefit of hindsight, have been cautionary.

All very familiar to scholars of England's first break with Rome though. There would need to be a statute, in 'restraint of appeals' to the European Court of Justice. A 'Great Repeal Act', as Cameron's successor, Theresa May, preferred to term it. And before that, some negotiations, most likely of the tetchy variety. Or maybe not. Perhaps the United Kingdom could leave the Union by the simple sweep of the Prime Minister's pen? Without all the bother of securing Parliament's approval. Article 50 of the EU Treaty suggests that any Member State can withdraw from the Union 'in accordance with its own constitutional requirements'. A sensible provision provided someone knows what, in each circumstance, such requirements might be. Otherwise, a facility for dissimulation and deceit and a recipe for chaos. But tempting. So much so that May decided to give it a go. And was duly challenged in court, by anti-Brexit campaigner Gina Miller.[34] At which point, it is time to reorient ourselves, and get ready for our second venture. Which in fact takes us back home.

A Morning in Middlesex

Defoe's home at least. London, 'the great centre of England'.[35] And getting greater, physically at least. 'New squares and new buildings rising up every day to such a prodigy of buildings'.[36] He compared it to the growth of Rome under the Emperor

---

[29] A winning margin of around 700,000 in a population of around 64.5 million.

[30] See Tombs (2022); and also Adam (2020) 195, referring to a country of 'embittered animosities'.

[31] A conceit that plays on the fact that the original agreement to establish a European Community was sealed by the Treaty of Rome in 1957.

[32] Burton (2021) 193–94, 210.

[33] Of the kind that might have required a 'super-majority' of those voting, or a certain percentage of the entire adult population. Or perhaps have required a confirmatory vote, once the terms of a final 'deal' had become apparent. For the significance of this error, see Bogdanor (2021) 264–65.

[34] *R (on the application of Miller) v Secretary of State for Exiting the European Union* [2017] UKSC 5; [2018] AC 61; 1 WLUK 387 (SC).

[35] An apposite descriptor, he supposed, given that his account of the city appeared at the 'centre' of his *Tour*, the fifth of the thirteen 'letters'.

[36] Defoe (1986) 286–87.

Trajan, only absent the planning. Defoe was born in St Giles, Cripplegate, and it is evident in his account of the 'City of London' that his greater interest lies about here, in the place of 'commerce and wealth'.[37] Our closer location is, however, a few miles to the west, in Westminster, where Parliament sat, along with the great courts of law. Not that Defoe was much impressed with what might be discovered there in 1726. All a bit shabby, a pervasive 'air of venerable, though ruined antiquity', Palace-yard now reduced to 'little offices for clerks, rooms for coffee-houses, auctions of pictures, pamphlets and toy-shops'. As for the great abbey church, frankly a bit of a 'heap', whilst Westminster Hall 'resembles nothing so much as a great barn'.[38] He did not describe the area to the south-west of College Green; there was probably nothing then to describe.

There is today, though. For it is here, four centuries on, that we can admire the Middlesex Guildhall, acclaimed by Pevsner as a prime example of '*art nouveau gothic*' architecture. And now the home of the UK Supreme Court. Established under the terms of the 2005 Constitutional Reform Act to serve as a constitutional court, in everything but name. It is here that Gina Miller's case was decided in 2016, and it was here that another case brought by Miller would be decided three years on. Directly concerned with the legal circumstance of Brexit, both cases tested core 'principles' of British constitutional law. In the words of one of the Justices, the second *Miller* case more especially invited the Court to resolve 'a question as fundamental as any that a British court' has 'ever had to answer'.[39]

As we have already indicated, the first *Miller* case moved around the possibility that Crown prerogative might be used to pull the United Kingdom out of the European Union without the bother of Parliament. It could not, the Supreme Court decided. Repeal of the European Communities Act would require primary legislation. It could not be implied, nor resolved by the exercise of Crown prerogative alone. There was nothing surprising in this opinion.[40] Prerogative vests a power in ministers to sign foreign treaties. It does not vest a power to implement them in UK law, or the converse. Parliament is supposed to do that. A 'major change to UK constitutional arrangements', as Lord Reed confirmed, cannot 'be achieved by ministers alone'.[41] A precedent found in the *Case of Proclamations* indeed. And then confirmed in Article 1 of the Bill of Rights, the 'pretended power of suspending of laws or the execution of laws by regall authority without consent of Parlyment is illegal'. As well, of course, as the very statute that the government was hoping to repeal.

Here again we might imagine the ghost of Sir Edward Coke smiling, however grimly, in the shadows. Just as we can imagine that of James Stuart scowling and

---

[37] Defoe (1986) 306.

[38] Defoe (1986) 323–25.

[39] See Sumption (2021) 196–97.

[40] More 'vanilla' than 'thriller', as Alison Young puts it (2017). Mark Elliott takes a broadly similar line (2017).

[41] Para 82.

muttering dark oaths. The ruling was certainly met with a predictable fury amongst Brexit supporters. The judges, the headline of one far-Right tabloid read, were the 'enemies of the people'.[42] Too much 'craturity', far too much. Ranting aside, it did leave the government in something of a predicament. 'Brexit means Brexit', Prime Minister May declared helplessly, as her government fell about her.[43] Two and half years of thrashing about and May gave up, resigning in July 2019.

To be succeeded as Prime Minister by Boris Johnson. And a decision a few months later to have another go at trying to circumvent Parliament in order to get Brexit 'done'. The idea this time was to prorogue Parliament for an extended period, principally so that it could not pass legislation intended to block the United Kingdom leaving the Union without a 'deal', when the clock wound down on the last day of the calendar year. Brexit by fait accompli. Hardly subtle, but then subtlety was no more part of Johnson's skill-set than honesty or bare competence. And there is nothing in the constitution which determines the length of parliamentary prorogations. Convention supposes three to four weeks to be the norm; but it is only convention.

There again there is nothing much in the British constitution which determines anything; which is perhaps the problem. Indeed, it can be argued that Alexis de Tocqueville's famous quip is just as pertinent today as it was two centuries ago. In England 'the constitution can change constantly, or rather it does not exist at all'.[44] It is why governments can order random referenda, regardless of whether anyone knows how to run them, or what to do with their resolution.[45] The constitution of 'nods and winks' that Kipling perceived half a century after Tocqueville, 'largely inarticulate, being void of self-expression'.[46] Johnson winked, the Queen nodded, and Parliament was closed for five weeks.

At which point attention turned once again to the courts, and the resolution of the second *Miller* case. Proceedings commenced in Scotland, with an action brought by Joanna Cherry, an SNP MP. The Inner House of the Court of Sessions held that the 'principal reason' for the extended prorogation was to 'impede Parliament' and declared the prorogation unlawful. The English High Court however reached a different decision in an action brought by Miller, accepting

---

[42] Headline in the *Daily Mail*, an ardent supporter of Brexit, on 14 November 2016, in response to the initial High Court judgment. Amongst the many things it seemed to dislike about Sir Terence Etherton, who was one of the three judges who gave judgment, was the fact that he was an 'openly gay ex-Olympic fencer'. Berating disobliging judges would become something of a habit over the coming years, both in the right-wing press and amongst government ministers. As childish as chilling. See Rozenberg (2020) 32–33.

[43] There were various possible 'withdrawal' models around which negotiations with the EU might have moved, describing different kinds of beneficial trading regimes. But party political exigencies preventing Theresa May from countenancing any. After a series of parliamentary defeats, May resigned in June 2019; blaming everything on a Parliament which had caused 'potentially irreparable damage to public trust'. In Adam (2020) 181–82.

[44] Tocqueville (1994) 101.

[45] See Bogdanor (2021) vi, on the *Miller* cases revealing the fragility of an 'unprotected' constitution.

[46] 'The Puzzler' in Kipling (1946) 533. For the reference to a constitution of 'nods and winks', see Colls (2002) 84.

the argument that the exercise of prerogative power is 'intrinsically one of high policy and politics'.[47] At which point the cases were joined and remitted to the UK Supreme Court.[48]

Which announced its decision on 24 September 2019. The judgment, read out by the President of the Court, Baroness Hale, was unanimous, and concluded that the decision to prorogue was indeed 'unlawful, null and of no effect':

> A decision to prorogue parliament (or to advise the monarch to prorogue parliament) will be unlawful if the prorogation has the effect of frustrating or preventing without reasonable justification, the ability of parliament to carry out its constitutional functions as a legislature and as the body responsible for the supervision of the executive. In such a situation, the court will intervene if the effect is sufficiently serious to justify such an exceptional course.[49]

By asking the Queen to prorogue Parliament at that moment, and for an extended period, the Prime Minister had sought to 'impede the essential function of Parliament in holding government to account'.[50] An evident threat to the sovereignty of Parliament. Whilst the fact that the prorogation convention was executed by means of Crown prerogative meant that it became a matter of constitutional 'legality', rather than mere 'political sentiment'.[51] Prerogative powers, Lady Hale emphasised, that have been justiciable since the days of Sir Edward Coke.

The decision to prorogue was accordingly void, which in turn meant that Parliament had never been prorogued at all, merely 'adjourned'; the sort of legal fiction of which Jeremy Bentham later despaired. In practice it had been forcibly shut down, for three weeks. Not any more though. Shortly after the judgment had been delivered, John Bercow, the Speaker of the House of Commons, appeared on College Green sporting an exceptionally bright tie, and a still brighter smile. Parliament, he confirmed, would reopen for business the following day. Nothing less than a 'constitutional coup', the arch-Brexiteer Jacob Rees-Mogg trilled. An opinion shared by the conservative jurist John Finnis, who announced that the Court had reached a ruling which 'would unhesitatingly have been rejected by all previous generations of judges back to the Bill of Rights'.[52] Nonsense of course, but it was an excitable moment.

The Brexit-supporting press defaulted once again to fulmination. Hale was a 'quintessential liberal blue-stocking' hell-bent on preventing the 'will' of the people; or 36 per cent of them at least.[53] Her choice of brooch, that fateful morning, did not go unnoticed. A spider-design, in silver; a tangled-web seemed the obvious allusion. Or perhaps a feminist icon. The ancient Egyptian spider-goddess Neith

---

[47] [2019] CSIH 49; and [2019] EWHC 2381 (QB). The decisions of the two courts are reviewed in *Miller 2*, paras 24–25.
[48] *R (on the application of Miller) v Prime Minister* [2019] UKSC 41, paras 50 and 61.
[49] Para 50.
[50] Sumption (2021) 219.
[51] Sumption (2021) 197.
[52] Finnis (2019) 5, 18, 11.
[53] Quoted in Rozenberg (2020) 47.

sprang to some minds, the spinner of destiny, good at dealing with crocodiles, and other slimy reptiles too. Johnson took it personally. Having added a botched response to the Covid-19 pandemic to his prime ministerial curriculum vitae, he left office in spring 2022, taking the opportunity in his resignation speech to launch an attack on Hale, who he had apparently 'seen off'. Ignoring the prosaic fact that she had reached retirement age, and he had simply lost.

That the decision in the second *Miller* case seemed to catch the government by surprise is again surprising. There are certainly plenty of precedents regarding the jurisdictional contention. Courts have long reviewed the operation of Crown prerogative. As Lord Diplock had noted in *ex parte Lain*.[54] Lord Scarman likewise in *CCSU*.[55] And then again Lord Browne-Wilkinson in the *Fire Brigades Union Case*.[56] In each instance making recourse to the same seventeenth-century precedents which Reed and Hale revisited in their respective opinions. Most pertinently Coke's renowned injunction in the *Case of Proclamations*, that 'the King hath no prerogative, but that which the law of the land allows him'. 'Time and again', as Hale noted, English constitutional history confirms that the 'limits of prerogative powers were set by law and were determined by the courts'.[57]

And there was nothing especially surprising about the resolution of the substantive question either, that of government accountability. Prescient though, for in many ways accountability is the animating controversy of contemporary constitutional debate.[58] In deference to Dicey, orthodoxy supposes that the UK courts cannot assume a capacity for constitutional review, at least not of primary legislation. That would be a threat to parliamentary sovereignty. A century on, however, modern government has become altogether more complex, whilst losing none of its instinctive authoritarianism. We noted this tendency in the previous chapter. So much so that executive overreach is now 'hard-wired', as Peter Hennessy puts it. In which circumstance the thought that political 'conventions' might serve as a sufficient check becomes dangerously naïve. Nothing more than 'parliamentary gossip', as Disraeli long ago observed. More immediately, it has become ever more starkly apparent that the age of the 'good chaps' is now passed, if indeed it ever existed; to be superseded by that of the liars and the cheats.[59] All of which makes the case for courts holding government to basic 'standards of decency, honesty' and 'competence' compelling.[60]

---

[54] *R v Criminal Injuries Compensation Board, ex parte Lain* [1967] 2 QB 864.

[55] *Council of Civil Service Unions v Minister for the Civil Service* [1985] AC 374, 418.

[56] *R v Secretary of State for the Home Dept, ex parte Fire Brigades Union* [1995] 2 AC 513.

[57] At para 32, citing in addition the authority of *Entick v Carrington* (1765) 19 How ST 1029; 95 ER 807, and then again at paras 41 and 49.

[58] See Rozenberg (2020) 1–4.

[59] Hennessy (2018). For the passing of this age, see Esler (2021) 242. See also Judge (2021) 285, 291, suggesting that the present age is characterised by a political morality of 'circumspection' rather than 'candour'.

[60] In the words of the former Lord Chancellor, Lord Falconer, quoted in Rozenberg (2020) 172.

Which brings us back to the *Miller* cases. In both instances animated by 'bad chaps' trying to circumvent Parliament. In this context, both cases can be read as defences of parliamentary sovereignty, even if, to borrow from Walter Bagehot, it is a matter of saving Parliament from its own 'caprice'.[61] To allow the government to sequester Crown prerogatives to personal use and political convenience would have been an affront to the very idea of a sovereign Parliament. Time now for the final leg of our 'tour'.

The High Road

Which will take us up the 'high road', to the 'north part of Great Britain'.[62] Edinburgh more precisely, which Defoe described in his eleventh 'Letter'. The first of three in which he sought to convey to his English readers what Scotland was like. Not as bad as they might think, was the gist. All it needed was better 'husbandry', and a 'change in the disposition of the common people'.[63] Defoe had been to Scotland before, despatched in late 1706 by Lord Harley to gather intelligence on the mood of the capital as the prospect of union loomed.[64] The merchants and their lawyers seemed keen, Defoe had reported back, but no one else much.[65] On his return to Edinburgh in 1725, Defoe focused rather more on topology, and dodgy sanitary conditions.[66] Built in the wrong place, the 'city suffers infinite disadvantages and lies under such scandalous inconveniences as are, by its enemies, made a subject of scorn and reproach'. A city which seems to have become inured to 'stench and nastiness'.[67] That said, Defoe thought the Royal 'Mile' one of the most 'handsome' streets in the kingdom, from its 'impregnable' castle, past the 'great church' of St Giles, and down to 'Haly-Rood' palace. The latter a 'handsome building, rather convenient than large', and a bit neglected, the Chapel Royal notably 'decayed'. And the stables were in the wrong place, stuck

---

[61] Bagehot (2001) 156–57, speaking more closely to the convention of dissolution.

[62] Defoe was following the terminological precedent set in the 1604 Merchant Shipping Proclamation, which distinguished 'our subjects of South Britain' from 'our Subjects of North Britain'. See Defoe (1986) 446.

[63] By husbandry Defoe meant farming. At the cusp of the agricultural revolution, improvements in farming techniques is a common refrain throughout Defoe's various 'letters'.

[64] Necessary, Harley jovially informed Parliament, because he knew no more of Scotland 'than of Japan'. A little disingenuous. Harley had already implanted a sophisticated intelligence network across the border. West (1997) 125–26.

[65] Hardly a night seemed to pass without the 'rabble' wandering the streets of Edinburgh, smashing windows and cursing the English. Only 'providence' keeping him alive, or so he reported. Glasgow was even worse. In truth, Defoe seemed happy enough to continue shuttling between Edinburgh and London for the better part of four years, his discomforts alleviated no doubt by a very nice stipend. See Richetti (2015) 115–21.

[66] The lack of political commentary, given his previous sojourn in Scotland, and the context of Union, is striking. See West (1997) 372–73.

[67] Defoe (1986) 557.

in front. He liked the 'physic' garden though, a pleasant spot to pass a couple of hours.[68] After which, it was off to Leith.

We, though, will stay in the immediate environs of Haly-rood. Because it is here, three centuries on, that the Scottish Parliament sits. An institution established to satiate Scottish nationalism under the terms of the 1998 Scotland Act, and thereby keep the Union intact. Not that Defoe would have acknowledged the need. In his opinion, the Union was anyway 'indissolvable'.[69] So far, history has proved him right. It might, though, be about to prove him wrong, for the prospect of dissolving the 'union' of crowns has rarely seemed greater than it is today.[70] The pending 'problem' of dissolution, which started with the overwrought imperial aspirations of James Stuart in the early seventeenth century, and the failure to properly comprehend from that very moment what a 'greater' Britain was supposed to be. Aside, that is, from an insider-dealing scam; the rationale of 1707.[71] The lack of purpose and planning, the 'walking shadow' that has haunted the Union since its inception.[72]

The Scotland Act was one of three devolution statutes enacted in the last years of the twentieth century. Along with re-establishing a Scottish Parliament, the Act determined certain 'reserved' matters that remained in the exclusive competence of Westminster. Imputing that all other matters, by default, fell within the competence of Holyrood. Along with the Scotland Act came a Government of Wales Act, which established an Assembly in Cardiff. The third devolution statute addressed Northern Ireland. Different again, conscious of historical sensitivities, and stipulated under the terms of the 'Good Friday Agreement', the Northern Ireland Act reinvested a devolved Assembly at Stormont, the governance of which is subject to 'power-sharing' arrangements, designed to ensure the functioning support of various unionist and nationalist constituencies. In terms of legislative competence, the Northern Ireland Act distinguished 'transferred', 'excepted' and 'reserved' matters, the Assembly enjoying discrete competence regarding the former.[73]

The three statutes thus confirmed that devolution is an asymmetrical process and is likely to remain so. Statutes in 2012 and 2016 saw the devolution of further powers to the Scottish Parliament, in the latter instance granting significant fiscal competences. Likewise, statutes in 2006, 2014 and 2017 enhanced the legislative competence of the Welsh Assembly.[74] Governance in Northern Ireland has

---

[68] Defoe (1986) 584–85.

[69] Defoe (1986) 580.

[70] See Bogdanor (2021) 171.

[71] See Wormald (2021) 378–82.

[72] *Macbeth* 5.5. 26. See also Wormald (2021) 420.

[73] Excepted matters remain within the exclusive competence of the UK Parliament. Reserved matters fall to Westminster by default, but can be 'transferred' to Stormont with the agreement of the Secretary of State.

[74] The 2006 Government of Wales Act devolved authority to legislate on certain Assembly 'measures', whilst statutes in 2014 and 2017 did similarly for fiscal, and transport and environmental matters respectively.

also been adjusted on various occasions, principally to sustain power-sharing arrangements and keep Stormont functioning.[75] The devolution statutes did not, however, do much to 'contain' the nationalist genie; in any part of Britain.[76] Further referenda would be held in both Scotland and Wales, in the former instance taking the shape of a full-blown independence vote in 2014. The fact that 45 per cent of those who voted in 'indyref', as it became known, expressed a preference to leave the Union, implies that Scotland is just as torn as the rest of the United Kingdom. Political sensitivities have precluded anything similar in Northern Ireland, as yet. But it is very evident that the EU Withdrawal Act has done nothing to stabilise governance at Stormont.[77]

In a famously muddled metaphor, Ernest Bevin advised against accession to the then European Coal and Steel Community in 1950, on the grounds that 'If you open that Pandora's box, you never know what Trojan horses will fly out'.[78] Prescient still. Except that it is not the joining, but the leaving. There is every likelihood that Brexit will hasten the dismemberment of the United Kingdom, constituent nations shearing off sequentially. Leaving behind the 'little England' prophesied by JB Priestley in his *English Journey* in 1934.[79] Still elusive, still in search of an identity. 'Of any people in the universe', David Hume declared in 1741, the English have the 'least of a national character, unless this very singularity may pass for such'.[80] An opinion echoed by the radical socialist Herbert Read, writing in the same moment as Priestley. 'Alone of national ideals', Read proclaimed in suitably cryptic terms, the 'English ideal transcends nationality'.[81] An attitude of patronising whimsy which has hardly lessened with time. A 'simple and politically unsophisticated people', Simon Heffer says of his compatriots.[82] No wonder they seem so confused. And still, famously, quieted: 'Smile at us, pay us, pass us; but do not forget;/ For we are the people of England, that never have spoken yet.'[83] GK Chesterton's England, imagined amidst the horrors of the Great War.

Not any more though, for 'little England' had decided that the time had come to make a very big statement. Every single English region, except London, voted to leave the European Union in the 2016 referendum.[84] Misshapen fruit and veg might have something to do with it, along with an irrational fear of foreigners. Nostalgia too, the debilitating 'ghetto of sentimentality' identified by Geoffrey Howe in the Commons speech which precipitated the fall of Margaret Thatcher

---

[75] Most significant here is the 2006 St Andrew's Agreement.

[76] Nairn (2002) 83–85.

[77] For discussions of the peculiar problems which Brexit has created in Northern Ireland, and more especially for the sustainability of the Good Friday Agreement, see Bogdanor (2021) 232–44; and Murray (2022).

[78] In Adam (2000) 221.

[79] Priestley (1977) 389.

[80] 'Of National Character' in Hume (1987) 207.

[81] In Young (1998) 8.

[82] Heffer (1999) 13.

[83] 'The Secret People' ll. 1–2 in Colls (2002) 289.

[84] Bogdanor (2021) 200.

in 1990.[85] At the end of the day, though, it was the plainer grievance intimated by Chesterton. Neglect. Not just because the English were denied a referendum in 1997, and much of a voice amidst the surrounding debate, but more generally. For the Brexit referendum was not, again, about the European Union. At least not much, and certainly not so much in the collective mind of 'little England'. Rather it was, to echo Carlyle's prophesy, about the 'condition' of this England.

Which was, in the Brexit moment, bad; and getting worse. The 'great' recession, triggered by the credit crisis of 2008, had bitten deep.[86] The strength of the Leave vote was found amongst the English working-class. More especially the male, the elderly, the white and the less well-educated.[87] Carlyle's constituency of the perpetually aggrieved. The 'just about managing', as Theresa May would later term them, the 'left-behind'.[88] Who expressed their frustration at not being able to detach themselves from the United Kingdom, by instead detaching themselves from the European Union. Their 'simmering rage' redirected away from Westminster, and themselves, towards a diabolic Brussels.[89] The anti-Christ and all his Hunnish minions. A second reformation.

Failing to appreciate the depth of grievance, and the virulence of a Eurosceptic press, the 'Remoaners' allowed themselves to be similarly demonised.[90] The poetics, of course, was always going to give succour to the little Englanders. The time-honoured rhetoric of Gaunt's 'sceptred isle', of Crecy and Agincourt and Waterloo; all victories, as one prominent Brexiteer put it, against 'Europe'.[91] The English love a poetic war; it is after all the 'seat of Mars'.[92] The England of 'ancient time' celebrated in William Blake's paean; still 'the greatest nation on earth', as another similarly excitable Brexiteer chirruped.[93] The England of 'gloomy Sundays, smoky towns and winding roads', as Orwell imagined it, in slightly hazier, and warier, terms.[94] Warier still in Defoe's *True-Born Englishman*. A different paean to the same pretended 'antiquity'. This time, though, nurturing an 'ugly, surly, sullen, selfish spirit', its perennially 'discontented' citizens forever inclined to blame the 'neighbours' for every 'pother' (3, 44, 161, 673). A poignant rhyme. The self-denying 'mongrel' (340), cowering behind his 'moat

[85] In Tombs (2022) 44.
[86] Up until 2008, campaigns to leave the EU had gained very little traction. For an extensive commentary on the 'great recession', see Burton (2021) 9, 25–27.
[87] 55% of Leave voters were male; 84% of younger voters, aged 18–24, voted Remain, as did 57% of those with university degrees; 67% of Asians; 70% of Muslims; and 73% of Black voters. For a statistical overview, see Tombs (2022) 61–63.
[88] Not that she seemed inclined to do much to help them along; the demands of getting Brexit 'done', and saving the Conservative Party, mattering so much more. Burton (2021) 43–46, 222, 229.
[89] Esler (2021) 40–43, 100.
[90] Not just 'moaning', but also inert. 'Leave' supposed movement, change, dynamism. 'Remain' supposed the converse. See Adam (2020) 72–73; and Burton (2021) 15, 166.
[91] Jacob Rees-Mogg at a Conservative Party conference in 2017, closing with the assurance 'We win all these things!' See Esler (2021) 24.
[92] Shakespeare (1961) 2.1. 41.
[93] Esler (2021) 108, quoting Andrea Leadsom.
[94] Orwell (1984) 116–17.

defensive', anxiously scanning the Channel for rubber dinghies crammed with dark-skinned people.

There was still time, of course, to heal the wounds, and the Union. But the exigencies of party 'pollitricks', to borrow from Bagehot, militated conversely. The second responsibility of a British Prime Minister is to save their party. The first is to save themselves. Saving the country comes, at best, around third. For which reason there could be no compromise, no healing; just purgation.[95] 'Brexit means Brexit', and, if need be, 'no deal', or so Prime Minister Johnson kept threatening. Bluff, of course. Thwarted by the Supreme Court and a Parliament that refused to countenance 'no deal', Johnson was forced to back down. There would be a deal, the weakness of which could become quickly apparent, and a European Union (Withdrawal Agreement) Act. By then, though, the damage was done. Britain had, as foretold, become a 'pariah' nation.[96] And a little closer to falling apart. Each of the devolved assemblies, in Edinburgh, Cardiff and Belfast, passed motions condemning the terms of the Agreement.

The more urgent concern was felt in Belfast. The Good Friday Agreement, reinforced by the Northern Ireland Act, had ended a century of sectarian violence on the island of Ireland. But then came Brexit, and the conundrum of how to reinstate a border between the United Kingdom and the European Union, whilst not reinstating a border between the United Kingdom and Ireland. The former was deemed necessary by the Union in order to protect the *acquis communitaire* of its 'single market'. The latter was necessary to forestall the risk of renewed violence. The solution written into a Protocol created a fictive border down the Irish Sea, which effectively left Northern Ireland subject to EU law in matters relating to the regulation of the market.[97] And, as a consequence, considerably richer too. It was not, however, a solution that sat comfortably with the unionist community in the Province, at least not their leaders.

Nor with those politicians back in Westminster who were reluctant to see what was left of the Anglo-British empire further diminished. In due course, the UK government took unilateral action in the shape of an Internal Markets Act, designed to ensure 'unfettered' trade throughout the United Kingdom. Article 16 of the Protocol permits such actions if 'strictly necessary'.[98] But Article 5 also requires parties to have first negotiated, in 'good faith', to resolve their differences.[99] Muttering vaguely about the failure of the European Union to do so, the UK government claimed that it was left with no alternative but to breach the terms of the Agreement in a 'specific and limited way'. More particularly by removing the

---

[95] Burton (2021) 190, 195, 220.

[96] Nairn (2002).

[97] For a discussion of the Protocol, noting the social as well as economic consequences of Brexit in Northern Ireland, see Murray and Rice (2021) 281. Section 2 of the Protocol includes certain human rights and equalities provisions.

[98] If the application of the Protocol threatens 'serious economic, societal or environmental difficulties that are liable to persist, or to divert trade'.

[99] Using the offices of the Joint Committee established in section 164 of the Agreement.

possibility of any legal challenges to the Act which sought to enforce rights and remedies enumerated in the Withdrawal Agreement.[100] Another act in 'restraint of appeal'. Criticism, at home and abroad, was unsurprisingly fierce. Not least because it, rather more than the Protocol, seemed to threaten the 'delicate balance' achieved in the Good Friday Agreement.[101] And thus, by intimation, the integrity of the 'united' kingdom. The future of the Northern Ireland Protocol remains in the balance, as does the future of Northern Ireland, and the 'united' Kingdom. The most recent development is the so-called 'Windsor Framework Agreement', designed to ease the flow of goods across both the United Kingdom and its border with Ireland. As yet, however, the Agreement has not persuaded unionist parties to re-enter power-sharing government at Stormont. There is still, it seems, a lot more Brexit to 'get done'.

Home Alone

We opened this 'epilogue' with a deceptively simple question; four centuries on, is there anything about England in 1616 which resonates today? There are, of course, various possibilities. Driven by our peculiar interest in reformation, we have focused on only one; our most recent 'break' with Rome. We might just as easily have revisited Defoe's writings on climate change, or the continuing gullibility of those who liked to believe in witches, the 'wokery' of its moment.[102] We might also have gone back to some of the various plagues which regularly afflicted early modern England, obviously resonant with our recent experience of the coronavirus pandemic. Defoe famously accounted for the 'great' plague of 1665 in his *Journal of a Plague Year*. Plenty there to ponder; the importance of securing external borders, the difficulty of enforcing lockdowns of anyway uncertain efficacy, the shortage of medical facilities, the mendacity and the venality of those who were supposed to provide political leadership.[103] Every plague has its profiteers. Defoe wrote his *Journal* as a caution for future generations, in the hope that they might be more vigilant.

Our greater concern is though with constitutional resonance. And it is for this reason that our attention has been drawn inexorably towards Brexit and its unfolding consequence. For it presents, without doubt, the greatest constitutional, as well as political, challenge in a generation. Not simply because it

---

[100] So the Secretary of State for Northern Ireland, Brandon Lewis, admitted. Other government ministers, most notably Michael Gove, appeared to take a different view. The breach related more closely to section 47 of the Act, which specifically disapplies the principle of direct effect in any such disputes.

[101] The conclusion of the House of Lords Committee reviewing the prospective Internal Markets Bill. See European Scrutiny Committee, *Fourteenth Report of Session 2022–23* (HC 119-xiii) ch 4.

[102] In his essay 'The Storm' Defoe recounted the effects of a week-long 'tempest' which hit parts of England in November 1703. Whilst there was no need for panic, there was a case for noting some strange weather patterns and devising some practical means to alleviate their consequences.

[103] For a commentary on Defoe's *Journal* in the context of Covid-19, see Ward (2022a).

required Parliament to repeal a so-called 'fundamental' statute, the European Communities Act of 1972, but because it has revealed, once again, a series of fissures in what passes for the Anglo-British constitution. The limitations of government accountability, most obviously, but also the functionality of Parliament and the constitutional responsibilities of the judiciary. It has become quickly apparent that the claim that Brexit is now 'done' has no greater credence than Macaulay's famous assertion that the 1832 Reform Act would bring 'finality' to the question of franchise reform. If the last half millennium of English history proves anything, it is that reformations are never really 'done'. They simply mutate.

Any maybe rhyme. There is no reason to suppose that our most recent break with Rome will be any different from those figured in our past. On the contrary, given how quickly its shortcomings have become apparent. That Brexit has been a failure in economic terms is barely arguable. The Centre for European Research calculates a retraction in the UK economy of around 5.5 per cent since the end of 2019, with a headline reduction in inward investment at 11 per cent.[104] The cost in terms of lost tax revenue alone amounts to around £750 million a week, or £40 billion a year. The overall on-cost of Brexit, from year to year, is around £100 billion.[105] The value of the pound sterling is 19 per cent lower than it was in 2016; a startling figure. Of course, Brexit is not the only cause for the deeper economic crisis in which the United Kingdom presently finds itself. There is a decade of longer-term under-investment, and a fateful 44 days of wild financial experimentation during the short-lived Truss–Kwarteng administration in autumn 2022. The latter costed at another £40 billion. The botched response to Covid-19 is estimated to have cost in the region of £240 billion, for now. The consequence of being the only European country to be obliged to endure four lockdowns, as opposed to three or two or, in some cases, just one.

A series of significant political and economic misjudgements then, of which Brexit is only the most patently self-eviscerating. An exercise which, as the *Financial Times* concluded in late 2022, leaves the United Kingdom at a 'permanent disadvantage' in global markets, and thus 'unable' to experience the 'recovery' evident in other Member States of the European Union. The only G7 member with an economy which, at the beginning of 2023, was still smaller than it was pre-Covid.[106] The Office for Budget Responsibility (OBR) reaches the same conclusion, that Brexit continues to exert a 'significant adverse impact' on the UK economy and is likely to do so for an indeterminate future. In its most recent report, the OBR confirmed that the 'increase in non-tariff barriers' represented an 'additional impediment to the exploitation of comparative advantage' which is likely to reduce long-term productivity by around 4 per cent. Imports and exports remain 15 per cent lower than pre-Brexit, whilst new trade deals, commonly trumpeted

---

[104] Springford (2022).
[105] A figure confirmed by *Bloomberg* (31 January 2023).
[106] Giles (2022).

by the Johnson government, will not in reality 'have a material impact'.[107] There is, as the Organisation for Economic Co-operation and Development confirms, only one major economy shrinking faster than the British: the Russian.

All of which might suppose that there is an obvious means of relieving the pressure. Whilst the future is harder to model than the past, logic would suppose that rejoining the Union would reap immediate economic dividends, at the least reversing the annual tax-take loss of £40 billion. But politics is not really about logic, as Defoe well knew. If it was, the United Kingdom would never have left the Union in the first place. Politics is about feeling and sentiment and putting up with stuff. The first reformation was couched in precisely these terms. Breaking with Rome was never going to be easy, but it would in time define the English, a people 'chosen' for their resilience, their preparedness to suffer for Him. This 'other Eden'. The seventeenth century would witness a series of constitutional crises as a direct consequence of this providential 'election'. Animated by a fear amongst the more zealous that the building of the 'new Jerusalem' was being inhibited by all the closet 'Remoaners', busying themselves decorating chancels, erecting altar-screens, and drafting books of 'common prayer'. And populating the prerogative courts of the most insidious 'Remoaners' of all, King James I and his son Charles.

Our longer history, if we recall, supposes that the crisis of 1616 might be revisited as a prologue to coming events of 1642 and 1649, and then 1689. A century and a half of torment until the settlement, finally, of a 'glorious' revolution. The moment when, it might be supposed, the resolution of 1616 was reversed; the moment when the English exceptionalism of Coke overcame the Roman absolutism of Bacon and his King. The destiny of the 'chosen' people realised. So generations of Whiggish historians would have us suppose. Except, of course, that we now cast a more sceptical eye towards histories versed by 'strolling minstrels'. Or at least we disdain those which neglect the contingencies and inconsistencies, and all the weird stuff lurking in the verges. Thus, our greater interest in histories that might be termed ironic and anecdotal, and which prefer to rhyme rather than repeat. Repetition assumes a certain determinism, whereas rhyme is something we discern for ourselves. Thus, our closer interest in reformations, breaks with Rome, and more particularly with our most recent and what the past might suggest of its future. An exercise not just in catching resonances, but in tracing them.

Having revisited some of the constitutional resonances of our latest reformation, courtesy of our whimsical 'journey' through Brexit Britain, we are left to conjure the likely consequence. Recent polling supposes that upwards of a quarter those who voted to 'Leave' are now experiencing buyers regret, with overall

---

[107] As a government body, the OBR is generally recognised as being the most reliable and impartial analyst of the UK economy. The most recent OBR report is dated 17 April 2023. The reason why the 'new' trade deals will have little impact is because the vast majority are not new at all; merely existing pre-Brexit deals 'rolled over'. Three years on, the UK government is still trying to negotiate a 'new' deal with India. The dream of such a deal with the US, the Holy Grail of many pro-Leave campaigners, has long passed.

support for Brexit stuck at around 30 per cent. The figure for those believing Brexit to be a mistake is now consistently in excess of 50 per cent.[108] Generational evolution will only exacerbate the disparity. But the same polls confirm that there is no greater enthusiasm to rejoin, at least not imminently. And no major 'Anglo-British' political party is prepared to vouch for the idea. The Scottish Nationalist Party loudly proclaims its support for reversing Brexit, but hardly anyone else dare even speak of it. So great is the trauma that Brexit has been cast beyond the margins of political debate; no more acceptable in polite conversation today than discussion of a mooted return to Rome would have been in the England of 1616. The talk of the devil and the 'Remoaners', the witches and the 'woke'.

It is the so-called 'apathy trap', familiar enough to behavioural scientists; close cousin to the 'irreversibility' myth.[109] Faced with the consequence of a shattering trauma, personal or collective, the instinctive recourse is to retreat inwards, to disengage, in the heated moment to deny. The risk in the political context, as in any other, is patent. 'The tyranny of a prince in an oligarchy', as Montesquieu noted, 'is not so dangerous to the public welfare, as the apathy of a citizen in a democracy'. An apathy, moreover, that originates in greed and gullibility and which, with a curious prescience, Montesquieu suspected might be a peculiar characteristic of the English.[110] Culturally, perhaps even genetically, predisposed to believe fatuous assurances of salvation. The reformation English hoped to save their souls; Brexit Britain slavered at the prospect of saving £350 million a day. At least the former was dignified, and just about credible. The current fatuity is the belief that the greater threat facing Brexit Britain is not trade deficits but inflatable dinghies; an 'invasion' of starving Yemeni children as terrifying as an armada of Jesuit missionaries. 'Nothing', Wittgenstein suggested, 'is so difficult as not deceiving oneself'.[111] But some deceptions are more easily forgiven than others.

John Kenneth Galbraith has broadened Montesquieu's aspersion, identifying an insidious 'culture of contentment' which pervades 'Western' society. Comfortable enough to disdain the future until it arrives, only then do we conceive our disappointment.[112] After which, 'surly, sullen, selfish', our instinctive response is to look for someone to blame; ideally someone else, for the healing of a self-inflicted wound is always more painful. And protracted, as Shakespeare, our recurring companion, appreciated: 'How poor are they that have not patience! What wound did ever heal but by degrees?'[113] Healing takes time, the more traumatic longer still. If there is a consolation to be had, it is the thought that salvation through suffering is the essence of reformation. 'Affliction is a treasure, and scarce any

---

[108] See, for example, polls published by *Ipsos* (30 June 2022); *YouGov* (17 November 2022); and *Statista* (8 December 2022).

[109] See Jacoby (1999); Govedic (2006); and Zhelnina (2020).

[110] Having located the most compelling example hitherto in late imperial Rome. See Montesquieu (1989) books 2, 8 and 20. For further commentary, see Boesche (1990).

[111] Wittgenstein (1980) 34.

[112] Galbraith (2017).

[113] *Othello* 2.3. 60–61 in Shakespeare (1965).

man hath enough of it'; the words of John Donne, Dean of St Paul's and suspected closet 'Remoaner'.[114] Suffering is what a chosen people is supposed to do. Oliver Cromwell, someone who learned from the bitterest experience how difficult it was to 'heal and settle' a fractured nation, consoled himself with the thought that there is 'always discord in Zion'. Churchill gave the sentiment an earthier spin, 'KBO': just 'keep buggering on'.[115] The motif of reformations, past and present.

[114] *Meditation* 17 in Donne (1987) 126. On Donne's suspected Catholic sympathies, see Morrissey (2023).

[115] The phrase has shaped its own provenance. The first recorded use of 'KBO' was recalled by his private secretary, John Peck, on Churchill receiving news that Japanese warplanes had sunk two British battleships three days after Pearl Harbor, on 10 December 1941.

BIBLIOGRAPHY

Printed Primary

Aristotle (1976) *Ethics* (Penguin).

Austin, J (1885) *Lectures on Jurisprudence or the Philosophy of Positive Law* (R Campbell ed) (John Murray).

—— (1995) *The Province of Jurisprudence Determined* (W Rumble ed) Cambridge University Press).

Bacon, F (1968) *Gesta Grayorum* (D Bland ed) (Liverpool University Press).

—— (1974) *The Advancement of Learning and New Atlantis* (A Johnston ed) (Oxford University Press).

—— (1985) *The Essays* (Penguin).

—— (1998) *The History of the Reign of King Henry VII* (B Vickers ed) (Cambridge University Press).

Bagehot, W (2001) *The English Constitution* (P Smith ed) (Cambridge University Press).

Bartlett, M (2014) *King Charles III* (Nick Hern).

Baxter, R (1994) *A Holy Commonwealth* (W Lamont ed) (Cambridge University Press).

Bentham, J (1982) *An Introduction to the Principles of Morals and Legislation* (J Burns and H Hart eds) (Methuen).

—— (1988) *A Fragment on Government* (R Harrison ed) (Cambridge University Press).

Blake, W (1977) *Complete Poems* (Penguin).

Bodin, J (1962) *Six Books of a Commonweal* (K McRae ed) (Harvard University Press).

Bohn, H (ed) (1854–56) *The Works of the Right Honourable Edmund Burke* (Chicago University Press).

Brenton, H (2010) *Anne Boleyn* (Nick Hern).

Burke, E (1985) *Reflections on the Revolution in France* (Penguin).

Byron (1980) *Complete Poetical Works* (J McGann ed) (Oxford University Press).

Clarendon, Lord (1978) *Selections from the History of the Rebellion and the Life by Himself* (H Trevor-Roper ed) (Oxford University Press).

Defoe, D (1986) *A Tour Through the Whole Island of Great Britain* (Penguin).

Donne, J (1987) *Selected Prose* (N Rhodes ed) (Penguin).

Fortescue, J (1997) *On the Laws and Governance of England* (S Lockwood ed) (Cambridge University Press).

Geobel, J (ed) (1969/1981) *The Law Practice of Alexander Hamilton: Documents and Commentary* (Columbia University Press).

Hobbes, T (1971) *A Dialogue Between a Philosopher and a Student of the Common Laws of England* (J Cropsey ed) (Chicago University Press).

—— (1985) *Leviathan* (Penguin).

Howell, T (ed) (1816) *A Complete Collection of State Trials* (Hansard).

Hume, D (1778/1983) *The History of England from the Invasion of Julius Caesar to the Revolution in 1688* (Liberty Fund).

—— (1987) *Essays Moral, Political and Literary* (E Miller ed) (Liberty Classics).

Kesselring, K (ed) (2016) *The Trial of Charles I* (Broadview).

King James (1924) *Daemonology and News from Scotland* (Bodley Head).

—— (1994) *Political Writings* (J Sommerville ed) (Cambridge University Press).

Kipling, R (1946) *Rudyard Kipling's Verse* (Doubleday).

Kramnick, I (ed) (1972) *Historical Writings of Lord Bolingbroke* (Chicago University Press).

Lipscomb, A (ed) (1903/04) *The Writings of Thomas Jefferson* (Jefferson Memorial Association).

Locke, J (1924) *Two Treatises of Government* (JM Dent).

Macaulay, Lord (1837) 'Lord Bacon' 66 *Edinburgh Review* 132.

Machiavelli, N (1995) *The Prince* (Penguin).

Milton, J (1991) *Political Writings* (M Dzelzainis ed) (Cambridge University Press).

Montesquieu (1989) *The Spirit of the Laws* (A Cohler et al eds) (Cambridge University Press).

Hooker, R (1989) *Of the Laws of Ecclesiastical Polity* (A McGrade ed) (Cambridge University Press).

Orwell, G (1984) *Essays of George Orwell* (Penguin).

Pope, A (1978) *Complete Poetical Works* (H Davis ed) (Oxford University Press).

Selden, J (1716) *Table Talk* (Jacob Tonson).

Seneca (2007) *Dialogues and Essays* (T Reinhardt ed) (Oxford University Press).

Shakespeare, W (1954) *King Henry V* (Routledge/Arden).

—— (1958) *The Tempest* (Routledge/Arden).

—— (1961) *King Richard II* (Routledge/Arden).

—— (1964) *The Merchant of Venice* (Routledge/Arden).

—— (1965) *Othello* (Routledge/Arden).

—— (1966) *King Henry IV part 2* (Routledge/Arden).

—— (1967) *Measure for Measure* (Routledge/Arden).

—— (1984) *Macbeth* (Routledge/Arden).

—— (1987) *King Lear* (Routledge/Arden).

Shelley, P (1971) *Complete Poetical Works* (Oxford University Press).

Sheppard, S (ed) (2003) *The Selected Writings of Sir Edward Coke* (Liberty Fund).

Sidney, A (1996) *Discourses Concerning Government* (T West ed) (Liberty Fund).

Sidney, P (1989) *A Critical Edition of the Major Works* (Oxford University Press).

Smith, P (ed) (1907) *Letters of Henry Wotton* (Oxford University Press).

Spedding, J (1857/2011) *The Works of Francis Bacon* (R Ellis and D Denon Heath eds) (Cambridge University Press).

—— (1861) *The Letters and Life of Francis Bacon* (Longman).

Spenser, E (1980) *Complete Poetical Works* (Oxford University Press)

Starkey, T (1989) *A Dialogue between Reginald Pole and Thomas Lupset* (T Mayer ed) (Royal Historical Society/Camden 4 ser 37).

Suetonius (2000) *Lives of the Caesars* (C Edwards ed) (Oxford University Press).

Tennyson, A (2009) *The Major Works* (A Roberts ed) (Oxford University Press).

Tocqueville, A de (1994) *Democracy in America* (Fontana).

Turner, K (1998) *Selected Poems of Thomas Gray, Charles Churchill and William Cowper* (Penguin).

Walker, L (1950) *The Discourses of Niccolo Machiavelli* (Routledge & Kegan Paul).

Webster, J (1986) *Three Plays* (C Gunby ed) (Penguin).

Wilkes, G (ed) (1999) *Ben Jonson: Five Plays* (Oxford University Press).

Wiggins, M (ed) (2008) *A Woman Killed with Kindness and Other Domestic Plays* (Oxford University Press).

Yale, D (ed) (1961) *Lord Nottingham's Chancery Cases* (Selden Society).

Secondary

Ackroyd, P (1998) *Sir Thomas More*, Chatto & Windus).

—— (2002) *Albion: The Origins of the English Imagination* (Chatto & Windus).

Adam, R (2020) *Brexit: Causes and Consequences* (Springer).

Allan, T (2001) *Constitutional Justice: A Liberal Theory of the Rule of Law* (Cambridge University Press).

—— (2011) 'Questions of Legality and Legitimacy: form and substance in British constitutionalism' 9 *International Journal of Constitutional Law* 155–62.

Allison J (2007) *The English Historical Constitution: Continuity, Change and European Effects* (Cambridge University Press).

Andrade, T (2011) 'A Chinese Farmer, Two African Boys, and a Warlord: Toward a Global Microhistory' 21 *Journal of World History* 573–91.

Anson, W (1980) *The Law and Custom of the Constitution* (Oxford University Press).

Baker, J (2017) *The Reinvention of Magna Carta 1216–1616* (Cambridge University Press).

Barroll, L (1988) 'A New History for Shakespeare and His Time' 39 *Shakespeare Quarterly* 443–54.

Bate, J (1993) *Shakespeare and Ovid* (Oxford University Press).

—— (2019) *How the Classics Made Shakespeare* (Princeton University Press).

Bergeron, D (2000) *Practising Renaissance Scholarship: Plays, Pageants, Patrons and Politics* (Duquesne University Press).

—— (2002) 'King James's Civic Pageant and Parliamentary Speech in March 1604' 34 *Albion* 213–31.

Berman, H (1994) 'The Origins of Historical Jurisprudence: Coke, Selden, Hale' 103 *Yale Law Journal* 1652–738.

Bernard, G (2005) *The King's Reformation: Henry VIII and the Remaking of the English Church* (Yale University Press).

Bingham, T (2010) *The Rule of Law* (Allen Lane).

Blakemore Evans, C (1988) *Elizabethan and Jacobean Drama* (A&C Black).

Boesche, R (1990) 'Fearing Monarchies and Merchants: Montesquieu's Two Theories of Despotism' 43 *Western Political Quarterly* 741–61.

Bogdanor, V (1998) *The Monarchy and the Constitution* (Oxford University Press).

—— (2021) *Beyond Brexit: Towards a British Constitution* (Tauris).

Bowen, C (1963) *Francis Bacon: The Temper of a Man* (Little Brown).

Braddick, M (2009) *God's Fury, England's Fire: A New History of the English Civil Wars* (Penguin).

Brennan, W (1988) 'The Quest to Develop a Jurisprudence in Times of Security Crisis' 18 *Israel Yearbook on Human Rights* 11–21.

Breward, C (2009) 'Fashioning the Modern Self: clothing, cavaliers and identity in van Dyck's London' in K Hearn (ed), *Van Dyck and Britain* (Tate Publishing) 24–37.

Briggs, J (1997) *This Stage-Play World* (Oxford University Press).

Brooks, C (1986) *Pettyfoggers and Vipers of the Commonwealth: The 'Lower Branch' of the Legal Profession in Early Modern England* (Cambridge University Press).

Brown, R (2003) 'Microhistory and the Postmodern Challenge' 23 *Journal of the Early Republic* 1–20.

Burgess, G (1992) *The Politics of the Ancient Constitution: An Introduction to English Political Thought 1603–1642* (Macmillan).

—— (1996) *Absolute Monarchy and the Stuart Constitution* (Yale University Press).

Burns, J (1996) *The True Law of Kingship: Concepts of Monarchy in Early Modern Scotland* (Oxford University Press).

Burton, M (2021) *From Broke to Brexit: Britain's Lost Decade* (Palgrave).

Butterfield, H (1931) *The Whig Interpretation of History* (Bell).

Carr, E (2001) *What is History?* (Palgrave).

Chandler, J (1998) *England in 1819: The Politics of Literary Culture and the Case of Romantic Historicism* (Chicago University Press).

Chrimes, S (1956) 'Richard II's Questions to his Judges' 72 *Law Quarterly Review* 365–90.

Churchill, W (1956) *A History of the English-Speaking Peoples* (Cassell).

Clark, S (1974) 'Bacon's *Henry VII*: a case study in the science of man' 13 *History and Theory* 97–118.

Coing, H (1955) 'English Equity and the *Denunciatio Evangelica* of the Canon Law' 71 *Law Quarterly Review* 223–41.

Colley, L (1994) *Britons: Forging the Nation 1707–1837* (Vintage).

Collinson, P (1987) 'The Monarchical Republic of Queen Elizabeth I' 69 *Bulletin of the John Rylands Library* 394–424.

—— (1988) *The Birthpangs of Protestant England: Religion and Cultural Change in the Sixteenth and Seventeenth Centuries* (Macmillan).

Colls, R (2002) *The Identity of England* (Oxford University Press).

Cook, H (2004) 'Against Common Right and Reason: The College of Physicians v Dr Thomas Bonham' in A Boyer (ed), *Law, Liberty and Parliament: Selected Essays on the Writings of Sir Edward Coke* (Liberty Press) 127–49.

Coquillette, D (1992) *Francis Bacon* (Edinburgh University Press).

Craig, W (2008) 'Hampton Court Again: The Millinery Petition and the Calling of the Conference' 77 *Anglican and Episcopal History* 46–70.

Cressy, D (2015) *Charles I and the People of England* (Oxford University Press).

Cromartie, A (1995) *Sir Matthew Hale 1609–1676: Law, Religion and Natural Philosophy* (Cambridge University Press).

Crow, M (2019) *Thomas Jefferson, Legal History and the Art of Recollection* (Cambridge University Press).

Cust, R (1985) 'Charles I, the Privy Council, and the Forced Loan' 24 *Journal of British Studies* 208–35.

Darwin, C (1974) *The Descent of Man* (Chicago University Press).

Derrida, J (1994) *Specters of Marx* (Routledge).

Dicey, A (1959) *An Introduction to the Study of the Law of the Constitution* (Macmillan).

Donaldson, I (2011) *Ben Jonson: A Life* (Oxford University Press).

Elias, N (1939) *The Civilizing Process and Psychogenetic Investigation* (Oxford University Press).

Elliott, M (2017) 'The Supreme Court's Judgment in *Miller*: In Search of a Constitutional Principle' 76 *Cambridge Law Journal* 257–88.

Elmer, P (2016) *Witchcraft, Witch-Hunting and Politics in Early Modern England* (Oxford University Press).

Elton, G (1973) *Reform and Renewal: Richard Cromwell and the Common Weal* (Cambridge University Press).

Esler, G (2021) *How Britain Ends: English Nationalism and the Rebirth of Our Nation* (Head of Zeus).

Evans, R (2000) *In Defence of History* (Granta).

Evrigenis, I (2019) 'Sovereignty, mercy, and natural law: James VI/I and Jean Bodin' 45 *History of European Ideas* 1073–88.

Ferris, I (2006) 'The "Character" of James the First and Antiquarian Secret History' 37 *The Wordsworth Circle* 73–76.

Fincham, K and Lake, P (1985) 'The Ecclesiastical Policy of King James I' 24 *Journal of British Studies* 169–207.

Finnis, J (2019) 'The unconstitutionality of the Supreme Court's prerogative judgement' (*Policy Exchange*, 28 September 2019).

Fortier, M (2005) *The Culture of Equity in Early Modern England* (Ashgate).

Galbraith, J (2017) *The Culture of Contentment* (Princeton University Press).

Gardiner, S (1886) *History of England* (Longman).

Garton Ash, T (2004) *Free World* (Penguin).

Gest, J (1909) 'The Writings of Sir Edward Coke' 18 *Yale Law Journal* 504–32.

Ghobrial, J-P (2019) 'Seeing the World Like a Microhistorian' 242 (supp 14) *Past and Present* 1–22.

Giles, C (2022) 'Brexit and the Economy' *Financial Times* (30 November 2002).

Ginzburg, C (1992) *The Cheese and the Worms: The Cosmos of a Sixteenth Century Miller* (Johns Hopkins University Press).

—— (1993) 'Microhistory: Two or Three Things That I Know About It' 20 *Critical Inquiry* 10–35.

—— (2002) *The Judge and the Historian: marginal notes on a late-twentieth-century miscarriage of justice* (Verso).

—— (2003) 'Latitude, Slaves, and the Bible: An Experiment in Microhistory' 31 *Critical Inquiry* 665–83.

—— (2012) *Threads and Traces: True, False Fictive* (California University Press).

—— (2013) *The Cheese and the Worms: The Cosmos of a Sixteenth-Century Miller* (Johns Hopkins University Press).

—— (2015) 'Microhistory and World History' in J Bentley and S Subrahmunyam (eds), *The Cambridge World History part 4* (Cambridge University Press) 446–73.

Gooch, G (1959) *History and Historians in Nineteenth-Century England* (Beacon Press).

Gossman, L (2003) 'Anecdote and History' 42 *History and Theory* 143–68.

Govedic, A (2006) 'The Trauma of Apathy' 77 *Revue des Etudes Slaves* 203–16.

Green, J (1997) 'I My Self: Queen Elizabeth I's Oratory at Tilbury Camp' 28 *The Sixteenth Century* 421–45.

Greenblatt, S (1985) 'Invisible Bullets: Renaissance authority and subversion in *Henry IV* and *Henry V*' in J Dollimore and A Sinfield (eds), *Political Shakespeare: New Essays in Cultural Materialism* (Manchester University Press) 18–47.

—— (2005) *Renaissance Self-Fashioning: From More to Shakespeare* (Chicago University Press).

Greenfield, L (1992) *Nationalism: Five Roads to Modernity* (Harvard University Press).

Guy, J (1982) 'Henry VIII and the Praemunire Manoeuvres of 1530–1531' 97 *English Historical Review* 481–503.

—— (ed) (1985) *Christopher St German on Chancery and Statute* (Selden Society).

—— (1988) *Tudor England* (Oxford University Press).

Gwyn, P (1990) *The King's Cardinal: The Rise and Fall of Thomas Wolsey* (Barrie & Jenkins).

Haigh, C (1984) *The Reign of Elizabeth I* (Macmillan).

—— (1993) *English Reformations: Religion, Politics, and Society under the Tudors* (Oxford University Press).

Hailsham, Lord (1976) *Elective Dictatorship* (BBC).

Haivry, O (2017) *John Selden and the Western Political Tradition* (Cambridge University Press).

Hale, M (1971) *History of the Common Law of England* (Chicago University Press).

Hamilton, D (1992) *Shakespeare and the Politics of Protestant England* (Kentucky University Press).

Hare, D (2005) *Obedience, Struggle and Revolt* (Faber and Faber).

Harris, J (2015) *Hume: An Intellectual Biography* (Cambridge University Press).

Hart, G (2002) *Restoration of the Republic: The Jeffersonian Ideal in 21st Century America* (Oxford University Press).

Hart, H (1961) *The Concept of Law* (Oxford University Press).

Haseler, S (1996) *The English Tribe: Identity, Nation and Europe* (Macmillan).

Haskett, T (1996) 'The Medieval English Court of Chancery' 14 *Law and History Review* 245–313.

Heffer, S (1999) *Nor Shall My Sword: The Reinvention of England* (Weidenfeld & Nicolson).

Hennessy, P (2018) 'Britain's good-chap model of government is coming apart' *The Economist* (18 December).

Holdsworth, W (1903) *A History of English Law* (Methuen).

—— (1938) *Some Makers of English Law* (Cambridge University Press).

Holmes, R (1994) *Shelley: The Pursuit* (HarperCollins).

Hopkins, D (2021) 'Reconsidering the Boredom of King James: Performance and Premodern Histories' 51 *Journal of Medieval and Early Modern Studies* 477–86.

Howsam, L (2004) 'Academic Discipline or Literary Genre? The Establishment Boundaries in Historical Writing' 32 *Victorian Literature and Culture* 525–45.

Hulsebosch, D (2003) 'The Ancient Constitution and the Expanding Empire: Sir Edward Coke's British Jurisprudence' 21 *Law and History Review* 439–82.

Hutton, R (1996) *The Rise and Fall of Merry England: The Ritual Year 1400–1700* (Oxford University Press).

Hutton, W (1995) *The State We're In* (Jonathan Cape).

Hutton, W and Giddens, A (2000) *On the Edge: Living with Global Capitalism* (Jonathan Cape).

Ives, E (1998) *Anne Boleyn* (Blackwell).

Jack, M (ed) (2011) *Erskine May: Parliamentary Practice* (LexisNexus/Butterworths).

Jack, S (2004) 'A Pattern for a King's Inauguration: The Coronation of James I' 21 *Parergon* 67–91.

Jacobs, F (2007) *The Sovereignty of Law: The European Way* (Cambridge University Press).

Jacoby, R (1999) *The End of Utopia: Politics and Culture in an Age of Apathy* (Basic Books).

James, H (1997) *Shakespeare's Troy: Drama, Politics and the Transformation of Empire* (Cambridge University Press).

Jardine, L and Stewart, A (1998) *Hostage to Fortune: The Troubled Life of Francis Bacon* (Gollancz).

Jenkins, K (1995) *On 'What is History?' From Carr and Elton to Rorty and White* (Routledge).

Jones, E (1971) *Politics and the Bench: The Judge and the Origins of the English Civil War* (Allen & Unwin).

Judge, D (2021) 'Walking the Dark Side: Evading Parliamentary Scrutiny' 92 *Political Quarterly* 283–92.

Kantorowicz, H (1957) *The King's Two Bodies: A Study in Medieval Political Theology* (Princeton University Press).

Kelley, D (1974) 'History, English Law and the Renaissance' 65 *Past and Present* 24–51.

Kernan, A (1995) *Shakespeare, the King's Playwright: Theatre in the Stuart Court* (Yale University Press).

Kim, K (1996) '*Calvin's Case* (1608) and the Law of Alien Status' 17 *Journal of Legal History* 155–71.

King, A (2007) *The British Constitution* (Oxford University Press).

Kishlansky, M (1999) 'Tyranny Denied: Charles I, Attorney-General Heath and the Five Knights Case' 42 *Historical Journal* 53–83.

Klinck, D (2010) *Conscience, Equity and the Court of Chancery in Early Modern England* (Routledge).

Klotz, L (2011) 'Ben Jonson's Legal Imagination in *Volpone*' 51 *Studies in English Literature* 385–408.

Knapfla, L (1977) *Law and Politics in Jacobean England* (Cambridge University Press).

Kumar, K (2003) *The Making of English National Identity* (Cambridge University Press).

Larner, C (1984) *Witchcraft and Religion* (Blackwell).

Latham, R (1993) *The Shorter Pepys* (Penguin).

Lepore, J (2001) 'Historians Who Love Too Much: Reflections on Microhistory and Biography' 88 *Journal of American History* 129–44.

Levack, B (1987) *The Formation of the British State: England, Scotland and the Union 1603–1707* (Oxford University Press).

Levi, G (1992) 'On Microhistory' in P Burke (ed), *New Perspectives in Historical Writing* (Pennsylvania University Press) 97–119.

—— (2019) 'Frail Frontiers' 242 (supp 14) *Past and Present* 37–49.

Loades, D (2009) *Henry VIII: Court, Church and Conflict* (Bloomsbury).

Lockwood, S (1997) *Sir John Fortescue: On the Laws and Governance of England* (Cambridge University Press).

Loewenstein, D (2001) *Representing Revolution in Milton and his Contemporaries: Religion, Politics and Polemics in Radical Puritanism* (Cambridge University Press).

Loughlin, M (2019) 'The Contemporary Crisis of Democracy' 39 *Oxford Journal of Legal Studies* 435–54.

Lumby, J (1995) *The Lancashire Witch-Craze: Jennet Preston and the Lancashire Witches 1612* (Carnegie).

Lyotard, J-F (1989) *The Differend: Phrases in Dispute* (Minnesota University Press).

Mack, J (1962) *Jeremy Bentham: An Odyssey of Ideas* (Heinemann).

Macleod, B (2021) 'So Exact His Text: Reading into the Margins of *Sejanus*' 28 *Ben Jonson Journal* 1–36.

Maitland, F (1898) *Roman Canon Law in the Church of England* (Methuen).

McCaffrey, W (1993) *Elizabeth I* (Arnold).

McConalogue, J (2020) *The British Constitution Resettled: Parliamentary Sovereignty Before and After Brexit* (Palgrave).

McEachern, C (1996) *The Poetics of English Nationhood* (Cambridge University Press).

McIlwain, C (1947) *Constitutionalism: Ancient and Modern* (Cornell University Press).

McKnight, L (1996) 'Crucifixion or Apocalypse? Refiguring *Eikon Basilike*' in D Hamilton and R Strier (eds), *Religion, Literature and Politics in Post-Reformation England 1540–1688* (Cambridge University Press) 138–60.

Millar, O (2007) 'Rubens' Whitehall Ceiling' 147 *The Burlington Magazine* 101–04.

Mincoff, M (1961) '*Henry VIII* and Fletcher' 12 *Shakespeare Quarterly* 239–60.

Monateri, P (2018) *Dominus Mundi: Political Sublime and the World Order* (Hart Publishing).

Montrose, L (1983) 'Shaping Fantasies: Figurations of Gender and Power in Elizabethan Culture' 1 *Representations* 61–94.

Morley H (ed) (1888) *Isaak Walton: Lives* (Routledge).

Morrill, J (1985) *The Scottish National Covenant in its British Context* (Edinburgh University Press).

—— (1993) *The Nature of the English Revolution* (Longmans).

Morrissey, M (2023) 'Was John Donne a Catholic? Conversion, Conformity, and Early Modern English Confessional Identities' 74 *Review of English Studies* 64–77.

Mowl, T (1996) *Horace Walpole: The Great Outsider* (Faber and Faber).

Murray, C (2022) 'From Oven-ready to Indigestible: The Protocol on Ireland/Northern Ireland' 73 *Northern Ireland Legal Quarterly* 8–36.

Murray, C and Rice, C (2021) 'Beyond Trade: Implementing the Ireland/Northern Ireland Protocol's human rights and equalities provisions' 72 *Northern Ireland Legal Quarterly* 1–28.

Nairn, T (2002) *Pariah: Misfortunes of the British Kingdom* (Verso).

Neale, J (1934) *Elizabeth I* (Harcourt and Brace).

O'Brien, C (1996) *The Long Affair: Thomas Jefferson and the French Revolution 1785-1800* (Sinclair Stevenson).

O'Mahoney, K (2009) 'The Witch Figure: The Witch of Edmonton' 24 *The Seventeenth Century* 238–59.

Orr, A (2016) 'God's Hangman: James VI, the Divine Right of Kings and the Devil' 18 *Reformation and Renaissance Review* 137–54.

Paine, A (1912) *Mark Twain, a Biography: The Personal and Literary Life of Samuel Langhorne Clemens* (Norton).

Palmer, R (1993) *English Law in the Age of the Black Death 1348-1381* (North Carolina University Press).

Pearson, M (2008) 'A Dog, a Witch, a Play: The Witch of Edmonton' 11 *Early Theatre* 89–111.

Plunkett, D and Shapiro, S (2017) 'Law, Morality, and Everything Else: General Jurisprudence as a Branch of Metanormative Enquiry' 128 *Ethics* 37–68.

Pocock, J (1960) 'Burke and the Ancient Constitution: A Problem in the History of Ideas' 3 *Historical Journal* 15–43.

—— (1967) *The Ancient Constitution and the Common Law* (Norton).

Porter, R (2000) *Enlightenment: Britain and the Creation of the Modern World* (Penguin).

Postema, G (2019) *Bentham and the Common Law Tradition* (Oxford University Press).

Price, P (1997) 'Natural Law and Birthright Citizenship in *Calvin's Case* (1608)' 9 *Yale Journal of Law and Humanities* 73–145.

Priestley, J (1977) *English Journey* (Penguin).

Putnam, L (2016) 'The Transnational and the Text-Searchable: Digitized Sources and the Shadows They Cast' 71 *American Historical Review* 377–402.

Pye, C (1990) *The Regal Phantasm: Shakespeare and the Politics of Spectacle* (Routledge).

Radcliffe, C (1952) *The Problem of Power: The Reith Lectures 1951* (Secker and Warburg).

Raffield, P (2004) *Images and Cultures of Law in Early Modern England: Justice and Political Power 1558-1660* (Cambridge University Press).

—— (2005) 'Contract, Classicism and the Common-Weal' 18 *Law and Literature* 69–96.

—— (2010) *Shakespeare's Imaginary Constitution: Late Elizabethan Politics and the Theatre of Law* (Hart Publishing).

—— (2017) *The Art of Law in Shakespeare* (Hart Publishing).

Richetti, J (2015) *The Life of Daniel Defoe* (Wiley Blackwell).

Robertson, G (2006) *The Tyrannicide Brief: The Story of the Man who Sent Charles I to the Scaffold* (Vintage).

Romm, J (2014) *Dying Every Day: Seneca at the Court of Nero* (Vintage).

Rorty, R (1989) *Contingency, Irony, and Solidarity* (Cambridge University Press).

Rozenberg, J (2020) *Enemies of the People? How Judges Shape Society* (Bristol University Press).

Rumble, W (1981) 'The Legal Philosophy of John Austin and the Realist Movement in American Jurisprudence' 66 *Cornell Law Review* 986–1031.

Russell, C (1990) *The Causes of the English Civil War* (Oxford University Press).

Salmon, J (1989) 'Stoicism and the Roman Example: Seneca and Tacitus in Jacobean England' 50 *Journal of the History of Ideas* 199–225.

Sandel, M (1996) *Democracy's Discontents: America in Search of a Public Philosophy* (Harvard University Press).

Sands, P (2022) *The Last Colony: A Tale of Exile, Justice and Britain's Colonial Legacy* (Weidenfeld & Nicolson).

Scarisbrick, J (1956) 'The Pardon of the Clergy 1531' 21 *Historical Journal* 22–39.

—— (1997) *Henry VIII* (Yale University Press).

Schoenbaum, S (1987) *William Shakespeare: A Compact Documentary Life* (Oxford University Press).

Sedley, S (2015) *Lions Under the Throne: Essays on the History of English Public Law* (Cambridge University Press).

Seeley, J (1971) *The Expansion of England* (Chicago University Press).

Sellar, W and Yeatman, R (1993) *1066 and All That: A Memorable History of England* (Sutton).

Shapiro, B (2019) *Law Reform in Early Modern England* (Hart Publishing).

Sharpe, J (1997) *Instruments of Darkness: Witchcraft in Early Modern England* (Pennsylvania University Press).

—— (2001) *The Bewitching of Anne Gunter* (Routledge).

Sharpe, K (1992) *The Personal Rule of Charles I* (Yale University Press).

Shaw, G (2004) *Man and Superman: A Comedy and a Philosophy* (Penguin).

Siedentop, L (2011) *Democracy in Europe* (Penguin).

Simpson, A (1975) *A History of the Common Law of Contract: The Rise of the Action of Assumpsit* (Oxford University Press).

—— (1981) 'The Rise and Fall of the Legal Treatise: Legal Principles and the Forms of Legal Literature' 48 *Chicago Law Review* 632–79.

Smith, D (1994) *Constitutional Royalism and the Search for Settlement c. 1640–1649* (Cambridge University Press).

—— (2014) *Sir Edward Coke and the Reformation of the Laws: Religion, Politics and Jurisprudence* (Cambridge University Press).

Somerset, A (1997) *Unnatural Murder: Poison at the Court of James I* (Weidenfeld & Nicolson).

Sommerville, J (1986) *Politics and Ideology in England 1603–1640* (Longman).

Springford, J (2022) 'The Cost of Brexit to June 2022' (Centre for European Research, 21 December 2022).

Stampnitzky, L (2013) *Disciplining Terror: How Experts Invented 'Terrorism'* (Cambridge University Press).

Stewart, A (2003) *The Cradle King: A Life of James VI and I* (Chatto & Windus).

Stewart, G (1959) *Pickett's Charge: A Microhistory of the Final Charge at Gettysburg, July 3 1863* (Houghton Mifflin).

Stone, L (1967) *The Crisis of the Aristocracy 1558–1641* (Oxford University Press).

Strachey, L (1971) *Queen Victoria* (Penguin).

Sumption, J (2020) *Trials of the State* (Profile).

—— (2021) *Law in a Time of Crisis* (Profile).

Sunstein, C (2005) *Laws of Fear: Beyond the Precautionary Principle* (Cambridge University Press).

Syme, H (2019) 'The Jacobean King's Men: a reconsideration' 70 *Review of English Studies* 231–51.

Talbert, E (1962) *The Problem of Order* (North Carolina University Press).

Tamanaha, B (2001) *A General Theory of Jurisprudence* (Oxford University Press).

—— (2011) 'What is "General" Jurisprudence? A Critique of Universalistic Claims by Philosophical Concepts of Law' 2 *Transnational Legal Theory* 287–308.

Taylor, A (1965) *English History 1914–1945* (Oxford University Press).

Thompson, E (1991) *The Making of the English Working Class* (Penguin).

Tittler, R (1998) 'Civil Portraiture and Political Culture in English Provincial Towns 1560–1640' 37 *Journal of British Studies* 306–29.

Tombs, R (2022) *This Sovereign Isle: Britain In and Out of Europe* (Penguin).

Trevor-Roper, H (1967) *The Crisis of the Seventeenth Century: Religion, the Reformation and Social Change* (Liberty Fund).

Tricomi, H (2004) 'Historicizing the Imagery of the Demonic in *The Duchess of Malfi*' 34 *Journal of Medieval and Early Modern Studies* 345–72.

Trivellato, F (2023) 'What Difference Makes a Difference? Global History and Microanalysis Revisited' 27 *Journal of Early Modern History* 7–31.

Tuori, K (2016) *The Emperor of Law: The Emergence of Roman Imperial Adjudication* (Oxford University Press).

Twining, W (2000) *Globalization and Legal Theory* (Cambridge University Press).

—— (2002) 'Cosmopolitan Legal Studies' 9 *International Journal of the Legal Profession* 99–108.

Underdown, D (1987) *Revel, Riot and Rebellion: Popular Politics and Culture in England* (Oxford University Press).

Usher, R (1903) 'James I and Sir Edward Coke' 18 *English Historical Review* 664–75.

Vogenauer, S (2005) 'An Empire of Light? Learning and Lawmaking in the History of German Law' 64 *Cambridge Law Journal* 481–500.

Wade, W (1955) 'The Basis of Legal Sovereignty' 13 *Cambridge Law Journal* 172–97.

Waller, G (1994) *Edmund Spenser: A Literary Life* (Macmillan).

Walsham, A (2012) 'History, Memory and the English Reformation' 55 *Historical Journal* 899–938.

Ward, I (1999) *Shakespeare and the Legal Imagination* (Cambridge University Press).

—— (2000) 'Casting Down Imaginations: Politics and Poetry in the English Republic' 21 *Journal of Legal History* 101–14.

—— (2018) 'The Matter of Henry VIII' 9 *Journal of International Dispute Resolution* 83–102.

—— (2019) *English Legal Histories* (Hart Publishing).

—— (2021) *The Play of Law in Modern British Theatre* (Edinburgh University Press).

—— (2022) 'The Last Roman King' 34 *Critical Survey* 67–92.

—— (2022a) 'Henry Foe's Dilemma' 18 *International Journal of Law in Context* 175–95.

—— (2023) *The Trials of Charles I* (Bloomsbury).

Watt, G (2008) 'The Law of Dramatic Properties in *The Merchant of Venice*' in P Raffield and G Watt (eds), *Shakespeare and the Law* (Hart Publishing) 237–52.

—— (2009) *Equity Stirring: The Story of Justice Beyond the Law* (Hart Publishing).

Wedgwood, C (2011) *A King Condemned* (Tauris).

West, R (1997) *The Life and Strange Surprising Adventures of Daniel Defoe* (HarperCollins).

Weston, C (1991) 'England: Ancient Constitution and Common Law' in J Burns and M Goldie (eds), *The Cambridge History of Political Thought 1450–1700* (Cambridge University Press) 374–411.

White, H (1978) *Tropics of Discourse: Essays in Cultural Criticism* (Johns Hopkins University Press).

Willms, S (2006) 'The Five Knights Case and Debates in the Parliament of 1628: Division and Suspicion under Charles I' 7 *Constructing the Past* 92–100.

Winston, J (2016) *Lawyers at Play: Literature, Law, and Politics at the Early Modern Inns of Court, 1559–1581* (Oxford University Press).

Wittgenstein, L (1980) *Culture and Value* (Blackwell).

Worden, B (1996) *The Sound of Virtue: Philip Sidney's Arcadia and Elizabethan Politics* (Yale University Press).

Wormald, B (1993) *Francis Bacon: History, Politics and Science 1561–1626* (Cambridge University Press).

Wormald, J (2021) *James VI and I: Collected Essays by Jenny Wormald* (John Donald).

Wortham, C (1996) 'Shakespeare, James I, and the Matter of Britain' 45 *English* 97–122.

Wright, S (2006) 'Nicholas Fuller and the Liberties of the Subject' 25 *Parliamentary History* 176–213.

Yandle, B (1993) 'Sir Edward Coke and the Struggle for a New Constitutional Order' 4 *Constitutional Political Economy* 264–69.

Young, A (2017) 'R (Miller) v Secretary of State for exiting the European Union: Thriller or Vanilla?' 42 *European Law Review* 280–95.

Young, H (1998) *This Blessed Plot: Britain from Churchill to Blair* (Macmillan).

Zagorin, P (1998) *Francis Bacon* (Princeton University Press).

Zhelnina, A (2020) 'The Apathy Syndrome: how we are trained not to care about politics' 67 *Social Problems* 358–78.

INDEX

When Rome fell to barbarian invaders, there were less than five hundred qualified Centurions. Not because Rome had fewer people but because it had fewer willing to make the sacrifices. And the last Centurions left their shields in the heather and took a barbarian bride...
—John Ringo, *The Last Centurion*

Prologue

From: *Marius Drake and Roman Garibaldi: Two Lives, Two Loves, One Empire* (4502 A.D)

Ah, what is to be said of Marius Drake and Roman Garibaldi that hasn't been said a thousand times already?

They were the two most famous men of their generation, perhaps the two most famous men since the "Band of Brothers" punched through the Asimov Point and won the final battle of the First Interstellar War. They are the subjects of countless biographies, ranging from works claiming that one was the true hero and the other was the villain to works suggesting they were both deeply corrupt, symptoms of the decline and fall of the Federation. There are works that suggest they were victims, helpless to do anything but play their roles, and works that suggest they were playing a game with each other that cost billions upon billions of innocent lives. And last, but far from least, there are works that suggest the two men were actually lovers and the final war between them was a tragedy on a far greater scale than *Romeo and Juliet*.

Indeed, history has truly hidden both men behind a shroud of nonsense.

That said, certain claims *can* be made with a fair degree of certainty.

The Federation was dying. Its government — the aristocratic and corrupt Grand Senate — was steadily sucking the lifeblood out of the countless innocent worlds in its thrall, destroying the economy that kept the Federation alive. Worse, the military had become deeply divided, with officers building little fiefdoms and patronage networks that were steadily corrupting the once-great Federation Navy. The purges that followed the Blue Star War only made it clear, to the smarter officers, that the only hope of permanent safety was in power. It should not have surprised the Grand Senate when one of them, Admiral Justinian, kicked off a civil war by mounting an attack on Earth.

Admiral Marius Drake rose to prominence during the attack, commanding the defense of Earth. Despite his own shabby treatment by the Grand Senate, Drake remained a noted Federation loyalist, a man who refused to accept the sundering of the Federation or the thought of claiming power for himself. His loyalties were noted; Drake was placed in command, eventually, of the fleet that would seek out and destroy Admiral Justinian's little empire once and for all.

Less is known of Roman Garibaldi's early life; it is known he was the sole survivor of an attack on an asteroid settlement, one who joined the Federation Navy and graduated from the Luna Academy with a First, but much else remains a mystery. It is clear, however, that he briefly took command of *Enterprise* during the ill-fated Operation Retribution and, in the aftermath, was recognized as an officer of rare promise. Indeed, like so many other youngsters in these troubled times, his rise up the ranks was rapid. War was no respecter of deadwood; hundreds of older officers, men who had gained their postings through patronage and connections rather than merit, had been killed in the early stages of the Justinian War. By the time Admiral

Drake led his fleet into Justinian's home system, Roman Garibaldi had assumed command of a starship.

Unknown to either Drake or Garibaldi, the Grand Senate had come to fear Drake as much as they had feared Admiral Justinian and his fellows. Accordingly, as soon as Drake defeated Admiral Justinian once and for all, they ordered an assassin, attached to Drake's staff, to kill him. The assassin missed: Drake's closest friend died saving his life. In his anger and rage, Admiral Drake led his fleet back to Earth, deposed the Grand Senate and took power for himself. After declaring himself Emperor Marius, he killed the final members of the Grand Senate personally. It was an unusual move that underscored just how different the new regime was to be.

It did not bring peace. Unknown to the Federation, a powerful alliance of humans and aliens was lurking just outside the Federation's borders. The Outsider Federation had taken advantage of the Justinian War to lay its final plans for an offensive that would shatter the Federation, freeing hundreds of thousands of worlds from its grasp. As Roman Garibaldi assumed command of Fifth Fleet, the Outsiders moved, launching an invasion of Federation space.

Already weakened, the Federation reeled under their blows. The economy, pushed to the limits by the Grand Senate, started to collapse, despite everything an increasingly desperate Emperor Marius could do. Political unrest and strikes mushroomed through the Core Worlds, while thousands of out-worlds joined the Outsiders or declared independence. Indeed, given his example, there was no shortage of military personnel wondering if they could take power for themselves.

Hope shone, it seemed, when Admiral Garibaldi won the Battle of Boston, stopping the Outsider advance dead in its tracks. The Outsiders reeled in shock, contemplating — for the first time — that they might lose the war. Emperor Marius traveled to Boston, where he met Admiral Garibaldi; together, they led an offensive towards Nova Athena, homeworld of one of the Outsider Federation's known leaders. But there, faced with defiance, Emperor Marius ordered the bombardment of the enemy world, threatening to exterminate uncounted billions of lives. Admiral Garibaldi moved to stop him...

... And the maddened Emperor opened fire on Garibaldi's ships, then retreated.

The stage was set for the final confrontation between the two greatest men of their generation... and a war that would determine, once and for all, the future of the Federation.

Chapter One

In the end, personal loyalty proved to be more important to the Federation Navy than its ideals or the Federation Constitution. But then, perhaps that was not surprising. The only way to rise in the ranks was through joining a senior officer's patronage network. Being promoted on merit was a thing of the past.
—The Federation Navy in Retrospect, 4199

Nova Athena, 4101

The universe had turned upside down, once again.

"The Outsider shuttle is approaching, sir," Lieutenant Sofia Thompson reported. She looked up from her console in the CIC. "They'll land in the shuttlebay in five minutes."

"Have the passengers scanned *thoroughly* before allowing them to enter the ship," Admiral Roman Garibaldi ordered, numbly. "Once they're cleared, bring them to the briefing compartment under guard."

"Aye, sir," Lieutenant Thompson said. She frowned. "Sir... they might not like being scanned and searched."

Roman laughed, harshly. "And I don't like running the risk of someone bringing an antimatter bomb onto the ship," he said. "We're not going to take chances."

He looked up at the console, watching grimly as the boxy shuttlecraft approached the massive superdreadnaught. No matter what he said, he doubted the Outsiders would try anything so stupid — *Valiant* was hardly the only superdreadnaught in Fifth Fleet — but he wouldn't have believed that Emperor Marius would attempt to commit genocide either. A great many certainties had toppled since Admiral Justinian had launched his attack on Earth nine years ago, sparking off a series of increasingly-bitter civil wars. And the Outsiders, his enemies up until an hour ago, had to be almost as confused as he was.

The shuttle vanished from the display as it landed in the shuttlebay. Roman watched through the monitors as armed marines surrounded the craft, then motioned for the occupants to come out with their hands clearly visible. Everyone was jumpy, now that they were caught in the middle of yet another civil war. Roman had made a career out of knowing what to do at the right time, but he honestly wasn't sure what to do now. He and his fleet were renegades, to all intents and purposes; he wondered, absently, just how many of his crewmen were considering burying a blade in his back. Bringing his head back to Earth would be *certain* to earn his assassin a rich reward.

Or a date with a firing squad, he thought, mordantly. *The Emperor has become increasingly irrational.*

He shuddered at the thought. Emperor Marius — Admiral Drake, as he'd been at the time — had seemed a strong leader, the sort of person Roman could follow into the fire without hesitation. Roman had wanted to be *like* him, even as he'd started to build a legend of his own. And he'd followed Admiral Drake until he'd

been promoted and given command of Fifth Fleet. Even then, he'd wanted to make Emperor Marius proud of him. He would have done anything for his mentor...

Except commit genocide, he thought. In hindsight, there had been far too many worrying signs before Professor Kratman came to see him. God alone knew what had happened to the Outsider POWs, but after the Battle of Nova Athena he wouldn't have bet money on them surviving for long. *I couldn't kill billions of humans on his command.*

His intercom buzzed. "Admiral," Elf said. His Marine CO — and his lover — sounded efficient, as always. "We have two guests: Senator Chang Li, the former Representative from Nova Athena and General Charlie Stuart. The remainder of the crew are the shuttle's pilots."

"Have the pilots held for the moment," Roman ordered. "Is the shuttle itself safe?"

"Yes, Admiral," Elf said. "There's nothing more dangerous than a pair of fuel cells and a couple of pistols."

Roman let out a breath. An antimatter warhead would be shrugged off by the ship's shields, if it detonated outside the hull, but a bomb that detonated *inside* the ship would blow them all to atoms. The Outsiders had to know they'd lost the war — or that they had, before Emperor Marius opened fire on their world — and they might have taken advantage of the brief truce to destroy *Valiant*. What hope did they have, other than the vague prospect of clawing the Federation as they went down?

"Take Chang and the General to the briefing compartment," he ordered, tiredly. He wanted — needed — a rest, but he knew he wasn't going to get one. "I'll join you there in a moment."

He closed the channel, then looked at the display. Hundreds of icons were scattered around the system; Fifth Fleet, surrounded by a cloud of starfighters, kept its distance from the remaining Outsider ships and planetary defenses. God alone knew what would happen, if some jumpy idiot pushed a firing key. Roman knew, deep inside, that the only real hope for survival was an alliance. But even that wouldn't be enough to save them, if Emperor Marius acted quickly. Roman knew, all too well, just how easy it would be for the Emperor to snatch the fleet train, then Boston itself. Losing the fleet base would doom his fleet to eventual irrelevance.

Unless the Outsiders can supply us, he thought. *But they can barely supply themselves.*

"Inform Captain Palter that he has tactical command of the fleet," he ordered. "He is to hold position and wait for orders, unless we come under attack. If so, he is to break contact as fast as possible and head for the system limits."

"Aye, sir," Lieutenant Thompson said.

Roman sighed, then rose and walked through the hatch, passing the armored marine who stood outside. The corridor beyond was deserted, the crew at their combat stations... he wondered, suddenly, just what would happen when the red alert finally came to an end and crewmen started to talk. There would be crewmen, he was sure, who would think nothing of genocide, who would care little for Outsider lives if their deaths ended a pitiless war. And some of them would be loyalists, loyal

to Emperor Marius. A handful might even have been covertly inserted onto his crew to watch *Roman* himself.

His hand dropped to the sidearm at his belt as he walked down the empty corridor, even though he was sure he was alone. The crew was armed; they'd faced enemies intent on actually *boarding* starships several times in the past. If even a handful thought to mutiny against his authority, either in the Emperor's name or merely to prevent another round of civil war, there was going to be a bloodbath. He wasn't even sure he could count on the loyalty of the marines...

Elf will keep them in line, he thought. *But where will she stand?*

It was a bitter thought. The marines prided themselves on being loyal to the Federation, on standing up for its values even as everyone else abandoned them. He had no reason to doubt Elf's loyalty to the Federation, but what would she make of it now, after Emperor Marius had tried to commit genocide? It wasn't as if they'd fired on *aliens*!

She'd tell me if she thought I was wrong, he thought. They'd been lovers for almost a decade. *I can trust her.*

He paused outside the hatch, taking a moment to gather himself, then opened the hatch and stepped into the briefing compartment. Elf stood against the bulkhead, wearing her light combat armor and carrying a plasma rifle in one hand; two other marines, wearing heavier armor, stood against the far wall. Senator Chang Li and General Stuart sat at the table, both looking tired and wary. Roman couldn't help thinking, as he cast his eyes over Stuart, that the Outsiders preferred far more practical uniforms than the Federation Navy. Stuart's uniform looked to be almost completely devoid of fancy gold braid.

"Senator, General," he said. "I am Admiral Garibaldi. Welcome onboard *Valiant*."

He studied them both as they rose. Chang Li was shorter than he'd expected, from her file; her long dark hair framed a middle-aged Oriental face. She'd been a Senator on Earth, he recalled; she'd been the *sole* Senator from the out-worlds before Admiral Justinian had launched his attack on Earth. Roman reminded himself not to underestimate her or her people, even though the Federation Navy had won the engagement. The Outsiders had to have been plotting their campaign long before Admiral Justinian started a civil war.

And the Emperor had some inkling there were unfriendly alien races out beyond the Rim, he thought. *It couldn't have made it any easier to deal with the Outsiders when they finally showed themselves.*

General Stuart was a complete unknown, according to the files; indeed, only a handful of data packets from deep-cover agents had provided any information at all. He'd been the enemy commander at Athena and Boston, putting Roman to flight in his first major engagement; the Outsiders, it seemed, hadn't adopted the Grand Senate's policy of shooting defeated admirals out of hand. It would give Stuart a chance to learn from the mistakes that had led to defeat at Boston, assuming the war didn't end quickly. And Stuart *looked* reassuringly competent. Roman just hoped Stuart was competent enough to make up for his earlier mistakes.

"Admiral," Chang Li said. "Thank you for receiving us."

Roman shrugged, not entirely sure what to say. He'd assumed, prior to the battle, that he — or Emperor Marius — would be dictating surrender terms, hopefully ending the Outsider War once and for all. But instead... he was forced into an alliance with his former enemies, now that the Emperor had gone mad. Roman couldn't help feeling torn between two competing loyalties; Marius Drake, the man who had sponsored him, and the ideals of the Federation, the ideals he'd upheld even as others had abandoned them.

And the Emperor did try to kill us, he thought, grimly. If it had been just him, he would have taken a starship and fled beyond the Rim, but he knew he wouldn't be the only target of the Empire's wrath. *We don't have any choice; we must fight.*

"The Emperor has gone mad," he said, bluntly. He had never been a diplomat. "He was prepared to fire on your homeworld."

"I know," Chang Li said. Her voice was oddly accented, something that surprised him. "I thank you for saving my people."

"At the cost of putting *my* people into terrible danger," Roman said. He had no illusions about their chances of success. Even if the Emperor didn't take and hold Boston, forcing him into a direct offensive though the system's Asimov Points, they'd have problems battering their way to Earth before the Federation's superior industry took effect. "The Emperor has to be stopped."

"We agree," Chang Li said. She cocked her head, perhaps in recognition of his concerns. "I am prepared to offer your fleet all the support we can provide."

"That would be useful," Roman said. "But what *can* you provide?"

"Relatively little," General Stuart said. His voice was gruff. "We lost too many ships at Boston, Admiral. I believe that was your work."

Roman nodded, curtly. He wasn't about to apologize for winning a battle, even though the consequences had come back to haunt him. He'd baited a trap and the Outsiders had fallen into it, giving him an excellent chance to tear their fleet apart. And he'd weakened them so badly that the counterattack hadn't met any serious challenge until it had crossed the stardrive limits and attacked Nova Athena itself.

"There's no point in dredging up the past," Chang Li said. "We must look to the future."

"Of course," Roman said. "What can you offer us?"

"Right now, four battle squadrons and a few hundred smaller ships," General Stuart told him, shortly. "Our fleet train, thankfully, remains largely intact."

"Assuming the crews don't desert when they realize just what they're facing," Chang Li added.

"The Federation is unlikely to show any mercy to independent freighters supporting the Outsiders," Roman pointed out. "Tell them that all will be forgiven if they help us win."

He sighed, inwardly. In hindsight, the Grand Senate's policies — their semi-legal monopoly over interstellar shipping within the core worlds — had driven hundreds of thousands of independent shippers out to the Rim. They'd signed up with the

Outsiders and started hauling supplies for them, while the Federation Navy was forced to depend on a badly weakened fleet train. The Grand Senate had chosen to concentrate on building warships, rather than the logistics the navy needed to support them. But then, until recently, the Federation Navy had been able to depend on a network of bases throughout explored and settled space.

"And what will happen," General Stuart asked warily, "if we *do* win?"

Roman understood, just for a second, the maddening problem facing Emperor Marius. The Federation's problems were impossibly vast, far too great for a single man to fix. And yet, tearing the Federation apart would be just as bad. Humanity hadn't survived a number of alien threats by being disunited.

And, come to think of it, he thought, *what do we do about their alien allies?*

He cursed under his breath. Humanity had long since abandoned the curse of racism, at least against their fellow humans, but it was a rare human who would agree that aliens should have equal rights. The memories of the First Interstellar War ran deep, even though it had been almost two thousand years ago. Aliens weren't welcome on human worlds; hell, they were rarely welcome on their *own* homeworlds. And the Outsiders had managed to drum up at least two alien races that were willing to fight alongside them against the Federation. It would be easy for Emperor Marius to turn the war into a crusade against aliens and their human dupes...

Of course he can, he thought, grimly. *The process was already underway by the time we won the Battle of Boston.*

"I think we should settle that after the fighting is over," he said, flatly. He didn't want to rule, but was there any choice? Sundering the Federation would be disastrous. "The Emperor still has a great many advantages. We may wind up merely prolonging the war."

"Agreed," Chang Li said. She shot her comrade an unreadable look. "We can determine how the future will look once we *know* we will *have* a future."

Roman nodded in agreement, then leaned forward. "How quickly can you get your ships here?"

General Stuart looked uncomfortable, sweat prickling on his forehead as his eyes darted around the compartment. It couldn't be easy, Roman knew, discussing classified information with someone who'd been on the other side until literally two hours ago. Hell, *he* didn't find it easy. He just knew there was no choice; his crews would die unless they won the war and saved themselves. It crossed his mind, as he waited for Stuart to answer, that Admiral Drake had faced the same problem after the Grand Senate had tried to kill him.

And they did kill his closest friend, he thought. Emperor Marius had never been quite the same afterwards. *Did losing Tobias push him off the deep end?*

"We should be able to assemble most of the remaining ships within a month, perhaps less," Stuart said, carefully. "But that will open up some of the systems we hold to counterattacks."

"There's less danger of that than you might think," Roman assured him. "We massed most of the Federation ships in the sector at Boston for the counteroffensive."

"Unless the Emperor sends out new orders on the way home," Stuart pointed out.

Roman shrugged. There were hundreds of stage-one colony worlds along the Rim, dozens of which had changed hands several times since the war began. None of them were useful, save perhaps as a source of untrained manpower; there was little to be gained by wasting time and effort capturing them for the umpteenth time. The Asimov Points, on the other hand, *would* be useful, but the Emperor didn't have the mobile forces — yet — to secure them.

He expended too many of the stockpiled fortresses to secure the routes to the core, he thought, darkly. It would be a headache he'd have to deal with, if he lived that long, but for the moment it was a blessing. *We were planning to secure the other Asimov Points as we consolidated, after winning at Nova Athena.*

"It shouldn't matter," he said, out loud. "The key to victory has been what it always has, ever since the First Interstellar War. The capture or destruction of the enemy's productive capabilities."

He looked straight at Chang Li. "How much can you produce, and how quickly?"

"Our missiles and ships are better, ton for ton, than their Federation counterparts," Chang Li assured him. Roman nodded, impatiently. He'd been on the receiving end of Outsider technical ingenuity more than once. "However, we simply cannot match the Federation's sheer weight of production. I'll give you the complete figures, if you wish, but... well, we can only produce a tenth of the missiles they can produce in the same time period, even though our facilities are more efficient."

"Assuming that their production nodes don't suffer from more disruptions," Stuart offered, ruefully. "There were a *lot* of strikes over the last two years."

"Which were broken," Chang Li reminded him.

"Even so, the workers weren't exactly enthusiastic about the whole affair," Stuart said. "I suspect their production has been quietly nose-diving for months."

"They'll do whatever it takes to get it back up again," Roman said, quietly. "We need to move fast."

He keyed a switch, displaying a starchart. "I'm going to take Fifth Fleet back to Spinner," he added, after a moment. "If the Emperor has secured Boston, retaking the system will be an incredibly costly battle. I don't dare give him the time to dig in."

"Understood," Stuart said.

"You two can return to the planet, then organize your ships to meet us at Spinner," Roman said. "Assuming we can retake Boston, we can push onwards to Earth as quickly as possible, before the Emperor has a chance to rally his defenses."

Chang Li blinked. "You intend to take the offensive so quickly?"

"There's no choice," Roman said. Stuart nodded in agreement. "If we don't take the offensive now, he'll take advantage of his production capabilities and crush us like bugs."

Chapter Two

This tended to ensure that officers stayed with their patrons, even when their patrons threw themselves into rebellion against their superiors — or the Federation itself.
—The Federation Navy in Retrospect, 4199

Von Doom System, 4101

Betrayed.

He'd been betrayed.

Marius Drake, Emperor of the Federation, Chief Naval Officer of the Federation Navy, sat in his darkened cabin, brooding. He'd been betrayed. Roman Garibaldi, his protégé, the young man whose career he'd mentored until Garibaldi had finally reached flag rank, had betrayed him. And, in doing so, had saved the Outsiders from defeat. The chance to burn them out of existence, once and for all, had been lost. Garibaldi had ensured that the war would go on and on...

I thought I could trust him, Drake thought. He'd believed in the younger man's loyalty to the Federation and Marius personally. God knew Garibaldi had been a mere cadet, if one of considerable promise, before the Justinian War had begun. Lacking connections, he should have put the Federation before political concerns. But instead he'd betrayed the Federation to its enemies. *I thought I could trust him!*

Raw, bitter anger welled up within Marius's heart. The Federation's unity was sacrosanct; human unity was all that stood between the human race and the hundreds of alien threats lurking beyond the Rim. He could not — he *would* not — tolerate any thought of sundering the Federation, of granting the Outsiders the independence they sought. It would only weaken humanity against the true threats. And indeed, had the Outsiders not made common cause with two alien races? In doing so, they had sold out the rest of the human race. They were beyond redemption!

They have to die, he thought, too tired to sit upright, let alone stand. It was hard, so hard, to muster the energy not to fall back into the darkness. He knew he should eat, get some proper sleep, but his thoughts were too agitated to allow himself to rise. *They have to be destroyed before they destroy us.*

He cursed under his breath, wrapped in a mixture of hatred and self-loathing. What had he been *thinking* when he'd made himself Emperor? Surely, he could have done something — anything — else, something that would have spared him the task of grappling with the falling Federation, of trying to save something from the ruins. But it wasn't in his nature to abandon a task, once started; he knew he had no choice but to keep fighting. The Outsiders had been badly weakened, after all. Even the addition of Fifth Fleet to their forces wouldn't save them in the long run.

Unless they have more allies out there, he thought. *And unless Roman manages to pull off a miracle.*

Drake shuddered in anger. Roman Garibaldi had a talent, a positive *talent*, for finding ways to get into and out of trouble. No doubt his talent would continue to work, even as he switched sides... had he wanted to be Emperor himself? Or had he

been a covert Outsider sympathizer all along? He'd certainly raised doubts about taking the POWs back to Earth for interrogation, then public execution. Had he been working for the Outsiders even then?

It didn't feel right, somehow, but it felt like hours before he reasoned it out. Roman *couldn't* have been working for the Outsiders, not before the Battle of Boston. A talented admiral — and Marius knew Roman to be a talented admiral — would not have found it hard to *lose* the battle, perhaps even by surrendering remarkably easily. No, Roman wasn't driven by love for the Outsiders, but a desire for power himself. No doubt he was already convincing the Outsiders to support him in his own bid for the throne.

The nasty part of Marius's mind contemplated that thought with no little amusement. Marius had thought himself used to command — he'd been commanding starships and fleets for decades — but being Emperor had been very different. The Grand Senate had left the Federation in a terrible mess and, no matter what he tried, the economy continued to collapse. Perhaps, if he'd had time, he could have saved the Federation, but the Outsider War had put a stop to that. The irony was almost amusing. He'd taken power at least in part to stop the Grand Senate from destroying the rest of the Federation, only to have no choice but to use the same policies himself.

That was why I wanted to end it, he thought, grimly. Destroying Nova Athena and its population would have ended the war. Too many lives had already been lost, sacrifices to the greater good. *A victory now would give us a chance to breathe.*

He looked up, sharply, as a low chime rang through the cabin. Someone was on the other side of the hatch, someone he didn't know... the marines wouldn't let someone hostile into the cabin, would they? He thought not; he trusted the marines, but then he'd trusted Roman Garibaldi too. Tobias, his former Marine CO and closest friend, was dead... who knew which way the marines would jump, when push came to shove? They'd already balked at some of the grisly tasks necessary to get the economy back up and running, including a moderate purge of trouble-makers...

The hatch hissed open. Marius winced, a second later, as the lights brightened. If someone on the ship had decided to switch sides... he relaxed, very slightly, as Commander Ginny Lewis came into view. She already knew there was something wrong with him and hadn't betrayed him, unlike so many others. But how long would that last?

"Emperor?"

Marius almost smiled at the alarm in her voice. The young redhead had shown rare promise — almost as much as the young Garibaldi — but it wouldn't save her if she were blamed for his condition. Captain Watson wouldn't hesitate to turn her into a scapegoat, although it wouldn't save his hide either. God alone knew what would happen to the Federation once Marius was gone. It wasn't as if there was a clear successor waiting in the wings. Marius had no children, and his wife, for all of her many talents, lacked the military skills to keep the fleet loyal to her. And the civilian government had been crippled decades before Marius's birth.

"I'm alive," Marius croaked. He forced himself to sit upright. If Ginny intended to kill him, he could at least meet it with some dignity. "Commander — status report?"

"You need to eat and drink something, if you won't let me call the medics," Ginny said, carefully. "Emperor... sir..."

"Not now," Marius said, stiffly. He didn't like anyone seeing him so weak; hell, he hated the thought of taking Ginny into his confidence. But there was no choice. "Status report?"

"We've just entered the Von Doom system," Ginny said. "Captain Watson was wondering how you wished to enter Boston."

"I'm sure he was," Marius muttered.

He cursed under his breath. Captain Watson was a solid man, but completely lacking in imagination or initiative. Even in the midst of a war, with deadwood admirals and captains being killed at an unprecedented rate, his rise had been suspiciously slow. But then, he did need authorization in triplicate to go to the head, let alone take command of his superdreadnaught and set course for the nearest star. And to think he'd thought that a lack of imagination was an asset!

"Tell me," he said. It was hard to think clearly, but he had no choice. "Have we detected any courier drones racing past us?"

"No, sir," Ginny said. "Fifth Fleet hasn't attempted to communicate with Boston."

"Unless they sent the drones the other way," Marius commented. There were *two* possible routes to Boston, after all, and Roman Garibaldi would have no trouble deducing which one Marius had taken. "And we have no way of knowing what we'll encounter at Boston."

He closed his eyes as a stab of pain burned through his head. Boston had been the linchpin of the Federation's defenses in the sector. Fifth Fleet had been based there for much of the war and, by straining the already-tottering logistics network to the limits, the navy had built up a powerful network of fixed fortifications. If his fleet had to punch their way into the system, it was going to cost them dearly. They'd expended most of their assault missiles during the flight to Nova Athena.

And if Roman Garibaldi planned to betray me all along, he thought, *whoever he left in command is likely to be ready and waiting for us.*

There was no choice, of course. If he wanted to get back to Earth in less than five *years*, he had to use the Asimov Point network. And if he wanted to do *that*, he had to enter Boston and hope...

"Inform Captain Watson that we are to enter the system as normal, announcing a victory over the Outsiders," he said. It was time to gamble. If the system's defenders had no idea what had happened at Nova Athena, they'd hesitate to open fire on his ships. "I do not believe we will be fired upon. Once we're in the system, head directly for the next Asimov Point."

"Aye, sir," Ginny said. "And the system itself?"

Marius took a moment to think. Boston *had* to remain in friendly hands, if it were at all possible, but he knew he didn't have the firepower to impose his will on the

system. If the local CO — who would be a Garibaldi loyalist, he was sure — put up a fight, all hell was likely to break loose. He dared not die, not now. The Federation he loved would not survive his death.

"Once we enter the system, detach Commodore Palin with orders to take command of the system's defenses," he said, carefully. Commodore Hassan Palin had a working brain, which put him ahead of Captain Watson; he should be smart enough to understand the dangers of trying to switch sides now the battle lines had been redrawn. "He is to send messages through the ICN... no, belay that. I'll write the messages myself."

"Yes, sir," Ginny said. "There are gaps in the ICN, though."

Marius nodded, impatiently. The Outsiders, damn them to hell, had targeted ICN platforms specifically, making it harder for the Federation to coordinate defensive operations on a galactic scale. *They* had the same problem, of course, but they'd been on the offensive and their homeworlds were largely unknown. The Federation could capture every world that had willingly joined the Outsiders, once the war had begun, and yet get no closer to final victory.

"The messages can also be relayed on the base's courier boats," he said, tartly. He tried to stand, but his body betrayed him and fell back into the chair. "They can take it to worlds and systems outside the network."

"Yes, sir," Ginny said. She held out a hand. "Should I help you up?"

"No," Marius said. He gathered himself and tried to stand again. His legs felt weak, as if he was about to fall over at any second, but somehow he managed to remain balanced. "I'm not a cripple..."

"You should eat, sir," Ginny said. "How long has it been since you ate or drank anything?"

Marius couldn't remember. Hell, he wasn't sure just how long he'd been in the cabin, just how long it had been since they'd blasted away from Nova Athena. The mere thought sent another jolt of pain stabbing though his head. His body had been enhanced thoroughly, first as a naval officer and then as an emperor, but he needed food and rest, perhaps not in that order. Ginny was right; he *should* go see the medics... yet he was too stubborn. The old distrust of starship doctors, the fear that they would relieve him of duty for not attending his physical exam, rose up in his mind. He knew he didn't dare show weakness to anyone outside his trusted circle.

And how many of them, his own thoughts mocked him, *can you trust?*

He shuddered, almost losing his balance as he tottered over to the desk. He'd trusted Blake Raistlin and the young man had nearly killed him, on orders from his familial superiors. And he'd trusted Roman Garibaldi, who'd shared the same graduating class as Blake Raistlin. He made a mental note to check what had happened to the others from that class — given the attrition of two wars, there was a good chance that most of them were dead — and he sat down, feeling his legs buckle underneath him. It was unlikely he could have remained standing for much longer.

"I'll find some food for you, sir," Ginny said. "There's normally something held in stasis..."

"Pass on the orders to Captain Watson first," Marius ordered. He didn't need food *that* quickly — besides, it would be a mistake to let the captain think he was incapable of command. Watson's subordinates might have their own ideas about the future. "And *then* go fetch something to eat."

He watched Ginny go, trying not to notice how her tight trousers showed off her behind. He was married, married to one of the few people he trusted... but could he trust her, really? If Tiffany was planning to betray him, too...

You have to trust someone, his own thoughts reminded him. *And Tiffany could have betrayed you to her family years ago, if she'd wanted you dead.*

It wasn't a pleasant thought. Tiffany was only his because her family had pushed her into marrying him, since they believed he needed a link to the Grand Senate. They hadn't realized that Tiffany and he would wind up in an alliance to survive, or fall in love, that their marriage would become far more than just another marriage of convenience. But now, if Roman Garibaldi had betrayed him, would Tiffany do the same?

I have to get back to Earth, he thought. *It's the only way to win.*

Every instinct, honed by decades of fighting the Federation's wars, told him to take command of Boston, replenish his ships and meet Roman Garibaldi's offensive when it came. Roman knew the laws of interstellar combat as well as Drake did; Garibaldi would *know* the only hope for victory was to overrun the Federation before Marius could rebuild the economy and deploy newer and better weapons from the research stations. He *had* to move quickly if he wanted to survive...

But if he stayed at Boston, he risked losing control of his flank.

He cursed, savagely. His attention was required in too many places, too many for him to handle personally... and yet, he couldn't delegate responsibility to anyone else. Who could he trust? He'd promoted Roman Garibaldi over the heads of officers with more seniority, more time in grade, because he'd trusted the younger man. Now, Roman had betrayed him and... and there were no others he dared trust. He'd have to double and triple-check his precautions, just to make sure no one else could stick a knife in his back...

It struck him, suddenly, that the Grand Senate must have felt the same way. The thought made him giggle, realizing that matters had come full circle. *He* was now playing the same role as the Grand Senate, trying to protect the *status quo* while young and ambitious officers sought to destroy it. And if Roman Garibaldi had his way, Marius would be removed, just like the Grand Senate.

And Roman might even shoot him in the head — personally.

The hatch hissed open again, revealing a harassed-looking Ginny carrying a tray. "The guards insisted on me tasting everything first," she said, as she put the tray on the table and removed the cover. Marius's stomach rumbled as he smelled the food. "Don't they trust me?"

"They don't trust anyone," Marius said, as he picked up the fork. It was unlikely that anyone had managed to slip poison into his food, but too many unlikely things had happened recently. A toxin keyed to Marius personally, thankfully, would be

well beyond the reach of most would-be assassins. "But with food like this, I wonder why anyone would bother adding poison."

He smiled as he took a bite of the food. Naval rations had never been very good, thanks to the Grand Senate ordering foodstuffs from the lowest or most-favored bidder. Indeed, he'd heard of hundreds of crews that had been discontented, before the Justinian War, because their commanding officers had been selling off the rations and, somehow, buying even worse food supplies on the black market. That, at least, had been *one* thing he'd been able to fix once he'd assumed control of the Federation. Making sure that captains and flag officers had to eat the same food as the lowest of crewmen had probably helped.

But you did host a feast for your officers before you departed Boston, his own thoughts reminded him. *Did you make sure the lower decks got the same food then?*

"It's a great improvement," Ginny said, carefully. "Although I'm not exactly sure what it *is*."

"As long as it's edible and reasonably tasty, it doesn't matter," Marius said. He'd spent most of his adult life on one starship or another. Most spacers preferred to draw a veil over *precisely* where most recycled food came from. "All that matters is that it will help keep you alive."

"I still think you should go to sickbay, sir," Ginny said. "You're not well."

"I can't afford to leave my post," Marius said. He cursed under his breath. Captain Watson could handle a transit through an Asimov Point, but if even a handful of ships tried to bar their path... he doubted the captain could deal with it. "And I have too much work to do."

He finished his meal, then reached for his console. "Inform me when we are two hours from the Boston Asimov Point," he ordered. "Until then, I have planning to do."

"You should sleep," Ginny said. "Sir..."

Marius felt a hot flash of anger. "I don't have time," he snapped. "Dismissed."

Ginny saluted, then hastily beat a retreat through the hatch. Marius watched her go, then reached into his uniform pocket for the packet of pills. There were dangers in using them too often, he knew all too well, but there was no choice. He *needed* to stay awake.

Popping a pill into his mouth, he tapped the console and started to work.

Chapter Three

When a senior officer was deserving of such loyalty, it worked in their favor — but, when they weren't, it only made the problems facing the Federation worse.
—The Federation Navy in Retrospect, 4199

Nova Athena, 4101

"You're being very quiet," Roman observed.

"I wish I had something to say," Elf replied. They stood together in the CIC, looking up at the giant display. Fifth Fleet was reversing course and powering out towards the system limits, where it would slip into stardrive for the short jaunt to the nearest Asimov Point. "I wish I knew which way to jump."

Roman cocked his head at her. "Could you accept attempted genocide?"

Elf shook her head. "There's a difference between collateral damage, however unfortunate, and the deliberate slaughter of billions of innocents," she said, firmly. "But I just worry about the future."

Roman nodded, curtly. There was no point in trying to hide what they'd done. They'd gone into rebellion against the Federation, against the Emperor... just like Admiral Justinian and the other warlords. And if they didn't succeed in defeating Emperor Marius, they would be hunted down and killed as the Federation's vastly-greater war industry swamped them in production. He hadn't had time to sit down and properly simulate the war, although experience had told him that simulations were rarely useful, but he had a feeling he knew what the predicted outcome would be. The Federation would win the war.

"And then there's the Outsiders," Elf said. "Do you really trust them?"

"I trust them to act in their own self-interest," Roman said. It was easy to blame the Outsiders for kicking the Federation while it was down, but they'd probably suspected they would never have a better chance for outright victory. And they were probably right. "And what happens after the war..."

"You need a plan to determine what will happen afterwards, if we win," Elf said curtly, as his words tailed off. "You need to decide what you want to happen before someone else decides it for you."

Roman shook his head, although he knew she was right. He'd been a RockRat, then a Federation Navy officer... he wasn't a politician or a planetary governor. He'd thought Emperor Marius could handle the task of reforming the Federation, but it had evidently driven the older man mad. There was no way he wanted to spend the rest of his life as emperor, trapped on Earth while trying to fix the damage of centuries of mismanagement and deliberate malice.

"You need to think about these details," Elf pressed. "The Outsiders will certainly have a plan for the post-war universe."

Marius had said, back during one of their private meetings, that the Federation's great strength was its unity. They'd fought the Inheritance Wars to make it clear

that the Federation was not going to be sundered. Indeed, even Admiral Justinian had moved to claim the seat of power, rather than separate his sector from the Federation... although, towards the end of the war, he might have had other ideas. But the Outsiders... they wanted to break the Federation up completely, even welcome aliens into the fold.

And we won't know if we can trust the aliens, he thought, numbly. *We would have another civil war over the issue.*

"I can see why the problem drove Emperor Marius mad," he said, finally. "How are we supposed to handle it ourselves?"

He cursed under his breath as he looked at the starchart, showing the quickest route back to Boston. There were no precautions in place to keep Marius from taking control of the base, then turning its formidable defenses against Fifth Fleet. Roman knew the defenses intimately — he'd designed the defense grid himself — and there was no easy way to push through the Asimov Point. It would be a brutal engagement that would cost him dearly, yet there was little choice. The cold equations that had pushed the Outsiders into attacking Boston, despite knowing they were slamming into the teeth of his defenses, applied to him too. If he wanted to break through into the Core Worlds, he *needed* Boston...

... And Emperor Marius would know it too.

"We may not survive long enough to discuss the future of the Federation," he said, turning away from the display. "We can worry about the future after we win the war."

"A mistake," Elf said.

Roman nodded, ruefully. "We need to concentrate on winning the war first," he said. "I can't get distracted like Admiral Stilicho."

"I suppose," Elf said.

She looked doubtful, but he knew she understood. Admiral Stilicho had commanded the Federation Navy's invasion force during the early stages of the Blue Star War, a war the Federation should have won easily. Indeed, Admiral Stilicho had been so confident of a walkover that he spent more time planning the victory parade on Earth and handing out patronage to his junior officers than preparing for the war. His masterstroke had turned into a military disaster on a scale unseen since the Battle of Spider Bite and, fortunately for him, he hadn't survived the first engagement. Roman had no intention of repeating the same mistake.

Because Emperor Marius is a skilled officer who beat Admiral Justinian, even when taken by surprise, Roman thought. *He won't hesitate to take advantage of any of my mistakes.*

"And that leads to another problem," he said. "The loyalty of our crews."

"I've stationed marines throughout the decks, ensuring the lockdown stays firmly in place," Elf assured him. "I doubt anyone can put together a plan to mutiny before we're halfway to Boston."

Roman scowled. He hated the thought of enforcing loyalty at gunpoint. It would be easy, too easy, for his crewmen to work at a deliberate pace, even when the ship

was under fire. He couldn't allow it to risk their chances when push came to shove. Emperor Marius already held too many cards for it to be tolerated.

"I need to speak to them," he said. He keyed a console. "Record."

"Recording," the console said.

Roman took a moment to gather his thoughts, then began. "This is Admiral Garibaldi," he said, carefully. By now, lockdown or no lockdown, word of the brief and savage engagement would have spread through the fleet. There was no point in trying to lie. "Emperor Marius attempted to bombard Nova Athena with antimatter weapons, ensuring the destruction of all life on her surface. When I tried to talk him out of it, he opened fire on Fifth Fleet."

He scowled at the thought. Three years of warfare against the Outsiders — and their alien allies — had worn down the fleet's desire to remain true to the Federation's ideals. It was quite likely that a large percentage of his crew, even a majority, would think that exterminating the entire population of Nova Athena was a good thing, even though it would be a monstrous act. They'd psyched themselves up for a final battle, one that would end the war...

But it wouldn't. Even if Nova Athena had surrendered, even if Emperor Marius had accepted the surrender without bombarding the planet, the other Outsider worlds and bases were still a complete mystery. The war would have dragged on for years before every last Outsider was hunted down and killed.

"The Emperor has gone mad," he said, picking his words carefully. "He has already declared us — *all* of us — outlaws. Our only hope, to save both our lives and something of the Federation, is to overthrow him as quickly as possible. Towards this end, I have forged an alliance with the Outsiders."

He paused, again. There was no point in trying to hide the truth, but it was chancy. A crewman who would otherwise have supported him might think twice, after learning that he was meant to work with the alien-loving Outsiders. Or someone who had a more personal grudge... the Outsiders had killed hundreds of thousands of naval personnel in their war, all of whom would have left friends and family behind. And, with sidearms issued to all personnel, a bloody mutiny at the worst possible time might end the war.

"I know this won't be easy to accept," he added, "but I see no choice. The Emperor has to be stopped.

"Once we return to Boston, those of you who are unwilling to take up arms against the Emperor can make yourselves known to my officers. You will be shipped to Boston itself, to remain out of the fighting until the end of the war. If the Emperor wins, you will be held blameless" — he hoped that was true — "and can resume your duties. And, if we win, nothing more will be said about the matter."

He took a long breath. "I know this won't be easy for many of us," he concluded. "Please make up your mind during the voyage to Boston, then let me know what you want to do."

"Good enough," Elf said, as he stopped the recording. "Maybe not the *sweetest* speech I've heard, but one from the heart."

Roman nodded, curtly. He knew he'd have problems with manpower — far too many officers and crew thought the Emperor was the greatest thing that had ever happened to the Federation Navy — but he wasn't about to force men to go into battle against their will.

"I'll transmit it through the fleet," he said. "Do you foresee any other problems?"

"There will be agents inserted into the fleet," Elf said. "*They're* not likely to bow out and stay on Boston."

"I know," Roman said. "Can you ID them?"

"Not easily," Elf said. "Once, it would have been easy, but now... with so much manpower washing around the Federation..."

Roman winced. Manpower — skilled manpower — had been a major problem for years, thanks to the Grand Senate's policies on education. Emperor Marius hadn't even *begun* to fix the problems with the educational establishment, but at least he'd been able to ensure that skilled engineers and technicians were encouraged to train others in how to maintain starships. Even so, vast numbers of skilled officers had been moved from ship to ship, making it impossible for a counter-intelligence team to look for the signs of an infiltrator. There were just too many officers and men who fit the profile.

"Just keep an eye out for trouble," he said. He wasn't too worried about agitators — the chiefs would deal with them — but an operative who kept his head down while plotting trouble was far more dangerous. "And we'll do what we can to encourage them to switch sides."

He keyed the console, sending the recording into the communications network, then called Lieutenant Thompson back into the CIC. She looked refreshed — she'd managed to snatch a couple of hours of sleep, something that had eluded both Roman and Elf — and took her place at the console without hesitation. Elf nodded curtly to Roman and strode towards the hatch, which hissed open at her approach. Roman just hoped she found time to have a nap before they reached Boston.

"Admiral," Lieutenant Thompson said. "I have a full status report from the fleet."

"Show me," Roman ordered. "And then reshuffle our damaged ships to the rear."

The display updated rapidly, showing him the remains of Fifth Fleet. It was an impressive collection of firepower — thanks to modern technology, it was more powerful than the mighty fleet that had been sent off on Operation Retribution — but it had taken a beating, thanks to the Emperor. Only five battle squadrons could claim to be at full readiness, the remainder no longer capable of flank speed or raising shields. Repair crews were already swarming over their hulls, but it would take weeks — at least — to get them ready to go back into the fire.

I don't want to leave them here, with the Outsiders, he thought. He knew he didn't dare trust the Outsiders completely, not when they *were* allied with aliens. *We just have to hope we can move them back to Boston... and that we aren't greeted with a hail of missiles.*

"Captain Hammond and Captain Tromie both claim their ships are still capable of

combat operations," Lieutenant Thompson informed him. "However, their engineers disagree."

"Tell them they're assigned to protect the cripples," Roman said, curtly. He didn't want to send a damaged ship through a potentially-hostile Asimov Point, no matter what the commanding officer thought. "And make sure they can establish a combat datanet with the remaining ships. We need to maximize our advantages."

"Aye, sir," Lieutenant Thompson said.

Roman sat back, thinking hard. He didn't blame the captains for wanting to remain in the fight, even against ships that had been friendly a few hours ago. Far too many decent officers had been cashiered, or had their careers frozen, for not being aggressive enough in the eyes of their superiors. But there was aggression and then there was a foolhardy desire to take a crippled ship into the maelstrom of modern war. It could not be allowed.

He pushed the thought aside as he tapped his console. "Order nineteen courier boats readied for dispatch," he said. "I'll be recording a message for them personally, which they are to upload into what remains of the ICN as they pass through the sector."

"Aye, sir," Lieutenant Thompson said.

"And make sure their commanders are aware of the importance of avoiding contact with Emperor Marius and his ships," Roman added. "The last thing they want — or need — is to be caught by the Emperor."

"Aye, sir," Thompson said, again.

Roman bent over his console, trying to think how best to compose a message to the other fleet admirals scattered around the Federation. It was unlikely, to say the least, that any of them would declare war on Emperor Marius — he'd put most of them in command personally — but he had to try. Fifth Fleet was the most powerful formation in the Federation Navy — in raw tonnage, she was more powerful than Home Fleet — yet she was grossly outgunned. He hated to think of what it would cost him as he fought his way through one defended Asimov Point after another, bleeding his fleet white as he advanced slowly towards Earth. By the time he reached the Gateway, the Asimov Point that led to Earth, he'd have hardly any ships left.

And some of them may see value in attempting to revolt, he thought, grimly. *They may even see what I'm doing as just another revolt.*

He scowled at the thought. How trustworthy *were* the other fleet admirals? He'd only met a couple of them personally... Emperor Marius might have chosen them for loyalty, rather than competence. But then, Marius would have *known* the dangers of putting incompetents in command positions. He'd been the one who'd had to save the Retribution Fleet after Fleet Admiral Cuthbert Parkinson had led it into a trap. There was a war on, after all. He wouldn't have repeated the Grand Senate's mistake.

The Federation is at stake, he told himself. *I have to try to make contact, even if it fails.*

He tapped out a message on his console, reread it twice, then attached sensor records up to the moment Emperor Marius had swung his ships around and fled the

system. There was nothing there, he was sure, that the Emperor wouldn't already have, once his analysts went to work sifting through the vast fields of data collected by his starships during the battle. He briefly considered attaching a note of his intentions, then dismissed the thought. The courier boats might well be captured *en route...*

And yet he'll know what you have in mind, he thought. *The laws of interstellar combat leave me with few options and he knows it.*

Roman scowled as another thought occurred to him. If they were lucky, the courier boats would beat the Emperor to Boston, even though the Emperor had a head start. And if that happened... he could warn his second, inform Commodore Sonia Yu that the Emperor's ships had to be stopped. They could win in an instant, if they trapped or killed the Emperor himself. And yet, he knew it would cause a great deal of confusion. Sonia was a skilled logistics officer, but she was no fighter.

"Record," he ordered. "Sonia, things have changed."

He ran through a brief explanation of what had happened, then uploaded it to the courier boats before they made it out of communications range. It was a gamble — Sonia might side with the Emperor, or waffle long enough for the Emperor to take control of the defenses — but it had to be tried. He just had a nasty feeling the courier boat wouldn't reach Boston in time to make a difference. The pilot wouldn't be able to take a least time course if he or she encountered the Emperor's fleet.

"Message sent, sir," Lieutenant Thompson said.

Roman nodded, then forced himself to relax. There were no emergency alerts, nothing to suggest that his crews were on the verge of mutiny... perhaps, just perhaps, he'd managed to sway most of them to his side. Or, perhaps, they were waiting until the fleet was at Boston before deserting him. What would he do, he asked himself silently, if the fleet lost most of its crewmen? The war would come to an end before it had even fairly begun.

He shrugged, looking up at Nova Athena. The planet's population knew just how close they'd come to total destruction, but would the rest of the Outsiders? How far could he trust them, too? They had to know he was their only hope for winning the war...

We just have to push on and hope, he told himself, firmly. *Because if we stop, the Emperor will have his chance to secure his position and win the war.*

Chapter Four

This was not, to be fair, a problem faced by the Outsiders. They handled the vast majority of their promotions purely on merit. Accordingly, their starship crews tended to be more efficient than their Federation counterparts.
—The Federation Navy in Retrospect, 4199

Nova Athena, 4101

"I think I hate you," Chang Li said.

She glared at General Stuart, who seemed unimpressed as she stepped into his stateroom, the hatch hissing closed behind her. Maybe it was a minor matter, given how sure they'd been that they were about to die, but she was still annoyed. He had defied her direct orders and, even though he'd been trying to save her life, there still had to be a reckoning.

"You had me kidnapped," she snapped. "And then the shuttle's power failed, midway through the flight. If the battle had gone differently..."

"I believed you would have died if you'd remained on Nova Athena," General Stuart said, calmly. "Your death would certainly have upset the fragile coalition —"

"The Outsider Federation is bigger than one woman," Li insisted. "My death would not have made a difference."

Carefully, she placed firm controls on her temper. She didn't *like* the thought of dying, even in a good cause, but she'd accepted it. Running from danger was bad enough; leaving hundreds of millions of others trapped on the planet's surface was worse. She might have been the sole survivor of her homeworld, if the Federation had bombarded the planet's surface. She'd certainly have been the only person to escape the battle.

"I believe your death would have been catastrophic," General Stuart said. His voice gentled, slightly. "We lack the long history of the Federation, Li. Our defeat at Boston was bad enough to rattle *everyone's* cage. We could easily have fragmented after losing you and your homeworld."

Li scowled. He had a point, but she didn't want to admit it. She certainly didn't want to admit that the only reason she would have survived was because her orders had been disobeyed. And yet, she had to admit it had worked out in their favor. She'd been in space, close enough to link up with General Stuart and travel with him to *Valiant*. They now had hope when, only a few hours ago, they'd had none.

And yet, they also had one hell of a mess.

But at least we have hope, she reminded herself. *I should cling to that.*

She sighed inwardly, forcing herself to think. She'd been stunned throughout her stay on the shuttle, but she'd reviewed the files once she'd been awakened. The Federation Navy, on the direct command of their Emperor, had been poised to fire antimatter warheads at her homeworld. She'd have lost her entire family in a handful of seconds. And the only thing that had saved her homeworld from complete destruction had been a mutiny in the enemy's ranks. Or something.

She honestly wasn't entirely sure what had happened. And she didn't really want to look a gift horse in the mouth.

"Very well," she said. "Do you think we can trust Admiral Garibaldi?"

"I've never met him before this moment, not face-to-face," General Stuart said. "I thought *you* were supposed to be the one who was good at reading people."

Li said nothing, merely raising her eyebrows.

"I think he's young and earnest," General Stuart said, after a moment. "And I think he was honestly shocked after the Emperor tried to commit genocide. But he could be very good at masking his thoughts and feelings. Don't forget, he was a serving officer during the days of the Grand Senate. He wouldn't have risen in the ranks without the ability to dissemble."

"Maybe," Li said.

She scowled. There was frustratingly little in the files her intelligence staff had collected on Roman Garibaldi — and almost none of it had been gleaned from any method more complex than reading the Federation's press releases. *Ensign* Roman Garibaldi had assumed command of *Enterprise* during Operation Retribution, suggesting either heavy casualties or *very* powerful connections. But his name didn't suggest any strong ties to the Grand Senate; indeed, the only patron he had was Marius Drake.

Command of a cruiser at a surprisingly young age, she thought, mentally reviewing what she'd read. No doubt patronage had played a role, but Marius Drake wasn't — hadn't been — the type of man to value loyalty over competence. *And then a commodore, commander of an entire fleet, and then an admiral. And he tricked us at Boston and kicked our asses right across the system.*

"He is competent," General Stuart said. "But politically... I don't know *what* he is."

Li shook her head. "Can he win the war?"

"With our support, perhaps," General Stuart said. "Without it, probably not. And then... I don't know what he'd want to do with the Federation."

"True," Li agreed.

She'd hoped, once upon a time, that the Federation could be reformed, that a modicum of justice and fairness could be restored to the system. But she'd found herself blocked at every turn, even when she'd beaten the Grand Senators at their own game and managed to get herself elected to the Grand Senate. She'd thought she'd won a great prize, yet it hadn't taken her long to sort out just how badly the entire system was rigged. The collected voting power of the out-worlds was of no consequence, compared to the might of the core. And even the destruction of the Grand Senate hadn't been enough to save the system.

The irony was chilling. She might not have met Roman Garibaldi before the Battle of Nova Athena, but she *had* met Marius Drake. He'd struck her as a grim bulldog, determined to burn his way through everything standing in his path, yet destruction was no way to reform the Federation. If the reports she'd read were correct, Drake — Emperor Marius — had become the monster he'd sought to kill. He'd found himself forced to destroy the Federation in order to save it.

And after we win the war, she asked herself, *what then?*

The Outsider Federation had settled on a federal structure for the post-Federation universe, an attempt to keep both human unity and grant hundreds of thousands of worlds autonomy, preventing them from becoming the victims of the federal government. But she knew, all too well, that not *every* Outsider supported the plan. They hated and feared Earth; they wanted, deep in their hearts, to burn the entire edifice to the ground. And there were times, far too many times, when she found herself agreeing with them. Earth was so far beyond salvation that destroying it was the only option.

But now, with the addition of Roman Garibaldi to their ranks, who knew where he would stand?

"I have a suggestion," General Stuart said. "We need time — months, at least — to repair our damaged ships and bring the next generation of superdreadnaughts online. Admiral Garibaldi can use that time to secure Boston, hopefully securing his fleet train and the immense stockpile of supplies in the fleet base. It would also get him control of a number of pathways deeper into the Federation."

Li nodded impatiently. Boston's importance was no great surprise to her. They'd discussed the system's role in the enemy's defenses, back when she'd authorized the attack on Boston that had ended so badly. If Admiral Garibaldi failed to secure the system, all hope of an offensive deeper into enemy space would be lost.

"We provide him with what limited support we can, while waiting for the remainder of our fleet to come back online," General Stuart added. "If his forces get worn down to a nub... that will make it easier, in the aftermath of the war, for us to determine the future of the Federation."

"You mean, use his forces to soak up enemy fire," Li said, flatly. "And turn him into a martyr, if necessary."

"Yes," General Stuart said. "He may be too dangerous to be allowed to live."

Li felt her eyes narrow. She could see the cold-hearted logic of it. The Outsider Navy had been badly weakened after the Battle of Boston and, even with their technical advantages, the Federation Navy would still outgun them rather badly. And even if they won the war, they might just be trading one emperor for another. Worse, a potential *Emperor* Roman would know the Outsiders far better than Emperor Marius could ever hope to do. He would have had plenty of opportunity to locate every last production node, then send ships out to destroy them. Allowing Garibaldi to weaken himself battering against the enemy's defenses might work in her favor.

But it was dishonorable.

She had no illusions of just how much Garibaldi had sacrificed, just to save her homeworld from genocide. He ran the risk of being knifed in the back by his own crew — or, perhaps, of being hunted down and shot like a dog. It was no favor, to such a man, to abandon him to the whims of his enemies. Or to use him, praise him, and discard him. She couldn't allow it to stand.

And he will see what we are doing, too, she thought, bitterly. *Nothing could be more certain to harden his heart against us.*

"No," she said. "We will treat him as a full ally, with all the rights and duties that that implies."

General Stuart frowned. "The risks..."

Li cut him off. "If we lose the war, perhaps because we withheld reinforcements that might have swung the tide of battle in our favor, there will be no point in worrying about the future," she said, firmly. "And if he believes we are deliberately sending him and his men out to die... well, he might have a very strong incentive to switch sides once again or declare himself an emperor in his own right. I don't think he's one of the bad guys."

"He took our fleet on and beat it," General Stuart said.

He took your *fleet on*, Li thought. General Stuart had been in command of the forces that had attacked Boston, only to be lured into an ambush and driven away from the system. It had to sting, losing a battle to a younger man... but then, the Outsiders had had almost no experience of full-scale fleet battles before the war, at least outside simulations. *Are you arguing to expend Garibaldi because he's dangerous or because of your injured pride?*

"That doesn't make him a bad guy," she said, instead. "Besides, if we refuse to accept him, don't we have to throw out all the former Federation Navy personnel who've joined our ranks?"

"That's different," General Stuart said.

Li met his eyes. "How?"

General Stuart took a long breath. "We recruited hundreds of thousands of former naval personnel — and mercenaries — before the war began," he said. "In all such cases, the personnel were scattered amongst the fleet and, when they were being offered posts in sensitive locations, tested thoroughly for disloyalty or hidden programming. Their ability to cause problems was minimized. The handful of spies or deep-cover personalities we did find were unable to take any information back to their masters before they were... dealt with."

He paused, significantly. "In this case, we have over a hundred thousand naval personnel, spread out over two hundred warships," he added. "More, in fact, if Admiral Garibaldi convinces Boston to join us without a fight. They are, if you will pardon the expression, an indigestible bulk; they have a fleet, they are loyal to Admiral Garibaldi rather than the cause and, if push comes to shove, I imagine they will follow him, rather than us.

"In short, Admiral Garibaldi will be in a very good position to betray us and do some very real damage."

"You don't know that will happen," Li pointed out.

"No, I don't," General Stuart agreed. He met her eyes evenly. "But it is my duty to make you aware of the dangers. There may come a time when you wish you expended his ships rather than have them hurling missiles at you."

"Yes, there may," Li said. "But we will not deliberately set out to betray him."

She pressed her fingertips together as she turned to look up at the display. The Federation Navy's Office of Naval Intelligence — or whatever had replaced it, given

how badly ONI had dropped the ball — would have sold its collective soul for a chance to inspect the display, knowing it showed a network of bases and settlements that were unknown to the Federation. If there had been more time, perhaps five or ten years, she was sure the Outsiders would have won the war easily. Their weapons research was easily two or three years ahead of the best the Federation could offer...

But it was not to be, she thought. Emperor Marius had already been planning survey missions deep beyond the Rim by the time the war had begun. *And now, we have to depend on someone who risked everything to save my homeworld.*

"He is not to learn of the bases," she said, making a swift decision. "The information must *not* reach the Federation."

"Understood," General Stuart said.

"But otherwise, we will support him to the hilt," she added. "I'll discuss the future of the Federation with him, after he secures Boston."

General Stuart frowned. "You intend to stay on the front lines?"

"It's not *quite* the front lines," Li corrected him. "But if we lose, we may as well start packing our bags and heading further into the Beyond."

"Very well," General Stuart said. "I must insist, though, on you having bodyguards with you at all times. You cannot, you *must* not, be risked."

Li snorted, then nodded reluctantly.

"Very well," she said. "I suppose those men you sent to kidnap me would be good for the job, wouldn't they?"

"We'll see," General Stuart said. "Mercenaries are not *always* reliable."

౭౦ಐ

"Well," Sanderson said, "I think we're probably going to be sent to the ice mines somewhere."

"Shut up," Lieutenant Caleb Roebuck muttered. "I thought she was going to have us all executed at once."

Uzi kept his amusement and frustration to himself as he studied the updates from the planetary defense network. His plan with the shuttle had been perfect, *completely* perfect; he'd kill the two Outsiders and signal for help, ensuring that the Federation Navy took Chang Li into custody before she recovered from the stun bolt...

... and then it had failed, simply because he hadn't even *begun* to consider that Admiral Garibaldi would switch sides. He'd ruined everything.

For the first time in a long career, Uzi found himself seriously considering abandoning his mission and just retreating into the shadows. It would hardly be impossible to steal a courier boat or find passage on a freighter, even though it meant admitting defeat. Admiral Garibaldi had *seen* him, back when he'd been inserted on Hobson's Choice; he'd know Uzi by sight if they encountered one another again. And even if he didn't, it wouldn't be long before *someone* started asking questions about the shuttle's power failure. *That* would be more than enough to reveal the presence of an infiltrator.

And yet, he *was* a loyalist. The Federation needed him. He didn't want to just back out and escape when he still had a job to do.

"Uzi?" Roebuck asked. "What do you think they'll do?"

Uzi glanced at the younger man. He'd practically been *mentoring* the Outsider, teaching him how to be a more effective commanding officer, all the while measuring Caleb Roebuck's back for the knife. Roebuck had promise, he acknowledged inwardly; he wouldn't have been too out of place in the Federation Marines, even if it *was* as just another stupid greenie lieutenant who had to be mentored before he got a bunch of men killed. And Roebuck was smart enough to ask for advice...

"We *were* ordered to stun the Senator and take her to the shuttle," he said, simply. It had definitely been the *oddest* set of orders he'd been given, up to and including the orders to sneak into a planetary rebel's office and kill his cats. "They can't hold us accountable for what we were ordered to do."

"She's the boss," Sanderson said, mournfully. "She can order us killed on the spot."

"I don't think she will," Uzi said, as reassuringly as he could. In the Federation, during the days of the Grand Senate, being worried about getting the blame for following orders wouldn't have been too bad a reaction. If a senior officer had made a mistake, his first instinct would be to search for a scapegoat. "She might be angry, but she'll be angry with the person who issued the orders, not with us."

"I hope you're right," Roebuck said. "But what do we do now?"

"We wait and see what our orders are," Uzi said. They'd docked the shuttle on the space station, then been herded into a private compartment and told to wait. "I don't know about the pair of you, but I could do with a nap."

"Yeah," Sanderson agreed, morosely. "And I bet the Senator thinks we should be taking a permanent nap."

"I can stun you, if you'd like," Uzi offered, only half in jest. Stunning them both would at least allow him to think in peace. He needed to do something about that shuttle before a technician took a close look at the drive failure. "You'd be sure of a good sleep."

"And a banging headache the morning afterwards," Sanderson said. "I'll sleep the natural way."

"Look on the bright side," Uzi called, as Sanderson rose to his feet and headed for the bedroom. "You'll have one hell of a story to tell the girls on Nova Athena."

Sanderson gave him a one-fingered gesture and stepped through the hatch. Uzi smirked, then returned to his silent contemplations as Roebuck also headed for bed.

What the hell should he do *now*?

Chapter Five

This was not their only advantage. Indeed, thanks to a far superior educational model, the average Outsider crew might have two or three times the efficiency of its Federation counterpart.
—The Federation Navy in Retrospect, 4199

Spinner/Boston, 4101

There was no way in hell, Marius had already decided, that he was going to miss watching from the CIC as his battle squadrons readied themselves to return to Boston. Commander Lewis had objected, of course, but he'd ignored her. If they were about to run into a blocking force, if they had to fight their way through, he was damned if he was lying in his cabin while Captain Watson directed the battle.

If only because we'd lose, he thought, as the final status reports flashed up in front of his display. The fleet's engineers had done what they could to repair the damage his starships had taken, but they were still critically short in a number of areas. In hindsight, firing off so many missiles might have been a mistake. *Punching our way into the system would be tricky even if we had a full weapons load.*

"Send the drones through the Asimov Point," he ordered. Commodore Yu hadn't left anything on station on the near side of the point, as far as his sensors could tell, although *that* meant nothing. A cloaked starship could have noted his arrival in the system and jumped back through to Boston to prepare a hot reception. "And stand by to send the first ships through."

"Aye, sir," Ginny said. She peered down at her console. "Drones launching... now."

She paused. "Sir, a courier boat has just come into sensor range, heading towards the Asimov Point," she added. "Its IFF marks it as being attached to Fifth Fleet."

Too late, Marius thought, vindictively. *Unless, of course, another courier boat traveled the other chain of Asimov Points...*

He pushed the thought aside, sharply. "Order her to shut down her drives and prepare to be boarded," he said. There was no time for wool-gathering. "If she refuses to answer our hails, fire on her the moment she enters weapons range."

"Aye, sir," Ginny said.

Marius nodded to himself as the new icon flashed towards them. Courier boats were the fastest things in space, but their crews were still largely dependent on the Asimov Point to get from place to place. The courier boat Roman Garibaldi had dispatched could either surrender or reverse course and try to run back to Nova Athena, he thought; there was no way it could get through the Asimov Point without entering his engagement envelope. And a courier boat was practically defenseless.

"She's altering course," Ginny snapped. "Sir, Captain Angstrom is requesting permission to give chase."

"Denied," Marius said. The courier boat wasn't a problem, as long as she didn't have a chance to pop through the Asimov Point before it was too late. "Order Angstrom

and his ships to hold position on this side of the point. If the courier boat returns, they are to blow her to atoms."

He turned his attention back to the display as Ginny started to issue orders to the fleet. The drones had returned, telling him things he didn't want to know about the brooding fortresses on the far side, but they *did* seem to be on standby, rather than ready to repel an offensive through the Asimov Point. No doubt, in the wake of the crushing defeat the Outsiders had suffered the *last* time they'd tried to punch their way into the system, the crews were taking the opportunity to do some maintenance while the threat of attack was very low. Unless it was all a trick...

No, he told himself, firmly. *We have to go through the Asimov Point.*

Ginny turned to look at him. "Your orders, sir?"

"Send the first elements through the Asimov Point as planned," he ordered. It was a gamble, one hell of a gamble, but there was no choice. The only alternative was skulking around the Rim until they were finally run down and destroyed, if their ships lasted so long. "And ready the remaining assault pods for deployment."

He tensed, despite himself, as the first starships approached the point and vanished. If the defenders *did* intend an ambush, they'd spring it... now. And his ships didn't carry anything like enough assault pods to force their way into the system. His mind raced, considering hundreds of desperate attack plans, before the next set of drones popped back into existence on the near side of the point. The first starships had entered the system without trouble.

"Take the rest of the fleet through," he ordered, curtly. "And stand by all weapons and defensive systems."

His stomach gave a twinge of unease, just one, as the superdreadnaught passed through the Asimov Point and entered Boston. Hundreds of new icons flared to life on the display; twenty-one heavy fortresses, thirty-seven support cruisers, hundreds of starfighters and thousands of mines and automated weapons platforms. If Commodore Yu had wanted to block his path, he knew, she might well have succeeded. But his fleet was already through the Asimov Point and heading out of her engagement range...

"Picking up a signal from the command fortress, sir," Ginny said. "They're asking what happened at Nova Athena."

Then Roman didn't manage to get a message back in time, Marius thought. He felt a wave of relief, followed by a flicker of the old confidence. *Sloppy work, young man.*

He smirked to himself as he leaned forward. If Commodore Yu *didn't* know what had happened, the prospect of violent resistance was minimal. But it would still be unwise to push her too far, particularly if she was loyal to Roman Garibaldi instead of the Federation Navy or Marius himself. He cursed the Grand Senate under his breath — they'd done so much to wear down the navy's loyalty to the Federation — and keyed his console.

"Commodore Yu, this is Emperor Marius," he said. He'd spent a great deal of time trying to decide what lie to tell her, knowing that his words would be spread across the Federation and — perhaps — used against him. "The fleet successfully secured

Nova Athena. Admiral Garibaldi is currently preparing an offensive deeper into enemy space."

He paused. "I'm detaching an officer to assume command of the system," he added, "but the remainder of this fleet needs to return to Earth immediately. Dispatch every fleet replenishment unit you have to rendezvous with my battle squadrons prior to our transit through the Asimov Point. We'll replenish while in transit."

Tapping the console again, he sent the message to Boston. Commodore Yu was a logistics officer, according to her file; she wouldn't be in command of any of the fortresses, regardless of tradition. And, hopefully, she'd send the replenishment ships without question. The thought of depriving Roman Garibaldi of the logistics he'd need to push onwards to Earth amused him, particularly as Roman wouldn't be able to punish Commodore Yu for her actions without undermining his own position. She'd merely followed legitimate orders from her superior officer.

He leaned back in his chair, studying the system display. Roman and his officers had done a good job, he had to admit. Boston had always been in a good position for industrial development — there were no less than *five* Asimov Points in the system, three of them leading into new Asimov Point chains — but Roman had built the system up into a formidable fortress during the war. Hell, it looked as though the local industrial base was *more* efficient than the Core Worlds, although that shouldn't have been a surprise. The planet's inhabitants had no doubt their system was on the front lines of a war.

I should take them all back to Earth with me, he thought, sourly. *They'd actually do good work, unlike the whining bastards on Luna.*

It was tempting, very tempting, to try to just take control of the system himself and make a stand. Roman Garibaldi couldn't be any better prepared for an Asimov Point assault than his own ships, even if he drew supplies from the Outsiders. They'd blown through their own supply of assault pods, he was sure, during their ill-fated attack on the system. But far too many officers and crew on the base would owe their careers to Roman Garibaldi. Their loyalties would be in doubt at the worst possible time.

Commodore Palin may not be able to hold the system, he told himself. *Even though we sent him additional troopers, he'll be trying to keep thousands of men under control while fighting off an Asimov Point attack*

"Sir, we picked up an acknowledgement from Commodore Yu," Ginny said. "She's dispatching the replenishment units now, sir, and she's requesting permission to dispatch additional supplies to Admiral Garibaldi."

Marius smiled, rather coldly. It *was* a reasonable request, given what Commodore Yu knew, but not one he was inclined to grant. The only problem was that refusing permission, for whatever reason, might arouse her suspicions. As far as she knew, Roman Garibaldi was holding an enemy system after a battle that would have cost his ships hundreds of missiles...

"Tell her that Commodore Palin will handle such matters," he said. Once Palin was in command of the Asimov Point, he could tell Yu the truth and force her to

decide who she was going to support. "And add a private note. I want Professor Kratman found and returned to the fleet."

Oddly, the thought cost him a twinge of pain. Captain Kratman had been his first commanding officer, back when the *Matterhorn* had led the charge that had sparked off the Blue Star War; *Minister* Kratman had been one of his first appointments to his cabinet. But there were too many unanswered questions about the Professor and the Brotherhood he served. Who knew *what* he'd said to Roman Garibaldi, back when Marius had brought him to the system...

And he taught Blake Raistlin, too, Marius thought. The Brotherhood had played a role in promoting him, back when the Grand Senate was still in power, but it had been surprisingly quiet since he'd become Emperor. And, in Marius's experience, silence meant that someone was plotting something. *How many other young men were seduced into serving the Brotherhood?*

He scowled down at his hands as his fleet crawled across the system, a handful of new icons on the display showing the replenishment ships as they left the planet and headed towards the Asimov Point. Every Federation officer knew to develop a healthy dose of paranoia concerning their superiors — even paranoids had enemies; they knew their superiors wouldn't hesitate to use them as scapegoats if necessary — and watch them carefully. And yet, he hadn't thought Professor Kratman *needed* watching. He'd been one of the few superior officers Marius had genuinely trusted...

But I was an Ensign, he reminded himself. *The idea of the captain bothering to actually notice me was absurd.*

The thought made him smile. Very — very — few ensigns *wanted* to attract the captain's attention. They certainly didn't share downtime with their commanding officer. But he'd trusted Captain Kratman, even after he'd taken up a teaching post at the academy. And yet, now, who *knew* what he'd been doing? Two members of his class had betrayed Marius's trust and turned on him.

"Sir," Ginny said, nervously. "Professor Kratman is nowhere to be found."

Marius blinked. They'd left the professor on Boston, hadn't they? Had he somehow sneaked onboard *Valiant*, with or without her commander's permission? Or had he taken a transport back into the Core Worlds? It was far from impossible, even though he would have needed permission from Commodore Yu to depart. A Brotherhood member in the right place and Commodore Yu wouldn't have known anything about it. Or he might simply have gone underground. Boston was large enough for a careful man to hide indefinitely.

"Order her to put out an alert for him," he said. There wasn't any time to take the planet and organize a search, not when there was no certainty Professor Kratman was still on the surface instead of heading away from the system. "When he's found, he is to be held in stasis and shipped back to Earth immediately."

"Aye, sir," Ginny said.

Marius scowled, making a mental note to have the remainder of the Brotherhood hunted down and arrested. He knew at least two others, back on Earth, and neither of them would be able to go on the run without surrendering their influence. Once

they were caught, they could be interrogated, revealing the names of their comrades. Or, if they were treated to keep them from spilling the beans, they could become ONI's test subjects in its endless attempts to break the conditioning and discover the truth.

He put the matter aside for the moment and turned his attention to the replenishment units, drawing closer to his ships. They'd have to accompany his ships through the Asimov Point — he hoped the crews would be loyal — and on the way to Earth. If they thought better of it, he wouldn't hesitate to have the marines invade the ships and take control. There was just too much at stake for half-measures.

"Commander," he said. "Have you readied the secure datapack?"

"Yes, sir," Ginny said. "It's ready for dispatch."

"Order the base to launch four courier boats," Marius said. "Once they're nearly at the Asimov Point, send them the datapack on tight-beam and tell the crews to take it straight to Earth, priority-one. Make sure they have the right codes to get through all the defenses and chokepoints without being halted."

"Aye, sir," Ginny said.

Marius looked up at the display, silently calculating travel times. It would take at least three months for his fleet to return to Earth, three months during which time anything could happen. But if he sent a warning on ahead, via a courier boat, Tiffany would be alerted within two months, perhaps less if they redlined their drives. He briefly considered boarding a courier boat himself — he'd endured worse, as a young ensign — before dismissing the thought. There were too many opportunists who wouldn't hesitate to take advantage of his weakness, if he turned up in a courier boat rather than a superdreadnaught. And then there would be another civil war...

And then the Outsiders will just walk in and take over, he thought, darkly. *How could so many people be so stupid?*

But he already knew the answer. People, particularly politicians, *were* stupid. They were so fixated on their own power, so insulated from the consequences of their decisions, that they put their own advantage ahead of the good of the Federation. He might have been able to nip the Outsiders in the bud, he was sure, if the Grand Senate had given him the firepower he needed and the authority to use it. Instead, they'd ignored a festering problem along the Rim until Admiral Justinian had forced them to fight for survival. And even then, they'd *still* put their own advantage first. They could have crushed Admiral Justinian like a bug if they hadn't put a political admiral in command of the fleet.

He felt his head start to pound and rubbed it, silently grateful that there was only one other person in the CIC to see his weakness. It wasn't something he could allow, during a major battle, but for the moment it would have to do. Thankfully, they should have more than enough warning if Commodore Yu decided to turn on them or reject Commodore Palin's authority. But even then...

The hours crawled by, far too slowly, as they approached the Asimov Point. There was no further update from the planet, no assurance that Professor Kratman had been captured or his departure confirmed... Marius fretted over it, despite his best

efforts. His old commanding officer was a sneaky devil. Who *knew* what he was doing? And who knew what he'd said to Roman Garibaldi, the night before the fleet had left Boston? Marius's intelligence officers hadn't been able to slip bugs into Roman's superdreadnaught.

Because I trusted him, Marius thought, bitterly. *I trusted him enough not to insist.*

"Sir," Ginny said, breaking into his thoughts. "We're cleared to pass through the Asimov Point. The replenishment ships have fallen into formation, as per instructions."

"Good," Marius said. Unless, of course, the fortresses surrounding the Asimov Point — weaker here, as there was no real threat of attack from the far side — intended to fire on the ships when they entered point-blank range. "Take us through as planned."

He looked up at the system display, silently calculating the odds. Commodore Palin would try to hold the system, he was sure, but would it be enough to stop the system's former master? His crews might turn on him when they realized just *who* was attacking. But there was no choice. He had to let Commodore Palin do his job and pray it was enough. He braced himself as the ship entered the Asimov Point, gritting his teeth as he felt the gut-wrenching unease as they passed through the tear in space and time.

"Transit complete, sir," Ginny said. There was nothing on the far side, save for a roving picket of gunboats. "The replenishment ships are asking for orders."

"Continue on course towards Earth," Marius ordered. "We'll replenish along the way, as planned."

He couldn't help a sigh of relief as he rose. They'd made it through the bottleneck and, hopefully, delayed Roman Garibaldi. Even if he retook the system without a fight, he'd still have problems replacing the replenishment ships. It would take him months, probably, to adapt older freighters to do the job...

... And, in that time, Marius knew he would have plenty of time to prepare his own forces for the final battle.

Chapter Six

Unsurprisingly, questions regarding loyalty tended to dominate the Federation Navy's concerns during the last years of the civil wars.
—The Federation Navy in Retrospect, 4199

Spinner/Boston, 4101

"I just picked up a message from the courier boat," Lieutenant Thompson said. "The Emperor's fleet passed through two days ago, sir, and detailed a squadron of destroyers to cover the Asimov Point. There was no way to slip a message through to Boston."

Roman cursed under his breath. Emperor Marius must have redlined his drives as soon as he entered the Asimov Point chain leading to Boston. Given how badly damaged some of the refugee ships had been, it was a considerable risk. Roman had hoped the courier boat would beat Marius Drake to Boston, but evidently it was not to be. And that meant... what? Who was in command of Boston? Commodore Yu, Emperor Marius... or someone else? If the latter, it would definitely be one of the Emperor's loyalists. Somehow, Roman doubted he would be willing to let himself be talked out of making a stand.

He studied the tactical display for a long moment, thinking hard. It wouldn't be impossible to sneak up on the destroyers, if they were just sitting atop the Asimov Point, but he rather doubted it would work. Almost all commanding officers had actual experience, these days; he had a feeling the enemy commander would have detailed half his squadron to run patrols while the other half stood ready to jump back to Boston. Hell, it was quite possible that a cloaked ship had observed their arrival at Spinner and a warning was already flickering back to Boston. It was what *he* would have done.

"Take us directly to the Asimov Point," he ordered. There was no point in playing games, not when the enemy commander had to know where he was going. "Launch a shell of sensor drones and hold them in position around our formation, watching for cloaked ships. I don't want to be caught by surprise."

"Aye, sir," Lieutenant Thompson said.

Roman settled back in his chair as the fleet began the slow crawl towards the Asimov Point, contemplating his options. There were just too many unknowns for him to come up with any real plan, which meant he would probably have to improvise when they jumped into Boston and discovered what was lying in wait. All he could do was prepare for everything he could, up to and including a full-scale assault on the Asimov Point, even though it would be terrifyingly expensive. His fleet had expended most of its assault pods during the advance on Nova Athena.

And why not? he thought, bitterly. *We weren't expecting to continue the advance beyond there, were we?*

Pushing the thought aside, he reached for the latest set of reports from the engineers and quickly skimmed through them. Most of his starships were combat-ready,

but there were limits to what the engineers could do without a proper yard and some downtime. Roman hoped Emperor Marius hadn't tried to destroy the facilities at Boston, although he knew it was a strong possibility. But then, the yards were necessary to rebuild the Federation as well as supporting the war effort. It was just possible that the Emperor had left them alone.

"Admiral, long-range sensors are picking up seven destroyers orbiting the Asimov Point," Lieutenant Thompson said. "I can't get a positive ID on them at this distance."

Seven destroyers, Roman thought. A standard destroyer squadron had nine ships. Had two of them cloaked to keep an eye on his fleet? Or had they jumped back through the Asimov Point to alert the defenders? Or had they been destroyed during the engagement, leaving the squadron understrength? *And presumably not starships attached to Boston's local defenses.*

"Keep us on course," he ordered. "Inform me the moment you get a positive ID."

"Aye, sir," Lieutenant Thompson said. She paused. "One of the destroyers just jumped into the Asimov Point and vanished."

"Understood," Roman said. It was possible that *someone* was planning a clever ambush, but they'd stripped Boston clean of assault pods prior to departure. "Prepare to transmit the pre-recorded message as soon as we enter our long-range missile envelope."

"Aye, sir," Lieutenant Thompson said.

Roman forced himself to relax. It was vanishingly unlikely that seven destroyers — six now — would put up a fight, not against the immensity of his fleet. They'd be incredibly lucky to score a single hit before they were blown to atoms. But if the ships were commanded by loyalists, they'd do anything for their Emperor. Roman himself would have done anything for Emperor Marius, once upon a time. Now...

The man you knew is gone, he told himself, sternly. *And in his place, there's a monster.*

"Sir," Lieutenant Thompson said. "We're entering missile range."

"Transmit the message," Roman ordered. "And then prep the courier drones for launch."

"Aye, sir," Lieutenant Thompson said.

Roman glanced at the fleet's status display and braced himself. Fifth Fleet had been through hell under his command, building up a level of experience and *esprit de corps* that few other Federation formations could claim, but it had never really anticipated having to turn on the admiral who'd led the Federation Navy to victory over Admiral Justinian. Roman couldn't help but think that they'd lost something of their innocence, even though he knew that the prospects for civil war had been looming before Admiral Justinian had attacked Earth. His crews had signed up to keep humanity safe, not fight wars against their fellow humans...

"The destroyers have jumped back through the Asimov Point," Lieutenant Thompson reported. "They made no attempt to reply."

Loyalists, then, Roman thought. *He* wouldn't have deigned to reply, if he'd still been a loyalist himself. *And that means we may have to fight our way into the system.*

"Launch the drones," he ordered. "And then take us straight towards the Asimov Point. It's time to jump into the fire."

And hope to hell we don't get burned, he thought, grimly. *Because even a successful assault on the system will cost us dearly.*

ဆ⍥ભ

Commodore Hassan Palin had the uneasy feeling he'd been staked out, like a goat, to lure a tiger into a trap. He and a handful of his men, scattered through the vast fortress, were the only men truly loyal to the Emperor in the system. Boston *belonged* to Admiral Garibaldi, he'd discovered in the two days he'd spent as system commander, and even though Garibaldi had been declared a traitor many were still loyal to him. He was grimly aware that stationing armored troopers throughout the station might be the only thing that was preventing a mutiny and keeping him alive.

I wish there was time to bring more crews up from the Core Worlds, he thought, although he knew reinforcements weren't going to arrive before it was too late. Even if the Federation hadn't concentrated on building starships and training their crews, there were just too many other demands on Fortress Command's tiny reserve of trained manpower. *And additional warships to ensure the system remains loyal.*

Hassan sighed to himself as he sat back in his command chair in the CIC, watching the destroyers as they snapped back into existence. He'd done everything he could to ensure the defenders remained loyal — and that any who remained *disloyal* had no chance to interfere — but he knew it wasn't good enough. The prospect of having a knife slipped into his back by one of his officers was all too real. Hell, it had been hard enough to disarm the majority of the crew before they did something stupid. Fortresses had been boarded before, during the war, and unarmed crewmen were just lambs to the slaughter. But again, there had been no choice.

"Commodore, the remaining destroyers have transited," Lieutenant Commander Rollins said, quietly. She was young, so young he thought she should still be at the academy, but it wasn't uncommon for talented youngsters to rise rapidly in the ranks these days. And her tone was *barely* on the right side of insubordination. "Fifth Fleet is approaching the Asimov Point."

"Bring the defenders to red alert, stand by to engage," Hassan ordered. If they triggered off the first shots, the crews would likely find themselves fighting desperately to save their lives, even if they *were* on Garibaldi's side. "Slave the command datanet to this fortress and override commands from the other fortresses."

"Aye, sir," Rollins said. Her back was stiff, her tone resentful. "Command datanet engaged."

Hassan glowered at her back. He could have her taken out and shot, yet that would almost certainly spark a mutiny. Unarmed the crews might be — although he suspected the sweep hadn't found *all* the weapons — but they weren't helpless. All he could do was hope to push them into the fight before they found a way to overthrow him.

He blinked in surprise as the first courier drones popped into existence, transmitting their message as soon as their systems recovered from the brief transit. A

moment later, he realized what the enemy commander had in mind. He was deliberately signaling his loyalists, inviting them — *begging* them — to take a stand against the Emperor. It could not be tolerated.

"Order the CSP to take those drones out," he snapped. There was no point in wasting single-shot automated weapons platforms on the drones. "Now!"

"Aye, sir," Rollins said. Her hand danced over her console. "CSP has been informed..."

She broke off as red icons flickered onto the display, each one representing an enemy superdreadnaught. For a moment, Hassan could only stare in disbelief. Admiral Garibaldi was sending the superdreadnaughts through the Asimov Point too quickly, running the risk of two or more of his ships colliding or interpenetrating. He had to be out of his mind... even if the fortress crews refused to engage his ships, the automated weapons systems would have no such hesitation.

He keyed his console, ordering the automated systems and minefields to engage. Let Admiral Garibaldi get slapped back, let him come in shooting. Hassan's crews would have no choice, but to fight to save their lives. He smiled, darkly, as the enemy superdreadnaughts began to vanish, their shields still too weak to save them from the bombardment. And yet, more and more of them were appearing... he might just win the new civil war in one fell swoop.

"Order the fortresses to open fire," he ordered. The inner minefields had been almost completely expended, while the automated weapons platforms were recharging. And yet, the enemy were *still* sending superdreadnaughts though the Asimov Point. "Take them out..."

It struck him a second later, as yet another superdreadnaught blinked into existence. If he went by sensor records alone, his forces had killed over fifty superdreadnaughts, a loss rate that no sane commander could afford. And yet, he *knew* Admiral Garibaldi didn't have more than seven squadrons of superdreadnaughts, assuming his engineering crews had worked miracles. Admiral Garibaldi had just thrown away over a hundred thousand lives...

... Or had he?

The Outsiders had produced a fleet, he suspected, that was nothing more than ECM drones... and Admiral Garibaldi had *allied* with the Outsiders. He checked the sensor readings himself, looking for the by-products of destroyed ships. There was nothing, nothing at all. It was possible, he supposed, that antimatter warheads simply hadn't left very much for his sensors to detect, but there should have been *some* debris. They'd been conned.

He swore, savagely. Admiral Garibaldi had pulled a fast one...

... And now, his only *reliable* defense systems had been completely wasted.

⋈

"The drones have reported back, sir," Lieutenant Thompson said. "They've cleared the enemy minefields and automated defenses."

Roman nodded, grimly. Using the ECM drones had been yet another gamble, but one he'd been fairly sure would work. The prospect of blowing apart a stream

of superdreadnaughts, one by one, had been simply too great a chance to miss. And besides, only an idiot would risk allowing a superdreadnaught to start opening fire at what was, effectively, point-blank range. The enemy commander, whoever he was, had done everything by the book — and still been thoroughly screwed.

"The fortresses," he said. "Have they opened fire?"

"Their fire is slack, apparently," Lieutenant Thompson said. "But they may just have been relying on the automated weapons and the CSP."

"All right," Roman said. "Send in the first wave, Lieutenant."

He took a breath. If the fortresses had decided to oppose him, most — perhaps all — of the first wave of actual starships were doomed, even if they *were* escorted by yet more ECM drones to soak up enemy fire. He'd briefed the crews carefully, warning them not to target any fortresses that didn't fire on them first, but he knew it was asking for trouble. At point-blank range, a fortress could switch from friendly to unfriendly in a split second and the first his crews would know of it would be when the missiles started slamming into their shields. And the fortresses fired heavier missiles than anything smaller than a superdreadnaught...

Please, God, he thought, with a grim earnestness he hadn't felt since he'd been a very small child. *Please let this work.*

⁝Ω

"Another wave of starships has arrived," Rollins said. "A number of superdreadnaughts, but also cruisers and destroyers."

Hassan sucked in his breath. He was *almost* sure the superdreadnaughts were nothing more than sensor ghosts — according to the sensors, they'd destroyed Fifth Fleet's entire superdreadnaught strength twice over — but if he was wrong...

"Target the cruisers and destroyers," he ordered. They, too, might be there to do little more than soak up his fire, but he couldn't afford to ignore them. "External racks only; I say again, external racks only."

"Aye, sir," Rollins said. "Firing now..."

There was a long pause. Only five fortresses opened fire.

Hassan came to his feet. "Report," he snapped. He had an awful feeling that he already knew. "What happened?"

"The remaining fortresses have isolated themselves from the command network," Rollins said. There was an edge of amusement in her voice as she glanced up at him. "They did not receive the command to fire."

Or they chose to ignore it, Hassan thought. By isolating themselves from the datanet, the mutineers had crippled his defense plan. The chances of victory had gone downhill and crashed into rubble. *The bastards...*

He unsnapped his holster and drew his sidearm, pointing it straight at Rollins's head. Her face paled, noticeably, as he made a show of clicking off the safety. She would have spent time in the shooting range, of course — naval regulations demanded that crewmen know how to clean and fire their weapons — but she probably wouldn't have actually seen a weapon used in combat, let alone have one pointed

right at her. Chances were, she still thought of warfare as something nicely bloodless. The blood and guts of an infantry battlefield would chill her to the bone.

"Target the treacherous fortresses," he ordered. There was no hope of stopping Admiral Garibaldi now, nor was there any real chance of escape. All he could really do was claw the enemy good and proper before he was killed. "Target them or I'll blow your head off, right here and now."

Rollins stared at him, her mouth moving soundlessly. Hassan felt an odd flush of exhilaration, mixed with a strange horror that chilled him to the bone. What sort of monster had he become? What sort of monsters had they *all* become? He'd been in the navy for twenty years and he had *never* had to threaten one of his crewmembers with death before, even during the early stages of the Justinian War. But now, he saw no choice.

"Do it," he hissed, willing her to believe. He *was* ready to kill her, if necessary. "Do..."

The power failed. Hassan watched in horror as the displays faded to darkness, the emergency lights coming on barely in time to keep the compartment from plunging into darkness. He clutched his pistol tightly as the artificial gravity failed, unsure what to do now that the entire battle had been lost. His troopers had clearly failed to prevent sabotage on a terrifying scale.

"It's over, sir," Rollins said. There was a hint of panic in her voice. Her face was pale as she clung to her seat, using one hand to strap herself down. Normally, few bothered to strap themselves into their chairs, no matter what regulations said. Now, with gravity gone, the logic behind the regs made sense. "Give up. I'm sure the Admiral won't treat you badly."

Hassan glared at her, but he knew she was right. Without main power, the fortress was a sitting duck. Even if reinforcements were dispatched from Boston, or the other Asimov Points, there was no hope of them arriving in time to save the day. All he could do was stand down and hope Admiral Garibaldi wasn't feeling merciless. There was nothing to be gained by trying to fight any longer.

"Very well," he said, snapping his pistol's safety catch back on. The shock of the motion sent him drifting upwards. "I hope you have a way to contact him, though. How is he going to know we've surrendered?"

He felt a flicker of pride as he bounced off the overhead and pushed himself back to the deck. It had been years since he'd had to work in a null-gee environment. Gravity was often the last thing to fail, along with the internal compensators; normally, the ship taking such a beating meant certain destruction. But now... he just hoped the mutineers *did* have a way to raise Admiral Garibaldi. The shields were down, the point defense was offline... a handful of antimatter warheads would be more than enough to blow the station into atoms, armor or no armor.

"We do," Rollins assured him. She watched him take a firm hold of the command chair, then produced a small marine-issue communicator from her belt. The mutiny had clearly been planned in advance. "And I'm sure he will be very relieved to hear from us."

Hassan snorted. He didn't know what Admiral Garibaldi might think, but he knew *precisely* what Marius Drake would think. There was no room for failures in his universe...

... And if Hassan fell into the Emperor's hands, his life would be worth less than nothing.

Chapter Seven

And the wave of mutinies that ran through the Federation Navy, as the ties that bound crewmen to the Federation finally snapped, did a thorough job of ripping the fleet's unity apart.
—The Federation Navy in Retrospect, 4199

Boston, 4101

"The fortresses have been secured," Elf reported, through the intercom. "We've taken seventy-five prisoners, all troopers and officers off-loaded from the 345th Battlecruiser Squadron. Commodore Palin has surrendered himself into our hands."

"Have them moved to the superdreadnaughts and held for the moment," Roman ordered. Thankfully, the fortress crews had mutinied. If they hadn't, he knew things would have been a great deal harder. "Ask Palin if he's willing to broadcast a stand-down signal to the rest of the system."

"Palin has refused to talk," Elf said. "But Lieutenant Rollins, one of the ringleaders of the mutiny, insists that the loyalists didn't try to dominate the planet. They just didn't have the manpower."

"Understood," Roman said. He was surprised the Emperor hadn't tried to make a stand, although if he had the war would have ended very quickly. Or would he have been better at appealing to the loyalty of Roman's crews? "What happened to the Emperor himself?"

"Left the system two days ago," Elf said. "He took the replenishment ships with him."

Roman swore. Emperor Marius hadn't missed a trick. He'd taken the ships Roman needed to give pursuit. His ships would need to be repaired and replenished at Boston, rather than on the way to a final confrontation. The Emperor had won himself far too much time.

"Understood," he said, again. "Have Lieutenant Rollins shipped over to *Valiant*, then see to it that the fortresses are secured. We may need to relocate them to the other Asimov Points."

He closed the connection, then looked at Lieutenant Thompson. "Send the pre-planned signal to Boston and the other Asimov Point defenders," he said. "And to the 345th Battlecruiser Squadron, too. Tell them to decide which side they're on."

"Aye, sir," Lieutenant Thompson said.

Roman nodded. The 345th Battlecruiser Squadron would probably refuse to join him, but her new commander wouldn't be able to run the gauntlet of the fortresses to pass through one of the other Asimov Points. Her only real hope of survival would be to head out beyond the system limits and drop into stardrive, rendering herself largely irrelevant for the foreseeable future. Unless, of course, her CO decided it would be better if he skulked around the edge of the system and awaited a chance to do the rebels some real harm. It would be a major headache for Roman if the enemy commander ever got the chance.

But, for the moment, a single squadron of battlecruisers was a very minor problem. "Set course for Boston," he ordered. "Best possible speed."

He sucked in his breath sharply, cursing — not for the first time — the speed of light delay. At best, assuming she responded at once, it would be at least four hours before he received a reply from Commodore Yu. There was no way to be sure what he would encounter on the planet, no way to be *certain* that the Emperor's goons hadn't already started to prepare a trap... hell, there was no way to be sure that *Yu* hadn't started to prepare a trap herself. Roman had been too young to be implicated in any of the Grand Senate's witch-hunts, after Admiral Justinian had betrayed the Federation, but he thought he understood how they'd felt. It was impossible to *know* just who to trust.

Fighting the Outsiders was a great deal easier, he thought, as he forced himself to relax and study the display. Thankfully, it didn't look as though the Emperor had bombarded the planet or its industries before fleeing through the Asimov Point... although *trying* would probably have doomed his entire fleet. *Back then, we knew who was on what side.*

"The 345th Battlecruiser Squadron has refused to respond to hails," Lieutenant Thompson informed him. "They're altering course and heading out of the system. The remainder of the system defense force has signaled that it wishes to join us."

"Tell them to rendezvous with us at Boston," Roman said. It didn't *look* as though the Emperor had had time to turn a few of his officers, but it was impossible — again — to be entirely sure. Civil wars were nightmares. "And inform me if there's a response from Commodore Yu."

It took nearly four hours for a response to arrive. "Admiral Garibaldi, Commodore Palin informed me that you had turned traitor," Commodore Yu's recorded message said. "I did not believe him, but I was in no place to intervene in his plans to meet you when you returned to the system. I'm very relieved that you have successfully entered the system and wish to inform you that Boston is firmly under control. The repair yards remain intact and will be ready to work on your ships as soon as you arrive."

Roman relaxed, slightly. It could still be a trick.

"Record," he ordered. "Commodore Yu, this is Admiral Garibaldi. Thank you for your welcome to the system. We should enter orbit in" — he glanced at the console — "five hours from this message. Please have a full report ready for me when I arrive."

He sent the message, then checked the datapacket Yu had sent along with the recorded message. There had been a handful of slow-downs on the planet's surface, but other than that there had been almost no activity at all. The Emperor, it seemed, hadn't bothered to land troops, although he'd had no reason to expect trouble. Boston *knew* it was on the front lines of a war.

And now it's on the front lines of another war, he thought, as he looked up at the planet's icon on the display. *Who knows which way the planet's population will jump?*

ॐ

"It's good to see you again, Admiral," Commodore Sonia Yu said, once she'd been

welcomed onboard *Valiant* and shown into Roman's quarters. "I must confess that the Emperor tricked me."

"It's understandable," Roman assured her, as she took the seat he indicated. He poured them both a mug of coffee, then sat down facing her. "I suspect I would have done the same myself."

It was hard to be so generous, but he had to admit that Commodore Yu had had no reason to suspect trouble, let alone refuse orders from her lawful superior. Losing the replenishment ships was a major headache, but one he'd have to cope with. She might expect to be relieved of her post, if not taken out and shot, but he was certainly not going to have her executed for a simple mistake. It would set a very bad precedent.

Commodore Yu relaxed, slightly. "I'm sorry, sir," she said. "I didn't expect to have to... to decide which side to support."

"Nor did I," Roman said. He looked up, meeting her eyes. "And are you sure you want to stay on my side? You could go into an internment camp on Boston, if you wish."

"I want to stay with you, sir," Commodore Yu said.

Roman wished, suddenly, that he could read minds. Did Commodore Yu feel loyalty to him and his fleet? Did she feel that genocide was beyond the pale? Did she think him the certain victor of the coming war? Or did she merely want to keep her power and position? It was the one question he knew he couldn't ask.

"Very well," he said. There hadn't been any resistance on Boston when his fleet had arrived and the marines secured the orbital defenses, then the shipyards. "Give me a status report, please."

"The Emperor took the replenishment ships, but he made no attempt to capture or destroy our shipyards and our vast stockpiles of spare parts," Commodore Yu said. There was a hint of pride in her voice. She'd battled logistics problems on a scale unseen since the Inheritance Wars and done a very good job. "Our manpower levels remain untouched. I believe that repairing the majority of your ships will take no more than a month."

She paused. "The bad news is that we stripped ourselves clean of assault pods and other such weapons, sir," she added. "Replenishing them may take more than a couple of months, at best."

Roman cursed the irony under his breath. He'd signed off on transferring all of the assault pods to the fleet, knowing they'd be necessary for the advance on Nova Athena. For once, they would have the Outsiders in a place where they would have to fight or give ground, allowing him to bring the sheer mass of Fifth Fleet to bear against them. But, given everything that had happened since, it had been a terrible mistake. Two months... what could the Emperor do in two months? His imagination provided too many answers.

And if it's longer than two months, we may have some real problems, he thought. *Our logistics are going to be fragile for a very long time to come.*

"Then get started on replenishing the assault pods," he ordered. It was annoying,

but there was no point crying over spilt milk. "What about the picket forces?"

"None have been informed of the... changing situation," Commodore Yu told him. "The 432nd Heavy Cruiser Squadron passed through two weeks ago for replenishment and then headed back to her patrol grounds."

Roman shook his head in tired disbelief. Thanks to the crazed laws of interstellar war, forces nominally under his command might be attacking the Outsiders for weeks to come, even though he'd come to an *agreement* with the Outsiders. He hoped they'd be understanding, when the reports finally came in; they'd understand, wouldn't they, that he couldn't call his ships back at once?

"Send a handful of courier boats to alert them and order an immediate return to Boston," he ordered. The Outsiders would have the same problem, but almost all of the systems that had changed hands in the last few years were useless, at least in the short term. They certainly couldn't give their holder a new fleet of starships. "Tell them to avoid contact with the Outsiders as much as possible and, if they do get detected, break contact if they can."

He winced at his own words. Cruiser commanders were *taught* to be aggressive, all the more so in the midst of a war. None of them would *appreciate* being told to avoid contact with the enemy, particularly when they'd been given orders to press their advantage where possible, but they'd obey. He hoped. It would be hard for many of them to accept an alliance with the Outsiders, yet it would be harder if there were a string of incidents that looked like mutual treachery and backstabbing...

"Yes, sir," Commodore Yu said. She took a breath. "The majority of the fleet train remains intact, sir, but we are still quite short on freighters. Supplying the offensive pushed us to our limits."

"We should be able to get more freighters from the Outsiders," Roman said. He didn't know if he could trust them completely, but he saw no other choice. "They won't be configured for naval service, though."

"We have workarounds in place, already," Commodore Yu assured him. "I've been pressing captured freighters into service for years."

Roman nodded, and turned to look at the strategic display. It was at least two months out of date — more, perhaps, given that *Earth* had been several months out of date when the information had been compiled — but it told a grim story. Emperor Marius, falling back towards Earth, could gather a formidable mobile force to challenge Roman, while using fixed defenses to slow his advance. There was no way to circumvent them either, no matter *what* Roman did. He'd committed himself to at least four assaults through Asimov Points he *knew* to be heavily defended.

Unless...

He studied the display for a long moment, thinking hard. There *was* a way to avoid contact with those defended Asimov Points, but it would be risky. Risky as hell. He'd have to fight his way across half the Federation, just to find a place where he could cross interstellar space and attack Earth through the Dead End, Earth's *second* Asimov Point. It was tempting, but the more he looked at it, the more he saw the weaknesses. His fleet would be running short on supplies by the time it finally

reached its destination, while the Emperor would have plenty of time to prepare his defenses and cut Roman off at the knees. No, the only true hope of victory was to complete those assaults as fast as possible.

"Admiral?"

He blinked, remembering Commodore Yu. "Yes?"

"There's one other detail that should be brought to your attention," Commodore Yu said, carefully. "Before he left, the Emperor issued a search warrant for Professor Kratman, an APB demanding his arrest and extradition to Earth under federal law."

Roman stared at her. "Professor Kratman?"

"He vanished — or, at least, there's no trace of him on the planet's surface from a point two weeks after the fleet's departure," Commodore Yu said. "The planetary police have been attempting to locate him, as per request, but without success. He's dropped out of sight completely."

"Then he took a ship out of the system," Roman said.

"I don't think so," Commodore Yu said. "We did check, but there's no trace of Professor Kratman passing through any of the orbital chokepoints before boarding an interstellar ship and departing the system. A smuggler might be better at getting him off the planet without passing through any of the chokepoints, yet it would have to be an incredibly brave smuggler..."

"True," Roman agreed. Boston hadn't *quite* entered lockdown, but all ships arriving and departing the planet had been carefully scrutinized. Quite a number had been caught with military-grade sensor suites they shouldn't have had, unless they were spies. "You think he's still here?"

"I believe so," Commodore Yu said. "This isn't an uninhabitable world, sir. A careful person could live off the grid, without being detected, for quite some time. There's been a black market in everything from living goods to luxury items ever since the war began. I believe, sir, that farmers have been producing more foodstuffs than they've bothered to report and selling the surplus on the black market."

Which is why I never liked living on a planetary surface, Roman thought. *It's so... disorganized.*

He leaned forward. "Did the Emperor say *why* he wanted the Professor caught?"

"No, sir," Commodore Yu said. "A federal warrant doesn't need a reason."

Roman nodded, thoughtfully. Professor Kratman had visited him, shortly before the fleet had departed Boston, warning Roman that the Emperor was no longer stable. And he'd been right, tragically right. The signs had been there for all to see, if they dared look.

"Put out a statement, inviting the professor to turn himself in," he ordered, finally. The Emperor might have been acting out of vindictiveness — he *had* shot the remaining Grand Senators personally — but somehow Roman doubted it. Hadn't Marius Drake once served under *Captain* Kratman? "And if he does, have him shipped to *Valiant*."

Commodore Yu frowned. "Is that wise?"

"I think I'd like to know what the Emperor thinks he's done," Roman said. "And

besides, he *was* a minister in the Emperor's government. He probably knows a great deal *we* should know."

"Aye, sir," Commodore Yu said. "If he turns himself in, I'll have him shipped back to you."

Roman dismissed her, and turned back to the display. He'd have to send a courier boat back to Nova Athena, asking the Outsiders to bring their ships and supplies forward as quickly as possible, then send another group of courier boats to the other admirals. If they turned on the Emperor, it *would* shorten the war... he refused to think about the deaths it would cause, if the civil war expanded. There was no choice.

And put a set of pickets through each of the Asimov Points, he thought, tapping orders into the console. *The enemy might just try to counterattack while we're desperately preparing an offensive of our own.*

He sat down, hastily reviewing Emperor Marius's possible options. Any *normal* admiral would launch a counterattack as soon as possible, just to keep Roman from getting too comfortable, let alone launching a further attack. It was what *he'd* done, back when the Outsiders had announced their existence by attacking Athena. But Emperor Marius would have to worry about securing his rear, something *Roman* hadn't needed to consider. He might just keep going until he had his fleet safely back at Earth.

But he can send other squadrons to counterattack, or harass my supply lines, Roman reminded himself. It *was* a fairly standard tactic. The Emperor wouldn't need any real imagination to think of it. *I need to worry about my rear now.*

The hatch chimed. He keyed a switch, opening it. Elf stepped inside, looking tired.

Roman smiled, rising. "Welcome back to Boston."

"It seems to be fairly stable," Elf said, as she gave him a tight hug. "But there could easily be underground cells just waiting for the order to cause trouble."

"I know," Roman said. He'd ordered stay-behind cells to be formed, just in case Boston fell to the Outsiders. The irony of having one of those cells carry out an underground war against him was chilling, but he had to admit it could happen. "I have every confidence in your ability to secure the fleet."

"I just wish it wasn't another civil war," Elf said. "It's impossible to judge just where *everyone's* loyalties lie."

Roman opened his mouth to answer, but the intercom buzzed. "Admiral, this is Lieutenant Thompson," a voice said. "We've just received a message from the planet. Professor Kratman has been located and is currently *en route* to the ship."

Elf blinked. "That quick?"

"He just walked in and announced himself," Lieutenant Thompson said. "Admiral?"

"Inform me when he arrives," Roman said. He closed the channel, then looked at Elf and smiled. "Answers, finally."

"Yes," Elf agreed. "Now tell me, do you know the questions?"

"I hope so," Roman said.

Chapter Eight

Once scattered, the Federation Navy lost all contact with its long history, its long traditions and, eventually, its reason for existence.
—The Federation Navy in Retrospect, 4199

Boston, 4101

Roman had first met Professor Kratman when he'd been a young cadet, struggling to earn high marks through nothing more than sheer merit. The Professor had never been dull; he'd opened their minds, taught them to think and, sometimes harshly, rebuked them for parroting what they learned in books and files. Roman had respected him deeply, even though he hadn't always *liked* him. But the man before him now was a shadow of the professor Roman remembered. He looked thinner and paler, his white hair reduced to a faint wisp covering his head. Being on the run for several weeks had evidently not agreed with him.

"I can have food and drink brought in, if you wish," he said, as the Professor took a seat in Roman's quarters. He keyed his terminal, sending the food order. "What *happened* to you?"

"Suspected it would be better to absent myself for a while," Kratman said. His voice, too, was raspier than Roman remembered. "Marius, I fear, was starting to suspect me. I'd acted too openly against him."

Elf leaned forward from where she sat on the sofa. "In doing what?"

"Talking to you, for a start," Kratman said. "The Emperor's paranoia was growing stronger, much stronger. I believe it wouldn't have been long before I was removed, on one pretext or another."

He met Roman's eyes, a hint of the old fire sparkling to life. "What happened at Nova Athena?"

"The Emperor attempted to commit genocide," Roman said, bluntly. He ran through a brief explanation, ending with the return to Boston. "Why? Why did this happen?"

"I believe I explained the problem to you, the last time we met," Kratman said. "The task of running a military is very different from the task of running an entire government, even without the stress of a major war. Marius Drake, sole ruler of the Federation, was cracking under the pressure. I suspected trouble a long time before I obtained proof that he was growing dangerously addicted to drugs and alcohol."

Elf snorted. "What was he *meant* to do?"

"Not get addicted, for one," Kratman said, shortly. "He knew the dangers; he was one of the smartest young officers I ever met..."

"And you helped put him in power," Elf said.

"I wish I'd had a better solution," Kratman admitted. "A period of military rule — ten years, as he promised us — seemed the ideal solution. We could streamline the regulations, pare the bureaucracy down to the bone and end the many — many — injustices perpetrated in the name of the Federation. We could loosen the bonds

on our industries, making them more competitive and, at the same time, expand our industrial base. The conditions that allowed for the rise of the Grand Senate would take longer to re-emerge, I hoped.

"Instead, we had a major war to fight," he added. "And the Emperor was utterly unwilling to compromise with the Outsiders. Instead of recovering, our industry has started to collapse; instead of growing, our economy has continued to decay. And the bureaucracy, the bane of billions upon billions of people, has actually managed to *grow*."

"The Outsiders appeared at a very bad time," Roman observed.

"Yes," Kratman said, flatly. "They did."

The hatch opened, revealing a pair of stewards carrying trays. Roman watched as they put the food on the table and retreated, then motioned to Kratman to eat. The Professor tucked in with considerable enthusiasm, suggesting he'd been going hungry for the last couple of weeks. Whatever he said, Roman doubted that dropping off the grid had been easy, even on a heavily-populated world like Boston. The war economy kept much of the planet under tight control. He nibbled companionably and waited, as patiently as he could, for Kratman to finish.

"Marius Drake is not a man accustomed to failure or frustration," Kratman said, when he'd eaten half of the reconstituted scrambled eggs and bacon. "Indeed, I believe trouble was brewing, deep within his mind, as Operation Retribution set off on its ill-fated voyage. The... agreement... he reached with the Grand Senate may have helped, a little, but their attempt to kill Marius pushed him over the edge. Now, he is forced to come to terms with the limits of absolute power at the same time as he has to fight a major war. He simply can't get blood from a stone."

"It doesn't matter how many orders he issues," Elf said, quietly. "All that matters is how many of them can be obeyed."

"Correct," Kratman said. "He's been taking drugs and drinking too much, sleeping too little and eating a very poor diet...

"And he's been lashing out at people he sees as potential threats to his plans, apparently unable to see how his actions are counter-productive. The strikers, for example, were pushed to strike because their working conditions were intolerable. Marius, in crushing the strikes and making examples of the ringleaders, has only made matters worse for the economy. The workers may not be on strike, but they sure as hell aren't working very hard."

He shook his head. "And his new security apparatus is out of control," he added. "I don't know just how much *Marius* knows about what they're doing, but they've been arresting journalists, commentators and generally casting a long shadow over public debate. Fear is spreading, Roman, and it's destroying us."

Elf shot Roman a sharp look. "Wasn't that true of the Grand Senate?"

"The Grand Senate, for all of its flaws, enjoyed a certain legitimacy," Kratman said. He shrugged. "If only because it remained in power for so long, no one could remember anything else. And, until the Imperialist Faction self-destructed, it *did* manage to do a fairly decent job of running the Federation."

"There are many who would disagree with that," Elf pointed out.

"Yes, there are," Kratman agreed. "No system of government is perfect, Major. There has never been a time in human history where there *weren't* discontented people of one stripe or another, people who had grudges against the system or merely thought *they* were the ones who should be in charge."

"A fairly common delusion," Elf noted.

Kratman nodded as he took another bite of his food. "Most of the problems facing the Grand Senate — and Marius Drake — came from the simple fact that the Federation is really too *colossal* to be micromanaged effectively. Marius, I suspect, really should have understood that from the start."

"Because micromanaging a military operation across thousands of light years is simply impossible," Roman said. He'd studied the problem at the academy a long time before he had to face it for himself. "By the time messages reach Earth and return with new orders, the situation has moved on."

"Correct," Kratman said. He tapped the table, meaningfully. "Lacking legitimacy, Marius needs to secure his power through other means. And those methods, Roman, are alienating the Core Worlds from him."

"But if he didn't," Roman said, "he couldn't fight the war."

"I know," Kratman agreed. "The timing was unfortunate. And now Marius Drake is going mad."

"You could have stopped him," Roman said. "You could have tried to warn him..."

"He didn't listen to me," Kratman said. "By the time I realized there was a major problem, Roman, he'd already concluded I wasn't saying anything he wanted to hear." He shook his head. "It isn't that he doesn't understand the problems," he added, after a moment. "It's that he sees defeating the Outsiders as the ultimate priority, with everything else second to that goal. His loyalty to the Federation, the same loyalty that kept him from becoming a warlord in his own right, drives him forward on a single-minded crusade to restore the Federation's unity. And anyone who stands in his way is, by definition, a traitor to the Federation."

"And you can do *anything* to traitors," Elf said.

"Exactly," Kratman said. "I don't think it will be long, Roman, before Marius starts using the military to *force* reform. And the results are likely to be disastrous. Earth, for example, requires patient handling, not dictatorship. Or, for that matter, being cut off from all government support and told to actually *earn* itself a living."

Roman leaned forward. "Very well," he said, tartly. "We've agreed the Emperor is a madman. We have to overthrow him before it's too late."

"Removing him from power isn't the only issue," Kratman said. "The question is what comes next? What do we put in his place?"

"There *is* Lady Tiffany," Elf offered. "She's the *Empress*, to all intents and purposes."

Kratman shook his head. "She has no authority, no influence, that doesn't come from Marius Drake," he said. "She certainly doesn't command any fleets in her own right. The best she can hope for is to be ignored by those who do."

Roman nodded, reluctantly. After Admiral Justinian and Marius Drake, the only people with power were the ones who controlled military formations. Even if Lady Tiffany hadn't been the last surviving member of the Grand Families — at least, the last one on Earth — she wouldn't have any power herself. If something happened to her husband, she'd fall with him.

He sighed. No wonder Marius Drake had started to slide down the slippery slope.

"Shouldn't we win the war *first*?" He asked. "This might all become academic if we wind up facing a firing squad."

"Marius did not have a plan of transition," Kratman said, frankly. "To my certain knowledge, Roman, he was making it up as he went along. He couldn't have planned for the Outsiders, I know, but still... he had little more than good intentions. And the pathway to hell is *paved* with good intentions."

"I don't want to take power for myself," Roman insisted.

"You may not have a choice," Elf said. She gave him a sharp look. "Without a strong central authority, the Federation will not survive."

Kratman looked up. "*Should* the Federation survive?"

Roman blinked in shock. He'd never been *wedded* to the concept of the Federation, not like Marius Drake, but he'd served it all his adult life. The idea of simply *allowing* the Federation to disintegrate into chaos was horrific. Billions upon billions of lives would be lost, through everything from starvation to military action, as galactic civilization crumbled into dust. The Outsiders would not hesitate to take advantage of the chaos, nor would rogue warlords intent on building up empires of their own. One colossal state would be replaced by dozens of others.

"At least, should it survive in its current form?" Kratman added. "The system the founders created was tailor-made for abuse. On one hand, the out-worlds had very little influence in federal policy; on the other hand, there were so many voters in the core that their votes were concentrated in a small number of hands. The rise of the Grand Senate, an aristocracy in all but name, was inevitable.

"Marius tried to reform the system from within and failed. The effort of *trying* drove him mad. You may need to replace the system with something else, something more durable, something that learns from the mistakes of the past."

"And something that pushes the Core Worlds to become more than just parasites on the rest of the Federation," Elf added. "A system that rewards actual *work*."

Roman held up a hand. "Right now, I have to concentrate on preparing the fleet for our push towards the Core Worlds," he said. "Professor, the Outsiders should be arriving within three weeks to a month, now we've secured the system. I want you to sit down with them and sort out an effective plan of transition, one that takes us to a successor state that will salvage human unity without creating another nightmare."

"It might take longer than you think to hammer out something that will be moderately acceptable to everyone," Kratman warned. "There are far too many issues that need to be addressed. For a start, Roman, what do we do about aliens?"

"Tricky one," Elf said. She sounded darkly amused. "Keep them in bondage, risk uprisings and interstellar wars; let them have their freedom, risk having the Emperor

declare a crusade against the alien-lovers. What do you think, Professor, that the Brotherhood will think of that?"

Kratman sighed. "The truth, Major, is that the Brotherhood may well be a spent force," he said. "Our ability to influence events has been weakening over the last five years."

Roman blinked. "I thought the Brotherhood was all-powerful?"

"Smoke and mirrors," Kratman admitted. "Oh, we were in position to shape public opinion, even to influence decisions made at the very heart of the federal government. We had people emplaced in the bureaucracy, the media, the military... but our ability to take direct action was always very limited. It was better, we felt, to gently shape public discourse rather than put a dam in its path. And, as long as no one started a purge, we were able to punch well above our actual weight."

"Because no one had any real idea of your true strengths and weaknesses," Elf said. "They allowed themselves to be intimidated by you."

"Yes," Kratman said. "And, to be fair, they found us useful. We played a vital role in ensuring that aliens remained firmly under control.

"Now, though, the ruler of Earth is a man who won't be intimidated, a man who pays no attention to public opinion or our spokesmen. I suspect, when he finally returns home, that the Emperor will take strong action against us. He knows we're no longer on his side."

"Brilliant," Roman said, sarcastically.

He looked down at the table, fighting to keep the disbelief off his face. The Brotherhood had cast a long shadow over humanity ever since the First Interstellar War, when the newborn Federation Navy had discovered just what the Snakes did to their human prisoners. An anger had been awakened, matched with a steely determination to ensure that no alien race was ever in a position to threaten humanity ever again. And the Brotherhood, a secretive organization to push for human supremacy, had been born.

And yet, it had all been a bluff?

"For the moment, then, we will leave the alien problem off the table," Roman said. He rubbed his forehead, wondering if Marius Drake had felt the same way when he'd contemplated the problem of reforming the Federation. "We..."

"The Outsiders have alien allies," Kratman reminded him. "They're unlikely to tolerate a continuation of the old policy."

"You mean crushing all threats, keeping the aliens firmly under control and dropping KEWs at the slightest hint of trouble," Elf said, flatly. "And exploiting alien labour on their own homeworlds."

"Yes," Kratman agreed.

Roman cursed under his breath. The problem hadn't changed. If they supported alien freedom, even aliens confined to their homeworlds, they'd be handing Emperor Marius a guaranteed propaganda coup. There was nothing — *nothing* — that galvanised the great mass of public opinion in the Federation more than the prospect of

aliens being granted even *limited* independence. The Brotherhood had played a major role in keeping public opinion firmly turned against the aliens.

And yet, *not* granting aliens rights and freedoms would alienate the Outsiders. Even if the *human* Outsiders accepted it, their alien allies would not. And then the civil war would only become worse.

Elf cleared her throat. "What does it actually matter?"

Kratman tossed her a sharp look. "What do you mean?"

"If some of the reports I've heard through the grapevine are accurate, the industrial workforce is having major problems keeping up with the Emperor's demands," Elf said. "You suggested as much yourself. So they get convinced we're going to free the aliens, with scenes out of a bad low-budget movie... so what? Even if he were assured of total support, could the Emperor translate it into something *effective*?"

Roman had to smile. Elf was right. Public opinion, outside of the workforce, mattered very little. What were they going to do? Hold protests against alien rights? And even if the workforce suddenly became far more motivated, it wouldn't slow the steady decline of the Federation's industry. Hell, it might make it a great deal worse.

"It might also motivate his military personnel," Kratman said. "How often do they watch those low-budget movies?"

"It may not matter," Roman said. "The Emperor... the Emperor can be very inspiring, when he chooses to be."

He looked back at the table. "We'll agree to withdraw troops and fortifications from alien homeworlds, granting them independence," he said. "Alien worlds that exist beyond the Rim will be left alone, provided they leave *us* alone; if they don't leave us alone, we'll smash their militaries and confine them to their homeworlds. And if they want to trade with us... maybe we'll let them."

"That won't go down well with everyone," Kratman warned.

Roman shrugged. "In my entire career, Professor, I've only ever seen a handful of living aliens, all from the same race," he said. "How often does the average citizen *see* an alien? I don't think there are any *real* aliens in any of those stupid movies."

"There aren't," Kratman confirmed.

Roman looked at him, sharply. "Work out the basics for a post-victory Federation," he said, "and have them ready to present to the Outsiders. I imagine they'll want to haggle for hours over the details..."

"Days," Kratman said. "If not months."

"But if we lose, it won't matter in the slightest," Roman said. "And you'd better make it clear to them that Nova Athena was a human world... and the Emperor was willing to fire on it anyway. I rather doubt he'd hesitate to scorch an alien world clean of life."

"It has been done before," Kratman said. He rose, then hesitated. "I assume I have a cabin?"

"You'll have plenty of space to work," Roman assured him. He keyed his terminal, calling a steward. "The steward will show you to your cabin. I'd suggest a shower and sleep before you actually *do* anything."

Kratman smiled. "In the words of a very old philosopher, Roman, when you get to my age, 'look as good, you will not.'"

Elf smiled. "How *did* you survive so long on Boston without being caught?"

"Big world," Kratman said. "And there's *always* an underground, if you know where to look and have the money to convince them you're worth helping."

He shrugged, then followed the steward out of the compartment.

"It's not going to end," Roman said. "Is it?"

"Probably not," Elf said. She leaned forward and patted his knee. "Nothing *ever* ends. All you can do is try your best."

"I know," Roman said. He sighed, wishing he had time to take her to bed. "And now I have to get my ships ready before the Outsiders arrive."

"Or before the Emperor counterattacks," Elf added. "*That* would put the cat amongst the mice."

Chapter Nine

The Outsiders, by contrast, remained a reasonably united force even after the defeat at Boston and the near-defeat at Nova Athena.
—The Federation Navy in Retrospect, 4199

Boston, 4101

Chang Li vaguely remembered passing through Boston, back when she'd left Earth after Admiral Justinian had started a civil war. She hadn't stayed long, unsure of just which way the system's commanding officer was planning to jump. He'd stayed loyal in the end, she recalled, but she'd had some nasty moments before she finally returned home. The Grand Senate, having granted itself colossal powers to ensure the security of the Federation, might well have sought to arrest her on trumped-up charges.

Now, she couldn't help feeling oddly conflicted as the superdreadnaught *Freedom* transited through the Asimov Point and entered the Boston System. She *had* returned, but as a diplomatic envoy rather than a conqueror. And, no matter how she looked at it, there was no way to avoid the fact that she would have to convince the system's population to join her, rather than taking their hatred of the Federation for granted. Boston had not only survived two rounds of war, it had prospered... and it was loyal to Admiral Garibaldi. If it hadn't been, the war might have come within shouting distance of being lost.

"Fifth Fleet is currently holding position midway between Boston and Asimov Point One," General Stuart said, as he stood beside her in the CIC. "It isn't a bad choice, really. Gives Garibaldi a mix of possible options if the Feds show themselves."

Li nodded and turned her attention back to the display. Boston was heavily industrialized, far more than ninety percent of the other systems along the Rim; it would have been a valuable prize, if her forces had taken it and its industry intact. Dozens of ore miners made their way through the asteroid belt, transporting raw materials to the industrial nodes orbiting Boston itself, while countless freighters headed to and from the Asimov Points or out into interstellar space. Throughout the system, powerful fortifications orbited the planet and guarded the Asimov Points. It was impossible to escape the impression that Admiral Garibaldi had an invulnerable fortress, if he chose to use it.

And yet, she knew that was an illusion. Given sufficient firepower, *any* system could be taken, either through direct assault or a careful campaign of isolation before dispatching a fleet across interstellar space to finish the job. The fortresses that dominated the display could be left to die, once they were cut off from their supply lines, while the planet itself was an immoveable target. If the Emperor had been willing to bombard Nova Athena, she asked herself, was there anything stopping him from targeting Boston? A single antimatter bomb would be more than enough to lay waste to the entire planet.

And I wonder, she thought, *just how many of the people on the planet understand the risk?*

"We've picked up a communication from the command fortress," General Stuart said. "They want us to join the main body of the fleet for discussions."

Li nodded. "Take us there," she said. She wished, despite herself, that she knew more about Admiral Garibaldi. What would *he* want from the Outsiders — and what would *he* see as the ideal post-war universe? "I'll be in my cabin. Please inform me when we reach shuttlecraft range."

"Of course, Senator," General Stuart said. He paused. "They are also asking for us to share classified information on our ships, so they can be slotted into their command network. The risks are quite high."

"I know," Li said. She looked back at the display, then shook her head. If Admiral Garibaldi had intended a trap, he'd have opened fire on her ships as they transited the Asimov Point and entered the system, one by one. "But the risks have to be borne."

She nodded again, then strode through the hatch and down the corridor to her cabin. It was smaller, by far, than the stateroom she'd been allocated on the liner she'd taken to Earth, decades ago, but she didn't mind. Her importance wasn't measured by the size of her quarters or the quality of her food. She closed the hatch behind her, checked the timer and lay down on the bed. There should be more than enough time for a quick nap before she needed to board the shuttlecraft.

Her lips curved into a smile. General Stuart would have been surprised, she was sure, to know she was napping, but she'd reached a point where constant revision was more likely to harm than help. There was nothing to be gained by going over the talking points, again and again; it would just drive her mad when she needed to relax and center herself for the coming discussions. She closed her eyes and started to take deep breaths. All she could do now was wait and sleep.

੪⃝ଔ

"Welcome back, Senator," Admiral Garibaldi said, as she and General Stuart were shown into his cabin. "I'm glad you could make it."

"Thank you, Admiral," Li said. Admiral Garibaldi wasn't alone: he was flanked by the young female marine she recalled from their first meeting and an older man who looked to be in his late seventies, although that could be an illusion. A person with access to rejuvenation treatments might remain the same physical age even as they entered their third century. "I'm very relieved that you managed to secure the system."

"So am I," Admiral Garibaldi said. "And that most of my crews remained loyal."

"I wanted to ask about that." Li said. "Have you had any trouble?"

"A couple of thousand officers and men were shipped to internment camps on Boston," Garibaldi said, as he motioned for them to sit down. "Most of them were reluctant to fight against the Emperor, either because they were loyal to him or felt that another round of civil war would shatter the Federation. They will, of course, remain unharmed."

General Stuart leaned forward. "Can you be *sure* there are no sleeper agents still present on your ships?"

"No," Admiral Garibaldi said, bluntly. He didn't seem annoyed by the question, but Li would have been surprised if he wasn't. "There's no way to be sure of anything."

Li winced. Spies were bad enough, but programmed sleeper agents were far worse. They could fool lie detectors because they didn't know they were sleeper agents; they knew themselves to be loyal. And yet, they might be pushed into taking action by commands they didn't know had been inserted into their brains, if the alternate personality didn't simply wash the original personality aside.

"We don't have time to brain-scan everyone who might have been turned into a sleeper agent," Admiral Garibaldi said, flatly. "All we can do is take precautions and hope."

He shook his head. "But that's not what we're here to discuss," he said. "First, we need to decide on a plan of campaign; second, we need to discuss the future of the post-war universe."

"That is correct," Li agreed. "I was under the impression, however, that you wanted to win the war before haggling over the peace."

"Professor Kratman insisted that I should have a plan for managing the transition," Admiral Garibaldi said. He nodded to the older man. "You'll be negotiating with him, later. For the moment..."

He keyed a switch. A starchart sprang to life, displaying the shortest route from Boston to Earth. Li, somewhat to her surprise, had no difficulty in understanding it, although — in hindsight — she knew she shouldn't have been surprised. The Outsider Navy had largely copied the Federation Navy's protocols, just to make life easier for experienced officers who joined the cause. Or, for that matter, to command captured warships.

"There are thirteen Asimov Points between Boston and Earth," Garibaldi said, "and two interstellar gulfs that will have to be crossed in FTL. Assuming we don't have to do any actual *fighting*, it would take around three months to reach the Gateway and enter the Sol System. As it happens, there are formidable defenses emplaced at Ruthven, Marble, Tara Prime and the Gateway itself. The latter two, in particular, are formidable indeed."

Li frowned. "None of the other Asimov Points are defended?"

"There were a handful of minefields and automated weapons platforms, as of the last set of updates," Garibaldi said. "However, the *defended* Asimov Points are *chokepoints*; we have to go through them or spend years trying to reach our destination via stardrive. There are alternatives — we can go through a different Asimov Point at Astrid and enter Tara Prime through the New London Asimov Point — but we'd still have to tangle with formidable fixed defenses."

He sucked in a breath. "Making matters more complicated, Senator, is the simple fact that the Tara Sector is controlled by Admiral Theodore Vincent," he added. "I don't know him, but he wouldn't have been left in command of the sector if he

hadn't been regarded as both competent and loyal. I'm hoping he will switch sides, which will make getting through the Tara Prime chokepoint a great deal easier, but there's no guarantee of anything. He might stay with the Emperor or he may declare independence as a rogue warlord."

"I assume he has a file," Li said, after a moment's thought. She hadn't met Admiral Vincent either. "Does it say anything useful?"

"Very little," Professor Kratman said. "He left the Luna Academy ten years before the Justinian War and cut his way to a captaincy, purely on merit. His career stalled afterwards as he had no powerful connections; he only became a commodore after his superior officers were killed during the war. Marius must have known him, I suspect; Tara Prime is not exactly a place to park someone you don't trust. But there's no hint of where they actually *met*."

Li's eyes narrowed. "They didn't serve together?"

"Captain Vincent's ship was assigned to Operation Retribution and fought in the Battle of Boskone," Admiral Garibaldi said, quietly. "They may have met in the aftermath, Senator. I certainly met the Admiral after Boskone. But they didn't serve together after that, as far as we can tell."

"Which means that the Emperor either made a snap judgement," the female marine said, "or they worked together on something that *wasn't* included in the files."

"There's no way to know," Admiral Garibaldi said. "I've sent messages to Vincent, but he hasn't had time to reply. We're proceeding on the assumption he's going to be hostile until proven otherwise."

He tapped the display. "I intend to leave Boston and proceed to Ruthven within two weeks — ideally, as soon as we have the latest sets of assault pods loaded onto the ships," he said, curtly. "The fleet train will have to work hard, unfortunately, as we will be forcing the Emperor's ships to fall back on his own supply bases. Worse, we will have to proceed from Ruthven to Marble as soon as possible, forcing us into another engagement with a heavily-defended system."

"Attacking Marble should be easier," General Stuart pointed out. "You'd be attacking the defenses from the rear, instead of punching through an Asimov Point."

"There are fortresses on both sides of the Asimov Point," Admiral Garibaldi said. "I imagine one group of fortresses will rush to battlestations as the second group holds out as long as it can. I'm not sure what the planners were thinking..."

He shook his head. "We must assume that the Emperor has also detached forces to harass our supply shipments," he added. "Convoying enough assault points to Maben to prepare for an attack on Tara Prime will be difficult, all the more so as Tara Prime would be a very good place for the Emperor to make a stand."

"You mean it's just like Boston," General Stuart said. "Only *you* are faced with the task of taking the system, rather than defending it."

"I'm afraid so," Admiral Garibaldi said. "If you have any wonder weapons that can blow a fortress into atoms with a single hit... now would be an excellent time to produce them."

"We don't," General Stuart said. "The Marsha have been quite happy to fly suicide missions, piloting cutters crammed with antimatter, but I suspect the Feds will be ready for such tricks."

"I know," Admiral Garibaldi agreed. "You used them on me."

He took a moment to gather himself, then leaned forward. "I don't think I need to tell you just how important it is that we preserve as much as possible of our mobile fighting power," he warned. "Home Fleet is still the single most powerful fleet element in the entire Federation, Senator, and it is backed up by the immense fortifications surrounding the Gateway and Earth itself. We could punch our way through to Sol and still lose the war."

"There is an alternative," General Stuart suggested. "Once we secure Tara Prime, we could launch raids through the Core Worlds, devastating their industrial base. The Emperor's ships would eventually grind to a halt through lack of maintenance and supplies."

"We could try," Admiral Garibaldi said, "but we'd have to tangle with dozens of other fixed defenses, wearing down our fleet too."

He looked directly at Li. "How many additional ships can you supply?"

Li nodded to General Stuart, who cleared his throat. "Though the magic of actually streamlining the whole process, Admiral, it takes us around six months to turn out a whole new superdreadnaught. Add another month or two to work the ship up... overall, give us a few years and we can replace all of our superdreadnaught losses. Smaller ships take less time, as you might expect; we've managed to get destroyer build times down to a month, assuming all the parts are on hand.

"Crewing is, of course, a weakness," he added. "Our training programs are far superior to the Federation's" — Li winced, inwardly, at the gloating note in his voice — "but our manpower base is nowhere near as extensive. However, we are recruiting more crew from the stage-one and two colony worlds that have joined our union. I suspect we will be churning out double or triple the amount of trained manpower within the next two years."

He paused, dramatically. "Right now, we have the battle squadrons we brought with us and several hundred smaller ships," he concluded. "Give us a couple of years and we will have a far superior fighting force."

"Except the Federation can still out-produce you," Admiral Garibaldi said, carefully. "It may take them a full *year*, perhaps longer, to build a superdreadnaught, but they can lay down five or six times as many ships as you can."

"It depends," General Stuart admitted. "Our industrial base is weaker, but our manpower is far superior and we are willing to use considerably more automation in the construction yards. And one of our superdreadnaughts is worth two or three of yours... sorry, of *theirs*."

"General," Li said.

General Stuart had the grace to look abashed. "We are working on expanding our industrial base too," he said. "Our projections show many different results, of course, but we believe that if the war lasts another five years, we should gain a decisive

advantage. However, the Federation may solve some of its own problems in the same time. If they manage to improve their educational base by a mere twenty percent, they — not us — will gain a decisive advantage. We can't risk giving them time to steady themselves and start work on improving their own systems."

"Which would give the Emperor more time to consolidate his power and plot a counteroffensive," Admiral Garibaldi said. "Marius Drake is not an idiot, General. He understands his military weaknesses very well."

He nodded to the display. "Are you willing to commit your forces to this operational plan?"

"I see no alternative," General Stuart said. "Leaving him in control of the Core Worlds will, at the very least, prolong the war."

"Agreed," Li said. She shuddered at the thought. The wars — the Justinian War, the Outsider War — had killed millions, perhaps *billions*, of humans. Merely trying to force their way into Boston had cost the Outsiders over a hundred *thousand* lives... and at least fifty *thousand* on the other side. "We have to end this war as soon as possible."

"We'll test your datalinks against ours," Admiral Garibaldi said. He looked at General Stuart. "Will you serve as second-in-command of the fleet?"

"If you'll have me," General Stuart said. His lips quirked in wry amusement. "I lost the last two battles I fought."

"You fought well," Admiral Garibaldi said. "And your trick with the ECM was very well timed."

"Yeah," General Stuart said. "It drove the Emperor mad."

"We'll move to the ops room and discuss our options," Admiral Garibaldi said. "Professor Kratman and the Senator can discuss the post-war universe. Assuming, of course, that we win the war. We could still lose."

He opened the hatch and led General Stuart out of the compartment, followed by the female marine. Li watched him go, feeling an odd flicker of respect. Admiral Garibaldi hadn't *needed* to invite General Stuart to serve as his second, even though Stuart commanded a sizable fleet in his own right. It was a diplomatic gesture that, she hoped, would go some distance towards integrating the two fleets.

And we're going to need it, she thought. She'd seen the projections too, noting just how many people were going to die even if the war stayed relatively clean. If the Emperor started bombarding planets at random, and he'd already tried to cross the line once, billions of innocent civilians would be added to the death toll. *This war isn't for the future, not any longer. It's for survival.*

"Senator," Professor Kratman said. "I've taken the liberty of preparing a set of proposals for our discussions."

Li nodded and dragged her attention back to the here and now. "I look forward to them," she said. "And I have some proposals of my own."

Chapter Ten

No one really expected Lady Tiffany, born Tiffany Eleanor Diana Katherine d'Artagnan, to be a serious player on the galactic stage. It was why she was practically given away to Marius Drake, forming a blood tie between him and the Grand Senate. In hindsight, of course, that was a terrible mistake.
—The Woman in Black, 4199

Earth, 4101

It hadn't been a comfortable night.

Lady Tiffany was loath to admit it, but she missed her husband. Marius Drake might be older than her — much older — yet he'd treated her as a person from the very start, rather than an unwanted wife or a nicely-shaped piece of meat. Tiffany hadn't been able to keep herself from responding to his courtesy; she'd hated the very thought of being forced into a marriage with a much older man, but she had to admit that it had worked out. Marius Drake, she thought, was truly deserving of her loyalty.

And he'd trusted her. It felt *wrong* to be apart from him for nearly seven months, but she knew just how much power he'd placed into her hands when he'd appointed her as his second on Earth. He trusted her enough to take the risk of betrayal that she would turn on him, appoint her own people to powerful positions throughout the Federation and, eventually, declare herself Empress in his stead. But the thought had never crossed her mind. She was loyal to the man who'd made her more than an isolated member of a very minor family, so isolated that she could be given away at the whims of her seniors. And besides, she knew, Marius Drake commanded the loyalty of his cabinet, something she doubted she would ever have.

She sat up in bed and rubbed her eyes, unsure *just* what had woken her. Seven months of solitude would have seemed a dream come true, once upon a time, but now it felt odd. She was the ruler of Earth, to all intents and purposes; she could surround herself with people, if she wanted, yet they wouldn't include the person she *needed*. Besides, she spent half of her working day answering petitions and listening to complaints from hundreds of people, all of whom insisted that their petty little problem was so urgent that it had to be dealt with immediately. Solitude at night seemed a welcome blessing.

The intercom buzzed, again. "My Lady, *Thunderbird* just passed through the Gateway," Johan Carmichael said. She'd taken pains to get to know her husband's staff, not just the men and women who tended the President's House. "The Emperor is on his way home."

Tiffany felt her heart leap, despite the foreboding she felt deep inside. A courier boat had arrived only a week ago, bearing grim tidings. The Battle of Nova Athena had been won, then lost, thanks to the treachery of Admiral Garibaldi. Tiffany had met the young man — he was only a few years her senior — during the final campaign against Admiral Justinian; she hadn't considered him a potential traitor. But

then, no one had considered Admiral Justinian a potential traitor, either. No wonder he'd gotten away with it for so long.

"Thank you," she said. "When will he arrive?"

"*Thunderbird's* ETA in orbit is thirty-seven minutes," Carmichael said, nervously. He had never seemed to be in awe of her birth, she'd noted with some amusement, but he definitely was in awe of her husband. "Assuming he boards a shuttle at once, My Lady, he'll be on the ground twenty minutes afterwards."

Tiffany grinned, feeling almost as giddy as a schoolgirl. "I'll be at the shuttlepad to meet him," she said, as she pulled back the covers and sat up in bed. "Please inform me when he is ten minutes from landing."

"Of course, My Lady," Carmichael said.

"And thank you," Tiffany added.

She smiled as she swung her bare legs over the edge of the bed and stood. Too many of her fellow aristocrats, male or female, cared nothing for the men and women who served them. Tiffany had seen servants insulted, molested, or even beaten bloody by their masters, none of whom had really considered the servants to be *human*. Tiffany's father, however, had told her to remember that the servants *thought*, and they could nurse resentments as well as any Grand Senator... *and* that they had a great deal more than merely losing a coveted trade deal to resent. She'd done her best to treat the servants kindly, even before she'd married Marius Drake...

... And, unlike so many others, she hadn't been betrayed by her own servants when the Grand Senate finally fell.

The thought chilled her to the bone as she stepped into the bathroom and removed her robe, studying her reflection in the mirror. Long red hair splashed down around a heart-shaped face, just a little *too* imperfect to attract a young buck from the aristocracy. Not that any of them *would* have married her, she thought, even if they'd *wanted* her. Her family lacked the wealth and connections to be of interest, certainly not to the old folks who determined who married whom. She'd resigned herself to being a spinster long before the old bastards had turned out to have a use for her, after all. Had Marius Drake ever *known* he'd been attached to a family of little real value?

Not that it matters any longer, she reminded herself. *The world has changed beyond repair.*

She pushed the thought aside as she hurriedly washed and dried herself, then stepped back into the bedroom and hunted for a dress. Normally, she would wear a suit and tie her hair back to appear professional, but she wanted to look good for her husband. It took her several minutes to locate everything she needed and get dressed before sitting in front of the mirror starting to apply make-up to her face. The green dress, she felt, set her hair off, while hinting at her curves rather than revealing them for all to see. Thankfully, no one expected her to set fashions right across the Federation. *That*, at least, was something she'd been spared.

Smiling, she hurried out of the door and into the antechamber. Her bodyguards, two men who had worked for her father before being assigned to Tiffany herself, rose to their feet and followed her as she walked into the corridor. Their presence

was more of a formality than anything else — the Presidential House was heavily defended by armored marines — but Marius had insisted, telling Tiffany that it would provide an extra layer of security for her. She couldn't help being touched by his concern for her safety as she walked up the stairs, men and women in uniform saluting her as she passed. No one else, save for her father, had given much of a damn about her.

She stepped out onto the shuttlepad and frowned, in sudden discontent, as she saw General Standerton Thorne standing at the edge of the pad. What was *he* doing, waiting for her husband? She didn't *like* General Thorne, if only because he gave her the creeps far worse than some of the aristocratic bucks she'd been supposed to mingle with at parties. *They'd* spent far too long drooling openly over her breasts, but Thorne gave her a very different impression. There was something in the way he looked at her, at everyone, that told her he wouldn't give a damn if she lived or died — and, that if she got in his way, he'd kill her without a second thought. She knew such people were necessary, sometimes, but Thorne still scared her. And she had no idea why Thorne had been entrusted with Earth's security.

A cold wind blew across the shuttlepad as the shuttle came into view, dropping rapidly towards the Presidential House. Tiffany was no expert, but it looked very much as though the pilot was expecting to run into trouble, as if there was something lurking just outside the security cordon with a HVM launcher. Her heart almost stopped at the thought, just as the shuttle came to a halt and hovered over the pad. Moments later, it lowered itself to the ground, a sudden flush of hot air causing Tiffany to take a step backwards. She caught herself and took a step forward as the hatch cracked open, revealing...

For a long moment, she didn't recognize her husband. War — and the stress of being Emperor — had taken a toll on Marius Drake, but now he had changed so much that it took her several seconds to be *sure* she was looking at him. He looked to have aged decades in a mere handful of months! His hair had turned white, his skin was lined and he looked as though he was on the verge of collapse, held up only by sheer willpower. She took a step forward, wanting to take him in her arms, but he held up a hand, stopping her.

"General," he said. Even his *voice* had changed! She fretted, just for a second, that he'd actually been *replaced* before reminding herself that a clone would never have made it through the security monitors. "Have the cabinet meet me in the conference room in ten minutes."

"Yes, sir," General Thorne said.

"Commander Lewis has a chip for the processor," Marius continued. "Escort her down to the conference room and wait with her."

Tiffany felt her eyes narrow as Commander Lewis emerged from the hatch, looking downright nervous. A flicker of suspicion crossed her mind, which vanished as she read the signs of fear — if not outright terror — on the officer's face. Tiffany prided herself on being a good reader of faces and there was something deeply, *deeply* wrong with the young woman. She was scared of something more than being caught

having an affair, Tiffany was sure. It might be worth inviting the young officer for a chat, once things had settled down a little. But now, all she could do was watch as Commander Lewis followed General Thorne down the corridor and out of sight.

"Tiffany," Marius rasped. "You're looking well."

"Thank you," Tiffany managed. This wasn't how she'd envisaged his homecoming. She'd planned a private dinner, then a night together, before they settled down to business. She didn't want to ask what had happened, but she needed to know. "I..."

"I'll discuss the keeping of Earth after this conference," Marius said, cutting her off. "We have a great deal to discuss."

"Of course," Tiffany said, deeply hurt. Had he no time, even, to tell her he loved her? What had happened at Nova Athena to steal her husband and put this stranger in his place? "I will, of course, attend the conference."

For a second, she thought Marius would object and started gathering arguments to convince him otherwise, but he merely nodded and swept off down the corridor. Tiffany trailed in his wake, fighting back the urge to cry. Once, he'd trusted her; he'd listened to her opinion and allowed her to change his mind. But now... what had happened to change her husband so much?

⅜⅓

There was no time, as much as Marius would have liked it, for a pleasant homecoming with his wife. He'd downloaded the latest updates from Earth as soon as his fleet transited the Gateway and it was obvious, blindingly so, that rumors were already out and spreading across the Core Worlds. There was nothing he could do, he suspected, to keep the rumors under control. All he could do was make damn sure he showed no sign of actual *weakness*.

"Admiral Garibaldi betrayed us," he said simply, as soon as the doors to the conference room were closed. His cabinet had assembled, save for Professor Kratman — another betrayal, although nowhere near as painful — and Commodore Arunika. The former Head of Intelligence's Brotherhood ties would not be enough to save her from being taken into custody and interrogated. "He has almost certainly joined the Outsiders."

He gave them no time to recover. "Worse, the Brotherhood was clearly involved," he added, curtly. In hindsight, the chain of events was all too clear. "I have no idea what passed between Admiral Garibaldi and Professor Kratman, but the Professor vanished shortly after the fleet departed from Boston and, somehow, managed to evade one of Garibaldi's hand-picked officers.

"We must face up to the fact that the war situation has taken a decided turn for the worse.

"I've spent the last three months running simulations and working my way through every last piece of data we collected over the past years of fighting," he continued. "I believe that Roman Garibaldi intended to take power and present himself as the man who saved the Federation *and* the Outsiders. With the Outsiders almost whipped, gentlemen, they are in no state to dispute this version of events. Garibaldi, therefore,

will bring his fleet back to Earth as quickly as possible. His goal will be to repeat my steps when I took the Grand Fleet to Earth after Tobias was shot."

He felt a sudden stab of pain. Tobias Vaughn had deserved better than to die that way...

"But, in doing so, he will almost certainly shatter the Federation. We cannot allow it to succeed. We *will not* allow it to succeed."

Marius allowed his voice to harden. "This is a bitter blow," he warned. "I will not try to hide just how badly Admiral Garibaldi's defection will shake the navy. We went through a long succession of purges after Admiral Justinian launched his offensive against Earth, people, and going through it again could destroy us. But we have no choice. The destiny of the human race cannot be put in the hands of either Admiral Garibaldi or the Outsiders."

He swung around to look at General Thorne. "What's the current situation on Earth?"

"Uneasy," Thorne said. "All vital installations, industries and housing complexes have been secured, but large parts of the planet are restless. The parasites who suck at the government's teat are still demanding the resumption of their support payments, rather than doing something useful with their lives. They, however, are not a serious problem."

Marius felt a sudden stab of pain in his head. "And the *truly* serious problem?"

"There haven't been any new strikes, Emperor," General Thorne said. "However, our industrial production has been dropping sharply over the last four months. I believe a number of workforces are deliberately slowing down, after we crushed the strikes."

"They're suffering from worn-out equipment," Tiffany said. "No matter how hard you push them, Marius, their ability to meet your demands is falling. It will take years to repair the damage we've inflicted on our own industry."

"They can meet our demands long enough to win the war," Marius said, dismissively. Hadn't there been a time when he'd *listened* to Tiffany? Was she trying to take their side? "General?"

"Yes, Your Majesty?"

"I want you to start conscripting additional personnel from Earth," Marius said. He'd hated the Earthers, back when he'd grown up on Mars. Ninety percent of the population was useless, yet they controlled the destiny of half the galaxy. "Everyone is to be given the standard aptitude test, then assigned for training as workers, spacers or security personnel. No more objections, General, no more protests about the right to suckle at the government's teat. I want all protests crushed with extreme force."

"Yes, Your Majesty," General Thorne said.

He'd do it too, Marius knew. Thorne had no morality, no sense of right or wrong; he'd follow orders to the bitter end. And if he killed a few thousand people who were technically innocent... well, one couldn't make an omelette without breaking a few eggs. Admiral Garibaldi and the Outsiders *had* to be stopped.

"They'll hate us," Tiffany said. "Marius…"

"It has to be done," Marius snapped. "There's no choice!"

"I want a full media campaign," he added, turning to Lawrence Tully. "Everyone is to know that Admiral Garibaldi has allied himself with the Outsiders, with aliens. He has to be stopped."

Tully looked doubtful. "Your Majesty, we spent the last two years *promoting* Admiral Garibaldi…"

"The idiots who watch the slop the media puts out will believe anything," Marius said. He shrugged, expressively. "Just make sure the story is convincing. Break out all the old propaganda and use it."

He took a breath, wishing for a pill or a drink, then went on.

𝄞𝄢

It took nearly three hours to bring the meeting to a close, Tiffany noted, three hours during which her husband proved he wasn't the man she remembered any longer. Marius had always had a ruthless streak, but now… now he was giving orders to have protesters shot and families taken hostage, just to keep the industrial workers in line. She had no illusions just how bad things would become, once it became clear that the government had abandoned all pretense of respecting Earth's long-held rights. There was going to be a nightmare.

She watched him, nervously, as they walked back to their bedroom. There were several new security guards outside, all wearing black uniforms copied from the original Blackshirts. It would have amused her, once upon a time, but it didn't now. Marius — and General Thorne — had resurrected the Grand Senate's security troops and put them to work.

"It's going to be fine," she said, as the hatch closed behind them. She wondered, suddenly, if she should light the candles or give him a massage. "What happened?"

Marius turned to look at her. There was something cold and dangerous in his gaze. For the first time since she'd met him, she couldn't help feeling frightened.

"I was betrayed," he snapped. He strode over to the drinks cabinet and opened it, removing a bottle of Caledonian Scotch. "Roman betrayed me. And Kratman."

"But what happened?" Tiffany asked. She watched in alarm as Marius put the bottle to his lips and took a long swig. "I thought…"

"I thought he was loyal," Marius hissed. "I won't make that mistake again."

Tiffany felt her heart break, just a little. She'd planned a romantic reunion, not… not being alone with a monster who wore her husband's face. But what could she do?

Better think of something quick, her own thoughts mocked her, as Marius took another long swig and then reached for her. *If this goes on, how long will it be before he comes to suspect you of treason?*

Interlude One

From: *The Chaos Years* (5023)

Word spread across the Federation, carried by starships and courier boats, as Admiral Garibaldi and Emperor Marius struggled to rally support for their cause. The out-worlds, already caught in the middle of the Outsider War, hastened to pledge their support for the Outsiders and Admiral Garibaldi, while the inner worlds hesitated, unsure which way to jump. No one wanted to back a loser.

The Core Worlds, already restless under Emperor Marius's rule, were deeply divided. Many feared losing control of the out-worlds, of what the Outsiders might do if they gained absolute power, while others deeply resented Emperor Marius's measures to boost and diversify the economy. Earth itself, homeworld of the human race, teetered on the brink of civil war. Many of its inhabitants would have liked to enter the workforce, if there had been jobs for them. Others, though, feared for the future, regardless of who won the war. Marius might be bad, some said, but the Outsiders would be hell incarnate. *They* had no reason to treat Earth with anything, apart from scorn.

Both sides fought desperately to prepare their forces for a further round of war. Roman Garibaldi mustered a joint fleet of Federation and Outsider ships, while Emperor Marius struggled to reinforce Home Fleet and prepare ambushes along the bloody route to Tara Prime. And, caught in the middle, once-loyal officers wondered who they should support, if they should support anyone. Why *not* set up as an independent warlord? The Federation they'd served was long gone, but, in its death throes, it might take the galaxy down with it.

And so the stage was set for war.

Chapter Eleven

The complexities of an Asimov Point assault were, by 4101, well known to the Federation Navy. Indeed, barring the lucky discovery of an unknown Asimov Point chain that would allow a navy to slip a fleet into the enemy's rear, they were still important despite the invention of the stardrive.
—The Federation Navy in Retrospect, 4199

Hammond/Alexis, 4101

"We seem to be alone, Admiral," Lieutenant Thompson said. "The system appears to be deserted."

Roman nodded, although he knew better than to take that on faith. The Emperor might well have detached a handful of cloaked cruisers as his ships passed through Hammond, either to provide advance warning for the defenders of Alexis or ambush his supply lines as his battle squadrons inched away from their bases. It was, after all, a standard tactic, honed in the years before anyone had invented the continuous-displacement stardrive. Even an officer as unimaginative as Admiral Ness would have thought of it.

"Detach a squadron of battlecruisers and order them to race to the Alexis Point, as planned," he ordered. He doubted he could *surprise* the defenders, but he could *try*. "If their CO sees an opportunity to destroy any picket ships, he is to take it."

He sat back in his command chair and studied the display. Hammond had been classed as worthless, when the first survey ships had passed through the system; the later discovery of a third Asimov Point hadn't changed the system's ranking, as the third Asimov Point led to a dead end. Unsurprisingly, the handful of rocky planets and single gas giant hadn't received much in the way of investment from the Federation. The system hadn't even had a cloudscoop until *Roman* had provided one, as part of buttressing the defenses of Boston. He would have been surprised if the population of the system's sole inhabited world knew what was happening beyond their thin atmosphere, or gave much of a damn if they did.

"Deploy an additional shell of recon drones," he ordered, absently. "I want to know about it if anyone tries to sneak up on us."

"Aye, sir," Lieutenant Thompson said.

Roman nodded to himself. Earthers — and other planet-dwellers — found it hard to grasp the sheer *vastness* of interstellar space, but as an asteroid-born he understood all too well. The entire Federation Navy could be hidden somewhere within the system and his sensors wouldn't see it, as long as her crews were relatively careful. Each superdreadnaught might be two kilometres long, yet they were grains of sand against the immensity of the interstellar desert. It was hard to escape the sense that he was leaving safety and security behind, heading out on a voyage that might lead him to rocky shoals. Part of his mind wanted to abort the mission and flee back to the warmth of Boston.

He smiled, dismissing the thought. He'd wanted to join the Survey Service, as a younger man, but the war had put a stop to such ambitions. Roman wondered, afterwards, if he'd be able to take command of a survey squadron and head out beyond the Rim, if only to see what was waiting for humanity in the darkness. He certainly met the qualifications required for survey officers now...

But the Outsiders may object to us poking through their territory, he thought, as his ships continued their stately crawl towards their destination. *And they may wind up with their independence, if the war allows it.*

Long hours passed before a new icon popped up in the display. "Admiral, the battlecruisers have detected an escort carrier sitting on the Asimov Point," Lieutenant Thompson reported, grimly. "She has a shell of fighters surrounding her."

Roman cursed under his breath, although he knew he shouldn't have expected the enemy to do something *stupid*. Escort carriers were largely defenseless — they were really nothing more than modified freighters — but with a fighter shell patroling local space there was no hope of getting his battlecruisers into missile range before the escort carrier detected them and launched drones back through the Asimov Point. The defenders would have ample warning of his arrival.

And they'll pick up my ships when we enter sensor range, he thought. *Even with ECM, they'll have a good chance to assess our strength before popping back through the Asimov Point.*

He shuddered, inwardly. The escort carrier was no treacherous warship serving a warlord, no Outsider or alien battleship that needed to be destroyed in open combat... her crew had been his allies, a mere three months ago. Who knew? If they understood what had happened, if they understood why Roman had realized the Emperor needed to be removed, they might *agree* with him. But the iron laws of interstellar combat decreed that the ship had to die, with as little warning as possible. There was no alternative.

"Order the battlecruisers to engage," he ordered. Surprise was already gone, but perhaps he could keep the enemy in doubt as to his total strength. The Emperor would already have a good idea of Fifth Fleet's total strength, but he would give a great deal, no doubt, to know just what the Outsiders had added to his fleet. "They are to kill her as quickly as possible."

He kept his face impassive, fighting down the wave of disgust and guilt at his decision. A crew had been sentenced to death, just for being trapped on the wrong side. And the crew might already be dead. The time-delay between sending messages and receiving them meant that his battlecruiser commanders might already have had to engage, if one of the fighters came too close to their ship. And he wouldn't *know* for at least two hours...

Damn you, Marius, he thought, bitterly. *What have we become?*

The hours crawled by, slowly, before the final update blinked up in front of him. Roman read it, quickly; the battlecruisers had killed the escort carrier, but she'd managed to get off her drones before she'd been blown to atoms. His commanders

had had no choice; they'd *had* to engage at long-range. And that had ensured the escort carrier had had time to do her duty before she died.

"Order the fleet to increase speed," he said. The enemy CO, trapped on the other side of the Asimov Point, would know about the battlecruisers, but hopefully he wouldn't have any real idea of just what was bearing down on him. "And signal the battlecruisers. Anything that pokes its nose through the Asimov Point is to be slapped back, hard."

He forced himself to relax as the Asimov Point appeared on the display, surrounded by his battlecruisers. The real-time update popped up in front of him; he breathed a sigh of relief as he realized the enemy CO had only launched drones through the point, rather than actual starships. Drones were hard to hit — the battlecruisers would have bare seconds to engage before they reversed course and plunged back through the Asimov Point — but most of their sensors were decidedly short-range. It was possible, reasonably possible, that the enemy CO had only seen the battlecruisers...

"Launch the first set of drones," he ordered, as the fleet sorted itself into assault formation. "I want them summoned to surrender."

"Aye, sir," Lieutenant Thompson said.

Roman gritted his teeth as the drones approached the Asimov Point and vanished. There had been three fortresses on the far side, according to the last update; Alexis hadn't been deemed important enough for heavier defenses, not given the far greater defenses of Ruthven. He doubted that could have changed, not in the three months since the Battle of Nova Athena, but he knew better than to underestimate the Emperor. Marius Drake hadn't had half the tactical flexibility Roman had enjoyed, simply by having access to new weapons systems, yet he'd been more than capable of using what he had in a creative manner.

The first set of drones popped back into existence, their numbers sharply reduced. Roman scowled — that almost certainly meant that the gunners and starfighter pilots on the far side were well-trained and experienced — and then frowned as their sensor records appeared in front of him. There were no additional fortresses, but the Asimov Point practically crawled with minefields and free-floating missile pods. It looked as through the enemy CO had actually started expanding his defenses long before the Battle of Nova Athena.

Smart guy, Roman thought. He'd checked the files, but there was no clue which way the CO would actually jump. *He'd bleed us white if we weren't ready for him.*

"There was no response from the fortresses," Lieutenant Thompson reported. "They didn't try to surrender."

"Send through a second flight of drones," Roman ordered. He wondered, absently, if the fortress commander was reluctant to surrender to a single squadron of battlecruisers. No sane battlecruiser commander would try to force an Asimov Point if there was any alternative. "I want them to have a chance to surrender."

He watched the drones vanish, but none returned. The enemy CO, it seemed, hadn't given any stand-down orders to his crews. Roman cursed under his breath

— over fifteen thousand trained personnel were about to die — then keyed his console.

"Launch the assault pods," he ordered. "And then ready the first assault squadrons."

ℬℭ

Commodore Leon Brinkman had no intention of surrendering. He'd made the mistake of allowing a sweet-talking superior officer to lure him into Fortress Command only to discover, too late, that Fortress Command was very much the despised ugly stepsister of the Federation Navy. He might reach flag rank, if he were lucky, but he would never command a fleet in action — and, because of that, he would never climb to the very highest ranks. The thought of surrendering without a fight to an officer a full four decades younger than he — and a traitor, to boot — was too much.

"Sir," Commander Hadfield said. "Enemy assault pods are transiting the Asimov Point."

"Order the CSP to engage," Leon said, although he knew it was unnecessary. Everyone in the navy knew just how important it was to kill as many assault pods as possible before they could open fire. Indeed, no one, not even the most anal superior officer, would complain if the pilots opened fire without waiting for orders. "And stand by to repel attack..."

He braced himself as the remaining pods opened fire, unleashing a tidal wave of missiles on his fortresses. A handful were picked off by the CSP, but the remainder kept coming, automatically shifting into sprint mode as they closed in on their targets. Hundreds died as his point defense crews picked them off; dozens survived to slam into the fortress's shields and detonate, shaking the fortress violently. Red icons flared up on the status display as the damage began to mount.

"Sir, we've lost four shield generators," Lieutenant Redbird called. "They were *antimatter* warheads!"

"We have been at war for the last seven years," Leon snapped. There was no time for *surprise.* Any reluctance to deploy antimatter warheads had vanished as soon as Admiral Justinian had attacked Earth, back in the mists of time. "Get repair crews on the task, now!"

He swore under his breath as a new cluster of red icons appeared on the display; destroyers, frigates and escort carriers, the latter already launching starfighters into the maelstrom. The former orientated themselves, then opened fire, launching mine-clearance missiles into the minefields as a second wave of assault pods materialized. Leon gritted his teeth as they started to launch, their warheads no doubt receiving updated tactical data from the rebel destroyers. It looked chaotic, but he was experienced enough to see a well-practiced team at work.

"Target the ships," he snapped, as the wave of missiles roared towards his command. "And fire!"

The fortress barely shuddered as it unleashed the first spread of missiles. Not having to cram the hull with engines gave it a throw weight a superdreadnaught would envy — and shields a superdreadnaught commander would sell his soul to have wrapped about his ships. The escort carriers had already reversed course and

plunged back into the Asimov Point, but the remaining ships were holding position, systematically sweeping the mines out of space. He had to admit their crews were *very* well trained...

... And yet, no destroyer could hope to stand up to capital shipkiller missiles.

"Four enemy destroyers have been destroyed," Commander Hadfield reported. "Two more have been badly damaged..."

"The escort carriers have returned," Lieutenant Robinson called. "They're launching a second wave of fighters!"

"Commit the remainder of the CSP," Leon ordered.

૪૦૦૪

"The enemy position has been badly weakened, sir," Lieutenant Thompson reported. "But their defenses are holding."

"Send in the third wave of assault pods, then the first battle squadron," Roman ordered. It was risky — the smaller ships had done an excellent job of clearing the minefields, yet there were hundreds of mines and automated weapons platforms still intact — but there was no choice. "Go!"

"Aye, sir," Lieutenant Thompson said.

Roman cursed under his breath as the third set of assault pods popped through the Asimov Point and vanished from the display. He'd hoped to blow through the defenses, not get bogged down into a long drawn-out engagement. But the enemy CO had put up a brutal fight, rather than surrendering, with or without firing a handful of shots to uphold his honor first. He hadn't thought too highly of the concept of sowing every Asimov Point with a handful of fortresses, when it had been proposed to him, but in hindsight it might just have been a good idea after all. If nothing else, it had certainly cost him three waves of assault pods. He'd have to slow his advance to resupply before he tried to force his way into Ruthven.

And the enemy will have plenty of time to prepare, he thought sourly. *They'll know what they're facing.*

"The first superdreadnaught is entering the Asimov Point," Lieutenant Thompson said.

"Good," Roman answered. He wanted to be on that ship; he wanted to lead his crews into the fire personally, just to make it clear that he would share the dangers. But he knew he couldn't risk his own life any more than strictly necessary. "Ready the second battle squadron to advance as soon as the first is deployed."

He closed his eyes for a long bitter moment. How many of his people were about to die?

૪૦૦૪

"Sir," Commander Hadfield snapped. "An enemy superdreadnaught — unknown class — has just transited the Asimov Point!"

"Release all remaining weapons," Leon ordered. An unknown class of superdreadnaught meant Outsiders... unless Roman Garibaldi had been secretly building up his own fleet at Boston. It wasn't completely impossible — Admiral Justinian had

certainly built up his own fleet — but ONI wouldn't miss the signs of a second secretive build-up. "Fire at will."

The enemy starship belched missiles at the same moment, without waiting for its tactical systems to recover from the shock of transit. Leon stared in disbelief, unsure *quite* what he was seeing. There was no way for anyone to be *precisely* sure just *where* a ship would appear, when it popped out of an Asimov Point; it took time, sometimes as long as a minute, for a ship to orientate itself, locate its enemies and open fire... and, in that time, the enemy had already had a free shot at its hull. But the Outsiders had opened fire at once...

They must have set up a dedicated tactical net, relayed through the destroyers, he thought, as another swarm of missiles roared towards the fortresses. *They took their targeting data from the destroyers, rather than the superdreadnaught.*

"Missiles away, sir," Commander Hadfield said. He cursed as another red icon popped into existence. "Sir, another superdreadnaught..."

"I have eyes," Leon said, cutting him off. The first superdreadnaught's point defense was good, but she was almost certainly doomed... even so, her weapons had already swept far too many of his remaining defenses out of space. "Retarget the second missile barrage on the newcomer."

"Aye, sir," Commander Hadfield said. "I..."

He broke off as a green icon vanished from the display. "Sir, Fortress Two is gone," he reported. "They took her out."

Leon winced. The fortresses were designed to soak up damage, even after their shields failed, but the enemy had simply overwhelmed Fortress Two with antimatter missiles. It was a standard tactic. And his remaining fortresses were on the verge of losing their shields too, while three more enemy superdreadnaughts had crawled out of the Asimov Point to add their fire to the assault. No matter what he did, he couldn't hope to hold out for much longer.

Resistance has become futile, he thought, bitterly. He *hated* the thought of surrendering, particularly after he'd put up such a savage fight. Who *knew* just how badly the rebels — and the Outsiders — would react to his attempt to surrender? *But what other choice do I have?*

He shook his head, swallowing his pride. There was *no* choice. The enemy were just piling on the pressure, accepting their own losses to wear him down... and they seemed to have an unlimited supply of assault pods. No matter what he did, he knew all he could really do was scratch them before they tore his fortresses apart. And the remainder of his crews would die for nothing.

"Launch courier drones to the Ruthven Asimov Point," he ordered, "then transmit a complete copy of our tactical records to both Ruthven and Alexis itself."

"Aye, sir," Commander Hadfield said.

"And then cease fire," Leon added. He felt a sudden vindictive glee as the first superdreadnaught blew apart, bare seconds before he would have had to let her go. "Inform the enemy CO that we'd like to surrender."

He felt the shock running through the compartment at his words. The Federation Navy rarely surrendered, certainly not to alien-lovers. But they all knew the truth. Resistance had *definitely* become futile.

"And prep the databases for destruction," he ordered. "I don't want them drawing a scrap of information from our files."

He sat back and waited. He'd done all he could, all he could think of, but right now his part in the war was over.

Chapter Twelve

In theory, prisoners taken by the Federation Navy were supposed to be well-treated. In reality, their treatment tended to be determined by circumstance. Pirates, rebels, traitors and aliens knew better than to expect mercy from the Federation's officers.
—The Federation Navy in Retrospect, 4199

Hammond/Alexis, 4101

"Admiral," Lieutenant Thompson said from her console. "The remaining fortresses are requesting permission to surrender."

Roman felt his eyes narrow. "Is this a trap?"

"They've deactivated everything but their shields and point defense," Lieutenant Thompson assured him, calmly. "I don't think they're doing anything to hinder our advance."

"Order the assault fleet to hold their fire, then inform the defenders that they are to shut down everything but emergency power," Roman ordered. No matter what he did, it was unlikely he could *completely* pre-empt the prospect of treachery. "Have boarding parties assembled and launched to take possession of the fortresses. Once the control systems are secured, the prisoners are to be removed from the station and prepped for dispatch back to Boston."

He scowled, inwardly. Emperor Marius had wanted to slaughter the Outsider prisoners, making it very clear to their comrades that they could expect no mercy. Roman knew he didn't dare repeat that mistake, whatever else he did. He had to make it clear that surrendering to his ships wasn't an automatic death sentence. And yet, he also had to guard against the prospect of a lone holdout condemning his comrades to death.

"Have the battlecruisers power past the fortresses and into the system," he added. "One squadron is to approach Alexis and inspect the defenses, the other two are to be dispatched to the Asimov Points. The defenders of Asimov Point Three are to be invited to surrender; the defenders of the Ruthven Point are to be monitored from a safe distance."

"Aye, sir," Lieutenant Thompson said. "And the planet itself?"

Roman shrugged. "We'll cross that bridge when we come to it," he said. Alexis was a stage-three colony; her industries were nowhere near ready to turn out starships, but she could certainly provide food and small components for the fleet. "As long as she doesn't have independent starships of her own, she's a very minor problem."

He looked back at the display as the next battle squadron slowly made its way through the Asimov Point. His squadron would be going through next, hopefully in time to see the fortresses before they surrendered. The risk was minimal, but it gnawed at him to be watching from safety as young men and women fought on his behalf. He had no idea how Emperor Marius had handled it, back when he'd sent Roman and his fellows into the storm.

"I have a preliminary damage report," Lieutenant Thompson said. "One super-dreadnaught — *Death to Tyrants* — was destroyed outright, although a number of her crew managed to get to the lifepods before it was too late. Another superdread-naught, the *Freedom's Call*, will require at least a month in the yards before she's fit for duty again. Two more superdreadnaughts took mild damage and will need basic repairs."

Roman nodded. "And the smaller ships?"

"Twelve destroyers and four frigates were lost with all hands, along with four-teen starfighter pilots," Lieutenant Thompson reported. "Nine more small ships took varying levels of damage, sir; preliminary reports suggest two would be cheaper to scrap rather than try to repair. Their crews are currently being prepped for transfer back to the personnel pool."

"See if they can find slots with the fleet first," Roman ordered. They didn't have time to send the crewmen to Boston, then have them brought all the way back to the fleet. "And have the fortress personnel checked for potential allies. We may pick up some new crewmen."

"Aye, sir," Lieutenant Thompson said.

ଚଠ03

Uzi couldn't help feeling a flicker of *déjà vu* as the shuttle disconnected from the makeshift troopship and raced across the void of space towards the fortress. It was hardly his first assault on a Federation Navy fortress, although it was definitely the *oddest* assault. His worst nightmare might not have *entirely* come true, but it was pretty damn bad. There was almost no hope of getting a message out without risking his position...

"Prep your weapons," he ordered, coolly. "And remember, you are not to fire unless fired upon."

It was hard, so hard, to keep his amusement off his face. He'd been promoted in the wake of kidnapping Chang Li, an irony that made him want to forget himself and giggle insanely. They'd put him in charge of an assault squad instead of asking a number of very pointed questions! But then, he *had* managed to cover his tracks reasonably well. It would take a very paranoid engineer to go over the shuttle with a fine-toothed comb, then stake his reputation on the suggestion that it had failed due to sabotage, rather than a freak incident.

He looked at the armored men in the shuttle and felt an odd blend of kinship and contempt. They were Outsiders, sworn enemies of the Federation, yet they were also soldiers, preparing themselves for combat as soldiers had done since the very first days of organized warfare. He could practically read their minds and understand what was going through their heads; they were nervous, fearful of screwing up, terri-fied that one of their mistakes would lead to the deaths of a friend or a comrade. And to think, they had it lucky! The Federation's officers had a habit of second-guessing their soldiers on the ground after the fighting was finally over.

"Remember, these people are to be treated with respect, provided they behave themselves," he added. He'd given some thought to triggering an atrocity, but he

hadn't been able to think of a way of evading the blame. Besides, word would probably not be allowed to get out of the system. "Any one of you who abuses a prisoner will answer to me and my fists long before you face anyone higher up the food chain."

He turned his attention back to the pilot as the shuttle closed in on the massive fortress, its armored hull pitted and scarred where the shields had failed, allowing the weapons fire to burn into the metal. The fortress could have survived worse, he was sure, but their position had been hopeless the moment the first superdreadnaught had joined the assault wave. He didn't really blame them for surrendering, even though they could have taken a bite out of the assault force before they were blown to atoms. It would probably not have inflicted enough damage to make up for getting so many crewmen killed.

"Approaching the forward hatch," the pilot said. "Docking in twenty seconds."

Uzi checked his suit, making sure his HUD was showing the right fortress diagram. The Federation standardized everything; it was unlikely, very unlikely, that there were any major differences between the standard fortress and the one facing him. He made a mental note to check which sections had depressurized, if *any*, as soon as they boarded, then caught hold of the seat as the shuttle latched onto the airlock. As soon as the shuttle stabilized, he was on his feet and heading for the hatch. His men followed him, weapons in hand.

"Atmosphere match," the pilot said, as the shuttle hatch hissed open. "No atmospheric contaminants."

"Glad to hear it," Uzi muttered. The fortress crew would have to be out of their minds to poison their own air — his men wore suits, making the whole exercise worse than pointless — but the prospect of fanatical resistance couldn't be *completely* ignored. "Open the inner hatch."

The hatch hissed open. Uzi stepped forward, feeling the gravity field shifting slightly as he stepped from the shuttle's to the fortress's, then smiled as he saw an older man wearing a commodore's uniform waiting for him. The commodore had removed his belt completely, he noted, just to make it clear that he wasn't carrying a sidearm. It would have been more impressive if Uzi hadn't known a hundred different ways to carry a weapon without making it obvious.

"Welcome," the man said, coldly. Uzi had no trouble hearing the bitter anger in the commodore's voice. "I am Commodore Brinkman."

"Thank you," Uzi said. "I trust you have prepared your fortress for surrender?"

"I have ordered my crews to disarm and wait in the designated spaces, save for a number of injured and the medics, who are in sickbay," Brinkman said. "The fortress is currently operating on emergency power and basic subroutines."

Because you purged the databases before surrendering, Uzi thought.

He smiled to himself. It would annoy the Outsiders, but he found it hard to care. The Federation Navy would have put Brinkman in front of a court-martial if he'd allowed the fortress's computer databases to fall into enemy hands. If nothing else, it would make it harder for them to put the fortress back into action in less than a month.

"Understood," he said. "Once the fortress is secured, junior officers and crewmen will be transferred to Boston, where they will sit out the war. Senior officers will be held with the fleet and, if necessary, turned into couriers to carry messages back to Earth."

Brinkman nodded, shortly.

"I am obliged to warn you that any resistance, any attempt to impede my men in the performance of their duties, will result in the application of lethal force," Uzi added. "Please ensure that your personnel are kept under control."

The commodore, thankfully, offered no resistance as the assault force searched the fortress from top to bottom. They'd taken quite a beating, he noted; ninety-seven crewmen had been badly injured in the fighting and a further seventy-four were either dead or lost somewhere in the ruined sections of the fortress. Once the station was secure, the prisoners were hurriedly loaded onboard a transport and sent back to Hammond, while the engineers searched the station for anything useful before shutting it down completely.

"They've wiped the missile warhead programming," one of the engineers reported. "Firing the missiles will be impossible without some reprogramming."

"Just be glad they didn't turn off the containment chambers," Uzi said dryly, as his squad explored the lower levels of the crew quarters. One distinct advantage of serving on a fortress was having larger cabins, even for the junior officers, although a civilian would probably have regarded them as impossibly cramped. "That would have really ruined our day."

He smiled inwardly at the thought. Draining the antimatter into a new warhead would be tricky, but far from impossible. Or, if the engineers felt lucky, they could try reprogramming the old warheads from scratch. Hopefully, if they tried, he would be well away from the fortress.

"Picking up something interesting, sir," one of his troopers offered. "It reads out as a low-level transmitter."

"Odd," Uzi said, checking the readings. It certainly *looked* like a transmitter, although whoever had set it up had been a little careless. The signal scatter was more than enough to lead them right to it. "Let's go see what it is."

He tensed as they passed through a pair of airlocks, into a small cabin on the outer hull. It was large enough to suggest it belonged to a senior officer, although Brinkman and his senior staff had all been housed near the command core. Indeed, whoever had lived in the cabin would have been thoroughly screwed if a missile had struck the hull near the transparent portal. If the blast didn't get them, the radiation certainly would.

"This is odd," the trooper said. "Sir, what *is* this?"

"Maybe it's for senior officers they disliked," Uzi speculated. He'd never actually *served* on a fortress, merely boarded them. "Or it could have been a privacy cabin. Making love can be quite romantic with the stars orbiting over your head."

He stopped as he saw the transmitter, pulsing a laser signal through the transparent canopy and out into space. There would be a stealthed recon platform nearby,

he was sure, relaying the signal to the forces protecting the Ruthven Asimov Point. It was too makeshift a device to have been set up in advance, he was sure. Brinkman certainly wouldn't have known anything about it. Hell, if whoever had set it up had made even a tiny mistake with his calculations, the entire effort would be worse than useless.

A federal undercover agent, he thought, as he looked up. The Grand Senate had been fond of covert agents, monitoring their officers and men, and Emperor Marius had learned his lessons well. *Someone like me.*

"Go fetch the engineers," he said, a plan forming in his head. "I'll stay and guard the device."

As soon as the hatch had closed behind the trooper, Uzi opened his internal datanodes and searched for a processor. Deep-cover agents weren't full cyborgs — it tended to raise eyebrows when implants showed up on medical exams — but they might well have a basic neural link... he smiled to himself as one popped up, linked into the transmitter. Given how little time they'd had, whoever had set up the transmitter had done an excellent job. He uploaded a compressed and encrypted message into the transmitter, watched it flicker off into the ether, then primed the self-destruct system as he stepped backwards. The engineer was in for a nasty surprise when he tried to take the transmitter apart.

The hatch opened, revealing two engineers and his trooper. Uzi watched, dispassionately, as the engineer immediately tried to shut the transmitter down, only to have it disintegrate into dust. There would be no evidence of his transmission, let alone whatever his unknown counterpart had sent... the recon platform, unless he missed his guess, would have either altered position or self-destructed itself once the signal stopped. Assuming, of course, that there *was* a recon platform.

"Someone on the station must have set it up," the engineer said. "This needed a skilled technician to assemble."

Uzi didn't — quite — roll his eyes. "Then we'll have to be careful who we invite to join us," he said, dryly. "This person was very clearly a watchdog."

୫୦୯ଷ

"The planetary government is none too pleased with us," Roman commented, four hours later. "But they have reluctantly agreed to grant us control of their orbital defenses and surrender the industrial nodes to us."

"They didn't have much choice," Elf pointed out. "If they hadn't surrendered the orbital defenses, Roman, what would you have done with them?"

Roman frowned. "I'm glad I didn't have to find out," he said. "As it was..."

He allowed his voice to trail away. Taking the planet's industries by force would have been easy enough, but actually putting them to work would have been a great deal harder. There might not have been any strikes, yet there would definitely have been slowdowns and production headaches, if not outright sabotage. And besides, he didn't *like* the idea of forcing people to support him. The Outsiders would certainly have wondered if he was copying Emperor Marius.

But Alexis is going to wonder if the Emperor will mount a counterattack within days, he thought, grimly. It was hard to blame the planetary government for being worried about being too enthusiastic about supporting Roman and the Outsiders. *They won't want to be caught supporting the wrong side during a civil war.*

"You won a fairly easy victory," Elf said. "Congratulations."

"It's not over yet," Roman said, shaking his head. The defenders of Asimov Point Three had surrendered without a fight, but the defenders of the Ruthven Asimov Point were evidently made of sterner stuff. They'd not only ignored all challenges to surrender, they'd fired long-range missiles at his battlecruisers whenever they'd come within range. "We need to take Ruthven before we can risk slowing the offensive."

He cursed Commodore Brinkman under his breath. The man might have a chip on his shoulder the size of a superdreadnaught, but he'd fought a stubborn defense and cost Roman dearly. Losing a superdreadnaught was quite bad enough; losing the assault pods, irony of ironies, was far worse. By now, he suspected, whoever was in charge of Ruthven would be towing every fortress in their system into position to stand off an assault through the Asimov Point. Breaking through would be immensely costly...

... And it would take months to rebuild his forces to the point where he could cross the interstellar gulf and enter the Tara Sector.

"True," Elf agreed. She rose and started to pace the cabin, turning her head to keep him in view. "When do you want to move?"

Roman sighed. "Ideally, I'd like two weeks to restock," he said. Hell, he would have liked a month, just to make sure his fleet was as strong as possible. "But I think we're going to have to move as soon as we get the next shipload of assault pods. Merely getting into a missile duel with the fortresses on *this* side of the Asimov Point will be quite bad enough."

"The fortresses can't dodge," Elf pointed out, wryly. She stopped pacing and turned to face him. "And you have some other advantages."

"We're still going to be hurt badly," Roman predicted. Outsider technology was all very well, yet they had yet to invent something that rendered the Federation Navy completely obsolete. He'd racked his brain for something — anything — that might save the lives of his crewmen, but nothing had come to mind. "Unless..."

He reached for the datapad and picked up the latest report from the engineers who'd inspected the fortresses. The databases were gone, they'd said, but reprogramming them wouldn't be *too* hard. Indeed, they'd claimed they could have the fortresses up and running again within a week. Roman rather doubted it, but...

"If the fortresses are capable of even minimal operations," he said, "I might just have an idea."

"That sounds bad," Elf said. "Is anyone going to *like* the idea?"

"Probably not," Roman said. He keyed through the intelligence reports, checking that he'd read an earlier outline of the system's assets correctly. "But at least, thanks to the Marsha, we have plenty of volunteers for what is effectively a suicide mission."

Chapter Thirteen

One of the major problems facing the Federation Navy, as a result of the patronage system, was that few junior officers were willing to confront their seniors, even when their seniors behaved abominably. For example, Admiral Stevenson, despite being a known rapist, remained in position until 4098, where he was removed from his post and shot by the direct command of Marius Drake.
—The Federation Navy in Retrospect, 4199

Earth, 4101

Tiffany had never really believed that a person could change rapidly, certainly not over such a short period as seven months. She'd had few *true* friends in her life and none of them had changed so quickly, even when they'd married or set out to take control of their family's interests. But her husband... he was distant, almost as if he was unaware of her existence, his moods shifting so suddenly that she was *sure* something was terrifyingly wrong.

She sat at her dressing table, methodically brushing her long red hair. Her mother, dead long before the rest of the Grand Senate, had taught her to brush her own hair when she was stressed, insisting it would help to calm her thoughts. Tiffany had thought her mother was being absurd until she'd realized just how few of her peers brushed their own hair. Why would they bother when they had maids to do it for them? But Tiffany had never seen the point...

I wish my mother was still alive, she thought, *I could ask for her advice. She'd know what was wrong, what I needed to do.*

It was a bitter thought. Her mother had given her a great deal of advice for the day Tiffany finally married, although she hadn't expected very much. Tiffany didn't know if her mother would have laughed or cried if she'd heard that Tiffany had married the Emperor, let alone had ruled the Sol System in his name. And almost none of her mother's advice had proved remotely useful. But then, Tiffany had been expected to be nothing more than a decorative piece of arm candy when someone finally offered to marry her.

She scowled, brushing her hair time and time again. It would be better, almost, if she *were* being treated as a piece of arm candy. At least then, she was sure, her husband would show a *little* interest in her. As it was, he'd barely touched her in the week since his arrival at Earth, their love-making so perfunctory as to be nothing more than a joke. Her mother had told her that some men could be selfish, that some men cared nothing for the pleasure of their partners, but Marius hadn't shown any interest in his *own* pleasure, let alone hers. He barely even kissed her any longer.

He'd always been a workaholic, but now it was worse. He barely slept. It was all she could do to keep him in bed for a couple of hours a night; his sleep was labored and broken. And he only ate enough to keep himself going, in-between reading reports, issuing orders, and supervising the revamping of the entire fleet. Tiffany was no military expert, but she couldn't see how shifting thousands of officers and crewmen

from ship to ship helped efficiency, nor how stationing Blackshirts on every ship ensured their loyalty. Hadn't the *Grand Senate* put Blackshirts and Commissioners on its own starships, after the start of the war?

He's going mad, she thought.

It wasn't a thought she wanted to face. She *loved* him, more deeply and truly than she cared to admit. He'd been the one who'd raised her up and out of her existence, who'd treated her as a human being, who'd given her the chance to actually do something useful... of *course* she loved him! And yet...

She looked over towards the bed, towards the terminal she'd been allowed to keep. Her authority had vanished the moment Marius had returned, of course, but she still got the intelligence reports from Earth. Marius's methods to get the population back to work were sparking off riots, each nastier than the last, yet he didn't seem to give a damn. She'd tried to talk to him, but he hadn't listened. He was so driven to extract revenge on Roman Garibaldi and everyone else who stood in his path that he didn't care about anything else, not any longer. The man who'd taken power, who'd set out to save the Federation from itself, was gone.

The intercom chimed. "My Lady," Operative Oslo said, "Commander Lewis is here, as you requested."

Tiffany swallowed. She had never — never — before gone behind her husband's back. None of her friends had been scared of their husbands, even if the marriages hadn't worked; they'd known their families would support them if their husbands treated them too badly. And the husbands would face their *own* families if they pushed the marriage bonds too far. But there was no one to protect *Tiffany* if her husband turned on her.

And there's no one to protect Commander Lewis, either, she thought. *I shouldn't have invited her...*

Angrily, she pushed the thought aside. She had to do something. And finding out what was wrong — what was truly wrong — was the first step.

"Send her in," she ordered. "And then hold my calls."

She snorted at the thought. Her life had dried up when Marius had returned home, but she hadn't welcomed the respite for long. Marius was trying to deal with everything, she saw; he simply didn't have the *time* to handle everything, let alone study a situation long enough to be sure he knew what was actually happening. Chances were, he wouldn't return to their suite until late at night, if at all. The staff had told her that they'd found him asleep at his desk, several times.

The door opened. Tiffany hesitated, unsure how to proceed, then put her hairbrush down and rose as Commander Ginny Lewis stepped into the room. She was a big girl, Tiffany noted, her red hair cropped close to her skull. The uniform she wore was surprisingly shapeless, but it clung close enough to her body to allow Tiffany to see she was almost mannish. Her file had made it clear that she was a tactical officer, not anything else. Tiffany wasn't sure if she should be relieved or worried by the fact that Ginny wasn't competition for her husband's attentions.

"My Lady," Ginny said. Her voice was quiet, but deeply worried. "You wanted to see me?"

"Yes, I did," Tiffany confirmed. As if Ginny would have been let through the security checkpoint without an invitation! "I wanted to talk to you about many things."

She led the way into the lounge, motioned for Ginny to take one of the comfortable seats and called the maid. She'd already been briefed; she stepped into the room carrying a tray, which she put down on the table. It was customary, in High Society, to begin any serious discussion with tea and cakes, but Tiffany had no idea how Ginny would react to it. Her file clearly stated that she'd been born on Mars.

Which might be why Marius trusts her, Tiffany thought, as she poured the tea rather than wait for the maid to do it. *They grew up on the same world.*

"I should tell you," she said, as she passed one of the cups to Ginny, "that this room is completely secure. You may speak freely."

Ginny gave her a long look. It wasn't hard to see the fear in her eyes. "Are you sure?"

"My people scanned it only an hour ago," Tiffany assured her. "And I won't repeat anything you say to me."

"There are bugs that are almost completely undetectable," Ginny said. "And equipment can be programmed to miss bugs, if the bugs are emplaced by the owners."

"My people are loyal," Tiffany said. She hoped that was true. If not... who knew what her husband would do? "If there is trouble because of this, Ginny, I'll try and make sure it all falls on me."

Ginny's eyes widened at Tiffany's use of her first name. "I hope you're right," she said, finally. She took a sip of her tea, peering down into the brown liquid. "What do you want from me?"

Tiffany hesitated. She knew how to dance around a subject with a girl from High Society, but she had no idea how Ginny would react. Marius had certainly never shown the patience for an involved conversational dance. And besides, it might spook the girl more than she was already. She had a nasty feeling that Ginny was already considering just how far it was to the door.

"The truth," she said. "What happened to my husband on *Thunderbird*?"

Ginny shuddered, suddenly. In relief? Or fear? Tiffany couldn't tell.

"He made me swear not to tell," Ginny said. Her file had stated that she was a tactical officer of rare promise, but she sounded like a scared little girl. "I gave him my word..."

"I'm his wife," Tiffany said, gently. She needed Ginny to trust her, but how could she do that? They came from very different worlds. "Please. I want to help him."

She studied Ginny for a long moment, trying to parse out the multitude of expressions flickering across her face. It spoke well of Ginny that she wanted to keep her word, but at the same time... there was a strong suggestion that she wanted to help, too. Tiffany forced herself to wait, praying silently that Ginny would talk herself into making the right choice. There was nothing else she could do.

"I'm not quite sure," Ginny said, finally. She glanced at the walls nervously, then back at Tiffany. "We were two days out of Boston, My Lady, when he had an attack of some kind."

Tiffany blinked. "An attack? What did the doctor say?"

"He didn't go to the doctor," Ginny said. "I tried to talk him into going, but he flatly refused and swore me to secrecy. He... he practically fell asleep on the command deck!"

"Oh," Tiffany said. "Is that bad?"

Ginny gave her an odd look. "A captain would be quite within his rights to *execute* any of his crew who fell asleep while on duty," she said. "It would, at the very least, be cause for instant demotion. The Emperor..."

She shook her head. "I helped him to his cabin and did what I could to make sure he ate, drank and slept normally," she added. "He left control of the assaults in the hands of his captains, officially as a test of their skill. And... he was drinking heavily and... I think he was taking something else, too."

Tiffany leaned forward. "Taking what?"

"I don't know," Ginny said. "He never let me see the packet, My Lady. It could have been anything from painkillers to illegal drugs."

And a man in his position could have anything, just by ordering it sent to him, Tiffany thought. There had been quite a few young men, born to High Society, who'd been quietly encouraged to indulge themselves to death. Being addicted to hard drugs, or neural stimulation, or... or *anything*... would render a man unsuitable to assume a high position, after his parents died. *And who knows* what *Marius is taking?*

"I see," she said. "How many did he take a day?"

"I don't know," Ginny said. "I only saw him take them a handful of times."

But that doesn't mean there weren't times you didn't see, Tiffany thought. It was clear, now, that her husband hadn't lured — or forced — Ginny into his bed. What did it say about the whole situation that that would almost have been preferable? *If he was taking those pills once a day...*

"All right," she said. "What — precisely — happened at Nova Athena?"

"We recombined the fleets, then advanced into the system," Ginny said. "The Outsiders put up a brief fight, but we kicked their asses until another fleet arrived. Your husband ordered the bombardment of the planet; Admiral Garibaldi refused to carry out the order. And then we opened fire on his ships."

Tiffany swore, aloud.

"He wasn't the same on the long route home," Ginny added quietly. "There were days when he was intensely focused on his task and days when he just sat in his cabin, staring into space. I think one of his guards must have found a still, because the Emperor was drinking heavily..."

"And now he's mad," Tiffany said, flatly.

"He's not stable," Ginny agreed. She glanced up at the ceiling, nervously. "And now I don't know what he'll do next."

"We have to calm him down, somehow," Tiffany said. "If we can get him off the drugs..."

"My Lady, you don't know what he's taking," Ginny said. "If he's already addicted to the pills, whatever they are, stopping them may merely make the situation worse. He may even have taken something that he *cannot* be weaned off from, no matter what we do. That's how drug suppliers used to work on Mars."

Tiffany nodded. It was rare for someone from High Society to encounter a drug he couldn't shake, but it had happened in the past. The victims tended to be treated as pariahs: given access to the drug they needed, yet otherwise shut out of High Society. She had no idea how such matters were handled outside High Society, but she doubted it would be very pretty. A commoner had few rights where such dangerous drugs were involved.

"So we find out what he's taking, first," she said. "Where does he keep the pills?"

"In his uniform jacket," Ginny said. "I don't think I've ever seen him without it."

"Oh, *goody*," Tiffany said, deadpan.

Ginny blinked, then flushed bright scarlet.

"I'll have to get my hands on one of the pills," Tiffany said. She scowled down at the cup in her hand. "How do you identify a pill?"

"If it's from a legal supplier, there will be a mark on the pill you can check against the datanet," Ginny said. "But if it's from an illicit supplier, it will probably require a laboratory to identify it. Your guards should probably be able to find somewhere discreet that will handle the task."

"You've been thinking about this," Tiffany said, wryly.

"Drugs are a persistent problem on the lower decks," Ginny said. "It wouldn't be the first time I've had to have something strange identified, My Lady. If we were back on the ship, it would be easy."

Tiffany nodded. "Why did he bring you down to the surface?"

Ginny paled. "I think I knew too much," she said, after a moment. "He allowed me to tend to him while he was unwell, My Lady."

"That should have been my job," Tiffany said, without heat. She met the other woman's eyes. "I want you to tell me, as soon as possible, if he suffers another attack."

"If I can get free," Ginny said. "It was hard enough to make time to come see you now."

Tiffany lifted her eyebrows. "What does he have you doing?"

"Reviewing operational plans," Ginny said, frankly. "He believes, reading between the lines, that the decisive battle will be fought in the Tara Sector. He's been looking at ways to ensure a preponderance of force that will ensure his victory."

"I see," Tiffany said.

"It won't be enough, My Lady," Ginny added. "And I've tried to tell him so, but he won't listen."

Tiffany looked up, sharply. "It won't be enough?"

"No," Ginny said. "My Lady... how much do you know about the logistics of interstellar war?"

"Almost nothing," Tiffany said, not entirely truthfully. She had picked up quite a bit, just by watching Marius, but she knew she was no expert. "What do you mean?"

"Space is *vast*," Ginny said, flatly. "The Federation alone is unimaginably huge, My Lady, and the galaxy far larger."

She placed her cup on the table and pointed to it. "If you imagine the cup as the Federation," she said, "and the table as the rest of the galaxy, you start to get some idea of the scales involved."

"I think I see," Tiffany said.

"We blunted the Outsiders at Boston," Ginny said. "If they'd had more ships, they would have sent them. They gain nothing from making a half-assed attempt at taking the system, even if—" she hesitated, noticeably "—the Emperor is starting to give vent to paranoid fantasies. ONI's best guess — and it *is* a guess — is that the Outsiders cannot reinforce Fifth Fleet by more than two or three battle squadrons.

"But even if Fifth Fleet *had* remained loyal, we wouldn't know where to target next," she continued. "The Outsider shipyards were *not* located at Nova Athena. Finding them would have taken months, perhaps years, during which time the Outsiders would have hastily rebuilt their fleet and incorporated all the lessons of the last two years of war. Now, even if we smash Fifth Fleet to rubble at no cost to ourselves, which is not going to happen, we'd still have the same problem of locating the enemy shipyards."

"And rebuilding our own ships," Tiffany said.

"Correct," Ginny said. "My Lady, we could win the coming battle and lose this war."

"I think we need to help Marius, then," Tiffany said, stiffly. "If I can find a pill, we can have it analyzed and then decide how best to proceed."

"Understood," Ginny said. She swallowed. "I'll do my best to help, My Lady."

"Call me Tiffany," Tiffany said. "I think we're too far gone to care about formalities, not now."

"Yes, My... *Tiffany*," Ginny said. She leaned forward, nervously. "But what are we going to do if we *can't* help him?"

"I wish I knew," Tiffany said. She loved Marius, really she did. The last thing she wanted to do was betray him. "Let us hope it doesn't come to that."

Chapter Fourteen

In the end, the Brotherhood had created a monster that eventually destroyed it.
—A True History of the Brotherhood, by the Sole Surviving Brother, 4200

Earth, 4101

"The prisoner is secure, sir," the marine said. "Do you require an escort?"

"No," Marius said, absently. Old memories rose up around him as he contemplated the detention block. "Once the door opens, shut down all monitors and recorders until I emerge."

The marine blinked. "Sir, standing orders..."

"Are overridden," Marius said. "You have new orders now."

He stepped through the hatch, feeling a tingle run over his skin as he walked through the protective forcefields. Inside, a naked dark-skinned woman lay on a table, her hands and feet shackled to the cold metal and a pair of tubes attached between her legs. Thin wires, barely visible, ran down from the overhead processor and into her skull; another restraint was wrapped around her neck, keeping her almost completely immobile. Marius studied her dispassionately, even though he knew he would once have been horrified to watch someone — anyone — being prepped for a full interrogation. But now... anything he had to do to save the Federation was justified.

"Emperor," General Thorne said. "She's been quite uncooperative."

Marius nodded, looking down at Commodore Arunika as she glared at him. He'd met her after the Battle of Earth, when she'd warned him that Admiral Justinian might well be stronger and better-prepared than the Grand Senate assumed. And then she'd become his intelligence officer, leveraging her Brotherhood connections to serve him. And *now* she was a prisoner, one of the few members of the Brotherhood to be captured alive. The others had either been killed while trying to escape or committed suicide when they discovered that escape was impossible.

"I'm not surprised," he said. "She was always stubborn."

Arunika twisted her head. "Rot in hell," she whispered, hoarsely. "Rot..."

Marius ignored her. "Can you defeat the suicide programming?"

General Thorne nodded to a technician, who looked doubtful. "It may be possible, sir," he said, "but we will not have a chance to correct any mistakes."

"They do prepare their people for the prospect of capture," General Thorne added. "But I think we rounded up most of the *known* Brothers."

Marius nodded, curtly. The Brotherhood had survived, he suspected, because its existence had suited the Grand Senate, but they'd always been *careful*. Like pirates, terrorists, and intelligence operatives, the Brotherhood had conditioned its senior members — the ones who knew more than just the members of their own cell — to make it impossible for them to talk, no matter what methods of interrogation were used. ONI tried, every time a conditioned pirate was captured, to break the conditioning, but it rarely worked. The pirate normally ended up dead on an operating table.

"We still haven't managed to track down Grand Senator Rupert McGillivray," General Thorne admitted. "He may well be the closest thing the Brotherhood had to a leader."

"His mansion was destroyed," Marius reminded him. Grand Senator Rupert McGillivray had been the last of the Imperialist Faction, their sole surviving representative in the Grand Senate. In hindsight, the Brotherhood might well have played a role in how he'd held on to power. "Are you sure he isn't dead?"

He kept an eye on Arunika, wondering if she would react to the question, but her face barely changed.

"I've had teams sifting through the rubble for the past two weeks," General Thorne said, walking around the table. "They have found no trace of his body. A man as paranoid as McGillivray would be sure to have a way out, even as the troops were storming his home."

"Dead in his house," Arunika said. Her voice was raspy, as if she'd screamed herself hoarse when the wires had been inserted into her skull. "He wouldn't allow himself to be captured."

"Ah, but we can't be sure you're telling the truth," General Thorne said. There was a nasty glint in his eye as he looked down at the prone woman. "Allow us to de-condition you and..."

Marius cut him off. "You served me well, I thought," he said. "Serve me one final time and you will be allowed to retire, perhaps to Paradise."

Arunika laughed, harshly. "Is it so much a paradise, now?"

Marius shrugged. He'd sent the remaining members of the aristocracy there, after he'd taken Earth and shot their leadership personally. They'd been Tiffany's relatives, after all, and they were harmless, without the money and patronage networks that had allowed them to rule the Federation. But would they survive without the hordes of servants who'd kept the terraformed planet in good shape? Marius neither knew nor cared. They had a better chance for survival than most of their victims.

"If we start drilling into your head," he told her, "you may not survive, even if we *do* break the conditioning."

"Fuck you," Arunika said.

"Erudite as ever," General Thorne murmured. "Emperor?"

"You won't win," Arunika said. She struggled to sit up, but the restraints kept her firmly pinned to the table. "And we will recover."

"We will see," Marius said. Her defiance was pointless. The Brotherhood's power had been decisively broken. "General, you're with me."

"We've prepped a new way of accessing her memories," General Thorne informed him, as they stepped through the door and walked to the elevator. "It's impossible to be sure, of course, but we think we have a fairly good chance of downloading her brain before the conditioning kills her. Even if it doesn't work *completely*, sir, we may get something."

"Let me know if you succeed," Marius said. "And McGillivray?"

"If he's still alive, he's gone into deep cover," General Thorne said. "We're probing through his finances now, but they're a complete mess. He may well have obtained some accommodation on Earth and kept it completely off the books. My teams will dig him up eventually, sir..."

"If he's still alive," Marius repeated. McGillivray was an old man, but he'd never struck Marius as someone who would simply commit suicide. "There's no way to be sure."

"No, sir," General Thorne said. "The self-destruct in his mansion might have been configured to wipe out DNA traces."

Marius cursed under his breath. It was hard to see how McGillivray could cause problems — even if he were still alive, he was cut off from his fortune and most of his supporters — but there was no way to know for sure. A few precautions would ensure that McGillivray would still have access to hard cash and unregistered bank accounts. The thought nagged at his mind, mocking him. He'd been tormented by the Grand Senate for much of his adult life, even though he'd been one of their most capable servants, and even now, after the Grand Senate was gone, one of its members was *still* tormenting him.

He glanced at General Thorne, rather darkly. Thorne was unlikeable, a man with no conscience or morals; he'd switched sides very quickly when the Grand Senate had fallen, hoping to escape certain death in a purge of the former patronage networks. And yet, he was useful... Thorne, at least, would have no qualms about exterminating the Outsiders, root and branch, for daring to oppose the Federation.

"Then keep searching for McGillivray," Marius ordered, although he knew it might be nothing more than a wild goose chase. Dead, McGillivray would be more of a headache than he'd been when he was alive. They'd never know for *sure* he was dead. "Leave no stone unturned."

"Yes, sir," General Thorne said.

Marius nodded. It was nice to have *someone* ready to do as they were told, without backtalk or pointless quibbling. And Thorne was definitely useful...

"We have located a number of other potential Brothers," Thorne added. "However, we would have to check their brains for conditioning before we knew for sure."

"See to it," Marius said, absently. The elevator door opened. "I'll see you at the briefing tonight."

"Yes, sir," General Thorne said.

Marius rubbed his forehead as the elevator door closed behind him. Useful or not, he didn't dare show weakness in front of General Thorne, even though he doubted the man would be able to overthrow him and survive. Marius didn't dare show weakness in front of anyone; he'd dragged Commander Lewis to Earth, without asking what *she* wanted, just to make sure she couldn't talk out of turn. And she, too, was useful...

It was hard, so hard, to do *nothing*. He'd made a career out of going where the fire was hottest and taking command, but now... now all he could do was wait, read

reports, and make plans, moving starships around the display and hoping — praying — that their movements in real life were as smooth. It was frustrating, yet he was starting to think he *understood* the Grand Senate's habit of micromanaging everything, even though it had been irritating at best and actively dangerous at worst. They'd been forced to wait at home, knowing battles could have been fought and won — or lost — months before they heard anything.

He stepped past the guard and entered his office. The latest set of reports were already blinking up on the main display, as he'd ordered. He *needed* to know what was going on, even if it meant spending hours each day digesting the reports, rather than allowing his subordinates to handle them. He'd been betrayed too many times – by Roman Garibaldi, Commodore Arunika — to take his subordinates loyalty for granted. And yet, without being with the fleet himself, all he could do was assign commissioners, watchdogs, and spies in the desperate hope he could stop another mutiny.

Home Fleet shouldn't mutiny, he thought as he sat down. *They're the most important military force in the Federation.*

He keyed a switch, calling up a starchart. It was dominated by icons, each one representing a starship, an orbital fortress, or an industrial node, but the information was already badly out of date. Roman Garibaldi wouldn't let the grass grow under his feet, Marius knew; he'd *trained* the younger man. By now, Garibaldi would have reached Ruthven, if he wasn't already crossing the gulf of space between Ruthven and Marble. But then, Marius had picked the CO of Ruthven personally. He was *sure* she would have taken a bite out of the enemy fleet before being forced to surrender, if she didn't fight to the last...

The door opened behind him. Marius jumped, one hand reaching for the pistol at his belt, before he remembered the only person who could enter his office without passing the marine on guard or being announced. He sighed inwardly — he didn't have *time* for his wife — and turned around. Tiffany was wearing a short black dress that showed off her breasts and long bare legs.

"You need to rest," Tiffany announced, firmly.

"I don't have time," Marius said. It was hard to keep his eyes off her. "There's too much to do."

Tiffany came forward and looked him in the eyes. "Is there anything, anything at all, that will *not* wait for a couple of hours?"

Marius hesitated — and was lost. There *wasn't* anything that couldn't wait, not even the revised deployment plans for the defense of a dozen sectors. They were already checked and rechecked; they didn't need to be checked a third time before they were sent away to the various sector commanders. And the hunt for Rupert McGillivray would proceed with or without his supervision. He could leave that in General Thorne's hands.

"I thought not," Tiffany said. She stepped up to him, then started to massage his shoulders gently. "You really *do* need to relax, Marius. You're far too tense."

Marius lifted his head and kissed her on the lips. "There's too much to do," he protested, weakly. The frustration kept boiling up at the back of his mind, making it hard to think clearly. He honestly had no idea how the Grand Senators had found time to lead a life of debauchery while ruling the galaxy. "I'm..."

"Taking the rest of the day off," Tiffany said. She pulled him to his feet, pressing her body against his. Marius was suddenly very aware of her heartbeat, of her firm breasts touching him, yet his body felt old and weak. "Come with me."

She pulled him into the bedroom, her hands unsnapping his uniform buckles and dropping his clothes on the floor. Marius shivered — very slightly — as she pushed him onto the bed, straddled his back and started to massage the tension from his muscles. He had no idea where Tiffany had learned how to soothe his tormented mind, but it seemed to be working even if his body wasn't responding properly. He yawned before he could stop himself — Tiffany giggled — and gave himself up to her ministrations.

I can always work late tonight, he reassured himself, as she helped him turn over. She'd removed her dress at some point, leaving her naked. *And no one will care if I miss the nightly briefing...*

☍ↃↃ

Tiffany watched her husband as he slept, praying that he hadn't picked up on her growing concern. Marius hadn't been *normal* since he'd returned from Nova Athena, but all her instincts were telling her that something *more* was wrong. He'd been passionate when they'd first married, even after becoming Emperor; now... he'd been almost lethargic, as if his age was finally catching up with him. Tiffany had had to work hard, once she'd worked the kinks out of his muscles, to prepare him for sex.

Something was deeply wrong.

She sat upright carefully, willing herself not to make any noise. Marius had been jumpy too, ever since he'd returned; he'd once practically *leapt* out of bed when she'd accidentally kicked him at night. There wasn't any weapon within reach, she thought, but she had no illusions about his strength. Indeed, his near-impotence was all the more worrying when she realized that he was still in good physical shape.

Because he's been engineered to remain healthy until the end of his life, she thought, as she stood and padded over to the small pile of clothing. Marius's jacket lay where she'd placed it, separate from the rest. *What the hell is he taking?*

Picking up the jacket, she stepped into the office, activated the sound-barriers and started to rummage through the jacket pockets. There was nothing in the outer pockets, save for a secure datachip, but she found a small bottle of liquid — it smelled like alcohol, although nothing like anything she'd smelled before — and a tiny packet of pills. One glance at the tiny grey pills was enough to tell her they weren't standard; there were no markings stamped into the medicine, nothing to say what might have gone into the pills. She took one out and sniffed it, but smelled like nothing at all.

Placing the pill in a tiny packet she'd prepared already and hiding it in her lingerie drawer, she returned to the bedroom, placed the jacket back on the ground and

climbed back into bed. Marius hadn't moved at all, although his breathing seemed normal, certainly more relaxed than it had been for several weeks. Tiffany wondered, absently, just how much of that was due to her ministrations. Her aunts had taught her a great deal about looking after men — no one had expected *her* to inherit any real power — but she'd often wondered if they were just pulling her leg. God knew only one of the four women had ever actually *married*.

And the other three held men in absolute contempt, she recalled, as she wrapped her arms around Marius. *I don't know why they spent so much time chasing men when they hated them.*

It was nearly four hours later when Marius finally stirred, sitting upright so sharply he nearly dislocated Tiffany's arm. She jerked awake, yanking her arms back, then forced herself to relax as Marius started hunting around for his watch before remembering how to turn the display back on. Tiffany had taken the precaution of deactivating it before she'd slipped into his office and started to seduce him.

"It's late," he protested. "I need to be at the briefing..."

"Yes, but you need to bathe first," Tiffany said. One of the few advantages of living in the Presidential House was a bath large enough to pass for a small swimming pool. They could share a bath, if they wanted. "And then you can get dressed properly."

She watched, warily, as Marius picked up his jacket and belt, then hurried into the bathroom for a shower. Clearly, he didn't think he had the time to bathe with her. She would have been offended if she hadn't been so nervous, but Marius didn't seem to notice that one of his pills was missing. Instead, he changed into a new uniform, donned the belt and jacket and headed for the door.

"I'll have dinner sent to you," Tiffany said. "And the stewards will have strict orders to make sure you eat."

"Very well," Marius said. "But I may not have time to eat everything."

He left the room. Tiffany waited ten minutes, then slipped on a dressing gown and headed through the connecting door to her suite. Operative Oslo and his men were based there, waiting patiently for something to do now that Emperor Marius had returned home. Tiffany hoped Operative Oslo was right, when he said her rooms weren't bugged. If he was wrong — and Ginny's warnings hung in her mind — she was about to get into deep shit.

"Lady Tiffany," Operative Oslo said, when she called him into the room. "What can we do for you?"

Tiffany held out the pill. "I want you to find out what this is and give me a full report," she said. "You have to be completely discreet about it. No one, and I mean *no one*, is to know what you're doing."

Operative Oslo gave her a sharp look, then nodded. "It may take some time, My Lady," he warned. "A discreet check always takes longer."

"That's fine," Tiffany said. She'd hoped for an immediate answer, but she knew one was unlikely to come. "Please try and *keep* it between us."

Chapter Fifteen

When an officer, like Marius Drake, could call on reserves of loyal subordinates, it ensured that the final spat of civil wars would be indefinitely prolonged.
—The Federation Navy in Retrospect, 4199

Alexis, 4101

"This is a daring offensive," General Stuart noted. "I would never have considered it."

"I don't think you ever attacked an Asimov Point that was defended on both sides," Roman said. He had come to like General Stuart, but he had the sense that the older man didn't return his regard. Perhaps it was simple annoyance — Roman was half his age, yet he'd soundly beaten him at Boston — or perhaps it was the awareness that the Outsiders had lost a superdreadnaught in the earlier battle. "This one poses a rather odd tactical problem."

"One you will face again and again," General Stuart said, "as you hammer your way towards Earth."

Roman nodded. Ruthven was heavily defended, but her defenses were miniscule compared to the towering fortifications defending Earth. The Gateway was fortified on both sides, despite arguments — put forward by penny-pinching politicians — that there was no need to worry. And the thought of tackling *those* fortresses, even in a straight missile duel, was enough to make Roman shudder. The fleet was going to be crippled if they didn't find another way to punch through the defenses and break into Sol.

Admiral Justinian must have been planning his offensive for years, he thought, as he turned back to the display. *And we can't repeat his feat without adding several months to our voyage.*

He closed his eyes as he contemplated the tactical picture. In theory, a combination of long-range sniping and constant jamming should have made it impossible for the defenders to know what was coming at them, but there was no way to be absolutely certain they'd eliminated *all* of the stealthed platforms within the system. The more Roman contemplated the problem, the more he knew they were embarking on a desperate gamble. Only the awareness that the crews before him had volunteered for the mission, had literally *begged* to be allowed to go, kept his conscience from pestering him.

"Task Force 5.1 reports that it is ready to depart," General Stuart said. "With your permission, Admiral, I'll return to my flagship."

"Granted," Roman said. Keeping the fleet's two most senior officers on the same ship was just *asking* for trouble. "I'll see you on the far side."

He sat back in his command chair, his eyes searching out the icons representing Task Force 5.1. If nothing else, he was sure the defenders were about to get one hell of a fright. It was impossible to build an *actual* warship much larger than a super-dreadnaught, but their displays would show them five stupendous warships cruising

towards them. He wondered, absently, just how long it would take them to realize that he'd pulled all of the captured fortresses off the other Asimov Points and turned them into makeshift assault vessels. The tugs, hidden behind their mighty armor, would keep them moving forward until they hit their targets or fell into the Asimov Point.

Which would be interesting to watch, from a safe distance, he thought. *Can something so large transit safely?*

"Admiral, the General's shuttle has undocked," Lieutenant Thompson said.

"Good," Roman said. "Signal the fleet. We commence operations in twenty minutes."

☙ ❧

Commodore Tracy Rosslyn paced her fortress's command deck, trying not to show her tension to the crew. Marius Drake himself had put her in command of Ruthven's defenses, telling her that he needed a loyal and competent officer to control the sector capital. And, after *Admiral* Drake had saved her from the unwanted attentions of another senior officer with more money and connections than sense, there was very little Tracy wouldn't do for him.

She scowled at her display, cursing the rebels in the privacy of her own head. Their ECM was good, *alarmingly* good, and their persistent jamming made it hard to be *sure* what lurked more than ten light-seconds from the Asimov Point. She'd assigned a handful of destroyers and patrol boats to sweep the outer edge of detection range, but after losing two starships to enemy ambushes she'd been forced to rethink that policy. Ruthven didn't have a large mobile force covering it and she simply couldn't afford to waste her ships.

Shouldn't have sent so many ships forward, she thought, darkly. Admiral Garibaldi, back when he'd been a loyalist, had called many of her ships to Boston to stem the Outsider advance. And it had worked, at a terrifying cost. *If they break through the Asimov Point, we will have no end of trouble stopping them.*

"Commodore," the tactical officer said. "I'm picking up something approaching from the direction of the planet."

Tracy nodded as she strode over to his console. Perhaps it was just another probe, another long-range missile attack to keep her people off balance, but her instincts were suggesting otherwise. Federation Navy doctrine called for pressing the offensive as hard as possible and the Outsiders evidently agreed, knowing that allowing the enemy time to prepare their defenses was a deadly mistake. She'd been expecting an attack ever since the system had fallen to the rebels. Indeed, she was surprised it had taken so long.

"I see," she said. There was a great deal of jamming, but not enough to cover the turbulence produced by dozens of starships. It looked almost as if the rebels weren't trying to hide, merely to minimize the time between detection and weapons range. And yet, there was something very odd about the pattern. "Order all fortresses to red alert."

"Aye, Commodore," the officer said.

"And bring active sensors online," Tracy added. There was no point in trying to hide the fortresses, not when the enemy had had ample time to draw a bead on them. It *did* run the risk of degrading her sensors, if she kept them active for more than a few days, but she had a feeling it wasn't going to matter. "Let's see what's out there."

The sensor officer swore. Tracy turned, opening her mouth to rebuke him, and froze as she saw the icons on the display. For a long moment, her mind simply refused to accept what she was seeing. There might be a handful of gigantic bulk freighters that were over ten kilometres long, but *no one* could produce a warship that size... and *no one* would build a warship with such a pathetic acceleration curve. Why, she could be outrun by a battleship from the First Interstellar War...

"Fortresses," she said, as it dawned on her. No *wonder* the drive signature had been so odd. The rebels had taken all five surviving fortresses, assigned a dozen tugs to provide motive power and pointed them at the Asimov Point. "They've assigned fortresses to clear our defenses."

She cursed under her breath. Two of the fortresses had been badly damaged — and, she hoped, shot themselves dry — in the first battle, but the other three hadn't seen any action. She had four fortresses of her own, yet however she looked at it she was definitely outgunned. And even if she blew the fortresses apart, it would weaken her for the rest of the rebel fleet. She silently tipped her hat to Admiral Garibaldi, then turned to the tactical officer.

"Target the fortresses as soon as they enter engagement range," she ordered. The fortresses would take a lot of killing... and she didn't want them any closer to *her* fortresses than strictly necessary. "Launch the reserve starfighters, then order the CSP to engage the tugs. They are to try to slow the fortresses."

"Aye, Commodore," the tactical officer said.

Clever bastard, Tracy thought, with an unwilling flicker of admiration. She'd only met Admiral Garibaldi once, but he wouldn't have been Emperor Marius's protégé if he hadn't been *very* good at his job. Unless she missed her guess, the *intact* fortresses would have their own starfighters... and the rebel carriers could be following close behind, ready to jump her starfighters when they ventured out to strike at the tugs. But what else *could* she do? *Very clever bastard.*

"The reserve starfighters are launching now," the CAG reported.

"Good," Tracy said. She glanced at the communications officer. "Send the drones through the Asimov Point. Inform Commodore Houseman that he is to prepare to defend his position — and that, if I don't return, he is to assume command of the system defenses."

"Aye, Commodore," the communications officer said. She worked her console for a long moment. "Drones away."

Tracy walked back to her command chair, bracing herself. She had rejected the first surrender demand, simply because she was loyal to Marius Drake. He was her patron, after all. And even if he hadn't been, she refused to accept that rebellion against the Federation was the only answer. For all its flaws, and she knew it had many, the Federation was all that stood between humanity and threats from beyond

the Rim. Alien-lovers were too dangerously naive to be allowed to dictate policy, not when the human race itself was at stake. If aliens refused to submit, they needed to be destroyed. Better them than all of humanity.

She sighed, inwardly, as the starfighters raced towards their targets. The enemy fortresses, as she'd expected, were already launching their own starfighters as they inched forward, slipping into missile range. It wouldn't be long before they opened fire, weakening her position quite badly. No matter what she did, she had a nasty feeling her existence had narrowed down to killing as many rebels and traitors as she could before they killed her.

"Missiles locked on target, Commodore," the tactical officer reported. "They are slipping into missile range."

"Fire," Tracy ordered.

She knew he didn't approve of her tactics, even as he keyed the switch that launched the first salvo of missiles. They were wasteful. The flight time was nearly five minutes, more than long enough for the enemy point defense to work out a targeting solution and pick the missiles off before they reached their targets. Indeed, *standard* tactical doctrine called for her to hold fire until the enemy targets moved closer. But there was no choice. The enemy couldn't be allowed to get their fortresses any closer to their targets than strictly necessary.

"Enemy starfighters are moving into attack position," the CAG noted. "Our pilots are requesting reinforcements."

"Denied," Tracy said. She didn't dare strip her fighter cover any further. "Tell them... tell them to do the best they can."

༜ᑫ

"The enemy starfighters are moving in on attack vector," Lieutenant Thompson said. "I think they're targeting the fortresses."

"They're more likely to be targeting the tugs," Roman said. Unless the defenders had some kind of weapon he'd never heard of, firing their plasma guns at the fortresses would be about as much use as shouting insults through a megaphone. "Order our starfighters to cover them."

"Aye, sir," Lieutenant Thompson said. She paused. "The enemy fortresses have opened fire."

Roman blinked in surprise. He'd expected the enemy fortresses to hold their fire until *his* fortresses got closer. It wasn't as if the fortresses could *dodge*. Merely getting five fortresses moving in the right general direction had been quite hard enough. But the enemy CO might want to stop the fortresses as soon as she could, rather than risk letting them get any closer. It did make a certain kind of sense.

"Order the fortresses to open fire, but continue along their current course," he said. If nothing else, convincing the enemy fortresses to shoot themselves dry would make taking the Asimov Point a great deal easier. "And prep the rest of the fleet to move up in support."

༜ᑫ

"They're coming for the tugs, boys and girls," Commander Rogers said. "I want you to keep the bastards busy!"

Lieutenant Shanna Robertson gritted her teeth. She'd joined up a year before Admiral Justinian had attacked Earth and she was getting tired of civil wars, of never quite knowing which side she was supposed to be on. First, she'd fought Admiral Jackson and his rogue fleet, then she'd been assigned to Fifth Fleet just in time to fight the Outsiders and, now, she was *allied* with the Outsiders and waging war on the Federation. She'd actually given serious thought to leaving the fleet, back when the Admiral had offered to allow anyone to leave if they wanted, but she couldn't leave her wingmates to fight alone.

"Here they come," Commander Rogers snapped. "Go!"

Shanna gunned her engine and threw her starfighter forward, opening fire as she flew into the wave of enemy craft. They were flying the exact same starfighters as her squadron, part of her mind noted, but they didn't have the experience *she'd* picked up in seven years of near-continuous fighting. Their reflexes were just a hair too slow for the task facing them... she smirked, despite herself, as enemy starfighters began to die. And then the loyalists altered course and started to dogfight. She swung her craft around, avoided a blaze of plasma fire that would have blown her to atoms and reversed course. There was barely a fraction of a second to note that her target had been trained to fight in an atmosphere before she blew him to dust.

"They're closing in on the tugs," Commander Rogers barked. "Intercept them."

"On my way," Shanna said, echoing her other wingmates. The fortresses were effectively indestructible, as far as the starfighters were concerned, but the tugs barely had any protection at all. "We'll sweep them all clear."

ଈଔ

"We've lost one of the tugs," Lieutenant Thompson reported. "Another tug has taken heavy damage and may have to disengage."

"Tell her to stay as long as she can," Roman said. He didn't like the idea of sending a human crew to their deaths, but there might be no choice. "And order the fortresses to keep firing."

He allowed himself a moment of relief as the fighting grew hotter. Both sets of fortresses were switching to rapid fire, even though only one missile in ten was getting through the point defense to strike against the target's shields. Starfighters were buzzing around desperately, often being picked off by the point defense when they flew in a predictable path for more than a few seconds. Roman hoped the IFFs held out long enough to prevent blue-on-blue strikes, when a starfighter was shot down by friendly fire, but there was no way to guarantee it. The loyalists had probably started trying to mimic rebel IFFs by now. It was what *he* would have done.

"Two more tugs gone, sir," Lieutenant Thomas said. "Fortress Three has lost acceleration and is just coasting towards her target."

Roman gritted his teeth. The enemy might not have known it, but Fortress Three was one of the intact fortresses. At least she was still in missile range. The remaining fortresses were inching towards their targets, soaking up fire as they forced their

way forwards. He checked the sensor records, trying to determine just how close the enemy fortresses were to shooting themselves dry, but it was impossible to be sure. Chances were, the defenders had shipped additional supplies through the Asimov Point while Roman had hastily prepared his fortresses.

Or they might have done the opposite, he thought, grimly. *Stripped the fortresses bare on this side to prepare a stronger defense on the far side.*

He forced himself to watch, grimly, as the enemy starfighters broke off. Two-thirds of them had fallen to *his* starfighters, but it hadn't been enough to keep them from picking off another tug. Indeed, if they'd had reinforcements, he suspected their offensive would have been rather more successful. But there was no time to allow them to rethink their operational deployments.

"Order the reserve starfighters to launch their attack," he said. "And send in the gunboats!"

ဆဝလ

Tracy cursed, savagely, as the display blossomed with red lights. The enemy fortresses might not be inflicting much damage, but they *were* keeping her forces jumpy. Now, hundreds of additional starfighters and gunboats had joined the offensive. And their timing had been excellent. She'd had to recall her fighters to rearm, which meant they had to choose between turning and fighting or trying to rearm and return to the fray while the enemy craft were surrounding the fortresses.

"Order the starfighters to turn and engage with plasma guns," she ordered. Their life support would hold out for a while longer, she thought. "And then direct the CSP to cover us as the gunboats close in."

She forced herself not to lean forward as the two groups of starfighters converged. Her pilots were tired and it showed, while the enemy starfighters had clearly had plenty of time to prepare themselves for the mission. One by one, starfighters started to vanish from the display while the gunboats roared onwards, trying to get into position to launch missiles towards the fortresses. And then they started to spit missiles at the starfighters...

"Order the CSP to back off," Tracy snapped, although she has a nasty feeling that it was already too late. "Now!"

"Antimatter warheads," the tactical officer said, as dozens of green icons vanished from the display. "They're using shipkillers against starfighters!"

"It seems to be working," Tracy snarled. The gunboats had just swatted dozens of starfighters out of space, for nothing. And now they were swinging around to resume their charge at the fortresses. "Blow them out of space!"

Her eyes narrowed as the gunboats came closer, overloading their engines to give them an additional burst of speed. The radiation would be instantly lethal to humans, but aliens? She hadn't seen any data on the aliens who'd joined the Outsiders... could they handle such radiation in small doses? Or were they just trying to get themselves killed...?

"Watch those ships," she snapped, as they raced closer. She'd studied the reports from a hundred skirmishes with the Outsiders. "They're trying to ram!"

Chapter Sixteen

The Marsha, it should be noted, were fighters, plain and simple. They had no conception of any victory that did not end with their foe being beaten into submission, nor could they escape the idea that retreat was something shameful. A glorious defeat was more to be feted, they thought, than a retreat that would allow them to fight again another day.
—The Federation Navy in Retrospect, 4199

Alexis/Ruthven, 4101

"The ramming ships have entered attack range," Lieutenant Juneau reported. "They're closing in on their targets."

General Charlie Stuart sat back in his command chair, fighting down a growing sense of *respect* for Admiral Garibaldi. It was easy to nurture a grudge against the officer who'd done so much to beat the Outsiders — and come alarmingly close to winning the war outright. And yet he had to admire someone who was willing to draw the line — and switch sides, if necessary — to prevent his former commander from committing genocide.

Who knew? Maybe there was hope for the alliance after all.

"Keep monitoring them," he ordered. Sending the Marsha out to die no longer troubled him, not when they *wanted* to carry out the mission. And besides, weakening the Marsha might help in the long run. "And ready missiles for when we enter missile range."

"Aye, sir," Lieutenant Juneau said.

Charlie nodded, watching grimly as the Marsha gunboats closed in on their targets. Four gunboats were blasted out of space, the explosions wiping out five more, but the remainder slammed into their targets and detonated, removing two of the defending fortresses. The remaining three held together, barely; he couldn't help noticing that the enemy shields had weakened and their fire had slacked badly. They had taken heavy damage.

"Signal the flag," he said. "The missions were completed successfully."

∞

Tracy clung on to her command chair for dear life as the fortress shuddered around her. It was rare, vanishingly rare, for *anything* to shake a fortress, even when she fired a full salvo from her missile batteries. And to think, only *one* gunboat had made it through the point defense! It had to have been crammed to the gunwales with antimatter.

"Report," she barked. Red lights were flaring over the system display, warning her that her command had taken heavy damage. "Status report!"

"We've lost all but two of our shield generators," the engineering officer reported. "Major damage throughout the structure, including the loss of our command datanet. We're isolated, Commodore! Point defense is down to thirty percent!"

Tracy looked down at her console, then back at the tactical display. The enemy fortresses were still crawling forward, save for one that appeared to have stalled; the

enemy starfighters were regrouping, readying themselves for another offensive. And there was a formidable force of capital ships coming into range, no doubt readying themselves to add their missiles to the swarm closing in on her remaining fortresses. The defense of the near side of the Asimov Point had come to an end, but she had seven *more* fortresses on the other side, just waiting for the enemy to poke their nose into Ruthven.

"Pass the word," she ordered. "We're evacuating the fortresses."

She took a breath. It wouldn't be easy, not in the midst of a battle. Lifepods were taken for weapons all the time and swatted out of space before the shooter realized the mistake. She'd taken the precaution of evacuating as much of her crew as possible, once the rebels had invaded the system, but she still had over a thousand men and women to get through the Asimov Point to safety.

"Switch weapons to automated firing mode, designate the warships as primary targets," she added. It was unlikely the enemy could get a fortress through the Asimov Point, although she wouldn't put it past the rebels to *try*. They'd lose nothing worth mentioning if the fortress was torn apart by gravity tides. "Add the fortresses as secondary targets."

"Aye, Commodore," the tactical officer said.

Tracy nodded as she rose from her seat. There was the option of surrendering — she was fairly sure her crews would be treated decently, whatever propaganda said about how the Outsiders fed their prisoners to alien cannibals — but she knew her duty to Marius Drake. As long as there was a chance to delay the enemy, to wear the traitors down, she had to take it. She doubted the automated firing systems would do more than cost the rebels whatever it took to complete the destruction of her remaining fortresses, but at least it would cost them *something*.

And delay their advance to the Asimov Point, she added. *That's worth doing, I fancy.*

"Send an updated drone to Commodore Houseman," she ordered. "Tell him... tell him to prepare to receive refugees."

୫୦୬

"I think they're evacuating the fortresses, sir," Lieutenant Thompson said. "They're launching a number of shuttles into the Asimov Point."

Roman nodded. The enemy fire had slackened, after the gunboats had rammed home, but even after they restored much of their firepower it lacked a certain *something*. Unless he was very wrong, the enemy had switched to automated firing systems to keep him busy while they fled through the Asimov Point. The Federation Navy's computers were among the best of the galaxy — the Outsiders didn't seem to have made any significant advances — but they lacked the initiative and insight of human intellect. After a handful of near-disasters, the human race had lost all interest in trying to manufacture a genuine AI.

"Contact the fortresses," he ordered. "They are to continue firing at the enemy fortresses until they are destroyed. Our ships are to hold position here until the fortresses are crippled."

Captain Yuma looked up. "Sir," he said. "Wouldn't that give them time to prepare an ambush on the far side?"

"I doubt it will matter," Roman said. Captain Yuma — the Outsider liaison officer — had an irritating habit of questioning Roman's decisions, although this was the first time he'd done it in the heat of battle. "They've had—" he glanced at the timer "—over two hours to get ready to meet an offensive. Very few tactical planners can count on having so much time."

He considered, briefly, attempting to target the shuttles... and then damned himself to hell for losing perspective. There was no way he'd lose sleep over killing enemy spacers who were trying to kill him, but slaughtering helpless men and women would be a step down the slippery slope. Besides, he rather doubted any of them were *important*, certainly not to the Emperor's war effort. Cold logic might argue that they should die, but cold logic could go take a flying leap out the airlock.

"We gain nothing by expending the missiles to destroy the fortresses quicker," he added, as he settled back in his command chair. Belaboring the obvious got old very quickly. "And we risk losing the battle when we plunge onwards into Ruthven."

Long minutes passed as the two groups of fortresses converged. Lacking a damage control team, along with human-directed point defense, the enemy fortresses started to take increasingly heavy damage until antimatter warheads were striking directly into their armored hulls. A human crew would have been trying to surrender at this point, unless they believed there was no hope of anything other than a quick execution, but the electronic loyalists kept firing until the stations were damaged well beyond any hope of repair. In the end, missiles detonated inside their hulls and completed their destruction.

"Take us to the Asimov Point," Roman ordered. They had only minutes before the first of their fortresses sought to plunge *into* the Asimov Point. "And alert all ships to be ready for a coordinated assault."

"Aye, sir," Lieutenant Thompson reported. "Starfighters are reloading, sir, but the remainder of the fleet reports that it's ready to jump."

"Good," Roman said. He braced himself as the first of the fortresses reached the Asimov Point. "Let's see what happens, shall we?"

སྤྱ

"Commodore, I'm picking up major disturbances in the Asimov Point," a sensor officer reported. "Something *big* is coming through!"

"They're actually trying to plunge one of the fortresses into the Asimov Point," Tracy said, torn between wonder and a kind of grim horror. She'd barely had time to board the battlestation on the far side before the enemy pushed the offensive through the point. "Stand at the ready."

She sucked in her breath. An oversized bulk freighter, complete with a working drive, was hard enough to steer through an Asimov Point; a fortress, which had barely anything beyond manoeuvring thrusters, had to be an absolute nightmare. And yet, they were *still* trying to get the immense structure through in one piece. She hoped,

absently, that the sensor records would be beamed to Ruthven and the courier boats before the fortresses were destroyed, if they failed to keep the enemy from gaining a toehold in the system. There was genuine, *original* science to be explored.

"Good grief," Commodore Houseman said. He'd surrendered command to her without a fight the moment she'd disembarked from the shuttle. "They have to be out of their minds."

Tracy couldn't disagree as the fortress emerged from the Asimov Point. Its shields had failed, half of its hull seemed to have been mangled and the tugs that had pushed it into the Asimov Point were gone. Behind it, the gravity tides whirled in and out; she wondered, just for a second, if the fortress was going to be sucked back *into* the Asimov Point. And then the fortress opened fire with its remaining weapons.

"Kill it," she snapped.

She shook her head in disbelief. The rebels, deliberately or not, had turned classic Asimov Point assault doctrine on its head. They'd sent a heavier unit through first, allowing its weapons a chance to sweep space clear of mines while gathering targeting data for the assault pods... no, she realized as a second fortress lumbered out of the Asimov Point, they'd sent *two* heavier units! And the cascade of debris that followed it suggested that the *third* fortress she'd seen hadn't made it through the Asimov Point.

"Impossible," Commodore Houseman muttered.

Tracy was tempted to agree. No one in their right mind would build a *warship* the same size as a fortress, yet she could see some advantages. Maybe, when peace returned to the galaxy, it would be time to consider the possibilities. If, of course, they could overcome the many problems in actually making such a warship...

And the bastards are even sucking in our mines, she thought. As tough as they were, the fortresses wouldn't last forever, but it wouldn't matter. Their mere presence was clearing the way for dedicated assault units. *This battle may have been lost before it even began in earnest...*

"The enemy fortresses are launching drones," the tactical officer snapped.

"Warn all of our fortresses," Tracy said. "Assault pods are about to start transiting the Asimov Point. Order the CSP to be ready to intercept."

ಐಗ

"That's the enemy location," Lieutenant Thompson said. "They're holding a pretty strong position."

Roman shrugged. "Signal all ships," he ordered. "Download targeting instructions from the datanet, then deploy assault pods on my mark."

"The assault pods are ready, sir," Lieutenant Thompson said.

"Deploy," Roman snapped.

ಐಗ

"Assault pods, unknown class!"

Tracy winced, unsurprised. The CSP was already rocketing forward, trying to kill as many of the assault pods as they could, but she knew their efforts wouldn't be enough. There were just too many pods, spread out over too wide an area of space.

And then the pods started to unload, launching hundreds of missiles towards their targets.

"Stand by point defense," she ordered, grimly. Having knocked all her plans out of alignment, the enemy was now going to smother her in missiles. They could afford to fight a conventional war now. "Fire at will; I say again, fire at will."

"A second bunch of assault pods have materialized," the tactical officer warned. "They're spawning already."

"Engage the missiles when they come within firing range," Tracy ordered. One of the two surviving fortresses was dying, its hull finally shattering as it was ripped apart by her missiles, but it hardly mattered. The damned fortress had done its job. "And..."

"Commodore," the tactical officer interrupted. "A *third* wave of assault pods has transited the Asimov Point!"

"Send a full tactical download to Ruthven and the courier boats," Tracy ordered. "And copy it to Commodore Ross. Tell him... tell him to prepare to assume tactical command."

She turned back to the display as the wall of missiles raged towards her fortresses. Hundreds fell to her point defense, but hundreds survived to slam into their targets. She braced herself, knowing there was nowhere to run, as the missiles pounded the station, systematically weakening the shields. One by one, the shield generators started to fail...

"Commodore," the tactical officer said. "They're throwing *another* wave of assault pods through the Asimov Point!"

They must have found a way to use the first set of missiles to update the later waves, Tracy thought, numbly. *And they seem to have unlimited reserves...*

"Send a final download up the chain to Earth," Tracy ordered.

"Incoming," the tactical officer said. "Shields failing..."

Tracy closed her eyes. "It's been an honor serving with you all," she said. Survival was no longer possible. "I thank you."

℗ ⊂⅌

"Five of the seven fortresses have been destroyed," Lieutenant Thompson reported. "The remaining two have taken heavy damage."

"Start sending through the first assault wave," Roman ordered. Given the number of pods he'd deployed, more than enough to smother the defenses, he was surprised that two fortresses had survived. "And tell them to attempt to get the remaining fortresses to surrender, if they can."

"Aye, sir," Lieutenant Thompson said.

Roman forced himself to wait as the first wave of ships vanished through the Asimov Point, wondering just how long the enemy would choose to hold out. They had to know their position was untenable, even though the Asimov Point had wiped out two of the four fortresses for them. But Ruthven was heavily defended in its own right. They might fear watching helplessly as the fortresses were turned against the planet they were supposed to defend.

"Admiral, the final Marsha fortress has been destroyed," Lieutenant Thompson reported, shortly. "Neither of the enemy fortresses are responding to our hails."

"Send through a final wave of assault pods," Roman ordered. He studied the status display for a long moment, noting the hundreds of mines floating outside the enemy fortresses, and then made his choice. "And then move the first battle squadron through into the system."

He settled back in his command chair as the assault pods vanished into the Asimov Point, completing the task of destroying the enemy fortresses. The minefields alone wouldn't pose a major threat, not when they could be swept by starfighters or starship-mounted energy weapons. But the real question was just what had happened to the enemy ships. Ruthven didn't have any superdreadnaughts — God knew he would have raided the system for superdreadnaughts during the early stages of the war — but she had a small fleet of battlecruisers, heavy cruisers and destroyers. Where were they?

"The first battle squadron has transited," Lieutenant Thompson said. "They're sweeping the mines now."

"Order them to launch a full shell of recon drones," Roman ordered. The time delay was irritating, but there was no way to avoid it until *Valiant* went through the Asimov Point herself. "And angle a number towards the planet. I want the starships found."

He frowned as the next set of updates popped into view on the display. The records *claimed* that over forty ships had been assigned to Ruthven, but long-range scans hadn't picked up anything apart from a handful of freighters heading into deep space and a number of asteroid miners. Not that that meant anything, he reminded himself. *He'd* kept his fleet concealed in Alexis for two weeks while preparing his attack on Ruthven. It didn't take a particularly skilled commander to keep forty ships hidden while trying to decide what to do next.

If I were in command, I'd stay hidden and wait for a chance to hit the enemy supply lines, he thought. There were at least forty starships unaccounted for, but only four of them were battlecruisers — and none of them were any match for a single battle squadron. *That would give me a chance to make an impact out of all proportion to my size. But would I be allowed to do that?*

The thought nagged at his mind as *Valiant* slowly advanced forward and transited through the Asimov Point. He braced himself, half-expecting to be greeted by a swarm of missiles, then checked the display. The minefield had been destroyed, leaving nothing but chunks of dust and debris. A handful of enemy starfighters were trying to surrender, their pilots ejecting into space to make it impossible for them to launch a sneak attack. But there was still no sign of the enemy starships.

And they could have simply retreated back to Marble, he thought. *If the Emperor left them in place...*

"Send a signal to the planet," he ordered. The enemy fleet would show itself eventually, he was sure, either by hitting his rear or linking up with a more powerful force. "Invite them to surrender."

"Aye, sir," Lieutenant Thompson said.

Roman took a moment to assess his fleet's position. Ammunition expenditure had been lower than expected, save for the assault pods. Thankfully, the fortresses had absorbed much of the enemy's firepower before he had to send his ships into the maelstrom. The only downside was that he would have to detail starships to guard the Asimov Point or run the risk of the enemy using it to mount a counterattack.

And that is the problem of victory, he reproved himself, sharply. As bad as it had been, he knew very well that it could have been a great deal worse. *How bad would it be if I were trying to cope with a defeat?*

"Order the damaged ships to return to Alexis," he said. They'd done well, but the battle wasn't over yet. There would be time to mourn the dead on both sides later. "The remainder of the fleet is to form up on the flag and prepare to advance."

Chapter Seventeen

The belief that planets were important, in some ways, was a millstone around the necks of naval planners. Very few planets were important unless they had formidable defenses or industrial bases.
—The Federation Navy in Retrospect, 4199

Alexis/Ruthven, 4101

Commodore Theodore Ross was convinced, as he peered up at the battlecruiser *Hammer's* tactical display, that he was seeing his worst nightmare unfolding in front of him. He had no illusions about his bravery — or about the simple fact that the Emperor had left him in place because everyone knew Theodore didn't have the mindset to become a potential threat. Besides, Ruthven was a *loyal* planet. Theodore couldn't have hoped to set up an empire of his own, even if his immediate superiors had somehow been removed — and he knew it. All he really wanted to do was see out the rest of his career in peace and quiet.

Then they stripped me of half my crew for the fortresses, he thought. *Now I have to command the ship as well as the squadron.*

The hell of it, he considered, was that he was in the perfect position for an ambush, if he'd had a handful of battle squadrons attached to his fleet. But the largest ship under his command was a battlecruiser and, even with external racks, he couldn't hope to match the firepower of a single enemy battle squadron. It was frustrating: a long-range engagement would see his missiles expended for nothing, while a short-range engagement would get his ships torn to ribbons by the enemy. His precaution of taking the fleet into cloak once the enemy had started to push through the Asimov Point would have seemed a brilliant move, *if* he'd been able to capitalize on it.

"Commodore," the tactical officer said. "The rebel fleet is advancing towards the planet."

"Noted," Theodore said, grimly. There were three Asimov Points in the system, but none of them were particularly important. The planet itself, on the other hand, was home to a growing industry that the rebels needed, desperately. "How badly did the fortresses hurt them?"

"I don't think their battle squadrons were badly hurt, sir," the tactical officer said. "It's impossible to be sure, but they're making a good clip towards the planet."

Attacking a target they know I have to defend, Theodore thought. *And they have to know I'm lurking somewhere within the system.*

He cursed under his breath as he checked the latest update from the planet. The evacuation and demolition plan had run into snags, unsurprisingly; the workers didn't want to leave their families *or* destroy the industrial plant they'd built up over the last decade. Theodore knew he should force them to leave, at gunpoint if necessary, before destroying the industrial plant, but he didn't want to do either. The former would leave him with a mob of angry and resentful workers, while the latter would

leave the planet's population open to retaliation from the rebels. Ruthven might be loyalist, but there were limits.

"We'll go with Plan Gamma," he said, finally. "Send a signal to the planet, ordering them to speed up the evacuation, then take us into engagement range—" he tapped a location on the display "—here."

"Aye, sir," the tactical officer said.

"And inform the remainder of the fleet," Theodore added. "There are to be no heroics. I want to get into missile range, land a blow or two, and then get out."

He kept his face expressionless as the fleet altered course, stealthily slipping into attack position. It was unlikely they'd manage to land a blow — or do anything, really, beyond giving the rebels a few nasty moments. The rebel point defense would probably be able to handle a full barrage from his ships, even if they were targeted on one or two superdreadnaughts. But at least he wouldn't have abandoned the system without a fight. The Grand Senate had shot officers who'd surrendered star systems to warlords and, even though Emperor Marius had been a military officer himself, Theodore was unwilling to take the chance of just pulling out of the system and joining the defenses at Marble.

Not that we will be staying there, he thought. Forty smaller ships weren't likely to tip the balance one way or the other, but they *might* make a difference if they were raiding behind the lines. Possession of Ruthven would give the rebels access to two new Asimov Point chains, which might make their logistics a little easier. *We can sneak out and hit the enemy where they're weakest.*

"Entering extreme missile range, sir," the tactical officer said. "Passive sensors are tracking the enemy ships. They're not trying to hide."

"Hold us steady," Theodore ordered. Unless the rebels had some new piece of sensor gear — in which case the war was on the verge of being lost — it was unlikely they'd pick up his ships for a few minutes longer. Besides, the shorter the range, the greater the chance of scoring a hit. "Fire on my mark."

He watched the display, feeling a churning unease in his gut. Rebels — Admiral Justinian as well as the Outsiders — had shown an alarming inventiveness, fueled, at least in part, by the imagination to actually *rebel*. The pace of change had slowed to a crawl, long before the war; military technology had practically frozen in place before Admiral Justinian had shown the Grand Senate just how many options remained for exploration. And now... he wondered, deep inside, if he had the mindset to adapt to an ever-changing universe.

Before the war, hitting one's enemies would have been impossible at this distance, he thought. *They're still outside the pre-war engagement range.*

"Stand by," he ordered. The closer his ships came to the enemy, the greater the chance of detection... and the lower the odds of escaping in one piece. "Prepare to fire."

"Missiles locked, sir," the tactical officer said. "Ready to fire."

Theodore braced himself. "Fire!"

Hammer shuddered, violently, as she emptied her external racks, then fired a full barrage from her missile tubes. Loading the external racks with antimatter warheads had been a gamble — it would never have been tolerated before the war — but it would give her some additional punch in the opening moves of the engagement. Theodore watched, grimly, as the other ships fired too, the smaller vessels launching a relative handful of missiles towards the enemy fleet. The rebels didn't flinch, but it was evident they'd been caught by surprise; they weren't in position to establish a *full* point defense formation. Even so, there was nothing wrong with their reactions.

"Enemy ships have opened fire," the tactical officer reported. "They're trying to lock on to us now."

They must have improved their missile warheads, Theodore thought. *But then, they wouldn't have any difficulty tracking our missiles back to their launch tubes.*

He shook his head in grim astonishment. He'd read the reports from the earlier engagements, but he hadn't really believed them, even when the analysts had drawn his attention to the salient points. Now, it was clear the enemy had *vastly* improved their seeker heads and command datanet. The never-to-be-sufficiently-damned speed of light delay wasn't such a problem for them any longer. And if they'd had five or ten more years before the war, part of his mind yammered, it might have been a walk-over.

"Fire the second barrage, then reverse course," he ordered. There was no point in trying to go toe-to-toe with seven battle squadrons, not when he'd already thrown the heaviest punch he could. "Get us out of here."

"Aye, sir," the helmsman said. "Reversing course now."

"Enemy ships are launching starfighters," the tactical officer added. "They're sweeping in behind the missiles."

"Stand by point defense," Theodore ordered, harshly. They might *just* get out of missile range before that barrage arrived, but they couldn't hope to outrun the starfighters. "Engage the missiles as soon as they enter firing range."

"Aye, sir," the tactical officer said.

Theodore felt a moment of hope, as a number of missiles started to burn out, but it flickered and faded as the remaining missiles kept coming. His point defense did what it could, burning hundreds of missiles out of space, yet hundreds more closed in on their targets and attacked. He watched, refusing to allow the pain to show on his face, as a dozen starships were blown to atoms, their point defense overloaded and their shields knocked down. A list of destroyed ships scrolled past him...

Hammer rang like a bell as two missiles made it through the point defense and slammed into the shields. The rebels had somehow managed to increase the quantity of antimatter crammed into their warheads, part of his mind noted; they'd hit his ship significantly harder than they should have been able to do. He worried at the problem for a few minutes, then dismissed it as he realized the missile bombardment had come to an end. But the starfighters were still coming.

"Enemy starfighters entering point defense range," the tactical officer said. "They're concentrating on our smaller ships."

Theodore's eyes narrowed. The *standard* tactic was to concentrate on the *larger* ships, although *he* wouldn't complain if *Hammer's* crew were allowed a chance to repair the damage the ship had taken before the starfighters turned their attention to her. But it made no sense... or did it? Destroyers, light cruisers... even *heavy* cruisers... they wouldn't make much difference in the defense of Marble, let alone Tara Prime, but they could do *real* damage operating behind the lines. The rebels *had* to want to smash as many of the smaller ships as they could before they scattered and fled into interstellar space.

He found himself caught, suddenly, on the horns of a dilemma. If he kept the remainder of the fleet together, he could concentrate his point defense... at the risk of losing too many of his smaller ships to the rebel starfighters. But if he ordered the fleet to scatter, he'd lose a handful of ships at the risk of being unable to defend himself if the enemy warships came after him. Hell, the starfighters themselves would need to rearm, sooner or later.

And if we present a tempting target, the enemy ships might come after us, he thought.

He turned his attention to the display. It didn't look as though he'd inflicted much — if any — damage on the rebel formation. Their jamming and ECM was first-rate, but they hadn't slowed or altered course. It was possible, he supposed, that their CO had decided it wasn't worth the effort to try to chase down his ships — his lighter units could outrace a battlecruiser, let alone a superdreadnaught — not when he needed to secure Ruthven as quickly as possible, before anyone could have any bright ideas about destroying the system's industrial base. Or he might just be relying on the starfighters...

But if they're not coming after us, he thought, *there's no point in trying to present a tempting target, not if they're not going to take the bait.*

"Send a signal to all ships," he ordered, as the enemy starfighters pulled back. "All ships are to scatter, then proceed with contingency plan theta-one; I say again, all ships are to scatter and proceed with theta-one."

"Aye, sir," the communications officer said.

"Ramp up the drive to full power, then take us straight to the system limits," Theodore ordered, tartly. "Launch one final set of tactical drones at the enemy formation and then link into the stealthed recon platforms. I want an up-to-date report when we leave the system."

"Aye, sir," the helmsman said. The tactical officer echoed him a second later. "We'll cross the system limits in seven hours."

Theodore nodded. It was risky, but better than losing his ships in a general engagement. And *he*, at least, needed to report to Marble. It was possible he'd be relieved of duty, even cashiered, but he'd done as much as he could. The remainder of the squadron would raid enemy shipping for as long as their supplies held out. He had no illusions about how long they'd last, even with a handful of pre-placed supply dumps, yet at least it was *something*.

And anything that delays the enemy can only be welcome, he thought. The Federation had taken a beating in two successive wars, despite the Grand Senate's attempts to

rebuild and expand its industrial base. *This new war may bring us to our knees, even if we win.*

He settled back in his command chair, watching the damage reports as they scrolled up in front of him. Seventeen ships destroyed outright, four more damaged so badly they'd need to be abandoned and scuttled... it was better than he'd dared hope, given the firepower on the other side. But he doubted he'd delayed the enemy long enough for it to matter. Making them expend a few thousand missiles hardly counted if there was nothing in place to take advantage of the shortfall.

They'll need time to gather themselves before leaping across the Void to Marble, he told himself firmly. *And, if nothing else, they will need to replace the missiles they fired.*

"Continue on our present course," he added, as the remaining enemy starfighters returned to their carriers. "And take us into stardrive as soon as we cross the system limits."

"Aye, sir," the tactical officer said.

⁎x℟

"The starfighters are rearming, sir," Lieutenant Thompson said. "Do you wish to launch another strike?"

Roman shook his head. The enemy squadron had launched a brief attack, perhaps for the honor of the flag, then broken off. There didn't seem to be any other motive; they'd fired thousands of missiles right into the teeth of his defenses, rather than trying to pick off one or two of his flanking units. Maybe the enemy CO hadn't *quite* realized that Marius Drake was in command, rather than an ignorant lout from the Grand Senate. Emperor Marius would have no trouble recognizing that the enemy CO was badly outgunned, that he'd had no choice but to retreat instead of dying for nothing.

But it did force us to expend some of our missiles, he thought, as he studied the reports from the long-range probes. *And it may cost us if we have to take the planet.*

He cursed inwardly as his fleet advanced on the planet. Ruthven had five fortresses in high orbit, protecting dozens of industrial platforms and habitats as well as the planet itself. Someone had clearly been taking advantage of Emperor Marius's incentives to develop new industries, he noted; in happier times, Ruthven would definitely be counted as a success story. But now, she was nothing more than a target. And one he had to take largely intact.

"Transmit the pre-recorded demand for surrender," he ordered. He'd gone to some trouble to guarantee the lives and property of the planet's residents, even though he had a nasty feeling there *would* be trouble once the Federation garrison surrendered. "And inform me the moment we receive a response."

"Aye, sir," Lieutenant Thompson said.

Roman gritted his teeth. Attacking a planet was far simpler than attacking through an Asimov Point, but there was the considerable danger of accidentally striking the planet itself with an antimatter warhead. Killing billions of humans would give Emperor Marius a propaganda victory, if only because mass slaughter was generally

believed to be the pastime of uncivilized aliens. The fact that Marius *himself* had attempted to commit genocide would probably go unmentioned.

And we could simply seal off the planet, if we didn't need it, he thought. Having the ability to produce new missiles and assault pods hundreds of light years closer to their next target would be very helpful. Ruthven's production rates were low, compared to Earth or the Outsider industrial nodes, but it hardly mattered. *And they might have ships they could send out to harass us when our backs are turned.*

"Picking up a signal from the planet," Lieutenant Thompson said. "It's a recorded message."

Roman smiled. "No doubt they recorded it before we broke through the Asimov Point," he said. With seven light minutes between the fleet and Ruthven, holding a real-time conversation would be impossible. "Put it on."

He looked up as a face appeared in the display. "Admiral Garibaldi, this is Colonel Knox," a voice said. A line of text below the screen confirmed his identity and noted, somewhat to Roman's relief, that Knox was planetary militia rather than a Federation officer. "Please state your terms of surrender."

"Record," Roman ordered. "Colonel Knox, my terms are very simple. My forces will assume control of the orbital fortresses, industrial nodes and select locations on the planet to guarantee our security. Any Federation personnel on the planet are to be handed over for internment, although we will provide security forces for any internment camps. Your planetary militia is to disband and return home, at least for the moment. The future disposition of Ruthven will be considered after the war."

"Message sent," Lieutenant Thompson said.

Roman nodded, hoping that Colonel Knox would be reasonable. His position was hopeless and he had to know it, but *not* putting up a fight would look bad if the Federation resumed control of the system. Besides, the Outsiders might be just as bad as the Grand Senate and try to suck the planet dry.

Goddamned civil war, he thought. *Wouldn't it be so much easier if we were fighting aliens?*

He had to wait another thirteen minutes for his reply. "Admiral, we are prepared to surrender on terms," Colonel Knox said. "However, we cannot guarantee that all Federation personnel will be rounded up."

"Understood," Roman said. There would probably be a multitude of stay-behind agents in place, given that the defenders had had months to prepare. "My forces will assume control of the high orbitals shortly."

He keyed a switch. "Elf? Did you get all that?"

"Yes, sir," Elf said. On duty, she was all business. "I'm readying the landing force now."

Chapter Eighteen

Ironically, one of the many problems of the pre-war Federation Navy — the rise of alcohol and drug abuse — was largely eliminated by the pressures of actual war.
—The Federation Navy in Retrospect, 4199

Earth, 4101

"I don't know where you got that pill, My Lady," Operative Oslo said, after she had walked into his office and closed the door. "But I sincerely hope you're not planning to take them yourself."

"I'm not," Tiffany said. Oslo and his men had protected her since she was a little girl. She had no idea what they'd do if they thought she intended to damage herself. "What can you tell me about it?"

Oslo eyed her for a long moment, perhaps wondering just *what* was going on. "I took the pill to a chemist I know and had it analyzed," he said. "I'll give you the full report, if you wish, but it's basically a combination of a very strong military-grade painkiller and a powerful antidepressant. The chemist noted that such combinations are, in fact, illegal, if only because of the dangers of two strong drugs interacting."

Tiffany swallowed. "And if I took the pill now," she said, "what would happen to me?"

"You'd go numb," Oslo said. "The painkiller side of the pill, My Lady, is normally only found in military emergency kits. You could cut off your own arm and feel nothing, even as you are bleeding to death. Combined with the antidepressant, you might start bouncing off the walls or find it hard to think clearly. The chemist was at some pains to insist that the ultimate end result is dangerously unpredictable."

He met her eyes, evenly. "The military insists that only one or two doses of such painkillers are to be handed out, regardless of the situation," he added. "That's because the painkillers are addictive. Three doses within a short period of time might well cause addiction, My Lady, and getting such pills outside the military is extremely difficult. The antidepressants, too, can get someone hooked on them. I should add that the military has a policy of rejecting any candidates who have used such drugs, even for a short period of time."

"I see," Tiffany said. Was Marius addicted? How many of the damned pills had he taken? "If someone were to be addicted... how could they be cured?"

"It would depend, according to the chemist, on just how badly they were hooked," Oslo told her, flatly. "Eliminating the physical dependency would not be too difficult, I was told, but curing the *mental* dependency would be a great deal harder. Not to put too fine a point on it, My Lady: anyone who takes these pills more than once or twice in their lifetime is going to have some *real* problems breaking free."

"Shit," Tiffany said. She shook her head. "What *else* do they do?"

"The chemist wasn't clear," Oslo said. "Anyone hooked on the drugs may lose his appetite, his enthusiasm for life... even become impotent. These are not *legal* pills, My Lady; they're not produced according to a standard recipe. The exact side effects

may vary depending on the precise combination of painkiller and antidepressants. If you know someone who has been taking them, the chemist concluded, they need immediate medical help."

He held out a folder. "This is the full report," he added. "There's a summary at the front, stripped of all the medical gibberish. I suggest you make sure it's carefully hidden, if you don't want to feed it into a shredder after you read it. Someone who found it could easily draw the wrong conclusion."

Or the right one, Tiffany thought, as she waved him goodbye and settled down to read through the folder. *Who's giving Marius the pills, and why?*

Her father had taught her, years ago, that bureaucrats and military officers liked burying bad news in the files, on the largely accurate assumption that their superiors rarely bothered to read more than the executive summary before signing off on the reports. Tiffany had pointed out, at the time, that reading a full report could take hours, hours she didn't have; now, she opened the folder and started to read from the beginning. The chemist had *loaded* the report with medical jargon — she had to look some of the words up on her terminal — but, if anything, Oslo had understated the situation. Excessive use of the painkiller alone would lead to heart attacks, as well as a host of other problems.

The final section of the report was nothing more than a detailed plan for *treating* the addiction before it got out of hand. Tiffany read through it, unsure if she should laugh or cry; she rather doubted she could talk a doctor, even a military doctor, into committing the Emperor to a medical ward for a year. And yet, without it, Marius's time was quite limited; he was running the risk of a massive heart attack or a stroke. He'd been an old man, despite rejuvenation treatments, long before the Justinian War had begun.

She closed the report and rose, looking around for a place to hide it. There *was* a safe in the suite, but Marius had the keycode; she didn't dare leave it there. She briefly considered shredding it, before deciding — instead — to bury it in her underwear drawer. Marius was unlikely to go poking through, she thought, and no one else would dare. She'd made it quite clear, back when they moved into the Presidential House, that her drawers were off-limits to the household staff. She hated the thought of anyone digging through her clothes.

Her intercom beeped. "Tiffany, please come to the conference room," Marius said. His voice was surprisingly strong. "We have much to discuss."

Tiffany blinked, hastily hid the folder and hurried out of the room, hoping it would remain undisturbed until she'd had a chance to show it to Ginny. Perhaps *she'd* have an idea of what to do about it. A pair of guards nodded to her as she hurried into the conference room and sat next to Marius, who gave her a sidelong look as she sat down. She studied him closely, wondering just which of the symptoms she should be looking for. The chemist had openly stated, after all, that the side effects were *definitely* unpredictable.

"Gentlemen, be seated," Marius said, once the last of the cabinet had entered the room and the doors were sealed. "Commander Lewis?"

Ginny rose to her feet, looking pale. Tiffany didn't know *much* about the military, but she was fairly sure Ginny was being loaded with responsibilities that were well above her pay grade. She wasn't sure if Marius was making a gesture of trust or if he found it too hard to care, these days, about military protocol. He could easily have arranged for Ginny to be promoted up a rank or two.

"Emperor," Ginny said. She sounded nervous, too. "We have received the first major set of updates from Alexis. According to the reports, the system fell to a major offensive through the Asimov Point."

Tiffany glanced at Marius. His left hand was shaking, slightly, but otherwise he showed no reaction. He would have known, she suspected, that the defenses of Alexis wouldn't hold, when Admiral Garibaldi came knocking. He'd had months to prepare himself for a piece of bad news.

"I see," he said, finally. "And the attackers have already invaded Ruthven?"

"We assume so, but we don't have any updates from Ruthven," Ginny said. "The last report stated that the enemy was sniping at the defenders while securing the planet."

"We shall assume the worst," Marius said. He cocked his head. "Is there any good news?"

"Yes, sir," Ginny said. "Major Jackson?"

Major Jackson, Commodore Arunika's successor, leaned forward. "We picked up a number of messages from the defenders as they were overwhelmed," he said. "One of them was an encrypted message from a deep-cover agent within the Outsiders. It contained a short update on the situation, including confirmation that Roman Garibaldi and most of his crew have indeed joined the Outsiders."

Marius's face darkened, ominously. "And what have they been doing?"

"Attempting to batter out a post-war plan, apparently," Jackson said. "There were few details, sir, but whatever it was seems to have been acceptable to both the Outsiders and Garibaldi himself."

"He agreed to split the Federation," Marius said, flatly.

"It's possible, sir," Jackson agreed. "We don't have any updates from the front lines. I hope we will receive more messages, as the rebel fleet pushes its way towards us, but there's no way to be certain."

"They'll certainly try to split *us*," General Thorne commented. "The Outsider propaganda was surprisingly effective, even within the Core Worlds."

Because the Grand Senate abused everyone who didn't have a title, Tiffany thought. What was the point of slaving when the choice was between the Grand Senate and Admiral Justinian? But now, the Outsiders were offering the prospect of freedom, of living in a universe where there were no aristocrats. *Who wouldn't want to join the Outsiders?*

"We must make ready to counter the next barrage of enemy propaganda," Marius said. "They will be sneaking messages to their supporters, even now."

"Yes, sir," General Thorne said. "My department is already preparing a media offensive that will overshadow their attempts to spread the word. We cannot deny

that we lost Alexis, sir, but we can make it clear that we bled the enemy badly. And that it's all part of a plan to force them to overextend themselves before we cut them off at the knees."

Tiffany leaned forward. "Wouldn't that be giving away the plan?"

General Thorne gave her a cold look that sent a chill running down her spine. "They will have no difficulty in *deducing* our plan, My Lady," he said. "It is, after all, the same thing we did at Boskone and Boston."

"And the time delay will make it harder for them to get word, even if they haven't deduced our plan," Marius added. "Where do we stand with reinforcements?"

General Yusuf Maringa, Head of the Joint Chiefs of Staff, looked worried. "Sir, we have sent orders to a number of fleets to detach battle squadrons to reinforce the defenses of Earth and the Tara Sector," he said. "However, we have run into considerable problems. Several of the fleets have not yet received their orders, *cannot* yet have received their orders, while others are proving reluctant to let go of their ships. And even if they do, we're looking at months before we get any significant reinforcement in place."

Marius clenched his fist. "Are the admirals I put in place turning on me?"

Maringa paled. "I... I don't know, sir," he said. "They do have good reason to be reluctant to let go of their ships."

Because those ships are their only guarantee of remaining alive, Tiffany thought. Once, mutiny and rebellion would have been effectively unthinkable. Certainly, the Inheritance Wars had taught the Federation Navy a number of sharp lessons about making sure the crews were indoctrinated in Federation precepts. *But Admiral Justinian let the genie out of the bottle and those admirals have to be wondering what will happen to them, if Marius's protégé could turn on him.*

She scowled, inwardly. Naval officer or not, she understood the time delay caused by the limitations on communications. An admiral on the other side of the Federation might not have received the message yet... and, even if he had, he might have problems of his own to worry about. And, by the time he dispatched the ships, orders for his arrest might already be racing out from Earth. They would probably send him into rebellion.

"So we are dependent on the forces we already have in place — and Home Fleet," Marius said, coldly. "And we have very little in the pipeline to replace them?"

Larimore Hammond, Minister of Economics and Production, looked down at the table. "We have thirty-seven superdreadnaughts and nineteen fleet carriers under construction," he said, keeping his voice tightly under control. "However, the problem of finding good workers and sourcing all the material we need is slowing production down, alarmingly. We are actually looking at ways to concentrate our efforts on a handful of ships, but that will only delay the others further. Worse, enemy propaganda is spreading amongst the crews..."

"Then crack down on it," Marius snapped.

"The workforce understands the problems it's facing," Hammond said. "I've been hearing complaints for months, sir. Workers are putting in seventeen-hour shifts

daily, making them tired and prone to mistakes... some of those mistakes have been quite serious. Over the last two weeks, twelve trained workers have been killed in accidents..."

"I don't want a list of problems," Marius said. "I want *solutions!*"

"There are none," Hammond said, so quietly it was hard to hear his words. "I need more trained manpower, sir, but I can't spare the workers to *teach* the recruits how to work in a shipyard. And I need to give my crews more rest time, sir, yet that too will slow down production. And morale is in the shitter, *sir*, because everyone *knows* they're being worked to death. How many strikes do you want to have to break?

"That isn't the only set of problems," he added. "There are over ten thousand components to a superdreadnaught, everything from heavy armor to life support units and... well, *everything.* We have been having major delays in *sourcing* those parts, sir; we need additional production plants, but again we don't have the time to set them up."

Marius leaned forward. "Why the delay?"

"Some of the plants have been having their own problems," Hammond said. "The same problems we've been having in the shipyards. Others... well, one plant had a foreman who supported the Outsiders. By the time we realized the problem, every last item produced by that plant was tainted by chaos software."

"Then we need to tighten security," General Thorne said.

"Security is too tight for any real good," Hammond said. His voice grew louder. "Do you realize just how many man-hours we're losing just through security measures alone?"

"It has to be done," General Thorne snapped.

"Your trained apes don't have the slightest idea how to comport themselves in an industrial plant," Hammond snapped back. "Seventy-four security officers have died in the last three months, mostly through stupidity. This isn't some nice safe city-block on Earth, General; *stupid people die in space!* And that doesn't include the idiots who thought it would be a good idea to rape a couple of workers! We found them drifting out in space with their underpants nailed to their heads!"

"You let the murderers get away with it," Thorne said with uncommon intensity. "They should be found..."

"They're more valuable than your thugs," Hammond said. "You have an infinite supply of idiots on Earth!"

Tiffany glanced at Marius, wondering if he would stop the argument. But Marius was just sitting there, looking between the two ministers with a slightly bemused expression on his face. Had he zoned out? Or was he allowing them to argue to keep them from taking sides against him? Or...

"Enough," Marius said. "Have you found a trace of McGillivray?"

"No, sir," General Thorne said. "There's still no proof he survived the destruction of his home, let alone managed to find safety. He could well be dead."

"A man like McGillivray will always have an escape plan," Marius said. He scowled across the table. "And he will not be content with finding a safe place to die."

Tiffany couldn't really disagree. Last survivor of the Imperialists or not, McGillivray had cast a long shadow over the Grand Senate. She was sure, from what her father had said, that he'd played a role in arranging her marriage, just as the Brotherhood had played a role in turning Marius Drake into the Grand Senate's last best hope for survival. Old he might be — he'd been in his seventies during the Blue Star War, nearly a century ago — but there was nothing wrong with his mind. And yet, if he were nearing two hundred years old, could he really survive on Earth?

It depends, she thought. *Just how much of the Brotherhood survived the purge?*

"I have located a number of other potential Brothers," Thorne said. "Unfortunately, as we discussed before, actually proving it without a brain scan is impossible."

"Have them checked," Marius ordered. "If they happen to be innocent... well, we can release them without delay."

"Sir," Tully said. "Snatching innocent civilians on Earth will not go down well."

Thorne snorted. "We've crushed riots before," he said. "Give the scum a taste of the lash, Comptroller. I *guarantee* they'll be better-behaved the rest of their lives."

"It's not like they can do much else with their lives," Tiffany said, before she could stop herself. "Even if they all wanted jobs, General, where would they get them?"

"They can at least stay quiet as we conscript them," Thorne said. "It's high time we started sending more Earthers out to the colonies."

"We don't have the logistics," Hammond snapped. "Our freighters are pushed to the limits already!"

"And even if we did," Tully said, "how would the colonies absorb a bunch of useless workers who don't have the slightest idea how to survive?"

"Whips and chains," Thorne said. His face twisted into a leer. "The strong will survive and prosper, once all coddling is removed. As for the weak... let them die."

Tiffany felt sick. Thorne... was *Thorne* the one supplying the pills? The report had made it clear, more than once, that no sane doctor would prescribe such pills. And any doctor Marius asked could have supplied *proper* pills. Thorne, on the other hand, might benefit if Marius slowly became dependent on the drugs.

"We can deal with that problem after the war," Marius said. Tiffany was relieved to hear that he sounded almost like his old self. "For the moment, let us concentrate on preparing ourselves to meet Garibaldi and his traitors."

And, on that note, the meeting came to an end.

Tiffany wanted to speak with Marius as the others left, but he swept out before she could say a word. She cursed under her breath, then headed back to their rooms. She needed time to think.

Chapter Nineteen

The perverse irony of the final war is that if more planets had been treated like Ruthven, if Emperor Marius had had more time to break down the former monopolies, the Outsiders would never have reached Boston. But then, if the Federation had approached the problem wisely, the war would never have begun in the first place.
—The Federation Navy in Retrospect, 4199

Ruthven, 4101

Chang Li had thought herself used to a hostile crowd, but the stares from the locals as she was driven through the streets towards the Planetary Hall were far from pleasant, all the more so for being unforced. She'd tried to give speeches that were interrupted by hired rioters, men paid to disrupt her performance, yet here... the people watching her acted as though they were under occupation, their expressions sullen as they followed her car. It bothered her, more than she cared to admit; Ruthven, no matter how one looked at it, had had a pretty good decade. By boosting the planetary economy, Emperor Marius's officers had done an excellent job of winning hearts and minds.

She braced herself as the car drove through the gates and came to a halt in front of the Planetary Hall. The President — democratically elected, as far as the analysts could tell — was standing there to greet her. She climbed out of the vehicle, shook his hand firmly and allowed him to show her into the Planetary Hall. Ruthven's government was democratically elected, at least in part, *because* the system knew that loyalty to the Federation would be rewarded. She couldn't help wondering, as she walked up to the podium, just how many of the assemblymen facing her knew what it was like to grow up along the Rim.

And they have three Asimov Points to play with, she thought. *Who knows what they'll become in a century, if they survive the war?*

"Thank you for allowing me to speak," she said, once the President introduced her. It was sincerely meant, although she knew there was no way they would have barred her with Admiral Garibaldi controlling the high orbitals. "I won't keep you long.

"The Federation has been decaying for years. Authority and power were slipping towards Earth for centuries, even before the collapse of the Imperialist Faction. And, as the Grand Senate grew more powerful, it sucked the life out of the Rim even as it undermined the ideals of the Federation Navy. Admiral Justinian was merely the straw that broke the camel's back.

"You must see this, I think, from your own economic boom. It would not have taken place, I suspect, if the Grand Senate hadn't been removed. But what took its place was, in many ways, far worse. Admiral Drake — Emperor Marius — is responsible for a whole string of crimes, up to and including attempted genocide. He came within minutes of ordering the antimatter bombardment of my homeworld. Nova Athena, a *human* world, would have died under his fire.

"We — the Outsiders — believe that the system needs radical and fundamental reform," she continued. It was impossible to gauge the effect of her speech on her sullen and suspicious audience, but she plunged on regardless. "The Federation was never really designed to handle the problems of half the galaxy, or trillions of humans. Indeed, the system was badly sullied from the start because it gave too many advantages to those who based themselves on Earth. Unsurprisingly, they made rules that worked in their own favor, and to hell with the rest of us."

A low titter ran through the room, but there was no other reaction.

Li smiled. "We have a plan for reform, if you will join us," she finished. "And if you want to be left alone, we can abandon your world once the war is over and the Federation has fallen. All we ask, now, is that your government stays out of the war."

It was a little more complex than that, she knew. The planetary industries would be used to support the war effort, but it would be very clear that the locals weren't being offered a choice. Li had no idea just how far Admiral Drake had fallen from the man she remembered, yet she was sure he'd understand the problems facing the planetary government. They were, after all, powerless to keep the Outsiders from reducing their planet to rubble.

"Thank you for your time," she concluded. "Details of our plan have been uploaded onto the planetary datanet. If you want to discuss membership in *our* Federation, you are more than welcome to do so."

She nodded politely, then left the podium.

ᛃᛈ ᛈᛃ

Uzi had been on more unfriendly worlds than he cared to count, ranging from planets caught in the grip of bitter civil wars to worlds that hated the Federation and would cheerfully set fire to the whole structure and piss on the ashes. And yet, there was something about Ruthven that perplexed him. The locals had to know they'd been lucky, that only a freak combination of events had kept them from being drained as dry as some of the worlds along the Rim... and that the destruction of the Grand Senate had powered their economic boom.

And yet they view us with hatred, he thought, as he stood outside the spaceport gates and watched the small crowd of protesters on the other side of the road. The higher-ups hadn't bothered to listen to his suggestions about shutting down road and rail traffic, even near the spaceport and the handful of other occupied facilities. *What did we do to deserve it?*

He silently gathered information as he watched the protesters, knowing he'd have to make a report sooner or later. But how? He *might* be able to pass on a message when the fleet entered the Marble System — he'd done his best to ensure his unit would return to the ships when they departed — yet he knew it was a risk. It was quite possible that *some* records had survived the battle and that one of those records might contain a copy of the message he'd sent from Alexis. And then... the Outsiders would know they had a spy somewhere within their personnel. What would they do then?

A shuttle screeched overhead, coming to a halt over the spaceport and slowly dropping to the ground. More reinforcements, Uzi hoped; they weren't trying to hold the entire planet, but they barely had enough mobile firepower to cover the spaceport and the handful of other installations. It was amusing — and yet distressing — to realize that the Outsiders had started to develop the same "sensitivity" that had plagued some of the Federation's more controversial operations, the reluctance to deploy too many troops because it might be "provocative," even though high troop numbers were often better at keeping a lid on trouble. The stupidest insurgent could still tell the difference between a hundred soldiers and a thousand... and calculate that fighting the former was easier than the latter. But then, he had to admit, the Outsiders had good reason to be on their best behavior. Ruthven's value wasn't just measured in its location.

They'll be going to Marble next, he thought. *The defenders have to know they'll be coming under attack soon.*

He smiled at the thought. It was a logical assumption — and, indeed, the only way for the treacherous Admiral Garibaldi to *win.* Even in its weakened state, the Federation Navy possessed vastly more firepower than the Outsiders. Given time, Emperor Marius would assemble a fleet capable of kicking the Outsiders all the way back to Nova Athena — and there would be no traitors, this time, to keep the planetary population from getting what it deserved. No, Marble would be targeted next and then... and then, Tara Prime. But by the time the Outsiders reached *that* system, they would already be worn down.

"Outsiders out," someone shouted. Others, moments later, took up the cry. "Outsiders out!"

Uzi gritted his teeth as the shouting grew louder, as if someone had flipped a switch. He had a nasty feeling someone probably *had.* A handful of stay-behind units could cause some real trouble by splashing money around, even if they did nothing else. No doubt someone had bused the first set of protesters to the spaceport, just to see how the Outsiders would respond. And now, it wouldn't take much for an incident that would spark off a massacre.

And I have to stop it, he thought, ruefully. An... *incident* would help the Federation, but it would come at the cost of his career. And he *needed* to remain with the fleet. *I don't have a choice.*

He keyed his radio. "This is Uzi," he said. The dispatcher would know who he was — and, more importantly, *where* he was. "I need reinforcements at the North Gate, now!"

"Understood," the dispatcher said. Another pair of shuttles screamed overhead, heading up to the fleet. Their passage seemed to drive the protesters wild with anger; they shouted and screamed at the shuttles, as if their bad temper could knock the craft out of the sky. "Do you require armored vehicles?"

"Probably not," Uzi said. "Try and get the planetary police out here."

He closed the connection and glanced at his men. The general confusion had seen him landed with command of ten new soldiers, rather than the squad he'd worked

with from the moment he'd joined the Outsiders as a mercenary. They looked nervous, fingering their weapons as the howling mob grew louder. Even experienced soldiers feared mobs, Uzi knew from bitter experience; a mob could soak up machine gun fire and just keep coming, if it were mad enough to disregard its own safety.

"Stand at the ready," he ordered, "but I'll have the hide of anyone who fires without a specific order."

He allowed his gaze to pass over them, then turned his attention back to the mob. Mobs were fickle things; they might shout themselves hoarse and do nothing else, or they might turn violent at any moment. A handful of protesters were already slipping out of the crowd, trying to sneak back into the city; clearly, he noted, they'd had enough of the prospect of sudden violence and death. But the remainder would be more focused on what they were doing.

"This is Overlook," a new voice said. "I've got a set of buses making their way off the ring road and heading to the spaceport."

"Keep them back," Uzi said, cursing the planet's government under his breath. If they'd bothered to install an automated traffic control system, those buses could have been redirected somewhere safer. Instead, they'd be on his position within minutes. "Do we have any word from the planetary police?"

"They're refusing to budge," the dispatcher said. "Half their policemen have reported sick!"

Uzi cursed, savagely. *This* was why planetary policemen couldn't be trusted. They were too damn close to their populations to do what was necessary. As bad as the police would have been, his forces would be a great deal worse if they had to put down a riot. And he and his men were dangerously exposed.

He gambled. "Open the gates," he ordered. "Once they're open, we'll move through the gates and slam them closed. Let them howl themselves silly outside."

"Yes, sir," the dispatcher said.

Uzi gritted his teeth as he heard the gates opening behind him. Showing weakness to a baying mob was a dangerous move, but he didn't have any non-lethal weaponry. Some bright spark on the fleet had probably reasoned that it wouldn't be necessary, that the planetary police would provide all the support the fleet could possibly need. And, thanks to that idiot — who he would have regarded with complete satisfaction if he hadn't been on the front lines — he and his men were about to be attacked.

"Move," he snapped. "And get those gates closed the moment the last of us is inside."

He turned and ran through the gates, hearing the sound of footsteps behind him as the mob lunged forward. The gates were already closing, but the mob slammed into them with staggering force. Uzi turned, motioning for his men to form a skirmish line, as the gates hissed closed. He had a brief glimpse of a young man — it was always the young men — being crushed by the gates before he fell out of sight. Uzi had seen enough mobs to know that the poor bastard was probably already dead.

"If they push down the gates, open fire," he ordered. He'd played the only card he could, but would it be enough? The gates were solid, yet he had a nasty feeling the

mob would just keep pushing on them until something broke. "We can't let them ransack the spaceport."

A thought struck him as another shuttle zoomed overhead. "Ask the pilot to make a low pass over the crowd," he added, calling the dispatcher. "It might disperse the idiots."

He covered his ears as the shuttle reversed course and flew low, as low as the pilot dared. The sound was deafening, but did the trick; he watched, in relief, as the mob broke and ran. A handful of men and women were lying on the ground, moaning; they'd been injured in the crush and left to fend for themselves. A number of them looked dead.

"Get the medics over here," he ordered, wearily. Who knew *what* the mob would do? It might just continue to break up, scattering as its individual members made their way home, or it might reform and return to the spaceport. "See what they can do for the poor bastards."

He sighed, suddenly feeling very tired. They'd been promised reinforcements, troops raised in the Outsider worlds and dispatched through the captured Asimov Points, but he doubted they would arrive in time. The locals weren't friendly, and that was the end of it, for the moment. And really, why was that a bad thing?

Because you have to play a role, he reminded himself. There were times, he was sure, when it would be easier just to put the mask aside, once and for all. *And because you have to stay in that role until you can act decisively.*

"Fifteen people injured, nine dead," one of the medics called. "I'm moving the injured to the spaceport infirmary."

Uzi nodded. It might make more sense, from a logistical point of view, to transfer the injured and dead to a local hospital, but it would only inflame public opinion. Quite why the planetary government permitted such free discourse was beyond him, yet he had to admit it was working nicely for the stay-behind agents. Either the Outsiders took care of the wounded themselves, wasting some of their resources, or they risked sparking off a second set of riots.

"Colonel Mooncalf is on his way," the dispatcher said. "Once he arrives, you're to report back to the shuttles."

"Understood," Uzi said. Maybe the Outsiders wanted a scapegoat. He *had* been the person on the spot, if nothing else. "I'll be on my way once he arrives."

∞∞

"So," Li said. "Just what happened?"

"According to the planetary police, a number of protesters tried to force the gates of the spaceport," General Stuart said. "They were turned back when a quick-thinking officer had the presence of mind to order a shuttle to fly low over the crowd, driving them away from the spaceport. I believe the officer in question should be commended."

"Indeed," Li said. She'd make sure of it, personally if necessary. A massacre would have given their enemies a propaganda bonanza. "And how did the protesters get there?"

"The wounded say the protests were organized from start to finish," General Stuart said. "I read their reports very carefully. They were paid to attend, forced to listen to long speeches on how we were going to take away their rights, and then herded into buses for the trip to the spaceport. The planetary police, so far, have turned up no leads. I suspect an enemy stay-behind force. Even a relative handful of people can cause some real trouble."

Li nodded. "Is there anything we can do about it?"

"Probably not," General Stuart said. "I've ordered the deployment of riot-control gear to the spaceport, but our troops aren't really trained in handling riots. We assumed an opposed landing, not... not a riot on the surface."

"Then we'll just have to hope matters remain peaceful," Li said. She scowled. She'd had some interest in joining the Outsiders from the planetary government, but it would be lost if their population turned on them. "Do you have anything to add?"

"Merely that you need better bodyguards," General Stuart said. "The stay-behinds would definitely risk life and limb to get at you — and you're down here, protected by the planetary police."

"They take their jobs seriously," Li protested.

"But they're also caught in the middle," General Stuart warned. "I think — I really think — that you need some additional bodyguards attached to you. They'll stay out of your way..."

"Hah," Li said. She hadn't forgotten what the *last* set of bodyguards had done, even though they'd meant well. But General Stuart was right. Ruthven had yet to decide which side it was on. "If you feel it's necessary, General, see to it. But I have no intention of treating this planet as hostile terrain."

"There were collaborators even on the worst planets along the Rim," General Stuart reminded her. "People who somehow benefited from kissing the Grand Senate's ass. And here... well, I wouldn't be surprised to discover there's an Emperor Marius Fan Club. I want to make sure you're well-protected for the remainder of your stay here."

"Very well," Li said. "But only when I'm on the ground. I don't have anything to fear on the ships."

Chapter Twenty

Throughout human history, logistics have been the bane of military operations. Thus the saying "amateurs study tactics; professionals study logistics." This was unfortunately true for the Federation Navy, a problem made worse by poor contingency planning and excessive reliance on a network of bases rather than supply ships.
—The Federation Navy in Retrospect, 4199

Ruthven, 4102

"Happy New Year," Elf said.

Roman allowed himself a smile as she pinned him to the bed, pushing herself down on him as she leaned down and kissed his lips. The fleet couldn't allow itself more than a brief pause for New Year — a holiday celebrated throughout the Federation — but he could, just for a few minutes, relax and enjoy himself. Their love-making was a reminder, in some ways, that there was a world beyond the war, even if they would never have been thrust together *without* it. How long had it been since they'd first met on *Enterprise*?

"Happy New Year to you too," Roman said, as his head filled with all the problems and concerns that had bothered him over the last two weeks. He pushed them aside with an effort and smiled. "Do you have anything planned?"

Elf elbowed him, none too gently. "Only dinner with you and the... *others*," she said. The fleet's senior officers had planned a dinner, followed by a conference. "How about you?"

"Nothing too serious," Roman said. He shook his head as he sat upright. "There are just too many things to do."

"Supply problems still worrying you?"

"Just a little," Roman said.

He scowled. Supply problems worried him a great deal, and she knew it. The enemy had had a remarkable stroke of luck when one of their battlecruisers intercepted a convoy running through Alexis and blown all four freighters into flaming debris, along with their escorts. Roman would have cheerfully strangled the convoy CO himself, if he hadn't died in the brief engagement. The idiot could have avoided the encounter if he'd followed SOP and deployed drones to sweep space ahead of him for traps.

"We can't go back on the offensive until we receive more assault pods," he said. "The defenses around Marble are formidable, but the defenses around Tara Prime are worse."

"True," Elf agreed. "No wonder weapons on the way?"

Roman shook his head, then stood and hurried into the shower. There wasn't enough time to chat with her, to relax... he cursed, inwardly, as he turned on the water. He was far too young to be an admiral, even if the wars had eliminated most of the deadwood in high command. There were just too many issues he had to handle on the fly.

At least I have a working staff, he thought. He'd picked his officers carefully, judging them by competence rather than loyalty. It was something, weirdly enough, that he'd picked up from Marius Drake. *And we're learning the ropes as we go along.*

Elf joined him in the shower; Roman picked up a sponge and washed her back, then turned to allow her to return the favor. It felt wrong, somehow, to be enjoying himself with her, even though he knew it was unlikely that any of his crew who wanted companionship would be deprived. The last two months had seen thousands of his people rotated through the spaceport on Ruthven, allowing them to have at least *some* shore leave. Roman had fretted at the time, fearing kidnap or worse, but there had only been a handful of minor incidents, mainly over the value of their money. The Federation Credit had been declining in value over the last decade, and it showed. And no other currency was considered acceptable.

Because the Grand Senate refused to allow local systems to establish their own currencies, he thought, as he stepped back out of the shower. He didn't pretend to understand economics — as a science, it seemed woefully imprecise — but it was easy enough to see the problems it caused. *And because no one knows if Earth will pay its debts.*

He dressed slowly, then checked the daily fleet update as he waited for Elf. There was nothing of great significance, save for a report from a starship patroling the edge of the system that it had detected another starship dropping out of stardrive and vanishing into cloak. Roman wasn't too surprised. The Federation Navy's raiders had been probing the edge of the system ever since he'd taken it, watching and waiting for a sign of weakness. It would be a long time coming.

Nothing to be done about it, he thought, nodding to Elf. She'd donned her dress blacks, accompanied by a medal she'd won during one of the more intensive battles of the Justinian War. *All we can do is keep our guard up and wait for them to show themselves.*

The ship's cooks, he discovered as he entered the officer's lounge, had outdone themselves in their efforts to make a proper dinner. Traditionally, New Year was celebrated with roast turkey and all the trimmings, which they'd sourced from the planet below and cooked in the galley. Roman nodded politely to Chang Li and General Stuart, then turned to greet his captains as they joined him. It was odd, and yet heartening, to realize that the Outsiders shared so many of the Federation's customs.

"We are all human," Chang Li said, when he commented on it. "And besides, New Year is a nice *politically-correct* holiday."

"One we can all agree on," General Stuart added. "Although, of course, we don't agree on what date marks the turning of the year."

Roman smiled, although he'd grappled with the problem himself as a young officer. The planetary year was different for each planet; Earth might have 365 days in the year, but Mars had 687. Just to complicate matters, the Martian day was longer than an Earth day, which meant that the Martians counted a year as 669 days. The

Federation had solved the problem by decreeing that the galactic standards would take their cue from Earth, but even so there was a great deal of confusion. He was surprised the system had worked as well as it had.

I suppose the First Interstellar War showed us the value of having a united system, he thought, as the conversation turned to other matters. *Having the Snakes breathing down our necks must have concentrated a few minds.*

"The war won't last forever," Chang Li commented. "What do you plan to do, Admiral Garibaldi, after the war?"

Roman shrugged. "I've spent my entire adult life in the navy," he said. It struck him, suddenly, that Marius Drake had done the same. "I don't think I'd be comfortable anywhere else. Taking a survey ship and seeing what's out there... maybe that's what I'd want to do."

He smiled. "How about yourself?"

"I always planned to retire to Nova Athena," Chang Li said. "But *someone* really needs to be the ambassador at large for the Outsiders."

"Speak for yourself," General Stuart grunted, curtly. He took a sip of his wine as he leaned forward. "I plan to retire, after the war, and spend the rest of my life somewhere nicely isolated. The rest of the galaxy can go amuse itself without me."

Roman blinked. "You'd be happier living on a planet?"

"I'd prefer not to live in a place where an air leak would be enough to kill me," General Stuart said. "I can see the value of raising one's children in such an environment, but I don't agree with the logic."

"He has a point," Elf agreed. Roman gave her a surprised look. "Stupidity killing wouldn't be so bad if it was only the stupid person who got killed."

He *did* have a point, Roman conceded, reluctantly. *Roman* had grown up in an environment where the slightest mistake could get someone killed, teaching him what was important from a very early age. But his mistakes could easily get someone *else* killed along with him, no matter what precautions were worked into the system. It hardly seemed *right*. And yet, growing up in a cocoon of safety explained a great deal about the Grand Senate's odder decisions. They were completely insulated from the reality of the universe surrounding them.

"I suppose," he said, shortly.

They reached the end of the dinner without incident, although Roman was careful to avoid the traditional toast to the Grand Senate, the Federation Navy, and the Federation Constitution. One was gone, one was torn asunder and one had been used as nothing more than toilet paper for generations. Indeed, he had to admit that the Outsiders were more faithful to the Constitution than the Grand Senate. But then, they'd never had the opportunity to gain wealth and power by violating it.

"The supply problem has yet to be solved," he said, once the stewards had cleared away the table and produced after-dinner drinks and chocolates. "We cannot advance towards Marble until we have a ready supply of assault pods."

"I would have thought you had enough," Chang Li commented.

"It isn't just Marble that's the problem," General Stuart explained, quietly. "We'd need to press on to Tara Prime as quickly as possible, rather than wait for the freighters to bring us more assault pods."

"And we'd need a huge reserve, just in case we run into something we can't handle," Roman added. "Astrid and Maben aren't heavily defended — or weren't, according to the last set of updates we received — but Tara Prime definitely is. I wouldn't be surprised if they'd received reinforcements by now. The Emperor knows his best chance to stop us short of the Gateway is at Tara Prime."

"You youngsters have it easy," Kratman observed. "In my day, we charged through Asimov Points, all guns blazing."

"That would explain the high casualty rates," Roman commented, mischievously. He wouldn't have dared say that, back when they'd been professor and student. "How many people died during the Inheritance Wars?"

"Millions," Kratman said, simply. Without assault pods, the only way to win was to send hundreds of small starships through the Asimov Points and tolerate truly *staggering* loss rates. "In sheer numbers, Roman, it beat every other war ever fought by humanity. But in frightfulness... the First Interstellar War still has the edge."

Roman nodded in agreement. *He* was used to aliens — or, at least, he'd grown up in a universe where aliens were common. But for the humans who'd discovered the Graveyard, who'd eventually made first contact with the Snakes, it must have been a terrifying shock. *And* they'd believed, for reasons that had never made sense to him, that aliens had to be peaceful as well as civilized. Surely, a single look at humanity itself would have put the lie to *that*.

"This war may grow worse," Chang Li said. "What happens if the Emperor starts scorching worlds at random?"

"I don't think he will," Roman said, although he wasn't entirely sure he was right. No *rational* mind would start destroying entire worlds, if only because it would be terrifyingly easy for the Outsiders to retaliate in kind, but Emperor Marius had already tried to cross that line once. "There are officers who would mutiny rather than carry out such an order."

"Don't underestimate how easy it can be to convince someone to violate their morals," Kratman warned, sternly. "Many of the worst people in history, Roman, didn't see themselves as monsters. They came up with elaborate justifications for carrying out vile atrocities just to escape the awareness of what they'd done."

He shrugged. "And there's no shortage of sociopaths to be found on Earth," he added. "I sometimes think the planet breeds them."

"It's easy to lose your concern for others if others show no concern for you," Elf offered, darkly. "What sort of life does the average person on Earth lead?"

Roman shuddered. He'd heard stories, of course, although the only time he'd been to Earth had been after the end of the Justinian War. Earth was a nightmare, he'd been told, even though the Grand Senate had feted the planet as the cultural and industrial heart of the Federation. But then, he'd seen some of the art that came from

Earth and it had turned his stomach. He liked to think of himself as a broad-minded man — growing up on an asteroid was a good way to learn to mind your own business — but some things were just disgusting.

He cleared his throat. "Be that as it may, we need to press forward as soon as possible," he insisted. "We don't, as yet, have any up-to-date intelligence on Tara Prime."

Chang Li frowned. "There were no updates here?"

"The defenders purged their databases before retreating," Roman said. It was understandable, but irritating. Officers had been put in front of a court martial board and then shot for allowing intact databases to fall into enemy hands. "The data we have is four months out of date."

He scowled. The Federation's vast stockpile of prefabricated fortresses had been drained by the demands of the war, but Emperor Marius should have had no problems moving the remainder to Tara Prime. Unless, of course, he had his doubts about Admiral Vincent. But if he had, Roman was sure, Marius would have removed Vincent by now. Indeed, he might have done so already, leaving someone else in his place. There was no way to know.

"We do have some tactical information from Marble, but nothing through the Asimov Points in the system," he added. "There's no way to know what's lurking in the systems between Marble and Tara Prime. They may assume we will take the shortest route to Tara Prime... or they might be keeping ships in reserve at Tara Prime, ready to intercept us once they know our likely course."

"Chancy," General Stuart observed. "They'd be better off aiming to fight a decisive battle at Tara Prime."

Roman nodded in agreement. Trying to be tactically clever was one thing, but trying to be clever on an interstellar scale — as had been drummed into him from his first day at the Academy — was quite another. Marius Drake — the Marius Drake he remembered — would know better than to over-commit himself. Better to force Roman to assault Tara Prime, where the defenders held most of the cards, than risk a running battle in the outer systems.

And yet...

"The Emperor may not agree with us, though," he said. "It depends on just how far he trusts Admiral Vincent."

Chang Li leaned forward. "He hasn't sent you any reply?"

"None," Roman said. "But then, there would be a very real risk of any message being intercepted."

He wasn't too surprised at the silence, as irritating as it was. The files hadn't been too detailed, but Admiral Vincent wouldn't have been appointed to Tara Prime if he hadn't been considered reliable. Admiral Justinian had been given control of a similar system and he'd launched a rebellion that had nearly brought the Federation to its knees. If Emperor Marius had the slightest doubt over Vincent's loyalty, Roman was sure, he would have been summoned home and brutally executed.

Unless he's too strong to be cowed easily, Roman thought. *Or...*

He shook his head, dismissing the thought as he turned his attention to other matters. "If the most recent update holds true," he said, "we should have a stockpile of assault pods by the end of next week. At that time, unless the situation changes, I intend to cross the interstellar gulf and attack Marble. We'll proceed from there as the situation dictates."

General Stuart snorted. "Do I assume you don't intend to move down the shortest route to Tara Prime?"

"It depends on what we find when we get there," Roman said, patiently. He closed his eyes for a long moment, recalling the starchart. "They may have rigged up defenses in Astrid or Maben, General. We may find it a better idea to proceed via an alternate route."

Chang Li gave him a sharp look. "Do you believe they will have rigged up defenses?"

"We were bringing forts online at the rate of one per week, back when we were setting up the defenses of Boston," Roman said. "Fortress Command is *very* experienced in unloading a freighter full of prefabricated components, then slotting them together and building a working fortress. They're nowhere near as complex as starships, true, but still..."

He shrugged. "I expect minefields and automated weapons platforms, at the very least," he added. "Anything they can do to slow us down and force us to expend assault pods will be considered worthwhile."

"True," General Stuart agreed. "But you might also get bogged down."

"It's a possibility," Roman acknowledged, coolly. "But it's also possible that we will get to our destination fast enough to beat the Emperor's reinforcements."

He keyed his console, activating the starchart. "There's only one gulf between Tara Prime and Earth," he said. "It won't take longer than two weeks to get a message from Tara Prime to Earth, once we attack Marble. I imagine, General, that Emperor Marius will send reinforcements, if he hasn't already. He may even come himself."

The intercom chimed. "Admiral, this is Sanderson at Tactical," a voice said. "A courier boat has just entered the system and announced itself. Her passenger is requesting permission to speak to you personally."

Roman frowned. "Who *is* the passenger?"

"It doesn't say," Sanderson said. "But the courier boat's IFF places it as one of the ships attached to Tara Prime."

"Have the vessel boarded and searched," Roman ordered, after a moment. A ship from Tara Prime could be very good news... or a potential disaster in the making. "Once it's confirmed safe, have the passenger transhipped to *Valiant*."

"Yes, sir," Sanderson said.

Elf frowned as the connection broke. "Who could this be?"

"I don't know," Roman admitted. "But I think we're about to find out."

Chapter Twenty-One

Naturally, as respect for the ideals of the Federation decreased, individual officers started to look to their own power rather than their duty. Indeed, despite the lesson of Admiral Justinian, the lure of supreme power remained strong. Why not? Marius Drake had made himself Emperor.
—The Federation Navy in Retrospect, 4199

Ruthven, 4102

Roman couldn't help feeling an odd mixture of excitement and concern as the shuttle settled down to the deck. The marines, once they'd boarded the courier boat, had reported the name and identity of the passenger, Commodore Hannalore Vincent. Roman had glanced at her file, while waiting for the marines to transfer her to *Valiant* and noted that she was very definitely Admiral Vincent's oldest daughter. Her father, it seemed, had smoothed her advancement through the navy.

And let's hope she deserves it, Roman thought. The shuttle's hatch hissed open, allowing two marines to step onto the deck. *She might have no real talent of her own.*

He sucked in his breath as Commodore Hannalore Vincent followed the marines out of the shuttle, feeling an unwanted flush of arousal. She was stunning, her long blonde hair falling in ringlets down to her shoulders, her uniform expertly tailored to show off her curves without revealing a hint of flesh below her collar. Her face was perfect, too perfect; Roman would have bet half his salary that she'd either been enhanced while in the womb or spent time in a bodyshop, once she'd grown old enough to decide what she wanted. She was thirty-three, according to the file, but she barely looked old enough to drink.

And that makes her dangerous, Roman reminded himself, sternly. He took a moment to compose himself, keeping his reactions under control. *She's smart enough to use her sexuality as a weapon.*

"Admiral Garibaldi," Hannalore said. Her voice was a rich, warm contralto. "I've heard *so* much about you."

"Thank you," Roman said. Elf, thankfully, was standing right next to him or he might have done something stupid. It was possible, he'd heard, to engineer phero-mones into one's body to enhance attractiveness... had Hannalore done something along those lines to herself? Or was he merely reacting to the presence of a beautiful girl? It was hard to be sure. "If you'll come with me, Commodore, we can talk in the briefing room."

Hannalore said nothing as they walked through the corridors, but her eyes kept flickering from side to side, taking in the giant superdreadnaught. Roman had a feel-ing she was looking for pieces of Outsider technology, but there was little of that inside *Valiant*. He couldn't help noticing that Hannalore sucked in attention from the crew, their eyes following her as she strode past with nary a care in the world. There was definitely something about her that caught the eye.

"I'm glad you agreed to speak with me," Hannalore said, once they were in a conference chamber and the hatch was firmly closed. "My father sent me with a message — and power to negotiate."

"I guessed as much," Roman said. These days, only a fool would rely on someone outside the family for sensitive negotiations. It explained a great deal about the Grand Senate, he felt. "I confess I don't have much patience for bullshit, Commodore. Can we get right to the point?"

If Hannalore was surprised by his tone, she didn't show it. "My father would like to make a deal with you," she said, simply. "He wants to switch sides."

"How... *convenient*," Elf said, dryly.

"The Emperor is going insane," Hannalore said. "My father feels the Federation will be much better off without him."

Which is precisely what I want to hear, Roman thought. He found it easier to think when he wasn't looking at Hannalore. *So I should be wary.*

"I'm glad your father has recognized the problem," he said. "Can we rely on him to attach his forces to my command?"

"If we can come to an agreement," Hannalore said. She gave him a brilliant smile. "As you said, let us cut through the bullshit."

She leaned forward, her hair shimmering under the light. "My father has been in command of the Tara Sector for three years," she said. "In that time, he has promoted the development of local industry, assisted the growth of a self-defense force and expanded the defenses quite considerably."

"And made a hefty profit for himself into the bargain," Elf commented.

Hannalore didn't bother to deny it. "My father wishes to retain his position," she said. "He doesn't believe the Emperor will leave him alone permanently, regardless of his loyalty to the Federation. The price for him joining you — and bringing both fleet and industry to aid your war effort — is recognition of his permanent possession of the Tara Sector."

"He wants to be king," Roman said.

"Crude, but essentially accurate," Hannalore said. "He wants a position akin to the monarchs of Albion."

Roman forced himself to think. On one hand, Admiral Vincent commanded three battle squadrons, hundreds of smaller ships and over forty fortresses. Getting that force on his side was worth almost any price. But, on the other hand, it would be a betrayal of everything the Outsiders — and the Federation — stood for. Who knew *what* the local population thought of their Admiral, a man imposed on them by Earth. Did they love him... or were they just waiting for the Outsiders to arrive before they launched an uprising?

"Albion had a great deal to offer the Federation, back when they were integrated into the fold," Elf said. "Does your father have enough to make the price worthwhile?"

Hannalore smirked. "Would you prefer to batter your way through the defenses of the sector?"

"Point," Roman conceded.

He ignored her smile as he dug through his memory for what little he recalled of the monarchs of Albion. They'd set up a network of colonies of their own, funded without recourse to federal funds... the same funds the Federation used as its excuse for dominating the outer colonies. And they'd embedded themselves so thoroughly at the heart of their system that digging them out would ruin the economy completely. The Federation had agreed to recognize their position, if he recalled correctly, in exchange for Albion joining the Federation. Perhaps, on some level, the Grand Senate had recognized a set of kindred souls.

And they were largely autonomous, he thought, grimly. *But then, they did enjoy a degree of popular support.*

"Your father intends to set up a dynasty of his own," Roman said.

"Correct," Hannalore agreed. "He believes that the Federation failed because the Grand Senate, in the end, did not inspire love. The Emperor, by contrast, threw *away* his love as he turned into a tyrant. Father... has other ideas."

"So did Marius Drake," Roman commented. "And good intentions led him right into hell."

He sighed, inwardly. There was no way he could avoid feeling out of his depth. His sole experience with interstellar politics, before the Battle of Nova Athena, had been Emperor Marius's determination to reunite the Federation. There had been no need for negotiation with others, let alone an awareness that the Federation would be profoundly changed by the war. And now he had to negotiate, with Admiral Vincent as well as the Outsiders. The hell of it was that Vincent's offer was *extremely* good.

"It will have to be discussed by the council," he said. "Do you have anything else you wish to say?"

"Just this," Hannalore said. "Father was very interested in sealing this alliance the old-fashioned way. He wishes to offer you the hand of his daughter, *my* hand, in marriage."

Roman stared at her in disbelief. Admiral *Drake* had been forced to marry into the network of families that made up the Grand Senate, but it hadn't saved him from an assassination attempt after Admiral Justinian's death. He could see the logic, yet he found it repulsive. He wouldn't be able to put down his burdens after the war if he had a family tie to the newest dynasty. And besides, there was Elf. He didn't dare look at her, to see how she reacted, but he was damned if he was dumping her for *political* reasons.

And did your father send you in the hopes you would seduce me, Roman thought darkly, *or is that merely a bonus?*

He found it hard to grasp why *anyone* would arrange their daughter's marriage. Or their son's, for that matter. The parents weren't the ones who would have to live with the unwanted spouse. But then, from what little he'd heard of the Grand Senate, some husbands and wives didn't even live together. All that mattered was that they had children and *that* could be done in an exowomb.

"That won't be necessary," he said, firmly. "If we accept the offer, Commodore, we will stick with it."

"My father believes a blood tie can only be beneficial," Hannalore said.

"But we don't," Roman said. He bit down several nasty comments that came to mind. She'd be better off marrying someone from the Tara Sector, really. "I thank you for the offer, Commodore, but we won't need a blood tie to make us keep our word."

He couldn't help feeling a stab of sympathy for Hannalore. Her father would have groomed her to be the perfect daughter, to marry well to help his career. It *was* one way of getting ahead, even though Roman found it sickening. But it was equally possible, he reminded himself, that she might be playing a role. There would be a definite advantage in being underestimated by her enemies.

"Assuming we do accept your father's offer," he said, "how do you plan to proceed?"

"You would need to take Marble," Hannalore said. She reached into her jacket pocket and produced a datachip. "There are four Asimov Points within the system, three of which can start you off on your voyage to Tara Prime. My father suggests that you punch through the defenses covering the Yellowstone Point, then head via Folkestone and New Redeye to Tara Prime. He's been establishing a blocking choke-point at Maben."

"I see," Roman said. On paper, it was good... but leaving the other fortresses at Marble would allow them to send messages through the Asimov Points to Tara Prime. If the whole scheme was an elaborate trap. Admiral Vincent would know precisely where to find his fleet when the time came. "And then?"

"You enter Tara Prime and my father joins you," Hannalore said, simply. "He has his loyalists on the entire fleet. Switching sides would be relatively simple. You'd then have ample time to restock, using the supplies at Tara Prime, before proceeding to Howarth and Maidstone."

"And from there, proceed to the Gateway and Sol," Roman mused. It was *very* tempting, he had to admit. Getting through Tara Prime without a fight, alone, would *definitely* be worth just about any price. But there were limits. "It will have to be discussed with the council."

He rose. "I've taken the liberty of having a cabin prepared for you," he said. "The marines will escort you there."

"And you want me to remain there until you have an answer," Hannalore said. She rose and smiled, cheekily. "I do understand."

Roman nodded. It was possible that Hannalore was nothing more than what she seemed, but it was equally possible that she was a spy, that her father was trying to play both ends against the middle. Trying to play games with Marius Drake was risky, Roman knew, regardless of how much the Emperor valued audacity. But, just in case she'd *earned* the rank she carried, he'd take precautions to make sure she didn't see anything that might offer the Emperor a tactical advantage.

"Interesting," Elf said, once Hannalore was out of the compartment. Her voice was very cold. "Just what we've been waiting for."

"Yeah," Roman agreed. "I don't trust her. And I definitely don't have any interest in her."

"Good," Elf said.

Roman nodded. "It might be better to look this gift horse in the mouth."

He looked up as the marines showed Chang Li and General Stuart into the compartment, then motioned for them to sit down.

"You'll want to watch this," he said, keying the console. "I took the precaution of recording the whole conversation."

"Good grief," Chang Li said, once the recording had finished. "Is she serious?"

General Stuart had a different question. "Is she really Admiral Vincent's daughter?"

"Her DNA was checked against the code on file," Elf said. "It checks, General. There are some ways to subvert the system, but they require massive genetic modification that would be instantly recognizable, if it was there. I had the marines do a *very* deep scan."

Roman cleared his throat. "It is possible it *could* be a trap of some kind," he said, flatly. "I don't think we can afford to take her message on faith. Emperor Marius could be pulling the strings, making sure Admiral Vincent put forward the right offer."

"He knows you," Elf said, quietly. "He'd know how to make you an offer you couldn't refuse."

"True," Roman agreed, feeling a stab of bitter pain. He'd trusted and respected the older man, even viewed him as a mentor. The thought of watching helplessly as his mentor prepared to kill billions of people still terrified him. Emperor Marius would *definitely* know how to tempt him. "And yes, this *is* an offer we can't refuse."

General Stuart smiled. "Does that mean you're going to marry her?"

Roman shook his head. "No," he said. Better to dismiss that idea before someone tried to talk him into it. "Do *you* want to marry her, General?"

Stuart snorted. "I think not," he said.

"Hah," Roman said. He cleared his throat, loudly. "But can we accept their offer?"

"We have recognized other autonomous governments before," Chang Li said. "But can we allow him to dominate one of the richest sectors outside the Core Worlds?"

"Military necessity commits us to accepting his offer, once we're sure it isn't a trap," General Stuart said, flatly. "The chance of getting through the Tara Sector without having to fight alone is too good to let pass."

"At the price of condemning the local population to slavery," Chang Li pointed out. Her voice was very cold. "We wouldn't be liberating them from their ruler."

"We don't *know* he's a bad ruler," Roman said. He gestured towards the holographic image of Ruthven. "The Federation is still surprisingly popular on Ruthven."

"We don't know he's a *good* ruler either," Chang Li reminded him. "And whatever the merits of his rule, we built our federation on the principles of freedom and self-determination."

"And, if we take those principles as fixed, we have to fight our way through Tara Prime," General Stuart said. "Even if they *haven't* done any improvements to the defenses since the last update, it's still going to be a nightmare."

"That's true," Roman agreed. "Our best simulations agree that we'll lose at least a third of our battle line, merely entering the system."

"And the local population might just overthrow him," Elf said. She smiled as they looked at her in surprise. "You assert that your economic policies lead to economic booms."

"They do," Chang Li said. "It's astonishing what people can do without interference from Earth."

"Well, *yes*," Elf said. She leaned forward. "If we win the war, because of this, Tara Prime will find itself surrounded by systems enjoying an economic boom, purely because of your lack of meddling. I suspect Admiral Vincent will find himself pressured to adopt a very similar political platform, purely out of expediency. And if he doesn't... well, I imagine the best and brightest will soon start leaving the system for good."

"Or we could simply stab him in the back once we win the war," General Stuart added. He smiled, rather thinly. "It isn't as if we owe him anything."

"Keeping our word is important," Chang Li said. "We'd be committed to whatever deal we made until Admiral Vincent is overthrown or otherwise compelled to change his ways."

Roman hid a smile. Did General Stuart intend to discard *him*, too, after the end of the war? It would be hard to blame him, although Roman had no real intention of doing anything beyond taking a ship past the Rim and out into the Beyond. Marius Drake, after all, had turned himself into a monster by trying to run the Federation.

He put the matter aside as he looked down at his hands. "There's no time to send word back to Boston, let alone Nova Athena," he said. The remainder of the council couldn't be consulted in less than two months, perhaps longer. "The decision rests with us. Do we accept or not?"

Chang Li frowned. "I have always hated the idea of making decisions because they're *expedient*," she said. "Because it's easier to do what's *expedient* than what's *right*. But in this case, we don't seem to have a choice. It's take up the offer, while it's on the table, or face a far harder struggle for the sector."

"And perhaps weaken ourselves fatally," General Stuart said. His face darkened as he contemplated the odds. "The Federation still outguns us."

Roman nodded. He had no idea how long it would take Emperor Marius to muster the remaining border fleets — it would be dangerous to thin the naval patrols too much — but the Emperor wasn't a man to let the grass grow under his feet. He'd be straining every sinew to reinforce the Tara Sector, to say nothing of Home Fleet and Earth. And time, in a sense, was on his side.

"So we accept," he said. He made a mental note to demand pieces of information, either from Hannalore or her father, that would help prove their trustworthiness. It hadn't escaped his attention that they wouldn't be able to keep Hannalore as a hostage either. "And advance once the pods have arrived."

"Just in case they're planning something," General Stuart said. "We'll be watching carefully, I assume?"

"Of course," Roman said. With the right IFF codes, he should be able to sneak a ship into Tara Prime before the main body of the fleet arrived. It would help detect any planned ambush before the jaws of the trap could swing closed. "And if this is a trap, we can make sure that Admiral Vincent regrets it."

Chapter Twenty-Two

Matters were not helped, in the final years of the Federation Navy, by a growing corps of spies, informers and political commissioners. The first two made it impossible for anyone to know when a remark would be taken out of context (and used as proof of disloyalty), while the latter ensured that military operations would be dictated by political concerns, often directed by commissioners whose actual military experience was minimal.
—The Federation Navy in Retrospect, 4199

Ruthven, 4102

It had always struck Uzi as ironic, even as he slipped out of the spaceport's shore leave facility and headed towards the city, that planetary cities were almost always the same, at least in general terms. There would be a section of the city that was populated solely by the rich and influential, a slightly-larger section that belonged to the middle-class and a handful of districts that were increasingly poor and crime-ridden. A decade of relative affluence hadn't changed Ruthven's criminal underground at all, Uzi was sure. It had merely driven parts of it underground.

Because humans are still humans, he thought, as he kept walking. *And there's always someone willing to make a fast buck out of someone else's misery.*

He braced himself as he reached the city's boundaries and slipped into the streets, hoping he'd remain unnoticed. Ruthven had slowly come around to *accepting* the rebel presence, even though they hadn't *quite* agreed to commit themselves to joining the Outsider Federation, but the prospect of running into a half-drunk mob wasn't one to take lightly. A pair of idiots might recognize him as a rebel and attack, without thinking of the likely consequences. He'd changed into an unmarked shipsuit before leaving, yet — with interstellar traffic sharply reduced — it wouldn't be hard for someone to deduce how he'd reached the planet. Cyborgs were relatively rare outside the military or the spacer community.

The trick, he reminded himself, was to find someone who could and *would* carry out his orders, without question. A smuggler would be ideal, but he doubted he would find any in the bars, not when a giant fleet was hovering over the planet. Admiral Garibaldi had a certain reputation along the Rim for being the commanding officer who'd sent a colossal fleet to Hobson's Choice, years ago, just to clean up the wretched hive of scum and villainy. Smiling inwardly, he slipped into a bar, ordered a beer and settled back to listen to the surrounding crowd of spacers. His implants were *very* useful at recording their conversation and picking out important keywords. But even so, it took him thirty minutes to locate a possible candidate for his mission.

"Just remember, you have to be sober tomorrow," a female voice said. "We're leaving at 0900 sharp!"

Uzi turned, just enough so he could see the speaker. A middle-aged black woman, wearing a merchant captain's uniform, was lecturing two younger men, both of whom looked to be barely out of their teens. Judging from their shared features,

the young men were brothers — or perhaps half-brothers — and probably quite experienced spacers in their own right. Their ship would be a family enterprise, Uzi guessed. There were thousands of family-owned starships plying the shipping lanes between stars. He took a photograph of the captain with his implants, uploaded it to the local processor nodes and searched for a match. Seconds later, one came back. Captain Shanna Rollinson, freighter captain, proud wife of two husbands and mother of nine children. And also, according to a mark in her file, due to depart for New Moscow the following morning.

And nothing to suggest she might be a smuggler, Uzi thought. *If I ask her to take a datachip for me, will she take it?*

He kept one eye on the captain as he hastily scanned through the other spacers at the bar. It might be better to have two candidates, but who'd be the second? He didn't *have* to speak to a captain, he knew, but in his experience freighter captains tended to get pissy if their subordinates accepted private commissions. It would add a complication he didn't need.

"Now, go get your rocks hauled," Captain Rollinson ordered. "And report back to the shuttle by 2330!"

"Yes, mother," the young men said.

Uzi concealed his amusement as they rose and hurried towards the door at the far end of the bar. Spacer bars were all alike; there was drinking downstairs, an entertainment complex on the middle floor and a brothel on the top floor. Ruthven might be more prosperous than worlds where women entered prostitution *en masse*, but there was probably no shortage of fresh meat for the industry. He wondered, as he rose, if the government was supervising the prostitutes and decided it was highly likely. They wouldn't be able to tax the brothels otherwise.

"Captain," he said, approaching Rollinson. "May I take a seat?"

"It's a free planet," Rollinson grunted. Her voice suggested she was a native of Earth, although it was rather more likely she'd been born on one of the asteroid colonies. "What can I do for you?"

"My name is Jones, Spacer Christopher Jones," Uzi lied. If she wanted ID, he had a couple of fakes he'd picked up from the Outsiders. "I need..."

"I don't have any free billets," Rollinson said, cutting him off. "I'm sorry for whatever got you dumped here, but I can't take you away."

Uzi allowed himself a moment of surprise, then relief. Someone who jumped to the wrong conclusion was often easier to manipulate than someone who reserved judgement, if only because they were too wedded to a particular theory.

"I don't need passage out of here," he said. "I need someone to take a datachip to an import office on Astrid. Are you passing through the system?"

He watched her for a long moment, silently gauging her reaction. A physical datachip, as opposed to an electronic packet, would almost certainly be something the sender wanted to keep concealed. And that suggested... what? A spy? Or a trader, trying to take advantage of changes in local prices? Spacers *were* paid commissions

for up-to-date information on such matters, without risking the wrath of an orbiting fleet.

"We are passing through Astrid," Rollinson said, slowly. "I wasn't planning to stop."

"I can make it worth your while," Uzi said.

He waited, feeling his heart starting to race, as she considered it. Paying wasn't a problem — he'd made sure to get his hands on unsecured cashchips — but there was a certain reluctance to divert her entire ship to Astrid, even though docking wouldn't cost more than a hundred credits for a few hours. And she wouldn't have to go down to the surface. The import-export office was on a station orbiting the planet.

"Two thousand credits," she said, finally. She held up a hand. "And that's the only offer you'll get."

"One thousand," Uzi said, ignoring her last remark. A spacer who refused to bargain was a very odd spacer indeed. "And there may be another reward on the far side."

"Oh," Rollinson said. "Really?"

"Yeah," Uzi said. "I cannot go in person, you see."

He saw the flicker of greed on her face and smiled, inwardly. A message to an import-export office *had* to be something to do with trade prices... and such data was time-sensitive. She could demand another two thousand credits on Astrid and she'd be paid, too. But she didn't know that the import-export company was a cover for ONI. The datachip, once scanned, would be immediately forwarded to Earth.

And she gets it all for herself, he thought. *There's no need to share with her crew.*

"Very well," she said. "Where do you want the message to go?"

Uzi gave her the address, then the first chip. "I should warn you that the encryption is unbreakable without the key," he said. "Trying to access the data without permission will have... unfortunate consequences."

"I will keep my word," Rollinson said, stiffly. She might not get into legal trouble if she took his fee and didn't keep her side of the bargain, but the spacer community would remember, and she'd find it harder to get charters in future. Or she would, if he was a genuine spacer. "And I trust that you'll keep yours."

Uzi passed her a pair of cashchips and waited as she checked the balance. The cashchips were almost completely untraceable, despite the best efforts of the Federation's banking industry. There were too many small banks outside the Core Worlds. Uzi was privately surprised the system hadn't fallen apart years ago.

"Thank you," he said, rising. "My friends will be very relieved to get that data."

And they would, he told himself, as he left the bar. *They have to know about Admiral Vincent.*

Uzi was no stranger to treachery. Betraying insurgent groups that had trusted him was his job, after all. But Admiral Vincent had no *motive* to betray the Federation, save his own wealth and power. It was *disgusting*.

And when the Emperor found out, Uzi was sure he'd make the bastard pay.

He wandered down the street, looking for his second target. Another captain was a possibility, but he would have preferred someone lower on the social scale. Like

it or not, captains tended to draw a great deal of attention from planetary security forces. Rollinson should be fine, as long as she kept her mouth shut at the right time... he was just passing another bar when the door opened and a middle-aged man was thrown out into the street.

"Come back when you've got your stinking paycheck," the bartender called after him, before slamming the door. "And not before."

Uzi almost smiled as he wandered over to help the man to his feet. A spacer — the marks on his uniform identified him as a Spacer Second Class — without much hope of rising higher, not given the stench of booze wafting up from his mouth. It was possible he'd been abandoned on Ruthven — it wouldn't be the first time a spacer was dumped when he proved unable to fit into the crew — but it was equally possible he was having one final bender before returning to his ship.

"You're all right now," he said, keeping one arm supporting the spacer before he could collapse. "Run out of cash?"

"Bastards won't give me an advance on my pay," the spacer said. His thick accent suggested he came from somewhere along the Rim. "Need more beer before we go."

"Oh?" Uzi said. The spacer was so drunk he couldn't think clearly, although he was definitely used to drinking his beer. "Where are you going?"

"Captain wants us to head to Riley before all hell breaks loose and we can't get through the point," the spacer slurred. "Fucking war getting in the way of our fucking profits."

"Soldier boys just want to make everyone else unhappy," Uzi agreed. He helped his newfound friend down the road towards a late-night cafe. A handful of people sat inside, drinking coffee and trying not to look miserable. "When are you going?"

"Two days," the spacer managed to say, after a long period of thought that would have been comical if it hadn't been annoying. "Got to leave before the grand offensive."

Uzi smirked as he ordered two steaming mugs of coffee. The rebels would be unhappy to know that word of the planned offensive had already slipped out — although, to be fair, it didn't take a genius to realize that the fleet *couldn't* stay at Ruthven forever. Someone had probably gone to a bar, got drunk and bragged to an interested audience. He made a mental note not to mention it to the rebels, just to see who spilled the beans first, then watched as the spacer drank his coffee. As he'd expected, the warm liquid helped him sober up.

"There's nothing at Riley for us," he said, finally. "But the captain thinks we can go there."

"I'm sure he has something in mind," Uzi said. He checked his internal datanodes, just to be sure. Riley was a strongly conservative world, dedicated to one of the many religions that had established off-world colonies during the first expansion into space. No booze, no drugs, no casual sex... it sounded hellish. "Are you going to stop at Tara Prime along the way?"

"Probably," the spacer said. "You want to come with us?"

Uzi considered it, very briefly. He'd smuggled himself onboard warships before, back when he'd been serving as a mercenary. It wasn't hard, provided one took the

right precautions... but it would take him away from his duty at the very time he needed to stay close to Senator Chang and General Stuart. The risk of being recognized by Admiral Garibaldi — and he'd done what he could to minimize the likelihood — was a small price to pay.

"No," he said. "But I do have an offer for you."

He produced a trio of cashchips from his pocket and dropped them on the table. "Yours, if you'll do one thing for me," he said. "Take a chip of mine to an office on Tara Prime."

The spacer picked up the first cashchip and stared at it, lovingly. "You are really prepared to pay me a thousand credits?"

"There'll be more at the far end," Uzi said. He had a feeling the office's staff might have something else in mind, but it hardly mattered. The message would reach its destination and that was all he cared about. "And don't show it to anyone else, or you'll have to split the bonus."

"You don't have to tell me that," the spacer sneered. "I've been on starships for years, you young bastard."

Uzi shrugged. The spacer might be drunk as a lord, but he retained enough of his wits to understand the cost of opening his mouth at the wrong time. He wouldn't want to share his unexpected windfall with anyone else, certainly not a commanding officer he disliked. Uzi suspected he wasn't long for the universe, anyway, but again it didn't matter. What was one life against the entire Federation?

"That's good," he said. He passed over the second datachip and a note of the address. A drunk — one who'd learned to function while drunk — shouldn't have any real problems finding the office and reporting in. "Thank you."

"Thank *you*," the spacer said. "You want to go find a girl and have some fun?"

"No, thank you," Uzi said. "I have to get back to *my* ship. The captain's a right asshole."

"As long as he doesn't kick you out the airlock, he's a damn good man," the spacer assured him, taking a final gulp of coffee. "Mine threw me out the airlock naked, but I was too drunk to notice, and eventually they reeled me back indoors."

Uzi resisted — barely — the urge to snort. Unless the spacer was a cyborg, and there were none of the tell-tale signs, he wouldn't survive more than a few minutes in space without protective gear. It sounded more like a drink-fueled hallucination than anything else; he knew, all too well, that some captains could be absolute monsters, but throwing crewmen out the airlock tended to lead to mutiny. Unless the rest of the crew hated the victim...

"You must have been very cold," he said, dryly.

"I've had worse," the spacer assured him. "And now I need to take a leak and then go find a girl."

Uzi watched him stumble towards the toilets, crashing into a pair of empty seats on the way, then paid the waitress and headed for the door. The spacer would be fine, probably; he wouldn't be fool enough to tell anyone about the cashchips *or* the

datachip. And if he spent the next two days getting drunker, his memories would be unreliable anyway.

And now there are two chips on their way out to my superiors, he thought, as he walked through the door and down to the road. *One of them will make it home.*

He pushed the thought aside as he made his way up the road. A handful of drunken men were walking past on the other side, singing a song Uzi vaguely remembered as having been top of the charts ten years ago, before Admiral Justinian had kicked off the civil wars, but it was depressingly clear they didn't know half the words or how to sing. Behind them, a set of women followed, almost certainly prostitutes plying their trade. A couple of spacers would probably wake up tomorrow in hotel rooms and discover, to their horror, that they'd been left with the bill. No one would give much of a damn if they complained.

A hand caught his arm and yanked him into an alleyway. "Give me all your money," a voice hissed, "or I'll cut you."

Uzi almost laughed. The would-be mugger would be in deep shit if the planetary police laid hands on him. Charging thirsty spacers twice the going rate for beer, prostitutes, and whatever else caught their fancy was one thing, but openly mugging spacers was quite another. It would discourage other spacers from visiting, which would cut into the system's tax revenue...

"Don't be a fucking idiot," he said. He yanked the knife out of the man's hand, snapped it in two with augmented strength, and dropped the pieces in the gutter. "Go home and sleep it off."

The mugger stared at him, then turned and fled. Uzi hesitated — for the sake of his own safety, he really should make sure the man was in no condition to talk — then let him go, rather than burying half the blade in his back. Maybe it was a mistake, but the mugger didn't deserve to die.

And besides, he told himself, as he returned to the road, *he may yet cause problems for the rebels.*

Interlude Two

From: *The Chaos Years* (5023)

It had finally begun to happen.

In one sense, of course, Admiral Justinian was the first true Federation Navy officer to rebel against his rightful superiors. In another, Admiral Drake not only rebelled, but *succeeded* in putting himself into power. But both men believed passionately in the idea of the Federation, even if it was a Federation with themselves at the head.

Admiral Vincent — and many other admirals in the waning years — was more concerned with his own power and glory. He was willing to sell the remainder of the Federation to the Outsiders, if they agreed to leave him in control of his sector. There was no bid for supreme power, no attempt to take control of the entire Federation... his goals were strictly limited, even selfish. His rule might be better for his sector, but not for the rest of the galaxy.

But, even as the final cataclysm began to build, Emperor Marius had yet to run out of tricks.

Chapter Twenty-Three

It says something about Admiral Vincent that he underestimated the cunning of Emperor Marius, and overestimated the power of his own hand.
—The Federation Navy in Retrospect, 4199

Earth, 4102

The tiny apartment *stank.*

Rupert McGillivray, no longer a Grand Senator, sat on the bed as he fiddled with the terminal, trying to access the datanet. He'd spent quite a bit of time outside his mansion — his parents had often reprimanded him for leaving their community and wandering through the nearby cities — but he'd been younger at the time, young and healthy. Now, in his second century, his old bones ached and groaned whenever he lay on the bed. He didn't want to *think* about what it might have been used for before he'd rented the apartment.

Too used to fucking servants, he thought, tiredly. If he'd known all hell was going to break loose, he would have taken more precautions. *And too used to not looking after myself.*

He cursed under his breath as the datanet connection broke. Earth was the one world in the Core Worlds where the datanet wasn't smooth, at least outside the government buildings and richer residential areas. The network of datanodes that built up the system on every other developed world simply didn't exist; instead, there was layer upon layer of older systems, going all the way back to the early space age. Rupert had heard, once, that there were even archivists who were constantly trying to track and store data that had been uploaded to the network over a thousand years ago. It was, he suspected, quite possible.

But it's also possible they don't want the proles revolting, he thought, darkly. Earth had been the one place, until comparatively recently, where the power of the Grand Senate could be challenged. The Grand Senate had supplied entertainments on one hand, to keep the masses quiet, and cracked down on any thought of political dissent on the other. *Keeping them from organizing a mass movement would be the first step to keeping the proles firmly under control.*

He reached for his pistol as he heard someone walking down the corridor outside, wondering if he'd have to sell his life dearly. The landlord had taken his money without demur, but Rupert was all too aware that the Emperor would have placed a price on his head. If the landlord recognized him, if the landlord wanted to ensure his rise out of the slums and into a far better place to live, he only had to call the police. And then, there was no shortage of human animals wandering the streets. He might be raped, killed, and eaten by someone who had no idea who he'd been.

And that might be better than what the Emperor has in mind for me, he thought. Marius Drake's increasing instability had been obvious... and it was clear that, whatever Professor Kratman had said to Roman Garibaldi, that it had been enough to

push Drake over the edge into full-blown paranoia and madness. *He won't be satisfied with my head if I fall into his hands.*

He eyed the door as the footsteps grew closer, understanding — finally — the fear that gripped Earth. The door was nothing more than a sheet of plywood. A single kick would bring it down, allowing robbers, rapists and murderers to break into the apartment. Earth's crime rates, based solely on reported crimes, were the highest in the Federation. He honestly didn't understand why the emigration rate wasn't higher. Life on a colony world might be hard, particularly if an immigrant didn't have the money to pay his way to the new world, but it was still better than life on Earth. But, perhaps, the all-pervading fear explained it.

It was easy to pour scorn on the poor when I was in my mansion, he thought, relaxing — slightly — as the footsteps echoed away. *They were nothing more than a voiceless mass.*

It was a bitter thought, but he was too honest to refuse to face it. He'd believed, despite his explorations, that the poor were poor because they *deserved* to be poor, because they did nothing to better themselves. But the corrosive effects of life on Earth, of being dependent on the government and helpless against thugs, wore them down. They were helpless to control their lives. Indeed, they didn't believe they *could* control their lives.

He put the terminal to one side — he'd have to try again later and hope the local processors were feeling more accommodating — and rose, staggering over to the window. His body had been enhanced, before and after his birth, but the cold was still seeping into his old bones, reminding him that winter was coming. He had a nasty feeling he wouldn't survive the next few months, even if he remained hidden from the Emperor's patrols. The cold would kill him as surely as a plasma pulse through the head.

Outside, night was falling over Chicago. Countless people thronged the streets, drained of life. Most of them were men; women tended to hide in their apartments or do what they could to keep themselves hidden. There were no children in sight. A handful of young men strode down the middle of the street, displaying a confidence that had everyone else scurrying for cover. Gangsters, Rupert thought; men who dominated the area, men who had no hesitation in taking what they wanted from the rest of the population. And yet, their lives were nasty, brutish and short. A gangster never knew when he'd be knifed by one of his comrades in a fight over a woman, or killed in one of the endless turf wars between street gangs.

And his life is as worthless to his leaders as the life of a woman on the streets, Rupert thought, morbidly. He couldn't help recognizing the similarity between the Grand Senate and the gangsters. The leaders lived lives of luxury, or what passed for luxury on the streets, while their footsoldiers fought, bled and died on their behalf. *They have nothing to live for, nothing but the certainty of death.*

He wondered, as he stepped away from the window, just how much of the poverty below was the government's fault. The Imperialist Faction had never really cared about Earth, beyond keeping the defenses strong; the Conservative Faction

had merely wanted to maintain the status quo. Only the Socialists had given a damn, and most of *their* leaders had been more interested in power than actually *helping*. Indeed, in some ways, they'd made the problem worse. They simply hadn't understood the beast they'd created.

And now, I may die here too, he thought, as he sat back down on the bed. The landlord had probably assumed that Rupert *would* die in the apartment, that he'd been kicked out by his family when he turned into a burden. Hell, he'd probably assumed that Rupert was only fifty years old, rather than well over a century. *And if I die here, everything I have done will be for nothing.*

It had been *his* decision to back Marius Drake, nine years ago. And it had been *his* decision to support *Emperor* Marius's bid for power. But now... the warning signs had come too late for him to do something about the Emperor's growing madness before the Brotherhood was crushed and broken. All he had been able to do was run and hide...

... And pray that he would still have the chance to make a difference.

℘℧

There was paperwork, Marius had once known, and then there was *paperwork*. The reports and briefings he had to read contrasted with the reports and briefings that could be safely passed on to subordinates. But now he had to read everything, just to make sure he knew precisely what was going on. It was hard, almost impossible, to prioritize, even between intelligence reports from Tara Prime, logistics reports from AlphaCent and personnel management reports from Home Fleet. They all seemed important.

He felt his head starting to pound, again, as he reached for yet another report and skimmed it quickly, looking for the key words. Not one useful damned thing from the Cairngorms Industrial Complex, he noted rapidly, and over fifty pages to tell him so. Production rates were still falling, go-slows were becoming more common... it didn't seem to matter what the workers were threatened with, they just kept slowing down. And the writer spent most of his time coming up with excuses for the slowdown rather than putting forward suggestions for solving the problem. Marius would happily have given him the authority to at least *try* to solve the problem if he'd come up with a possible solution.

I should have him shot, he thought, putting the datapad down. Bad news was one thing, but a lack of optimism was quite another. *And tell his successor not to waste my time.*

Gritting his teeth, he rubbed his forehead, then reached into his pocket and produced the small packet of pills. He needed them, he told himself, as he swallowed two of the grey pills and washed them down with a swig of coffee. The headaches were nothing more than a distraction, a distraction he couldn't allow himself. But, even with the pills, the headaches were growing worse. Frantically, he searched through the small pile of datapads, each one crammed with reports, looking for good news. Surely, there had to be something going his way.

The doorbell chimed. He glanced up, irritated.

"Sir, General Thorne requests an immediate audience," the marine guard said. "Do you have a moment to see him?"

Marius glanced at the reports, then nodded curtly. General Thorne, at least, brought him solutions as well as problems. They might not always be the best solutions, but at least he was *trying*, Everyone else seemed content to have *Marius* come up with the solutions, as if there was no one else with a spark of initiative. And he was *tired* of it. The date he could retire, the date Tiffany and he could walk off into the sunset together, seemed further and further away every time he looked.

"Send him in," he ordered. His stomach rumbled. "And ask the steward to bring us fresh coffee."

The door opened. General Thorne entered, looking surprisingly well turned out for someone who should have been awake for most of the day. Marius felt a stab of envy, remembering the days when he'd been on his command deck for over forty hours at a stretch, then reminded himself sharply that he was no longer a young man. Besides, the drugs and stimulants they'd taken during that battle had nasty side effects. They'd been useless for days after the battle had come to an end.

Pity, he thought. *There just isn't enough time in the world to sleep.*

"Sir," General Throne said. He pulled himself upright and saluted smartly. "I have interesting news."

"Sit," Marius ordered.

He rubbed his forehead, once again. His headache hadn't faded, despite the pills. He cursed under his breath as the steward arrived, carrying a tray of fresh coffee and sandwiches. Tiffany again, he noted, with a flicker of mixed love and irritation. She'd been nagging him to eat — and making sure the staff nagged him too. But there was little *time* to eat. There were just too many goddamned reports to read, orders to issue...

"Very well," he said, as he took his cup of coffee. "What's the interesting news?"

"A courier boat arrived from Tara Prime," General Thorne said. "It was chartered, specifically, by ONI."

Marius lifted his eyebrows. "Go on."

"The courier boat carried a datachip earmarked with a specific code, a code belonging to one of our deep-cover agents," General Thorne continued. "Thankfully, the local branch of ONI couldn't get past the priority codes, so they forwarded the chip to Earth. And *there* it was decrypted. It's both bad and good news."

"I see," Marius said. "And what *is* the bad news?"

"Admiral Vincent has been cuddling up to Admiral Garibaldi," General Throne said. "He approached Garibaldi on New Year's Day with an offer of an alliance."

Marius swore, running through a collection of words he'd learned on his first cruise from the formidable Chief Petty Officer. He'd trusted Admiral Vincent, at least as much as he trusted anyone with two battle squadrons under his command. But then, he'd trusted Admiral Garibaldi too, and Roman had turned on him. Why wouldn't Vincent do the same?

"I see," he said, again. He wanted to take Home Fleet and lay waste to Tara Prime, after snatching Admiral Vincent for cruel and unusual punishment, but caught himself before issuing orders. "And the *good* news?"

"He doesn't know we know," General Thorne said. "The deep-cover agent only found out through sheer luck."

Marius closed his eyes in silent contemplation. If Admiral Vincent *was* trying to play both ends against the middle... it was possible, he had to admit. Roman Garibaldi had always been an idealist — Marius had admired that in him — but Admiral Vincent was more of an opportunist. No doubt he wanted something in exchange for switching sides, or he wouldn't have risked opening negotiations. He could just have surrendered, rather easily, when the rebels flowed into Tara Prime.

"Which leads, I suppose, to the obvious question," he mused. "What does he *want?*"

"Permanent control over the Tara Sector, apparently," General Thorne said. "In exchange for his support, the rebels are to concede the sector to him as a permanent fiefdom. His heirs will inherit it and the will of the people, for what it's worth, will count for nothing. Apparently, the rebel leadership were quite uncertain about accepting the offer."

Marius snorted. In his experience, politicians and traitors saw nothing wrong with going back on their word — or stabbing a former friend in the back — as soon as their friend was no longer needed. Hadn't the Grand Senate tried to kill *him* after he'd saved their collective ass from Admiral Justinian? The rebels, led by a bunch of turncoats, would probably turn on Admiral Vincent after they took Earth, no doubt claiming they were liberating the Tara Sector from a tyrant. Unless, of course, Admiral Vincent was savvy enough to take precautions...

He probably is, Marius thought. *He's not bidding for the whole shebang.*

His face darkened as he contemplated the possibilities. Admiral Vincent had always struck him as an unimaginative sort, but that very lack of imagination might have saved Admiral Vincent from making a bid for empire. Instead of trying to grab Earth and declare himself Emperor — as Admiral Justinian had tried — he merely wanted a sector. Given enough time to dig in, Vincent might well make it impossible for *anyone* to dig him out without expending vast amounts of war material. The rebels might just concede the sector and allow Admiral Vincent his kingdom.

He won't overextend himself, Marius added, mentally. *And whoever wins the civil war will be too exhausted to fight for Tara Prime.*

"He doesn't know we know," he said, out loud. "And we *were* planning to move reinforcements into the sector, to stage a decisive battle..."

He allowed his voice to trail away as he contemplated the possibilities. Admiral Vincent — like Roman Garibaldi — had had plenty of time to place his loyalists in key positions all over the sector and its defending fleet. It was unlikely Marius could count on a mutiny when Admiral Vincent came out in support of the rebels, even though there *were* a handful of deep-cover agents on the Admiral's ships. At most, he suspected, there would be a great deal of confusion, which would render it impossible to defend the sector. The rebels might even take advantage of the chaos to put

an end to Admiral Vincent there and then.

He's sure he can get away with it, he thought. *I don't think he would have taken the risk otherwise.*

"We could move Home Fleet forward, into the sector," he mused. "And then shut Admiral Vincent down before it's too late."

"He might not surrender," General Thorne pointed out.

Marius nodded in irritation. If Admiral Vincent knew — or suspected — that Marius knew what he'd been planning, he wouldn't come quietly. His ships would put up a fight, depleting the supplies Marius needed to fight the Outsiders. And the rebels, presumably already inching down from Marble, would intervene before the shooting came to an end, capitalizing on dissent in his camp. No, Marius couldn't afford to do anything too overt. But, at the same time, he couldn't just *allow* Admiral Vincent to get away with treachery. Losing Tara Prime would make ultimate victory far harder to achieve.

Get the fleet to Tara Prime, he thought. *Invite Admiral Vincent to board my flagship for dinner and grab him. Then take control of the planet and the system's defenses...*

"There is a possibility," General Thorne said. "I took the liberty of reading Admiral Vincent's file."

Marius looked up, suspiciously. If there had been something in the files relating to possible treachery, he would have noticed. The Grand Senate would certainly not have tolerated a bottom-feeder like Admiral Vincent if it had a reason to doubt his loyalty. God knew they'd had enough problems with Justinian and his ilk. And Vincent, careful which cards he played, might prove a more dangerous threat.

"He had political ambitions, I believe," General Thorne said. "His two eldest children have entered the navy, but his four youngest children were dispatched to Blyton Towers and remained there, despite the... upset."

Marius blinked in surprise. Blyton Towers was, officially, a finishing school for young adults. In reality, it specialized in teaching the kind of manners and deportment favored by the aristocracy. Tiffany had told him that she'd been lucky to escape; the school, she'd said, specialized in turning brains into mush. Admiral Vincent must have hoped to marry his children into prominent families and use their new connections to further his career.

And now he's planning to create his own kingdom, he thought, sourly. *His children will be the highest in the land.*

"We could grab the children," General Thorne said. "It won't be long before he recalls them, I suspect. And then we could use them..."

"Very true," Marius agreed. He smiled, rather coldly. Everyone brought him problems, but only General Thorne brought him solutions. "Snatch the children now, before they can be recalled. And then we will see what use we can make of them."

Tiffany would be appalled, part of his mind noted as General Thorne turned to leave. The thought cost him a pang, which he ruthlessly pushed aside. It didn't matter. All that mattered was preserving the Federation and stopping the traitors before it was too late.

Chapter Twenty-Four

Like all elite groups, the Grand Senate — and the aristocracy that surrounded it — had developed its own manners, its own way of living, that was profoundly alien to the rest of the Federation. Newcomers to the group, be they as illustrious as Admiral Drake or rich as Director Hamilton (CEO of Falcone Corp), found themselves profoundly out of place, their etiquette marking them as newcomers. Even the wealthy, who traded social respect for money, were looked down upon by those born into the aristocracy.

Unsurprisingly, it proved harder for newcomers to replenish the Grand Senate than it should otherwise have been.
—The Grand Senate in Hindsight, 5123

Earth, 4102

"You know how much it costs to come here?" Lieutenant Gartrell asked. "More than I'll make in a lifetime."

Lieutenant Kevin Sanderson shrugged as the aircar approached Blyton Towers, its automated beacon already requesting and receiving permission to land. The school was halfway up a mountain in what had once been Switzerland, surrounded by white snow that cast an eerie sheen over the towering building. A hot zone at the rear puzzled him — his sensors could shed no light on it — until he realized it was a swimming pool. He couldn't help thinking that the students, scions of some of the richest families in the system, had to have easy lives.

"I looked it up," Gartrell added. "The fees for one term here, three months of schooling, are over two *million* credits. And five years ago, before the Emperor, they were over *five* million credits. None of the students here are worth less than ten billion apiece."

"I shouldn't worry about it," Kevin said. He'd loathed the Grand Senate's children as much as the next officer of Senate Security, but the Emperor had killed or exiled the worst of them before folding the survivors of Senate Security into Planetary Security. "The children here... now... are the families of men and women who actually *earned* their wealth."

He tapped a switch on the console and the aircar began to descend towards the roof, where the landing pad was waiting for them. It was hard to be sure, but it looked as though there was no easy way to reach the school *without* using an aircar. There was certainly no road leading up to the walls, no way for the proles in the cities to get to Blyton Towers. Gartrell was right, at least in one respect. No one got anywhere near Blyton Towers without having a shitload of money and political connections.

But there was no point in getting angry, he reminded himself. He'd been lucky enough to escape the lower class ghetto he'd been born and raised in, lucky enough to earn a chance to attend a security training course. It still surprised him, at times, that Senate Security had hired him, but they'd been having a real problem with recruiting enough manpower to handle their duties. But that, at least, wasn't a surprise. There

was only so much abuse one could take without requesting reassignment to an easier station, signing up for a tour of duty on the Rim, or going mad and brutally murdering one's charges. Indeed, he had a feeling he'd only won the position because he'd scored highly when he'd been assessed for self-control.

The little shits who tormented me are now on Paradise, he thought, as the aircar touched down on the landing pad. *And now they have to work for themselves. They probably think they're in hell.*

He glanced back at his three officers. Lieutenant Gartrell was bitter and resentful; he'd bear watching, particularly once they entered the building. Lieutenant Fletcher wasn't much better — she wasn't pretty, but that hadn't saved her from being molested — leaving Lieutenant Garcon as the sole truly reliable officer. He would have preferred to have taken longer to choose his back-up, but he hadn't been given the time. Their orders allowed for no delay.

"I expect you to remember that most of the students in this place have powerful families," he said. "The Grand Senate may be gone, but there're a great many industrialists and military officers who've taken their place. Do *not* lose your temper, whatever they do. Our superiors will not be happy if there's an... incident."

"Little snots deserve it," Gartrell muttered. He'd probably have snapped, sooner or later, if the Grand Senate hadn't been toppled. "Really, sir..."

"These are not *those* little snots," Kevin reminded him, sternly. He'd met a few men and women who'd married into quality, paying out vast sums of money in exchange for a name and an unwanted partner. They'd always struck him as deeply unhappy, as though they hadn't *belonged*. "And we will not be protected if we slap a couple of them around. Do you understand me?"

"Yes, sir," Gartrell said, sullenly.

Kevin eyed him for a long moment, then opened the hatch. The cold struck him like a physical blow, but at least there was no snow on the landing pad. He stepped outside, feeling a low warmth emitting from the pad, and led the way towards a door. A wave of heat greeted them as he pushed the door open and stepped inside. Behind him, the others followed. Gartrell, bringing up the rear, closed the door firmly behind him.

"Greetings," a snooty voice said. "Welcome to Blyton Towers."

It was all Kevin could do to keep his face under control. He'd heard that snooty accent daily for five years and he'd grown to hate it. And then, when the Emperor had taken the planet, the accent had vanished. He hadn't realized how deep an impact it had made until he heard it, once again, for the first time in *years*. The speaker, a man wearing a tailored suit, looked bland, utterly unassuming. Kevin couldn't help noticing that he seemed to lack a chin.

"Thank you," he said, reminding himself — firmly — that he no longer worked for the Grand Senate. He might be a small cog, but the Emperor was the unquestioned ruler of Earth — and their orders came directly from him. "Escort us to the headmistress, at once."

"Of course, sir," the man said. "It would be my pleasure."

Kevin had spent more time than he cared to admit in the homes of the great and good — the *former* great and good. He'd expected Blyton Towers to be more of the same — and it was — but there was something indefinably *different* about it. He looked from side to side as they walked through the elaborately decorated corridors, paintings lining the walls and frowning disapprovingly at the proles who had dared to enter the building, yet he couldn't put his finger on it. The handful of students he saw stared at the troopers in surprise, then hurried away as fast as they could. He smiled at their reaction — at least there was fear, if not respect — and then put it out of his mind. It hardly mattered.

"Heh," Gartrell muttered.

Kevin followed his gaze, through a window that opened onto a beach. It was disturbingly lifelike, as if someone had plucked a beach from the tropics and planted it in the middle of the school, but that wasn't what caught his eye. Lying on the beach, wearing nothing, were a dozen girls, sunning themselves in the artificial light. Their bodies were young, healthy, supple and thin; their hair shone under the yellow glow. They looked as though they didn't have a care in the world.

Bitches, he thought, although he knew it was unfair. *They have everything, and yet they're satisfied with nothing.*

He pushed the thought aside as their guide stopped in front of a larger wooden door and knocked, then opened it without waiting for a reply. The office inside looked like something out of the past; the walls were lined with wooden bookshelves, surrounding a real fire in the grate. A large wooden desk dominated the room, with a middle-aged woman sitting behind it and studying the newcomers with a gimlet eye. The dark dress she wore, with a golden broach placed just above her right breast, only added to the severity. Kevin felt a sudden stab of pity for the woman's students, then straightened to attention. The office, he suspected, was probably designed to impress visitors, rather than serve as a workplace. There wasn't a single computer terminal or datapad in sight.

"Good afternoon," the woman said. "I am Madame Grey."

"Lieutenant Sanderson," Kevin said. "I'm here with a warrant from Planetary Security."

Madame Grey's mouth twisted, just for a second, as if she'd bitten into something nasty. She probably had. Blyton Towers had its own security force, according to the files. No outsiders, not even Senate Security, had been allowed to enter. But now there was nothing she could do to stop the intrusion, not when they were backed by the authority of the Emperor himself. If marines could clump through the mansions of the Grand Senators, what was stopping them from smashing down the gates of Blyton School?

"A warrant," she repeated. "And may I ask who it's for?"

"Talia, Kamala, Bill and Andrew Vincent," Kevin said. He removed the datachip from his jacket and placed it on the desk, wondering if she'd bother to check. "Please have them summoned to the office immediately."

Madame Grey opened a drawer, produced a standard datapad and inserted the chip, skimming through the warrant with a surprising amount of care and attention. Kevin wondered, absently, if she would try to find an excuse to deny it, but she had to know it wouldn't get her anywhere. The Emperor had spoken, and that was that. His subjects had no choice but to obey.

"I will call them," Madame Grey said. "Are they in trouble, themselves?"

"I do not believe so," Kevin said, finally. They *hadn't* been given specific orders to treat the kids as potential criminals, merely take them into custody. "But I don't know for sure."

"Then please don't drag them through the school in cuffs," Madame Grey said. "It would only humiliate them upon their return."

Kevin bit down a hot flash of anger. Anyone arrested in his hometown would have been marched off in cuffs, even if it had been for non-payment of debts rather than "harmless" little pranks like rape, murder or child abuse. Indeed, anyone guilty of not paying their debts was more likely to be arrested than someone guilty of a far more serious crime. The little brats in the school didn't deserve any special treatment. He could cuff all four of them and no one would give a damn...

But they were young, he reminded himself, and there was nowhere to run.

"As you wish," he said. He wondered, absently, if Madame Grey would go so far as to have the corridors cleared, just to make sure no one knew what was happening. "Please call them now."

Madame Grey tapped the broach on her chest. "Sophie, please call Talia, Kamala, Bill and Andrew Vincent to the office," she said. "And then inform their housemothers that I will speak with them after classes."

She tapped the broach again, then looked up. "Do you have any idea when they will be returned?"

"No," Kevin said. "We're just the messenger boys."

He waited, counting the minutes in his head, until the door finally opened. He'd seen pictures of the four children, but he had to admit that Talia and Kamala — their father had named them after great naval heroes — looked prettier in person. Talia, at eighteen, still had the aura of innocence that so many slum children lost before they were legally adults, something her teachers would have tried to hone. But then, her father had presumably intended to marry her off to an older man. He didn't seem to have realized that the universe had changed.

"Madame Grey," Talia said. Her voice held the same damnable accent, but lacked the entitlement or self-righteousness of someone born into the very highest levels of the aristocracy. It was almost pleasant. "You summoned us?"

Kevin cleared his throat. "Talia, Kamala, Bill and Andrew Vincent," he said. "By direct orders of the Emperor, we are taking the four of you into custody. I must inform you, here and now, that while you are not technically under arrest, you are obliged to cooperate with us until you reach your final destination. Should you misbehave or attempt to escape, we will use all necessary force to keep you under control. There will be no further warnings."

Talia stared at him in shock. Beside her, Kamala's eyes rolled upwards and she slumped to the floor in a faint. Kevin resisted, barely, the urge to kick her. He'd seen too many High Society girls pretend to faint to allow himself undue concern. The two boys looked equally stunned and angry, bunching their fists as if they wanted to throw themselves on the officers, even though they had to know it would be futile. None of the students were taught how to fight.

Wouldn't want them fighting off their partners, he thought, coldly. *No one cares about their happiness in marriage.*

He knelt down and checked Kamala, then twisted her nose. She yelped in pain, then sat upright, her dark eyes burning with sullen resentment. Kevin snorted — it had been a pretty pathetic attempt to fake a fainting fit — and helped her to her feet. The look in her eyes told him he'd better keep a close eye on her.

"There isn't anywhere to run," he said, patiently. Better to make their position clear to them, regardless of their feelings, than run the risk of chasing them all over the school. "Please cooperate, or we'll have to carry you through the building."

He glanced at Madame Grey. "Thank you for your assistance."

"The school's lawyers will be in touch," Madame Grey informed him, tightly. "We do not appreciate visits from outside security forces."

"I would advise you to save your money," Kevin said, "but I think you won't listen to me."

He glanced at the four children. "Come with us."

Talia gave him a nasty look, then accompanied him through the door and down the long corridor. Kevin could hear her three siblings following them, with his officers bringing up the rear. The corridors were almost deserted, but as they passed a classroom all eyes turned to follow them. He couldn't help thinking, as the students began to chatter in unison, that it would have been *less* striking if he'd cuffed all four of them and carried them out.

Maybe we should have insisted on the corridors being cleared, he thought, as more and more students appeared. It didn't *feel* like a brewing riot — most of the students would be sheep, rather than wolves — but he tensed anyway. The Emperor would not be pleased if they accidentally hurt or killed the child of one of his supporters. *We need to move faster.*

Andrew bolted, suddenly. Kevin had no idea where he thought he could go — there was no way to leave the school and, if necessary, Kevin could have called for reinforcements and swept the school from top to bottom — but it hardly mattered. Lieutenant Fletcher gave chase, her legs pumping madly as she ran the teenage boy down and tackled him. Andrew hit the carpet, face-first; Kevin heard a crunching sound that suggested, very strongly, that he'd broken his nose. Lieutenant Fletcher produced a pair of cuffs from her belt, secured Andrew's hands behind his back and yanked him to his feet. A trail of blood, dripping from a twisted nose, confirmed Kevin's impressions.

"The silly bastard is in shock," Lieutenant Fletcher said, as the students drew back.

Anyone would think they hadn't seen *blood* before. "You want to do something about his nose?"

"We'll deal with it in the car," Kevin said. "He'll survive until then."

He glanced at Gartrell and Garcon, who'd grabbed Kamala and Bill respectively. Judging from the look on Kamala's face, Gartrell had taken advantage of the situation to cop a feel as well as keep her from running. Making a mental note to tear a strip off him later, Kevin led them the rest of the way towards the aircar. Thankfully, the remaining students kept their distance, staring in horror rather than doing anything stupid.

We'll have to work hard to put a positive spin on this, Kevin thought, as they walked through the cold to the aircar. Andrew was shackled in the rear of the vehicle; the others, somewhat to his relief, showed no inclination to fight. *Breaking someone's nose would be meaningless down below, but here...*

Talia cleared her throat as Kevin started the drives. "Sir... where are we going?"

"The Presidential House, at least at first," Kevin said. It was annoying that Gartrell hadn't realized the implications. The Emperor might be annoyed at his behavior. "And then... I don't know."

He took the stick and steered the aircar up into the sky, allowing the children to take one last look at the towers below. It was unlikely they'd ever be allowed to return, even if they were released tomorrow. Madame Grey clearly hadn't liked the idea of anyone bringing political entanglements into her school.

"Why?" Talia asked. Her accent seemed to have vanished completely. "Why us?"

"A very good question," Kevin said. He had a theory — the files had made it clear that the four children were related to Admiral Vincent — but he didn't know for sure. As annoying as Andrew had been, there was no point in worrying them. "I dare say you'll find out when you get to your destination."

He checked the autopilot as the aircar picked up speed. They'd be there in a couple of hours, barring accidents. It was annoying — he would have preferred to switch to a bigger vehicle — but there was no room for 'accidentally' misinterpreting his orders. Someone clearly wanted to keep matters as quiet as possible.

Ours not to reason why, he thought, as he settled back in his chair. *Ours merely to carry out orders and hope for the best.*

Chapter Twenty-Five

In retrospect, Admiral Vincent's power-grab seems to have been a catalyst for Emperor Marius's final mental and physical decline.
—The Federation Navy in Retrospect, 4199

Earth, 4102

Tiffany wasn't quite sure when Marius had returned to their suite. She'd waited up for him as long as she could, then climbed into bed, hoping he'd disturb her when he arrived from the office. He was always better, always more like his old self, after they made love... or even after a massage. But when she'd woken the following morning, he'd been lying on the couch in the living room. He hadn't come to bed at all!

"You'll have to eat something," she said, as he sat up. She was wearing one of her special nightgowns, a wisp of silk that concealed nothing, but he wasn't even *looking* at her. Hell, he hadn't climbed into bed with her, now that he knew she was awake. "When did you last eat?"

Marius shrugged.

Tiffany eyed him for a long moment, then called the steward and ordered a full-sized breakfast for both of them. She expected an argument, she expected to have to practically force-feed him, but Marius ate with surprising gusto. His body knew it was hungry, even if his mind refused to bow to the necessities of living. Or, judging by the sudden change in behavior, something else was preoccupying him.

"There's going to be a full meeting of the cabinet this morning," Marius said, as he finished the last piece of bacon and wiped up the remains of the fried eggs. "You are, of course, expected to attend."

Of course, Tiffany thought. She'd had the impression, over the last few months, that Marius didn't care if she attended or not. He hadn't forced her to leave, but he hadn't solicited her opinion either. *And what is this about?*

She watched him carefully as they showered and dressed. Marius looked normal, suspiciously normal. She couldn't help thinking he looked like a man who was patiently waiting for his opponent to discover the booby trap, even though she wasn't sure just who he considered his enemy. Had he turned against her? She doubted it, although she suspected that Marius knew how to dissemble. He'd survived ninety years as a naval officer before becoming Emperor, after all.

"You look good," Marius said, as she showed off her dress. The long green outfit clung to her body and showed off her hair to best advantage. "Shall we go?"

Tiffany smiled as she took his arm, though it bothered her. Marius had said she was beautiful when they'd become partners as well as husband and wife, but he hadn't really seemed to notice her or anyone else when he'd returned from Nova Athena. Oslo had said the pills he was taking caused impotence, as well as a number of other side effects. Marius might not be *quite* impotent, but he wasn't paying much attention either. She kept her worries to herself as they walked through the corridor

and into the conference room. Somewhat to her surprise, there was fresh coffee and cakes on the table.

He's acting more like his old self, she thought, as Marius let go of her arm and pulled a chair out for her. *Why does that bother me?*

She said nothing as the rest of the seats started to fill. General Thorne, looking like the cat that ate the cream; Comptroller Tully and Larimore Hammond, both looking worried; General Maringa and Admiral Singh, their expressions schooled into masks that revealed nothing. And, at the rear of the table, Ginny Lewis. Tiffany caught her eye and winked, even though she knew it was risky. They hadn't been able to find much time to talk since New Year's Day.

"Ladies and gentlemen," Marius said. He *sounded* like his old self too, but there was a harder edge that worried her. "This may turn out to be a long meeting, so feel free to eat, drink, and request breaks to go to the head."

There were some smiles, but Tiffany couldn't help thinking that too many members of the cabinet looked concerned. The only one who didn't was General Thorne. He had regular private meetings with Marius, Tiffany knew all too well. What had the two of them cooked up together?

"Major Jackson," Marius said. "Perhaps you could tell us what your agent reported?"

Major Jackson shot General Thorne an unreadable look, before leaning forward. "The basics of the report, sir, were that Admiral Vincent is planning to switch sides, in exchange for being recognized as the undisputed ruler of the Tara Sector. It would seem the rebel leadership is planning to accept this offer, assuming that Admiral Vincent keeps his word and allows them to pass into Tara Prime without delay. Our agent, sir, noted that the rebels would definitely *prefer* to avoid tangling with the defenses of Tara Prime."

"So they would," Marius agreed.

Tiffany stared at him. If the betrayal of Roman Garibaldi had been enough to tip Marius into a fit of rage, why wasn't he so angry with Admiral Vincent? She knew enough about the military situation to understand that Admiral Vincent switching sides would open up a chink the defenses, allowing Roman Garibaldi to bring his fleet to AlphaCent before he encountered anything that could stop him from proceeding further. And yet Marius seemed almost *amused*.

"I think you can all understand why this has the potential to be massively disruptive," Marius continued, after a long moment. "But ah... *we* know and *he* doesn't know *we* know. We can turn this to our advantage."

He sat back, pressing his fingertips together. "It is, I admit, a situation that could turn dangerous with frightening speed," he added. "My first thought was to recall him, but without a valid reason, he was quite likely to smell a rat. And then I thought about sending out another fleet, yet his people would probably resist any attempt to winkle him out of his orbital fortress. The rebels might force their way into the system while we were fighting yet another civil war. It looked as though our best bet was to offer him a *better* bargain than the rebels.

"And then it struck me. Admiral Vincent has made one tiny, but fatal, error."

His voice hardened. "His youngest children are still on Earth," he said. "And, by all accounts, he loves them."

Tiffany felt her blood run cold as all the pieces fell into place. Family ties were *important*. It was why she'd been married off to Marius in the first place, creating a blood tie that should have kept him from contemplating rebellion against the Grand Senate. And it would have worked, too, if the Grand Senate hadn't decided he needed to die anyway. She knew very little about Admiral Vincent, but threatening a man's children to get him to do as one wanted was horrific...

... And she *knew* them. She'd met his kids, back before Marius had left Earth for Nova Athena. She knew them...

She glanced at General Thorne and knew, with a sickening certainty, just who was responsible for the idea.

"Our original plan was to dispatch three battle squadrons from Home Fleet to reinforce the defenses of Tara Prime," Marius was saying. Tiffany dragged her attention back to him with an effort. "Those forces would have been placed under Admiral Vincent's command. I believe he would have delayed matters long enough for those squadrons to arrive, knowing it would give him a chance to capture an extra twenty-seven superdreadnoughts to strengthen his hand. Instead, I will dispatch seven battle squadrons and take command of them personally. We will not, of course, give Admiral Vincent advance notice of my coming."

"Sir," General Maringa said. "That will leave the defenses of Earth quite thin."

"The remainder of Home Fleet can hold against any reasonable threat," Marius assured him, kindly. "Right now, the major threat is the combination of the rebels and Admiral Vincent's ships. They must not be allowed to pass through the Tara Sector unmolested!"

"Yes, sir," General Maringa said, reluctantly.

"Once I arrive at Tara Prime, Admiral Vincent will be informed about his children and *precisely* what will happen to them if he refuses to do as I say. He will not be given any chance to come up with a plan to warn Garibaldi and the Outsiders, or to come up with a way to evade my orders. Instead, he will invite the rebels forward, as planned, and lure them directly into a trap. The rebel fleet will discover, too late, that they are facing ten battle squadrons and thousands of starfighters."

Tiffany fought to keep her face impassive. She believed firmly in the Federation, she believed in the unity of the human race... but at what cost? Kidnapping *children* and using them as hostages...? What had her husband become? And how far would he go to accomplish his aims?

"They won't be able to avoid an engagement," General Maringa said.

"No, they won't," Marius agreed. "They will, in fact, be allowed to enter the system without being molested. The fortresses covering the Asimov Points will allow them in, as if they were friendly ships. And then the gate will slam closed behind them, trapping their ships at Tara Prime. Even if they set out at once for the system limits, they'll still find it hard to avoid a missile duel."

He smiled at them all. "Once the rebel fleet is smashed, I will detach five battle squadrons to fight their way back up the chain and reoccupy every system as far as Nova Athena. The loyalists will, of course, be rewarded for remaining loyal; the rebels will be put in front of a wall and shot. And once our survey units report the location of the Outsider worlds, we will send units to those systems and scorch the planets clean of life. The threat will come to an end, ladies and gentlemen, in less than a year."

Tiffany couldn't keep herself from shuddering. How many innocent people were about to die?

"Victory in the war," Marius added, "will win us the time we need to rebuild our industrial base, put our economy on a sounder footing, and correct the mistakes of the past. The population of Earth, as riotous as always, will be brought under firm control, with mass emigration encouraged to thin the herd. The contraceptive program will be enhanced, ensuring that the birth rate will be cut sharply. And we will use similar programs, if necessary, to prevent the other Core Worlds from falling into the same trap."

He paused. "Comments?"

Tiffany wanted to ask what he intended to do with Admiral Vincent and his children, once the coming battle was fought and won, but she didn't quite dare. In truth, she wasn't sure she *wanted* to know. Marius might understand the value of mercy, yet he'd watched helplessly as Roman Garibaldi betrayed him. He'd see Admiral Vincent as just another traitor, an asshole who turned on him at the worst possible moment. Admiral Vincent would be lucky if he and his family were merely banished to Paradise, rather than tortured to death and thrown out of the airlock.

"I have a question," General Maringa said. "What happens if Admiral Vincent refuses to cooperate?"

"Then we overwhelm his command fortress as quickly as possible, before the rebels can intervene," Marius said. "I doubt there are many rebel sympathizers amongst them, not when Admiral Vincent will have crammed their ranks with his own supporters. Once Vincent is dead, we'll offer amnesty to any of his supporters who switches sides. After the war is over, they can be scattered amongst the navy or offered settlements on newly-opened colonies."

"There is another concern," Tully said. "My office has been fielding calls from various parents over the removal of Admiral Vincent's children from Blyton Towers. The version of the story they heard was that the kids were brutally beaten, then dragged out of the building and into the snow by their hair."

Tiffany blanched.

"That isn't true," General Thorne snapped.

"That may be immaterial," Tully said. "What matters, General, is what people *believe*."

"No one is going to give a shit about a bunch of rich kids getting a kick up the backside, let alone a beating," General Thorne said. "I assure you that most of Earth's

population would cheer if we threw the little assholes into the arena and told them to fight for their lives."

"But the percentage of the population that *does* believe it, General, happens to include men and women of ability and talent, men and women we happen to need," Tully insisted. Beside him, Hammond nodded. "This is their *children* who reported the whole affair to them."

"Then they should be told that good little children don't tell lies," General Thorne said, coldly. "I can send you the medical report, if you wish."

Tiffany cleared her throat. "Why was there a medical report if there was nothing wrong with them?"

"All of our... clients are given a full medical examination when they enter our facilities," General Thorne said. "It's standard procedure. In this case, we have four little brats, aged fourteen to eighteen, one of whom hit the ground hard enough to bloody his nose. No significant damage, no reason to panic. And, as they're not actually criminals, they're being well treated. I dare say having a chance to drop that repulsive accent is doing wonders for their morale."

"No doubt," Marius agreed. "Is this likely to be a significant problem?"

"Of course not," General Thorne said, before Tully could open his mouth. "Blyton School has outlived its usefulness. Any parent stupid enough to send his kids there deserves everything he gets."

"An attitude they will not share," Tully said. "Blyton School isn't known for strict routine, harsh discipline, or anything beyond teaching children how to behave in High Society. There have been complaints about children being told that they're not to do something, even if it's something actively harmful — or criminal. Apparently, being told not to pick on others is traumatizing."

He looked directly at Marius. "I can reassure them, as best as I can, but it would be better to keep the matter under wraps as much as possible," he added. "The last thing we need is industrialists thinking they're disposable."

"Make sure they receive copies of the medical report," Marius ordered. He cleared his throat, loudly. "Is there any other business?"

No one said a word. Tiffany looked at him and then around the table, wondering who would show the nerve to question his decision. But Thorne had probably thought of the idea in the first place, Jackson, Singh and Maringa understood the danger of Admiral Vincent switching sides, Tully and Hammond were too exposed to risk an open disagreement with a tyrant and Ginny was far too junior to open her mouth without a direct invitation to speak.

And I can't disagree with him, not openly, she thought. Her father had made her attend enough classes on how to be a good wife. *A man hates being contradicted by his wife in public.*

"Then we will hold one final meeting before we depart," Marius said. "Dismissed."

He rose. Tiffany followed him, feeling numb. She understood the realities of the universe far better than many of the girls she'd known in High Society, but...

Dear God, she thought, as Marius led the way into their suite. *I don't love you anymore.*

It was a chilling realization. She'd thrown her lot in with Marius, at least in part, because she had nowhere else to go. Her family had sold her to the Grand Senate for a pittance, for the confirmation that they were still important... Marius had been kind to her and she'd loved him for it. But now, he'd crossed the line. She wasn't naïve enough to think that peace could come without bloodshed, that the Federation couldn't be reunified without a fight, yet there were limits. Her husband — and General Thorne — were planning mass genocide. And while the millions who'd been casually sentenced to death had no faces, she could imagine the faces of Admiral Vincent's children.

"We can win this," Marius said, once the door was closed. He swung around, took her in his arms and kissed her with his old fire and passion. "The war can come to an end."

Tiffany almost pushed him away. A day or two ago, she would have wanted it, demanded it... now, she hated the thought of touching him. And yet, she knew she had no choice. He might be hurt if she refused him, he might lash out... or he might ensure she had no chance to do something, anything, to stop his plans. She could kill him, she reminded herself as she pressed her lips against his, but the result would be chaos. The Federation *needed* someone in place to take control.

At least I was taught how to fake it, she thought with grim amusement. His hands tore at her dress, pulling it down and allowing her breasts to bob free. *And he won't be able to tell the difference.*

Afterwards, she held him tightly as she contemplated her options. "Are you going to leave me on Earth?"

"Someone has to remain in charge of the planet," Marius said. "And you did a good job before."

Tiffany felt sour. She would have given anything, one day ago, for such honest praise.

"I would prefer to come with you," she said. She'd been advised to be subtle — she'd been told it was better to manipulate a man into deciding to do whatever you wanted him to do — but she wasn't sure how. "I've handled negotiations for you before and these... these will be the most complex and vital negotiations of your career. One mistake, and Admiral Vincent will turn on you."

Marius gave her a long considering look. Tiffany held herself still. Marius was easily three times her age and an experienced naval officer, old enough to know how to read people. Did he suspect her loyalties, now? Or was he so short on trustworthy people that he couldn't decide where to leave her?

"Very well," Marius said, finally. "You'll come with me."

Tiffany kissed him, gently, and then headed for the shower...

... Trying, all the while, to think of a plan.

Chapter Twenty-Six

Timing was everything, of course. The cursed time-delay between systems, as always, messed up the very best of plans.
—The Federation Navy in Retrospect, 4199

Marble, 4102

"The scouts have returned, sir," Lieutenant Thompson said.

"Download their readings and put them on the display," Roman ordered.

He leaned forward as the Marble System appeared on the CIC's display. Hannalore Vincent's briefing hadn't been inaccurate, he noted; the system's defenders had established powerful defenses around the Astrid Point, as well as smaller defenses around the Yellowstone and Harper Points. The McQueen Point didn't seem to have received anything like as much attention, but it was a *cul-de-sac*. There was little point in wasting resources guarding a system that had little worth taking, let alone no strategic value.

"They're going to see us coming, sir," Lieutenant Thompson said.

Roman nodded in agreement, feeling oddly uncertain how to proceed. If Hannalore was telling the truth, if her father could be trusted, they could proceed through the Yellowstone Point to make their way to Tara Prime. And yet, every instinct called for him to go through the Astrid Point instead, shortening the journey down to two transits. Speed was vital, after all, particularly if Admiral Vincent wasn't as trustworthy as they hoped. But, at the same time, he did know the defenses of Astrid and Maben were strong. Battering them down would cost his fleet dearly.

"And they're going to have plenty of time to send an alert up the chain," he agreed. "Are there any starships on duty?"

"A squadron of destroyers, sir," Lieutenant Thompson said. "There's nothing else."

"That you can see," Roman reminded her, absently. Admiral Vincent could hide a thousand cloaked superdreadnaughts within the vastness of the system and, as long as their crews were careful, there'd be no hope of seeing them until it was too late. "But they'd be wary of making a fight for Marble."

He scowled as he studied the display. He'd been taught, time and time again, that trying to be clever was a good way to lose the battle. Admiral Vincent, assuming he was untrustworthy, would understand the dangers as well as himself. And if he was trustworthy, there was little to lose by following his suggestions. But then, Roman knew all too well, there was something to be said for trying to be clever, if only because the enemy wouldn't expect any flexibility. Orthodox naval tactics really consisted of nothing more than finding a target the enemy had to defend and charging at it.

There's no way to keep the alert from heading up the chain, he thought, grimly. *And there are too many loyalists in Astrid and Maben who will try to make a fight of it. Or so we've been told.*

He cursed, not for the first time, the true nature of a civil war. No one could be relied upon, not even the most loyal and faithful of crewmen. Admiral Vincent's officers would fight to repel the Outsiders, he was sure, or a marauding alien fleet, but would they fight *him*? Or would they turn on their superior instead, when *he* tried to surrender? It was impossible to be sure which way people would jump when push turned to shove.

But if there's no way to prevent them from sending a message up the chain, he added mentally, *we have no choice but to live with it.*

"Order the fleet to prepare to head for the Yellowstone Point," he said. "The defenses of the other points can be left to die on the vine."

"Aye, sir," Lieutenant Thompson said.

Roman nodded to himself, slowly. Unless the defenders wanted to repeat his trick of pushing their fortresses through the Asimov Point — a trick that had cost him two out of four fortresses with the others heavily damaged by the stresses of transit — they'd be irrelevant to the overall war. There was nothing to be gained by killing thousands of crewmen who couldn't harm him, no matter how loyal they were to the Emperor. And he would be damned if he allowed himself to turn into a mass murderer on the bloody road to Earth.

"We'll depart in one hour," he added. "Until then, continue to monitor the situation."

He rose and stalked through the hatch, heading down to the guest suite. It was unlikely in the extreme that anything *would* happen, as the fleet hovered nearly half a light year from the primary star, well outside detection range, but it made sense to be careful. Roman had heard rumors about *extreme* long-range sensors for years, along with a host of other pieces of technology that had never come into general use. But then, Emperor Marius had once told him that the Grand Senate generally discouraged technological research. *They already ruled the galaxy*, he'd said. *Why take the risk of accidentally inventing something that would completely destroy their power?*

But the Outsiders didn't come up with too many improvements, Roman thought, as he keyed the hatch. There was a low chime, then the hatch hissed open. *The long-range missiles were the only real surprise and it didn't take the Federation more than six months to duplicate them, once we knew it was possible.*

"Admiral," Hannalore Vincent said. "Welcome to my humble abode."

Roman's lips twitched. The Federation Navy, for some reason that was probably buried in the files, insisted on guests being given the very best of everything. Hannalore's suite was huge, large enough for a game of zero-gee soccer. Roman would have killed, when he'd been an ensign, to have such lavish quarters. Or perhaps he would have found them a little disconcerting. During his last year as a cadet, he'd shared quarters with *five* other cadets and considered himself lucky that he wasn't sharing a dorm with ten.

"We're on the outskirts of Astrid now," he said, choosing to forgo any pleasantries. "Are you ready to depart?"

Hannalore rose, the movement drawing his attention to her curves. "I can leave at any moment," she said, cheerfully. "Are you proceeding through the Yellowstone Point?"

Roman nodded, silently giving her points for being ready to leave at a moment's notice. It wasn't common among aristocrats — or civilians. Maybe Hannalore had earned her rank after all. He'd looked her up, in the files, but they hadn't been very enlightening. He'd privately concluded that Hannalore had been assigned to her father's command as soon as she'd graduated, leaving her with no chance to carve out a career of her own.

"We'll be leaving in an hour," he said. "I trust that will give you enough time to make it through the Astrid Point?"

"It should, barring disaster," Hannalore said. "The crews won't bat an eyelid when I return from my inspection tour."

Roman studied her for a long moment. He hadn't met many aristocrats, save for Lady Tiffany and Blake Raistlin — and the latter, of course, had tried to kill Marius Drake. But Hannalore seemed remarkably composed for someone who'd stuck her head in the lion's jaws. Perhaps she had *definitely* earned her rank after all.

"Good," he said. She *was* her father's oldest child, after all. She'd be his heir when the old bastard finally died. He had a feeling he'd be dealing with her several times in the future. "I thank you for coming."

"I dare say my father will be pleased," Hannalore said. "He's quite interested in meeting you, Admiral."

"I'll try and make time to see him once we have the fleet moving through the Tara Prime system," Roman said, as he led the way to the hatch. "But right now our concern is getting to Earth as quickly as possible."

Hannalore followed him through the hatch and down to the airlock, where her courier boat was docked. Roman's technicians had gone over the tiny craft with a fine-toothed comb, eventually concluding that there were no surprises, save for the fact that Hannalore had flown the craft herself, without assistance. It was an impressive feat, Roman had to admit. The couriers practically flew themselves, but being alone in such a tiny cabin could be terrifying.

He keyed his wristcom as Hannalore stepped through the airlock, which hissed closed behind her. "Bridge, this is the Admiral," he said. "Prepare to release the courier boat."

"Aye, sir," Captain Lancelets said.

Roman waited until the courier boat had separated itself from the fleet, then slowly walked back to the CIC. The die was cast now, he knew; they'd be committed to making their slow way to Tara Prime through a route he knew to be predictable. But then, they'd lose the element of surprise the moment the other defenses within the system reported their arrival and transit through the Asimov Point. He considered, briefly, attacking the system's defenses after all, but it wouldn't give them any worthwhile advantage. Admiral Vincent would have New Redeye under observation as well as Maben.

"Admiral," Lieutenant Thompson said. "The courier boat has dropped into FTL."

"Very good," Roman said. He glanced at the display, silently calculating the vectors. It shouldn't take Hannalore more than twenty minutes to reach the system limits, with another four hours to reach the Astrid Point. As long as she didn't alter course, there shouldn't be any real risk of accidentally running her down. "And the fleet?"

"All units report ready, sir," Lieutenant Thompson said. "*Tyrant's Test* reported an unexpected harmonic in her shield generators, but Captain O'Brian insists that his ship is fit for battle."

Roman had to smile. No one questioned the bravery and competence of Federation Navy crews, not now that the Justinian War had burned away a great deal of deadwood, but the Outsiders were practically fanatics. But then, their ancestors *had* been driven away by the Federation, during the Inheritance Wars. They knew, all too well, that Emperor Marius intended to restart surveying and settling the Beyond once he had a few years of peace and quiet to rebuild the Federation. The Outsiders would have to choose between fleeing again, or submitting.

"As long as he's sure," he said. The Federation Navy gave a great deal of autonomy to starship captains, but the Outsiders gave more. "But keep an eye on her, just in case. We don't want to take a superdreadnaught into battle with a faulty shield generator."

He sat down in his command chair, then leaned forward. "Our course is set?"

"Yes, sir," Lieutenant Thompson said. "Least-time course to the Astrid Point."

"Then take the fleet into stardrive," Roman ordered. "And drop us out at the system limits."

Valiant shuddered, slightly, as her stardrive came online, pushing her into FTL. Roman forced himself to relax, even as the fleet dropped back out of FTL, reminding himself that the odds of being detected and ambushed were incredibly low. Even if Hannalore intended to betray them, she simply wouldn't have the time to organize an ambush. Or so he hoped...

"No contacts, sir," Lieutenant Thompson said. "Local space is clear."

"Launch a shell of recon drones," Roman ordered, as the fleet advanced into the system. "I want to know if a single *atom* of dust is out of place."

He leaned back in his chair as the fleet slowly proceeded towards the Asimov Point. There was no attempt to hide — there was no hope of keeping the other Asimov Points from sounding the alert — and so he waited, as patiently as he could, until they slid into weapons range. The Asimov Point was defended by three fortresses and hundreds of mines, but the latter would be more effective against ships coming through from Astrid. He couldn't help wondering if the defense planner was inexperienced, incompetent, or if there was something else involved. There was, after all, little worth fighting for at Marble.

A civilian might have thought the minefield to be a good idea, he thought, dryly. *But an experienced officer would know it was a waste of resources.*

"Send a surrender demand," he ordered. "Inform the fortress crews that they will be treated honorably, if they surrender without a fight."

"Aye, sir," Lieutenant Thompson said. There was a long pause. "No response, sir."

An alarm sounded. "They're locking weapons on our formation, sir," she added. "I think they're preparing to fight."

"Idiots," Roman muttered. The fortresses weren't even the *latest* model — it certainly didn't look as though they'd been refitted since the Justinian War — and even if they had been, they couldn't have done more than delay him. "The Emperor isn't going to be here to save them."

"Yes, sir," Lieutenant Thompson said. She paused. "They may be hoping the minefield will suck up enough of our missiles to give them a fighting chance."

"Then they're idiots," Roman said, firmly. It *might* have worked, if the fortresses had been mobile units, but no missile heads were going to be diverted when they *knew* where their targets were. The mines might soak up a few missiles, he figured, yet the remainder would definitely get through. "Signal the fleet. Open fire."

Valiant shook, violently, as she unleashed a full broadside from her external racks, then her missile tubes. Roman wondered, as the other ships added their own weight to the barrage, if the enemy was trying to convince him to expend his missiles, but he had plenty of time to reload before proceeding through the Asimov Point. And, if there *was* something in the system big enough to fight him, he had more than enough space to evade it while making his way back to the system limits. It would be embarrassing, but better a retreat than a missile duel with a superior force.

He watched, grimly, as the missiles ploughed through the minefield as if it wasn't there. As expected, the mines soaked up a handful of missiles, but the remainder kept going. The fortresses returned fire, of course, yet *they* weren't shooting at fixed targets. And their missiles were definitely second-rate, dating all the way back to the Justinian War. It didn't *look* as though they'd been refitted with the latest ECM, let alone replaced altogether.

Oh, you stupid bastard, Roman thought, wondering just who was in command of the fortresses. *What did your men do to deserve having you as their commanding officer?*

"Direct hits," Lieutenant Thompson reported. "Fortress One has taken heavy damage, sir; Fortress Two has lost power and is spewing lifepods..."

She paused as an icon vanished from the display. "Fortress One has been destroyed, sir," she added, correcting herself. "The minefield is still active."

"Launch minesweeper missiles," Roman ordered, curtly. "And then dispatch shuttles to pick up the lifepods."

He paused, considering. "Try to raise Fortress Two, if you can," he added. "Offer to take their surviving crew off."

"Aye, sir," Lieutenant Thompson said.

Roman nodded, then glanced at the status display. Missiles from the Justinian War had been deadly, once. But advances in defensive technology and point defense rendered them far less dangerous to starships. Hell, merely updating the fire control

sensors had stripped the missiles of half their long-range effectiveness. He was surprised no one had seen fit to upgrade the fortresses, although Yellowstone was far less important than Astrid. It was quite possible they'd run into something far more dangerous before they reached Tara Prime.

Although not if Hannalore was telling the truth, he mused. *Tara Prime is the chokepoint, after all. They might not choose to waste effort fortifying the side-systems.*

"Admiral," Lieutenant Thompson said. "I have been unable to raise anyone on Fortress Two, but the marine shuttles are prepared to try to force a docking."

Roman hesitated. Common humanity called for an attempt to save lives, despite the risk. If there was anyone still alive on the powerless hulk, they'd die when they ran out of air. But, at the same time, they might try to resist, violently, when his men came to rescue them. Who knew what they were thinking?

But they didn't do any damage, beyond forcing us to waste our missiles, he thought. *We'd have no reason to take revenge.*

"Order them to try," he said, finally. "And launch drones into the Asimov Point as soon as possible. I want a clear picture of everything awaiting us on the far side."

"Aye, sir," Lieutenant Thompson said.

Roman settled back in his chair, quietly reviewing the contingency plans he'd made over the last week. Maybe Hannalore and her father were telling the truth, maybe everything would be sunshine and roses once they reached Tara Prime, but he dared not take it for granted. It was quite possible that one of their officers would overthrow them, either out of loyalty to the Emperor or a simple desire for promotion. And then all hell would break loose.

"The drones are returning, sir," Lieutenant Thompson said. "There's nothing on the far side, beyond a minefield and a number of automated weapons platforms."

"Odd," Roman said, out loud. "No covering units?"

"There're no active starships within the system at all, at least as far as the drones can tell," Lieutenant Thompson said. "The minefield is just sitting there."

"Dispatch a handful of assault pods to clear it," Roman ordered. It was *definitely* odd. Every tactician knew that minefields were only reliable if covered by mobile units or fortresses, even when guarding an Asimov Point. "And then ready the first assault units to move through the point. I want the entire area swept for hidden surprises."

"Aye, sir," Lieutenant Thompson said.

Roman nodded, grimly. It had been easier, far easier, when he'd known he could expect nothing but brutal resistance. Now... now there was no way to know who was on what side — and who might change sides, given the incentive. Admiral Vincent *should* have had more than enough time to pack Tara Prime with his loyalists, but what if he'd missed a handful of deep-cover agents?

And if the game was easy, he told himself, as the superdreadnaught inched through the Asimov Point, *anyone could play.*

Chapter Twenty-Seven

And so began a game of treachery, bluff and counter-bluff.
—The Federation Navy in Retrospect, 4199

Tara Prime, 4102

Marius couldn't keep himself from feeling a flicker of grim anticipation as he watched Admiral Vincent's shuttle approaching *Enterprise*. The superdreadnaught, named for the now-defunct supercarrier that had once been the flagship of the Federation Navy, had entered the system through the Asimov Point, followed by sixty-two other superdreadnaughts and over two hundred smaller ships. He had to smirk at the shock the system's defenders would have felt, when they saw the fleet... and, perhaps, the panic running through Admiral Vincent's mind. Sixty-three superdreadnaughts were quite enough to lay waste to the system, particularly if the defenders were having a crisis of loyalty.

But at least he came, Marius thought, glancing at Tiffany. She'd been beside him for most of the voyage, providing what comfort and support she could. *He doesn't know that we know.*

The thought almost made him laugh out loud. If Admiral Vincent knew what *Marius* knew, he would have boarded a shuttle and fled through the Maben Point in hopes of linking up with Admiral Garibaldi before it was too late. Not that it would have worked, of course; he'd have fled to the rebels with nothing, save for his own skin. Admiral Garibaldi would probably have interned him, rather than giving him a command. Unless, of course, he'd managed to take his battle squadrons with him.

"Sir," Commander Lewis said. "The Admiral's shuttle has landed."

"Have him escorted to the briefing compartment," Marius ordered, unable to keep the childlike glee from his voice. He was going to *enjoy* himself, by God. *This* time, the damnable traitor would dance to Marius's tune. "I'll meet him there soon."

Normally, he would have been punctual. The Grand Senate's custom of making someone wait to see you, just because you were more important than your guest, had never failed to annoy him. But this time he waited, knowing it would make Admiral Vincent more unsure of himself. He'd be fretting like a boy sent to see the headmaster, or an ensign facing the captain, before Marius chose to enter the compartment. His uncertainty would make him far easier to control.

He gave it twenty minutes before nodding to Tiffany and leading the way down to the briefing room. A pair of armed marines stood outside, wearing light combat armor and carrying plasma rifles. Marius rather doubted that Admiral Vincent would pose any threat — he was shockingly overweight in a universe where removing excess fat was hardly a problem — but their presence would add to the uncertainty. Admiral Vincent had to be wondering, right now, just what Marius knew, if anything. It was certainly *unusual* for someone to be summoned to the flagship and then made to wait under armed guard.

The hatch hissed open. Marius pasted a smile on his face as he entered, spying Admiral Vincent sitting at the far end of the table. He'd grown fatter since Marius had last laid eyes on him; Marius couldn't help comparing Vincent to an overgrown walrus, complete with a moustache that had been fashionable years ago, back during the Blue Star War. His piggish eyes surveyed Marius nervously as he sat down, with Tiffany leaning against the rear bulkhead rather than sitting down herself.

"Your Majesty," Admiral Vincent said. "Welcome to Tara Prime."

Marius felt his smile grow sharper. *No one* called him 'Your Majesty,' save for people who were either trying to suck up or were desperately unsure of themselves. "Sir" was quite sufficient; besides, being addressed by any honorific would sound unnatural after nearly a century in naval service. And Admiral Vincent shouldn't have any *need* to suck up.

"The rebels are approaching this system," he said, watching Admiral Vincent closely. He'd be as experienced a dissembler as Marius himself, after years spent serving the Grand Senate, but there were limits. "I brought this fleet to meet them."

"Very good, Your Majesty," Admiral Vincent said. Marius could practically *see* the gears moving in his head. "I'm sure the rebels will be defeated."

"And so am I," Marius said. He briefly considered ending the game, then decided to play with Admiral Vincent for a moment longer. "Perhaps you could send a message to the rebels, Admiral. You could invite them into the system, perhaps..."

If he hadn't been watching the admiral closely, he would have missed the sudden twitch of fear, the sudden horrified realization as everything fell into place, leading to a very simple and inescapable conclusion. *Marius knew*. And now, Marius could see, Admiral Vincent was trying desperately to think of a way out of the mess. He had no allies on *Enterprise* and he knew it.

"Oh, cheer up, Theodore," Marius said, mockingly. "I'm not a *bit* angry."

He leaned forward, allowing his teeth to show as the game got darker. "You invited the rebels to enter the system, in exchange for being recognized as king of the sector," he said, flatly. "It was a brilliant move, no doubt, to lure them into missile range."

"Yes, Your Majesty," Admiral Vincent stammered. "I... I... wanted them to be lured into a false sense of security..."

"And you have succeeded brilliantly," Marius said, lightly. "My, you even fooled *me*. Of course, I suppose, allowing the rebels to actually enter the system in battle array could easily have gone wrong. The rebels might have been trapped, but they could fight their way out or carry forward against Tara Prime itself. Still, I dare say seven additional battle squadrons will tip the balance in our favor."

"Yes, Your Majesty," Admiral Vincent said. "The rebels will be trapped, unable to advance or retreat."

Marius allowed himself a moment to savor the dawning hope in Admiral Vincent's eyes, then crushed it as sharply as he could. "Indeed, I was fooled so badly that I actually took your children out of school and brought them with me," he added. "I do trust you're not going to do anything *foolish*?"

Admiral Vincent stared at him. "My children...?"

"Oh, come now," Marius said. "It was really very foolish of you to leave hostages in my grasp while you plotted against me. Did you send a message requesting their return to Tara Prime? Or are you so callous that you're prepared to write off your four youngest children?"

Marius leaned back in his chair. "This is what you are going to do," he said. "You're going to keep in touch with the rebels and do everything you can to lure them into the system. You can even tell them that you'll add your superdreadnaughts to theirs and accompany them to Earth, if you wish. And once they're in the system, you are going to slam the door shut behind them while the battle squadrons move into position to attack."

"Your Majesty..."

Marius ignored him. "If you cooperate, Admiral, you and your family can move to Paradise and remain there for the rest of your life," he said. It was a lie. He didn't really care about the children — let them go to an out-world, if they wished — but Admiral Vincent would *suffer* for trying to betray him. "If you *refuse* to cooperative... well, I imagine you can guess what will happen to your children."

Admiral Vincent blanched. He knew, as well as Marius himself, just what the Grand Senate had done to Admiral Justinian's relatives. And the relatives of the other warlords had been treated in the same way. There were limits to what Marius was prepared to condone, at least to innocent children, but there was no way for Admiral Vincent to *know* that. His imagination would fill in the blanks more effectively than any number of threats.

"You'll go back to your ship now," Marius said. "And you will do everything in your power to lure the rebels into this system."

He paused. "Do bear in mind," he added, "that your children are aboard this ship. If anything happens to *Enterprise*..."

"Please send them back to Earth," Admiral Vincent said. "I will cooperate..."

"I think not," Marius said. "I want them within easy reach."

He met Admiral Vincent's eyes. "There will be no further betrayals, Admiral," he said, sternly. "Fuck this up, and your children will pay the price."

Admiral Vincent wilted. "Yes, Your Majesty," he said. "I will do as you say."

৪৩৪৪

Tiffany trailed behind the two men as Marius led Admiral Vincent to the brig and allowed him, briefly, to speak to his children. Any doubts Admiral Vincent might have had about Marius's willingness to carry out his threats were dispelled by the presence of a pair of Blackshirts eying the teenagers with open interest. Tiffany knew Marius had placed them there to convey the right impression, but it was still horrifying. If everything went as Marius had planned, the rebels would be lured right into a trap and butchered.

She watched as Admiral Vincent was escorted back to his shuttle, then returned to her quarters as Marius headed to the tactical section. Operative Oslo had scanned the compartment and assured her that there were no bugs, although he'd warned her that nothing could be taken for granted. But then, who would dare to spy on the

Emperor and his wife? It was hard to imagine anyone, even General Thorne, having the nerve. She poured herself a cup of coffee — naval coffee tasted foul — and tapped her console. Minutes later, she was joined by Ginny Lewis and Oslo.

"I don't have long," Ginny said. She sounded nervous. Tiffany had sounded her out, as carefully as possible, during the long voyage, but the thought of betraying the Emperor scared her. "I'll be expected back in the tactical compartment in less than an hour."

Tiffany nodded. "How much time do we have?"

"The last update stated that the rebels had moved into the Yellowstone system," Ginny said. "Assuming they don't get slowed down by the defenses at New Redeye, they'll be here in approximately three days. Admiral Vincent, it seems, was making a sincere offer to them."

Oslo frowned. "How do you know?"

"The defenses at the Maben Point are considerably stronger than anywhere else in the system," Ginny said. "They'd be much more effective in trapping the rebels than the defenses at the New Redeye Point."

"I see," Tiffany said. She looked at Oslo. "Can we get the children off the ship?"

"I believe so," Oslo said. "But it will be chancy. The slightest advance warning, My Lady, and the marines would swarm us. And then there's the risk of being blown out of space once we steal the courier boat."

"That shouldn't be a problem," Ginny said. "I can work a macro into the point defense datanet that will keep it from targeting the courier boat. But that won't last long. Once they realize the problem, they'll either set up the firing solution manually or order one of the other starships to take the boat out."

Tiffany scowled. "You can't order the datanet not to *see* the courier boat?"

"I'd need to reprogram far too many critical systems," Ginny said. "And even if I did, the discrepancies would be noted. The datanet is *designed* to combine the viewpoints of hundreds of ships. They'd just assume the flagship couldn't see the courier boat for some reason and target it anyway."

"But if the datanet is linked together," Tiffany mused, "couldn't you block the courier boat out completely?"

"Not now, My Lady," Ginny said. "It might have been possible before the Battle of Earth, but computer security was tightened sharply after Admiral Justinian exploited our weaknesses. The firewalls would notice if I tried to reprogram another ship remotely and sound the alarm. At that point..."

"They'd start trying to find out what was going on," Tiffany finished. She nodded, slowly. "As long as you can give us a chance to break free, Ginny, it will be enough."

Ginny nodded, looking pale. She'd said she thought she could remain undetected — with a little effort, the blame could be placed on a glitch rather than deliberate malice — but Tiffany didn't envy her. Somehow, whatever Marius felt for Ginny, she doubted it would save her life if he knew she'd betrayed him. Or Tiffany herself, for that matter. If Marius was prepared to threaten the lives of innocent children to make their father do as he was told, she doubted he'd hesitate to kill her.

"We'd need to trigger the security alert too," Oslo added. "It would slow the marines down, particularly as they wouldn't know just what we were doing."

"I can set up an override, if necessary," Ginny agreed. "But the real danger lies in breaking the children out of prison. What if they don't come with you?"

"Then we stun the brats and carry them," Oslo said. He looked at Tiffany. "You will be coming with us, won't you?"

"Yes," Tiffany said, flatly. Marius wouldn't have any trouble realizing that her bodyguards had carried out the operation. He'd *know* she was the one who'd given them their orders. No one else could have commanded Oslo to take such a risk. "I'll be right behind you."

She took a long breath. "You don't want to try to move earlier?"

"I wouldn't advise it," Oslo said. "Courier boats are fast, My Lady, but we'd be lucky to get out of weapons range before someone puts the pieces together and opens fire."

"And Admiral Vincent will be in no position to switch sides for real," Ginny added. "The Emperor has a contingency plan to assume control of the system himself, if Admiral Vincent proves uncooperative. He might well succeed in beating Admiral Vincent, taking the system's defenses and *still* beating the rebels. The only hope for victory lies with convincing Admiral Vincent to switch sides... and the only time he can do that effectively is when the rebels arrive."

"Understood," Tiffany said. "Are we ready to move on a moment's notice?"

"Just about, My Lady," Oslo said. "We should have some warning, shouldn't we?"

"Yeah," Ginny said. "But just how much is an open question."

"I'll speak to the girl," Tiffany said. "Can you safeguard the interview compartment?"

"Not for long," Ginny said. "I suggest you speak quickly."

ಬಿಸಿಜ

The suite was a prison cell in all but name.

Talia Vincent sat on her bed, trying not to think about what had happened to her and her younger siblings — and what would happen to them, if their father refused to cooperate. The black-clad guards who kept an eye on them hadn't bothered to lie, when she'd asked; they'd made it clear that the best Admiral Vincent's family could expect, if all hell broke loose, was involuntary transportation to a stage-one penal world where no one knew who their father had been.

And that was the *best* option. Talia didn't want to think about the worst.

She looked up as the hatch hissed open, revealing two black-clad men. The guards always came in pairs, she'd noted, as if they were scared the children would somehow overpower a single guard and break free. Not that there was anywhere they could go, Talia was sure, even if they did. She knew nothing about superdreadnaughts, beyond the simple fact they were on one. Her brothers might talk of stealing a shuttlecraft and escaping back to their father, but none of them knew how to find the shuttlebay, let alone fly a shuttle.

"Talia," one of the men grunted. None of them had bothered to share their names. "Come here, now."

Talia sighed, rose to her feet and stalked over to the guards with all the dignity she could muster, despite the prison outfit she'd been given to wear. The guards looked her up and down, cuffed her hands behind her back and half-dragged her through the door. Talia rather doubted they thought she was a serious threat; instead, she suspected they cuffed her just to make it clear they were in charge. She held herself together, somehow, as they marched her through a pair of doors and into a small briefing room. The Emperor's wife was waiting for them.

"Leave us," she ordered, once the guards had plunked Talia down in a metal chair and snapped a cuff around her ankle. Talia found it hard not to smile bitterly. Escape, already impossible, was now even *more* impossible. "I'll call you when I need you."

Talia frowned as the guards retreated, closing the hatch behind them. The Emperor's wife — Tiffany — had spoken to her a few times, but their conversations had been largely pointless. There was nothing she could do, it seemed, to make their stay more comfortable. Talia wasn't even sure why the older woman bothered, unless it was through guilt or simple boredom. The hostages — the guards hadn't bothered to hide what their status now was — were powerless.

"Listen closely, as I can't stay long," Tiffany said, intensely. "Soon, perhaps within two days, there will be a chance to break you and your siblings free and get you off the ship. When that happens... we need you to be ready to leave."

Talia stared at her. "Really?"

Her mind raced. Was it a trap? But really, why bother? It wasn't as if there was anything to be gained by manipulating her siblings into incriminating themselves. Their only value lay in who had fathered them, not in themselves...

"Yes, really," Tiffany said. "There may be no time to warn you, either. Make sure your siblings are ready to go, but don't say anything out loud. You're being watched."

Talia flinched. "Even in the bath?"

"Yes," Tiffany said. "We can only talk here because my men have buggered the observation routines."

She rose. "Be ready, but be careful," she added. "One false move, and we're all dead."

Talia swallowed. How the hell was she meant to warn her siblings, without having one of them say something that would ruin the whole plan? But she didn't have a choice...

"I understand," she said. If nothing else, at least they had a chance. "Thank you."

Chapter Twenty-Eight

The core problem with trying to be clever, as naval cadets have been taught since time out of mind, is that an unimaginative enemy tends to be better prepared than one gambling everything on a cunning plan. One doesn't have to look any further than Admiral Baldric's defeat at the Battle of New Wellington to grasp the principle that trying to be clever can sometimes be really stupid.
—The Federation Navy in Retrospect, 4199

New Redeye/Tara Prime, 4102

"You've been rather quiet, recently."

Uzi groaned, inwardly. If there was one thing he'd noted about women, particularly after he'd been sleeping with them for a few weeks, it was that they wanted to talk about everything. Their problems, his problems, someone else's problems... it never seemed to occur to them that there were times when all a man wanted was sex and sleep, perhaps not in that order. Honestly, how could someone who'd reached the rank of lieutenant in the Outsider Navy — where there was almost no nepotism to speak of — be so stupid?

"It's just the new responsibilities," he lied, as he rolled over. Cleo Pearlman should have been more understanding, now she'd been assigned to *Valiant* as one of the embedded tactical analysts. "I feel a little out of place."

"You're doing fine," Cleo assured him. "The Senator hasn't kicked you back to the infantry, has she?"

Uzi shook his head, crossly. In some ways, being sent back to the infantry would be a blessing. He'd done what he could to change his appearance, without making it obvious, but there was still a very good chance of being recognized by Admiral Garibaldi or his marine lover. The bitch had sparred with him, once or twice, back when they'd been on *Midway*; she might recall his face. Indeed, if he hadn't been so keen to stay on the flagship, where there was a chance to do some real damage, he would have pulled strings and convinced General Stuart that a mercenary made a very poor bodyguard.

It's not like the Mercenary's Code is still in operation, he thought, mischievously. *And if it was, who's going to enforce it?*

"Besides, you're on a starship," Cleo added. "What sort of threats does she face?"

"Incoming missiles," Uzi said. He could have told tales about disloyal starship crews that would have turned Cleo's hair white, but there was no point in giving her ideas. "And enemy starfighters."

"Neither of which you can do anything about," Cleo pointed out, seriously. "Why not just relax and enjoy yourself?"

"Because I feel I need to be doing something," Uzi said, after a moment. It wasn't entirely true, but it *was* part of his established personality. He'd worked hard to make it clear that he would *keep* working hard, that he needed to keep doing *something* all the time. "Just lying around doing nothing drives me insane."

"You're not doing nothing," Cleo pointed out. She traced a line down from between her breasts to her legs. "You just made me very happy."

"Glad to hear it," Uzi said, stiffly.

"Tell me," Cleo said. She rolled over and climbed on top of him, her bare breasts dangling over his face. "What do you want to do after the war?"

Uzi groaned inwardly, again. He felt nothing for her. How could he? His life amongst the Outsiders was a sham, a tissue of lies built to cover his presence as he waited for the chance to strike. He could kill her, as easily as one might step on an ant, without feeling the slightest shred of remorse. The idea that they might have a future together, after the shooting was done, was absurd. Even if the Federation died, he knew he'd never be able to settle down and relax.

"I don't know," he said. It was honest enough; besides, he knew the danger of telling too many lies. "I like to fight, you see. I was kicked out of the service for fighting."

Cleo snickered. "And to think they *paid* you to fight."

"They did," Uzi confirmed. The cover story had held up to whatever scrutiny the Outsiders had focused on it, thankfully. He'd be dead if they had the slightest reason to suspect his true nature. "They just thought I wasn't fighting the right people."

He smiled, allowing her to see his teeth. His record, a carefully-crafted mixture of truth and lies, made it clear he'd been kicked out for picking fights with other service personnel. It was true enough, after all; it just didn't mention that he'd been recruited by ONI, which had falsified the dismissal to ensure no one questioned why he'd become a mercenary.

"I'd probably go back to the Rim and find someone else to work for," he added. It was what he'd *done*, after all, although in reality he'd taken control of resistance movements so they could be wiped out by the Federation Navy. "There are never any shortage of wars along the Rim."

Cleo raised her eyebrows. "You don't want to settle down?"

"I'd get bored," Uzi said. "There's nothing to do along the Rim, but farm, fuck, and raise a dozen children. I just don't have the patience to settle down and have a family."

He watched her, wondering absently just what she'd do. Slap him? Run off in tears? Or merely remind herself that neither of them had any guarantees of surviving the coming months? Whatever happened at Tara Prime wouldn't put an end to the war. Even if Admiral Garibaldi and Admiral Vincent completed their betrayal of the Emperor, the fighting would go on until Earth lay in ruins.

"You might think better of it, after you've had your fill of killing," Cleo said. "What do you fight *for*?"

Uzi pushed her off him, then rolled over and straddled her. "I'm a mercenary," he said, smiling down at her. "I don't fight for anything, but money and the thrill."

He kissed her, feeling a flicker of amusement as she tried to regain control by pulling him closer. It *was* a diversion, after all, and one he needed. Losing control now, so close to his targets, would be a dangerous mistake. And he might well have said too much. Cleo might think she could change him, or she might find his mercenary

status exciting... or she might start to wonder, deep inside, if he'd change sides on a whim.

Never get too involved, he reminded himself, as he spent himself inside her. *It makes it harder to do the job.*

Afterwards, he lay beside her, thinking hard. He hadn't expected a reply from ONI, not given the way he'd sent them the encrypted datachips, but it was frustrating. There was no way to know what was happening on the other side of the Asimov Point. No one had tried to fight the fleet, either, as it passed through Yellowstone and Folkestone. Uzi couldn't decide if Admiral Vincent had succeeded in his betrayal, which would be bad enough, or if the Emperor was setting a trap. There might *just* be enough time for the Emperor to do something about the treacherous bastard before it was too late.

And if it isn't enough, I may have to do something on my own, he thought. *And that will mean the end of my time here.*

†††

"No opposition," Roman said. "The system appears to be undefended."

He scowled, inwardly. A plan that worked well was one thing, but a plan that worked *perfectly* was suspicious. The defenses of Yellowstone had been wiped out within seconds, the pair of outdated fortresses covering the Folkestone Point had surrendered, without even trying to launch drones or send a message further up the chain to Tara Prime. And now the New Redeye system had surrendered the moment his fleet took possession of the Asimov Point.

"The records did say there were no defenses on this side of the Tara Prime Point," General Stuart pointed out. "Were you expecting that to change?"

Roman frowned. New Redeye wasn't Ruthven, let alone Tara Prime, but she did have a population of over two *billion* humans. Given the Outsider threat, reinforcing the defenses would have made a great deal of sense. But then, New Redeye might also have ideas about autonomy that Tara Prime wouldn't want to encourage. How long had Admiral Vincent been planning his bid for independence?

"It just bugs me," he said. He glanced up at the display. The fleet was advancing slowly towards the Tara Prime Point, where it would make the jump into Tara Prime itself. "It's going too well."

"The Admiral *is* meant to be clearing your way," General Stuart said. "And who in their right mind would put up a fight with outdated fortresses?"

"The defenders of Marble," Elf said. "Rock can beat laser, in the right situation."

"True," Roman agreed.

He scowled up at the display. There was nothing, as far as they could tell, barring their path to Tara Prime. And there had been nothing in either of the two preceding systems. It was possible, he supposed, that someone could race from Tara Prime to Marble, then follow them back through Folkestone to take them in the rear, but it would be a plan that relied on too much going perfectly. None of the other options he'd considered were any more workable, even when he'd discounted the normal limitations.

If there's a trap, it's waiting for us in Tara Prime, he thought. *And if there isn't a trap, we're being paranoid.*

"Detach two squadrons of battlecruisers with orders to probe the Asimov Point," he ordered, carefully. "Once they report back, we'll move the remainder of the fleet closer, secure the point, and then advance through as planned."

"Yes, sir," Lieutenant Thompson said.

"And then, once we have secured the point, I want to leave the battlecruisers behind, along with a stockpile of assault pods," Roman added. "It's time to make sure we can take a few precautions."

"Yes, sir," Lieutenant Thompson said.

Roman nodded, slowly. Maybe he was being paranoid, but even paranoids had enemies. If it was a trap, he promised himself silently, he'd make sure that Admiral Vincent would regret it. But then, what did Admiral Vincent gain? Emperor Marius would never condone the autonomy of an entire sector, certainly not one in such an important position. Albion had never been particularly important to the Grand Senate.

And are you reasoning like this, he asked himself, *because you want to believe you can secure Tara Prime without fighting... or because you don't want to believe you're being lured into a trap?*

"I want you on your superdreadnaught at least an hour before we reach the Asimov Point," he said, addressing General Stuart. "You may need to take command if something goes wrong."

"Aye, sir," General Stuart said.

Roman looked at Chang Li, then shrugged inwardly. She'd flatly refused his suggestion that she should remain behind at Ruthven, despite the prospects for luring the planet into joining the Outsider Federation. Roman had to admit she had nerve, for a politician. Emperor Marius had *commanded* one half of the two-pronged attack on Nova Athena, but Marius Drake was an experienced naval officer. Chang Li, as far as Roman knew, had no real experience of combat, at least outside debates in the Grand Senate.

"I would advise you to remain at the rear," he said, "but I don't think you'd listen."

"My being on your ship is a gesture of trust, Admiral," Chang Li replied. "For you — and for Admiral Vincent. There's no greater way to lose a man's faith in you than to prove you don't trust him."

"Right now, I don't," Roman said, simply. "The Federation Navy is no longer a united force — we prove that, even if Admiral Vincent doesn't. And I don't know which way he'll jump."

ꙮ

"The drones confirm it, sir," Lieutenant Lewis said. "The rebel fleet is within an hour of the Asimov Point."

Marius allowed himself a moment of amusement. Whatever else could be said about the treacherous asshole, Admiral Vincent had done an admirable job at making sure the defenders of Astrid and Maben didn't have to decide where their loyalties

lay. Instead, they'd have no choice, but to accept the *fait accompli* once the rebel fleet was solidly in control of Tara Prime. Astrid and Maben weren't exactly stage-one colonies, yet they couldn't hope to supply the defenders with everything they needed to keep blocking the way to Marble... if, of course, the rebels didn't simply keep outflanking them.

You must have been planning this for a while, he thought, looking at the icon of Admiral Vincent's superdreadnaught. He'd behave, Marius was sure, as long as his children were alive and well. *And yet, you didn't have the intelligence to realize that someone might outflank you.*

"Very well," he said, dryly. "Inform Admiral Vincent that he may send the welcoming committee through the Asimov Point."

"Aye, sir," Lieutenant Lewis said.

Marius allowed his smile to grow wider. Admiral Justinian had pioneered the technique for using StarComs to coordinate fleets across interplanetary distances, but Marius and Roman Garibaldi had both copied the idea. Marius had even expanded it by putting StarComs into freighters, despite the attendant risks. They were nowhere near an effective FTL communications method, but they did allow him to coordinate his forces with far greater efficiency than Roman Garibaldi could hope to match.

And a good thing too, he thought. *Admiral Stockholm is loyal enough, but his competence is somewhat questionable.*

It was a bitter thought. Hadn't there been a time when he'd put competence over loyalty, skill over connections? But he'd been betrayed too often by those he'd trusted. Roman Garibaldi had betrayed him, Admiral Vincent had betrayed him... his eyes slid back to the Admiral's icon as cold hatred flowed through his heart. There was no real hope of getting his hands on Roman Garibaldi — the young man was too skilled to allow his ship to be boarded — but Admiral Vincent would never have a chance to escape. Marius would see to it that his suffering was prolonged indefinitely.

And his children will not have a fun time on a stage-one colony, he reminded himself. He'd thought to kill them, just to make their father suffer, but Tiffany had argued for mercy and it had pleased him to grant it. Besides, they knew nothing of value in the real world. Life as a farmer, if they were lucky enough to be assigned to a farm, would be an endless series of unpleasant learning experiences. *No one will ever draw the connection between them and their father.*

"The courier boat has jumped through the Asimov Point," Lieutenant Lewis reported. "The messenger is on his way."

Marius nodded, curtly. He'd ordered Admiral Vincent to send his eldest daughter — again — but the bastard had argued that Hannalore knew too much, that she might reveal something to Admiral Garibaldi. Marius had been tempted to repeat his order — Hannalore would be sure to behave herself if her younger siblings were at risk — yet too much was at stake for his amusement. A junior officer, one unaware of the threat to the Admiral's family, could carry the can.

And Hannalore will not survive the final battle, Marius told himself. *She's just too dangerous to keep alive.*

It wasn't a pleasant thought. He'd read the young officer's transcripts from the academy, studying them with ninety years of experience in reading between the lines. Hannalore had been praised in glowing terms, of course, but there was enough solid evidence to make it clear she was a competent officer who'd graduated reasonably well. She might have made a very good officer, he considered, if her father hadn't directed her life and career for his own purposes. As it was, she'd missed the seasoning she desperately needed. A skilled mentor would have made much of her, given time.

"The courier boat has returned, sir," Lieutenant Lewis said, as more data appeared on the display. "The rebels are closing in on the Asimov Point."

"Very good," Marius said. He'd thought about mounting a defense of the Asimov Point itself, but Roman Garibaldi wasn't hot-headed enough to refuse to back off when it was clear he was losing the battle. "And now... we wait."

੪੦ ੦੪

"A courier boat just transited the Asimov Point," Lieutenant Thompson reported. "It's transmitting a message."

"Put it through," Roman ordered.

He frowned as an image of Admiral Vincent appeared on the display. "Admiral Garibaldi, welcome to Tara Prime," the recorded message said. Hannalore, it seemed, had not been returned to the fleet. "As per your requests, the defenses of the New Redeye Asimov Point have been placed in lockdown. Known loyalists have been rounded up and are currently being held under guard. I look forward to meeting you in person once you enter the system."

Roman frowned. "Lieutenant," he said, "do the drones confirm the message?"

"Yes, sir," Lieutenant Thompson said. Her eyes narrowed as she studied the readings. "The fortresses appear to have been largely depowered."

And now, we decide if we want to jump, Roman thought. The defenses of the New Redeye Point were puny, compared to the fortresses covering the Maben Point, but they were nothing to take lightly. *And find out if we're about to be greeted by the lady — or the tiger.*

He sucked in his breath. "Inform the fleet that we'll proceed with Plan Alpha," he said. The formation would bring his heavy ships through first, just in case the defenses weren't *quite* as defenseless as they seemed, but give him enough flexibility to break off if he ran into something he couldn't handle. "It's time to go into the fire."

"Yes, sir," Lieutenant Thompson said. Her hands danced over the console, sending orders through the datanet. "Transition in ten minutes."

Roman braced himself. One way or another, the uncertainty would all be over soon.

Chapter Twenty-Nine

Perversely, the idea of using StarComs to improve tactical flexibility came too late to prove a decisive advantage. All it did was prove that the Federation, even in the latter stages of its decline and fall, could still innovate.
—The Federation Navy in Retrospect, 4199

Tara Prime, 4102

Commander Ginny Lewis had never been so scared in her life.

She'd expected to spend a couple of years in the tactical section as she continued her steady climb to a captaincy of her own. Junior officers were supposed to know all they could about their ships, even if those on the command track rarely learned more than the basics of each department. Being assigned to work as the Emperor's personal tactical aide should have been a badge of honor, a guaranteed jump up the promotions ladder.

Instead, it was like working next to a dangerous animal. There was no way to know when the animal would turn and bite you.

Ginny was no innocent. She knew that corruption had been rampant through the Federation Navy, and that officers like the late unlamented Admiral Stevenson had been fond of forcing junior officers into bed. The Emperor had put a stop to that, simply by making examples of a few of the worst offenders, but she would almost have preferred to be sexually harassed, rather than work with an increasingly maddened Emperor. One word out of place, she suspected, and it would be the end of her. The Emperor's guards would be more than happy to put her out the airlock — or worse.

She flinched, inwardly, as the first enemy ship appeared on the display. The giant superdreadnaught lumbered out of the Asimov Point, its shields raised and its weapons at the ready. It looked as though the rebels were being careful; they might have forsaken the standard tactic of sending smaller and expendable units through the point first, but their ships weren't lowering their guard. Another superdreadnaught appeared, followed rapidly by two more. They were transiting as fast as they could without running the risk of accidentally interpenetrating one another. Federation Navy officers would have hesitated to run such a risk unless it was absolutely necessary.

"Sir," she said, "five rebel superdreadnaughts have made transit. They're moving away from the point."

"They wouldn't want to stay near the fortresses," the Emperor said. He sounded almost rational, surprisingly. "Can you get an ID on those superdreadnaughts?"

"Recon platforms class them as *Outsider-Ones*," Ginny said, after a moment. "There's no way to know what the *Outsiders* call them."

"Something witty or defiant, no doubt," the Emperor mused. Four more superdreadnaughts flickered into existence, then glided through the silent defenses to

rendezvous with their companions. "See if you can identify *Valiant* when she makes her appearance."

"Aye, sir," Ginny said.

She rather doubted it would be possible, thankfully. The Emperor might have noticed if she'd found the ship, then lied. Roman Garibaldi might not switch his flag to another ship, but he'd certainly be smart enough to ensure his flagship couldn't be picked out easily. He knew, just like every other cadet to pass through the academy, that having the flagship be the first starship blown out of space almost certainly guaranteed losing the battle.

"Five enemy battle squadrons have emerged, sir," she said. Three of them were definitely composed of Federation Navy superdreadnaughts. "They're sending through flanking units now."

"Let them have time to build up their fleet," the Emperor ordered. "We *want* them on this side of the point."

"Yes, sir," Ginny said.

She sucked in her breath. Standard tactics called for holding the Asimov Point, by fighting to the death if necessary. It was the one place where the defenders would have a colossal advantage, where the enemy would need to spend assault pods and starships like water to punch through into the target system. Just *letting* the enemy slip through one's defenses was the sort of tactic that would have earned an automatic fail at the academy, with the instructors pointing out that it nullified most of the advantages the defenders would have enjoyed. And yet, she could see the awful logic of the Emperor's plan. Roman Garibaldi's ships would be caught in a trap, unable to advance and unable to retreat. Even if he darted towards the system limits, he wouldn't be able to evade the thousands of starfighters and gunboats under the Emperor's command.

And it might just work, she thought. She cast her mind about for anything she could do, but there was nothing. Even if the Emperor were to suffer another attack of... whatever, his second would take over the battle. *The rebels will certainly be a great deal more careful about accepting more turncoats.*

The steady stream of smaller ships was replaced, suddenly, by yet another set of superdreadnaughts. Ginny closed her eyes for a long second, then opened them to see two more battle squadrons making their way to join the enemy fleet. A handful of carriers accompanied them, already launching starfighters to prowl the surrounding region of space for potential traps. It was unlikely that they'd pick up the jaws of the trap before they slammed closed. And even if they did, they'd be pushed into a close engagement with the fortresses while the two loyalist formations closed on the point.

It will be the sort of battle that never occurs outside simulations, she thought. Her tutors had told her, more than once, that real-life engagements tended to be messy. *The one where the enemy manages to trap himself.*

"I think that's the last of them, sir," she said, as the stream of red icons finally came to a halt. "They're launching probes..."

"They shouldn't be able to see us," the Emperor grunted. He smiled as she looked up at him, sitting in his chair and admiring the display. His expression boded ill for any rebels unlucky enough to be taken alive. "Inform Admiral Vincent that he may send the welcoming signal."

"Aye, sir," Ginny said.

She had no real love for Admiral Vincent — the man gloried in his appetites, waddling around like a beached whale — but she couldn't help feeling a flicker of sympathy. His children were hostages, after all; Ginny had no doubt the Emperor would have them killed if their father refused to cooperate. Treacherous asshole Admiral Vincent might well be — she suspected he would have turned on the rebels too, if it had proven expedient — but no one deserved to watch helplessly as his children were turned into pawns.

But they would already have been their father's pawns, Ginny thought. She liked and respected Lady Tiffany, yet *her* life had been that of a pawn. It must sting to realize that she'd sided with her husband over her family, only to have her husband turn into a madman. *Ginny* had enjoyed more freedom than she, even as a junior officer or cadet. *This time, they're someone else's pawns.*

She shook her head as she studied the display. "They're shaking down into a standard formation," she reported. "It doesn't look as though they're planning to fight."

"They'll have been drilled into switching into an offensive or defensive posture if necessary," the Emperor said. He sounded oddly wistful. "Roman Garibaldi, whatever his faults, is a firm believer in regular drills. I taught him that."

Ginny felt an unexpected stab of sympathy. In so many ways, Marius Drake had been good for the Federation Navy... and not just because he'd had Admiral Stevenson summarily shot for abusing his subordinates. Getting rid of the remaining deadwood, of officers who had been promoted because of their connections rather than their ability... if he'd had more time to make reforms, the entire navy might have been saved.

But instead, the Outsiders had struck and the Emperor had started to go mad. He had to be removed.

"Yes sir," she said, instead. She swallowed hard to get rid of the lump in her throat. "Time to engagement point, thirty-seven minutes at current speed."

"Bring the fleet to battlestations in twenty minutes," the Emperor ordered. "And inform Admiral Stockholm that he may start moving his ships into position."

"Aye, sir," Ginny said.

She couldn't help feeling impressed. Timing was everything, particularly when the rebels needed to be caught in a position that forced them to choose between doubling back or making a run for the system limits. And there were so many things that could go wrong. If the rebels saw the looming trap before the jaws snapped shut...

They'd still find it hard to avoid engagement, she thought, grimly. *The starfighters would catch them if they tried to run.*

"And keep a weapons lock on Admiral Vincent," the Emperor added. "We don't want him having a sudden change of heart."

Roman couldn't help feeling nervous as *Valiant* slipped past the brooding fortresses and made her way into the system. There was something oddly *unnatural*
about not clearing the way first, about merely being *allowed* to move through the
defenses without being molested. He'd flown past dozens of fortresses, of course,
when they'd been on the same side, but *these* fortresses were nominally held by the
enemy. And yet, it looked as though Admiral Vincent had kept his promise. The
fortresses were almost completely powered down.

"System scan," he ordered. "What do you see?"

"The system's in lockdown, I think," Lieutenant Thompson reported. "There's a
small fleet gathered at the pre-planned location, sir, but otherwise the system is
unnaturally quiet. Even the asteroid miners appear to have been told to go dark."

Roman nodded, curtly. Tara Prime had been industrialized for centuries, ever
since the Inheritance War had opened up a whole new region of space for exploration. And the settlers, being based in a system with no less than five Asimov Points,
had escaped the worst of the abuse that had made so many systems along the Rim
throw their lot in with the Outsiders. Admiral Vincent, it seemed, had done a
remarkable job of building up the system's industry, although it had yet to match
Admiral Justinian's work.

Or the Outsiders, for that matter, Roman thought. *But then, Admiral Vincent had
good reason to worry about attracting attention.*

"Keep us on course towards the RV point," he ordered. Lieutenant Thompson was
right. It *was* unnaturally quiet. But then, a single message escaping the system would
alert the Emperor *before* the joint fleet reached Howarth, let alone AlphaCent. "And
continue to deploy recon platforms and drones."

"Aye, sir," Lieutenant Thompson said.

Roman settled back into his command chair, trying to ignore the uneasy feeling in his gut. It looked as though the plan was working perfectly. Too perfectly.
And that bothered him... although, for all he knew, there were riots underway on
Tara Prime. Or perhaps not; the locals shouldn't have the slightest idea of what was
going on outside their atmosphere, at least until Admiral Vincent made some kind of
announcement. Absently, Roman wondered what the locals would *think* when their
admiral told them he was now their king. If they knew what had almost happened
to Nova Athena...

They'd worry about getting scorched themselves, he thought. Marius Drake *had* broken the taboo against indiscriminate planetary strikes, at least against human targets.
It wasn't *that* hard to imagine him doing the same to Tara Prime. *Or merely losing
contact with the industrial base near the Core Worlds.*

"Picking up a compressed signal," Lieutenant Thompson said.

"Put it on the display," Roman ordered.

He leaned forward as Admiral Vincent's face appeared in front of him. "Admiral
Garibaldi, welcome to Tara Prime," Admiral Vincent said. "I suggest we proceed jointly

to the Macaque Point and secure it, then meet for dinner and future discussions."

Roman frowned. It sounded reasonable enough, yet something was nagging at the back of his mind. Something important, something he'd missed...

Hannalore said he'd announce the system's change in loyalties once the fleet arrived, he thought, as it dawned on him. *And yet he hasn't done anything of the sort...*

"Launch another spread of recon probes," he ordered. "And record a message."

"Recording," Lieutenant Thompson said.

"Admiral Vincent, thank you for your welcome," Roman said. "I look forward to hearing your message to your people."

He keyed his console. "Send it."

"Sent," Lieutenant Thompson said.

›‹

No battle plan, at least in Marius's experience, had ever survived even the slightest contact with the enemy. War was a democracy, after all, and the enemy got a vote. But even so, he was pleasantly surprised by just how well the plan had gone. *He* would have made certain to have Admiral Vincent helpless before committing himself to entering the system.

Politics, he thought, as a new message blinked up on the display. *Roman cannot afford to bully someone he desperately needs.*

"Sir," Ginny said. "There is a new message from Admiral Garibaldi, addressed to Admiral Vincent."

"Play it," Marius ordered.

He smiled, coldly, as he listened to the message. He'd specifically ordered Admiral Vincent *not* to broadcast anything to the population, if only to keep them quiet while their fate was decided in combat. But, naturally, the admiral's reluctance to inform his people of the change in management had aroused Garibaldi's suspicions. Marius would have been annoyed, and frustrated, if he hadn't anticipated something more spectacular going wrong.

"No response," he ordered. "Time to engagement point?"

"Seven minutes to optimal engagement range," Ginny said. "Admiral Stockholm is advancing forward now."

Marius allowed his smile to grow wider. Garibaldi was suspicious, but was he suspicious enough to try to break out of the trap? Marius had a healthy respect for his young protégé — Garibaldi would act decisively, if confronted by a real threat — yet he'd be torn between taking steps to save his command and overreacting to a nonexistent danger. Doubt and indecision would work their will on his mind.

Which way would he jump? Or would he hesitate long enough for the jaws to spring closed?

"Inform the fleet," he ordered. "Prepare to launch starfighters and engage the enemy."

›‹

"There was no response?"

"None, sir," Lieutenant Thompson said. "If he'd replied at once, it would have reached us two minutes ago."

Roman bit his lip, thinking hard. Admiral Vincent might have a perfectly good reason not to announce his kingship before the two fleets united. For all he knew, there were enough spies and informers on the planet and its defenses to make issuing any such claim a dangerous move. And yet, it looked very much as though something wasn't quite right...

... But all he had to go on were his instincts. There was nothing he could point to, nothing he could say justified an immediate retreat. It was hard to know what to do.

"Admiral," Lieutenant Thompson reported. "One of the recon platforms is picking up turbulence. Computer analysis says it's a cloaking system."

Roman swore. "Where?"

"Behind us, past the Asimov Point," Lieutenant Thompson said. "But moving towards our rear."

"Shit," Roman said, as new icons appeared on the display. "Can you get an ID?"

His blood seemed to turn to ice. There was no legitimate reason for Admiral Vincent's ships to be sneaking around behind him, particularly when everyone was feeling jumpy. And besides, Admiral Vincent's ships were in front of him. It was hard to be sure at such range, but the Outsider-made sensors insisted those ships were real. And that meant that the ships *behind* him had come from somewhere else. Home Fleet?

"No, sir," Lieutenant Thompson said. "But judging by the displacement, there's at least one battle squadron out there."

"Bring active sensors to full power," Roman ordered. If there were ships moving up behind him, under cloak, it was a trap. And he'd walked right into it. "Order the fleet to prepare to engage."

&⊙&

"Sir," Ginny said. "The enemy fleet has started to bring its active sensors online!"

"Noted," Marius said. Roman hadn't *quite* fallen into the trap, but he'd come far too close to escape. And there was no point in trying to hide any longer. "Drop the cloaks, then launch starfighters and commence firing!"

"Aye, sir," Ginny said. She keyed a switch, triggering the firing pattern she'd programmed when the rebels had made their appearance. "Firing... now!"

&⊙&

"New contacts," Lieutenant Thompson snapped. "Two enemy forces..."

Roman gritted his teeth as yet more red icons popped into existence. Six super-dreadnaught squadrons in front of him, four more to the rear... backed up by at least ten fleet carriers and hundreds of smaller ships. And they had him neatly pinned. If he continued the advance, Force Two would take him in the rear while he tried to overwhelm Force One; if he reversed course, Force Two would hold him while Force One caught up with the fleet. Either way, he'd be crushed. The only realistic option was to head for the system limits, but the enemy would overwhelm him with starfighters, gunboats and long-range missile fire. Unless...

"Reverse course," he ordered. At least he had *a* contingency plan. It wasn't much, not against what he was facing, but it might just give them a chance to escape. "Take us back to the Asimov Point!"

"Yes, sir," Lieutenant Thompson said. She paused. "Sir, the fortresses are coming online!"

"I see," Roman said. *That* explained why Force Two was weaker than Force One. Admiral Vincent — and the Emperor, given that Home Fleet was the only formation that could have sent so many superdreadnaughts to the system — had to have counted on the fleet being supported by the fortresses. "They're slamming the door closed behind us."

He took a breath. "Launch starfighters," he ordered, as the display sparkled with deadly icons. Thankfully, the Outsider pilots had long since overcome the inexperience that had dogged them in the early battles. "Lock long-range missiles on Force One, then commence firing!"

Chapter Thirty

Of all wars, civil wars are the worst. They turn brother against brother, fathers against sons, wives against husbands... everyone needs to make a choice about where their duty truly lies when civil war breaks out. Friends can become enemies, enemies can become friends; nothing is ever truly what it seems. And, for some of them, the decisions they take can result in tragedy.
—The Federation Navy in Retrospect, 4199

Tara Prime, 4102

"Now hear this," the loudspeaker boomed. "Red alert; I say again, red alert. All hands to battlestations."

Tiffany braced herself, sweat pouring down her back. She'd been in combat before, technically, but she'd never been anything more than a helpless bystander. If her ship had been destroyed — and Marius had been at some pains to point out that there was no guarantee that her ship wouldn't be targeted — she would have died, alone and unremarked. All she'd been able to do was stay in her cabin, in one of the better-protected parts of the ship, and pray they survived. But now...

She glanced down at the weapon in her hand. Oslo had taught her how to shoot when she'd been young, claiming it was a useful skill for a girl. Tiffany couldn't say she'd kept up with it, even though she couldn't imagine Marius objecting if she'd wanted to use the shooting range on the superdreadnaught. However he saw her, it wasn't as just an attractively shaped piece of meat. And besides, he knew the danger of being unarmed if the enemy chose to board the ship.

Which doesn't change the fact that I'm about to commit treason, she thought, as she studied the terminal. Technically, freeing hostages held in defiance of Federation Law wasn't treason, but she'd been raised to understand that the law *really* meant what the Grand Senate said it meant. Marius could call her a traitor and no one would disagree with him, at least not openly. *I could die in the next few minutes.*

Her palms felt sweaty, as if the weapon would slip from her hand. There were men and women guarding the hostages who knew how to fight, men and women who had been in real danger. Oslo and his team, at least, had some experience, but they'd never had to do their duty in earnest until now. No one had ever considered her worth assassinating until her husband had become Emperor, and by then it had been too late. She could die, if one of the guards shot her... or she could be captured, caught in the act of high treason.

Somehow, she doubted Marius would forgive her betrayal. He'd been betrayed far too many times.

"My Lady," Oslo said. A dull shudder ran through the ship. Tiffany hoped that meant the ship was launching missiles, rather than taking incoming fire. "This is your last chance to change your mind."

It was tempting. She could pretend that nothing had happened, that she hadn't planned to liberate the prisoners and steal a courier boat. And if Talia Vincent said

otherwise... well, Talia was the daughter of a traitor, trying to lie to sow trouble between the Emperor and his loyal wife. Ginny wouldn't say a word. It would be so easy just to climb onto her bed and crawl under the covers, to pretend that she'd never been anywhere else.

I wouldn't be able to live with myself any longer, she thought. The whole concept of threatening children to make their father cooperative was too much. Perhaps, in hindsight, she should have acted on her doubts sooner. *And if I die here, at least I will have tried.*

She took a breath. "I'm coming," she said, firmly. "Please don't try to stop me."

Oslo gave her a long look, then nodded curtly. He must have been concerned for her safety, she figured; he wouldn't have agreed to take the immense risk of liberating the hostages and fleeing the ship if he hadn't felt she was in danger every day she spent with her husband. It was a depressing thought, but one she knew she had to face. Marius was no longer the man she'd married, the man she'd pledged herself to.

"Keep your weapon in your holster until we reach the guest quarters," he reminded her, as the rest of the team checked their equipment. "We don't want someone sounding the alert."

Tiffany nodded, then glanced in the mirror. Her dress, the one Marius enjoyed, was gone, replaced by a form-fitting shipsuit that just *had* to have been designed by a man. It was so tight she almost felt naked. And yet, with her make-up scrubbed off and her hair tied up in a bun, it was unlikely that anyone would recognize her. *Enterprise* had over two thousand crewmen, after all. She hoped — she prayed — that they didn't run into anyone who knew them all by name.

At least it's not a miniskirt, she thought, as they headed for the hatch. *I'd feel silly walking around in something so short.*

She smiled at the thought, then braced herself as the hatch opened. There was no one outside, not even the marine guards. They'd been called away to their duty stations. She took a breath as she followed Oslo down the corridor towards the sealed airlock keeping the Emperor's quarters separate from the rest of the ship. The super-dreadnaught was in lockdown, she reminded herself. Each compartment was supposed to be sealed off, in case of a hull breach. Oslo checked the telltales, then pushed a datachip against the bulkhead-mounted scanner. The airlock hissed open, revealing another empty corridor.

"Too many airlocks, sir," one of the bodyguards whispered.

"They need to keep the air trapped," Oslo muttered. He didn't sound nervous, merely focused on the task at hand. "If something happens to vent the air in the compartment beyond, the airlock won't open no matter what overrides you have."

And it will keep the marines from mounting an immediate response, Tiffany thought. Ginny had explained, in some detail, just how the system worked. The marines had overrides too, of course, but they'd still be slowed down as they opened and closed every hatch between Marine Country and the makeshift brig. *Unless, of course, there's a marine duty station closer than we know.*

She shook her head as they passed through yet another airlock. It would be hellish to find themselves caught before they'd even gotten close to the prisoners. She wondered, absently, if there was any excuse she could give, but realized there was no way anyone could put an innocent spin on her actions. They'd armed themselves, donned shipsuits to make themselves look like crewmen, and left her quarters. Even Public Information, which had somehow managed to make the Grand Senate look good, couldn't possibly have spun it into a believable story.

"This is the outer edge of the guest compartment," Oslo warned, as they reached yet another airlock. "We may encounter resistance beyond this point."

He glanced at Tiffany. "Stay in the rear."

Tiffany nodded, bracing herself as the guards drew their weapons and opened the airlock. A Blackshirt stood outside the door, looking visibly nervous as low tremors ran through the entire ship. Oslo lifted his pistol and pulled the trigger. Tiffany stared in horror as a green plasma bolt struck the Blackshirt's head and burned it clean off.

"You *killed* him!"

"Yes, I did," Oslo said. "We don't dare let anyone call for help."

Tiffany couldn't take her eyes off the body. She'd never seen anyone die so close to her before, not even Tobias Vaughn. Part of her wanted to kneel and beg the man's forgiveness, even though she knew it would be useless. If he'd still been alive, he would have tried to stop them from taking the hostages. She glanced up, sharply, as the hatch opened, revealing the guest quarters. Two more guards, on the inside, were caught by surprise and blasted down before they could grab their own weapons.

"They may have rigged the room to set off an automatic alert if someone fires a weapon," Oslo muttered. He nodded to the hostages, hidden behind the forcefield, as he started to work on the security systems. "But if we're lucky, they didn't have time."

The forcefield snapped out of existence, leaving only a faint taste of ozone in the air. "You need to come with us," Oslo snapped. "Don't do *anything* to slow us down."

Tiffany wanted to tell him he was being too sharp, but she was still stunned by the sudden violence. Three men were dead... and it was all her fault. She pushed her fear aside as Talia gave her a tight hug, tears streaming down her face. Meeting their father, if only briefly, had probably rammed home the seriousness of the situation in ways no words could hope to match.

"Come on," Oslo hissed. "We need to get moving before they realize something's wrong..."

A low hooting ran through the compartment. Oslo swore and hurried back into the corridor, just as an airlock started to hiss open at the far end. Tiffany followed him, hurrying the former hostages back the way they'd come. She glanced back, just in time to see a trio of Blackshirts behind the opening airlock. Oslo gunned them down, then threw a grenade down the corridor and into a side room. The resulting explosion almost deafened her.

"That's the intruder alarm," Oslo snapped. "One of the overrides must have failed."

Tiffany nodded, clutching her pistol as they hurried through the next set of air-locks, closing them in hopes of slowing down the enemy. *She* wouldn't have given the Blackshirts override keys, but the marines definitely *would* have overrides of their own. Maybe, just maybe, they'd assume the ship was being boarded and search for the hull breach... and yet, she knew it was too much to hope for.

Talia caught her arm. "Where are we going?"

"There's a courier boat docked to the hull," Tiffany gasped. She wasn't used to running so hard. "It's going to be cramped, but..."

She threw herself to the deck, dragging the younger girl with her, as the airlock behind them exploded with shattering force. Oslo and his men spun around, firing bolt after bolt of green plasma at the Blackshirts; Tiffany prayed, desperately, that they'd hold the enemy off long enough for the hostages to escape. She crawled forward as the guards held the line, pressing her override key against the scanner. The airlock hissed open, allowing them to make a break through the airlock and into the next section. Oslo threw another grenade down the corridor, then brought up the rear.

"Kenny and Sam didn't make it," he said, as the airlock hissed closed. "They're both dead for sure."

Tiffany felt as though she'd been punched in the gut. Kenny had been a sweet man, always ready to chat, while Sam had been engaged to a girl he'd planned to marry after completing his tour of duty. She'd liked them both. Hell, she'd intended to convince Marius to arrange for a sinecure for Sam, once his loyalties to her family were replaced by loyalties to his wife and children. But now she'd never have the chance. She wanted to slump against the bulkhead and cry...

"Come on," Oslo snapped. He hauled her to her feet, and pushed her forward. "There's no time to mourn!"

There was no sign of any resistance as they passed through the next set of compartments, but Tiffany could tell that Oslo was getting more and more concerned. The Blackshirts were a minor problem, compared to the marines, yet the marines hadn't shown themselves. Where were they? Ginny *had* promised to do what she could to delay pursuit, but she'd made it very clear that there were limits. Compromising the internal communications datanet was one thing, yet the marines had communicators of their own. Once they realized there was a problem, they'd make the switch and that would be that.

She fought her way forward, desperately. "How much further?"

"Three more compartments," Oslo said. "But do they know where we're going?"

Tiffany blanched. There weren't *many* ways to get off a superdreadnaught — and using the lifepods would guarantee recovery by the wrong side, if their pods didn't get mistaken for weapons in the confusion and destroyed by one side or the other. The marines would think of the courier boat at once, believing it to be a better option than the shuttlebay. It was certainly closer to the guest quarters.

On the other hand, we'd need the right codes to fly the craft, Tiffany thought. *Do they realize Ginny gave us the codes?*

She felt a sudden stab of guilt as the next hatch opened, revealing nothing. Oslo led the way forward, then swore as the next hatch snapped upwards. He unhooked a grenade from his belt and hurled it forward, just as four armored men appeared ahead of them. Tiffany hit the ground again as it detonated, but two of the men kept coming forward. She stared, in horror, as Mike fell to the ground, his chest smoking from where a plasma bolt had struck him dead center. The other two marines were picked off by Oslo and Stuart before they had a chance to kill any of the others...

"They must not have had time to set up a proper ambush," Oslo said. "I..."

He ducked backwards as another bolt of plasma fire burned through the air, striking Stuart in the head. Tiffany felt her gorge rise at the stench and swallowed hard. Oslo lunged forward and checked the next compartment, weapon in hand. Thankfully, there didn't seem to be anyone blocking their way to the courier boat.

"Get the kids onto the ship," Tiffany told him. "You're the only one who can fly her."

"I'm supposed to protect you," Oslo snapped, as Talia urged her siblings through the hatch and into the courier boat. "My Lady..."

Tiffany turned, holding her pistol at the ready. "If you don't get them off the ship, all of this will be for nothing," she snapped back. "I..."

Something slammed into her body and picked her up, hurling her down the corridor and straight into a bulkhead. She was unconscious before her body hit the deck.

⁖⁓

Oslo stared in shock, helplessly caught between two imperatives, as Tiffany was thrown away from him. On one hand, he was meant to protect Tiffany, the sole surviving member of the family he served. But on the other hand, he knew she was right. If he failed to get the hostages off the ship, the death of every other member of his team would be for nothing. He slammed the hatch closed, then ran to the console to start the flash-wake sequence. It would put a great deal of wear and tear on the courier boat's systems, but he rather doubted it would matter. There was a very good chance they'd be blown out of space in the next five minutes.

"Strap yourselves in," he barked at the former hostages. The older girl seemed to have a good head on her shoulders, but the other three were clearly panicking. "Don't even think about getting up until I say otherwise."

He disconnected the courier boat from the superdreadnaught, then triggered her thrusters and hurled her away from the mighty ship. If Ginny had succeeded, the targeting datanet should have problems locking onto the courier boat, at least long enough to give them a fighting chance to escape. But there was also the very real risk of being caught and killed by a rebel starfighter, the pilot merely seeing a loyalist courier boat fleeing to somewhere safe. Alarms sounded in the tiny compartment as he pushed the drives well past their safety limits, silently thanking the Emperor for overriding the Grand Senate's decrees. It would kill the Emperor, Oslo thought, when he realized that the courier boat would probably not have escaped if she'd been forced to operate within the Grand Senate's safety limitations.

"I need to speak to dad," Talia said. "If we're no longer hostages..."

Oslo hesitated. Emperor Marius had turned spiteful — it was why he hadn't argued too strongly against risking Lady Tiffany. He doubted the Emperor would hesitate to blow the courier out of space, once Talia revealed that the game was up. And Tiffany wasn't even on the ship!

"Do it," he ordered, grimly. He picked up a headset and tossed it at her, barely taking his eyes off the controls. "Hurry!"

Talia swore. "Are you sure this will reach dad?"

"Stay on the emergency channel and *everyone* will hear it," Oslo snapped. He had no idea which of the superdreadnaughts within range held Admiral Vincent; hell, he had no idea if Admiral Vincent was surrounded by Blackshirts or not. But they had to try. And everyone, according to regulations, was meant to monitor the emergency channel at all times. "And make it convincing!"

"Yes, sir," Talia said. She started to speak into the headset. "Dad, it's me. We got away from the Emperor..."

And let's just hope that's enough, Oslo thought. On the display, a trio of starfighters were turning towards the courier boat. He could have outrun them, if he'd had a head start, but as it was they'd catch him before he could make his escape. *We might not survive the next few minutes.*

He pulled back, studying the display. The Emperor's ships were advancing towards the rebels, firing so rapidly they had to be burning through their magazines at a terrifying rate. But if it worked, if the rebels were trapped, it would be more than worth it. Oslo feared the Emperor, yet he also respected him. Emperor Marius still had a very good chance of winning the war.

"There's no reply," Talia said. "I don't know what to do."

"Keep talking," Oslo said. There was no point in trying to hide. "That's all you *can* do."

And hope we can rescue Lady Tiffany, he added, silently. *Her husband will not be pleased with her.*

Chapter Thirty-One

It is ironic indeed that one of the greatest battles of the final civil war was also the whole civil war in microcosm.
—The Federation Navy in Retrospect, 4199

Tara Prime, 4102

"Force Two is opening fire," Lieutenant Thompson reported. "Force One's missiles are entering point defense engagement range."

"Order the point defense to engage at will," Roman said. The missiles were a problem, but the tidal wave of starfighters and gunboats were a nightmare. If he ordered his starfighters to attack the enemy ships, the enemy starfighters would have a clear shot at his ships. "And order the CSP to cover our hulls."

"Aye, sir," Lieutenant Thompson said. "Force One is impaling itself on our missiles."

Roman shrugged. Emperor Marius — and he was sure he was matching wits with his former mentor — would have arranged his ships to ensure the smaller craft soaked up most of the missiles. The range was closing all the time, of course, but it probably wouldn't matter now that he had to split his fire between two enemy fleets. And yet, there *was* a light in the darkness...

He left tactical control to the tactical staff and studied the overall situation. Force Two was reducing speed as it approached the fortresses, ready to combine its fire with the fixed defenses to overwhelm any incoming ships. It would be *Roman* who had to impale himself, if the battle played out the way Emperor Marius had clearly expected. Breaking through the Asimov Point was the only apparent hope of success, but it meant running a gauntlet of fire from Force Two and the fortresses, with Force One breathing down their necks.

Unless, of course, something happened to those ships first.

"Record a message for Commodore Hazelton," he ordered. "Commodore, the tactical situation has taken a turn that is quite definitely *not* to our advantage. You are hereby ordered to reprogram your assault pods to the following coordinates—" his fingers danced across his console "—and launch them on my mark."

"The courier boat we left at the Asimov Point is not responding," Lieutenant Thompson warned. "She's gone."

Roman wasn't surprised. The courier boat had been right next to the fortresses. She'd either popped through the Asimov Point as soon as she'd seen the trap or been blown to atoms at point-blank range. Either way, she was gone.

"Load the message onto a flight of courier drones," he ordered. "And prepare to fire them, along with a full protective ECM shroud."

Lieutenant Thompson started. "Sir," she said, "I am obliged to warn you that regulations..."

"To hell with regulations," Roman snarled. It meant giving up a barrage of missiles, but he didn't dare rely on one or two courier drones. The fortresses would do

whatever they could to keep him from signaling anything on the other side of the point. "Let's live dangerously."

He smiled, then gritted his teeth as the tidal wave of missiles broke over his command. The enemy had fired thousands — clearly, *someone* had been pushing Earth's industrial base to the limits — and hundreds broke through, closing in on their targets. Roman forced himself to watch as dozens of ships were damaged or destroyed; the superdreadnaught *Potemkin* blown into radioactive debris by nearly a dozen antimatter warheads, the superdreadnaught *John Paul Jones* only narrowly avoiding the same fate when the battlecruiser *Agrippa* took four missiles that were meant for the larger ship. The superdreadnaught *Sheridan* drifted out of formation, atmosphere streaming out of a dozen hull breaches; Roman couldn't help feeling a flicker of guilt at his own relief when her hulk absorbed five more missiles before she disintegrated into a fireball. At least some of her crew had made it off the doomed ship before it was too late.

"The courier drones are ready, sir," Lieutenant Thompson stated.

Roman hesitated. Emperor Marius was no slouch. If he saw the drones, he'd guess at what was coming. And yet, timing was everything. There should be almost no time for him to respond before it was too late.

He cursed under his breath as the starfighters and gunboats closed in, the latter launching three or four shipkiller missiles from practically point-blank range. Home Fleet's pilots lacked the practiced skill of Fifth Fleet's, but they'd clearly been training hard in the simulators. And there were a lot of them. Roman had a nasty suspicion they were staging starfighters from Tara Prime itself, rearming them in the carriers and then throwing the tiny craft straight into the battle. Clearly, Admiral Vincent had thought better of his attempted betrayal.

"Launch the drones," he ordered.

৪৩৫৪৩

"The enemy ships have just launched a cloud of drones," Ginny reported. Emperor Marius was barely paying attention to her — he was watching the crisis unfolding inside his ship — but he snapped back at her words. "They're aimed at the point."

"There's nowhere else they would be going," the Emperor snarled. One hand was toying with the flap of his holster, as if he intended to draw his pistol and shoot the next person who brought him bad news. "They have to have hidden additional forces behind the Asimov Point!"

He thumped the display, sharply. "Order the fortresses to shoot down the drones!"

It was too late, Ginny knew. Even with StarComs, the time-delay would ensure that the fortresses would engage — or not — on their own, without orders. And she had no idea just how trustworthy Admiral Vincent's people were. Their Admiral might have ordered them to stand beside Home Fleet and fight to the last, but how many of them knew his original plan?

"Aye, sir," she said, anyway. There was no point in arguing. "Message sent."

The Emperor nodded curtly, then returned to following the reports from below decks. It sounded, very much, as though a small mutiny had broken out, but the

Emperor didn't seem particularly impressed. The reports made the mutineers sound incompetent or ignorant. Taking control of a ship was easy enough, provided one snatched the bridge, engineering, and life support sections before anyone realized a mutiny was underway. But he hadn't yet realized that the mutineers had taken the hostages...

And none of his cronies have dared to tell him the truth, Ginny thought. Thankfully, the programs she'd inserted into the starship's datanet were making it harder for him to get a picture of the overall situation. *They know their lives are at stake.*

⁝⁞

"The fortresses killed seventy of the ninety drones," Lieutenant Thompson reported. "I think the remainder made it through the Asimov Point."

"Understood," Roman said. Statistically, at least ten of the remaining drones would survive transit through the point and start transmitting their message. And then... he glanced at the timer, trying to estimate just how long it would take Commodore Hazelton to reprogram the missile pods. "Continue firing."

"Aye, sir," Lieutenant Thompson said.

Roman forced himself to relax as a missile crashed against the starship's shields, sending shockwaves running through the hull. He wasn't blind to the dangers of trying to turn on Force Two, but if he were lucky his ace in the hole should make life interesting for the enemy personnel. Besides, it *did* give him the best chance of escaping through the Asimov Point, if he didn't think he could beat Force One...

Unless we kill him, he'll be able to build up a whole new fleet, Roman thought. *And if we do kill him, here and now, the power vacuum will plunge the remainder of the Federation into chaos.*

"Admiral," Lieutenant Thompson said. "Missile pods are transiting the point!"

⁝⁞

Commander Sven Kristopher knew it wasn't his place to question his superiors. He'd been put in command of the New Redeye Point defenders precisely *because* he knew better than to question his superiors. Admiral Vincent was his sole source of patronage, after all; anyone foolish enough to question one of his orders would be lucky if they were *merely* assigned to a garbage scow or some isolated asteroid mining shithole. But the orders he'd received over the last week had been the oddest he'd ever seen. First, he'd been ordered to shut his fortresses down, allowing the rebels to enter the system without a fight. It had looked, very much, as though Admiral Vincent intended to switch sides.

And then, the orders had been changed. He was still to let the rebels into the system, but then slam the door shut behind them. It just made no sense. Which side were they actually *on*?

He scowled down at his display as the rebel fleet slowly made its way back to the point, right into the teeth of his fire. Which way did Admiral Vincent *really* want him to jump? Should he fire on the rebel ships, or not? He'd already shot at their drones, but there had been too many to guarantee their complete destruction before

they plunged into the Asimov Point and vanished. Was that what he was meant to do?

"Commander," the tactical officer barked. "Missile pods! I say again, missile pods!"

Sven stared in horror. Missile pods, over a thousand of them, were materializing from the Asimov Point. A number interpenetrated and exploded, of course, but the survivors were already unleashing their deadly cargo. And they were all aimed at Home Fleet's superdreadnaughts!

He hesitated. What was he supposed to do?

"Switch point defense to alpha mode," he ordered. There was *just* enough confusion for that to seem a reasonable order. "And then open fire."

"Aye, sir," the tactical officer said.

☯

Roman allowed himself a moment of glee as the missile pods flickered into the system and opened fire, launching thousands of missiles directly at Force Two. The massive superdreadnaughts seemed to flinch on the display as they realized just how badly they were screwed, then their point defense opened fire with practiced efficiency. But they were too late to keep the missiles from raining havoc on their formation.

Shouldn't have stayed so close to the Asimov Point, he thought. Emperor Marius had clearly intended to tempt him with the prospect of crushing Force Two, then Force One, but it had been wasted effort. Even if he hadn't had to contend with the fortresses, he'd still have been mouse-trapped by Force One. *But you didn't want to risk me escaping, either.*

"Admiral," Lieutenant Thompson said. "There are some odd patterns appearing in the data."

Roman frowned. "In what way?"

"The fortresses didn't engage the missile pods," Lieutenant Thompson said. "They didn't shoot at anything that didn't pose a threat to them."

That *was* odd, Roman admitted privately. It was possible the fortress crews had been surprised, but their electronic servants should have reacted instantly. No one in their right mind would let someone shovel a thousand missile pods through the Asimov Point without doing everything in their power to thin the herd before it was too late. His missile pods could have engaged the fortresses as easily as they'd engaged the superdreadnaughts...

"Keep an eye on them," he ordered. There was no way to know what it actually meant — and he was damned if he was trusting Admiral Vincent's people any longer. "How badly did we hurt Force Two?"

"We killed at least seventeen superdreadnaughts," Lieutenant Thompson said. "I don't think there's an undamaged ship left in the formation."

Roman studied the display as the data rolled up in front of him. Force Two hadn't been defeated, but it was unlikely that it could put up a fight. But the fortresses were still a dangerous unknown. Had someone on the fortresses believed the original plan was still valid? Or did they have an ally they didn't know? Or...

And we might still run into real trouble if we have to force our way past the fortresses, he thought. He *hated* not knowing which way the enemy formations would jump, when push came to shove. *That only leaves us with one real option.*

"Alter course," he ordered. "Bring us about to face Force One."

ଞୠଓଷ

Marius stared in disbelief. "What... what happened?"

"They rammed missile pods through the point," Ginny said. She sounded as stunned as he felt. "They destroyed over seventeen superdreadnaughts! Admiral Stockholm is among the dead."

"Shit," Marius said. All of a sudden, things had changed — and changed badly. The rebels had been hurt, but the battle was suddenly a far more even contest. And Garibaldi, damn the man, knew it. "Order all ships to continue firing."

Ginny nodded. "Aye, sir," she said. "And..."

Marius glanced at his console as an emergency message appeared in front of him. "Sir," Lieutenant Rain said. "They got away!"

"Who got away?" Marius demanded. "And how?"

"They snatched the courier boat, sir," Rain said. He sounded panicked. "The brats, sir; they snatched the courier boat and fled!"

Marius rounded on Ginny. "Find that damned boat!"

"Aye, sir," Ginny squeaked.

"It's worse, sir," Rain said. "Sir, we recovered..."

"Spit it out," Marius ordered.

"Sir, we found your wife near the courier boat's airlock," Rain said. "Her security team was involved in the attack!"

Marius, just for a second, found himself utterly unable to move. The first reports hadn't been very clear, suggesting a minor outbreak of fighting amongst the crew rather than anything more serious. And the internal sensors hadn't reported a major incursion. He'd assumed it was minor, even if it was alarmingly close to the guest quarters. But now... if Tiffany's security team had been involved, they could have overridden the internal sensor network. They could have taken the hostages and made their way to the courier boat without being stopped...

... And Tiffany had been with them. She'd betrayed him.

She'd betrayed...

"Admiral," Ginny said. "I..."

"Shut up," Marius roared, shocked out of his trance. His head was pounding so hard he thought his brain would explode. "Shut up..."

The entire superdreadnaught rocked. Marius caught hold of his command chair, unsure if something had genuinely gone wrong or if he was imagining it. His vision was dimming, but red icons were flashing up on the display...

"Sir," Ginny said, "Admiral Vincent's ships have opened fire on us!"

Another betrayer! The wave of cold hatred, mingled with fiery rage, was enough to force Marius to pull himself back together. "Target his ship," he growled. "Blow it apart!"

"Sir," Ginny said, "the rebels are altering course and..."

"Target Admiral Vincent's ship and kill it," Marius ordered. His head was splitting open, but he was damned if he was letting Vincent get away with everything. There should be just enough time to kill him before they had to run. "And then..."

He forced himself to think, despite the pain. Admiral Stockholm was dead, along with far too many ships and men. Admiral Vincent's crews were unreliable, even if their commanding officer died. And Roman Garibaldi, the betrayer-in-chief, held an unbeatable advantage. His ships had been hurt, but not badly enough to keep him from finishing the war here and now.

"Alter course," he ordered. He'd lost the battle — he conceded as much — but he hadn't lost the war. "All loyalist ships are to head for the Macaque Point."

"Aye, sir," Ginny said. She sounded nervous, but still in control of herself. "Admiral Vincent's ship is taking heavy fire..."

Marius nodded, watching with cold glee as the superdreadnaught was blown into atoms. It wasn't the revenge he wanted — nothing short of a year of prolonged torture would have repaid the betrayer for his crimes — but it would have to do. At least *Tiffany* was in his hands. If she'd been seduced into betraying him...

"Take us to the point, best possible speed," he ordered. Admiral Vincent's ships would be confused, he hoped; they certainly didn't seem to have found a new leader. They'd solve that problem eventually, but by that time the loyalists would be gone. "And send a specific message to *Judgement*. Condition Black. I say again, Condition Black."

"Aye, sir," Ginny said.

80 CB

Tara Prime wasn't a bad-looking world, Captain Gilbert Cole thought. Four days of lying doggo in orbit, pretending to be an ordinary merchantman, had convinced him that Admiral Vincent understood the secret of economic success. There were none of the regulations that made visiting Earth or AlphaCent such a pain, none of the constant attempts by suppliers to screw every last credit from spacers that needed to use the planet's facilities. Indeed, under other circumstances, he would have enjoyed his time at Tara Prime.

But he knew his duty.

"Activate the missile launch codes," he ordered. Rebels could not be tolerated. And if a single large example needed to be made... well, it had to be made. "And prepare to fire."

"Aye, sir," his first officer said. "Missiles ready to launch."

There were no objections from the rest of the crew, but only three people on the ship knew the targets. Everyone else thought their mission was to attack the planet's orbital infrastructure. He couldn't help wondering if some of his crewmen had actually inferred the truth, given how few questions they'd asked. Spacers were naturally curious and nothing less than threats would normally keep them from trying to work out what was going on.

Gilbert didn't hesitate. "Fire!"

His ship didn't have any real targeting systems. A military-grade sensor system on the hull would have given them away to even the most cursory of inspections. By any reasonable standards, they shouldn't have been able to hit anything...

... But then, a planet *was* a very big target.

༄༅

"Admiral," Lieutenant Thompson said. "We just picked up... my God!"

"Report," Roman snapped. He'd never heard that note of horror in her voice, even when they'd been trapped. "What happened?"

"Antimatter detonations, *multiple* antimatter detonations," Lieutenant Thompson said, her voice shaking in horror. "The Emperor just scorched Tara Prime!"

Chapter Thirty-Two

It is no exaggeration to say that the destruction of Tara Prime, with an estimated death toll of well over four billion lives, was the act that finally shattered Emperor Marius's government beyond repair.
—The Federation Navy in Retrospect, 4199

Tara Prime, 4102

Roman was speechless.

The horror before him was almost beyond his ability to grasp. Tara Prime was a blackened wasteland. The ground had been scorched clean of life by the firestorms, which had in turn faded away as the atmosphere was burnt to nothingness. Dead ground surrounded them; there was no proof, ever, that there had been a city where they were standing. And yet, Roman only had to check his hardsuit's HUD to confirm that they were standing in the middle of Willow City, center of administration for an entire sector. The city was completely gone.

He swallowed hard, feeling his body start to shake. It was hard, so hard, to comprehend the sheer *magnitude* of the devastation. He'd been told, years ago, that one death was a tragedy while one million was a statistic, yet he hadn't really understood what it meant until he'd watched Tara Prime die. Four *billion* humans — men, women and children — had lived on the now-lifeless rock, living their lives as if what happened in the galaxy beyond didn't matter in the slightest. And now they were dead, wiped from existence so completely that there was no proof they'd ever existed. It was impossible for him to grasp just how vile a crime had been committed.

Four billion? He couldn't *imagine* that many people.

"The radioactivity is picking up," Elf said, softly. "And the planet itself is unstable."

Roman nodded, tears prickling at the corner of his eyes. In all of human history, antimatter had been used once, only once, to scorch a planet clean of life. And the inhabitants of that world hadn't been human. Few had mourned for the Snakes after they'd butchered millions of humans during the First Interstellar War, but humanity — common humanity — had insisted on a taboo against using antimatter warheads against planetary surfaces. Emperor Marius had broken that taboo and condemned billions of people to death.

He tried to do it to Nova Athena, he reminded himself, sharply. *Why wouldn't he do it here?*

In hindsight, it was obvious. Nova Athena was — had been — an enemy world. Roman had never considered the attempted genocide as anything other than a desperation measure, even though he'd refused to sit back and allow it to take place. But Tara Prime had been friendly... Roman still had no idea what Admiral Vincent had been plotting, yet he *had* allied himself with the Emperor to lure Roman's fleet into a trap. There should have been no *reason* to exterminate an entire world. And yet it had been done.

He caught his footing as the ground trembled below his feet. The hammer blows that had struck the planet had triggered off earthquakes and worse, threatening to complete the destruction of human civilization. Not that it really mattered, Roman suspected; if there were any survivors, they were in underground bunkers deep below the surface. The screech of static that had greeted the fleet's hails, when they'd finally entered orbit, suggested that no one had survived. Even the deepest of bunkers might not be able to survive earthquakes on a global scale. All the old certainties about which areas were safe and which weren't no longer applied.

"Roman," Elf said. "We can't stay here."

"I know," Roman said. "I'm coming."

He took one last look at the devastation and then turned to follow her back to the shuttle. His hardsuit blinked up more alerts, warning him that the wind — what little wind there was, now that most of the atmosphere was gone — was blowing radioactive fallout towards him. If any survivors, by some miracle, managed to emerge from hidden bunkers, they'd be poisoned before they realized it was already too late. Four billion people...

"The hatch is opening," Elf told him, as they reached the shuttle. "The shuttle can take off while we decontaminate."

Roman didn't argue as they stepped through the hatch. Water cascaded down, sweeping radioactive particles off the hardsuits; he watched, grimly, as the radiation counters continued to tick upwards. They were in no danger — the hardsuits were meant for even worse environments — but he still felt a shiver of fear running down his back. He was a brave man — he'd proved it often enough — yet the thought of being killed by invisible dangers was terrifying. One couldn't fight back against radiation poisoning.

He felt the shuttle take off as they entered the next compartment, where they removed the suits and scurried into the decontamination chamber. Elf picked up a portable scanner and waved it over his body, then did the same for herself while Roman showered, keeping his eyes closed against the chemicals in the water. He'd made fun of the whole process as an immature cadet — jokes about decontamination chambers had run through the whole installation — but he knew it wasn't funny. And there was nothing sexual about worrying if they were going to die of poisoning.

"Clean, sir," the doctor said, once he stepped out of the shower and into the final compartment. "You shouldn't be in any danger, I think."

"Thank you," Roman said. He removed his sodden shipsuit and dumped it down the recycler, where it would be broken down to its component atoms. Normally, it would be washed and returned to him, but there was no point in taking chances. "And Elf?"

"The Brigadier should be fine too, I think," the doctor said, as Elf followed him into the final compartment. "But neither of you would have lasted five minutes on the surface without hardsuits, sir."

"Yeah," Roman agreed. He'd wanted to launch rescue missions, but the radioactivity in the planet's remaining atmosphere had made it clear that trying would be

futile. The level was so high that every living thing on the planet would be dead, if the firestorms hadn't already killed them. "The entire planet is dead."

He changed into a clean shipsuit, then stepped into the lounge as the shuttle continued its steady flight towards the orbiting superdreadnaughts. The remainder of Admiral Vincent's formation had surrendered, as soon as the Emperor's ships had broken and run, but he had no idea if they could be trusted. And yet, they'd just watched their planet die. How many of them, Roman asked himself, had had family and friends on the surface? They'd want revenge, wouldn't they?

But who, he asked himself, *will they blame?*

His wristcom buzzed. "Admiral, we received a priority message from *John Stuart*," the pilot said. "They boarded *Admiral Petty*, sir, and captured Hannalore Vincent. She wishes to speak to you."

"I bet she does," Roman muttered. He cleared his throat. "Order them to have her transhipped to *Valiant*."

"Aye, sir," the pilot said. "They're also reporting that they picked up a number of the admiral's relatives and their rescuer."

"Have them transhipped too," Roman ordered. He wasn't sure what that meant, but he'd find out. "And then send a signal to Senator Chang and General Stuart. We need to decide on our next step."

Roman settled back into his seat, trying to think. Could they have averted the disaster? He didn't see how, save for unconditional surrender... and even then, he had a nasty feeling that Emperor Marius would still destroy Nova Athena. His former mentor knew how to bear a grudge, after all; he'd kept Governor Barony's criminal greed and outright treachery in mind for over five *years* before dealing with him at the first possible opportunity. Roman wouldn't have bet any of his once-princely salary on Nova Athena surviving, even if the Outsiders surrendered unconditionally.

"We have to carry on the fight," he said. News of the atrocity would spread through the Federation, but how would people respond? How many of them could truly comprehend what was at stake? "We can't let him get away with murdering so many people."

"No," Elf agreed, practically. "But we also have to keep him from murdering billions *more*."

Roman shuddered. *Earth* had a population numbered in the high billions and AlphaCent wasn't too far behind, while there was hardly a Core World that didn't have at least five or six billion humans on the surface. *All* of them were at risk, if their populations or their leaders chose to revolt against the Emperor... or even if the Emperor wanted to keep them out of Outsider hands. Was Emperor Marius willing to destroy the Federation in order to save it?

The thought nagged at his mind as the shuttle returned to *Valiant* and docked at the nearest airlock. Shuttles were coming and going in a flurry of activity as the system was secured, logistics experts counting stockpiles while engineers inspected the remaining starships and starfighters, trying to determine what could be repaired and

put back into service and what needed to be broken down and cannibalized for spare parts. Roman glanced at the ship's log, noted to his relief that nothing had happened that demanded his immediate attention, then led the way to the briefing compartment. Elf followed him, muttering into her mouthpiece as she checked in with the rest of the marines. Her once-proud force was scattered across the system, trying to secure every last fortification before someone decided to do something stupid.

"They've been searched, but they're not restrained," Elf noted, as they approached the solid hatch. Two marines stood on duty outside, wearing light combat armor. "Do you want to change that before you meet them?"

Roman shrugged. "Why bother?"

He keyed the hatch, which hissed open to reveal Hannalore Vincent and four teenagers sitting at the conference table. Hannalore looked as though she was trying to keep her face as immobile as possible — a sure sign of tension — but the youngsters looked terrified, as though they'd been put through too much too quickly. It was easy, judging by their faces, to tell they were probably related. They all had the same eyes and chins. Behind them, a grim-faced man in his early forties, wearing a shipsuit, leaned against the bulkhead. He looked tired and worn.

"Admiral," Hannalore said. Her face was a mask, but Roman had no trouble hearing the fear in her voice. "My father was blackmailed."

Roman sat down at the far end of the table. "Explain."

He listened, without saying a word, as Hannalore explained. It was hard to believe that Admiral Vincent had made such an elementary mistake, leaving his children where his enemy could grab them without any real effort, but it *did* fit the facts. Admiral Vincent's ships had turned on the Emperor, engaging his ships at point-blank range. And they'd done a great deal of damage before they'd been blasted out of space.

"And now your father is dead," he said, when she'd finished. Oslo had added a few comments, but he'd need to be debriefed properly later. "I don't bear a grudge against you."

Hannalore relaxed, visibly. She'd played a role in luring the rebels forward, after all, even if she hadn't known that her father would be unable to keep his side of the bargain. It would be human, very human, for Roman to take everything out on her, if not her siblings. But she'd been an innocent dupe and her siblings pawns in a political game...

He shook his head. "Your mother was on the planet's surface," he said, shortly. "I'm sorry for your loss."

"Thank you, sir," Hannalore said. "We — the remaining survivors of the fleet — want to join you. There's nothing else for us."

Roman studied her for a long moment. *He* was quite prepared to ransack Tara Prime's orbiting stockpiles for missiles and spare parts for his ships, but he was much less eager to add the remaining personnel to his fleet. There was too great a chance of accepting a sleeper agent or an outright loyalist — if, indeed, they remained *loyal*

after watching a planet die. And yet, who was he to deny the survivors their chance at revenge? They had little else to live for.

"If we do, your crews will be split up and newcomers will be assigned to your ships," he hedged. "I trust that will be acceptable?"

"It will be more than suitable, if we can just strike back at the bastard," Hannalore said. "He would have had my siblings raped and killed."

"Killed, certainly," Roman agreed. The Marius Drake he'd known would have hesitated, surely, before ordering a young girl to be raped. But he'd changed so much in the last three years that Roman honestly wasn't sure if he'd stop at anything now. "I'm sorry your father's dreams have come to an end."

"I just want revenge," Hannalore assured him.

"Very well," Roman said. "You'll have your chance. For starters, you can help convince the fortifications in Maben and Astrid to surrender without a fight."

He called the marines, gave orders for the former hostages to be treated as honored guests, and installed in a guest suite on *Valiant* as Chang Li, General Stuart and Professor Kratman were escorted into the compartment.

"Lady *Tiffany* helped them break free?" Elf asked. "I wouldn't have thought she had it in her."

"That's what Oslo said," Roman said.

He shook his head. "She's a strong-minded person," he added. He'd only met Lady Tiffany a handful of times and they hadn't really had a chance to chat, but she *had* allied herself with Marius Drake rather than remain with her family. "And maybe there were limits to what she was prepared to condone."

"She's also either dead or a prisoner," General Stuart said, curtly. "I don't think she's going to be in position to do much of anything in the future."

"Probably," Roman agreed. He cleared his throat. "Going by the preliminary reports from the fleet's engineers, we should be rearmed and ready to move in less than a week. I intend to press onwards to Macaque — if we can, I want to move sooner. Macaque is not heavily defended."

"You intend to push on to Earth," Chang Li said.

"I think we have no choice," Roman said.

"There will be people who will want revenge," General Stuart pointed out. "They'll want us to destroy one of *his* worlds."

"It would be pointless," Roman said, flatly.

"It might convince the Emperor not to commit another slaughter," General Stuart said.

"I doubt it," Professor Kratman said. "Marius... has committed genocide once. He'll find it easier to do it again."

"I will not be responsible for the mass slaughter of men, women and children who are powerless to affect the course of the war," Roman said, raising his voice just loud enough to make the point clear. He understood the General's reasoning, but he knew he couldn't step over the line. "And burning Earth or AlphaCent until the land is blackened or broken won't affect the Emperor's ability to make war."

He closed his eyes in pain, wondering just what had become of his mentor. In *his* place, Roman would have fired on the stockpiles, crippling Tara Prime's ability to resupply his ships and forcing Roman to wait while the fleet train hauled more supplies from Boston or Ruthven. It hadn't escaped his notice that they were putting more and more pressure on the fleet train, the further they moved from their home bases. Surely, an officer as experienced as Marius Drake could see the potentials? Roman himself had hacked away at *Outsider* supply lines during the middle stages of the war.

"Agreed," Chang Li said. She glanced at her companion, then nodded. "We will not be responsible for more atrocities."

"We'll probably get the blame for it anyway," General Stuart warned. "The Emperor's lie departments will be working overtime, just to convince the sheep that *we*, not the Emperor, burned Tara Prime to ashes. Admiral Vincent will probably be turned into a hero who died bravely, clearing the way for the Emperor to escape, and we destroyed his world in retaliation."

"No one will believe that," Roman objected.

"They might," Chang Li said. "The Grand Senate built up quite an infrastructure for lying to the population."

"I can try to slip a message back to Earth," Professor Kratman offered. "I don't know if there are any Brothers left, but if there are one or two still undiscovered... well, it might be possible to get the word out."

"They wouldn't be believed," Chang Li objected.

"They might be," Professor Kratman said.

He leaned forward. "You see, hardly anyone really *believes* a word put out by Public Information," he added. "The media largely exists in an echo chamber, where they tell themselves that they're important and the Grand Senators believe them, because if they weren't telling the truth it would be on the news. But if we can get out an alternate story, it will sound more believable because there's already a strong reservoir of distrust."

"I'm not sure that makes any sense," Roman said.

"You're an asteroid brat," Kratman reminded him. "You *have* to have a firm grasp of objective reality. The people on Earth... not so much. Convince them that the Emperor killed Tara Prime — and he might do the same to Earth — and the Emperor will have riots on his hands."

"Which he'll crush," Roman said.

"And that will only make the riots worse," Kratman said. "What's he going to do if every worker across the system puts down his tools?"

"Very well," Roman said. "Send the message, Professor, and hope it reaches someone who can make something of it."

He sighed, tiredly. "But right now we need to press on as hard as we can," he added. "We have a minimum of four more systems to crawl through before we reach Earth — and the Gateway is heavily defended. Getting there may mean accepting horrendous losses."

"We could try to sneak around the defenses," Chang Li said. "It worked for Admiral Justinian."

"Admiral Justinian had all the time in the world," Roman said. "We have none."

Chapter Thirty-Three

A strong man might have been able to turn the tide. But Emperor Marius, like so many other tyrants, was strong because he had allowed no one else to be strong. His insanity only made it impossible for him to get a proper grip on the situation.
—The Federation Navy in Retrospect, 4199

Howarth, 4102

Tiffany fought her way back to consciousness through a haze of pain.

"I think she's coming out of it," a voice said. She was barely aware of the speaker, standing on the verge of her awareness. "The damage wasn't severe, but she took quite a blow. I can give her something for the pain, if you like."

"No," another voice said. It was a very familiar voice. "Leave her to cope on her own."

Tiffany felt a shock as she realized the second speaker was her husband. He'd never hurt her — he would never hurt her... memory returned and she realized, to her horror, that while Oslo and the former hostages might have escaped, *she* hadn't. She opened her eyes and found herself staring up at a blaze of white lights. The sight sent a stabbing pain through her head and she hastily closed her eyes again.

"You can open your eyes now," the first voice said. "I've dimmed the lights."

Tiffany did as she was told, despite the growing headache. Marius stood alongside her, his cold eyes boring into her skull, while an older man wearing a doctor's uniform was holding a scanner against her arm. Her hands, she discovered when she attempted to sit up, were restrained, and someone had also wrapped a cloth tie around her neck and ankles, making it impossible to move. And, as cold air blew across her body, she realized she was naked.

"You banged your head pretty badly," the doctor said. There was a hint of warmth in his tone, although it was clear she was a prisoner. "Your left arm was also broken, thankfully after you blacked out. I've repaired the damage, but you're probably still in for a few rough days."

"Thank you," Tiffany rasped. Her voice sounded odd in her ears, as if she could no longer talk properly. "Water?"

"Here," the doctor said. He picked up a tube and held it to her lips. "You shouldn't need to eat for a while, but when you do, we'll do it through a tube, rather than ask you to eat lying down."

So I won't be allowed to sit up, Tiffany thought, as she swallowed the water. It tasted curiously flat. *And escape is impossible.*

"Thank you, doctor," Marius said. There was no warmth in his voice at all. "You may leave us."

"She's fragile," the doctor said. "Sir..."

"Leave us," Marius repeated.

Tiffany wanted to close her eyes as the doctor turned and headed for the hatch, but she knew there was no point. Marius's eyes followed the doctor as he stepped

through the hatch, then, as soon as the doctor was gone, snapped back to Tiffany. She had to fight the urge to look away or try to cover herself. The man staring down at her might wear her husband's face, but he wasn't the man she loved. That man was long gone.

"Over twenty thousand crewmen dead," Marius hissed. "Forty-seven superdreadnaughts and two hundred and seven smaller ships damaged or destroyed. An entire planet wiped clean of life. Was it worth it?"

Tiffany felt her eyes widen in horror. "An entire planet?"

"Tara Prime," Marius confirmed. There was so much certainty in his voice that it never occurred to her to doubt him. "Burned to a crisp for treachery."

"You... you killed an entire planet?"

"I destroyed a wretched hive of treachery," Marius said. "By now, everyone on the planet will be dead or wishing they were."

His voice hardened. "We could have beaten the rebels," he snarled. "We could have won the battle and restored the Federation. Instead... we lost. We had to retreat, leaving the battlefield to the traitors. And that was all your fault."

"Marius," Tiffany said. "I..."

Marius slapped her face, hard. Tiffany cried out in pain. She'd been raised in the aristocracy, where she'd never had to experience pain or discomfort. The shock of being struck was almost worse than the pain. No one had ever struck her before.

"We could lose this war," Marius said. "And all thanks to you!"

He slapped her again. Tiffany tasted blood in her mouth. Marius cocked his fist, pulling it back as if he intended to slam it right into her head, then relaxed very slightly. Somehow, Tiffany didn't think it was good news. Part of her almost hoped that Marius would kill her and finish the job.

"A planet is dead, Tiffany," he said. "And what will happen when the rebels storm the Gateway?"

"You have to listen to me," Tiffany said, despite the throbbing pain. "Marius, the Federation can't be held together by force..."

He slammed his fist into her chest, hard enough to make her retch. "What do you know about it? Spoilt little brat, raised by the Grand Senate... I had to *work* to earn *my* title, only to see everything I did thrown away by stupid little men who had never heard a shot fired in anger or arrived — too late — on the scene of a pirate raid. I could have saved millions of lives if I'd been given the power and responsibility I needed. Instead, they tried to kill me!"

Tiffany stared at him, hopelessly, as he started to pace the compartment. There didn't seem to be any point in appealing to logic and reason, not now. Marius had been betrayed so many times that he'd lost the ability to consider if the betrayer had a point. But then, so many of his betrayers had *no* point. The Grand Senate hadn't been in danger until it had tried to kill him. They'd created the monster that had destroyed them and was burning the Federation to the ground.

She tried, hard, to imagine what would happen as word spread through the Asimov Points, no matter what the Emperor did to stop it. Entire worlds would

quake in fear — or rise up against the Emperor, taking control of their own defenses and desperately preparing to resist his starships when they arrived. The glue that held the Federation together, already weakening, would melt for the final time. And nothing Marius could do would keep the Federation from shattering.

"Marius," she said, hoping she could get through to him one final time, "what would Tobias think of this?"

Marius whirled around and lunged at her, his hand coming down and grasping her neck, threatening to choke the life out of her. Tiffany tried to struggle free, but the restraints were too strong. She gasped, fighting for breath, as his grip tightened, unable to avoid staring up into his maddened eyes. He'd kill her with his bare hands...

"Don't mention his name," he snarled, as he let go. Tiffany wanted to rub her aching throat, but she couldn't move. "Don't you fucking mention his name!"

He stepped backwards, angrily, but when he spoke his voice was almost calm. "I haven't decided what's to happen to you yet," he said. "But I assure you that you will never be in a position to cause any more harm."

Tiffany watched, helplessly, as he strode through the hatch and out into the corridor, leaving her alone. She tested the restraints, once again, but no matter what she did she couldn't pull free. At least the hostages were free, she reminded herself, even though it had been no part of her plan to remain behind. Whatever happened now...

She closed her eyes as the darkness rose up again, threatening to overwhelm her. Part of her wanted to remain awake, but she knew there was no point. Deep inside, she knew she had come to the end of the line.

ᔥᔦ

Marius poured himself a glass of whiskey and swallowed it in one gulp, then poured himself another glass as he sat down on the sofa in his office. He hadn't been able to go back to his suite, not when it held far too many reminders of Tiffany... it was hard, so hard, to keep the anger under control whenever he remembered his wife. The final betrayal... and, perhaps, the one that hurt the most. He'd trusted Tiffany, even though she was from an aristocratic family. He'd even left Earth in her care when he'd gone to Nova Athena...

And maybe that is why there were so many problems, he thought, as he stared at the golden liquid. *Tiffany was sabotaging me all along.*

He scowled as all the pieces fell into place. Her clingy insistence on being close to him, her determination to make love every day... she'd been keeping him away from his work and ensuring the Federation would collapse into ruin. And she'd insisted on coming with him to Tara Prime purely to ensure that Admiral Vincent's plan to betray him succeeded. At least *that* bastard was dead, along with his homeworld and maybe even his family. It wasn't what he'd *wanted* to do to Admiral Vincent, but it would have to do. One of the betrayers had paid with his life — and the lives of everyone he'd ever cared about.

And Tiffany will pay too, he thought. How many times had she been next to him, curled up beside him in bed? Had she been betraying him all along? She could have been Blake Raistlin's handler, the one who passed the order to assassinate Marius

before he could turn into a threat. *Did she only want power for herself or for her family?*

He looked up as the doorbell chimed. For a moment, he considered merely ignoring it — there shouldn't be any problems Captain Watson couldn't handle before they reached the Gateway — but duty overrode the temptation to just sit in his suite and wallow. He snapped out a command and the hatch hissed open, revealing Ginny Lewis. Marius glared at her, then felt an odd flicker of shame as she flinched. Ginny, at least, had never betrayed him. She'd merely done her duty.

"Come in," he grunted. "Sit."

Ginny obeyed, looking nervous. Her uniform looked rumpled too, something that puzzled Marius until he remembered that he'd ordered the Blackshirts to search everyone who wanted to enter his office. No doubt Ginny had been groped quite thoroughly before she'd been allowed through the first checkpoint. If she'd been carrying anything that *might* have been a weapon, they'd have carted her off to the brig before she could say a word in protest.

"We just transited into the Howarth System, sir," Ginny said. "They know."

Marius *looked* at her. "Know *what?*"

"That Tara Prime has been destroyed," Ginny said. "And that we did it."

"Someone must have sent a message," Marius muttered. It wasn't impossible, even though he'd tried to keep a lid on the Macaque Point. Someone — probably someone still working for Admiral Vincent — would have snapped a courier drone through the Asimov Point and the secret would be out and spreading. "What do they know?"

"That we destroyed Tara Prime," Ginny said. "There was no attempt to bar us from entering the system, but they're clearly ready to engage if we try to approach the planet."

Marius considered, briefly, turning to flatten the planet's defenses, just to make it clear that resistance to legitimate authority was futile, before dismissing the thought. They *had* to return to Earth. God alone knew what problems General Thorne was facing, thanks to Tiffany and whatever remained of the Brotherhood. Howarth wasn't important, particularly not when an Outsider fleet was breathing down his neck. There would be time to teach the planet a lesson later.

"We proceed to the system limits," he said. "Do you have an updated status report?"

"Yes, sir," Ginny said. "We have barely two active squadrons of superdreadnaughts and flanking units. It will take at least two months, according to the engineers, to fix the damaged ships."

Marius breathed a curse. He'd taken seven squadrons of superdreadnaughts to Tara Prime, but losses had been heavy. Admiral Vincent's attack, at point-blank range, had done almost as much damage as the rebels, in far less time. He'd paid for it, but still...

"We need to return to Earth," he said. "Has word gone ahead of us?"

"Probably, sir," Ginny said. "If a ship happened to be leaving Howarth for Maidstone..."

"Then the Gateway defenders may know," Marius snarled. He'd picked the officers in command carefully, but he knew just how quickly a mind could turn to treachery. He certainly hadn't suspected Tiffany until it was far too late. "And they may try to bar our passage back to Earth."

Ginny blanched. "They wouldn't..."

"They might," Marius said. Her naiveté would have been amusing, if it hadn't been so serious. It was easy to forget she'd only been in the navy for five years. "And Home Fleet has been badly weakened."

He ran his hands through his hair. "And I never suspected Tiffany," he added. "Who knows what she might have done to the fortresses?"

"I'm sorry, sir," Ginny said.

Marius shook his head. "Inform Captain Watson that he is to maintain our best possible speed towards Earth," he ordered. "And then start going through the reports from the tactical analysts. I'll want your analysis this evening."

"Yes, sir," Ginny said. She rose. "And I'm sorry about your wife, sir..."

"Do your duty," Marius growled, too tired to be angry. He wanted to sleep, but he wasn't sure he dared. "And don't come back until this evening."

"Aye, sir," Ginny said.

Marius watched her go, feeling only a trace of guilt for admiring her buttocks in her tight uniform. Ginny was too young, too innocent, to be treacherous — and she was a navy brat, not an entitled officer who happened to be related to a Grand Senator. She'd be a better wife than Tiffany, he was sure, but he had no time to consider remarrying. He certainly couldn't allow himself to be distracted by sex when there was too much else to do.

He yawned, then leaned backwards onto the sofa. Perhaps he'd take a very short nap...

‽⎇

Ginny couldn't help feeling, as the hatch hissed closed behind her, that she'd just escaped by the skin of her teeth. The Emperor had looked a mess, his face purple and his hands twitching constantly... Ginny had no idea what he'd been drinking, or if he'd been taking more of those damnable pills, but he was clearly in a state. He needed a long rest and detoxification, not more stress...

And he doesn't suspect me, she thought, as the Blackshirts closed in. *If he did, I'd be dead by now.*

"Arms and legs apart, then stand still," the lead Blackshirt ordered. Ginny had no idea where the Emperor — or General Thorne — had found them, but the Blackshirts seemed to enjoy harassing crewmen, male as well as female. There was no logic in searching her *after* she'd left the Emperor's office, yet they didn't let that stop them. "Let's see what you're hiding."

She gritted her teeth as they ran their hands over her body, lingering over her breasts and buttocks, before finally sending her on her way with a casual slap to her behind. Their touch made her feel dirty; she'd endured searches before, back in the

academy, but they'd never been so thoroughly *vile*. It didn't seem to have occurred to the Emperor, or General Thorne either, that the Blackshirts would probably wind up provoking a mutiny. Their predecessors had certainly done the same thing, back before the Grand Senate had fallen.

They're not doing it because they're searching for guns or bombs, she thought. *They're doing it to make it clear they're in charge.*

Captain Watson turned to face her as she stepped onto the bridge, an odd look of respect in his eyes. He outranked her, but she was the *Emperor's* tactical aide. A word from her in the emperor's ears, when he was in a receptive mood, might put an end to the captain's career. She felt a flicker of sympathy for the man, but pushed it aside. Captain Watson had sat on the bridge and done nothing while the Emperor killed an entire world.

"The Emperor wants you to proceed to the Gateway as fast as possible," she said. "And he wants to keep the entire fleet in lockdown."

He didn't look surprised, she noted, but the orders wouldn't be particularly surprising. It wasn't as if they could make a stand before the Gateway. Maidstone had some defenses, but they were largely emplaced around the planet itself, rather than the Asimov Point.

"As the Emperor commands," Captain Watson said. "When will he grace us with his presence?"

Ginny hoped that was sarcasm. The Emperor, she'd learned, had little patience for flattery, let alone senior officers fighting over who had the right to kiss his buttocks. But Captain Watson hadn't survived so long without a sense for who best to flatter and who best to cut dead. His career certainly hadn't been based on tactical acumen.

"He has much work to do," she temporized. Captain Watson could be relied upon to carry out his orders and little else. There certainly wouldn't be any unexpected surprises from him. "I believe he feels that matters can be safely left in your hands."

She saluted, then walked back through the hatch and into the tactical compartment. The analysts were still hard at work, assessing every last moment of the engagement. Ginny picked up a datapad, downloaded a copy of the raw data, and started to go through it personally. It would take time, but she knew the Emperor wanted her assessment...

... And, while she worked, she contemplated ways to betray him.

Chapter Thirty-Four

And, because of the Emperor's clear madness, those who would have been his allies chose
to turn on him.
—The Federation Navy in Retrospect, 4199

Macaque, 4102

"We're picking up a signal from the planet, sir," Lieutenant Thompson said. "They want to surrender."

Roman lifted his eyebrows. The fleet had only transited the Asimov Point a few scant hours ago — indeed, Macaque must have decided to surrender within seconds of receiving the news, although the defenses surrounding the Asimov Point hadn't put up a fight. It looked, very much, as though the system had heard what had happened to Tara Prime and wanted to switch sides. By now, five days after an entire planet died, word had to be spreading through the Core Worlds.

"Inform them that we accept their surrender and will be taking possession of the defenses of the Howarth Point," he ordered. "If they have any warships, they are to be handed over; everything else can remain with them until we figure out the shape of the post-war galaxy."

"Aye, sir," Lieutenant Thompson said.

Roman nodded, and turned his attention to the display. Howarth's Asimov Points had never been heavily fortified, not when the system's only real attraction was being too close to Maidstone in realspace; they shouldn't have any difficulty breaking into the system and setting course for the system limits. Howarth itself was quite heavily defended, but Roman had no intention of attacking the planet. Like Macaque, the defenders could be safely left alone until the war was over.

Unless we happen to need something from them, he thought. *But what is there that we need?*

He frowned in contemplation. The latest update, secured from Tara Prime, insisted that the defenses of AlphaCent and the Gateway itself had been heavily updated, which was no surprise; the only real question was just how *loyal* those defenses would be to the Emperor. AlphaCent was perhaps the most loyal planet in the galaxy, at least to the Grand Senate, but would even *they* turn on a rogue Emperor? Or would they fight to keep his ships from entering the system?

They'll certainly know we've entered the Maidstone System, he reminded himself. *And by now, the Emperor might well have had a chance to make sure that any weaklings are removed from power before it's too late.*

He pushed the thought aside. He'd just have to see what happened when the fleet reached the system.

"Ask Senator Li and General Stuart if we can have a private chat after the diplomatic dinner," he ordered, instead. One advantage of holding Tara Prime, quite apart from the chance to resupply, was making contact with a number of worlds that weren't *quite* Core Worlds, but were certainly important enough to be worth

courting. A number of diplomats had insisted on accompanying the fleet. "We have much to discuss."

"Aye, sir," Lieutenant Thompson said.

೮೦೦೪

Uzi had honestly expected to die when the superdreadnaught had lumbered into Tara Prime... and straight into a trap. He'd thought himself prepared to make certain Chang Li, if no one else, didn't survive, only to recoil in horror as Admiral Vincent turned his coat for the second time and threw victory to Admiral Garibaldi. The destruction of Tara Prime didn't bother him, no matter how many times he'd faked crocodile tears for his comrades, but losing the battle the loyalists should have won nagged at him.

And now, utter disaster was staring the Federation in the face.

Macaque's surrender was a minor matter, but the arrival of diplomats from a dozen other worlds was far more serious. Some of them would have been primed by Admiral Vincent, he thought; others, perhaps the ones from richer worlds, had come on their own. And by choosing to throw their weight behind the rebels, they made Admiral Garibaldi's momentum almost unstoppable. Even if the fleet was destroyed, and it was still possible, the Federation was doomed. The Outsiders would win.

"It's a wonderful time," Cleo said, hugging him as they made their way back to their shared cabin. "Everything is finally falling into place."

"I suppose," Uzi mumbled.

He was barely paying attention to her as he contemplated the problem. Something would *have* to be done. He'd been out of place to assassinate either Chang Li or Admiral Garibaldi — and he'd received no orders — but his overall briefing included permission to act on his own initiative if there was no other option... and he saw none.

What should he do? Wait until the fleet hit the Gateway? Even if the Gateway held, even if the fleet died, it wasn't likely that the Federation could be restored.

No. The twin problems of Admiral Garibaldi and Senator Li had to be resolved as soon as possible.

"There's going to be a larger meeting tonight, after dinner," Cleo said. "Will you be attending?"

"I think I'll be on the outside," Uzi said. The idea of having a dinner that included junior officers was alien to him, at least when the junior officers were commoners, but the Outsiders were ruthlessly meritocratic. Besides, he had to admit it was a good way to gauge crew morale. "I'm a bodyguard, not her advisor."

Cleo glanced at him as she opened the hatch. "Don't you ever get asked for advice?"

Uzi shrugged. "What sort of advice could I give?"

He eyed Cleo's back, silently contemplating the most efficient way to kill her. She couldn't be allowed to sound the alert, not when he was going to be organizing his weapons for the assassination attempt. Playing with her had been fun, even if she had become annoyingly clingy, but time was now up.

"We do have time for some fun," he said, as he stepped up behind her. "And now..."

He pressed one hand over her mouth, using the other to snap her neck. She grunted in surprise, then went limp. Uzi held her in place until he was sure the life had drained out of her body, just in case she had some enhancements she'd never mentioned. Once he was sure, he placed her body in the corner of the tiny cabin, covered it with the blanket and opened his bag. One definite *advantage* to working along the Rim, or with the Outsiders, was that no one ever questioned why anyone would want to carry a small arsenal. You never knew when you might have to fight.

There was no time for a real plan, he told himself, as he removed a handful of explosive packs and buried them under his uniform. He'd have to cause an emergency, then take advantage of the chaos to carry out his mission. Survival was very unlikely — after Admiral Vincent's bastards had escaped, Admiral Garibaldi would have learned from the Emperor's mistake and the courier boats and shuttles would be guarded — but he'd just have to take his chances.

And no one will ever know what I did, he thought. He remembered, morbidly, just how much he'd done in the name of the Federation. *But perhaps that's for the best.*

☙❧

"It could have gone worse," Chang Li said, as she entered the small dining room and sat down next to Admiral Garibaldi. "They want independence, rather than membership in a new federation."

"You may find that it's impossible to convince them to slip all the way to join you," Garibaldi commented. "They're the ones who watched in horror as Tara Prime died."

Li nodded in grim agreement. The Federation had started life as nothing more than an overarching federal government, intended to coordinate humanity's ongoing expansion into space. But it had claimed more and more power until the Core Worlds had little in the way of true independence and the Rim became helpless to keep the Grand Senate from draining it dry. And now, after Tara Prime, it would be a long time before anyone willingly surrendered political power again.

She leaned back in her seat and watched the diners as they started to eat, chatting all the while. A number of the diplomats looked shocked by the sheer lack of formality, but willing to play along; a couple looked as though they were on the verge of being led to their own executions. Li smiled at their frustration, even though she understood their feelings. The rules they knew, the rules that had taught them how to act in every given situation, simply didn't apply.

No one cares which fork you use to eat the starter, she thought, remembering the etiquette lessons she'd had to endure when she'd become a Grand Senator. From what Talia Vincent has said, Blyton Towers was *still* teaching children how to pass for aristocrats even after the Grand Senate had fallen. *All that matters is that you know what you're doing.*

She sighed, inwardly. She'd never really believed the Emperor would commit genocide, even after he'd tried to destroy her homeworld. Tara Prime had been one of his worlds, after all; it certainly hadn't deserved to die for Admiral Vincent's crimes. But she knew, now, that the Emperor was no longer sane. He might start turning

antimatter weapons on AlphaCent — or even Earth itself — if he could no longer rule the Federation.

And that's why we have to win, she told herself. *We can fight over who gets to put the pieces back together afterwards.*

৪০ ৫৪

It was lucky, Uzi knew, that Admiral Garibaldi had decided to continue flying his flag on *Valiant*, rather than transferring to one of the Outsider ships. The Federation had made great strides in computer security, ever since Admiral Justinian had rubbed the Grand Senate's collective nose in its own weaknesses, but there were still gaps in the defenses. It wasn't enough to allow him to trigger the self-destruct system or detonate a warhead — that only happened in bad movies — yet he could still move around the ship relatively unmolested and spy on her crew.

They're at the High Table, he thought, as he slipped into the internal tubes and started to crawl towards the hatch. Civilians never grasped just how many hidden passageways there *were* through a superdreadnaught, let alone how easy it was to crawl between the bridge and engineering without being seen. He'd planned to kill anyone he met, but it hadn't been necessary. *And I can catch them by surprise.*

He reached his destination, a hatch right *above* the dining compartment, and glanced down at his terminal. There was no sign of a security alert, no sense that anyone knew he was in place to strike a major blow for the Federation. It was a relief, but still... part of him found it a little annoying. He keyed a security code into the terminal, and sent the signal.

Seconds later, the superdreadnaught rocked as a small explosive detonated just down the corridor. No one should be hurt, but it would be just big enough to put the entire ship into lockdown while the bridge crew scrambled to figure out what had happened.

He wondered, absently, just what they'd conclude, then opened the hatch and dropped down.

৪০ ৫৪

Roman hadn't been enjoying the dinner, although he'd kept a smile pasted on his face as he'd chatted to a number of diplomats. Some were good people, but others were more interested in their own personal power than the survival of the Federation and the defeat of the Emperor. He'd lost count of just how many of them had promised reinforcements in exchange for post-war concessions, when there was no guarantee of actually *winning* the war. Emperor Marius might still find a way to take the Federation down with him.

And then the entire ship shook, a dull rumble echoing through her hull.

He jumped to his feet as panic flickered through the compartment. It wasn't a missile hit, he was sure. Even if a cloaked ship had managed to get close enough to launch a missile without being detected, it just felt *wrong*. An internal explosion... but what? A single warhead would have done a great deal of damage, perhaps smashing the antimatter containment fields as it exploded and blowing the entire ship into atoms. Or...

"Get down," Elf snapped. She caught his arm and yanked him forward, throwing him facedown to the deck. "Stay down!"

And then the shooting started.

࿅࿅

He'd messed up, Uzi noted, as he hurled a pair of grenades towards the stunned diplomats and junior officers. The hatch *hadn't* been quite where he'd expected it to be, although he *had* managed to land on the high table. He swung around, looking for his targets, and smirked nastily when he laid eyes on Chang Li. The treacherous senator hadn't any real combat experience, despite commanding one side of a galaxy-spanning war; he put four shots into her, just to make sure she was dead. He jumped down as the grenades exploded, ducking low in case someone returned fire. The Outsiders, after all, refused to surrender their weapons to anyone.

Smart move, he thought, as he killed a diplomat and a uniformed officer he didn't recognize while hunting for his other target. *They know they're being hunted.*

He turned... and the hammer of God slammed into his body. A woman stood there, pistol in hand; it took him a second, a second too long, to recognize Brigadier Tanager. She might not have recognized him, but she'd probably realized, just from the speed he was moving, that he'd been enhanced. Uzi tried to lift his rifle, yet it was already too late. Five more bullets slammed into his body.

He crashed to the deck. Red icons flared up in front of him, warning him that he'd been too badly hurt to continue the fight. The bitch knew *precisely* how to kill him.

At least one of the targets is dead, he thought. Chang Li had held the Outsiders together, despite a war they'd been on the verge of losing before Nova Athena. General Stuart was a military man, not a diplomat; he'd be unable to hold the federation together. *And...*

Darkness came.

࿅࿅

"He's dead, I think," Elf said. "It would be better to evacuate this compartment."

Roman pulled himself to his feet, then swore. Chang Li's body lay on the deck, blood pooling beneath her. It was clear, even to his inexperienced eye, that there was no hope of resurrection. One of the bullets had gone right through her head and out the rear of her skull, leaving her brains leaking out onto the deck. Beside her, the assassin was a mangled ruin of a man, cyborg implants sticking out of his chest and head.

"Take everyone still alive out of the room," Elf ordered. "I'll make sure the body remains untouched — and immobile."

It didn't look as though the assassin *could* move, Roman thought, but he knew better than to take it for granted. Being promoted to admiral had given him access to a number of secret files, including ones covering enhanced soldiers. Marines weren't enhanced, yet if they could perform miracles... what could an enhanced soldier do? He looked at the bloody remains of a dozen officers, where the grenades had exploded, and felt sick. Starship combat was clean and tidy, unless one's ship was hit. This... this was something worse.

"Clear the compartment," he ordered, as the marines and medics burst into the chamber. "If you're injured, tell us now."

And hope we can survive this, he thought, privately. *Without Chang Li...*

                    ଚୢଓଷ

"The assassin was one of the mercenaries assigned to the senator as a bodyguard," General Stuart said, an hour later. "He killed his girlfriend, it seems, just before he set off on his final mission. His background was fully vetted, we thought, when we accepted him. And he served us well over the last three years. There was never any suggestion he might turn on us."

"He was an enhanced mercenary," Roman said. He'd seen some enhanced cyborgs when he'd been in command of *Midway*, years ago. In fact, he had a nasty feeling he'd seen this *particular* cyborg some time ago. "The Federation might have paid for his implants in exchange for loyalty."

"Or programmed it into his skull," General Stuart said. "He might not have had a choice."

"It doesn't matter," Roman said. He looked down at the blood splattered across his uniform, then up at the General. The mercenary might have acted out of his own free will or not, but it was irrelevant. All that mattered was what he'd done. "We have to carry on."

"She would have wanted it that way," General Stuart agreed. He shook his head, slowly, suddenly seeming much older. They'd been friends, Roman realized, perhaps more than friends. They'd certainly worked closely together for decades. "But... will there be anything left of us, either?"

Roman considered his answer for a long moment. "I think the Emperor still has to be stopped," he said. Had Emperor Marius issued the orders to kill Chang Li person-ally? It was possible, but unlikely. Surely, if there had been direct communication between the mercenary and the Emperor, the orders would have been to assassinate Roman on his own bridge. "And afterwards... well, we'll worry about that afterwards."

"Everything's falling apart," General Stuart said. "I don't know what will happen when word gets home."

"We'll have won or lost by then," Roman said. There was no way to keep word of Chang Li's death from spreading, but most of the Federation's citizens wouldn't know how vital she'd been to the Outsiders. "And the Emperor will never have the chance to dance on her grave."

He turned to look at the display. "We'll clear up the mess and continue our course towards Howarth — and the Gateway. And then we can put an end to this whole damned war!"

Chapter Thirty-Five

Chang Li's death, while unfortunate, came too late to make any real difference. The news of Tara Prime's destruction had already spread too far to be stopped.
—The Federation Navy in Retrospect, 4199

Earth, 4102

"Emperor," General Thorne said, as he entered Marius's office. "Are you not returning to the Presidential House?"

"I prefer to remain on *Enterprise*," Marius said, stiffly. He'd done what he could to keep himself busy, but the nightmares refused to fade, despite the alcohol and the drugs. "It makes it easier to coordinate the fleet."

"Understood," General Thorne said. "Rumors have been spreading through Earth, but most of them have been gravely exaggerated. I do not think they are being believed."

"Good," Marius said. "It will not be long before Admiral Garibaldi challenges the Gateway."

General Thorne rocked back in surprise. "The defenders of AlphaCent won't stop him?"

"I believe he will punch his way into AlphaCent and make a beeline for the Gateway," Marius said. It was a bitter thought, but one that had to be faced. "I intend to greet him with a full-scale defense. He will not pass."

"Yes, sir," General Thorne said.

"There is another matter," Marius added, after a moment. A pang of bitter grief and guilt ran through him. Was there no one who could be trusted completely? "My wife committed treachery."

"Yes, sir," General Thorne said, neutrally.

"I want you to find out if she acted alone," Marius added. "And if she was assisted by others, I want their names."

"Yes, sir," General Thorne said. "Do I have your permission for extreme measures?"

Marius hesitated. He wanted Tiffany to suffer for betraying him... and yet, he didn't want to go too far. She needed to look reasonably intact for her trial. This time, there would be no games; this time, her guilt would be conclusively proven for all to see.

"No," he said. "She needs to remain healthy for her trial."

"Sir," General Throne said. "Does she *need* a trial?"

Marius felt a hot flash of anger. "The universe has to see her guilt," he snapped. "They have to understand just what she did, General, and they have to understand why she was *wrong!*"

"Yes, sir," General Thorne said, bowing low. "I will see to it personally."

Marius watched him go, feeling an odd flicker of affection. Thorne, at least, hadn't betrayed him — and he'd kept Earth under control while Marius had been at Tara Prime. Maybe some of the rumors would be believed — Marius knew just how

fast rumors could spread from one end of the Federation to the other — but everyone knew he was still in control. Given time, he could turn the Gateway into an impregnable fortress and crush Admiral Garibaldi when he tried to force his way into the system. And then he could link up with the remaining admirals and drive the Outsiders back into the Beyond.

He sighed, then keyed the intercom, calling for Ginny. They had much work to do.

ଚଡ଼ଓଃ

Tiffany hadn't been too sure what to expect, after Marius half-strangled her before walking out and leaving her with the doctors, but she hadn't expected boredom. They'd kept her tied to the bed and fed her through tubes, ignoring her when she tried to strike up a conversation or request something — anything — to do. She'd begged for a computer terminal or an entertainment console, like the ones used to keep the proles occupied, but all she'd been allowed to do was lie there. They hadn't even drugged her back to sleep!

And how long have I been lying here, she asked herself, for the umpteenth time. It felt as if she'd been lying on the bed, practically immobilized, for years, but there was no way to *know*. The lighting never changed. *If they've been drugging me, I could have been lying here for months.*

She heard the hatch open and twisted her head, as far as she could, to see who had entered the small compartment. Her blood ran cold, a second later, as she recognized General Thorne, a man who'd been left behind on Earth. If he was here, they had to be back in the Sol System... she'd been on the bed for two weeks, then. Oddly, the thought gave her a feeling of bitter satisfaction. At least she now knew something they'd wanted to keep from her.

"Lady Tiffany," General Thorne said. "I must say you're looking well."

"Fuck off," Tiffany said. Her etiquette tutors would have been horrified, but she rather doubted her marital prospects mattered any longer. Besides, she'd been naked for too long to care about him seeing her nude body. "You twisted bastard..."

"There, there," General Thorne mocked. He patted her forehead, as one might pet a dog. "Is that any way to speak to the man who's going to save your life?"

"You're not here to save my life," Tiffany said, grimly. Ginny was the only person she knew she could trust on the ship... and she hadn't seen Ginny since they'd freed the hostages. Had she been caught? Marius would have killed her, mercilessly, if she had. "What do you want?"

"Now, *that* is a far better question," General Thorne said. He made a show of looking up and down her body, his eyes crawling over her skin. "What do you *think* I want?"

"I think you're so pathetic that you have to wait for a woman to be tied down so you can have your way with her." Tiffany sneered. She knew she couldn't stop him, if he wanted to climb on top and force his way into her, but she could at least lash out at his ego. And maybe she could pinch him too. Or urinate on him. He'd have to remove the tubes if he wanted to rape her anyway. "And forcing yourself on me won't change the fact you have a very small penis!"

"Such crude manners from one of High Society," General Thorne observed. "No *wonder* you were never married off until they decided they needed to keep the Emperor under control."

He smiled and went on before Tiffany could think of a rejoinder. "I've never had any trouble getting the girls and boys into bed, Lady Tiffany. They are lured to me by power, willing to do anything, no matter how degrading, in exchange for a scrap of influence. It's always interesting to watch just how many people are willing to compromise their principles, when there is power and prestige at stake."

"No doubt," Tiffany said. She'd expected torture, but hearing General Thorne prattle on was worse. "I'm sure you know all about it."

"Let me tell you a joke," General Thorne said. "There's this beautiful virgin, a nineteen-year-old society beauty who's the living image of female rectitude. Everyone wants her, but she's too demure to let them have her. And then a very rich man comes along and offers her a million credits in exchange for sleeping with him. She thinks about it; she doesn't want to open her legs for some old bastard with a penis transplant, but a million credits is a million credits. So she says yes."

"And then the old bastard offers her a single credit," Tiffany finished, sharply. "And when she protests, demanding to know what he thinks she is, he tells her that they've already established that she's a whore and they're just haggling over the price. I know the joke, General. It was hammered into my head as a child. My father taught it to me."

"Then he did you a great service," General Thorne said. "Not *all* of us are so lucky with our parents."

"And you're the old bastard who delights in making people compromise them-selves," Tiffany said. Understanding clicked. "You're the person who gave Marius those pills, aren't you?"

"I may have had something to do with it," General Thorne said. "Although, to be fair, the stresses of running the Federation were getting to your husband long before I clawed my way into his confidence."

"And you enjoyed watching him compromise *his* principles," Tiffany snapped.

"I don't think he really compromised anything," General Thorne said, after a moment of apparent thought. "It's evident that he always had the *mindset* to be a dictator, to do whatever he felt necessary to uphold the Federation... which also hap-pened to uphold his power base. But, at the same time, he lacks the pragmatism of Admiral Vincent. The idealism of an idealistic man can lead him to commit far more atrocities than a selfish bastard more interested in his own power than anything else."

"He wanted to remain an admiral," Tiffany said.

"And what do you think an admiral *is*?" General Thorne asked. "An absolute dicta-tor, in command of hundreds of ships and thousands of spacers."

Tiffany sighed. "What is your *point*, General?"

"The recorders are off," General Thorne said. "I've gone to some trouble to make sure that we will be unheard."

"How kind of you," Tiffany said, snidely. "I didn't think I could get into *worse* trouble."

"Marry me," General Thorne said.

Tiffany blinked in shock. "*What?*"

"The Emperor is mad," General Thorne said, flatly. "I think you know it as well as I do, Lady Tiffany. And trying to ally myself with Admiral Garibaldi would be a dangerous gamble. There's always a need for someone like me, someone who can do the dirty work without those inconvenient moral scruples, but Admiral Garibaldi probably has his own set of enforcers by now."

"Or he might just decide he has no use for you," Tiffany pointed out.

"There's always a need for someone like me," General Thorne repeated. "But you're the *Empress*, to all intents and purposes. Marry me, and I will free you and overthrow your former husband. And together we will rule Earth."

Tiffany fought down an insane urge to giggle. She knew — she *knew* — that General Thorne was being sincere, even though it seemed laughable. He might just be able to overthrow Marius, then declare himself the new Emperor. And, with Tiffany by his side, he might just be able to make it stick. Unless, of course, Admiral Garibaldi unseated both of them when he attacked Sol...

"You do realize that Admiral Garibaldi is unlikely to be impressed," she said. "What do you plan to do about *him?*"

"I don't ask for much," General Thorne said. "I — we — will remain in possession of Sol, perhaps AlphaCent and a handful of other Core Worlds. If Garibaldi was willing to make a similar deal with Admiral Vincent, he should be willing to make one with me. And your name will add a certain credit to my regime."

Tiffany shuddered. She wanted to be free, she wanted to escape Marius's grasp, but she knew she couldn't trust General Thorne. She'd exchange captivity in sickbay for a gilded cage, at best; she'd be lucky to have any freedom at all, if he didn't just implant her to ensure that she was an obedient wife. And even if he treated her as an equal, she doubted Admiral Garibaldi would leave Sol in the hands of a ruthless bastard. Earth was the homeworld of humanity, after all.

"No," she said, flatly.

General Thorne cocked his head. "You *do* realize there's no other way out?"

Tiffany shrugged.

"I'm serious," General Thorne warned. "You'll be interrogated, over the next few days, until you spill everything you know. And then you'll be put on trial, in front of a carefully-selected jury, and found guilty. And *then* you will be put to death. Or, if your husband is feeling sadistic, dumped on a penal world. What do you think would happen to a young woman like you, dumped amid thieves and murderers and rapists?"

"It would be better than lying with you," Tiffany said. "And what is to stop me telling everyone about *your* little ploy?"

General Thorne smirked. "You know the interesting thing about direct brain induction? A subject can have all sorts of hallucinations, without ever being entirely

certain what is real and what isn't. You might become convinced that aliens are eating your brain, Lady Tiffany, or that your father was actually a wizard with magical powers. And you'd tell the world those lies with total conviction. No one will believe a word of the truth."

"Then go to the devil," Tiffany said, tiredly. Marrying General Thorne, even if he *could* overthrow Marius, was too high a price to pay for freedom. And even if they did get her to tell them about Ginny... well, maybe they'd discount it as yet another hallucination. It wasn't much, but she clung to the thought anyway. "Get on with it."

"As you wish," General Thorne said. He patted her left breast, affectionately. "The next few days are going to be *really* interesting."

"Only for you," Tiffany said.

"Oh, for you too," General Thorne said. "Quite a few people learn interesting things about themselves just by seeing what hallucinations their minds produce."

ഇൽ

It was growing colder.

There was no thermostat in the tiny apartment, nothing to suggest what the temperature actually was, but Rupert McGillivray had no trouble realizing that it was getting colder and colder. It was so cold that he was having trouble sleeping. His bones ached and creaked as he struggled to keep himself busy. The landlord hadn't bothered to install heating elements, despite a number of governmental regulations insisting on keeping the building warm at all times. It wasn't as if anyone gave a damn, after all.

He poured himself a cup of powdered soup as he sat down at the table and inspected — again — the terminal. It was hard to maintain any sort of link to the planetary database, even though he'd spent the last month trying to access some of the hidden accounts buried deep within the banking system. It was galling to know he could have moved himself to a far superior apartment within hours, if he hadn't been sure it would attract attention. The Emperor's goons would be watching for him. And even if they weren't, it would be too easy to fall into bad habits.

Cursing under his breath — even buying food was tricky, in the slums — he logged into one of the message accounts and blinked in surprise. A message was waiting for him, marked with a code that only a couple of Brothers knew. Rupert hesitated — he'd assumed that Professor Kratman had been killed by the Emperor — and then opened the message. If someone had tracked it through the datanet, the mere act of logging into the account would reveal his location.

Assuming they can track me back through all the datanodes, he reminded himself. ONI was good — he had a healthy respect for their WebHeads — but Earth's datanet was a shambolic mess. He'd voted to repair or rebuild the network, or perhaps just install a new one, yet he'd always been outvoted. For once, his political isolation had actually worked in his favor, making it harder for the Emperor to track him down. *And even if they can...*

He opened the message and swore as he realized there were a whole series of attachments accompanying the text. Tara Prime had been destroyed — by the

Emperor. For a long second, Rupert's heart skipped a beat. The Brotherhood had backed Marius Drake, using its influence to ensure the Grand Senate couldn't simply marginalize him, but for what? If Tara Prime had been destroyed, and it had, it was impossible to escape the conclusion that they'd allowed a monster to take control of the Federation.

And when he opened the attachments, he knew, beyond a shadow of a doubt, that the Emperor was mad.

He shivered. If the Emperor was willing to butcher over four billion humans, what was he *not* willing to do? Destroy Earth? Or AlphaCent? Or resist to the last when — if — the rebels came to depose him? How many more people were going to die?

Rupert felt his hands shaking in shock. How much of the whole affair was his fault? He'd been the one to propose, to *insist*, that the Brotherhood use Marius Drake. And now the Brotherhood was effectively gone and Tara Prime was dead.

I can't stay in hiding any longer, he told himself. There *were* a handful of contacts left, he hoped, men and women who'd remained undiscovered because he was the only one who'd known their names and faces. Contacting them was a risk — the Emperor would redouble his efforts to find him — but he owed it to his conscience to take the chance. *I have to get the word out.*

It wasn't a pleasant thought. Like all Grand Senators, he'd feared the mob, even as he'd sought to placate it. But the Emperor would act to crush it, if the mob rioted on Earth after it learned what had happened to Tara Prime. Hundreds of thousands of people would die...

... And yet, they'd die too if the Outsiders retaliated in kind.

Gritting his teeth, he downloaded the last of the attachments to his terminal and went to work, putting together a news broadcast. There were censors in the news offices, he knew, but his contacts could circumvent them, if they tried. The government would act at once, of course, to stop the broadcasts, yet it would be too late. Word would be out and spreading.

God help us, he thought. He shivered, again. It was hard to escape the feeling that he wasn't long for the world, whatever happened. The cold was seeping into his bones. Millions of others, though, would be putting their lives at risk if they rioted against the Emperor. *But at least they'll have a fighting chance.*

Praying he was right, he tapped the terminal and sent the message.

Chapter Thirty-Six

Riots on Earth were not, in and of themselves, a major problem. Riots spreading to the industrial nodes, on the other hand, were a serious headache.
—The Federation Navy in Retrospect, 4199

Earth, 4102

"Emperor," Lawrence Tully said. "I think we have a problem."

Marius snarled at him. He had too many problems. His wife was a traitor, his former protégé was advancing on AlphaCent, and his other admirals were clearly showing signs of treachery themselves. Starships and personnel that he'd ordered back to Earth, to stand in defense of the homeworld, had yet to appear. It was clear some of the admirals he'd appointed were considering becoming warlords.

And now *Tully* had a problem? "*What* problem?"

Tully looked nervous, but stood his ground. "A broadcast just started to go out from all of the major entertainment companies," he said. "The *same* broadcast. They're showing images of the destruction of Tara Prime, sir, and blaming it on us."

Marius stared at him. "How?"

"I don't know, sir," Tully said. "The censors should have stopped the program getting out, but it's on all the major channels and it's spreading through the datanet. It'll be halfway to Mars by now!"

"I see," Marius said. He fought to control his temper. Someone — someone *else* — had betrayed him and they would pay, in time. But, for the moment, he had to cope with the disaster they'd unleashed. "Is the broadcast still going out?"

"Yes, sir," Tully said. "The media companies say they can't stop it."

Marius snarled in frustration. "Order the troops to take the broadcasting headquarters, then shut the transmission down by any means necessary," he said. "And then tighten up planetary security. I want the people responsible caught."

"Yes, sir," Tully said.

It was the surviving Brothers, Marius thought, as Tully scurried off to do his bidding. They had always known how to steer the media, and it was quite likely they'd embedded commands and hidden programming into the broadcasting networks. ONI was still picking apart the network of shell companies and corporations that masked the Brotherhood's activities, but it was clear that many of them did business with the media companies. No doubt they'd supplied software to the companies that had backdoors worked into the programming. And if the software itself had gone rogue, nothing short of physically destroying the transmitters would be enough to stop the broadcasts going out.

He closed his eyes as his head began to pound. Someone had betrayed him; someone had downloaded footage from the fleet and passed it to the Brotherhood. But who? Or... the timing was just about right for a message forwarded from Admiral Garibaldi, who was accompanied by the traitor Kratman. Marius had practically sealed the Gateway, but even *he* couldn't keep Earth isolated from the rest of the

Federation indefinitely. The bonds holding the Federation together were already far too weak.

A new alert popped up in front of him. He swore, bitterly, when he read through the handful of words. Crowds were already gathering on Earth, outside the media companies, government installations, and dozens of other public places. He'd banned public gatherings, but the bastards didn't seem to care. Hell, he was sure the universities were already fueling the fire by dispatching agitators to make the crowds angrier...

He tapped his terminal, feeling another flicker of bitter rage. Earth had betrayed him, just like everyone else. And it would pay.

"General Thorne," he said, once the channel had opened. "You are ordered to use all necessary measures to keep the planet under control."

"Aye, sir," General Thorne said. "I'll see to it at once."

ഇരുൽ

Lieutenant Kevin Sanderson gritted his teeth as the aircar dropped towards the giant complex on the outskirts of London, followed by a dozen more. Planetary Security had been hailing the media bastards ever since the first broadcast had gone out, but the directors of the complex hadn't bothered to answer, no doubt considering the greatest ratings of their career to be worth more than the lives of millions of people. The lies they were spreading — and Kevin's CO had made it clear they were lies — would get thousands of people killed in London alone.

"There are crowds gathering outside the complex," Lieutenant Gartrell reported. "Just *look* at the scum."

Kevin nodded. London was just like every other city on Earth; a handful of hard-working people, surrounded by thousands upon thousands of worthless leeches who did nothing beyond turning out the *next* generation of worthless leeches. It made his blood boil to think about just how many idiots were wasting their lives, while the taxpayers — men like himself — worked frantically to keep their heads above water. They preferred to drown themselves in drink or drug themselves into a stupor, rather than actually work to escape the horrors of their lives. It wasn't as if it was *hard* to sign up with a colonization firm or even join the military...

"We'll have to put ourselves down at the outskirts of the crowd," he said. It was possible the crowd would disperse when they realized the security forces had arrived, but he had a nasty suspicion that they'd stand their ground. Crowds were only ever as smart as the stupidest person in them, and most of the workshy were *very* stupid indeed. "Make sure you keep your weapons in your hands at all times."

"Yes, sir," Lieutenant Gartrell said.

Kevin checked his own weapon as the small flight of aircars dropped to the ground. Some of the crowd took the opportunity to run, but thousands more were pouring onto the streets to join them. Dozens of alerts flashed in front of him, warning the security forces that criminals were taking advantage of the chaos to loot. He shook his head in sardonic amusement, knowing that the only people who would

suffer were the Londoners themselves. Who would build a business in the city when it could be torn down and destroyed at any moment?

Children, he thought, dismissively.

He opened the hatch and led the way out, weapon at the ready. The crowd turned to face him, hundreds of faces blurring into a mass of seething hatred. He almost flinched, despite himself. Planetary Security wasn't popular — they'd had to clean up messes during the earlier set of strikes — but he'd never seen such hatred written on so many faces. He clutched his rifle tighter as the other aircars unloaded their troops. Ideally, he'd set up barricades and force the crowds away from the complex, but there was no time. One didn't advance in Planetary Security by creatively reinterpreting one's orders.

"ATTENTION," he said, through his mouthpiece. "THIS IS AN ILLEGAL GATHERING. YOU ARE ORDERED TO RETURN TO YOUR HOMES AND AWAIT FURTHER INSTRUCTIONS. THERE WILL BE NO FURTHER WARNINGS!"

The crowd murmured angrily, but didn't move. Kevin felt his chest contract in fear as the anger grew stronger, fighting down the urge to run or open fire. He didn't *want* to open fire, he didn't *want* to kill so many people... and yet it was starting to look as though he had no choice. Gritting his teeth, he took a step forward, but the crowd stood its ground. The remainder of the troopers followed him, moving too slowly for the crowd to believe they were trying to be intimidating. It was all too clear that they were nervous...

Someone threw a rock. Kevin barely had a second to register it before it struck Trooper Powell, sending him to his knees. Lieutenant Gartrell opened fire, aiming his rifle right into the heart of the crowd. Kevin opened fire himself, spraying bullets into the crowd. It flinched, then roared with anger and lunged forward. All of a sudden, Kevin was knocked onto his back, and there was nowhere to run. Hands tore at his uniform, feet stamped on his chest...

... And then there was nothing but darkness.

৪০ ৫৪

Tadd had never had any real ambitions in life, beyond surviving as long as possible. He'd left school at sixteen with a useless set of grades, then spent the next four years of his life drifting in and out of the gangs while drinking, whoring and taking drugs. Indeed, he couldn't be said to have any political ideas at all. He'd only joined the crowd because it looked like a good chance to do some pick-pocketing while shouting his disdain at the government's officers. The meddling scum deserved everything they got...

... And then the shooting had started.

Left to his own devices, Tadd would have run. He knew himself to be a coward; brave men died on the streets of London, trying to prove their manhood even as the last breath drained from their bodies. But the crowd pushed him forward, fueling his anger towards the security forces and everyone else who'd meddled with his life. He

slammed into one of the troopers, knocked him to the ground and stamped on his throat. Behind him, the crowd roared as it tore the troopers apart and then headed for the aircars. They were on fire before it occurred to anyone, even Tadd, that they might have been gainfully sold for beer money.

"To the streets," someone shouted. "Death to the pigs!"

The crowd lunged onwards. Tadd, somehow, managed to get to the edge of the street and drop down, curling up into a ball as the crowd raged around him. The shouting was terrifyingly powerful, a lure that threatened to pull him into the maelstrom; he covered his ears, trying hard to keep from surrendering to the call. He'd never been a gangster, not really; he'd never been committed to anything. And yet, the call reached for him, pulling him towards the crowd. It was all he could do to keep himself low until the crowd raged off towards the nearest police station.

He uncurled, slowly, and looked around. The street was littered with dead bodies; men, women and children, lying where they'd fallen. Tadd had gloried in watching the violent broadcasts on the entertainment channels, where gladiators died on the bloody sands to please their viewers, but this was something different. He looked down at a body and shuddered, fighting down the urge to vomit. The body was so badly mangled that it was impossible to tell if it was male or female, young or old. He looked away, then shuddered as he saw a young woman taking her final breath. The entire lower half of her body was missing.

Shit, he thought, numbly. It was impossible to avoid the sense that he was in hell. *What happened?*

Somehow, he managed to stumble forward. The sound of rioting in the distance was growing stronger, but there was another sound, someone pleading, much closer. He peered into the dark alleyway and winced as he saw a female trooper struggling desperately against two thugs ripping off her uniform. A third was already removing his trousers, preparing to rape her. Tadd found himself torn between an unholy desire to watch as one of the hated bitches was taught a lesson and the urge to flee. The gangsters wouldn't hesitate to kill him if they knew he'd seen their faces...

He glanced up as a pair of helicopters flew overhead, then started to hurry away from the alley and down the street. It didn't look as though there would be *any* safety for the next few hours, not after so many troopers had been killed. They'd want revenge, he knew; there was nothing more certain to upset the natural order than a trooper or two being killed. And there had been at least forty in the group that had been overwhelmed and battered to pieces by the mob.

Shit, he thought again. He'd seen enough movies to know how it would go down. The troopers would secure the area, then move in and arrest everyone. They'd all be sent to a colony world along the Rim, if they were lucky. *Now what do I do?*

༄༅

"The mob is attacking the police station, sir," Lieutenant Ruth Davis said. She peered down from the helicopter as it wheeled over London. Hundreds of thousands of people were swarming around the police station, trying to break through the

defenses. It didn't look as though they were having much luck, but it was only a matter of time. "I can't see any surviving troopers on the ground."

Sweat trickled down her back as she wheeled the craft around, hoping the noise of the rotor blades would scare off the crowd. She wasn't trained for this, damn it; she was a pilot, not a riot control specialist. But when she'd dared object, her CO had bawled her out in front of everyone before ordering her into the helicopter. There was an emergency, he'd said, and all hands were required on deck. And he was right, except Ruth wasn't remotely sure what to do. Her helicopter was armed...

"Check again," the CO ordered. "They can't all be dead?"

"I can see bodies," Ruth said, flatly. She guided the helicopter to where the riot had started and peered down, again. Six or seven aircars were burning, surrounded by hundreds of bodies, both civilian and military. "But none of them appear to be moving."

"Very well," the CO said. "You are authorized to open fire on the crowd."

Ruth felt her mouth fall open in shock. "Sir...?"

"You are authorized to open fire on the crowd," the CO repeated. "That is a direct order, which you may have in writing if you wish."

"Sir..." Ruth said again. "I..."

She swallowed, hard. She'd been a trooper long enough to know that no one, absolutely no one, requested or received orders in writing. Her superiors had no interest in creating a paper trail that might be used against them and anyone foolish enough to request written orders could kiss their careers goodbye. And yet... and yet, if her CO was actually *offering* written orders.

"They killed over a hundred troopers," the CO snarled. "They deserve to die."

"Acknowledged, sir," Ruth said. She tapped a switch, deactivating the safety, as she brought the helicopter back to the police station. The crowd hurled sticks and stones at her, but they might as well have been hurling spit-balls for all the good they did. "Weapons online..."

She gritted her teeth. Her comrades were dead and she wanted to avenge them, yet... yet she knew she was about to commit mass murder. But what choice did she have? Her career would be in the shitter if she failed to follow orders, no matter what the orders were. There was no room for whiners, naggers and shirkers in Planetary Security. And to think she'd thought it was an easy billet when she'd signed up.

"Targets locked," she said. She tapped a switch. "Firing now."

Her machine guns opened fire, yammering loudly as they flailed the crowd with thousands of bullets. She saw hundreds of people knocked to the ground, a handful of bodies disintegrating under the impact, then swore as her threat receiver pinged an alert. She'd flown low, without taking precautions, because she'd *known* she wasn't in any real danger...

She swore as she saw the missile — where the hell had that come from? — and yanked her helicopter up, too late. The missile slammed into the helicopter, sending the craft crashing towards the ground...

... And slamming down hard enough to explode in a colossal fireball.

ᛒᚩᚳ

"It's gotten worse, sir," Tully said. "General Thorne's measures have not succeeded. We now have fighting in half a dozen cities."

He paused. "And there's some quite heavy weaponry involved," he added. "We've lost four helicopters and a dozen drones to MANPADs."

Marius sucked in his breath. "Order in reinforcements," he said. There was no longer any time for half-measures. Admiral Garibaldi was less than a week from Sol, unless he failed to force his way into AlphaCent. "I want those cities crushed."

"Yes, sir," Tully said. He looked doubtful. "Do you wish to pass the orders to General Thorne in person?"

Marius nodded. "Concentrate on keeping the riots from spreading to the asteroids or the moon," he said. By now, word would have reached the Gateway and jumped through to AlphaCent. The damned message packet that had started all the trouble might have bootstrapped itself into AlphaCent's datanet. "Earth itself is immaterial."

ᛒᚩᚳ

Rupert McGillivray would have been excited, if he hadn't known the Emperor still held most of the cards. The media broadcasts had been taken off the air, but the original broadcast was still moving through the datanet, well ahead of any attempt to erase it once and for all. And shutting down the media had only made things worse — huge crowds had thronged onto the streets after their favorite programs had been cancelled — and rumors were spreading widely. A population that hadn't really cared when an entire planet died had turned to rioting after their entertainment had been cut off...

... But the Emperor could still crush the rioters.

It would be easy, Rupert knew. There were millions of illicit weapons in the cities, but the Emperor controlled the high orbitals and the fleet. He could bombard the cities into submission, one at a time, or simply destroy the entire planet. Rupert had no doubt Marius Drake could rationalize it to himself, if he tried. Sol might have a huge industrial base, despite centuries of mismanagement, but Earth herself was nothing but trouble. Why *not* let the population die?

I have to get a message back to the rebels, he thought. He wasn't an expert, but he had a fair idea just how long it would take for the rebels to reach Earth. *And tell them we need them here as soon as possible.*

Gritting his teeth, he went to work.

Chapter Thirty-Seven

In some ways, AlphaCent was more important to the Federation than Sol. Nine Asimov Points circled the star, allowing messages to be slipped up the chains faster than they could be dispatched from Earth. And the planet's population was often much more industrious than Earth's. Indeed, it was generally believed that losing AlphaCent would cost the Federation everything.

And, as it turned out, they were right.
—The Federation Navy in Retrospect, 4199

AlphaCent/Earth, 4102

"The drones are returning, Admiral," Lieutenant Thompson reported. She sounded rather perplexed. "The remaining fortresses are surrendering."

Roman frowned. "They are?"

"They're signaling surrender, Admiral," Lieutenant Thompson said. "Four of them aren't even *damaged* yet!"

"Odd," Roman muttered.

It made no sense. There had been twelve fortresses covering the Maidstone Point, backed up by hundreds of automated weapons platforms and thousands of mines. He'd launched two salvos of assault pods through the point, but he'd assumed that he'd need to fire off at least five more before he could start sending smaller ships into the fray. Instead, the seven surviving fortresses were trying to surrender, even though they could still have forced him to expend dozens of ships destroying them.

"Send the first attack ships through the point, then have them ready to send marines to secure the fortresses," he ordered, finally. Was it a trap? Maybe, but if they were faking a surrender to lure him in close, he'd have every legal right to slaughter every last one of them — and they knew it. "And ready a third flight of assault pods."

He waited, feeling the seconds ticking away, until the next set of courier drones popped out of the Asimov Point. "They surrendered," Lieutenant Thompson said, in disbelief. "The marines are on the fortresses, the minefield has been deactivated, and the crews are ready to be transferred to internment camps."

"Take us through the point," Roman ordered. He'd expected to have to *fight* to break into AlphaCent, let alone Earth itself. "What the hell is going on?"

There was no answer until the fleet secured the Asimov Point and started the long crawl towards the Gateway. "There's a civil war going on," Lieutenant Thompson said. "If some of the transmissions are to be believed, AlphaCent has risen against the Emperor. And there's another war going on in the Sol System."

"Shit," Roman said. He studied the display for a long moment. It looked as though AlphaCent's massive orbital defenses had turned on themselves. Fortresses were hurling missiles at other fortresses, rather than attacking starships. "Why?"

"I don't know, sir," Lieutenant Thompson admitted. "I can ask the marines to interview the prisoners, if you like?"

"Do it," Roman ordered. "And keep us well away from any local forces. I don't want to get tangled up in their civil war."

"Aye, sir," Lieutenant Thompson said.

The picture grew clearer as more data flowed into the starship's sensors, accompanied by hundreds of messages from various factions on the planet's surface. There had been riots on Earth, sparked off by a message about the destruction of Tara Prime... and rumors had spread, rapidly, that AlphaCent would be scorched clean of life too. Desperate men had bonded together, planned mutinies and launched them, in isolation. Now, AlphaCent was torn apart by fighting, while there was little keeping Roman from making his way across the system to the Gateway. It was, definitely, something of a relief.

"I picked up a message tagged for me," Professor Kratman said. "Rupert — Grand Senator McGillivray — is urging you to hurry."

Roman swore, inwardly. "Is it a trap?"

"I don't think so," Kratman said. "It looks very much as though Earth, too, has risen against the Emperor."

"They can't hold out for long," Elf said. "Not if the Emperor is willing to flatten the entire planet."

"We still have to punch our way through the Gateway," Roman said. He'd broadcast offers to accept surrender at the fortresses on the near side of the Gateway, but there had been no response. Maybe they just hadn't had time to reply... or maybe they were still loyal to the Emperor. "We can't speed up any further."

"They may let us pass through without delay," Kratman suggested.

Roman met his eyes. "Can you guarantee it?"

"No," Kratman said. "You *know* I can't."

"Then Earth will have to take care of itself until we can force our way through the Gateway," Roman said. He didn't have the ties to Earth that Kratman and Elf shared — they'd both been born on Earth — but he understood their feelings. And yet, he didn't want to risk any more of his ships than strictly necessary. "If they surrender, well and good; if not... we'll have to fight."

"Understood," Kratman said.

Roman glanced at the display. "We'll be within weapons range in seventeen hours, Professor," he added. "The alpha crews will need to get some sleep before then."

"So do you," Elf said, firmly.

"Understood," Roman said.

He was tempted, very tempted, to invite her to bed. The Gateway was a formidable obstacle, the most heavily-defended Asimov Point in the galaxy. There was no way Marius Drake would have put anything, but the most trustworthy of loyalists in command of the defenses, with strict orders to hold against all comers. They might be dead by the end of the day, no matter what happened to the battle...

... But she had work to do, as did he.

"I'll see you on the far side," he said, instead.

Ginny braced herself as she stepped into the Emperor's cabin, feeling dirty after the mandatory groping session. The Blackshirts had only grown more paranoid after the uprisings on Earth, and she was grimly aware that large parts of the crew were on the verge of mutiny. Only the simple fact that they'd been stripped of all weapons, she suspected, had prevented a mutiny from already taking place. *No one* liked to be poked and prodded by leering men, even if it *was* in the name of security.

The Emperor was sitting on his sofa, watching the images from Earth. Entire cities were burning, his soldiers advancing through the rubble and massacring anyone who dared to put up a fight. The datanet was crumbling, with rogue reporters broadcasting brief snapshots of violence from the heart of the inferno, snapshots that the Emperor seemed to enjoy watching even as they made the violence worse. It was almost as if the population *knew* it was the end, that Earth would never rule the galaxy again.

"Ginny," the Emperor said. He wore a bathrobe, rather than his uniform; his face was unshaven. A faint smell hung in the air, something she didn't want to identify. "What do you have for me?"

"A report from AlphaCent," Ginny said. She hated being the bearer of bad news. He hadn't had her thrown out of the airlock yet, but he'd banned Tully from his presence after the Comptroller had urged him to take a more merciful approach to the rebels on Earth. "The rebels have entered the system."

The Emperor looked up at her. "And they are on their way to the Gateway?"

"Yes, sir," Ginny said. "The last report stated that they'd be challenging the defenses in less than twelve hours."

"At last," the Emperor said. He stood; Ginny looked away as the bathrobe yawned open. "A final chance to win."

Ginny had her doubts. Nothing had been said overtly, but she'd grown practiced in reading between the lines and... well, it was clear that the defenders of the Maidstone Point had surrendered rather easily. With civil war on AlphaCent and communications between Earth and the rest of the Federation cut, it might be too late to save *anything.* And who knew if the defenders of the Gateway would feel the same way too?

The Emperor stepped into the bathroom, his voice echoing back to her. "Have the fleet moved to support the Gateway," he said. "We'll fight a conventional defense."

"Aye, sir," Ginny said, as she heard the shower coming to life. At least she hadn't been ordered to join him. "A classic pattern, or a modified one?"

"The classics are always the best," the Emperor said. "Besides, they can't refuse battle, not this time."

He was right, Ginny knew. The rebels *had* to punch through the Gateway if they wanted to win, particularly if they wanted to save something from Earth. Going the long way around might work, but it would also give the Emperor time to organize a stronger defense.

No, they couldn't afford to back off. The defenses would tear them to shreds, assuming the crews remained loyal, but giving the Emperor time would be a dangerous mistake. And if they didn't...

"I'll see you on the CIC before battle," the Emperor told her. "Now, go organize the fleet movements."

"Aye, sir," Ginny said.

☉CB

"There's still no response to our hails," Lieutenant Thompson reported. "I'm not even sure they're hearing us."

"They must be hearing us," Roman said, curtly. There were seventeen fortresses defending the near side of the Asimov Point, enough firepower to give him pause. But he had no choice. He *had* to clear them from his path if they refused to surrender. "Send one final demand, then prepare to fire."

"Aye, sir," Lieutenant Thompson said. There was a long pause. "No response..."

The display flickered with red icons. "They're opening fire, sir," she said. "Long-range missiles, Mark-IIIs by my count."

Roman nodded. It didn't *look* as though the defenders had Mark-IVs, unless they were just trying to lure him into a false sense of overconfidence. But all of the Mark-IVs had been earmarked for Fifth Fleet and Home Fleet, not the defenses of a system everyone had *known* to be secure. And production rates had been terrifyingly low right up until the Battle of Nova Athena.

"Order point defense to engage the missiles as soon as they enter range," he ordered. "And return fire."

"Aye, sir," Lieutenant Thompson said.

Roman gritted his teeth as the enemy missiles moved into his engagement envelope and started to vanish, one by one. He'd have preferred to close the range, but he didn't dare risk having one of the enemy missiles set off a chain reaction on a superdreadnaught's external racks, blowing the ship to atoms. The good news, as far as he could tell, was that the enemy hadn't had time to upgrade their sensors and ECM. Fifth Fleet's ECM was superior and the Outsider ECM better still. Hundreds of missiles were suckered away from their targets even though they made it through the point defense network.

"The fortresses are continuing to fire," Lieutenant Thompson reported. "The Marsha are offering to launch a suicide charge."

"Denied," Roman snapped. Aiming antimatter-packed shuttles at the fortresses, with the fortresses having plenty of time to realize the danger, was just asking for trouble. It would be better to hurl the shuttles through the Asimov Point and into the teeth of the Gateway's defenses. "Continue the missile engagement."

"Aye, sir," Lieutenant Thompson said.

Roman leaned back in his chair and watched, grimly, as the damage mounted. The superdreadnaught *Pashing* took several hits and drifted out of formation; the battlecruisers *Runner* and *Coyote* exploded into fireballs as their defenses were overwhelmed... but otherwise the fortresses seemed to be splitting their fire. It puzzled

him, until he realized that Emperor Marius would want to weaken his fleet before they faced the true challenge. The tactic might even work.

"They're not launching fighters," he mused. The fortresses were taking damage, but otherwise holding firm. "Why not?"

"They may be trying to shield the fighters," Lieutenant Thompson said. "The commander might not be very experienced..."

Roman shook his head. He'd been on *Enterprise* long enough to understand the danger of trying to keep the fighters in their launch tubes as long as possible, no matter the conditions outside the hull. One of the many — *many* — reasons the First Battle of Sapphire had gone pear-shaped was that the CO had tried to keep his fighters safely on the carriers, only to have the carriers caught in the ambush and destroyed before they could launch more than a handful of their starfighters. No CO worth his rank badges would try to keep his crews safe when they had a far better chance of surviving in their craft.

"I doubt it," he said. "They may not be *carrying* starfighters."

Or the starfighter crews are unreliable, he thought. *They might turn on the fortresses instead of our ships.*

It was plausible. Starfighter jocks tended to be among the most individualistic of officers, at least partly because they knew death could come at any time. Someone could have started a mutiny, or flatly refused to fight... he pushed the thought to one side as the fortresses belched another wave of missiles. It was what he wanted to believe, after all, and self-deceit was among the most dangerous mistakes a commander could make.

"Continue firing," he ordered. Four of the fortresses had taken heavy damage, but were still trying to fight. "Batter their shields down."

"Aye, sir," Lieutenant Thompson said.

ഇരു

"Sir, the far side of the Gateway is under heavy attack," Ginny reported, as Marius stumbled onto the command deck. "They're taking missile fire so far, but it could get worse at any moment."

"Or better," Marius noted. He sat down before his legs gave out from under him. Clearly, drinking so much had been a mistake — and taking the sober-up even worse. "They won't want to expend too much firepower on the outer defenses."

He studied the display, feeling an odd sense of exultation. Here, at last, was an enemy he could *fight*. No cowardly traitors, waiting to bury a knife in his back; no faceless rebels, lurking in the shadows; no numberless insurgents, where the dead were replaced as quickly as they fell. Nothing, but starships meeting for one final time in honorable combat.

He checked his fleet's formation, noting with satisfaction that Ginny had deployed them in a standard pattern. The invaders would clear their way through the fortresses, if they had enough firepower, only to run into the teeth of his fire.

And I won't need to worry about burning half of Earth, he thought. It had been hard, at first, to give the order to launch KEWs; now, he hardly cared *what* happened, as

long as he wasn't bothered. And yet, watching Earth burn had been almost *relaxing*. *Maybe it's time the planet was finally put to rest.*

"There's a new update coming in, sir," Ginny said. "Two more fortresses have been destroyed."

"Tell the remaining fortresses to fight to the last," Marius ordered.

He didn't know if the order would be carried out, but — in all honesty — he didn't much care, not since the uprisings on AlphaCent. He'd already had to strip the fortresses of their starfighter pilots after the grinning bastards had started to mutter about pretending to be sick, as if they were too important to be punished for attempted mutiny. All that really mattered, right now, was greeting Garibaldi when he poked his nose through the Gateway. There would be one final battle, and that would be the end.

"Aye, sir," Ginny said. She paused. "I'm picking up a communication from Earth..."

"Ignore it," Marius said. He had every confidence in General Thorne... and besides, if the General failed, it hardly mattered. Earth could burn. He no longer cared. "Concentrate on the impending battle."

He ran through the calculations in his mind. Roman would need at least thirty minutes to deploy enough assault pods to do real damage to the Gateway, unless he'd mounted the weapons on minelayers and used them to emplace the pods. And he'd also need to reload his external racks... it was a pity, really, that there wasn't any way to ambush his fleet while he was replenishing himself. But Marius no longer trusted anyone on AlphaCent.

"The last of the fortresses has been destroyed, sir," Ginny reported. "None of them tried to surrender."

"Good," Marius grunted. He cleared his throat. "And now to make sure their deaths count for something."

80 ○3

Roman watched the last fortress die with bittersweet feelings. Nineteen thousand men and women had died, unless the crews had been stripped just prior to the battle. It was possible, he supposed, but unlikely. Emperor Marius was no longer the father to his men that Roman recalled; he spent them freely, like water, as long as he thought he could win.

"There are no lifepods," Lieutenant Thompson reported. "They never even *tried* to escape."

Someone must have deactivated them, Roman thought. It was rare, vanishingly rare, for a fortress to be lost with all hands. They tended to survive long enough for the crew to jump to the pods, even if they were quite definitely doomed. *The bastards wanted the crews to die with their fortresses.*

He pushed the thought away, savagely. "Are the missile ships ready to go?"

"Aye, sir," Lieutenant Thompson said. "And the Marsha shuttles are ready to follow up."

Roman took a breath. This was it, the final battle. Either they broke into the Sol System, which would be the end of the war, or they were crushed.

There was no middle ground, not any longer. Either they won or they died.

"Signal the fleet," he ordered.

He tried to think of something to say, something that would inspire the crew, but nothing came to mind. He'd have to think of something later, something that could be added to the history books. It struck him, in a moment of amusement, that all the other admirals might have done the same thing. How many of the dramatic statements they'd been forced to memorise had really been made up on the spot?

"Signal the fleet," he repeated. "We're going home."

He took a breath. "Commence attack pattern delta," he added. "I say again, commence attack pattern delta."

Chapter Thirty-Eight

And so everything came down to one final battle...
—The Federation Navy in Retrospect, 4199

AlphaCent/Earth, 4102

"Admiral," Ginny said. "We have assault pods transiting the gateway... and shuttles."
Marius leaned forward, surprised. So quickly?

"Order the CSP to intercept," he snapped, although he knew it was wasted breath. The starfighters would swoop in to take out as many of the pods as possible before they opened fire, although the *shuttles* were an odd step. More suicide shuttles? Or... what? "And warn the forts to brace for attack."

He cursed under his breath as the pods opened fire, spewing an endless stream of short-range missiles into space. Their targeting sensors had clearly been improved, part of his mind noted; they'd orientated themselves far faster than he would have believed possible. He wondered, absently, if the Outsiders had managed to get a clear look at the forts before the system went into lockdown, but decided it was unlikely. Even if they had, the forts had shifted position before the attack began in earnest.

Should have kept our own pods, he thought, grimly. He'd thrust Earth's stockpile of assault pods forward for the drive on Nova Athena, then ordered the industrial node to focus on producing long-range missiles. In hindsight, it had been a mistake. *Given them a taste of their own medicine.*

"The shuttles are crammed with antimatter," Ginny reported, as one of the shuttles vanished in a blinding white flash. "They must have stuffed containment chambers into every last square inch of their hulls."

Marius frowned as the display fuzzed for a long moment, then came back into focus, informing him that a number of starfighters, mines and automated weapons platforms had been wiped out by the blast. It was no consolation to note that the blast had *also* wiped out a number of enemy missiles. Roman Garibaldi wouldn't have challenged the Gateway without a massive stockpile of assault missiles at his disposal. Hell, he might have been able to obtain *more* at Tara Prime. Admiral Vincent might have intended to secure control of a handful of other junctions by force.

"Or they just reengineered the craft with a single vast containment chamber," Marius observed. The part of him that still enjoyed puzzles toyed with it for a long moment — it wasn't as if a suicide craft needed anything more than engines and a simple control system — before putting the matter aside. "Order the fortresses to target the shuttles with long-range missiles."

He cursed as a second wave of assault pods materialized through the Asimov Point, followed by a flight of shuttles and gunboats. The shuttles flew off in all directions, some aiming at the fortresses while others seemed to be flying into empty space, as the gunboats opened fire on the CSP. Marius gritted his teeth, helplessly, as he realized what his former protégé was trying to do. The starfighters had to wipe

out the assault pods before they could open fire, but the gunboats were making it difficult. And the first wave of missiles was approaching its target...

"Gateway Three is reporting heavy damage, sir," Ginny said. "Gateway Five has lost communications. Gateway Six has lost her outermost shield generators..."

"Tell them to keep firing," Marius snapped.

His head started to pound, again, as wave after wave of assault pods transited the Gateway, throwing thousands of missiles against the defenses. Hundreds were wasted, picked off by the point defense or simply lost in the ongoing sea of electromagnetic distortion, but hundreds more found their targets. They were followed by shuttles, trying desperately to ram their hulls into the fortress shields. A single shuttle struck an almost-undamaged fortress and exploded so violently that the fortress was completely crippled. Another shuttle, hot on its tail, completed the destruction before a single crewman could escape.

"Gateway Nine has been destroyed," Ginny reported. "Gateway Six has taken heavy damage..."

Marius cursed, yet again. Those damnable shuttles hadn't *just* been aimed at his fortresses, they'd been aimed at his minefields and automated weapons platforms. Each antimatter blast had cleared great reaches of space, ensuring that Garibaldi would have plenty of room to manoeuvre his ships once he finally began the main offensive. Marius knew he'd come, unless the Gateway held; Garibaldi had no choice.

This was *the* battle.

He rubbed at his forehead, then reached for the packet of pills and popped two into his mouth. No matter what happened, he needed a clear head for the next hour or two. After that... depending on the outcome of the battle, it was unlikely to matter.

"Another wave of assault pods has just transited the gateway," Ginny reported. "They're accompanied by over a hundred shuttles."

Marius nodded, shortly. "Order the fortresses to attempt to engage," he said, as the shuttles picked up speed and flashed away from the Asimov Point. There was no point in trying to direct the CSP to handle the shuttles, not when it would mean mutual destruction. "And then send a message to Home Fleet. The enemy will make their appearance soon."

※ ※

Roman silently tallied up the latest set of reports with a profound feeling of dissatisfaction. He'd expended hundreds of assault pods and thousands of missiles — along with over five hundred shuttles and gunboats — but the Gateway was still formidable, despite the staggering damage it had taken. Earth's gateway to the galaxy was defended by no less than twenty-four fortresses and innumerable automated defenses; he knew, based upon the reports, that they had destroyed or crippled only seven of them. And he was running out of assault pods.

And we can't withdraw, he thought, numbly. *We have to go on.*

"Order the first wave to commence attack," he said. "And tell them they're authorized to deploy the latest ECM."

"Aye, sir," Lieutenant Thompson said.

Roman forced himself to watch as the next wave of icons reached the Asimov Point and vanished, accompanied by a swarm of assault pods, gunboats and shuttles. It was a shame the latest Outsider ECM couldn't be fitted to the pods, although there had been so many sensors surrounding the Gateway that the ECM would probably not have been as effective as the designers had promised.

And many of those young men and women are going to die, he thought. *And I'm not there with them.*

೮೦ᴄ೩

"The next wave of attackers has transited the Gateway," Ginny reported. "Sir, they're accompanied by smaller ships!"

Marius bared his teeth. This was it! The real attack had finally begun.

"Send in the reserves," he ordered, as the enemy assault pods began to spew yet more missiles. "Tell them they may fire at will."

"Aye, sir," Ginny said. "I..."

She broke off. Marius leaned forward in disbelief as the missiles on the display doubled, then tripled; hundreds of thousands of missiles, according to his sensors, were advancing on the remaining fortresses, an avalanche of missiles that could not possibly be stopped. For a moment, his heart seemed to freeze in his chest; he found it terrifyingly difficult to breathe...

"Sensor decoys," he choked out. "They have to be decoys..."

Ginny spun around to face him. "Sir..."

Marius forced himself, somehow, to breathe, despite his fading vision. "Tell the fortresses that they have to be decoys," he said. "Sensor illusions..."

He clutched hold of his command chair, feeling his heartbeat start to stutter erratically. They had to be ECM decoys — and, with the Gateway's sensor net so badly degraded by the earlier attacks, it would be impossible to separate the real missiles from the decoys. No *wonder* the rebels had seemed so unconcerned about the fate of their shuttles. They hadn't been trying to inflict damage so much as blind his sensors, in preparation for this moment.

"I'm calling the doctor," Ginny said.

"No," Marius said. On the display, the reserve starfighters were already racing towards the enemy ships. "I'm staying on the bridge..."

"You're going to collapse," Ginny said. "I need to get you to sickbay..."

"You're dismissed," Marius rasped. Had even *she* betrayed him at the end? "Go fetch Lieutenant Hashimoto. He can take over as tactical assistant."

Ginny stared at him for a long moment. Marius stared back at her with morbid fascination, wondering just what she'd do. Call the medics anyway, against his orders, or summon a replacement before leaving the CIC? Perhaps it had been a mistake to have only the two of them in the compartment, but he'd trusted her...

"Yes, sir," Ginny said, finally. "I'll have Lieutenant Hashimoto sent in at once."

She saluted, then left the compartment. Marius barely noticed as he switched tactical control to his console. It was far from ideal, but it would hold long enough

for Lieutenant Hashimoto to arrive. On the display, the fortresses were reeling under repeated hammer blows; their defenses hadn't been able to cope with the sudden multiplication of threats. Five more had been destroyed, while the remainder were badly damaged. And wave after wave of enemy ships were slipping through the Gateway, their carriers spitting out starfighters before hastily reversing course and vanishing back through the Asimov Point.

I taught him this, Marius thought, feeling an odd flicker of pride. He'd never had children, even though — as a man who'd married into the aristocracy — he'd been *expected* to have children. Tiffany and he had talked about it, but he'd known he wouldn't be a good father to a young baby. Roman Garibaldi was the closest thing he had to a son. *And look what's become of us.*

A new set of icons appeared on the display, one by one. Marius knew, long before the sensors identified them, that the newcomers were superdreadnaughts. Roman Garibaldi was sending them through in a tight stream, taking the risk of a collision in stride just to ensure he had plenty of firepower through the Gateway before Home Fleet or the remaining fortresses could intervene. They were accompanied by yet more shuttles, racing off to throw themselves at the fortresses. Marius wondered, absently, just how they could kill themselves so casually, then pushed the thought aside. Both sides knew there would be no second chance at total victory.

His console beeped. He opened his mouth to order the message displayed before remembering that he was alone. Where *was* Lieutenant Hashimoto? He keyed the switch, then blinked in surprise as General Thorne's face popped up in front of him. Somehow, he was sure it wasn't good news. Whatever had gone wrong, thanks to the curse of time-delayed communications, had taken place hours ago.

"Emperor," General Thorne said. "There have been a string of mutinies among the orbital defenses of Earth. Fighting has broken out on a dozen settlements on Luna and Mars. My forces on Earth have even been targeted from orbit..."

Marius clutched his chest as the full weight of the message sank in. He'd lost. Even if he stopped the rebels from taking the Gateway, there was no hope of rebuilding Earth's industry before a rebel admiral punched through the remains of the defenses and secured the system, destroying the Federation once and for all. And then another admiral would boot him out, and then another, and then another...

He'd lost. Everything he'd done had been for nothing. He'd...

His vision blurred. Darkness howled at the corner of his mind. He fought to remain conscious, but it was no longer possible...

ಬಿ ಲ

"Home Fleet is advancing to reinforce the Gateway," Lieutenant Thompson reported.

Roman nodded, curtly. Home Fleet had been badly weakened at Tara Prime, but there were still four squadrons of superdreadnaughts and thousands of starfighters. It looked as though Emperor Marius had commandeered every last ship in the system too, bolting weapons onto freighter hulls as if it would turn them into warships. Roman wondered just how enthusiastic the crews were about their missions,

then decided it probably didn't matter. If Emperor Marius was prepared to take Admiral Vincent's children as hostages, he probably wouldn't hesitate to do the same to freighter crews.

The economy is going to be fucked, he thought, numbly. There were freighters... but also ore miners, worker bees and hundreds of other civilian craft. Replacing them all would take years, even with an intact industrial base. *He's throwing everything he has at us, just in the hopes that some of those vessels will take a missile aimed at a superdreadnaught.*

"Start transmitting the surrender demand," Roman said. "And order all ships to assume attack formation."

"Aye, sir," Lieutenant Thompson said.

⁎C⁗

If there was one advantage to being the Emperor's most trusted tactical aide when the shit was about to hit the fan, it was the right to keep her sidearm when no one else was allowed such an advantage. Ginny hadn't let the weapon leave her side since the news from AlphaCent had arrived, despite angry mutterings from the Blackshirts. Who knew what would happen when — if — the superdreadnaught was boarded?

She gripped the weapon in her sweaty palms as she paused outside the brig, then keyed open the hatch and stepped into the compartment. A Blackshirt was on guard, sitting on a stool and reading a datapad. Ginny lifted her weapon and shot him before he had a chance to register her presence. She watched the body carefully for a long moment — she'd practiced extensively in the shooting range, but she knew she wasn't a natural — then hurried over to the sealed compartment. The hatch opened at her command, allowing her to step inside. Lady Tiffany was naked, lying on a bed, her hands and feet secured to keep her immobile.

"Ginny," Tiffany said. She sounded weak, but at least she was alive. "What's happening?"

"I'm getting you out of here," Ginny said. She was tempted to try to run — the shuttlecraft might be guarded, but stealing a lifeboat wouldn't be hard — yet she knew she had to try to do something to stop the coming slaughter. "Your husband has snapped completely."

Tiffany sat upright the moment Ginny removed the band covering her throat. "Just *completely?*"

"The rebels are attacking the Gateway," Ginny said, ignoring the comment. "And even if we win, we lose."

She hoped Tiffany knew what to do, even though she'd been a helpless prisoner for the last two weeks. Because... *she* didn't know what to do. Because she knew hardly anyone would listen to her. She was the Emperor's favorite, after all. She might as well have been the teacher's pet.

"Take me to him," Tiffany said.

⁎C⁗

"There's no response to our surrender demand," Lieutenant Thompson reported. "However, a handful of fortresses have stopped firing on us."

Roman frowned. Surrendering... disabled... or playing possum?

"Keep us well clear of them," he ordered, flatly. The fleet was already sweeping the remainder of the minefields out of space, while bracing itself to withstand Home Fleet's final charge. "I take it Home Fleet has not responded?"

"No, sir," Lieutenant Thompson said.

"Then inform the fleet," Roman said. "We will open fire once Home Fleet enters attack range."

"Aye, sir," Lieutenant Thompson said.

∞ Ↄ

Tiffany could feel her heartbeat racing as she stumbled through the maze of corridors, silently grateful that she'd had a chance to snatch a pair of trousers and a jacket even if they *had* come from a dead man. She had no doubt he would have killed Ginny and herself, if given the chance; General Thorne might well have issued orders to make sure Tiffany was never allowed to talk to her husband one final time. Who knew? Maybe she'd succeed in convincing him that Thorne was a snake in the grass.

"I didn't call another aide," Ginny said, as they approached the tactical compartment. "He should be alone."

There was no one on duty outside the hatch, somewhat to Tiffany's surprise. But then, her husband's paranoia had just been growing stronger and stronger. He'd probably decided to ensure that the entire crew, save for combat-essential personnel, were kept in their quarters, where they couldn't harm anyone. The fact that they couldn't escape, either, wouldn't bother him.

The hatch hissed open, revealing a darkened compartment, illuminated only by a giant tactical display. Ginny muttered a curse under her breath as she glanced at the display, then started to look around. Tiffany sucked in her breath as she saw her husband, lying on the deck; Ginny hurried to the tactical console while Tiffany stepped over to kneel down beside Marius. He was still alive, somehow, but his face was flushed and his breathing was erratic.

"The fleet is requesting orders," Ginny said. "There's no one who can take the Emperor's place."

Tiffany looked up. "There's no second-in-command?"

"None was appointed," Ginny confirmed. "We're currently closing in on the main body of the rebel fleet. In two minutes, perhaps less, we'll be in firing range. And the winner will be the person who has one or two ships left."

Tiffany took a breath. "Can you issue orders?"

"Yes," Ginny said. "They'd think they'd come straight from the emperor."

"Then tell the fleet to stand down and surrender," Tiffany said. She cradled her husband's head in her arms. It would be easy to let him die, but she found herself unable to just walk away. "And then call the medics."

This could be a mistake, her thoughts warned her. She'd never anticipated Roman Garibaldi turning on her husband, although she had to admit she understood why he'd switched sides and dedicated himself to overthrowing Marius. *The Outsiders may want revenge for everything the Grand Senate did to them.*

But at least the war will be over, she told herself. *And there are no other aristocrats left on the Sol System.*

"The rebels have accepted our surrender," Ginny said. "They're insisting that we cut all drives and lower our shields in preparation to be boarded."

"Do it," Tiffany ordered. "Where are those medics?"

"On their way," Ginny said.

Tiffany nodded. She just hoped they arrived in time.

Chapter Thirty-Nine

What did Marius Drake and Roman Garibaldi say to one another, when they met for the final time? No one knows... but generations of historians, writers and politicians have speculated endlessly.
—The Federation Navy in Retrospect, 4199

Earth, 4102

"You do realize this could be a trap?"

Roman nodded, shortly. Elf was right; it *could* be a trap. Lady Tiffany inviting — practically *begging* — him to meet her husband one final time, before his death, hadn't been on the list of things he'd anticipated. And the confusion gripping the system would make it easy for someone to carry out an assassination, if that was what they wanted to do. Home Fleet was barely under control, the remaining fortresses still menaced passage through the Gateway...

... And Earth, Mars and Luna were consumed with civil war.

And we now know that five admirals and over a hundred major systems have declared independence, he thought, darkly. *We can't stay here indefinitely or we'll be cut off from Boston and the Rim.*

"Yeah, I know," he said, as the shuttle made its slow way towards *Enterprise*. "But I have to see him. I have to *know*."

Elf gave him a sharp look. "Know what?"

"I wish I knew," Roman admitted. What *could* he expect from Marius Drake? And why did he expect *anything*? He'd respected the man, even seen him as a father-figure, but those feelings were long gone. Marius Drake had attempted to commit genocide months before he'd slaughtered billions on Tara Prime. "I just think I want closure."

"Hah," Elf said. She settled back into her seat, crossing her arms under her breasts. "You just want everything neatly wrapped up with a bow."

Roman wanted to deny it, but he had a feeling she was right. He scowled inwardly, then peered out of the portal as the superdreadnaught came into view. Seeing the superdreadnaught gave him an odd pang, if only because he still had no idea what had happened to the original *Enterprise*. The giant supercarrier had been his first command, although not one he'd been expected to hold for long. He'd only become her commander because everyone above him in the chain of command had been killed.

I could check the records when we reach Earth, if there's anything left by then, he thought, wryly. *Or simply chalk it up as a permanently unsolved mystery.*

He braced himself as the shuttle docked, a dull *thud* echoing through the tiny craft as she matched gravity fields with the superdreadnaught. There was a pla-toon of marines already onboard, carrying an antimatter mine just in case the crew intended to do something stupid, but it didn't make him feel *safe*.

Elf was right. If Marius Drake intended to launch an ambush, out of hatred or rage

or a bitter determination to see the galaxy burn, the marines were unlikely to be able to help. They'd all die together.

But I have to know, he thought, as the hatch hissed open. He rose, allowing Elf to lead the way through the hatch. *Even if it kills me, I have to know.*

A young redheaded woman wearing a commander's uniform met him as he stepped out of the hatch. "Admiral Garibaldi, I am Commander Ginny Lewis," she said. "The Emperor is currently held in a private compartment. He has expressed a wish to speak with you."

"Understood," Roman said. Marius Drake was no longer emperor, but there was no point in arguing over titles with a junior officer. "Please take us to him."

"Yes, sir," Ginny said. She turned to lead the way up the corridor. "The doctors say he doesn't have long to live, no matter what they do. Please don't push him too hard."

Roman heard Elf snort rudely, behind him, as they made their way through a set of sealed hatches. The entire ship was in lockdown and would remain so until the Blackshirts had been disarmed and the crew marched off to an internment camp, if they didn't volunteer to join his fleet. God alone knew what would happen afterwards, Roman thought. Reports of increasing frightfulness had been filtering in through AlphaCent as word of the battle and its outcome spread. To all intents and purposes, the once-mighty Federation no longer existed.

He closed his eyes for a long moment, wondering just what shape the post-Federation galaxy would take. The Core Worlds could no longer compete on even terms, but they still had a great deal of industry, even though Marius Drake had worked it half to death. He suspected that hundreds of warlords would fight to take control of the infrastructure, or head out to the Rim where there was a chance to build something new. The old economy was doomed. It would take decades, perhaps centuries, before interstellar trade returned to its pre-war heights.

"I'll wait outside," Elf said, as they entered the outer compartment. Lady Tiffany sat there, her face pale and wan. She looked up and gave Roman an unreadable smile, then returned to her thoughts. "You can go in whenever you're ready."

Roman nodded, slowly. He knew himself to be brave — he'd led assaults through Asimov Points and defied senior officers — but the thought of stepping through the hatch and meeting Marius Drake for the final time was terrifying. His mentor, his friend... his enemy... what could they say to one another before death separated them once and for all? And yet, he knew, all too well, that if he backed out now he'd wonder, for the rest of his life, what would have happened if he had taken the risk. Gritting his teeth, he stepped up to the hatch. It hissed open and he walked through.

The light was dim, inside. A handful of medical displays glowed on the far bulkhead, but Roman only had eyes for the bed in the center of the compartment. Marius Drake was there, a handful of tubes running down from high overhead and into his body. Roman frowned, wondering, just for a second, if he'd stepped into the wrong compartment. The profile was correct, but the face was flushed and bloated. He stepped closer, trying to see what had happened to the man he'd respected and admired... but that man was gone.

Marius Drake opened his mouth. "Roman," he rasped. He sounded as if he had to remember how to speak. "You came."

"Yes, sir," Roman said. "I came."

"You betrayed me," Marius Drake said. There was no anger in his voice, just a simple statement of fact. "You turned on me."

"You would have killed billions of people," Roman said. He felt a stab of guilt, mixed with anger. "You *did* kill billions of people."

"I needed to preserve the Federation," Marius Drake said. "The Outsiders would have destroyed it, given a chance."

"Perhaps they would have," Roman conceded. "But they didn't slaughter billions of humans."

"The aliens will, given half a chance," Marius Drake rasped. "Humanity is strong because humanity is united."

"And what did that unity get us?" Roman asked. "A Grand Senate so deeply corrupt that it was sucking the lifeblood out of the galaxy, a military where ambitious officers were plotting coups, a thousand colonies with desperate natives plotting hopeless rebellions against the Federation, because the alternative was to wind up dead. And now the Federation is coming apart at the seams!"

"You mustn't let it come apart," Marius Drake whispered. "I took care of the Grand Senate for you, Roman. You must deal with the other threats. Human unity must be preserved."

"It can't be preserved," Roman said. "Who trusts us any longer?"

"You can make them trust you," Marius Drake urged. His breathing grew louder as he tried to sit upright. "The war is over now. You can rebuild in peace."

He sagged back on the bed. "Would have won, if the Outsiders hadn't appeared," he said. "We could have saved the Federation, we could have rebuilt the economy. But they came and the war swallowed up all my work."

"I know," Roman said, gently. "But the war is over now."

"Don't let everything go to waste," Marius Drake pleaded. "Please!"

Roman looked down at him for a long moment, unable to untangle his feelings. Marius Drake had been his mentor, his friend, and yet he'd also been a monster who'd killed billions and slaughtered the Grand Senate personally, a man who'd triggered uprisings, civil wars and breakaways that had ripped the Federation he loved apart. Roman had no illusions about the difficulty of the task facing *anyone* who wanted to rebuild the Federation. The once-proud Federation Navy had been shattered, while Fortress Command and various system defense forces had declared independence. Putting it back together would require a war on the same scale as the Inheritance War, with far fewer resources at his command.

And what would it do to him, if he tried?

Marius Drake had started with good intentions. Everyone knew that, even his enemies. He'd killed the Grand Senate and started to work to restore freedom and rebuild the economy, only to be confronted with a war crisis that had destroyed all of his work. And the stresses of fighting the war had driven him mad. The decision

to destroy Nova Athena, Roman suspected, had been impelled by a desire to just put an end to the war.

"I won't," he said. The lessons of the war — the endless conflicts from Admiral Justinian to the Outsiders and Roman himself — wouldn't go to waste. "Marius..."

"I used to think I could do everything without resorting to brute force," Marius said. He sounded distant, as if he no longer knew where he was. "And now... look what's become of us."

"I'm sorry, sir," Roman said. He'd hoped for answers, but he knew — now — he'd never get them. Or perhaps he had. The Federation was Marius Drake's religion, after all; he'd been quite happy to do *anything* in her name. "I wish..."

"Don't wish," Marius said, sternly. Just for a second, he sounded like his old self. "Do your duty. Tobias *died* doing his duty."

And what, Roman asked himself, *would Tobias think of you now?*

He sighed, inwardly. He'd never believed in life after death — religion had never really been a big part of his life, before or after the attack that had left him the sole survivor of his asteroid settlement. Asteroid dwellers rarely believed in any form of life after death; indeed, he'd been astonished when he discovered just how many of his comrades at the academy prayed heavily before taking their exams.

Life was neither fair nor unfair, he'd thought; it simply *was*. And what you got in life depended on what you made of it.

But if Marius did believe in an afterlife, who knew who he'd meet? His friend, the man who'd died saving his life, or the billions who'd died on Tara Prime?

"I couldn't allow you to kill billions of people," he said. "It would have been horrific."

Marius, absurdly, smiled. "I always liked your idealism," he said. "Mine was lost along the Rim, Roman, lost when I had to struggle to keep the pirates from tearing the colonies apart. I could have saved millions of lives if I'd had the resources to patrol the sector properly. I could have done so much."

You've done more than enough, Roman thought. *But it would be cruel to tell you that now.*

"I did what I thought I needed to do," Marius said. His breathing grew ragged again; Roman winced as an alarm echoed through the compartment. "But everything I did only created new problems. I thought I could take the bull by the horns..."

He gasped, his entire body shaking. Roman looked around, wondering where the hell the doctors had gone, then realized they had been banished from the compartment. Marius Drake — or Lady Tiffany — had ordered them to stay out. Was Marius Drake lucid enough to realize he didn't want to live any longer? Or had his wife quietly arranged matters so he could die with some dignity?

"Save the Federation," Marius said. "And don't give up."

He shuddered, one final time, then fell still. The alarm shut off; the displays on the far side of the compartment went blank. He was dead, dead beyond all hope of resurrection.

Roman stared down at the body for a long moment, feeling oddly conflicted. Part

of him knew he should be relieved — alive, Marius Drake would be dangerous, even if it was only as a figurehead — and yet he felt saddened. Marius Drake had been a great man, once upon a time; if things had been different, he might have *died* a great man.

If Tobias Vaughn had survived, Roman thought. *Or if I'd stayed on Earth...*

He shook his head. There was no way to know what would have happened if something had been different. The Grand Senate had been tearing the Federation apart ever since the Blue Star War, their inherent greed and conservatism destroying all faith in the once-great society and ruining countless lives in its wake. Admiral Justinian hadn't been the only warlord, after all; he'd merely been the one who'd struck first. And it would have made very little difference, Roman suspected, if Admiral Justinian had taken Earth, so many years ago.

He sighed, once. And then he reached down and gently closed Marius Drake's eyes.

"I'm sorry," he said, softly. "Goodbye, Admiral."

Turning, he strode back through the hatch and into the outer chamber. Ginny was gone, but Elf and Lady Tiffany were waiting patiently, the former calm and composed while the latter was clearly worried. Roman wondered what, if anything, she'd said to her husband before the latter's death. She had had time, perhaps... or had she felt that *Roman* should be the only person to speak to him? Their marriage had been arranged, but it was clear she'd had strong feelings for him — and vice versa, as she'd survived the purge of the Grand Senate.

"He's gone," he said, flatly.

Lady Tiffany bowed her head for a long moment. Elf merely nodded.

"He would have wanted to be buried amidst the stars, I suspect," Roman added. It was customary among long-serving navy officers and he couldn't imagine Marius Drake being any different. "We will have his body prepared for burial, then conduct the ceremony before we leave the system."

Tiffany looked up. "You're *leaving*? The system is in chaos!"

"The strain of trying to hold the Federation together drove Emperor Marius mad," Roman said, "and the tools at his disposal were far greater than those at mine. I don't think we can hold the Federation together any longer."

"Millions of people will die on Earth," Tiffany protested.

"They'll die anyway," Elf said, coldly. Roman understood; she knew she couldn't do much, save perhaps rescuing some of her remaining family. "There's no way we can feed the entire planet, now the food production and distribution networks have been destroyed. I don't even believe we can save a tiny percentage of the population."

"There are far too many systems declaring independence and leaving the Federation," Roman added. "Trying to force them back into the alliance will spark off another long and bloody — and futile — war. I doubt the Outsiders will assist us in reuniting the Federation."

"Of course not," Tiffany said. "They'll just start snapping up worlds for the Outsider Federation."

"Would that be a bad thing?" Roman asked. "They *are* planning to offer autonomy to worlds, merely adhesion to a mutual defense and trade pact. It wouldn't be anything like as unpleasant as the Grand Senate."

He paused. "And even if it did evolve into something worse," he added, "at least they will have tried. The Federation failed. Rebuilding a failed structure would be nothing more than a waste of time."

"I hope you're right," Tiffany said. She looked up at him, meeting his eyes. "What now?"

"We will offer to take the trained personnel to Boston with us, when we leave," Roman said. He had no idea how many others would want to leave the Sol System, but with at least two warlords sniffing around he suspected millions of people would want to go. Boston would make a good place to build up a whole new civilization, then either join the Outsiders or remain independent. "And you too, if you wish to come with us. Or we can transfer you to Paradise..."

"It won't be a paradise for long," Tiffany said, shaking her head. "Even if the aristocrats survived their first year on the planet, one or more of the warlords would target them for revenge. I don't think they'll be left unmolested."

"Probably," Roman agreed. He was surprised that *Marius Drake* had left them unmolested, although they'd been out of his sight and mind. "Is there anyone there you want to save?"

"They never considered me one of them," Tiffany said. She shook her head. "Let them survive or fall, Admiral. I have nothing in common with them."

Roman nodded in understanding. "Elf and I will head back to *Valiant* and complete our work," he said. "Once you bid farewell to your husband, you are more than welcome to join us. I believe your surviving bodyguard and the hostages you freed are hoping to meet you again."

"Thank you," Tiffany said. She looked oddly pleased, then resigned. "Nothing is ever going to be the same again, is it?"

"Probably not," Roman said. He was used to change, but Tiffany — and Marius Drake — had been used to a stable universe. "Change is a universal constant."

Tiffany nodded, once.

"You were in there for twenty minutes," Elf said, once they were back in the shuttle. "What did he say to you?"

Roman hesitated. In truth, he wasn't sure he wanted to discuss it with anyone, even Elf.

"He told me to make sure his death wasn't in vain," he said, finally. "And I will make sure of it, personally. We'll never forget what giving one man absolute power can do."

Chapter Forty

It is funny, really, just how much effort has been wasted trying to determine the last resting place of Marius Drake. In the years since the fall of the Federation, hundreds of missions have been mounted in the hopes of locating his coffin and recovering his body, some dispatched by cultists and others sent by organizations who want to make sure the former Emperor is definitely dead. But none have ever located the corpse.
—The Federation Navy in Retrospect, 4199

Earth, 4102

General Charlie Stuart couldn't help feeling an odd mixture of emotions as the fleet prepared for departure, for a voyage that would take them back through AlphaCent and Tara Prime until they finally reached Boston. On one hand, the Federation had been broken and Earth itself was consumed by civil war. But, on the other hand, Chang Li was dead and the Outsider Federation had yet to recover from her loss.

She wouldn't have wanted to see Earth burn, Charlie told himself, as he stood in his office and studied the reports. *And she would have wanted to save as many souls as we could.*

The planet's security forces had died or scattered, leaving an increasingly desperate mob battling over the remaining scraps of food. Who would have thought Earth was so close to a complete breakdown?

He looked up as the hatch chime sounded. "Enter."

The hatch hissed open. Professor Kratman stepped through the hatch, looking surprisingly dapper in a civilian suit and tie rather than a shipsuit. Charlie's eyes narrowed in suspicion; Kratman was Brotherhood, perhaps the sole surviving Brother. And the Brotherhood had never been keen on the idea of sundering the Federation, let alone embracing aliens as allies and... *brothers.*

"Professor," he said, stiffly. "What do you want?"

Kratman didn't appear to be fazed by the rudeness. "A few moments of your time, General."

Charlie hesitated. It was tempting, very tempting, to tell the professor to go away. He didn't have the time to listen to sob stories, let alone political manipulation. And yet, he was curious. Kratman *had* to know the Brotherhood wouldn't be considered welcome in the Outsider Federation, so why was he here?

"Take a seat," he said. He deliberately did *not* summon the steward to provide tea or coffee, something that was more insulting to the Federation than the Outsiders. Kratman could not fail to miss the unsubtle implication that he was far from welcome. "What can I do for you?"

"To the best of my knowledge, I am the last surviving member of the Brotherhood," Kratman said, without preamble. Charlie was almost relieved. "There has been no communication from Grand Senator McGillivray since the fleet entered the Sol System. I believe, under the circumstances, that he is almost certainly dead."

"Rendering the Imperialist Faction extinct as well as the Brotherhood," Charlie observed, tartly. "I trust you won't object if I don't weep crocodile tears?"

Kratman leaned forward. "The Federation I swore to defend is gone," he said, simply. "That's a fact. There may be some warlords who dream of rebuilding the Federation in their own image, of converting their vest-pocket empires into something greater, but I doubt any of them have the resources to turn their dreams into reality. Even Roman, who commands the single largest force known to remain active, probably couldn't do it."

"He doesn't *want* to do it," Charlie said. It had been a relief. The Outsiders didn't need another war while they sorted out the issue of just who succeeded Chang Li as Speaker. "I don't see any reason to question his judgement."

"The bonds that held the Federation together have snapped," Kratman agreed, shortly. "And putting it back together is impossible."

He leaned forward. "But that does leave us with the problem of determining what happens *after* the Federation."

Charlie frowned. "I dare say we're looking at a number of warlord states," he said. "And us, of course."

"And you," Kratman agreed. A flicker crossed his face. "And your alien allies."

"Most aliens didn't start out hating us," Charlie pointed out. "They only turned into human-haters after they met the Federation."

"Something that was hardly true of the Snakes," Kratman said. "They shot first."

"Yes, they did," Charlie said. "But the crimes of one alien race can hardly be rested on another, totally separate alien race."

Kratman bowed his head. "Whatever happens afterwards... well, that's a young man's game," he said. "I'm well over fifteen decades old, General, and I would be surprised if I see out one more decade. But I have a gift for you, of sorts."

He reached into his jacket and produced a datachip, which he dropped onto the desk. "I never really expected to go into history," he admitted. "Studying history has always been quietly discouraged in the Federation, even when I could mine history for examples I could introduce to my cadets. The Grand Senate preferred the peons to believe that the Federation had always stood, that nothing had changed from the birth of the universe till now."

"Very few people would believe that," Charlie sneered.

"You might be surprised," Kratman said. "It's astonishing what people can be convinced to believe, if they have no reliable intellectual framework with which to assess new data."

He shrugged. "That—" he tapped the datachip "—is one of two copies of my own private historical research. The book would have been banned, without hesitation, if I'd submitted it for publication, so I chose not to make the attempt. It's an attempt to assess the last five thousand years of political history and draw lessons for the future."

Charlie frowned. "The last five *thousand* years?"

"History may not repeat itself, General, but it does rhyme," Kratman told him, flatly. "I suggest you and the Outsiders seek to learn before it's too late in order to

avoid repeating some of the Federation's mistakes."

"The Federation tolerated the Brotherhood," Charlie said, as Kratman rose. "*That* was a mistake."

"Perhaps," Kratman said. He didn't sound offended. "The other copy, for what it's worth, is going to Roman Garibaldi. Maybe he will draw some interesting lessons from it, too."

                                     ℬⲄ

"Is it wrong of me," Tiffany asked, "to feel that I betrayed him?"

Ginny shrugged as they stood together in *Valiant's* observation blister. "I don't think you had a choice," she said. "The Federation would have fallen far harder if Emperor Marius had remained in command. You know that to be true."

Tiffany nodded. Two weeks after the Fall of Earth, with Admiral Garibaldi preparing to leave, a warlord had seized control of AlphaCent and threatened to deny passage back through the Asimov Point to Maidstone. It hadn't lasted — the warlord had realized that Admiral Garibaldi outgunned him four to one — but it had been a sign that the future would be far from peaceful. If Marius had been in command, the warlord would have been obliterated instead of merely pushed out of the system.

"And yet, I feel like I did the wrong thing," she said. "Like I could have stopped him..."

"I don't think you could have," Ginny said. She reached out and rested a hand on Tiffany's shoulder. "He wasn't listening to anyone who tried to talk him down, me included. The drugs made sure of it, too."

"I know," Tiffany said. She'd wanted to murder General Thorne personally, but the mob on Earth had taken care of it for her. She still had no idea why General Thorne had moved his command center to Earth, yet she found it hard to care. All that really mattered was that General Thorne had been brutally murdered when the defenses failed and the mob had stormed the building. "But I did love him."

"Yes, you did," Ginny said. "And I think he loved you, too. But in the end, his love for you was outweighed by his love for the Federation."

Tiffany touched her chest, lightly. She'd thought long and hard, but she'd eventually ordered the doctor to preserve some of Marius Drake's sperm while he was unconscious. It would be easy, when she reached Boston, to have herself impregnated with his seed, even though she had no idea what her life would be like. It wasn't as if she had any skills the out-worlds would find useful. Maybe she could write a book about being married to the one and only emperor.

"I don't know if we did the right thing," Ginny said. "But all we can really do is give thanks that we're alive."

"I know," Tiffany said. She peered into the endless darkness of interstellar space, the shadows broken by the light of countless stars. "And his body is out there, somewhere."

"No one will ever find it," Ginny assured her. "And if there is an afterlife, maybe you'll see him again."

Tiffany shrugged. She'd hated and resented her fellow aristocrats for looking down on her family, so abandoning them and throwing her lot in with Marius Drake had been an easy decision. He'd taken her seriously, and he'd treated her kindly when he could have easily consummated the wedding and then never seen her again. She would always love him for that...

... And, at the same time, he was a mass murderer who'd committed genocide on a planetary scale.

And someone who might be indirectly responsible for more genocides, she thought. *Now the taboo has been broken, who knows what's going to happen next?*

She wrapped an arm around Ginny as the starships slowly made their way towards the Asimov Point and watched, numbly, as Sol faded in the background. It was unlikely she'd ever return, and even if she did, everything would be different. All she could do was look to the future and try to build a whole new life.

"Goodbye, Marius," she muttered. "And farewell."

৪৩ ଓଷ

Roman studied the display, thoughtfully, as the fleet slowly made its way towards the Gateway. There were thousands of ships, ranging from the remains of Home Fleet to countless freighters crammed with people who wanted to leave Sol and build a better life along the Rim. Roman had stripped the system of as much infrastructure as he could, including artefacts from Naval HQ and the Luna Academy, but he knew there was still a great deal to attract raiders. It wouldn't be long before the warlords started fighting over the Sol System — and AlphaCent — in earnest.

"Admiral," Lieutenant Thompson said. "We picked up a message from Lieutenant Ricer. He states that the special orders have been carried out."

"Good," Roman said. He'd given orders to have Marius Drake's coffin quietly aimed at the Dead End, Sol's other Asimov Points. Lacking either a drive field or sufficient mass, it would be ripped to atoms by the gravity tides and lost forever. No one would find the body, either as a cult relic or to gloat over his mortal remains. "Have them return to the ships and then we proceed through the Gateway."

"Aye, sir," Lieutenant Thompson said.

Roman turned his attention to the system display. Earth was still wrapped in a brutal civil war as the planet's inhabitants came to grips with the simple fact that they couldn't feed themselves without outside support, while Mars and Luna were still skirmishing. It wouldn't matter long, Roman thought; the warlords would probably put a stop to it when they took the system and started to loot in earnest. He wondered, absently, if they'd do anything about Earth.

But they can't, he told himself. *And nor can we.*

It was a bitter thought. He'd been raised to believe that there was *always* an option, while the academy had taught him to have the right attitude. And yet, and yet, there was no point in wasting the fleet's resources on Earth. He could put everyone on the fleet to work, discarding all other priorities, and it wouldn't be enough to feed even a tiny percentage of Earth's population. The nightmare gripping the planet was the end result of the Grand Senate's policies, policies that Marius Drake had

been unable to undo before the war overwhelmed him. There was nothing Roman could do...

... And yet it felt as though he was running away.

Marius Drake went mad trying to hold the Federation together, he reminded himself. *And I will go mad if I try.*

He looked at Lieutenant Thompson. "Has Lieutenant Ricer returned to the fleet?"

"Yes, sir," Lieutenant Thompson said.

"Then signal the fleet," Roman ordered. "Take us to the Gateway. It's time to go home."

He picked up a datapad as the fleet picked up speed and inserted the chip Professor Kratman had given him, and started to read. It wasn't *professional* to read while on duty, but he was fairly sure the journey home would be uneventful. The warlords knew better than to mess with his ships, particularly as they were abandoning Sol anyway. They could wait, like the petty scavengers they were, until the system was defenseless.

The problem with history, he read, *is that people who don't learn from history are condemned to repeat it. But it is also true that people who do learn from history are condemned to watch as the first group of people repeat it...*

Epilogue

From: *The Fall of the Federation* (4502 A.D)

It is generally agreed, amongst historians, that the Federation fell in 4102, ending an era that began in 2051. Historians have alternately praised Marius Drake as the last of the great men and cursed him for a usurper who ensured that the decline and fall of the Federation became inevitable, but there is little real argument over the date. However, there is a great deal of disagreement over the *why*. *Why* did the Federation fall?

The roots of the Federation's slow decline into civil war can be traced all the way to the Inheritance Wars, even though the wars ended in 3114. On one hand, the Inheritance Wars answered the question of whether a planet or an alliance of planets could leave the Federation — the answer was no — while, on the other hand, the Inheritance Wars made the Grand Senate, and the Federation as a whole, more authoritarian and less inclined to take concerns from the out-worlds seriously. The rise of the political triad that dominated the Federation until 4029 — the Conservative, Imperialist and Socialist Factions — only strengthened disturbingly illiberal trends in government. In short, the Conservatives wanted everything to remain frozen in place; the Imperialists wanted to control the entire galaxy and the Socialists wanted to fundamentally reform the Federation itself (although not, it should be noted, at the expense of their power).

Even before the Blue Star War, which discredited and destroyed the Imperialist Faction, the seeds of disintegration were sown. The Grand Senate wrote the rules to suit themselves, which inevitably ensured that the out-worlds were marginalized and ambitious but unconnected officers and officials were denied promotions and ranks they'd earned. Furthermore, the vast bureaucracy the Grand Senate created to run the Federation only made matters worse; it was impossible for smaller businesses to meet their reporting obligations, which had the unexpected consequence of ensuring that most industries were soon owned by only a handful of wealthy families. Finally, the educational infrastructure was allowed to decay; the students produced, particularly those without the drive to educate themselves, were barely good for anything. Unsurprisingly, the Federation's overall infrastructure began to decay — and a crash was only a matter of time.

These destructive trends only grew stronger after the Blue Star War. Peons, on Earth and the out-worlds, might have enjoyed the humiliation of the Imperialist Faction, but its fall removed the last restraints on the other two factions. Their grab for power — for more power — only made the growing crisis worse. Military officers fumed at being held back and plotted escape; colonials, their ranks swelled by able men who saw no future on Earth, plotted revolution. By the time Admiral Justinian made his own bid for power, it was clear that a final reckoning could not be long delayed.

And, by the time the Grand Senate fell, it was simply too late to recover.

Marius Drake was a great man, all agree. But the Federation had too many problems for any one man to fix, even with supreme power. The Outsider War only made
matters worse, in that it offered a chance for freedom to men and women who had
no reason to trust either the Grand Senate or Marius Drake. It is generally agreed that
there was nothing Marius Drake could do that would save the Federation, without
destroying it. The story might have had a different plot, but the ending would be
the same.

The Federation had simply declined too far to be saved. And if those who replaced
it had not learned from its fall, they too might have fallen into the shadow of the past.

THE END

Afterword

I don't think Bob won that election legally. I can't believe a convicted felon would get so many votes and another convicted felon would get so few.
—Lisa Simpson, *Sideshow Bob Roberts*

Why did the Roman Empire fall?

The question is more complicated than it seems because there were, in Roman history, two separate political entities (three, perhaps, if you include Byzantium), both of which eventually fell. On one hand, you have the Roman Republic and on the other, you have the Roman Empire itself. Just to complicate matters, it isn't actually easy to say when the Republic became the Empire. Was it in 83/82BC, when Sulla won the first civil war; 49/44BC, when Julius Caesar won the second civil war, only to be assassinated himself; 31/30BC, when Augustus Caesar defeated Antony and Cleopatra... or 14AD, when Tiberius Caesar succeeded Augustus as Emperor? The Romans did not, you see, point to a single moment when the Republic was finally dead, even in hindsight. They still thought of themselves as a republic long after Augustus became the first *true* Emperor.

To us, that may sound paradoxical. However, Augustus, learning from Julius Caesar's mistake, was careful not to portray himself as a dictator, even though he was practically unassailable. He consulted regularly with the Senate, worked hard to pose as a simple citizen and generally did what he could to keep the appearance of republican rule in place for as long as possible. His dominance was considered far more acceptable, therefore, than the dictatorships of either Sulla or Julius Caesar. For all of his genius, however, Augustus suffered from a run of bad luck when it came to his family. His sole practical successor was the dour Tiberius and, for all of his virtues, Tiberius was ill-suited to be Emperor. Not the least amongst his flaws was a simple failure to understand that the republic was beyond recovery.

And *his* successors — Caligula, Claudius and Nero — were far from great.

The Roman Republic fell, in short, because the governing system Rome had evolved was simply ill-suited to the task of governing an immense empire. Rome was ruled by stiff-necked aristocrats who preferred to allow problems to fester, rather than allow someone else to claim the credit for solving them. The system produced many larger than life figures — Marius, Sulla, Pompey, Cato and Julius Caesar — but it also tried to restrain them. A man who grew too powerful would be pulled down by the combined work of his peers back in Rome — a dangerous thing to do, when the Romans had been breeding men who were prepared to fight to the last over a point of pride. Julius Caesar was quite right when he asserted he'd been forced into war. Put in a position where he had to submit or fight, he chose to fight — and, upon reaching supreme power, was assassinated. However, by this point, the death of the dictator was not enough to automatically restore the republic. Too much damage had been done.

Largely thanks to Augustus, the early years of the Roman Empire showed a considerable amount of promise and even bad emperors — Nero in particular — were not enough to bring the structure toppling down. The civil wars of 69AD, which saw four emperors crowned in rapid succession, weren't fatal. However, as time wore on, successive problems began to emerge which rotted away at the heart of the empire. By the time the barbarians stormed Rome itself and dethroned Romulus Augustus in 476AD, Rome had weakened to the point where, again, recovery was no longer possible.

The principle causes of the collapse of the Roman Empire were many; in essence, however, I believe the core of the problem was that the Romans themselves no longer considered Rome to be worth fighting for. This should not have been surprising. The empire's citizens were no longer honored, but treated as serfs by their overlords. Taxed savagely, unable to meet their obligations, vast numbers of civilians were forced into debt-peonage or crushed under the immense weight of bureaucracy. Fairness and justice were no longer evident; runaway peasants were forced into banditry to survive. The Emperors themselves were so isolated from their own people that their attempts to come to grips with the scale of the crisis, when they bothered to take note, were largely ineffectual.

And, in the end, the Roman Empire died. It committed suicide.

It has always struck me as odd that Westerners, mainly Americans, have looked to Rome as a source of inspiration for their politics. George Washington, for example, held up Cato as an example of what a man should be. And yet, such comparisons are often misleading. A counterpart of Cato in 1777 would not be George Washington, but Lord North; a counterpart of Julius Caesar, Benedict Arnold. The Roman World was not the world of 1777 any more than it is our own.

But that shouldn't stop us learning from the mistakes of the past.

[People interested in a short look at the empire's failings would be well-advised to read *The Fall of the Roman Empire*, by Michael Grant. The best modern narrative history of the decline and fall of Rome is *The Fall of the West*, by Adrian Goldsworthy.]

ಬಂಡ

The problem facing the West today is centered around what has been generally called the "political class," men and women who have rarely been uninvolved in politics and *very* rarely have any experience *outside* politics and its related fields. Like the aristocracy of pre-revolutionary France, the political class has little in common with the people it rules, to the point where it doesn't have any real understanding of the problems they face. Existing in an echo chamber, they find more in common with politicians who are *nominally* on the other side of the political divide than non-politicians. It is hard for them to hear any dissenting voices and, when they do, it's easy to fall into the trap of believing the dissenters don't have any legitimate concerns.

This may seem paradoxical. Unlike the aristocracy of every state from Rome to the British Empire, the political class has no legal existence. A democratic state is not supposed to *have* an aristocracy with an inherent right to rule. However, the political

class controls a great deal of the political establishment, giving it the ability to promote its selected candidates over candidates who may be favored by the rank and file. The existence of political dynasties like the Kennedys, Bushes and Clintons — and their ability to push their children forward as their successors has been limiting the influx of new blood into the political arena. Indeed, given how savagely newcomers have been attacked by the establishment, it is easy to see how so many newcomers choose not to take part in politics.

Unsurprisingly, the results have been disastrous. A number of people who have no experience of anything outside politics — and a very specific kind of politics at that — are incapable of doing their job in anything like a reasonable fashion. Senators who don't understand the lives of the people they purport to rule are unlikely to pass legislation that actually *helps* the general population. Congressmen who have no contact with their constituents are hardly likely to understand their concerns. And Presidents who have never served in the military are unlikely to grasp what it can and cannot do. The real world rarely operates on political timescales.

And when the political class uses its power to escape the consequences of its actions, or to evade laws that apply to everyone else, it merely sows the seeds of destruction.

The political class, in a very real sense, is merely the tip of an iceberg that threatens to sink the ship of state. It is buttressed by a media establishment (the mainstream media) that supports its candidates uncritically, while hammering any outsider with charges that are simply inaccurate and yet maddeningly difficult to refute. A favored candidate can expect to have any problems in his life smoothed over — Obama's sheer lack of experience, for example, or questions raised about his academic standing or even nationality — while anyone who raises these issues gets attacked sharply. But a candidate who is unfavored can expect to be brutally attacked for even the tiniest of gaffes.

This too has been disastrous. President George W. Bush embarked upon a long and dangerous endeavour, but the media expected results at once. Small failures were treated as immense disasters, forcing Bush to play keep-up instead of merely learning from the problems and pushing forward. Much of Bush's early reputation was shaped by the media choosing to present a very unfavorable picture to the world. (A problem made worse by the media rarely understanding the issues.) Obama, on the other hand, was treated so favorably by the media that he developed a truly staggering level of narcissism. His policies have been disastrous because he appears to believe that his involvement is enough to make them successful.

As I write these words (February 2016), the race for the American presidential nomination is in full swing. It has already taken on the veneer of a revolt against the elites, with the Republican base eying Trump and the Democratic base considering Bernie Sanders while the elite tries to promote Jeb Bush and Hilary Clinton. Neither of the latter two are really appealing to voters, in times of trouble. They have been part of the political class for decades. (So has Bernie Sanders, to a quite considerable extent.) Indeed, Donald Trump's coarseness — his willingness to say what he thinks

and his complete refusal to apologize for anything — has made him astonishingly popular, because he appears to be standing up to the elites.

This does not mean that Trump would make a good President. But the skills needed to be a *good* President are *not* the skills needed to get elected.

The Roman Empire died, at least in part, because it rotted away from within. Our society is facing the same problems. The rise of the bureaucratic nanny-state is sapping our virility; the rise of unchallenged and unchallengeable political consensuses is stripping common sense from our world; the slow decline of education is turning our young men and women into morons; the cuts in our military make it harder for us to fight; political correctness is making it impossible to stand up and say, bluntly, that the emperor has no clothes.

And we are also facing many of the same exterior problems. Russia and China are both growing stronger, while we are at war against an Islamic ideology that seeks the complete destruction of every opposing ideology. The global economy is on very rocky ground, thanks largely to the carelessness of politicians who thought the good times would never stop. And economic migrants are flooding our borders, bringing with them ideas and cultures that cannot be tolerated, while our politicians do nothing. The situation is dire.

We are not Rome. We don't have to go the same way. But time is short.

Christopher G. Nuttall
Edinburgh, 2016

About the author

Christopher G. Nuttall is thirty-one years old and has been reading science fiction since he was five when someone introduced him to children's SF. Born in Scotland, Chris attended schools in Edinburgh, Fife and University in Manchester... before moving to Malaysia to live with his wife Aisha.

Current and forthcoming titles published by Twilight Times Books:

Schooled in Magic YA fantasy series
Schooled in Magic — book 1
Lessons in Etiquette — book 2
A Study in Slaughter — book 3
Work Experience — book 4
The School of Hard Knocks — book 5
Love's Labor's Won — book 6
Trial By Fire — book 7
Wedding Hells — book 8
Infinite Regress — book 9
Past Tense — book 10

The Decline and Fall of the Galactic Empire military SF series
Barbarians at the Gates — book 1
The Shadow of Cincinnatus — book 2
The Barbarian Bride — book 3

Chris has also produced *The Empire's Corps* series, the *Outside Context Problem* series and many others. He is also responsible for two fan-made Posleen novels, both set in John Ringo's famous Posleen universe. They can both be downloaded from his site.
Website: http://www.chrishanger.net/
Blog: http://chrishanger.wordpress.com/
Facebook: https://www.facebook.com/ChristopherGNuttall

Lightning Source UK Ltd.
Milton Keynes UK
UKOW04f1835011117

312031UK00001B/75/P

www.ingramcontent.com/pod-product-compliance
Ingram Content Group UK Ltd.
Pitfield, Milton Keynes, MK11 3LW, UK
UKHW020617231125
465212UK00025B/200